Clinical Handbook of
Pastoral Counseling, Volume 1

EXPANDED EDITION

Integration Books

STUDIES IN PASTORAL PSYCHOLOGY,
THEOLOGY AND SPIRITUALITY

Robert J. Wicks,
General Editor

Clinical Handbook of Pastoral Counseling, Volume 1

EXPANDED EDITION

Robert J. Wicks
Richard D. Parsons
Donald Capps,
editors

Integration Books

paulist press/new york and mahwah

The Publisher gratefully acknowledges the following: Use of the essay adapted from *Loneliness, Solitude and Companionship* by Robert E. Neale. Copyright © 1984 Robert E. Neale. Adapted and used by permission of The Westminister Press, 925 Chestnut Street, Philadelphia, PA 19107. (This work includes exercises for individual and study groups which can be used by pastors for care and counseling.) Bernard Tyrell's chapter on "Christotherapy: An Approach to Facilitating Psychospiritual Healing and Growth," first appeared as "Communicating Christ Through Christotherapy" in *Camillian* and is used with the permission of the National Association of Catholic Chaplains. Use of the American Association of Pastoral Counselors Code of Ethics. Reprinted by permission of the American Association of Pastoral Counselors.

Cover and interior logos used courtesy of the Graduate Program in Pastoral Counseling, Neumann College, Pennsylvania.

Library of Congress Cataloging-in-Publication Data

Clinical handbook of pastoral counseling/Robert J. Wicks, Richard D. Parsons, Donald Capps, editors.—Expanded ed.
    p. cm.—(Integration books)
  Includes bibliographical references and indexes.
  ISBN 0-8091-3351-2 (pbk.: v. 1)
  1. Pastoral counseling. I. Wicks, Robert J. II. Parsons, Richard D.
III. Capps, Donald. IV. Series.
BV4012.2.C54 1992
 253.5—dc20
                                    92-30017
                                        CIP

Published by Paulist Press
997 Macarthur Boulevard
Mahwah, New Jersey 07430

Printed and bound in the
United States of America

Contents

Contents

Robert J. Wicks

Introduction to the Expanded Edition

In general, persons engaged in ministry and pastoral counseling have responded enthusiastically to the broad range of practical and theoretical material published in the original edition of this *Handbook*. However, some comments and reviews also mentioned critical areas that needed attention but were left uncovered in the original edition. In response to reviewers' comments, chapters on *supervision, family systems, ethics, research*, and *spiritual direction* have been included in this Expanded Edition of Volume 1 of the *Handbook*.

In the chapter "Supervising Pastoral Counseling," David A. Steere (author of *Bodily Expressions in Psychotherapy* and editor of a book on supervision in pastoral care) offers a context, and practical information, on the process. He notes four major traditions in the current practice of pastoral counseling supervision, then offers a model (constructed from one used at Louisville Presbyterian Seminary for a number of years), which is an approach to integrating these traditions. And, finally, he presents and examines several dimensions of the supervisory task which he sees as being common to them all.

In the area of "Essential Elements of Family Systems Approaches to Pastoral Counseling" Carolyn J. Bohler (of United Theological Seminary in Dayton, Ohio) helps us move away from a traditional psychiatric focus on the "identified patient/client." She then helps us refocus on the connection between the family as a whole and the specific reported symptoms and visible signs about which people are offering complaints. With this as a backdrop and using "circular causation" rather than "linear thinking" as a theoretical vantage point, she offers clear and practical information on interventions, themes, boundaries, the use of metaphors and images for reframing, the employment of stories and homework assignments aimed at changing boundaries within the system, and an examination of family triangles/

secrets. Following this, Bohler also gives a brief overview of some of the major "schools" of family systems approaches and then ends this rich chapter by addressing ethnicity, gender, faith and societal issues as they relate to the work of pastoral counseling in this context.

In "A Philosophical Foundation for Professional and Ethical Issues in Pastoral Counseling" Melvin C. Blanchette (co-editor of *The Art of Clinical Supervision*) addresses the twofold question: What are ethics and why are they necessary? and then turns to the practical issue of how ethics are applied. Two aspects of this chapter make it especially valuable. The first is the Kantian philosophical foundation with which the author begins in order to provide us with a broad context for the topic. The second is the carefully-thought out and worded section "Pastoral and Practical Reflections" which he provides for our consideration. This chapter lends itself well for use in pastoral counseling centers in training discussion groups as well as for individual reflection. (An Appendix which contains the newly revised American Association of Pastoral Counselors Code of Ethics has been added to this Expanded Edition of the *Clinical Handbook of Pastoral Counseling, Volume 1* to supplement the information included in this valuable chapter.)

In "Research in Pastoral Counseling: Definitions, Methods, and Research Training," Joanne Marie G. Greer (the Director of Research for the Graduate Programs in Pastoral Counseling of Loyola College in Maryland) offers a number of pertinent questions and distinctions. Among them are: Can pastoral counseling be simultaneously "pastoral" and "scientific"? How does one define "pastoral counseling research"? What is "methodology"? Does correct methodology *really* matter? What do the results actually mean? or Did anything really happen? and Can all useful theories be proved? As well as providing a great deal of complex material in a clear, straightforward manner, Greer offers her position on a number of research-oriented topics which need to be addressed in pastoral counseling today. In summary, whether one is research-naive or has a sophisticated research background, this chapter offers a great deal on an often misunderstood and under-attended area: pastoral counseling research.

The final addition to this Expanded Edition of the *Clinical Handbook of Pastoral Counseling, Volume 1* is by one of the leading contemporary writers on spiritual direction, William A. Barry, S.J. In this chapter Barry's position connects spiritual direction with pastoral counseling and puts it within the overall context of pastoral care. The distinction he makes in this chapter will be of particular interest and use for those who have tended to see spiritual direction in an overly defined light. Particularly useful sections of this chapter are the ones on needed qualities in spiritual directors; how the spiritual director uses the skills of counseling to help people to develop their relationship with God; transference, countertransference and supervision; and (what I feel is an especially creative section) an analogue between the development of a relationship with God and a developing human relationship.

Given the fine quality of the original contributions to the *Clinical Handbook of Pastoral Counseling*, I am pleased to offer you in this Expanded Edition the addition of these five well-written pieces on topics which should further enhance the contents and value of this book. In requesting these new contributions to Volume 1 of the *Handbook*, my hope was that they would equal the quality level set by the authors of the original edition. They have more than fulfilled my expectations.

M. Scott Peck, M.D.

Foreword

I am honored to write this Foreword to *Clinical Handbook of Pastoral Counseling*. It is not merely a professional work of excellence; its publication is a significant historical event.

We are, by God's grace, moving out of an age of excessive specialization into an age of integration. Already we can recognize many features of this saving trend: the holistic medicine movement, the ecology movement, the bishops beginning to reach out from their churches to integrate our political and economic life with the gospels. This book is yet another. It represents the coming of age of the pastoral counseling movement.

I have described this profound movement from specialization toward integration as both graceful and saving. This is because it is a movement toward integrity. The noun integrity comes from the verb "to integrate."

We psychotherapists often use a verb which is the opposite of "to integrate": "to compartmentalize." By "compartmentalization" we refer to that remarkable capacity which we human beings have to take things which are properly related to each other and stick them in separate airtight compartments in our mind so they don't rub up against each other and cause any pain. An example would be the man who goes to church on Sunday morning, believes he loves God, God's creation and his fellow human beings, and then on Monday morning has no difficulty with his company's policy of dumping toxic wastes in the local river or lake. This is because he has put his business in one compartment and his religion in another and is what we call a Sunday morning Christian. It is a very comfortable way to operate, but integrity it is not.

Conversely, integrity is never painless. It requires that we do let things rub against each other—that we fully experience life's conflicting demands and attempt to integrate them into resolutions of integrity. For instance, what are we to do with the conflict that this country on whose

1

coinage is written the words "In God We Trust" is also currently the leading manufacturer and seller of weapons in the world? Should we think of these facts separately? Or should we experience their friction and seek a path of national behavior which is not hypocritical?

The way of integrity is a way of tension. But remember that the cross, among other things, is a symbol of tension: the tension of the horizontal ripping across the perpendicular. Indeed, if we experience fully the conflicts of life, there will be times that we will feel as if our body is being torn apart and our souls broken. But remember also that the cross is a symbol of integrity, of wholeness. The way of integrity is the way of the cross, and there is no other way to truth and healing.

It is inevitable, therefore, that this handbook in particular should have some tensions in it as it integrates the insights of psychology and religion. But this is not a fault. To the contrary, it is my hope that all mental health workers—psychologists, social workers, and psychiatrists as well as pastoral counselors—will come to this work precisely because they will find as a result of the integration that its discerning scope is generally wider and deeper than that of their own more specialized professional literature.

I have written elsewhere of the potential for evil that is inherent in excessive specialization,[1] which is why I exult in the fact that through their integration of psychology and religion pastoral counselors have become generalists. My only fear for the pastoral counseling movement is that it may slip backward into a more established and defined (and hence comfortable) specialized identity. I hope that pastoral counselors will continue to be willing to suffer the tension of an identity that is not always clear but remains open to new possibilities.

In fact, the only—and relatively minor—criticism that I have of this work is that it is not quite general enough. It lacks a chapter or section on "hard" research and scientific methodology. Many of the chapters use the findings of "soft" research, but there is little mention of statistics or control groups and the like. As I suggested in *People of The Lie* when I proposed the establishment of an Institute for the Study of Deliverance, the interface between psychology and religion is a wide open frontier for scientific research. The effectiveness of prayer in various forms of healing, for instance, is an area of study which would submit itself quite readily to the rigors of the scientific method. I do not mean to imply that "hard" science will ever be able to penetrate all the mystery of the human psyche. It will, on the other hand, always be one of the essential avenues toward truth. I worry that pastoral counselors might leave hard research to the psychiatrists. Conversely, it is my hope in the direction of integration and integrity that pastoral counselors will come to think of themselves not only as psychotherapists who are people of God but also as scientists.

Note

1. *People of The Lie: The Hope for Healing Human Evil* (Simon and Schuster, 1983).

Donald S. Browning

Introduction to Pastoral Counseling

To become oriented to the field of pastoral counseling, it is useful to make some fundamental distinctions. I find it helpful to distinguish between the activities of pastoral care, pastoral counseling, and pastoral psychotherapy.[1] These three sets of terms are commonly used to refer to three different types of pastoral practice, all of which can be addressed, and are in the chapters contained in this book, from an interdisciplinary perspective using both theology and the social sciences, especially psychology and psychotherapy.

These three forms of helping can be distinguished from one another by the extent to which the pastor distances himself or herself from an explicitly moral stance in working with people and focuses instead on the psychological dynamics involved. Hence, pastoral care is clearly the most inclusive pastoral activity of the three. It is the more or less unstructured general work with youth, couples, adults and other such groups in various types of informal and formal conversations, dialogues, and other communicative interactions. Pastoral care in this sense occurs on the street corner, at the end of a committee meeting, in the hospital room, in and around the funeral, and in many other more or less marginal situations. Pastoral care must hold together religious, ethical, and psychological perspectives. It brings the full witness of the Christian community—even the moral perspective—to each interpersonal exchange.

On the other hand, there are those occasions when individuals seem to need and even request the time and attention of the pastor in a structured relationship that may occur within the context of a specific time commitment in a designated place. These relationships are frequently referred to as pastoral counseling. Here the focus is more on the individual and his or her problems. In many such instances, the problem entails some conflict, ambivalence, or depression in the person's capacity to act freely and confidently. When this is the case, it is often thought that the pastor or religious counselor should bracket or temporarily set aside moral or normative concerns and concentrate instead on the psychological blocks and

5

developmental impediments which seem to be stifling personal growth. At other times, the problem does not seem to center primarily around the inability to take free and confident action, but deals more with the area of value confusion and/or questions of religious commitment. In some cases, the issues around which pastoral counseling occurs deal with both problems of free action and problems of moral and religious discernment. Insofar as they deal with the first, they are often thought to be more properly psychological and matters pertaining to mental health. Insofar as they are problems of moral values and religious commitment, they are often thought to be the more proper province of the minister and the wider pastoral care of the congregation. *The major new development that has motivated the founding of the pastoral counseling movement has been the insight that most human problems are various mixtures of both conflicted human freedom and moral and religious discernment.* This partially explains the new interest on the part of the professional minister in combining psychological-developmental understandings with moral and religious perspectives on human behavior.

Pastoral psychotherapy, however, is more specialized than pastoral counseling, at least as it is generally understood and practiced in the North American scene today. Like pastoral counseling, it entails some kind of time limited contracts covering length and frequency of pastoral conversation. But pastoral psychotherapy is generally seen as a more specialized activity, occurring in a more specialized setting and having more specialized goals. Its more specialized setting entails, generally, a specific institutional locale such as a pastoral psychotherapy center which is generally located at some distance, both psychologically and physically, from the worship and fellowship life of the congregation. But its goals are more specialized as well. It tends to concentrate more on the first of the two sets of problems mentioned above. It addresses more completely than does either pastoral care or pastoral counseling the psychological and developmental obstacles within a person's life which may be impediments to free and confident thinking, decision making, and action. Hence, pastoral psychotherapy resembles, as its name suggests, more nearly the goals of psychotherapy in general. That is why it is shaped so significantly by some of the analytic tools and interventions devised by secular psychotherapeutic theories.

But pastoral psychotherapy is still pastoral because it takes place within the moral and religious assumptive world associated with the Judaeo-Christian tradition. These assumptions consititute the faith of that tradition. There is a discernible moral tradition in this religious heritage. Although this moral tradition is under some crisis at more concrete levels, there is still wide agreement at higher levels of general principle and fundamental perceptions of the good. There are also within this tradition widely shared assumptions about the nature of human nature and the fundamental character of the world. These moral and religious attitudes constitute the assumptive background of pastoral psychotherapy. It is within a view of human nature and the world consistent with the Christian faith that the use of psychological understanding and interventions takes place. Hence, within the context of pastoral psychotherapy, psychological ideas become highly circumscribed and heuristic perspectives on human behavior. Psychological ideas help us to understand *some* of the developmental factors which incline humans to act and feel the way that they do. But within the context of pastoral psychotherapy, some of the world views and implicit moral commitments in many of the contemporary secular psychotherapies get relativized and subsumed to the moral commitments and world view of the Christian tradition. Within the context of pastoral psychotherapy, the psychologies should help us understand the way the individuals we are helping developed the personalities and characters that they have; but the psychologies alone should not, and indeed logically cannot if they are to remain scientific psychologies, tell either the therapist or the client what or who the client should become. That is, the psychologies cannot rightfully tell the client which moral and religious values he or she finally should hold once the freedom is gained to make these new commitments.

But for the purposes of the remarks that are to follow, I will use the phrase "pastoral counseling" roughly to refer to all these forms of pastoral help. In addition, I will use that phrase to refer to the total work of the church or congregation in caring for one another, especially when that care is under the guidance of a minister trained in the interdisciplinary use of both theology and psychology to enable the caring process. Although this usage is somewhat arbitrary and doubtless will not agree with the usage of all the authors in this book, it will serve the purposes of my contribution. In summary, then, pastoral counseling will refer to those caring acts of the church under the guidance of the minister that addresses issues of care from the perspective of both Christian theology and the modern social sciences, especially the modern developmental and psychotherapeutic psychologies.

Why Pastoral Psychology?

In the following pages, I will present six reasons why the church in particular and society as a whole should encourage the development of a pastoral counseling perspective on the care of individuals. In making this claim, I am using pastoral counseling in the broad sense as defined toward the end of the above discussion. The reasons that I will present are of several kinds and represent the interdisciplinary character that I believe pastoral counseling should take. I will present two theological reasons, two sociological reasons, and two psychological reasons for the importance of the pastoral counseling movement. These six reasons will not exhaust all the possible supports for the importance of this movement, but they will at least illustrate the kinds of defenses for the movement that can be advanced.

Theological Reasons

1. *Because human beings are a mixture or synthesis of spirit and nature, their behavior is a product of both free decision and various forms of conditionedness.* It is a fundamental affirmation of Christian theology found in the works of Augustine, Kierkegaard, Niebuhr, Tillich and others that human beings are viewed as fully a part of nature and subject to its finitude, necessities, and rhythms.[2] But at the same time, humans are seen to be creatures of spirit, by which it is meant that they have some capacity for freedom, self-reflection, and self-transcendence. By self-transcendence it is meant that they have limited but genuine capacities to transcend certain types of causal determination and, in some circumstances, even have the capacity to transcend their own immediate self-interests. For instance, humans are creatures of sexuality and subject to its inevitable arousals, rhythms, and satisfactions. But humans also have the freedom to direct, restrain, express, and develop their sexuality in a variety of ways and toward a variety of ends. Much the same can be said for the way they can respond to causal pressures stemming from their early childhood experiences and to the sociological, economic, class and historic determinations that shape their lives.

Insofar as this is true, most human problems are a mixture of an inappropriate use of freedom and the play of various psychological, sociological, and historic causal factors. Pastoral counseling, committed as it is to a bi-focal perspective on human behavior that emphasizes both spirit and nature (both freedom and conditionedness), can approach these problems from two perspectives. Pastoral counseling can look for the developmental and environmental causal pressures which work to distort optimal human growth. But at the same time, it can look for the subtle misuses of freedom, its orientation around inadequate moral and non-moral values, and the various ways that the human will center itself upon deeper untrusting and idolatrous attitudes toward the ultimate conditions of human life.

2. *Because pastoral counseling has as a part of its assumptive world*

a belief in a God who is both the author of a good creation and the ultimate agent behind all redemptive change, it can take a positive attitude toward the possibilities and resources for both general human growth and redemptive change. This is a way of saying that the deep attitudes of the pastoral counselor are founded on certain faith assumptions about the nature of the ultimate conditions of life. Because pastoral counseling believes in a God who creates and sustains the world in its natural forms, it is interested in general human growth, the development of basic human capacities and potentialities, and the elemental health and welfare of the human race. Pastoral counseling is not just interested in the redemptive change of persons; it is interested in their general human flourishing as part of the task of participating in the fulfillment of God's good creation. Hence, pastoral counseling is dedicated to the support of basic human goods such as strong families, healthy children, good working conditions, education, adequate nutrition, and good mental functioning.

But pastoral counseling is interested in more. It is concerned to help individuals and communities overcome inordinate self-interest or what Christians have ordinarily called sin. Hence, it is interested in redemptive change and not just the general fulfillment of human capacities, health, and well-being, although it is certainly concerned about these things as well. Furthermore, pastoral counseling, regardless of its appreciation for the skills of the counselor in promoting growth and redemptive change, always sees these human capacities as mediative. That is to say that it perceives the ultimate agent behind both growth and redemptive change as being the creative, sustaining, and redemptive power of God. This means that the growth-producing and curative powers of the pastoral counselor are finally always relativized and seen as at best reflecting deeper and more abiding forces that transcend the work of the counselor.

Sociological Reasons

3. *Because of the increasing secularization of Western societies, we tend more and more to see human problems as either a matter of causally-determined developmental and sociological problems or a matter of misused human freedom, and less as a matter of both.* The secularization process has had both conceptual and professional manifestations, and the two are closely related. As the professions of psychiatry, psychology, and social work developed, they also promoted their own conceptual tools and specialized frameworks for the interpretation of human behavior. These frameworks tended to accentuate psychological and sociological determinants behind human problems rather than the misuse of freedom around moral and religious commitments. This was both a gain and a loss for the

modern world. Insofar as it balanced the more traditional emphasis on the misuse of freedom as the primary cause of human difficulties, it was a definite gain. It helped us discern a whole host of factors contributing to human misery that were often overlooked or not carefully attended to in the older perspectives. But there was also a loss which followed from the ascendency of the more specialized social science perspectives. The contribution to human misery that comes from the misuse of freedom in both the moral and religious realms has become obscured. Pastoral counseling, due to its more complicated view of humans as both nature and spirit—and as both conditioned and free—is in a propitious position to retain the wisdom of the older views while absorbing the more differentiated understanding of the causal factors operative on human life that the modern sciences have developed.

4. *Because of the mixed nature of human problems, there are strong sociological reasons to develop a new pastoral counseling emphasis in ministry and possibly even a new professional sub-specialty called "pastoral psychotherapy."* This is a proposition first put forward with considerable power by Talcott Parsons in the concluding chapters of his *Social Structure and Personality* (Parsons, 1965). Because so many human problems have developmental deficiencies as a factor in their etiology, Parsons saw the value of the church creating a new sub-specialty of ministry that could address these dimensions of human problems but without becoming alienated or too far removed from the more normative standards and visions which it was the proper role of ministry to both discover and uphold. Hence, it is good, Parsons argued, to have a sub-specialty of ministry that could both develop some social-psychological distance from the normative center of the church as well as have some continuity with it. It was thought by Parsons that such a sub-specialty could help people bracket explicitly moral and religious concerns long enough to examine the developmental and social factors that may be inhibiting their sense of selfhood, freedom, and initiative. At the same time, because this specialty is an expression of ministry with clear continuities with the normative concerns of the church, this distance could be seen and experienced by the client as both temporary and heuristic and not permanent, dogmatic, or metaphysical.

Of course, such a specialized ministry has now emerged and is represented by the American Association of Pastoral Counselors as well as the Association of Clinical Pastoral Education. Although the professions represented by these organizations should not be seen as a model around which to pattern pastoral counseling as it takes place in the congregation, they can be a great support to parish-based pastoral counseling and care. In addition, the use of the psychological perspective by the minister within the congregation can help gain some of the distance necessary to look at the developmental factors behind human difficulties. To the degree that this is accomplished, the pastoral counselor within either the congregation or the counseling center can help distance temporarily the parishioner from these normative concerns until a greater degree of freedom and initiative is achieved. When this happens the person will have a heightened capacity to address these ethical and religious matters without being crushed by their challenging normative weight.

Psychological Reasons

5. *Because humans are creatures who are partially subject to the necessities of biopsychological development as well as the conditioning of the environment, pastoral counseling needs the assistance of psychological disciplines to aid in the retrospective analysis of these determinants of human behavior.* By retrospective, I mean the process of looking backward toward the causal factors conditioning human behavior. Without claiming that human behavior is totally conditioned by factors outside of human freedom, we can acknowledge the usefulness of the various psychological disciplines in helping the pastoral counselor to analyze the genesis of these biopsychological and environmental factors. Hence, the developmental psychologies of Freud, Jung, Erikson, Mahler, Kohlberg, Fowler, and Piaget should be a part of the resources available to the pastoral counselor. These psychologies help us gain the backward or historical perspective on an individual's life history. They help us answer the question: What were some of the factors that shaped the life of this person? However, these psychologies cannot rightly dictate what the person we are helping should become, especially in terms of more normative understandings of the moral and religious goals of life. I say that they cannot "rightly" dictate these goals. By this I mean that they cannot as scientific psychologies dictate the goals of life; if they do, they no longer are scientific psychologies but quasi-moral and quasi-religious systems which function as substitutes for religious faith. That many of the clinical psychologies can function this way is an argument made by a variety of contemporary writers—especially Rieff, Vitz, Halmos, Back, and myself.[3] But it would be precisely the task of pastoral counseling to critique the religious and moral horizon that sometimes accompanies the so-called modern psychologies and neutralize their value-laden commitments so that the more truly scientific aspects of these psychologies can be used within the moral and religious commitments of the Christian faith.

6. *Because all humans are shaped by developmental and environmental factors, the use of psychological analysis can greatly increase the accuracy of the efforts of pastoral counseling to mediate the transforma-*

tive resources of the Christian faith. Although it is a very complicated process about which much more can be written than I can say here, pastoral counseling presupposes that, in the end, it is God's activity working through the processes of creation and redemption that bring about growth and change in the helping relationship. It is finally God's activity, it is assumed, that undergirds the pastoral counselor's empathy, acceptance, reflections, constancy and interpretations. But we now know that these transformative qualities have much more potency and lasting effects if they are mediated with real psychodynamic accuracy. That is, pastoral counselors are more truly helpful in mediating these transformative qualities—more truly able to increase a sense of self-cohesion, initiative, and freedom in those they help—if they are sensitive to and able to address the actual developmental and environmental blocks, conflicts, and ambivalences that are undercutting a person's capacities. For instance, a particular person may need to accept himself more, but it helps a great deal to understand that his mother's sexual anxiety is part of the reason that he has difficulties accepting his own sensual feelings. Another person may need to take more initiative and control over her life. But it will help a great deal if she understands that it is partially because her parents withdrew their empathy whenever she expressed her early childhood aspirations and grandiosity that she is now afraid to take initiative for fear that it will lead to a loss of love from those to whom she is attached. Such insights help us to be more accurate in our mediation of care.

Pastoral counseling as defined as the interdisciplinary use of theology and psychology for the task of mediating care is an important new movement within the church. But it is also a synthesis of two important cultural resources—the Judaeo-Christian tradition and the modern psychologies. For this reason it has broad social and cultural implications which go far beyond the more immediate ministries of the institutional church. It may constitute an important new cultural synthesis that could go a long way in transforming the self-understanding of the citizens of modern nations.

Notes

1. For earlier discussions of these distinctions, see my *The Moral Context of Pastoral Care* (Philadelphia: Westminster Press, 1976), pp. 104–114; *Religious Ethics and Pastoral Care* (Philadelphia: Fortress Press, 1983), pp. 75–76.

2. St. Augustine, *The Confessions of St. Augustine* (New York: New American Library, 1963); Soren Kierkegaard, *The Concept of Dread* (Princeton: Princeton University Press, 1957); Reinhold Niebuhr, *The Na-*

ture and Destiny of Man (New York: Charles Scribner's Sons, 1941); Paul Tillich, *Systematic Theology*, I (Chicago: The University of Chicago Press, 1951).

3. Philip Rieff, *The Triumph of the Therapeutic* (New York: Harper and Row, 1968); Paul C. Vitz, *Psychology as Religion* (Grand Rapids: William B. Eerdmans Publishing Co., 1977); Paul Halmos, *The Faith of the Counselors* (Schocken Books, 1970); Kurt Back, *Beyond Words* (Russell Sage Foundation, 1972); Don Browning, "Psychology as Religio-Ethical Thinking," *The Journal of Religion* (forthcoming), and *Christian Thought and the Modern Psychologies* (Fortress Press, forthcoming).

Bibliography

Parsons, Talcott. *Social Structure and Personality.* New York: The Free Press, 1965, pp. 292–324.

Orlo Strunk, Jr.

A Prolegomenon to a History of Pastoral Counseling

Pastoral counseling is as old as the church and as new as the birth of psychoanalysis. This seemingly paradoxical notation cannot be overemphasized in a Zeitgeist frequently ahistorical, if not blatantly antihistorical. After all, the religious counselor was an integral part of the early Israelite courts. And in the New Testament times the notion of counselor carried enough importance to be used as a symbol for the activities of the Holy Spirit (John 14:16). Indeed, there has never been a time in the history of the Christian church when religious leaders have not had as one of their functions the counseling and guidance of the members of their congregations.

This old/new paradox is even more evident when we equate or fuse pastoral care and pastoral counseling—a tendency not completely absent even in modern times. Yet it is necessary to treat these modes separately when examining historical developments. At the same time, it is imperative to hold these two religious expressions at interface. Pastoral care is the more inclusive term. Traditionally, it referred to one of the offices of the church. Called *poimenics,* it was in contrast, for example, to *homiletics* (preaching) or to *catechetics* (religious instruction). However, in more recent times the general term pastoral care usually refers to the broad activities of a pastor in his or her relationships with parishioners. Although the sociologist Max Weber wrote of pastoral care as "the religious cultivation of the individual," that individualistic notion tends to be softened considerably in the contemporary life of the church where pastoral care includes caring for society and for other larger systems of life.

Pastoral counseling, on the other hand, has had a more limited focus. In its most direct and less controversial sense, it has tended to be viewed as counseling done by a pastor or a religious professional. However, with the professionalization of the field and its movement toward greater specialization, the term presently communicates considerably more than this simple definition. The Association of Pastoral Counselors, which accredits pastoral counselors at various levels, has defined it as "a process in which a pastoral counselor utilizes insights and principles derived from the disciplines of theology and the behavioral sciences in working with individuals, couples, families, groups, and social systems toward the achievement of wholeness and health."

What is particularly significant in this definition is the phrase "behavioral sciences" in that it ties *modern* pastoral counseling to a group of human sciences which were non-existent in much of the history of pastoral care and pastoral theology. This actuality helps to delimit an approach to pastoral counseling and to set it as an historical development of contemporary times.

At the same time, it is imperative to remember that modern pastoral counseling—no matter how specialized and how closely identified with current human sciences it may be—is deeply colored by the long and rich history of pastoral care. Fortunately, we have available a literature which ought to keep us attuned to this essential tie: F. Kemp's *Physicians of the Soul: A History of Pastoral Counseling* (1947), J.T. McNeill's *A History of the Cure of Souls* (1951), and W.A. Clebsch and C.R. Jaekle's *Pastoral Care in Historical Perspective* (1964) offer such reminders, as does the more recent volume by Holifield, *A History of Pastoral Care in America* (1983).

In this chapter, then, I will attend to saying a few generalizations about pastoral counseling in its very modern guise, that is, as a specialized form of ministry greatly influenced by the behavioral sciences of the twentieth century. As such, I cannot pretend to be engaged in writing a history of pastoral counseling. We stand much too close to the modern pastoral counseling movement to be "historical." Even the designation "prolegomenon" (a critical introduction) is a bit presumptuous. Still, I think we can come to get a feel for the recent background of this movement, and perhaps—remembering to hold firm to the much longer and richer history of pastoral care—gain something of a historical sensitivity to pastoral counseling's current manifestations.

I

In a general sense, the beginnings of contemporary pastoral counseling may be traced to the cultural and intellectual concerns contained in the dialogue between science and religion. That dialogue—both in its ancient and modern forms—became especially evident at the turn of the twentieth century. Although the science/religion conversations manifested themselves on many fronts, its presence in the rise of psychology and psychiatry holds a special place in the early notions of a pastoral counseling that, though built atop the long tradition of the pastoral arts, would graft to that tradition new and different ways of looking at humankind and of understanding it.

In part, then, the beginnings of a pastoral psychology whose praxis would come to be called pastoral counseling, even pastoral psychotherapy, were, like so many other "innovations," a reflection of wider cultural interests—in this instance, consciousness raising in regard to science and technology. And although the church and its theological seminaries frequently resisted this wave of modernism and the secular mentality associated with it, that resistance was softened in important ways.

First was the intellectual project of theological education itself. At the turn of the century theological education tended to be primarily an intellectual project with great concentration in the classical disciplines—biblical studies, theology, church history, biblical languages, etc. Where praxis held its place was usually in the areas of homiletics and religious education. Although Protestant theological curricula often contained courses in pastoral theology and pastoral care, and Catholic seminaries carried courses in moral philosophy, an examination of seminary catalogues in the early 1900's reveals very little of the praxis dimension; that is, the intellectual mode dominated the curriculum even in such areas as pastoral care and pastoral theology.

This historic reality takes on special significance when it is placed beside what was happening in the broader academic community, particularly in the establishment of departments of psychology in American universities. Even more significant as a sign of this relatively young science's growing influence was the publication at the beginning of the twentieth century of William James' *The Varieties of Religious Experience* (1902). The fact that an American scholar would choose such a topic for the prestigious lecture series was itself symbolic of the young science's ambitious agenda. But it was also a sign that religion—often an "untouchable" in the halls of respectable scholarship—was to be seen as fair game for this new human science.

James' excursion, coupled with the many writings of his contemporaries (now called the classists in religious psychology), initiated a field of inquiry called the psychology of religion (Strunk, 1971). Still essentially an intellectual pursuit without any direct praxis, it became a part, however minor, of many theological curriculums, particularly those in the liberal Protestant tradition.

Although such a subject could seep into the traditional theological curricula as another cognitive approach, it nevertheless contained per-

spectives which challenged certain practices of ministry and which introduced different ways of looking at the human condition. The notions of
health and disease, for example, began to question the strictly theological
meanings of such terms as sin and salvation. As one commentator noted in
drawing out the implications of James' "healthy/sick" religion categories:

> . . . the general and traditional judgments passed on man's sin-
> fulness by the word of God, by which a sinner becomes "con-
> victed," can now be supplemented by detailed diagnosis and
> prescriptions. The sharp lines that used to be drawn between
> crimes and diseases, morals and religion, eternal and temporal
> welfare have become shadowy . . . as the body-mind-soul com-
> plex is unified in the concept of the person or self, so the health-
> righteousness-salvation complex becomes a unified though com-
> plicated problem (Schneider, 1952, p. 186).

In no better way is this "academic" influx illustrated than in the works
of A.T. Boisen (1960), often counted the father of the clinical pastoral education movement (Powell, 1975). In one respect, the publication of Bois-
en's *The Exploration of the Inner World* (1936) represents most clearly the
way in which a psychosocial perspective tended to find its way into theological education, despite resistance. And at the same time, as we shall see
in reviewing later the role of therapeutic psychology in leading to pastoral
counseling, Boisen's academic/research thrusts carried with them an aura
of praxis which would indirectly lead to the formation of new emphases in
the area of ministerial training—the clinical pastoral education movements
and the pastoral counseling movement.

Mainstream psychology and psychiatry, however, did not enter theological curricula on their own terms or without marked modifications. As
Paul Johnson, one of the pioneers in the formation of the modern pastoral
counseling movement, noted:

> The conflict of theology with psychology intensified during the
> years when psychology was enjoying a crescendo of influence in
> the modern world. Earlier in the 20th century, theology was ac-
> commodating its perspectives to a modernism influenced by the
> natural sciences and secular culture. This seemed to endanger
> the supernatural revelation and unique authority of the Christian
> position. The conflict came to a dramatic crisis in Germany when
> Hitler was reaching out to engulf the church in Nazi statism and
> genocide. Then Karl Barth gave a ringing challenge to be faithful
> to the Word of God, with undivided allegiance to the biblical rev-

elation of Christ. Theologians of that generation rallied with Barth to proclaim a faith in the transcendent unapproachable God revealed in the Pauline Christ.

So there developed a cult of supernaturalism, in which theology recoiled from engagement with a scientific culture and retreated into other-worldliness. This was a productive awakening of biblical studies and historical theology. There was in fact a renaissance of classical theology in its prescientific grandeur. Charismatic leaders brought a glowing enthusiasm to this other-worldly supernaturalism which attained high authority over theological education. Esoteric vocabularies were debated endlessly like the medieval chanting of plain song.

By some slight of hand or black magic, psychology has become invisible in the halls of theology. Psychology of religion was displaced by existentialism and ontology. Pastoral psychology yielded to pastoral theology and pastoral care. Psychological studies were disguised as personality and religion or personality and theology (when religion also was discredited as the enemy of Christianity). There must be no lingering doubt that theology is the queen of the sciences.

Like the parable of the purist who swept his house clean of worldly dirt, this was not the end of the story. More devils moved in lustier than ever, including the other sciences and arts of man, such as sociology, anthropology, communications, field engagement in the community, and the theater, once out of bounds to puritans and evangelicals. Psychology has returned in our psychological testing, counseling, psychotherapy, psychiatry, personality and culture, human development and pastoral care.

The theologians are by this time vying with each other to employ psychology as an auxiliary science, to understand the nature of man, Christian education, pastoral theology, and Christian ethics. There is scarcely a theological doctrine that has escaped this searching and mounting dialogue with psychology (Johnson, 1969, pp. 58–64).

II

As academic psychology at the turn of the century struggled for its place in the intellectual sun, therapeutic psychology—particularly psychiatry—was having a similar struggle. The general history of psychiatry is relevant here, but given our intention and space limitations we cannot deal with it in any detail. Yet it is essential to remember that medicine, including that branch of it called psychiatry, has a long and rich tradition which runs deep and has influenced considerably the religion/science interface. Psychoanalysis, as part of that medical evolution, does not stand apart from that history and tradition any more than modern pastoral counseling stands apart from the history of pastoral care and pastoral theology (Ehrenwald, 1976).

Still, for our purpose it is necessary to note particularly the development of Freudian psychoanalysis because it does provide one of the life-giving roots in the modern pastoral counseling movement.

As we know, Freudian psychoanalysis has tended to evolve outside formal academic halls. Unlike American psychology proper, its life has been nurtured in the medical clinic and in its free-standing institutes. When psychoanalytic thinking entered the universities, it usually did so via the professional schools, especially schools of medicine and schools of social work.

G. Stanley Hall's invitation to Freud and Jung to visit and lecture in the United States in 1909 marks an important exception in the evolution of the psychology/psychiatry/praxis dynamic in that it was an invitation to an academic setting and came from an academic psychologist. Although the works of these two European psychiatrists and psychotherapists were known by a small cadre of American psychologists and psychotherapists, the impact of their radical notions—particularly their emphases on the unconscious—were not in any sense an integral part of higher education or of the professional education of either physicians or clergy. That visit, although primarily symbolic, initiated a wave of literature and praxis which would have an amazing impact on both medical and theological education, and, later, on pastoral counseling as a specialized form of ministry (Homans, 1970).

Two historic phenomena illustrate ways in which therapeutic psychology got itself firmly imbedded in the training of clergy—the Emmanuel Movement and the Clinical Pastoral Education movement. Both were attempts to bring together the forces of medicine and religion with the purpose of healing mind and body under the conviction that Christ heals in the contemporary as well as he did in New Testament times.

In 1904 Elwood Worcester, rector of the Emmanuel Episcopal Church in Boston, Massachusetts, in cooperation with several prominent New England physicians, established a clinic for "spiritual healing." In 1908 he, in collaboration with his ministerial associate, The Reverend S. McComb, and Dr. I. Cariat, a prominent physician on the faculty of Tufts Medical School, published *Religion and Medicine* (1908), a volume later included in the Surgeon General's *Progress of Medicine During the Nine-teenth Century*. Unlike many other healing cults being established at the time, the Emmanuel Movement built on enlightened and sophisticated notions of both medicine and religion. Although the movement recorded many successes and attracted a wide range of clergy and medical persons, in 1934 the movement began to subside, and by 1940 it was dead.

In interpreting the movement's decline, Thornton (1970) notes three reasons: (1) it failed to train ministers, (2) Worcester did not himself grow and change with the rapid developments in psychiatry, and (3) the rela-tionships between physicians and clergy, so essential to the life of the de-velopment, broke down.

Although the Emmanuel Movement was abortive, its historic signif-icance is evident since its spinoffs in regard to later developments in the mental hygiene movement were wide-reaching. Even more important in tracing the roots of modern pastoral counseling is the fact that the Em-manuel Movement was one of the preludes to the establishment of the clinical pastoral education phenomenon, a development with similar aims but one which did not fall prey to the same limitations which prevented the Emmanuel Movement from attaining full fruition.

In terms of the beginnings of modern pastoral counseling, it is difficult to underestimate the importance of the CPE movement. A full account of its beginnings has been given by Thornton (1970) and cannot be recorded here in any appropriate detail. Suffice it to say that its formal beginnings were initiated by two physicians and a minister. The physicians—W.S. Keller in Cincinnati, Ohio, and R.C. Cabot in Boston, Massachusetts—brought young clergy into the world of human crises where their theolog-ical studies, primarily classical at the time, could be grounded. In the case of Keller, the main objective was to train "social engineers" able to create a new and different world than what existed in the early 1900's. For Cabot the aim was to assist clergy in achieving professional competence in their pastoral ministry. Although both held different objectives, their methods were similar in that they agreed that the best way to learn is through in-volvement in the lives of suffering persons experiencing crises.

Somewhat ironically, the clergy part of this triad—Anton Boisen—saw his primary aim the facilitation and encouragement of research in the psychology of religion, not in the training of ministers as special counse-lors. His early work (Boisen, 1936) focused much more on understanding than on praxis, although he too felt strongly that close association with "the living human document" was the best way to acquire such understandings. Boisen's early contributions were deeply phenomenological and theoreti-cal, particularly in dealing with complex issues of religion and psychopath-ology. But in typical American style, the praxis implications were forcefully acknowledged by his associates, and as a result the Keller-Cabot-Boisen ethos soon took on a practical flavor and an organizational project that was to have a massive impact on theological education in America. As one historian notes:

> Cabot's and Boisen's disciples, along with various physicians, joined together to form the Council for Clinical Training of Theological Students, an organization which eventually split and evolved into two competing groups: the Council for Clinical Training, centered in New York City, and the Institute of Pastoral Care, based in Boston. A third stream of the movement developed within the Baptist and Lutheran traditions. By the mid-1940s it is estimated that as many as 2000 seminary students had received some form of clinical pastoral training, nearly 30 clinical training centers had been established, and at least 75 seminaries were affiliated with these centers to some degree (Van Wagner, 1983, p. 164).

Little wonder that this new development was called by some a "mid-century phenomenon" and that from it would come a new and enthusiastic specialization in ministerial service.

III

From this caldron of developments, both within and beyond the church, a new awareness of what a counseling ministry might mean began to emerge. The Swiss psychiatrist C. G. Jung's oft-quoted observations that a majority of persons seeking help from psychiatrists manifested essentially religious concerns and that a generation ago these same persons would have consulted a pastor or priest are stark, if overgeneralized, indications of the situation in the first half of the twentieth century. Clergy, seeing secular invasions into soul caring, became concerned. And, as is often the case, it was frequently individual practitioners, not their institutions, which began to take very seriously the new claims of the young sciences, especially as they were expressed in the care-giving professions.

Part of this concern, as already noted, was expressed in the development of such things as the Emmanuel experiment and, later, the CPE movement.

During this period—roughly between 1920 and 1940—the specific form for the expression of the theology/science/praxis projects was personal and organizational. Strong personalities frequently overshadowed principles and standards, although as one commentator (Aist, 1983) has noted, standards writing represents one important way of tracing and monitoring the professionalization of the movement. His observation on the relationships between visionizing and standard-setting is worth noting:

> The clinical pastoral movement was founded by men and women who wanted to revolutionize theological education for ministry. Their aim was not to change the subject matter, but to bring empirical methods of investigation into the theological curriculum. The chief method they proposed involved in-depth study of persons in crisis through personal encounter. The founders of the movement—Keller, Boisen and Cabot—did not spend a lot of time writing standards, at least not initially. They focused rather on the objectives, the methods, and the promising benefits to be derived from theological reflection in clinical settings. But when the objectives, method and intended results of an educational endeavor are seriously explored, concern about formal standards cannot be too long in following. They were in fact implicit in the value judgments being made in the process (Aist, 1983, p. 61).

Although this principle is noted here primarily in reference to the CPE movement, it is equally apropos in regard to the origins of the modern pastoral counseling movement. For by the late 1940's a marked interest in pastoral counseling as a specialized ministry became evident, particularly in the liberal Protestant tradition. Obviously stimulated by the secular psychotherapeutic developments, as well as the CPE establishment, a growing number of clergy were being trained as specialized counselors and therapists. In attempting to characterize this period, Van Wagner cites a report from California claiming that "guys were going around with turbans and crystal balls calling themselves pastoral counselors." In a more serious tone, he notes, ". . . any 'pastoral counselor' could charge whatever the market would bear in terms of fees; and any 'pastoral counseling center' could be responsible only to itself in terms of administrative structure, professional ethics, and its relationship to the institutional church" (Van Wagner, 1983, p. 166). Clearly, it was a time for structure and for standard setting.

It was in 1963 that pastoral counseling as a movement in its own right began to take an institutional form, for it was then that the first conference of pastoral counselors was held in New York City. Leadership for that meeting came mostly from members of the CPE movement. The result of that meeting was the establishment of the Interim Administrative Commission which worked to establish support and to develop membership criteria. Howard Clinebell, later to become president of the new professional association, extended a call beyond the essentially clinically-based and oriented parties to the seminary professors. Such persons as Carroll Wise, Paul Johnson, Seward Hiltner, and Wayne Oates created a vibrant theoretical dialogue, particularly centering on the pastoral vs. clinical orientations which permeated the movement at that time and in fact may still be found currently in the sundry streams of pastoral care and counseling literature (e.g., Oglesby, 1969; Strunk, 1973).

The first formal American Association of Pastoral Counselors conference was held a year later in St. Louis. In many respects (not all), the history of modern pastoral counseling in America *is* the history of AAPC. For over two decades it has struggled to formulate conceptual guidelines, to express such guidelines in professional standards, and to interpret them to a variety of bodies, especially the religious communities from which pastoral counselors hold membership.

However, the rapid growth of AAPC has not been without conflict. From its very inception, disagreements relating to the nature and function of the pastoral counselor have permeated the organization. In another place (Strunk, 1982), I have suggested four "issues" which generate the movement's élan and thus much of its history: the *identity* issue which often has taken form in questions dealing with the "uniqueness" of the pastoral counselor and the pastoral counseling process; the *theological* issue which confronts the matter of the place of theology in forming the pastoral counseling project; the *ecclesiastical* issue which has tended to concentrate on the nature of the relationship between the pastoral counselor as a specialist and her or his religious community or denomination; and the *paradigm* issue which, though usually tied closely to the theological question, has dealt especially with the technical and metapsychological backdrop of its praxis.

At this writing, the AAPC continues to experience considerable growth. It has established and operationalized levels of membership (Member, Fellow, Diplomate), conducts annual and regional meetings, accredits pastoral counseling centers, interfaces with government and religious bodies, and co-publishes *The Journal of Pastoral Care*, a quarterly professional journal in the areas of pastoral care, pastoral counseling and psychotherapy, chaplaincy, and clinical pastoral education. AAPC's executive director, James W. Ewing (1983), has aptly characterized the association's growth in terms of commitment, vigor, excitement, and intellect.

Current dialogue within the movement includes concerns over the need to recognize a wider range of issues than those traditionally associated with pastoral care and counseling—e.g., issues of women in ministry, minorities, nuclear arms and freezes, environmental responsibility, etc. In a word, the "prophetic" stream of religion is offering special challenges to a traditional "pastoral" stream. Also, articulate calls for another look at the older pastoral models are being aired, often raising the issue of whether indeed the "new" therapies really possess the power often ascribed to them by the scientific communities and too frequently and uncritically accepted by the pastoral counseling movement (e.g., Oden, 1983). And too the ecumenical nature of pastoral counseling is being reassessed with some intensity, particularly in regard to greater inclusiveness relative to the Roman Catholic community, the conservative evangelical movement, and the Jewish faith groups.

Clearly, pastoral counseling faces an agglomeration of issues beyond those of a praxis nature. Its future and directions—as the next chapter of this book demonstrates—suggest excitement and continued evolution.

Bibliography

Boisen, A.T. *The Exploration of the Inner World.* Chicago: Willet, Clark, & Co., 1936.

Boisen, A.T. *Out of the Depths.* New York: Harper and Row, 1960.

Clark, A.S. "Standards: A View from the Past and Prospects for the Future." *The Journal of Pastoral Care,* 1983, 37, 60–67.

Clebsch, W.A. and Jaekle, C.R. *Pastoral Care in Historical Perspective.* Englewood Cliffs: Prentice-Hall, 1964.

Ehrenwald, J. (ed.). *The History of Psychotherapy: From Healing Magic to Encounter.* New York: Jason Aronson, 1976.

Ewing, J.W. "Epilogue: Pastoral Counseling Issues: Current and Future." In B.K. Estadt, Melvin Blanchette, and John R. Compton (eds.), *Pastoral Counseling.* Englewood Cliffs: Prentice Hall, 1983, pp. 287–296.

Holifield, E.B. *A History of Pastoral Care in America: From Salvation to Self-Realization.* Nashville: Abingdon Press, 1983.

James, W. *The Varieties of Religious Experience.* New York: Longmans, Green and Co., 1903.

Johnson, P.E. "Pastoral Psychology in the Christian Community." *Spiritual Life,* 1969, 15, 58–64.

Kemp, C.F. *Physicians of the Soul: A History of Pastoral Counseling.* New York: Macmillan, 1947.

McNeill, J.T. *A History of the Cure of Souls.* New York: Harper and Brothers, 1951.

Oden, T. *Pastoral Theology: Essentials of Ministry.* San Francisco: Harper and Row, 1983.

Oglesby, W.B., Jr. (ed.). *The New Shape of Pastoral Theology.* Nashville: Abingdon Press, 1969.

Powell, R.C. *Fifty Years of Learning Through Supervised Encounter with Living Human Documents.* New York: Association for Clinical Pastoral Education, 1975.

Schneider, H.W. *Religion in 20th Century America.* Cambridge: Harvard University Press, 1952.

Strunk, O., Jr. (ed.). *The Psychology of Religion: Historical and Interpretative Readings.* Nashville: Abingdon Press, 1971.

Strunk, O., Jr. (ed.). *Dynamic Interpersonalism for Ministry.* Nashville: Abingdon Press, 1973.

Strunk, O., Jr. "The Role of Visioning in the Pastoral Counseling Movement." *Pastoral Psychology,* 1983, 31, 7–18.

Thornton, E.E. *Professional Education for Ministry: A History of Clinical Pastoral Education.* Nashville: Abingdon Press, 1970.

Van Wagner, C.A. "The AAPC: The Beginning Years, 1963–1965." *The Journal of Pastoral Care,* 1983, 37, 163–179.

Worcester, E., McComb, S., and Coriat, I.H. *Religion and Medicine: The Moral Control of Nervous Disorders.* New York and London: Moffat, Yard Company, 1908.

Clyde J. Steckel

Directions in Pastoral Counseling

Introduction

Modern pastoral counseling is moving in directions which promise a bright future. While the Christian community has always cared for the needy and counseled the perplexed, it is only since the middle decades of the twentieth century that modern clinical theories and methods have been widely employed in pastoral practice. For a time this appropriation seemed limited to liberal Protestant circles, and further confined to a highly professionalized understanding of pastoral practice. But in the late twentieth century it is increasingly clear that these limitations are breaking down, and that modern pastoral counseling is becoming *ecumenical* in many senses of that term. This chapter will attempt to illustrate and account for this ecumenical development, to anticipate its future, and to identify issues of particular concern for those who teach and work in pastoral counseling.

Theological Ecumenism

One sign of this growing ecumenicity in pastoral counseling is its acceptance in conservative Protestant churches and in the Roman Catholic Church. Liberal Jewish religious life also reflects the appropriation of modern pastoral counseling. It is more difficult to document its appearance in Orthodox Christian circles, but it is likely to be growing there as well.

This acceptance can be seen in the pastoral literature of these bodies, though their theological and moral reasoning remain distinct from that of liberal Protestant theorizing. But one can see it even more vividly in their embrace of Clinical Pastoral Education and other human relations training experiences for their clergy and lay pastoral leaders.

Whether this extension of modern pastoral counseling into such diverse religious communities represents genuine ecumenical growth, or the increasing secularization of all religions in modern culture, or the practical demands of caring for a bewildering array of human needs is difficult to assess. Whatever the reasons, this growth seems likely to continue, not recede. Its long-term influence on theology and ethics will be interesting to observe.

Global Ecumenism

Another sign of this growing ecumenicity in pastoral counseling is its extension over the globe. North American models of Clinical Pastoral Education and pastoral counseling training are now extensively developed in Europe, and growing on other continents. Newly indigenous churches in Africa and Asia are seeking clinical training for their pastoral leaders, either by sending them for study abroad or by establishing their own programs. The cultural and theological jolts can be severe in this process. European theological method with its dependence on careful text analysis and logical reasoning does not readily accommodate American pragmatic approaches. Nigerian Christians wonder whether boys grow up through the same developmental stages as those observed by Erikson in Western culture. Native American peoples value reticence as an expression of respect, and so it is difficult to persuade them to be "up front" about their feelings, or to engage in confrontation.

The risks of cultural imperialism seem high in these exchanges. Surely a better outcome would be the emergence of a variety of culturally indigenous Christian movements, in which Western contributions could be received without dominating. While there is evidence of sensitivity about these risks on both sides, modern Western pastoral counseling continues to be in demand around the globe. The question here, as with computers, television, or thousands of other Western exports, is whether such technology can be uprooted and transported without Westernizing the recipients. Perhaps in time we can look for a more distinctly Indonesian or Ethiopian or German pastoral counseling to emerge from these exchanges. But for the present, at least, Western pastoral counseling is sweeping the field.

Clinical Ecumenism

A different kind of ecumenism in modern pastoral counseling is to be found in its increasingly eclectic approach to therapeutic methods and theories. Not many years ago the Rogerians and the Freudians contended for the theoretical souls of the pastoral counseling movement. Then came the Jungians, the neo-Adlerians, Gestalt, Transactional Analysis, Logotherapy, Reality Therapy, Rational-Emotive Therapy, Behavioral Methods, and a host of others. Increasingly the literature of pastoral counseling reflected this diversity, and with Howard Clinebell's *Basic Types of Pastoral Counseling* in 1966, an eclectic approach to therapeutic methods received strong endorsement (Clinebell, 1966).

Since that time eclecticism has gained adherents in pastoral counseling. There are still vigorous advocates for particular therapeutic orientations, but they seem increasingly embattled. From the theoretical side, they are charged with expanding theory into ideology, or covert theology. And from the practical side, they are charged with procedural dogmatism and rigidity.

How are we to explain this trend toward eclecticism? Surely it has something to do with the transplantation of earlier European methods into the North American soil, where pragmatism has gradually prevailed over an emphasis on theory. Research on the outcome of psychotherapy has also made it increasingly difficult to argue that one therapeutic orientation is predictably more successful than others. Practitioners are increasingly acknowledging their own eclectic orientation, irregardless of the therapeutic orientation in which they were trained. And the growing emphasis on the theological foundations of pastoral counseling makes it increasingly clear that fundamental theory in pastoral counseling must be theologically framed, and that however helpful the various therapeutic orientations may be in that process, theological procedures must finally be used to articulate theory. As a result, practice is freer from theoretical orthodoxy, and open to a wider range of methods.

If this trend toward therapeutic eclecticism continues, teachers and practitioners of pastoral counseling will need to develop further their theological understanding of pastoral counseling so that eclecticism does not degenerate into the aimless pursuit of passing fads (there has been plenty of that!), and so that the criteria of pastoral objectives and methods become theologically articulated. Otherwise the norms of society regarding the healthy personality, or the norms implicit in a particular method, will govern pastoral practice. Not all of these norms are incompatible with Christian faith, to be sure, but many of them are. "Therapies" which advocate self-enhancement at the expense of others, or which try to teach mental control over emotions and actions, for example, would seem to harbor ideologies alien to Christian affirmations about service, community, and the wholeness of the person.

Plurality of Problems

An "ecumenism" of subject matter or problem areas is also growing in modern pastoral counseling. It seemed that in the earlier Freudian and Rogerian periods, typical cases in pastoral counseling concerned people who were bound up with neurotic repressions from which they needed to be released. "Presenting problems" were more varied, but the deeper issues were remarkably similar. There was dispute over whether the Freudian or the Rogerian personality theories and therapeutic methods were better able to account for this condition and cure it. But the condition itself was largely taken for granted.

Today that is all changed. The pastoral counseling literature[1] is now replete with books and articles on *many* problem areas—marriage and divorce, family life, aging, chemical dependency, sexuality, family abuse and violence, racism and sexism, suicide, learning disabilities and retardation, moral and spiritual development, anorexia and bulimia, assorted phobias and compulsions—the list goes on and on. This proliferation in the literature undoubtedly reflects the range of human problems which come to the pastor, who needs reliable information, at least about diagnosis and referral. But it is more than that. Each of these problem areas is now treated as a more distinct discipline, where the causes of the condition and appropriate therapeutic interventions are treated *in their own terms*, not as surface symptoms of a more generic human difficulty. A counselor requires specific knowledge of each problem area. The general "human relations skills" pastors and other helping professionals share in common may not be helpful, and may even become harmful in some circumstances. For example, a pastor whose general style is to facilitate communication may become a co-dependent with an alcoholic parishioner, rather than intervening to see that the parishioner gets treatment.

This explosion of new knowledge and treatment methods may overwhelm the pastor who is trying to remain a general practitioner. Surely one effect will be a heightened awareness of the need for enough knowledge of symptoms and community resources in order to make competent referrals. Another effect will be changes in the way pastoral counseling is taught. More teaching time will be spent on basic information and referral skills, less time on detailed therapeutic technique.

Even more important will be the consequences of this diversification for the place of theology and ethics in pastoral counseling. No longer able to rely upon a single personality theory and method of therapy, pastoral counselors will increasingly rely on theological and ethical reflection to guide both objectives and procedures in pastoral care. Already this shift can be seen in the literature. Oglesby's (1980) work on the bible in pastoral care and Browning's (1976) view that pastoral theology is a part of ethics reflect this new direction. That kind of work will also help pastoral counseling to become more free from cultural norms of adjustment and happiness.

Laicization of Pastoral Counseling

Yet another "ecumenism" is increasingly evident in modern pastoral counseling. That is a significant degree of de-professionalization, or, expressed more positively, the movement to educate laity as pastoral counselors. More CPE centers are offering such programs. And seminaries are increasingly offering lay theological education including counselor training.

This lay training in pastoral counseling seems headed in two directions: training for professional (or para-professional) staff positions in churches and chaplaincies where there are not enough ordained leaders, as in the contemporary Roman Catholic Church; and training for strictly lay roles in churches, where lay people become primary care providers, under the guidance of a pastor. This latter direction is fraught with both promise and peril. It is promising to give specific shape to the often vague challenge that laity be directly engaged in the ministries of the church. And it is also encouraging to imagine how the amount of competent care could be multiplied. But there are issues of confidentiality and "knowing too much" which may limit the development of lay pastoral care, as well as limits set by the unwillingness of the clergy to let go of the subtle kind of control which pastoral care provides.

A related lay development in pastoral counseling is the emergence of support groups, often based on the model of Alcoholics Anonymous, where people sharing similar experiences meet regularly for support and growth. These groups often meet in churches or are started in churches. Some have professionally trained leaders, but many do not. While not claiming to be pastoral counseling, these groups certainly extend the caring ministry of the church. As our society becomes even more aware of the healing power of sharing the pain and discoveries of life, there will surely be more such groups formed. Whether pastoral counseling can (or even should) adopt a more intentional relationship to these groups remains to be seen. If there can be support without interference and domination, that would seem the better direction to take.

The Larger Scale of Pastoral Counseling

An "ecumenism" of scope is also growing in pastoral counseling. Earlier the pastor-parishioner relationship was the primary unit of investigation. The individual counselor and individual client constituted the counseling process. Increasingly the primary unit is now the married couple, the family, the group, or, in a few instances, whole communities. At first it may simply have been a concern for greater efficiency which led in this direction. But as new theoretical formulations have emerged—family systems theory, for example—it is increasingly argued that one-to-one counseling is simply unproductive in many instances, since the relevant pathology is woven into the fabric of the entire system. Indeed the identified patient, in whatever way he or she is calling attention to the problem, may be trying to escape an intolerable situation and thus may be more ready for change than are other parts of the system.

But it is one thing to grasp systems theory and quite another matter to function successfully as a family or group systems counselor. Pastoral counseling, as a discipline, does not yet seem to have come to any consensus about how much of this skill is required of every pastor, and how much should be left to specialists. Every pastor does, in fact, work with groups and with families. So it would seem that some skills would be mandatory—the ability to identify systemic pathology and to intervene at the points of greater vulnerability and promise. But with their busy schedules, it does not seem humanly possible to expect the pastor to maintain extended group or family counseling relationships. Nor is it wise to expect it, since one of the discoveries in family counseling has been the value of a team of leaders, sharing and enriching the counseling process from the resources of differing ages, genders, styles, and life experiences.

Pastors in multiple staff settings have opportunities to develop counseling team approaches which would be more difficult in single pastor parishes. But there are also limits set by temperament and political wisdom. Successful family counselors are sometimes flamboyant, unpredictable, and very directive. Many pastors are not like that, nor would it be wise for them to be that way, given the complex leadership roles and relationships they must maintain in the congregation.

Ecumenism of Varied Experience

Finally there is an "ecumenism of outlook" growing in modern pastoral counseling. Partly this is a recovery of the theological and ethical character of the discipline, noted earlier. But it is more complex than that.

Newly recognized varieties of individual and communal religious experience and their symbolizations are finding their ways into our thinking about pastoral counseling. The experience of women provides a useful example. Feminist theology is recovering lost or suppressed dimensions of the religious experience and history of women. Feminist pastoral counseling is attempting to develop the implications of these recoveries for pastoral counseling, not rejecting the contributions of the modern clinical disciplines, but trying to be very clear about the hidden or overt sexism to be found there, and trying to construct a new kind of pastoral counseling combining feminist and clinical insights. Such developments are also underway among blacks, Hispanics, Native Americans, and in the churches of Africa and Asia.

Theology, Ethics and Practical Theology

In surveying the ways in which pastoral counseling is becoming more "ecumenical," one trend was noted at several points: the recovery of the theological and ethical character of the discipline. Some might argue that these were never lost. They might concede that in the heyday of psychotherapy and the clinical movement, it might have *seemed* that chaplains, pastoral counselors and clergy were doing exactly the same kind of counseling as that of the social worker, clinical psychologist or psychiatrist. But even then, this argument would continue, the office held by the counselor and the shared faith assumptions of counselor and client would make this counseling religiously meaningful, even if overtly religious symbols and concepts were absent. But even if that argument is granted, surely the adoption of the clinical disciplines in pastoral counseling has often not been accompanied by careful theological reflection or ethical analysis. Too many assumptions have gone unchallenged, most notably the assumption that the norms of health and pathology in the clinical disciplines can simply be accommodated to Christian theology and ethics.

The trend today is clearly in the direction of reaffirming the distinctively religious and theological dimensions of pastoral counseling. Chaplains and pastoral counselors emphasize this theme in their multi-professional dialogues. The literature of pastoral care and counseling is now rich with references to the religious resources for counseling to be found in scripture, theology, and devotional or spiritual literature (Oden, 1983). Everyone now seems to be in favor of more theology!

But it is not clear how far or deep this recovery of theology will run, or what directions it will take in the field of pastoral counseling. Don

Browning is arguing that pastoral theology and counseling belong in theological ethics, because of their obvious concern for norms and methods of Christian living. While the ethical dimension of pastoral counseling certainly deserves greater attention than it has received, Browning's view does not yet seem to be widely held in the pastoral disciplines. Oden and Lapsley (1983), among others, continue to argue for the foundational theological and methodological character of pastoral theology and counseling. The popularity and prestige of pastoral counseling in theological study (at least among students and pastors) would suggest that their practitioners will not be easily subsumed into the department of ethics.

Perhaps the recovery of theology in pastoral counseling will have to proceed in this piecemeal fashion. A better way, in my view, is to be found among those who are trying to recover *practical* theology, as the discipline of relating the various academic fields of theological study to the functional areas of ministry. For too long the so-called practical fields were regarded as disciplines which applied the truths discovered in traditional academic inquiry. Pastoral theology has been in the forefront of the practical disciplines in challenging this viewpoint. But alas this viewpoint still persists, and is strongly entrenched in many theological school curricula as well as in the folkways and customs of theological academe.

Farley's (1983) work and recent writing in practical theology by Tracey and Browning (1976) are hopeful signs that a more serious and substantive challenge to this old prejudice can be carried through. For this effort to succeed, changes in both attitude and the conception of the field will be required.

People in the practical disciplines will need to acknowledge and renounce attitudes of subservience and defensiveness regarding academic disciplines. This attitudinal recovery will come as the practical disciplines gain greater clarity and confidence about their character and methods. But it is partly a matter of consciously rejecting the biases and caricatures rife in the practical disciplines, which are more at home among practitioners out in the churches but which are forced to live in academe, where the power of reflective thought and logic prevail, not action. Being on foreign soil should be claimed as an opportunity for missionary work by those in the practical fields, not used as an excuse for building walls of isolation.

A new conception of the field of practical theology is also needed, along with attitudinal changes. This new conception will be created in two ways: (1) by becoming better academicians themselves (not, however, by aping academic style and jargon in the practical literature, but by more disciplined study in the academic disciplines); (2) by distinguishing between the methods appropriate to the academic disciplines (the interpretation of texts and the logic of inquiry) and those appropriate to the practical disciplines (the interpretation of complex situations and the logic of human action).

It would seem that this kind of methodological clarification has the greatest promise for the recovery of the theological character of all of the practical disciplines, including pastoral counseling. If the methods of interpretation of complex situations and the logic of human action are carried through adequately, all of the so-called academic disciplines will be brought into play, as necessary resources for understanding and action, but not as providers of abstract truth. Truth in practice will be created and will emerge from pastoral action itself, not deductively or propositionally.

Pastoral Counseling and Social Change

Along with the recovery of its theological and ethical character, it will be important for pastoral counseling in the future to clarify its orientation to social change. For too many years the dependence of pastoral counseling on psychotherapy has made it seem that the primary goal is a healthy or well-adjusted personality. Pastoral counseling did not often act as a social critic or question the assumption that social adjustment was a generally worthy aim. While it is no longer possible to hold this assumption (thanks to the social upheavals and emerging pluralism of recent years), pastoral counseling has not yet clarified its tasks in relation to social change.

If the aim of pastoral counseling, and indeed churches in general, is the formation of communities of people willing to love and care for their world, and to challenge those who would exploit rather than care, then a force for social change is implicitly grounded in pastoral counseling itself.

If people are to become loving and caring, they will not only need assistance in the expression of love, but in being able to resist and challenge those who follow other gods. In an affluent economy, this may mean learning how to live simply, without excessive consumption or the wasteful use of resources. It may mean working in politics to elect people who will develop programs for human relief and justice. In violent and oppressive political regimes, expressing love may take the form of revolutionary struggle.

Pastoral counseling will need to transcend its Western and privatistic assumptions if it is to extend its proper work into the formation of Christian character which can *resist* and *struggle* as expressions of love, along with the more familiar form of care. Other trends noted in this chapter will help—renewed theological and ethical concern, clinical eclecticism, cultural pluralism. But pastoral counseling will need a more explicit and intentional alliance with social ethics and theology at those points where the promise of God's new age judges all present social systems and points to the society which is to come. Pastoral counseling along with religious education and social prophecy should be preparing people for that new age, not primarily fitting people into the present age.

Conclusion

Throughout this chapter the "ecumenical" direction of modern pastoral counseling has been emphasized. Other characterizations might have seemed fitting—pluralism, fragmentation, disintegration into competing factions. But "ecumenical" seemed a better term, not only because it is more hopeful, but also because it expresses a commitment to "be together" while acknowledging authentic differences with respect and in a relationship of mutuality.

This analysis does, however, raise the question of how pastoral counseling will retain any sense of being a singular discipline in the face of all this diversification. This is the same question faced by theology, and by the ecumenical church. Pastoral counseling will share in the process of discovering the answers which will be eventually given to these questions. A new kind of discipline will surely emerge, with a new kind of singularity. Claims to understand or know how to treat human problems in general will be more modest and qualified than at present. Many definitions of the human condition will be considered, not just one rooted in ancient Athens and Jerusalem and elaborated in Western patriarchal civilization. These varied definitions will require varied therapies. So the singularity of the pastoral counseling discipline will rest on increased understanding of and respect for this variability.

That is a vital, necessary, but still minimal and insufficient degree of singularity. Pastoral counseling will also, like the other disciplines of theology, struggle with *shared human symbols and concepts*, which represent a Christian theological outlook for the *whole* church, East and West, North and South, men and women, persons of every color and culture. While they will still be variously symbolized and expressed, such affirmations as the value of every person, the right to just and humane treatment, the divine character of love and its transforming power in human lives, and the initiative God takes to transform through love will be foundational. Pastoral counseling will then seek to preserve modern and scientific understandings of the ways that love is received and given, and to reclaim traditional ways of understanding and manifesting that love.

Note

1. The series of volumes on pastoral counseling published by Fortress, for example.

Bibliography

Browning, D. *The Moral Context of Pastoral Care*, Philadelphia: Westminster, 1976.

Clinebell, H. *Basic Types of Pastoral Counseling*, Nashville: Abingdon, 1966.

Farley, E. *Theologia: The Fragmentation and Unity of Theological Education*, Philadelphia: Fortress, 1983.

Lapsley, J.N. "Practical Theology and Pastoral Care: An Essay in Practical Theology." In D.S. Browning (ed.), *Practical Theology*, San Francisco: Harper & Row, 1983.

Oden, T. *Pastoral Theology*, San Francisco: Harper & Row, 1983.

Oglesby, W. *Biblical Themes for Pastoral Care*, Nashville: Abingdon, 1980.

Joann Wolski Conn

Spirituality and Personal Maturity

What is the relationship of Christian spirituality and personal maturity? Doesn't Christianity promote self-denial and psychological maturity promote self-fulfillment? How can these two be reconciled? Isn't there an unbearable tension in pastoral counseling when the outcome of counseling should be personal autonomy and better control of one's life, while the aim of Christian discipleship is caring for others' needs and surrendering to God's will?

The most productive way to answer these questions, I believe, is to proceed in three steps.

First, the term "spirituality" will be defined and explained. Its relationship to a similar term, "religious experience," will also be noted. Spirituality as an academic discipline will be compared and contrasted briefly with James Fowler's faith-theory. Then I will summarize the Christian tradition's view of the goal of spirituality and the way to reach it.

Second, the goal of human development—personal maturity—will be examined. Although the most prevalent notion of maturity is that of personal autonomy, I will emphasize another persuasive view that suggests development beyond autonomy. This section will conclude by specifying the advantages for pastoral counselors of this view of maturity.

Lastly, furnished with a useful definition of maturity, we will be ready to answer the central question: What is the relationship between Christian spirituality and personal maturity? There will be two types of answers. General answers with some of their practical consequences for pastoral counselors are followed by specific issues. The latter will demonstrate the inseparability and reciprocal effects of spirituality and maturity.

What Is Spirituality?

Spirituality is a term often distorted by dualism or naive religious assumptions. When spirit is assumed to mean "the opposite of matter," then spirituality is only associated with invisible thoughts or feelings. When spirit is defined as "what God is," then spirituality becomes a narrowly religious term.

However, when spirituality is understood as a contemporary philosophical and psychological as well as religious term, these distortions are corrected. Philosophers such as Paul Ricoeur (1967) and Martin Heidegger (1962) explore our human capacity for spirituality, that is, for self-transcendence. Our ability to go beyond ourselves in truthful knowledge, loving relationship and free commitment exemplifies this self-transcendence. In psychology Gerald May (1982b, p. 32), for example, uses the term spirituality for the aspect of personal essence that gives it power, energy, and motive force. The religious meaning of spirituality is both general and specific. General or universal religious spirituality refers to the actualization of human self-transcendence (i.e., capacity for relating, knowing, committing ourselves) by whatever is acknowledged as the ultimate or the Holy: what is acknowledged as "religious." Rudolf Otto (1958) exemplifies this approach. Within religious spirituality are the specific spiritualities such as Jewish, Christian, Hindu. In each specific spirituality the basic components are the same: the human, and the Holy. Yet each is interpreted according to its own diverse anthropological and religious assumptions.

Christian spirituality involves the human capacity for self-transcending knowledge, love and commitment as well as the presence of the Holy to us. Christian theology affirms belief in the actualization of this human capacity through the experience of the Holy as God, in Jesus Christ, by the gift of the Spirit. As I explain more fully elsewhere (Conn 1980), because this God, Jesus, and the Spirit only come to us through body-community-history influenced experience and symbols, Christian spirituality includes every dimension of human life. Thus Christian spiritual development cannot legitimately be identified only with the soul, nor be exclusively associated with prayer, mysticism or institutional religion.

Does spirituality mean the same thing as "religious experience" or what James Fowler (1981) calls faithing?

In its philosophical sense, spirituality refers to a universal human capacity (i.e., drive for self-transcendence) which is not always interpreted religiously. When religious experience refers to the "depth" or "ultimate" dimension of all human experience and not to any specific experience, as John Smith explains (1968), it is analogous to general religious spirituality. What "spirituality" intends to add is emphasis on the human relationship to what activates or actualizes that experience: some relationship between the human and the Ultimate or Holy. Religious spirituality as an academic discipline deals with religious experience as experience, that is, in all its psychological complexity and cultural specificity, as well as in its cross-traditional manifestations and theological affirmations. Just as general religious experience may be focused or epitomized in a specific experience such as prayer or artistic expression, so general religious spirituality may be specified in the unique characteristics of Christian or Buddhist spirituality. Or even more specifically, Christian spirituality may be experienced or studied according to its nuance as Roman Catholic or Lutheran; or Catholic may be viewed in its emphasis as married or celibate, or as Carmelite or Franciscan. Religious spirituality, then, is closely related to religious experience.

Spirituality as an academic discipline is similar in many ways to James Fowler's faith-theory. By focusing on the structure of faith as an activity, Fowler (1981, pp. xii-34) describes faith as the way we make and maintain meaning in terms of a pattern of relationship to an ultimate center of value and power. Faith is a universal, fundamental, infinitely varied reality which grows in stage-like developmentally related styles, from early egocentrism to later universality.

Faith, like the term spirituality, has both a non-religious and a religious sense. It may refer to universal human faith in an ultimate that, like Tillich's (1957) "ultimate concern," need not be transcendent. However, Fowler (1981, p. 293) maintains that faith, at the most mature stages, will take essentially religious forms. Like spirituality, faith involves relationship to the Transcendent, its knowing is fused with affectivity, and it always has a social dimension. Relatedness to the ultimate qualifies relationships to persons and things. Like spirituality as an academic discipline, faith-theory is concerned with what promotes or inhibits mature relationship to the Transcendent, it examines the complex characteristics of God-images, and a primary source of data are women's and men's autobiographical statements about their beliefs and values.

Fowler himself (1976, pp. 203–206) has pointed out some differences between faith-stages and the levels or stages in the quest for spiritual growth found in traditions of spirituality. First, there is the issue of structure rather than content. Faith-stages are a matter of structure: the more general psychodynamic and psychosocial functions of a patterned process of knowing, valuing and acting. In spiritual paths, however, the goal is not the faith-structure of Fowler's Stage 5 or 6. Persons may, in fact, develop those structures in advanced spiritual paths, but that pattern would be the secondary by-product of their focused spiritual quest. But whereas faith-stage theory makes no claims to religious sufficiency, spiritual paths do claim to be truly tried and tested ways toward union with the Holy or the Transcendent. This second difference is not merely a matter of prescriptive (i.e., spiritual paths) and descriptive (i.e., faith-stages). For Fowler does envision stage theory as a kind of normative model against which other criteria for spiritual development may be tested.

Spirituality as an academic discipline differs from faith-theory in several ways. Whereas faith-theory is principally structural and psychological, spirituality includes content as well as structure, and it incorporates psychology yet is multi-disciplinary. Unlike faith-theory, spirituality can include, as proper to its discipline, accepting as valid the divine action toward humans that is affirmed in religious belief-traditions.

Growth in specifically Christian spirituality is our concern here. Is there a pattern or model that is characteristic of the way Christian spirituality develops? Yes, when there is agreement about the goal of spirituality, there is general agreement about the way to journey toward that goal. For example, when one is influenced more by dualistic philosophy than by scripture and the witness of holy women and men, or by a narrow view of "sin," the goal can be "the perfection of the soul." This goal, then, generates models of spiritual growth that stress purification from whatever is material and sinful, and are suspicious of anything "human," such as feelings or sexuality. On the other hand, whenever one relies on authentic sources (e.g., all of scripture; experience of lives open to God) another goal and pattern emerges.

A sampling of classical and contemporary writers demonstrates a common understanding of the goal of Christian spirituality. It also shows a common theme-with-variations regarding the way to reach this goal.

A classical author, such as Catherine of Siena, in her *Dialogue* (1980, pp. 65, 92, 100) hears God say, "I am their goal," and is advised that all should seek this goal by loving God's goodness in themselves and through all created things, avoiding all spiritual self-centeredness. Teresa of Avila (1980, pp. 53, 301) teaches that our aim should be conformity to God's will which is that we be God's friends, be the very image and likeness of God. We accomplish our aim through prayer that is rooted in love of neighbor, humility and detachment.

Contemporary authors repeat this classical vision of the goal: a loving, wholistic relationship to God that is Jesus' own relationship. However, their expression of the goal and the paths toward it use more explicitly psychological vocabulary. Sandra Schneiders (1983, pp. 52–55) defines the goal as "participating in the revelation dynamic centered in Jesus." Signs of growth in this process are integration, interior freedom, deepened faith commitment, and a balanced and intense apostolic involvement. For Henri Nouwen (1981), our aim is to be centered, to be rooted in the life of God's Spirit of love within us, just as Jesus was. How can we best do this? By careful listening and responding to God's presence in our lives. Incorporate silence and prayer into our actions of counseling and teaching. Develop a determination and capacity to be open and stay open to God's gifts. Stay attentive and free from compulsions so that the concerns of God's reign can be our personal center. Expressing the Reformed tradition, Rowan Williams (1980) focuses spirituality issues on the implications of the cross. Because Christianity demands dealing with the human history of Jesus in all its concreteness and complexity, the goal of Christian development is not enlightenment but wholeness. This means we must accept life's complicated experiences as the theatre for the hidden God who works in the cross; that is, God influences and supports us in ambiguity and contradiction, in human inadequacy and failure. Kenneth Leech (1980) also sees the goal as wholeness. But he means by that a wholeheartedness or a unified, free personality aware of and involved in the Spirit's way of leading one into deeper union with God in Christ. Given this goal, development is measured by one's ability to involve one's total self in God's own involvement in one's life, and others' lives.

In summary, then, both classical and contemporary sources demonstrate a common theme-with-variations. Relationship is the goal of spirituality and the pathways to it are means of developing and sustaining relationship. Ernest Larkin (1981) notices that a closer look reveals three relationships and two movements within each relationship. All the sources are really describing three basic relationships: to self, to God, to others. The relationship to self is primarily the acceptance of our limitations as well as our gifts, to God the attitude of trust and to others compassion and hospitality. Within each relationship there are movements of both renunciation and self-fulfillment. Christian spirituality is distorted when seen as primarily self-denial. Indeed, that aspect is as essential for spirituality as it is for mental health, but it has been exaggerated. The positive aspects of peace, consolation, personal fulfillment, and human joy are just as significant in the tradition as detachment and self-surrender. What must be emphasized is their proper balance at appropriate stages of spiritual growth.

Alerted by feminist concerns, I notice two other movements within each relationship: independence as well as belonging. The traditional themes of centeredness and inner freedom presume that one has sufficient self-identity and independence. Otherwise one would blandly conform to whatever enthusiasm was current. The traditional emphasis on self-surrender (belonging) is the advice and experience of persons in mature stages of prayer. At the appropriate moments of one's life with God this is good advice. At other moments the biblical emphasis is upon accepting God's empowerment in one's life; it is on sensing oneself as deeply accepted just as one honestly is before God. Like the movements of renunciation and self-fulfillment, the longings for both independence and belonging are integral to all the relationships of Christian spirituality. What must be emphasized is their proper balance at appropriate stages of spiritual growth.

Clearly, these concerns that Christian spirituality raises in religious terms are also psychological issues: the goal of human life and the process of development toward that goal. But how does psychology view these same issues? What is psychology's view of life's goal, its view of human maturity? How does psychology suggest we reach it? If we now explore this psychological issue, we can later draw out some practical implications for the relationship between Christian spirituality and human maturity.

What Is Human Maturity?

Although the most prevalent notion of maturity is one of psychological autonomy and independence, of taking control of one's life, another persuasive view is emerging that suggests qualitative development beyond autonomy.

Doubt about autonomy as the principal criterion of personal maturity has surfaced in the last decade (Miller, 1976; Gilligan, 1978, 1982). Robert Kegan, of Harvard University and the Massachusetts School of Professional Psychology, recently published a study (1982) which places these insights about autonomy and maturity within a comprehensive view of human development. What follows is a short summary of his explanation of maturity and the process through which we attain it. The summary then becomes the basis for noting the advantages of this approach for pastoral counseling.

Central to Kegan's theory (1982, pp. 1–21) is an understanding of development as meaning-making activity. This meaning-making is not only the unifying, but also the generating context for both thought and feeling, as well as self and other (subject and object). Evolutionary activity involves the very creating of the other (a process of differentiation) as well as our relating to it (a process of integration). Self-other relations emerge out of a lifelong process of development: a succession of more adequate differentiations of the self from the world in which it is embedded, each creating a more complex object of relation. Maturity in each phase of the process is a relative triumph of "relationship to" rather than "embeddedness in."

Psychoanalytic theory looks to infancy for its basic themes and categories. Kegan, however, in his constructive-developmental view (1982, p. 77), regards infancy as qualitatively no different from any other moment in the lifespan. What is fundamental is the activity of meaning-making evolution. The distinctive features of infancy are to be understood in the context of the same activity which is necessary throughout a person's life. Recurrence of these distinctive features in new forms later on in development is not seen as later manifestations of infancy issues, but contemporary manifestations of making-the-meaning-of "self" and "other," just as infancy issues are, in their own time, manifestations of meaning-making.

Kegan explains five developmental phases or stages which may describe—but not necessarily be—a person's life history (1982, pp. 85–110). Each stage involves a certain kind of balance between differentiation and integration, between the yearning for autonomy and inclusion. Each balance is a temporary solution to the lifelong tension between the yearnings for inclusion and distinctness. Each balance resolves the tension in a different way. At one phase the balance will tip slightly in favor of autonomy, while at the next stage it will favor inclusion.

Infancy is a transition from complete incorporation in the parent into the *Impulsive* balance (stage one) of two year olds. This transformation occurs through a process that is repeated: decentration, emergence from embeddedness. Gradually infants cease being their reflexes and, instead, have them. In disembedding themselves from their reflexes, two year olds come to have reflexes rather than be them. The new self is now embedded in impulses or wishes, in that which coordinates the reflexes. The new self is "hatched out" through a process of differentiation from that which was the very subject of personal organization and which now becomes the object of a new subjectivity which coordinates it. In this impulsive balance the meaning of the self *is* its impulses or perceptions which now *have* reflexes (the other, object).

A distinguishing feature of the *Imperial* balance (stage two) is a self-containment that was not present before. Now the self is its enduring interests or wishes, its needs. Therefore, a self-concept can emerge. The capacity to have one's impulses, rather than be them, allows a new sense of freedom, independence, agency. The transition out of this stage of embeddedness in one's needs brings into being that need (or interest or wish) mediating reality which we refer to when we speak of mutuality. From this perspective, it is clearer now that the evolutionary balance of stage two tilted toward independence and stage three will retain a certain freedom yet lean toward belonging. One consequence of moving the meaning of self from *being* needs to *having* needs is the ability to talk about feelings now *as* feelings rather than social negotiations. However, *during* the transition this change can be felt as perplexing. Its most common manifestation is adolescent moodiness.

Because stages three to five are the everyday experience of pastoral counselors, I will give a little more thorough explanation of them than I did of earlier stages. Later, this will permit me to correlate these processes toward maturity with issues in Christian spirituality.

In the *Interpersonal* balance (stage three) the self's feelings are, by definition, shared; someone else is in there from the beginning. Its strength is its capacity to be conversational, freeing itself from the imperial balance's frenzy-creating constant urge to find out what other people will do about how it feels and acts. Its weakness lies in its inability to consult itself about that conversation, that shared reality. It cannot because it *is* that shared reality.

At this stage my personal conflicts are not really conflicts about what I want and what someone else wants. On closer examination, they consistently turn out to be conflicts between what I want as part of *this* shared reality and what I want as part of *that* shared reality. To ask me in this evolutionary balance to resolve such a conflict by bringing both shared realities before me is to touch precisely the limits of this way of making my self and the other. "Bringing it *before* me" means not being subject to it, being able to take it as an object, which is just what this balance cannot do.

When I live in this balance as an adult I am a prime candidate for assertiveness training, for learning to stand up for myself, for allowing more "selfish" attitudes, as if these were skills to be added on to whoever else I am. Much psychological and spiritual literature will talk about me as lacking self-esteem, as being "easy" because I want other people to like me. But this does not really address me in my predicament, in what I hope for. It is not as if this self which supposedly lacks self-esteem is the same self that can stand up for itself independently of how other people feel. It is more that there *is* no self independent of "other people liking." This self is constructed differently. The difference is not an affective matter—how much I like myself or how much self-confidence I have. The difference goes to the fundamental ground, to the way I construct the meaning of my self. This balance lacks coordination of its shared psychological space "pieced out" in a variety of mutualities. It lacks the self-coherence in these varieties that is taken as the cornerstone of "identity" or the more public coherence ordinarily meant by "ego." For Kegan, (1982, p. 96) it would be incorrect to say that an ego or identity is lacking at stage three, or that here there is a weaker ego. What there is here is a qualitatively—not a quantitatively—different ego, a different way of making the ego cohere.

Although this balance is interpersonal it is not intimate. That is because what might appear to be intimacy here is the self's *source* rather than its aim. There is no self to share with another; instead the other is necessary to bring the self into being. This is fusion, not intimacy. This way of making the self generates much that can appear to be worthy of religious admiration: spending one's life caring for others, deferring to others' needs and interests. Precisely because these activities can appear to be Christian self-sacrifice, intimate love, or religious dedication they have significant implications for our overall concern with the relationship between spirituality and personal maturity. Let it suffice now simply to call attention to these religious overtones while the focus of this section is psychological. Later I will expand on the implications for spirituality inherent in Kegan's view of maturity.

Persons in stage three are uncomfortable with anger; actually they may not even *be* angry in situations which might be expected to make a person angry. Anger owned and expressed is a risk to the interpersonal construction of the self. My getting angry amounts to a declaration of a sense of self separate from my relation to you—that I am a person too, that I have my own feelings. It is also a declaration that you are a separate person who can survive my being angry, that it is not an ultimate matter for you. There are hundreds of reasons why people might hesitate to express anger when they feel it. But it seems that persons in this balance undergo experiences, such as being victimized by their husbands, which do not make them angry because they cannot know themselves apart from the interpersonal relationship; instead they feel sad, wounded, or incomplete. Again, the possibility that these responses can be praised by religious people as "patience," "long suffering," or even "carrying the cross," has significant implications for pastoral counselors.

In differentiating itself from embeddedness in interpersonalism, meaning-evolution makes a self which maintains coherence in relationships and so achieves an identity. This sense of self-ownership, self-direction is its principal characteristic. In moving from "I am my relationships" to "I have relationships," there is now someone who does this having, who brings into being a kind of psychic regulation, law, or *Institutional* balance (stage four).

Desire to "transcend the interpersonal" makes people uneasy who want to stress—and rightly, I believe—that other people should remain important to us throughout our lives. However, others are not lost by emergence from embeddedness in the interpersonal. On the contrary, now they are found. The issue is how "other people" are found. The *Institutional* balance includes other people in the new context of their place in the maintainance of a self-system.

A strength here is the new capacity of persons for independence to own themselves, rather than have all the aspects of themselves owned by various relationships. Feelings arising out of one's relationships no longer constitute the "self"; instead they are mediated by a self-system. Within this very strength lies a limit. The "self" is identified with the organization or system it is trying to run smoothly. Regulation rather than mutuality is now ultimate. Here the question is not "Do you still like me?" but "Does my control still stand?" This evolutionary balance allows one the stability and integrity of personal boundaries, of deciding, in a relationship, who will get in, and when. However, the primacy of control inhibits mutuality and is still far from intimacy.

The rebalancing that characterizes the fifth ego stage (*Interdividual*) is, finally, the achievement of human maturity. The self is separated from identification with maintainance of the self-system or institution; there is now a self which *has* control instead of *being* the control. Unlike the previous stages which tilted toward either independence or belonging, this rebalancing has both of them equally.

One's construction of human community is significant here. One now has the capacity to join others not as fellow-instrumentalists (stage two) nor as partners in fusion (stage three), nor as loyalists (stage four), but as individuals who are value-originating and history-making. Whereas the institutional self brought the interpersonal "into" the self, this new construction brings the self back into the interpersonal. There now is a "self" to be brought to others, rather than derived from others. Genuine "self" sacrifice is now a possibility. Intimacy can, finally, be a reality. There is a self which can surrender its counter-dependent independence for freely chosen interdependence.

The meaning of "work" and "dedication" are revolutionized at this stage. If one no longer *is* one's self-control, neither is one any longer the duties, work roles, career which maintaining a self-system gives rise to. Because one *has* a career rather than being a career, one is no longer vulnerable to performance-failure as an ultimate humiliation; one can "hear" negative reports about one's activities since one no longer *is* these activities.

Maturity is, then, the outcome of a process of balancing the lifelong tension between the yearnings for inclusion and distinctness. Maturity is, basically, the deep personal openness which comes from having an independent identity, yet recognizing the personal limitations of independence and autonomy as the goal of development. Valuing, instead, the intimacy of mutual inter-dependence, mature persons are those who can freely surrender themselves, who can risk a genuinely mutual relationship.

Because maturity as openness, as surrender, can too easily be counterfeit, criteria for evaluating authentic surrender are imperative. Gerald May, a psychiatrist with extensive knowledge of spirituality, provides some pertinent guidelines (1982b, pp. 307–308). First, surrender is conscious. One is aware of everything that is happening at the time; there is no robotic mindlessness. Second, it is intentional. It may be elicited from one's heart, but it is never forced or compelled in any way. Third, it is a responsible act. One is willing to accept responsibility for the act if it turns out to be a mistake, if in fact the surrender has been misplaced. Fourth, it assumes responsibility for the consequences as well as for the act itself. There can be no blaming of any other person, cause, force or entity. Fifth, it represents a willingness to engage the fullness of life with the fullness of oneself. It cannot be an escape or an avoidance.

Having summarized the process by which we may reach maturity and the criteria for evaluating its authentic presence, we can now appreciate some advantages of this position for a pastoral counselor. First, this view of maturity allows counselors to see themselves as involved in the same life process as the client; instead of seeing themselves as the "healthy" ones who help the "sick" person they see themselves as also striving to make the meaning of their self and others by balancing the tension between distinctness and inclusion. Second, it takes full account of the two greatest yearnings in human experience: to be included and to be independent. These yearnings are central to all accounts of religious experience which, like Kegan's approach, should always view these yearnings in relation to each other. Third, it recognizes the equal dignity of each yearning. Consequently, it is a corrective to all present developmental frameworks that are biased toward autonomy. The latter consistently define growth in terms of differentiation and increasing autonomy, and lose sight of the fact that adaptation is equally about integration and attachment. As sensitive women and men are recently pointing out (Gilligan, 1978; Kegan, 1982; May, 1982; Miller, 1976) the result of this bias has been that differentiation (the stereotypically male overemphasis in this human ambivalence) is favored with the language of growth and development, while attachment (the stereotypically female overemphasis) gets referred to in terms of dependency and immaturity. Kegan's inclusion of both aspects at every stage is less easily bent to this prejudice because it consciously listens equally to women's and men's expressions of their own experience. It is far different from Jung's theory of the complementarity of symbolically "masculine" and "feminine" characteristics in each person (1953). For Jung's notion of "the feminine" is extrapolated entirely from the theory of male ego development without ever testing its explanation of "the feminine" against women's own understanding of themselves. From the beginning Kegan listens equally to women's and men's experience. Therefore he can legitimately generalize (1982, p. 210) that if women are more vulnerable to fusion (balance three), it is also possible that they are more capable of intimacy (balance five). And if men find it easier to reach psychological autonomy (balance four)—not to be confused with human maturity—it is also possible that they find it harder to evolve to mature mutuality and relational inter-dependence (balance five). Lastly, Kegan always contextualizes the individual in two ways. Initially he reminds us that a person is continually settling and resettling this issue of precisely what is the self and the other; the relationship between the individual and the social is made and remade at each balance. Also, he reminds us that each of us is always in some culture of embeddedness that promotes or inhibits our development according to the way it confirms certain of our attitudes and actions, contradicts others, and stays put to allow us to reintegrate it into the new meaning of our self and others (1982, pp. 115–132).

What Is the Relationship Between Christian Spirituality and Personal Maturity?

Equipped with an understanding of maturity that envisions development beyond autonomy we are ready to explore our central question. What is the relationship between Christian spirituality and human maturity? I will approach the question in two ways—first some general answers, then some specific issues which concretize the way in which this relationship operates. In both approaches my concern will be with insights that could help pastoral counselors promote their own as well as their clients' spiritual and human maturity.

One general answer to our question comes from theology. Here the question about spirituality's relationship to human maturity is raised in terms of grace and nature. God's grace (i.e., God's offer of loving relationship) is sovereign and freely given. Because humans cannot earn it and do not deserve it, we wonder just what is our part in this relationship. Can we actively deepen or insure the relationship? Does the power of grace eliminate our human freedom? Through the years theologians have constantly debated these complex questions. However, out of these discussions two trends or emphases are clear: a Reformation emphasis (from Luther) on the primacy of God's action, and a Roman Catholic emphasis (from the Eastern Fathers and Thomas Aquinas) which affirms that grace builds on nature—grace constantly works through human nature. In contrast to the older antagonistic atmosphere between mainstream Protestants and Catholics in which these "emphases" became "opposing positions" our current ecumenical climate promotes mutual appreciation of both sides of the issue. Pastoral counselors can learn from their own experience that both theological insights are significant. For example, most often our "eyes of faith" are opened to God's gracious presence at the very times our ordinary human development opens us to appreciate human friendship, to ponder the cycle of death and birth, and to struggle with our own resistance to change or conversion of heart. Yet, the normal processes of our lives are not entirely predictable nor subject to our complete control. We are often gifted with what is seen eventually to be more than we could have desired or more than we thought we could stand. And we discover from experience that God works through our ordinary life-experiences yet acts in ways beyond our control or complete comprehension. From this perspective human maturity and Christian spirituality are inseparable but not identical.

Another general answer comes from psychology. Here spirituality and human maturity are aspects of the relationship between religion and psychology. Conclusions about their mutual antagonism or compatibility depend, of course, on prior assumptions about both components of the relationship.

Four conclusions are common. First, if one assumes that the human personality grows to fulfillment primarily by satisfying basic needs, by greater differentiation, and by self-directed control, and one also assumes that religion is basically authoritarian or that it is an extrinsic "higher" demand for conduct that human nature itself finds repugnant, then one conclusion is inevitable: religion and psychology are incompatible or are adversaries. However, if one can admit elements of exaggeration as well as kernels of truth in this first position, then a second conclusion is possible. Their relationship can be mutually beneficial precisely because each side is legitimately critical of some real inadequacies. Psychology helps religion by highlighting its persistent tendency to promote dependency and authoritarianism and its suspicion of legitimate pleasure. Religion can also be helpful when it criticizes psychology's tendency to reduce the human person to needs and satisfactions as well as its inclination to use an unsophisticated understanding of religion in its diagnosis of patients' problems. Yet another conclusion follows when psychology admits development beyond autonomy and when religion affirms autonomy as legitimate and necessary for authentic self-donation and genuine religious dedication. Under these conditions their relationship can be reciprocal; one can spur the other. Human maturity (i.e., differentiation in and through relationship) can facilitate deeper Christian spirituality (i.e., wholehearted relationship to God). Equally, an adult relationship to God (i.e., an experience of empowering love) can promote human maturity (i.e., the ability to move beyond the boundaries of independence to risk a genuinely mutual interdependence, the willingness to risk intimacy and commitment). A variation on this conclusion would see religion and psychology as parallel but not identical. Some holistic psychological positions (e.g., M.S. Peck, 1978; G. May, 1982a,b) include within their definition of humanity a dimension of openness to transcendence, of need for what is beyond human decision and scientific "natural law": an intimacy of the self with its Source. This view of humanity notices the parallels of human growth with religious development. Yet it cautions us about the consequent tendency to imagine that we can control spiritual growth because we can influence and promote human growth. These two types of growth are often parallel, but the unexpected breakthrough of spiritual insight and religious love in persons of limited human development demonstrate that God's spirit permeates humanity in ways beyond psychology's comprehension.

Practical consequences flow from these general answers to the question about Christian spirituality's relationship to human maturity. In each theological and psychological answer given above, I surfaced hidden assumptions which can now become keys to understanding their practical consequences. For example, pastoral counselors and counselees who speak of tension between psychology's concern with self-fulfillment and religion's call to self-sacrifice ought to examine their own assumptions. Does Christian discipleship call one primarily to self-denial or to love? If love is primary, then whatever promotes honest free adult self-donation to God and others is promoting authentic religion. Is concern for self-fulfillment incompatible with adult self-donation? Not if one envisions the legitimacy of both satisfying autonomy and challenging movement beyond autonomy to adult intimacy. If one can question prior assumptions, then one can consider alternative conclusions. In another case, if couples expect their marriage problems to disappear because they have experienced being "born again" in the Spirit, they ought first to examine the roots of this false expectation. Questioning their assumption can promote more patience with each other in the process of working out the long-term consequences of the new sense of forgiveness and mutual love which often arises from authentic religious experience.

Against this background we can now turn to specific issues which concretize the way in which Christian spirituality relates to human maturity.

Pastoral counselors often clarify this relationship by doing two things: noticing the common ground they share with Christian spiritual directors as well as distinguishing each one's unique angle of vision onto that common ground. By examining the relationship of these ministries which deal primarily with either spirituality or maturity, we can distinguish the unique focus on each side of the relationship as well as demonstrate their inseparability and their reciprocal effects.

As a recent study points out (Barry and Connolly, 1982) common to both counselors and directors is their involvement in a working alliance which will go against another person's "defended" personality. Secular counselors would interpret the source of that alliance simply as the human drive toward life and growth, or as the tendency to self-actualization and the will-to-health. Both pastoral counselors and spiritual directors would agree with their secular colleagues as far as they go, yet would extend the interpretation to include its ultimate source: the indwelling Spirit of the living God who desires that we experience life abundantly. The life-force and the Source of this life are absolutely inseparable. In seeking an ultimate source for this drive to life, appreciating it, and counting on it, both pastoral counselors and spiritual directors have still more common ground.

Both counselors and directors make a mutual agreement or contract regarding what their client/directee wants and what they as the counselor/director can do. Now each one's unique entry-point to this common ground emerges. What the directees want differs from the clients' desires. The former primarily seek help in developing their relationship to God; the latter primarily desire help in order to see and solve a problem. The former want to move to autonomy and beyond to surrender to God; the latter usually want to achieve self-control, autonomy, and the ability to satisfy their needs. The former may need to concentrate first on the autonomy needed for movement beyond that to authentic self-surrender to God; the latter may eventually utilize their self-directed freedom in religious dedication. These would be inseparable from their primary goals, but not identical with them. The former want to experience with understanding and commitment the presence of God in their life; the latter want to relate better to others and to themselves. Of course, each one may also implicitly seek what the other desires. But the explicit focus differs.

What directors can do is both the same and different from what counselors can do. Like counselors, the directors can, first of all, clarify what those who come to them really do want. For example, if one wants adult surrender to God, then one must also want—or learn to want—the self-direction and autonomy that are the prerequisites of authentic self-surrender. Women, especially, can be very unclear about their basic desires. Because women are socialized to notice and respond to everyone else's desires, they frequently repress their own desires so much that they do not or cannot easily contact them. Or they cannot admit a longing for autonomy because they assume it means selfishness or self-centeredness. On the other hand, women will sometimes resist autonomy because they wisely suspect that autonomy is not the appropriate goal of human or spiritual maturity. What is detrimental for women—their embeddedness in relationships—can also generate something positive: this appreciation for the way attachment and belonging are just as valuable for human growth as differentiation and autonomy. What is significant for both men and women is noticing and evaluating one's basic desires. If one wants adult surrender to God, then one will want to examine what can easily appear to be religious charity but can actually be immature immersion in others' lives. As I noted earlier in the section on psychological maturity, to give unquestioning praise to persons who spend their lives on others, who defer to others' needs, who do not express a justified anger can actually retard their religious development. For true religion is the donation of one's authentic self to God and to others. These persons may have little or no self-identity and so must develop this psychological self-coherence in order to promote their religious growth. Directors may unintentionally reinforce immaturity when they use religious insights divorced from appropriate psychological insights. Because spirituality and maturity are inseparable, the immaturity reinforced here is both religious and psychological. Also, like the counselor the director looks for religious delusion or pathology which, unlike genuine religious experience, is compensatory and extremely self-serving. Again, like the counselor the director acts without conflicting loyalties. Spiritual direction is not "used" to keep a person in the seminary or in an unhappy marriage, nor is counseling a vehicle for promoting the counselor's own moral values. In contrast to the counselor, however, the director does not directly use the relationship with the directee to achieve the goal of their conversations. The director/directee relationship is completely subordinate (though significant) to the primary relationship attended to in their conversations: the relationship to God, in Jesus, by the power of the Spirit. That relationship to God is absolutely inseparable from the directee's everyday relationship to himself or herself and to everyone else (which are topics of the conversation) but it is not reduced to those relationships and is not entirely the product of those relationships. Without a faith-vision of life and without personal experience of seeking God in personal prayer and surrender of heart one cannot grasp the distinction I am making here. What helps to draw out this distinction most sharply, perhaps, is the contrast between what the director and counselor are *primarily* doing in each session. Primarily, counselors are using their human maturity (i.e., freedom from self-preoccupation, loving concern for the client, the fruit of their own struggles for integrated self-awareness) to facilitate the clients' own insights and self-direction. Primarily directors are surrendering themselves to God so that their maturity (i.e., themselves) might be the free struggling, flexible, humanly involved "instrument" for helping the directees notice and respond to God's directing presence in every aspect of their life. As John Carmody reminds us (1983, p. 134), "The love of God . . . is at least latent in all the dimensions of human living."

The inseparability and reciprocity of Christian spirituality and human maturity are most evident when we examine the third area of common ground shared by counselors and directors. Both facilitate a process of sharing inner states. In both counseling and direction, thoughts and feelings are noticed, described and evaluated. In both cases there is a formal process involving the hard work of self-knowledge and self-acceptance.

Christian discernment of the Spirit's gentle guidance in the directee's life is possible only through a process that is clearly psychological. For it is in "the secrets of the heart" that God's presence and guidance are revealed. Christian tradition is unanimous on this point. This is not the only place, but certainly our inner and outer lives must be integrated. Sharing the movement of one's deepest feelings and thoughts in prayer is the organizing focus of conversation in spiritual direction. Every other aspect of life is attended to also; it is noticed, however, as a dimension of one's relationship to God. God's presence and guidance emerge in my consciousness in direction as I share the four aspects of prayer which Barry and Connolly describe (1982, pp. 69–79): (1) noticing my feeling-response to life situations, (2) how I express this to God, Jesus, the Spirit, (3) how I listen for God's response to my expression of feeling, (4) how I express my response to God's being this way toward me. A few examples can illustrate this basic connection. As I react to humans who hurt me, so will I respond to the Source of life if "life has hurt me." If my self-image is so poor and weak that I am preoccupied with defending myself from being hurt by other's rejection, then I will tend to defend myself (often unconsciously) from intimacy with the Holy Other who might also reject me. As I have explained elsewhere (1980, p. 298), if I am developing a sense of myself as free and self-directed, then I must relate to a God who affirms and empowers my freedom if I am to preserve that self-identity. If my prior religious education or experience does not provide me with such a God-image, then I will either sustain my current sense of self and "reject God" (i.e., the only God I know) or try somehow to reconcile these conflicting images. The latter results in unresolved developmental issues: development toward religious intimacy with God is retarded because a free adult self cannot be intimate with an authoritarian God; development toward adult self-direction is difficult or impossible when a person believes such a stance is "wrong" or "against scriptural teaching" or "contrary to God's will."

Because of the reciprocal relationship between maturity and Christian spirituality, pastoral counselors can assist their client's growth by helping them see how their Christian experience fosters or inhibits their psychological development. Does their own or their client's Christian vision make them suspicious about emotion and sexuality as "arising from their lower nature"? Does it make them apprehensive about expressing anger because "Christian charity is long-suffering," or uncomfortable with ambiguity on moral issues because "biblical teaching is clear and absolute"? Does it foster wives' acceptance of their husbands' neglect or abuse because they should "obey their husband" or "carry their cross"? Does it reinforce men's socialization to be workaholics and perfectionists because they are impressed with the force of "Gospel demands," or "God's discipline," or "Christian ideals"? Or does their Christianity support women's equality and self-direction because it proclaims what Elisabeth Schüssler Fiorenza (1983) demonstrates is "egalitarian discipleship" and what Bernard Cooke (1983) explains is "reversal of the patriarchal/heirarchical model of God's Fatherhood"? Does it legitimate attention to what Roy Fairchild (1982, pp. 88–89) points out is discovering of a deeper identity because "Christ lives in me" and "God's intention can be realized through surrender of one's current self-definition"? Does it legitimate valuing one's feelings as reliable indicators of God's call or direction in my life, as Thomas Hart (1980, p. 77) explains? Does it support viewing life crises or transitions as opportunities for risking new decisions and walking untried paths because, as Jon Sobrino reminds us (1978, pp. 87–103), Jesus' own faith developed by considering new possibilities, and because exodus and resurrection opportunities emerge from within normal life crises and transitions, as several recent studies demonstrate (Haughton, 1981, Whitehead and Whitehead, 1979)?

In summary, both counselors and directors commit themselves to a parallel, reciprocal and mutually fruitful process of assisting persons to notice and interpret their feelings and thoughts so that they may overcome their defenses for the sake of deeper life. Because the Christian experience of God in Jesus by the power of the Spirit comes only through body-community-history influenced experience and symbols, Christian spirituality embraces *every* dimension of human thought and feeling but cannot be reduced to human psychology because it is a relationship to God who is beyond all limits. There is no avenue to God, for me, except through my own and everyone else's human experience *of* God. As the Scripture scholar, Raymond Brown, reminds us (1981) there is no communication from God to us except through our human interpretation and expression of the revelatory insight from God we Christians call "the word of God." Whether that word (i.e., the insight from God expressed in human terms) be scripture or historical decisions or our own everyday lives, it is a matter of thoughts and feelings being expressed and interpreted. Pastoral counselors attend to these thoughts and feelings being convinced that greater Christian maturity yields greater human ability to perceive real problems and relate better to self and others. Directors attend to the same thoughts and feelings, convinced that greater human maturity yields the ability to perceive the "real" God, to relate better to self, others, and God and to surrender completely only to the Ultimate Mystery.

As we can see when we distinguish pastoral counseling from spiritual direction, pastoral counselors do not focus primarily and directly on a client's Christian relationship to God. However, I believe that counselors can directly promote that relationship. They do it, first, insofar as they assist and support human development toward and beyond autonomy. For that capacity is at the very essence of authentic Christian spirituality. Without something of that capacity for autonomy which goes on to risk intimacy, one's relationship to God is a variation on conformity, compulsion, or merely cultural religion. With at least the beginnings of that capacity, one has a self and can surrender; and the process of ever deeper surrender to God in all the complexities of life is precisely the definition of Christian spirituality. Counselors do it, second, insofar as they reinforce only a mature Christian vision in their clients. Mature Christianity is that persistent stream within the tradition which acknowledges two points. First, it recognizes that human autonomy is legitimate and necessary for authentic self-donation and holiness. Second, it understands Christian surrender and union with God not as loss of self but as complete mutuality with differentiation. Union with God does involve loss of self-image. However, Christian contemplatives distinguish this self-image from the "true self" which one is and remains even in the mystical prayer of union.

Pastoral counselors can easily think of practical ways to implement my first directive for promoting mature Christian spirituality. For counselors are skilled in ways to promote autonomy and self-direction. These same skills can be applied to development beyond autonomy if the counselor agrees with the vision of maturity set out earlier in this essay.

The second directive is not as easy. Pastoral counselors have general theological training but lack specific competence in the details of Christian spiritual tradition. My hope is that counselors' interest will be sparked by this discussion of Christian spirituality and they will study and use the resources mentioned here. For the more we can promote mature Christian spirituality, the more we are cooperating with God's bringing about the compassionate reign of God's justice and love.

Bibliography

Barry, W. and Connolly, W. *The Practice of Spiritual Direction.* New York: Seabury, 1982.

Brown, R.E. " 'And the Lord Said?' Biblical Reflections on Scripture as the Word of God." *Theological Studies* 42/1, 1981, 3–19.

Carmody, J. *Holistic Spirituality.* New York: Paulist, 1983.

Catherine of Siena. *The Dialogue.* Translation by S. Noffke. New York: Paulist Press, 1980.

Conn, J.W. "Women's Spirituality: Restriction and Reconstruction." *Cross Currents.* 30/3, 1980, 293–308.

Cooke, B. "Non-Patriarchal Salvation." *Horizons* 10/1, 1983, 22–31.

Fairchild, R. "Guaranteed Not To Shrink: Spiritual Direction in Pastoral Care." *Pastoral Psychology* 31/2, 1982, 79–95.

Fowler, J.W. "Stages in Faith: The Structural-Developmental Approach." In T.C. Hennessy (ed.), *Values and Moral Development*. New York: Paulist Press, 1976.

Fowler, J.W. Stages of Faith: *The Psychology of Human Development and the Quest for Meaning*. San Francisco: Harper & Row, 1981.

Gilligan, C. "In a Different Voice: Women's Conception of the Self and Morality." *Harvard Educational Review* 47 (4/1978): 481–517.

Gilligan, C. *In a Different Voice*. Cambridge, Mass.: Harvard University Press, 1982.

Hart, T. *The Art of Christian Listening*. New York: Paulist Press, 1980.

Haughton, R. *The Passionate God*. New York: Paulist Press, 1981.

Heidegger, M. *Being and Time*. New York: Harper & Row, 1962.

Jung, C.G. *Two Essays in Analytical Psychology*. New York: Bollingen Foundation, 1953.

Kegan, R. *The Evolving Self: Problem and Process in Human Development*. Cambridge, Mass.: Harvard University Press, 1982.

Larkin, E. *Silent Presence: Discernment as Process and Problem*. Denville, N.J.: Dimension Books, 1981.

Leech, K. *True Prayer*. New York: Harper & Row, 1980.

May, G. *Care of Mind Care of Spirit*. New York: Harper & Row, 1982a.

May, G. *Will and Spirit: A Contemplative Psychology*. New York: Harper & Row, 1982b.

Miller, J.B. *Toward a New Psychology of Women*. Boston: Beacon, 1976.

Nouwen, H. *The Way of the Heart: Desert Spirituality and Contemporary Ministry*. New York: Seabury, 1981.

Otto, R. *The Idea of the Holy*. New York: Oxford University Press, 1958.

Peck, M.S. *The Road Less Travelled*. New York: Simon and Schuster, 1978.

Ricoeur, P. *The Symbolism of Evil*. New York: Harper & Row, 1967.

Schneiders, S. "The Contemporary Ministry of Spiritual Direction." In K.G. Culligan (ed.), *Spiritual Direction: Contemporary Readings*. Locust Valley, N.Y.: Living Flame Press, 1983.

Schüssler-Fiorenza, E. *In Memory of Her*. New York: Crossroad, 1983.

Smith, J. *Experience and God*. New York: Oxford University Press, 1968.

Sobrino, J. *Christology at the Crossroads*. Maryknoll: Orbis, 1978.

Teresa of Avila. *The Collected Works of St. Teresa of Avila*. Translated by K. Kavanaugh and O. Rodriquez. Washington, D.C.: ICS Publications, 1976, 1980.

Tillich, P. *Dynamics of Faith*. New York: Harper & Row, 1957.

Whitehead, E. and Whitehead, J. *Christian Life Patterns.* Garden City: Doubleday, 1979.

Williams, R. *Christian Spirituality: A Theological History from the New Testament to Luther and St. John of the Cross.* Atlanta: John Knox, 1980.

Bernard J. Tyrrell, S.J.

Christotherapy:
An Approach to Facilitating
Psychospiritual Healing and Growth

Christotherapy (Tyrrell, 1975) and especially *Christotherapy II* (Tyrrell, 1982) seek to provide Christian counselors and spiritual directors with a concrete example of a balanced integration of psychological and spiritual principles and methods useful for facilitating holistic healing and growth. There is a direct and immediate relevance and application of the key insights and methods of Christotherapy to the area of pastoral counseling. *Christotherapy II* describes certain basic forms of conversion and fundamental attitudes which should be present in Christian counselors and spiritual directors if they are to be effective Spirit-guided instruments of the healing and life-giving Christ. These same conversions and attitudes need to be at work in pastoral counselors. In *Christotherapy II* Christian counselors and spiritual directors are invited to practice the methods of existential loving, diagnosing (mind-fasting), appreciative discerning (spirit-feasting), existential memory-enrichment and existential clarification. Due to the basic and foundational nature of these methods pastoral counselors should also find the use of these methods both appropriate and effective.

First of all, the pastoral counselor needs to be religiously or spiritually converted and in an ongoing state of religious or spiritual conversion. Some tend to think of religious conversion as a rather superficial adherence to a set of beliefs and ritual practices. For this reason it is important to understand religious conversion as a profound *spiritual* transformation effected by the Holy Spirit who floods the human heart with the love of God (Rom 5:5) and with a living faith and hope in God at work in Christ. The pastoral counselor in the state of ongoing religious conversion comes to love God more and more with all his or her heart and soul, mind and strength and to love all others with a Christly love.

The pastoral counselor in a state of ongoing religious or spiritual conversion comes to see all persons not merely from the limited perspective of the natural and human sciences and culture but within the context of divine love and providence as well. The pastoral counselor can honestly face and openly acknowledge the reality of radical human limitations and a sense of personal powerlessness without falling or causing others to fall into despair. He or she can do this because of the inward possession of a vibrant faith which acknowledges the reality of a Higher Power, the living God who offers gifts of restoration and growth to all those open to receiving them.

The pastoral counselor is called not only to be religiously converted and in an ongoing state of religious conversion but also morally converted and in an ever deepening state of ongoing moral conversion. Moral conversion is the fruit of authentic religious conversion. To be morally converted is to let one's life be effectively guided by authentic values and not by a self-centered quest for personal pleasures and satisfactions to be achieved at all costs. In Pauline terms the morally converted person rejects the works of the "flesh" such as strife, jealousy, and dissension and manifests the fruits of the Spirit such as peace, kindness, faithfulness, and self-control (Gal 5:16-24). The morally converted person is the one who is not content to say "Lord, Lord" but who actually does the will of the Father (cf Mt 7:21; 12:50). The pastoral counselor in a state of ongoing moral conversion seeks actively to pursue what is truly good and worthwhile. He or she constantly grows in the assimilation of authentic human and spiritual values and in cherishing these values draws others to embrace them.

The effective pastoral counselor also needs to be in a healthy psychological state and to be free of severe addiction. The pastoral counselor, of course, can be a wounded healer. In fact, the wounded healer can be a most effective instrument of the healing and life-giving Christ. But if the pastoral counselor has had to struggle with severe psychological woundedness or addiction it is important that he or she be in a dominantly recovered state or, in other words, in a condition of ongoing psychological conversion or conversion from addiction. There is a sense in which the recovered addicts or recovered neurotics are, like the sinner, always recovering. They are aware of their ongoing need for a deepening of their basic recovery and for continuous reliance on God's help to resist temptations to relapse or to settle into a false sense of security. Recovered and yet always recovering addicts and neurotics need to be deeply aware of the Pauline doctrine that if we weak human beings have the proper reliance on God we can glory in our weakness, knowing that God is glorified by sustaining us in our weakness. The pastoral counselor who is in a state of ongoing recovery from addiction and/or neurosis should also recall the teaching of Christ that it is impossible to give without receiving. This can be expressed in the form of a beatitude: "Blessed are the healers, for they shall be healed."

A most vital aspect of ongoing psychological and spiritual maturation is the constantly deepening presence in an individual of authentic self-respect and self-love. The pastoral counselor needs to have a healthy form of respect, reverence and love for himself if he or she is going to be able with God's help to have a healthy love and respect for others. The pastoral counselor needs to delight in himself or herself as a human being created in the image and likeness of God and as possessing the dignity of one for whom Christ lived, died and rose unto everlasting life. This means also that the pastoral counselor needs to be forgiving toward himself or herself for deficiencies and failures. To be authentically forgiving toward oneself is not to be a rationalizer or a denier that one has sinned and fallen short of his or her glorious calling. To be forgiving toward oneself is to be open about one's failures before oneself and before God and to accept the gift of divine forgiveness the Father has bestowed upon us in Christ and his saving work. The fact is that it is very difficult to be loving, respectful and forgiving toward others if one is not loving, respectful and forgiving toward oneself.

Besides the presence in the pastoral counselor of ongoing religious and moral conversion and, where necessary, of psychological conversion and/or conversion from addiction, there is also the need for the presence in him or her of a certain "intellectual conversion." Philosopher-theologian Bernard Lonergan coined the expression "intellectual conversion." He implies that St. Augustine underwent a certain type of intellectual conversion when he broke away from his materialism and came to acknowledge the existence of spiritual as well as material realities (Lonergan, 1957, xx). In a creative adaptation of the expression intellectual conversion I describe the pastoral counselor as intellectually converted who has a correct understanding of the basic meaning and interrelationship of the psychological and the spiritual and is able to recognize and critique false psychological and spiritual beliefs, especially as they relate to holistic healing and growth.

Clearly, the issue of intellectual conversion introduces us into a controversial area. There exist among psychologists and theologians sharp disagreements about fundamental psychological and spiritual issues. But the existence of contradictory positions and beliefs does not dispense the pastoral counselor from the need to take a stand on central psychological and spiritual issues. In what immediately follows I will take certain positions and offer some critiques regarding foundational psychological and spiritual issues. I do so recognizing that there are those who will disagree but I also do so in the hope that my comments will stimulate further reflection and discussion among pastoral counselors concerning these foundational matters of great importance.

As a means of clarifying the distinction and relationship between the psychological and the spiritual it will be helpful to consider briefly the adequacy of the oft repeated belief that "holiness is wholeness." First of all, most members of the major Christian denominations would reject the view that a person who was blind or lacking a limb could not be holy and deeply in love with God and his or her neighbor. In this perspective holiness does not of necessity imply physical wholeness. But what about the case where there is a lack of wholeness on the psychological level? Is it possible for a person who has experienced in early childhood and later as well deep human rejection to possess basic psychological feelings of being unlovable and yet to have God's gifts of faith, hope and love dwelling within his or her heart? Unless one identifies the spiritual with the psychological it does not seem necessary to hold that holiness by its very nature demands psychological wholeness. Moreover, for a pastoral counselor to tell his or her counselee that the latter's psychological feelings of being unlovable are a certain sign of a lack of faith and holiness would be severely damaging to the counselee. Certainly psychologically wounded individuals can at times have intense experiences of God's love which affect them in the very depths of their psyche but this does not necessarily occur in all authentic religious or spiritual experiences. Again, what about the case where there is a lack of wholeness on the physical or psychological level due to addiction? There are definitely cases where individuals through no fault of their own have become physically addicted to pain-killing medications administered to them in hospitals. Does the presence of this addiction in these individuals automatically exclude the presence of a deep love of God and holiness in them? It would not seem so. In like manner, if an addiction such as alcoholism can have its basic roots in a metabolic or physical condition it would not seem that the presence of active addiction necessarily excludes the presence of authentic religious or spiritual conversion.

This critique of the "holiness is wholeness" maxim rests on a particular understanding of the human person, the needs of the human person and how these needs are to be met. In my perspective the human person is viewed as an incarnate subject, created in the image and likeness of God, with a hierarchy of basic needs. Among these needs are physical needs, psychological needs and spiritual needs. As a rule physical needs are fulfilled through physical means, e.g., hunger is satisfied through nourishment; psychological needs are fulfilled through psychological means, e.g., the need for social intercommunion and affirmation is met through receiving human love; spiritual needs are fulfilled through spiritual means, e.g., the need for divine forgiveness is fulfilled through the experience of God's reconciling act in Christ. Yet, due to the close interaction of the somatic, the psychological and the spiritual it is possible for an experience of need fulfillment on one level to contribute in a certain way to the fulfillment of a need on another level. If, for example, a person has an ulcer due to psychological tensions, the healing of the psychological tensions can indirectly bring about the healing of the ulcer. Again, if a person has a deep psychological sense of being unlovable due to a profound experience of human rejection, at times— as I know through individual testimonies—a deep faith-encounter with Jesus Christ as loving redeemer and friend can fulfill not only the spiritual need for divine forgiveness and acceptance but the psychological need for a sense of being loved as well.

One result of the failure to understand the distinction and interrelationship between the psychological and the spiritual dimensions of human existence is the tendency to substitute psychology for religion or to psychologize religion in subtle ways. A few years ago psychologist Dr. Paul Vitz wrote a book entitled *Psychology as Religion* (Vitz, 1977). The thrust of Vitz's book was to demonstrate the thesis that for many psychology had become a new religion. Dr. Gerald May from another perspective has noted "a widespread tendency to over-psychologize spiritual direction both in its actual conduct and in the supervision of directors-in-training" (May 1979, p. 1). May also observes that early CPE and pastoral counseling were patterned in large part after the existing behavioral sciences and that unfortunately they too often tended themselves to become forms of behavioral sciences. May states with sadness:

> I have seen people in tears because their pastoral counselor "can't even hear my spiritual questions, let alone respond to them." Pastoral counselors refer people to me for "therapy" because their problems are "too spiritual." CPE students claim that "there is no room left for faith or compassion in their training" (May 1979, p. 1).

Dr. William Hulme in his *Pastoral Care and Counseling* (Hulme, 1981) adds his own nuanced confirmation to the views of Vitz and May in remarking that "as one becomes proficient in the use of counseling skills, a psychological base can subtly replace a theological one" (Hulme, 1981, p. 3). The remarks of Vitz, May and Hulme provide grounds for pastoral counselors to engage in a kind of examination of conscience and to ask themselves just how they function in their particular ministry. Are they operating as instruments of the healing Christ or merely as disciples of Freud, Jung, Adler, Rogers or some other psychologist?

If a failure to understand properly the distinction and interrelationship between psychology and religion can lead to the substitution of psychology for religion it can equally lead to the replacement of psychology with religion or spirituality of some type. For Christian Science practitioners, fundamentalist faith-healers and others it is a basic tenet that the tools of medicine and psychology are useless for the healing of any form of disease or lack of wholeness and that the use of spiritual or religious means alone can bring about the goal of real healing. For most pastoral counselors today, however, the danger does not lie in the direction of the replacement of psychology with religion or spirituality but rather with the replacement of religion by psychology.

The failure of the pastoral counselor to understand the central importance of spirituality in his or her ministry can also lead to the false belief that "my work is my prayer" and an adequate substitute for participation in the communal or sacramental life of the Church and for personal, solitary prayer. Certainly the daily work of mercy that is pastoral counseling is a most important means of glorifying God. But the pastoral counselor also needs to pray often and explicitly for those with whom he or she works. And the daily, ongoing prayer of the pastoral counselor for his or her counselees should have its wellspring in communal worship and in solitary meditation and contemplation as well. It is all too easy to say in effect to oneself: "I am too busy to spend time in private prayer or in communal worship." No one had more work to do than Jesus Christ and yet he was very careful to pray in the synagogues and often to spend whole nights in solitary prayer.

It is very important for the pastoral counselor to realize that God gives to each one of us a certain number of persons whom we are especially and uniquely called to serve. I like to speak of "the sacrament of the present person." Each day God gives us a certain number of individuals to encounter, and it is often the case that either we will console and bless these individuals or no one will. At times just a few words spoken from an attentive, caring heart can make all the difference in the suffering person's day. But we need the nourishment of communal and solitary prayer in order to dispose ourselves properly to be present with love to the particular individuals whom God will send to us on a given day.

A further result of the failure of the pastoral counselor to grasp the key importance of spiritual understanding in his or her ministry is the danger of yielding to the myth of self-sufficiency instead of acknowledging that our sufficiency is from God (2 Cor 3:5). Today there is a great stress on self-assertiveness training (though many could probably use a course in non-assertiveness training) and on the need to make the self as radically independent and self-sufficient as possible. Now, as I already indicated, there is most certainly a need in each of us for a valid self-love, self-acceptance and a capacity for self-forgiveness. But there is equally a need for a deep sense of our dependence on God in terms of our own proper self-development and of our work with others. Dr. Gerald May somewhere remarks that when an individual possesses a very strong, positive self-image this can often stand in the way of openness to God and to an acknowledgment of dependence on God. For this reason it is especially important for pastoral counselors who recognize in themselves strong self-assertive tendencies together with a strong, positive self-image to meditate often on those scriptural passages which remind us that apart from Christ we can do nothing of a truly salutary nature and that all we possess is gift.

Dr. Jonathan Lieff in an article entitled "Eight Reasons Why Doctors Fear the Elderly, Chronic Illness and Death" (Lieff, 1982) indicates that there is today a widespread prejudice against the elderly, the handicapped and the dying in American culture. Lieff, who has served as Chief of Geriatrics at Lemuel Ahattuck Hospital, as Director of Geriatric Fellowship at Boston University, and in similar positions, cites a study which indicates that first year medical students reveal a more strongly negative view toward the elderly than their prejudice related to race (Lieff, 1982, p. 49) and that their education in medical schools only serves to intensify this prejudice. It is apparently common in medical academic settings to refer to elderly patients with pejorative terms and names. Lieff suggests that part of the problem is that doctors have unresolved feelings about their own aging, that they have not come to terms with the issue of dying and that because they experience a certain impotence in the face of the complex psychosomatic and even spiritual difficulties of the old and the dying they tend in these cases to focus attention exclusively on medical details. Clearly, since pastoral counselors are called at times to work with the elderly, the handicapped, the chronically ill and those who have to face the reality of dying, e.g., terminal cancer victims, it is crucially important for them to possess as adequate a knowledge as possible of their own biases and prejudices. If they have strong self-images and self-assertive tendencies, for example, they need to ask themselves what their real attitude is toward weakness and impotence in others. Moreover, it is important for all pastoral counselors to ask themselves on occasion: "What are my own gut feelings regarding my own aging and the issue of my own eventual dying? Do I perhaps have a bias toward the aging, the handicapped and the terminally ill and does this show up in the way I deal with this type of individual?"

The failure of pastoral counselors to recognize the primary importance of the spiritual dimension in their ministry can also lead them to view the practice of counseling as a job rather than as a ministry. All Christians are called to be sharers in Christ's healing ministry. But there are special callings and charisms given to specific individuals. God gives some special gifts and talents for making use of medical means for aiding in the healing of individuals in need. God bestows on the pastoral counselor natural gifts of empathy and understanding and special spiritual charisms of wisdom, discernment, etc. Each pastoral counselor should at times ask himself or herself: "Do I really view my practice of pastoral counseling as a Christian ministry, a God-given calling, a charism and gift to be used for the building up of others and the glorification of God or do I view my counseling merely as a job or a secular involvement?

The pastoral counselor who is in an ongoing stage of religious and moral conversion and is intellectually converted in his or her attitudes regarding the spiritual and psychological dimensions of human existence is best prepared to utilize the various methods of Christotherapy both for Spirit-aided facilitation of personal healing and growth and in the assistance of others.

One of the most basic methods of Christotherapy is *existential loving*. To love existentially is to cherish the gift of unique existence which each human being possesses and incarnates. As I already indicated, pastoral counselors are called to love themselves in an authentic fashion, and this means most basically to delight in the gift of existence which they possess. It means also to rejoice in oneself as created in the image and likeness of God and as a redeemed brother or sister of Jesus Christ. Pastoral counselors are likewise called to love existentially those who come to them seeking healing or growth or a solution to a problem in some area. To love existentially is to love with a deep human love transformed by the gift of a Christly love which floods one's heart. It is very important for pastoral counselors to pray daily for the gift to love themselves and those who come for aid with an ever deepening existential type of love.

Drs. William Glasser (Glasser, 1965), Abraham Maslow (Maslow, 1970, pp. 43–46) and many other psychologists have shown that all human beings have basic needs for a sense of being lovable and worthwhile. Dr. John Evoy in his excellent book *The Rejected* (Evoy, 1981) makes a strong case for the view that the root source of a high percentage of neuroses lies in an experience of rejection or extrinsic valuation (the person is valued for what he or she can do rather than for himself or herself) on the part of the neurotically suffering person. This means that a very significant number of those who seek the aid of the pastoral counselor will possess in varying degrees of intensity unmet needs for a sense of being personally lovable and worthwhile. These individuals will, of course, approach the pastoral counselor with specific problems, e.g., difficulties in interpersonal relationships or requests for advice. Pastoral counselors must seek to meet the particular needs of the individuals who come to them, but it will be through the practice of existential loving that the ideal climate will be established for the solving of problems, for consoling, for advising and for reconciling.

It is important to emphasize that existential loving is not an exercise in sentimentality; it is a love which accepts but does not condone irresponsible types of behavior. It can and does confront when this is necessary. It is a holistic love which is at once affective, spiritual, volitional and contemplative. Existential loving is also the type of love which liberates rather than enslaves; it aids persons to realize a legitimate sense of autonomy and independence where these qualities are lacking. Finally, the pastoral counselor who loves existentially is aware of the psychological phenomena of transference and counter-transference and deals with them if and when they occur. But the pastoral counselor who works within the framework of Christotherapy does not seek to promote actively transference as do practitioners of some other forms of therapy.

Besides existential loving, the two most central methods of Christotherapy are *diagnostic discerning*, which culminates in a certain fasting of the mind, heart and/or imagination, and *appreciative discerning*, which blossoms in the feasting of the mind, heart and/or imagination. These are processes which pastoral counselors need first to practice in their own personal daily living. It is this personal self-engagement in these processes which brings pastoral counselors to understand and verify for themselves the true significance and value of these processes. The pastoral counselor is then able to make use of these processes in a fruitful way in working with others and in helping them to utilize these processes themselves.

Diagnostic discernment seeks to understand the meaning and unveil the self-destructiveness of erroneous attitudes, false beliefs, ignorant assumptions, evil or misguided choices and forms of behavior which underpin and generate illness on the spiritual, psychological and/or somatic level or disorders on the level of external events. Individuals at times deliberately and sinfully cling to certain beliefs and practices of a self-destructive nature. At other times individuals unconsciously or non-reflectively entertain and live out certain false assumptions, attitudes, beliefs, etc. about what true fulfillment and happiness consist in and how they are to be realized. Diagnostic discerning concerns itself with understanding and revealing in a graphic manner the self-destructiveness of any attitude, belief, assumption, decision, behavior (conscious or unconscious) which is, in fact, truly corrosive of authentic human existence and the source of deformation and disorders on the spiritual, psychological or somatic order or in negative external events.

The aim of diagnostic discerning regarding sin on the levels of thought, word or action can be shown by reflecting briefly on a text of St.

Thomas Aquinas. In his commentary on St. Paul's Second Letter to the Corinthians Aquinas remarks: "He who refrains from obeying a precept because God forbids it is not free; but he who refrains from evil because it is evil is free" (Murphy-O'Connor, 1977, p. 116). There are various degrees of freedom, and I believe that Thomas is here speaking of the highest form of freedom. I do not think that Aquinas is stating that a person who refrains from evil because God commands it is not exercising an act of free choice in some sense. But I believe that Thomas is saying that that person is most truly free who avoids evil because he or she perceives it to be evil. God is not a capricious God who arbitrarily decides to forbid one type of activity, calling it evil, and to command another type of activity, naming it good. God commands human beings to avoid certain things because they are truly evil and to embrace certain things because they are truly good and life-giving. The aim of diagnostic discerning, accordingly, is to unmask evil and see it for what it really is, namely, corrosive and self-destructive. And the culminating stage in the diagnostic discernment process is to fast in one's mind, imagination and will from what is understood and verified to be truly evil and self-destructive. There is a text in St. Paul's Second Letter to the Corinthians which expresses very well the aim of diagnostic discerning as I have just described it:

> We live in the flesh, of course, but the muscles we fight with are not flesh. Our war is not fought with weapons of flesh, yet they are strong enough, in God's cause, to demolish fortresses. We demolish sophistries, and the arrogance that tries to resist the knowledge of God; every thought is our prisoner, captured and brought into obedience to Christ (2 Cor 10:3-5).

Appreciative discerning seeks to discover and make manifest the life-enriching quality of various attitudes, beliefs, choices, behaviors, values which are a generative source of health and wholeness on the spiritual, psychological, and/or bodily level and bring about harmony on the level of external events. Appreciative discerning discriminates what is worthwhile, perceives what is true, savors what is excellent, delights in what is beautiful, unveils and rejoices in the deepest natural, spiritual and mystical life-enhancing realities.

To shed further light on the nature of appreciative discerning I would like to re-express creatively in a positive statement the quotation I cited above from Thomas Aquinas. "The person who does something good because God commands it is not free; but the person who does something good because it is good is free." We are speaking here, of course, of the richest form of freedom. Further, we must keep in mind that God does not command us to do and embrace good things out of mere caprice but because these good things truly are good and worthwhile. In the light of these comments it is most appropriate to say that that person is most free and God-like who does good and embraces good things precisely because he or she perceives that what is done or embraced is truly good and worthwhile. The aim of appreciative discerning then is to see the good for what it really is, namely, good, truly of value and life-enhancing and to cherish, cultivate and embrace it. The culminating stage of the appreciative discernment process is to feast in an ongoing fashion in one's mind, heart and imagination on what is truly good and of value. There is a text of Paul in the Letter to the Philippians which expresses very well the goal of appreciative discerning and spirit-feasting:

> I want you to be happy, always happy in the Lord . . . . Finally, brothers, fill your minds . . . with everything that is good and pure, everything that we love and honor, and everything that can be thought virtuous and worthy of praise . . . . Then the God of peace will be with you (Phil 4:4-9).

In *Christotherapy II* I demonstrate in a variety of contexts and with many examples the concrete applicability of the diagnostic and appreciative discerning processes. I show, for example, how diagnostic and appreciative discerning contribute to healing and growth in such basic feeling areas as fear, anger, sadness and guilt. I also demonstrate how the practice of these discernment processes leads to the healing of severe neuroses as well as to the facilitation of healing and growth in the day to day living of individuals. In applying these discernment processes to the healing of severe neuroses I use a rather subtle combination of psychological and spiritual means, e.g., techniques of existential and cognitive therapies combined with certain forms of prayer. I do so because the self-destructive beliefs and assumptions of the severe neurotic are largely non-reflectively or unconsciously held and lived out and hence very difficult to unmask and handle. In what immediately follows I will present for the sake of brevity a rather simple example of the diagnostic and appreciative discernment processes in action. The subject of the example will be the addict (recovered and yet always recovering) and the struggle with self-pity. Since self-pity is a rather universal phenomenon it should be easy for most to appreciate the example. I will first focus on the diagnostic discernment process which culminates in the fasting of the mind, heart and imagination and then on the appreciative discernment process which blossoms in the feasting of the mind, heart and imagination.

In Alcoholics Anonymous one occasionally hears the expression "stinking thinking." It is a rather crude expression but it makes its point well by "telling it the way it is." Self-pity is one of the more notorious forms of stinking thinking and fantasizing. It is a self-destructive form of reflection and imagining which tends to make the person indulging in it miserable and, when this person is a recovered addict, it endangers his or her sobriety as well. The recovered and always recovering addict needs to discern diagnostically the truly poisonous character of self-pity. Once the discerner understands and personally verifies at a gut level that self-pity is indeed self-destructive, then he or she is called to watch out for self-pity when it begins to arise in consciousness and then freely to release and let go of it in an ongoing fasting of the mind, heart and imagination. There is no danger of repression here because the act of mind-fasting is conscious, freely engaged in and the result of enlightenment.

It will be useful here to enumerate four stages in the diagnostic discerning process which culminates in the actual fasting of the mind, heart and imagination. First, I have an experience of some negative data, e.g., I am feeling miserable and am stagnating in this feeling of misery. Second, I pray for the gift of a diagnostic understanding through which I can get at the real meaning of the misery and pain I am experiencing. This second stage requires the use on one's natural power of reflection as well as a prayerful spirit of openness and humbleness of heart. Third, as a result of prayerful reflection I am gifted with the revelation/recognition, that is, with a verified understanding on my part that the meaning of the feeling of misery is that I am wallowing in self-pity and that this wallowing in self-pity is a very self-destructive, useless, corrosive type of activity. Fourth, as a result of my personally verified understanding on the gut level of the self-defeating, self-destructive character of self-pity I freely decide to begin to let go of my self-pitying thinking and imagining and to fast from it in my mind, heart and imagination. I ask the Holy Spirit to aid me in my ongoing fasting.

It is also useful to enumerate four stages that culminate in the actual feasting of the mind, heart and imagination. I should make it clear that the fasting of the mind, etc., needs to be complemented with the feasting of the mind and spirit. It is never enough just to drive out a "devil." One needs to replace the devil that is expelled with an "angel" that is invited in through prayer. It is necessary to complement the process of diagnostic discerning and fasting with the corresponding process of appreciative discerning and feasting. The first stage, then, in the process that culminates in the feasting of the mind and spirit is to place myself mentally, imaginatively or actually in the presence of something positive, good, life-enhancing, e.g., instead of engaging in self-pity I reflect on the fact that I am well, sober and in the presence of a nice day. In the second stage of the process I pray to God that he will help me to discern appreciatively the excellence and worthwhileness of the gift of sobriety and that he will also help me to open my eyes to the beauty of the day which greets me. In the third stage, as a result of my development of a spirit of receptivity and in answer to my prayer, God grants me the gift of a certain revelation/recognition in which I appreciatively discern the excellence of sobriety. I also come to recognize that there is real good in my life and that even such a simple thing as a nice day is something in which I can rejoice and for which I can be thankful. In a fourth stage I engage in an ongoing, Spirit-guided feasting in my mind, heart and imagination on the joys of sobriety and the beauty of the day. And I continue to praise and thank God for the many gifts I possess and continue to receive. It is, of course, most important to keep in mind that healing and growth are on-going processes and that it is consequently vital to engage daily in the psycho-spiritual exercises of diagnostic and appreciative discernment, of the fasting and feasting of the mind, heart and imagination.

As an aid in the practice of the fasting and feasting of the mind and heart I suggest the practice of what I call *existential memory-enrichment*. I name the method *existential* memory-enrichment because this practice enables individuals to *exist* in the world in a fuller, more vital way.

Today because of the easy availability of books, written materials of every type, tapes and TV we tend to neglect the use of memory, especially in areas which touch upon the deeper dimensions of our lives. People who need to remember facts and names due to the nature of their job often take courses in the development of memory. But if anything, in the area of the sacred, the spiritual and the religious there is almost a certain mistrust of the use of memory. Not too long ago Christian children were "forced" to memorize certain prayers, the list of the commandments and such things. More recently there has been a certain legitimate reaction against the rote memorization of prayers with no understanding.

But what I am suggesting through the exercise of existential memory-enrichment is that we seek to memorize prayers, poems, sayings, maxims, segments of literature which directly relate in a deeply felt way to the areas in which we need to practice the fasting and feasting of the mind, heart, imagination and spirit. Thus, for example, if a person tends to be fearful it can be very helpful to memorize Psalm 23:

Yahweh is my shepherd,
I lack nothing . . . .
Though I pass through a gloomy valley,
I fear no harm;

beside me your rod and your staff are there,
to hearten me (Ps 23: 1,4).

Individuals who are fearful can also find comfort and strength in Psalm 91:

I rescue all who cling to me,
I protect whoever knows my name,
I answer everyone who invokes me,
I am with them when they are in trouble;
I bring them safety (Ps 91:34–35).

Psalms, poems, sayings, passages from literature of a sacred or humanistic nature can be tremendously helpful when we feel the need to cleanse our consciousness of some negative element and also when we experience ourselves called to fill our minds and spirits with something good and beautiful. At times we find ourselves just too nervous or distracted to attempt spontaneous prayer. At times like these it can be of great help just to be able to draw some Psalm or saying from the treasury of our memory and to recite it slowly again and again. This practice can bring peace and inner tranquillity when everything else has failed. Thus, for example, when we have sinned or come to experience the weight of some past sin and darkness of spirit we can draw out of our memory Psalm 51:

Have mercy on me, O God, in your goodness,
in your great tenderness wipe away my faults;
wash me clean of my guilt,
purify me from my sin (Ps 51:1).

The recitation of this Psalm can greatly aid a person in his or her attempt to fast in heart and imagination from engaging in an orgy of self-defeating guilt recollections. Like the psalmist the person can simply acknowledge his or her sin and then turn to contemplate the tender mercy of the Lord. Again, when we experience a call to rejoice in God we can summon from the fountain of our memory Psalm 63:

God, you are my God,
I am seeking you,
my soul is thirsting for you,
my flesh is longing for you,
a land parched, weary and waterless;
I long to gaze on you in the sanctuary,
and to see your power and glory (Ps 63:1–2).

Each of us needs to know his or her particular weaknesses and needs and then to select those Psalms, sayings, poems which can aid us in our fasting and in our attempt to come to grips with what is negative in us. Likewise, each of us needs to know those strengths and virtues which are correlative to our weaknesses. We can then select and memorize those sayings, poems, narrative passages which will most help us to feast in a truly life-enhancing and enriching manner.

It is not necessary to have a "great memory" in order to use profitably the method of existential memory-enrichment. If, for example, an individual places a poem or scriptural passage on his or her desk and just commits to memory two or three lines a day, it does not take long before the whole passage is stored away in the treasury of the memory. The poem or passage can then be brought forth whenever there is an occasion to use it. And it is surprising how many situations present themselves where an individual can fruitfully make use of materials he or she has stored away in the memory. Thus individuals can call upon the riches of the memory when they are stuck in a traffic jam, sitting in a dentist's office, waiting for a friend, taking a stroll and in countless other situations. This recommendation of the practice of existential memory-enrichment may seem banal but I have received written and oral testimonies from various persons full of gratitude who have enthusiastically recounted how very beneficial they have found this practice in their daily living..

A final method of Christotherapy which the pastoral counselor is invited to practice is *existential clarification*. This method is particularly applicable to those who come to the pastoral counselor with sufferings or problems rooted in false beliefs and self-destructive behavior. The practice of this method flows out of the diagnostic and appreciative discerning which the pastoral counselor practices in reference to the counselee. Existential clarification is the dynamic process through which the pastoral counselor seeks to communicate to the counselee the diagnostic and appreciative understanding which he or she reached concerning the way of being in the world of the counselee. The pastoral counselor seeks to communicate the results of his or her understanding of the mode of being in the world of the counselee in such a way that the counselee equally comes to participate in and verify for herself or himself in a deeply felt way this diagnostic and appreciative understanding.

There are two basic phases of the dynamic process of existential clarification. In the first phase the pastoral counselor seeks to make clear for the counselee the true existential meaning of whatever self-destructive or growth-prohibiting factors the counselee is experiencing. Through the use of examples and vital descriptions the pastoral counselor seeks to help the counselee to grasp in a deeply felt manner the intrinsic connection between the problem experienced and some self-destructive belief, attitude, assumption, etc., which the counselee consciously or very likely non-reflectively embraces and lives by. The pastoral counselor needs to be capable of depicting for the counselee in a very graphic manner just precisely how his or her misery is flowing directly from certain patterns of belief and behavior. The pastoral counselor must be capable of demonstrating just how corrosive of human happiness and authentic fulfillment the destructive attitudes and behavior are, and he or she must do so in such a way that the counselee will come to perceive and verify at a "gut-level" the true destructiveness of these attitudes and behaviors and will then begin to let go of them in an ongoing fasting of the mind, heart and imagination. The pastoral counselor throughout the process of existential clarification should invite counselees to engage themselves in an ongoing prayerful quest for an unmasking of whatever is self-destructive in their way of living in the world. At times it will be in the moment of being understood that the counselee will come to understand. But as the process of healing continues the counselee will gradually come to a diagnostic understanding apart from the explicit aid of the pastoral counselor. The degree of dependence of the counselee on the pastoral counselor will be in direct relation to the psychological condition of the counselee, e.g., if the counselee is quite neurotic the dependence will be fairly substantial. The aim, of course, of the pastoral counselor is to lead counselees toward freedom and the development of the capability of practicing diagnostic discerning on their own, always, of course, with the aid of the Holy Spirit. I must add the cautionary note that pastoral counselors should be very aware of their professional limitations and should not undertake what Dr. Howard Clinebell, Jr. has referred to as "depth pastoral counseling" (Clinebell, 1966, p. 266) or long-term pastoral counseling unless they have the proper background and resources to do so. It is possible, of course, to utilize diagnostic discerning and existential clarification at many different levels, in varying degrees of intensity and in highly diverse situations.

As I mentioned above there are two phases of existential clarification. In the second phase the pastoral counselor seeks prayerfully to help counselees discover and rejoice in those truths and values which are especially life-giving and life-enhancing for them. Through an appeal to personal experiences and the use of Holy Scripture, poems and other means the pastoral counselor seeks to help bring the counselee to a heart-felt savoring and cultivation of whatever truths and values are integrative and wholesome. The second phase of existential clarification complements the first just as appreciative discerning complements diagnostic discerning. This is so because a person who is suffering from the living out of a self-destructive belief needs to replace this belief with a truth which will be the source of life-enrichment and authentic fulfillment. Thus, for example, if a person is dominated by an extreme possessiveness he or she needs to discover the beauty and value of letting-being-be. The pastoral counselor needs to seek prayerfully to clarify for the sufferer the excellence and worthwhileness of the ongoing practice of allowing people to be themselves. It is also the task of the pastoral counselor to invite the counselee to pray daily for the gift of discovering, appreciating and delighting in those truths and values which are the source of wholeness, integration, peace and joy.

Finally, the pastoral counselor will be an effective instrument of Christ and a communicator and clarifier of authentic truths and values precisely to the extent that he or she discerns and embraces truths that liberate and values which are the source of abundant life. The pastoral counselor is called to possess as God's gift an "inner eye" full of light. For "the lamp of the body is the eye. It follows that if your eye is sound, your whole body will be filled with light" (Mt 6:22). If the inner eye of the pastoral counselor is full of light, then he or she will radiate the healing and life-giving presence of God's love in the world. Jesus says to the pastoral counselor and, indeed, to all of us: "You are the light of the world . . . . Your light must shine in the sight of men so that, seeing your good works, they may give praise to your Father in heaven (Mt 5:14, 16). Each pastoral counselor is called by God to be a beneficial presence in the world, a light-giver who in her or his encounters with others lets the light of Christ shine forth so that all of God's human family can have life and have it in great abundance.

Bibliography

Clinebell, Jr., Howard. *Basic Types of Pastoral Counseling*. New York: Abingdon Press, 1966.

Evoy, John. *The Rejected*. University Park and London: The Pennsylvania State University, 1981.

Glasser, William. *Reality Therapy*. New York: Harper and Row, 1965.

Hulme, William E. *Pastoral Care and Counseling*. Minneapolis: Augsburg Publishing House, 1981.

Lieff, Jonathan. "Eight Reasons Why Doctors Fear the Elderly, Chronic Illness and Death." *Journal of Transpersonal Psychology*, Vol. 14, No. 1, 1982, 47–60.

Lonergan, Bernard. *Insight. A Study in Human Understanding*. New York: Philosophical Library, 1957.

Maslow, Abraham. *Motivation and Personality*. New York: Harper and Row, 1954.

May, Gerald. "Spiritual Direction, Pastoral Counseling and Psychotherapy—A Differentiation." An unpublished lecture presented at the Howard Chandler Robbins' Lectures at Wesley Theological Seminary in Washington D.C., March 23, 1979.

Murphy-O'Connor, Jerome. *Becoming Human Together*. Wilmington: Michael Glazier, Inc., 1977.

Tyrrell, Bernard. *Christotherapy*. New York: Seabury Press, 1975.

Tyrrell, Bernard. *Christotherapy II*. New York: Paulist Press, 1982.

Vitz, Paul. *Psychology as Religion*. Grand Rapids: William B. Eerdmans Publishing Co., 1977.

Robert J. Wicks

Countertransference and Burnout in Pastoral Counseling

Christians encounter many problems and pitfalls when in their pastoral counseling they employ a system of psychology in which the study of unconscious mental processes plays a major role. One way of handling these difficulties is by attempting to learn more about their own personalities in general and how to understand and deal with "countertransference" and "burnout" in particular (Wicks, 1983).

Countertransference

Our personality is responsible for the way we view ourselves and the world. No matter how well people know, love, or care for us, they will never view us or the world in quite the same way we do. No one can have the same personality as someone else because personality is a special singular product of heredity, pre-natal environment, and the formative relations we have had with significant others early in life.

These early important interpersonal encounters with the key figures in our life help us form a blueprint for dealing with the world. Naturally the blueprint needs constant revision. People we encounter now are not the same as those we interacted with early in life, nor are they in a position to meet our childhood needs. When we act as if they are, we are demonstrating "transference."

Transference is common because we all have ingrained learned patterns of dealing with the world. Likewise, everyone has at least some unresolved childhood conflicts which are beyond awareness. There is no such thing as the *totally* analyzed, personally aware individual. Anytime people interact there is some aspect of distortion in the way one person views the other.

In order to remain in touch with our own unresolved conflicts and needs, and to see reality as clearly as possible, it is important to monitor our transferences on an ongoing basis. There must be an effort to keep the interferences of the past to a minimum, while recognizing that it is impossible to screen them out altogether. The overall goal is to avoid superimposing personal needs and conflicts on the verbal and non-verbal messages we receive from others. This aim is particularly important when we function as pastoral counselor or pastoral psychotherapist.

Transference in the counselor is referred to as "countertransference." It is the counselor's transferential reaction to the patient or client. It is an unrealistic response to the patient's realistic behavior, transferences, and general relationship with us and the world. Langs (1974, p. 298) in his two volume treatment of psychoanalytic psychotherapy views countertransference in the following way: "We may briefly define countertransferences as one aspect of those responses to the patient which, while prompted by some event within the therapy or in the therapist's real life, are primarily based on his past significant relationships; basically, they gratify his needs rather than the patient's therapeutic endeavors."

Not everyone in the field of mental health views countertransference as Langs does. Countertransference has been portrayed in a number of ways over the years since Freud introduced the concept. For example, it has been seen negatively and narrowly as being solely a block to effective counselor-patient communication. In this light it was considered as something to be discovered and analyzed out of existence (Fenichel, 1945; Ruesh, 1961; Tarachow, 1963). Its presence was seen as evidence of weakness in the counselor. Those who followed this line of thought sometimes found it difficult to be natural and genuine in the counseling session. They feared that by relaxing or letting their guard down, they might accidentally show some of their countertransference. Needless to say, this resulted in quite stilted and unrealistic counseling sessions.

When this happens in a pastoral counseling setting, those who come for help are unpleasantly surprised. They are seeking a warm caring religious leader and instead find a distant, "professional," aloof person filling the role of "helper."

This is the result of a misunderstanding of how one works as a counselor. It is attributable to a failure to appreciate that therapeutic techniques are presented to help the pastoral counselors project their own personality in a healthy way, not bury or disguise it out of fear of demonstrating countertransference. In not allowing personal needs, conflicts, and personality style to interfere with the patient-counselor relationship, the pastoral helper must not become a robot in the process.

On the other end of the continuum with respect to countertransference, some in the field have elevated its importance to the point where it is seen as practically the cornerstone of treatment (Fromm-Reichmann,

1950) or as a source of prelogical communication which the helper must tap into if he is to appreciate the deep messages the patient is unconsciously trying to send out (Tauber, 1954). Such positions with regard to countertransference are still being looked at today. However, most theorists and practitioners now take more of a middle ground.

They accept the reality of countertranference. No matter how well analyzed a counselor may be, the occurrence of countertransference is seen as being a natural part of life, albeit to a lesser extent than in the unanalyzed person. With this position in place, most counselors or therapists don't adhere dogmatically to the principle that it must be feared and eliminated at all cost. Rather, they believe they should take all steps possible to reduce unruly countertransference. Along with this they recognize that the counselor's own transference will occur to some extent and that utilization of the knowledge it brings should take place as a means of furthering the patient's treatment.

The premise is that by monitoring the personal feelings patients elicit—initially and throughout the treatment—it is possible to learn about the patient's problems in living as well as about oneself. Consequently, in this light, countertransference is not something to be feared. Instead it is an inevitable process which needs to be recognized, uncovered, and dealt with in a useful direct fashion each time it appears.

Recognizing and Uncovering Countertransference. Self-awareness and use of a consistent therapeutic style are the best measures to prevent countertransference from developing and remaining hidden. Counselors who monitor personal feelings and thoughts on a regular basis while with clients can readily appreciate how they are responding to them. By using a consistent style in dealing with patients, counselors can become sensitive to those times that they for some reason (i.e., possibly countertransference) veer from their normal approach. Such variance would be a clue that something the patient is doing might somehow be eliciting an unwarranted response. This allows one to get a quick grasp on the situation before it goes on unnoticed and unchecked for a long—and possibly destructive— period of time.

Chessick (1974) says that helping agents should treat those who come for help in a courteous fashion, but one that has normal reserve. He suggests to secular therapists that they behave toward their patients as if they were guests in their home and their spouse were present. In another attempt to bring the point across he also suggests preventing countertransference from being acted upon by doing only those things in therapy that can easily be shared with one's colleagues without hesitation or embarrassment.

One of the most succinct listings of ways to recognize and quickly un-cover potential countertransferences is presented by Karl Menninger in his book, *Theory of Psychoanalytic Technique* (1962, p. 88):

The following are some (countertransferences) I have jotted down at various times during seminars and control sessions in which they appeared: I think that I have myself been guilty of practically all of them.

Inability to understand certain kinds of material which touch on the analyst's own personal problems.

Depressed or uneasy feelings during or after analytic hours with certain patients.

Carelessness in regard to arrangements—forgetting the pa-tient's appointment, being late for it, letting the patient's hour run overtime for no special reason.

Persistent drowsiness (of the analyst) during the analytic hour.

Over- or under-assiduousness in financial arrangements with the patient, for example, letting him become considerably indebted without analyzing it, or trying to "help" him to get a loan.

Repeatedly experiencing erotic or affectionate feelings to-ward a patient.

Permitting and even encouraging resistance in the form of acting-out.

Security seeking, narcissistic devices such as trying to im-press the patient in various ways, or to impress colleagues with the importance of one's patient.

Cultivating the patient's continued dependence in various ways, especially by unnecessary reassurances.

The urge to engage in professional gossip concerning a pa-tient.

Sadistic, unnecessary sharpness in formulation of comments and interpretations, and the reverse.

Feeling that the patient must get well for the sake of the doc-tor's reputation and prestige.

"Hugging the case to one's bosom," i.e., being too afraid of losing the patient.

Getting conscious satisfaction from the patient's praise, ap-preciation, and evidences of affection, and so forth.

Becoming disturbed by the patient's persistent reproaches and accusations.

Arguing with the patient.

Premature reassurances against the development of anxiety in the patient or, more accurately, finding oneself unable to gauge the point of optimum frustration tension.

Trying to help the patient in extra-analytic ways, for example, in making financial arrangements, or housing arrangements.

A compulsive tendency to "hammer away" at certain points.

Recurrent impulses to ask favors of the patient.

Sudden increase or decrease of interest in a certain case.

Dreaming about the patient.

Though Menninger is directing his comments to those involved in doing analysis, they can also help pastoral counselors or psychotherapists to appreciate when they are responding or acting in an unusual fashion during the session. Some religious counselors though may feel that the comments don't apply to them. For instance, some may say, "Well as part of my work I have to help persons with their finances, so his comments with respect to that area and similar ones just don't apply to me."

When pastoral workers are helping in this way they are involved in the process of social work. This certainly is an important part of ministerial work but at the same time such efforts may hinder the psychotherapeutic process. Active social work is difficult to undertake at the same time as counseling. So, at the very least, Menninger's comments can provide guidelines to help determine which role we are assuming with the person coming for help. Many roles are therapeutic in nature; social work is certainly one of them. However, one can't be everything to everyone, and counseling, of its very nature, has certain limits and structures built into it. Not seeing this may result in frustration for both the counselor and the patient.

Another reason this list is important for pastoral counselors is that it helps them to keep in mind the old maxim: "Give a person a fish, feed him for a day; teach him to fish, feed him for life." Training in the ministry may encourage *doing* in the sense of active intervention even when it isn't the best course of action.

In many cases direct intervention may be warranted, but reaching out to others in a social work fashion is not always called for and sometimes has negative results. Rather than helping the person to become independent our active efforts to intervene in their lives result in encouraging infantile dependence. Instead of learning how they may help themselves put their lives and situation in perspective on their own, their own coping abilities are undercut.

Some pastoral counselors would also vehemently and quickly dismiss the Menninger guidelines as being inappropriate for them on other grounds. They would argue that their pastoral role supersedes their purely therapeutic one and that such limits are only for secular therapists. For instance, Natale (1977) says, "When at the end of a long and tiresome day the pastoral counselor agrees to see yet another patient, the counselor is expressing a Christian acceptance which surpasses psychological theory" (p. 20).

This distinction would seem to be a questionable one. A good counselor or psychotherapist would see another patient at the end of the day *if it were an emergency.* If not, there is a questionable advantage in seeing yet another person. Counselors model healthy limit-setting for patients and help them learn to fulfill their needs within the givens of reality whenever possible. In addition, when a pattern of expending energies without an appreciation of personal limits exists, it may lead to burnout. Moreover, in falling into the trap of trying to meet every need that people bring to him no matter how great it is, the counselor is demonstrating the pattern referred to as the "savior complex."

This pattern results when individuals unconsciously accept the role of savior and believe they can produce results in all cases without the process taking a personal toll. From the Christian perspective it is a distortion of the belief that with Christ anything is possible.

Part of the reason why this is especially a problem for pastoral counselors is due to their obvious connection with the church. In being seen as aligned with religion, persons may transfer the feelings they have toward God onto the religious who is a counselor. The same problems pastors have with their parishioners, persons who are pastoral counselors can expect to have. In terms of the "savior complex," this may especially be so with very dependent types of individuals, as can be seen in the following comments by Pattison (1965, p. 197): "Infantile images ultimately affect the pastoral role. . . . The person who sees God as a protective, all-giving, warm mother may expect the pastor to be all-giving and ever-protective, and react with anger if the pastor does not fulfill these expectations. Those who react to authority with a passive-submissive stance may acquiesce to all suggestions as if they were commands. Or, they may react angrily if the pastor does not give them explicit guidance or commands to follow; they demand to be told what to do." It isn't any wonder then that many pastoral counselors give in to strong transferences and try to fulfill the unresolved needs of others by being God-like; the "advantage" is to avoid the immediate wrath and disappointment of those whose view of God and life is immature.

Menninger's guidelines, and the limits and norms of the therapeutic situation discussed here and later in the book, need to be modified in certain situations by the pastoral counselor; this much is true. However, too often these modifications of the therapeutic guidelines are indicative of countertransference on the part of the pastoral counselor, rather than as an example of a necessary exception which is an outgrowth of the fact that the therapist is answering a higher call to God. Therefore, whenever possible, counselors need to work hard to be aware of themselves and their normal style of helping others and think through any exception to the therapeutic rules they have set down. In this way, when a decision is made to make an exception and go the extra mile with the person, it will be to benefit the patient and not to satisfy the counselor's anxiety or unconscious needs in some way.

Dealing with Countertransference. Countertransference exists; though there are differing opinions, many now feel it can play an important facilitative role in therapy if dealt with properly. The following then is a logical question: How should countertransference be handled so it can be beneficial rather than counterproductive in the treatment?

Some of the primary methods for dealing with countertransference include:

1. Personal analysis/intensive psychotherapy and/or systematic self-analysis
2. Supervision
3. Case-by-case countertransference review
4. Consultation with a colleague
5. Reanalysis

All of these approaches except the last two are primarily preventive in nature. That is, they are designed to keep the countertransference from getting unruly to the point where it becomes destructive and resistant to use in the service of the patient. The final two approaches are interventions which may be necessary when a block cannot be overcome through the use of the other methods listed above.

Personal Analysis/Intensive Psychotherapy and/or Systematic Self-Analysis. The reasons for entering religious life, the fields of psychiatry and psychology, or becoming a pastoral counselor are quite varied. No one reason motivates each person who enters one of these special helping professions. Also, no decision made is a *totally* mature one.

Everyone brings to religious and mental health work primitive motives from childhood. Freud felt that much of people's search for happiness is based on a continuing desire to gratify childhood needs. The person who becomes a pastoral counselor is not exempt from this. Neither is the psychologist or person in ministry. Such immature needs may include the desire to work out personal problems in the process of helping others, a voyeuristic urge to see others in an intimate light, or a need to have the power of one who occupies a position of authority.

Everyone has seen instances of this. There is the psychiatrist who rationalizes being seductive to his patients—possibly to the point of even having sexual relations with them; the minister who uses the pulpit to increase his or her feelings of personal mastery rather than as a means of spreading the word of God; and also the person who enters religious life as a means of running away from his or her feelings of personal or sexual inadequacy at home. Unchecked and unanalyzed, these persons can move forward on a path which is self-destructive and harmful to those they are meant to serve.

Going through a process of personal therapy or systematic self-analysis is a necessary prelude to working as a pastoral counselor. There is no way around it. While working with others in an intense fashion, counselors must have a good grasp on who they are and how they are reacting to their patients. In expecting patients to be courageous and to look at themselves, the counselor must first go through the process personally. The more the counselor understands and has worked through childhood motivations, needs, and conflicts, the greater the chances are of being helpful to patients. The more maturely integrated one is as a person—or, in analytic jargon, the less fractious one's ego is—the less likely it is for that individual to stray into an immature arena of self-gratification at the expense of the patient.

A pastoral counselor then must look carefully inward and attempt to get in touch with unconscious issues. To accomplish this, entering into a contract with an experienced mental health professional for the purpose of a personal analysis or intensive psychotherapy is normally recommended. This is supplemented during and after the personal analysis is terminated with a structured systematic process of self-analysis. (In some cases, people feel that a planned, thorough self-analysis is sufficient of itself without undertaking a personal therapy as well. This is *not* a widely accepted position today.) William Glasser in his book *Reality Therapy* (1965) referred to therapy as "an intensified version of the growth process." Self-analysis is designed to take the knowledge achieved in therapy/analysis a step further out of the consulting room and into the world. Even when therapy is officially terminated, it is carried on by the patient (in this case, the pastoral counseling novice) throughout his or her life.

When a decision is made to go into therapy, the question subsequently arising is: Whom should I get for a therapist? Implied in this question are at least three others: Does the therapist have to be of my own faith? What kind of theoretical orientation should he or she have (i.e., must he or she be an analyst)? Is there some place I can go to find someone so I don't have to just look up a name in the phone book?

These are specific questions that need to be faced by a religious who is looking for a therapist. The answers to the more general ones would require too lengthy a treatment for inclusion here. Also, this information has been sufficiently covered elsewhere. (For a compact discussion, the reader is referred to Chapter 11 in the book *Helping Others*, Wicks, 1982; for a more comprehensive coverage, the reader is referred to the following authors who have recently published books entirely devoted to the topic: Ehrenberg and Ehrenberg, 1977; Kovel, 1976; Mishara and Patterson, 1977; Park and Shapiro, 1976.)

There remain, though, a number of specific questions which relate particularly to the pastoral counselor who is seeking a personal therapist. For instance, there has always been debate about whether a person should seek personal therapy with someone of the same faith. There is no clear answer to this question.

Some would indicate that it might be wise for the pastoral psychotherapy intern to seek a person of the same faith who would be attuned to his or her religious lifestyle. Others would take the opposite position. They would point out that a fresh point of view from someone not steeped in the same religious tradition is preferable.

A possibly more reasonable approach to the issue than either of the previous two extremes is to pick someone who believes in the existence of God and respects the religious way of life. Belief in God would seem to be a baseline since it would be difficult to attain enough empathy with the religious if the therapist did not see God as a relevant, important entity.

With regard to respect, unless there is an appreciation of the religious' way of life, bias could interfere. For instance, if there were a lack of respect for a Catholic priest's or sister's vow of celibacy, then the therapist might quickly assume the vow was the problem each time this type of religious came into therapy.

When respect and acceptance are there though, such difficulties can be avoided. A therapist who believes in God may not be someone who focuses strongly on having the Holy Spirit as an affective life-giving element of life. However, this same therapist could still treat pentecostals or charismatic Catholics and respect their type of worship and style of involvement with God.

In line with this respect, there must also be present an ability to question anything about the style of faith the religious holds. Respect for the way a person believes does not preclude this. This point is very important since religion like anything else can be employed defensively.

Therapeutic orientation is also important to ascertain. A pastoral counseling intern need not go into analysis which involves three to five sessions a week for a number of years with a professional whose theoretical base is Freudian or neo-Freudian. Some interns *may* choose this route, but it is not necessary or even the best approach for everyone. On the other hand, the therapist chosen should be someone whose professional orientation includes at least some psychoanalytic theory and practice—in other words, someone who does what we refer to as "intensive psychotherapy."

In reality, most therapists today are labeled as "eclectic." This means that they have integrated a number of schools of thought into their therapy. If the therapist has done this, yet still retains the primary features of psychoanalytically-oriented psychotherapy, then this individual would probably be suitable from a theoretical standpoint. Discussion regarding the therapist's orientation is certainly appropriate in the first session. By the same token, those desirous of doing intensive pastoral psychotherapy themselves someday (which by definition is in part based on depth psychology) are cautioned from having their own personal therapy done by a professional who is far afield from analytically oriented psychotherapy—i.e., Behavorist, Gestaltist, Transactional Analysis therapist, etc.

Help in choosing a particular therapist can be sought from the headquarters of the group to which the religious belongs. For example, many Catholic archdioceses maintain a list of approved therapists for Catholic religious/laity who request mental health assistance. Local theology schools and centers for pastoral counseling and psychotherapy can also provide assistance. Naturally, there is also the less reliable, but frequently helpful, source of other members of one's religious denomination who have had past experiences with therapists residing in the area. Whatever the method used though, this choice is an important one, so it should be made with care.

Supervision. The same principles involved in obtaining a healthy, well-trained, appropriate therapist are applicable in the choice of seeking a counseling supervisor. Supervision is the key to useful consolidation of therapeutic theories and skills. In working with patients, the pastoral counselor begins the delicate process of taking knowledge from lectures, readings, and tapes, and applying this information in actual encounters with other persons.

What may have seemed quite clear in a book can become quite confusing in an *in vivo* situation. Principles are guidelines; they form attitudes, but they do not provide a real understanding of what it is like to *be* a counselor. This comes with experience. Supervision provides help in becoming more attuned to one's personal approaches and countertransferences, and is a step toward integrating good theory and practice in a way that ultimately results in positive professional growth and formation.

Expense is often cited as a reason why a supervisor is not obtained after graduation. This is shortsighted since the tuition for a pastoral counseling/psychotherapy program or course is probably much greater than the fees that are paid for supervision. Yet, without supervision the value of having completed a pastoral program would be greatly limited.

Another reason for not obtaining supervision after completing a program is that some supervision is experienced as part of pastoral training. This help, though necessary, is not enough. The completion of formal training is an ideal juncture at which to seek supervision. It is at this point that professional formation and growth are accelerated and consolidated.

In the beginning of supervision there is much focus on countertransference. This information is invaluable. Even for the novice who has undergone a personal therapy, this is the case. After this focus on the countertransference has been given primary attention, a bulk of the time is then given to the technique and style of the counselor. Both of these phases of supervision enable the pastoral counselor/therapist to integrate, solidify, and elucidate a personal—probably eclectic—therapeutic philosophy to the point where it becomes vital and powerful.

Case-by-Case Countertransference Review. Counselors generally take the time to jot down notes on their sessions. This is usually done immediately after the session. The complex aspects of the interaction are fresh then. If time or circumstances do not permit, notes are made at the end of the day after all patients have been seen. Whichever method is chosen, such a time is an ideal opportunity to do a countertransference review as well.

Each session can be reviewed for process and content—the former being the theme and unspoken flow of the session, the latter being the specific issues that were addressed. The process is the music, the content the lyrics; both are important to examine and thus determine how the counselor felt and responded durng the session.

Even though immediate monitoring of reactions and feelings is done, a written review of thoughts, feelings, and anxieties felt after the session is also essential. In doing this for each session important revealing patterns develop. This makes it easier to see the consistent, particular technique ("countertransference structure"—Racker, 1968) one is developing and using with different patients.

In conducting a case-by-case review, the following questions are usually presented. What did the person say and how did he or she come across? How did I feel being with the person today? Did my attitude or affect change within, and possibly without (visibly), in my dealings with the patient during certain points in the session? What is my present attitude toward the patient as a result of this past therapeutic encounter with him or her? As these questions are answered the unconscious levels and nuances in the style the patient is using at this point in the therapeutic relationship come to light. By monitoring countertransferences, much can be learned about messages the patient is sending as well as about the therapist's response. As a matter of fact, the process can even aid in arriving at a preliminary diagnosis. This can be seen in the following chart for pastors by Lee (1980, p. 12).

Pastor's Feelings	**Possible Diagnosis of the Person**
Male pastor feels actually aroused by the female patient	Hysteria
Feeling used or manipulated	Sociopath or narcissistic
Feeling guilty	Passive-dependent
Feeling annoyed, frustrated and angry	Obsessive-compulsive or passive-aggressive
Feeling afraid	Schizophrenia, borderline syndrome or primary affective disorder
Feeling attacked or provoked	Paranoia

So, being in tune with countertransference from the very *first* contact can facilitate counseling and provide invaluable information from which original hypotheses can be developed. As the counseling proceeds, personal feelings should be continually monitored to see if the diagnosis as well as the thrust of the treatment needs to be altered.

Countertransferences represent not only the counselor's own unconscious communication to self, but the patient's unconscious communication to the counselor as well. In the above chart, when the male pastor feels actually aroused by the female patient, he is coming in touch with his own primitive sexual needs (i.e., the need to be loved and recognized, the need for status—to be attractive to others). However, he is also getting the unconscious message from the patient that she wishes to have control, to demonstrate her (sexual) power to win over (conquer) an important person like the pastor. For the patient, the issue is power, not sexual attraction; the hysterical person does not have a mature sexual interest, but is seeking to demonstrate personal mastery over someone else—albeit in an immature aggressive fashion.

This process is all on the unconscious level. Thus, if the pastor responded to the sexual overtones, or even was physically warm in gesture, problems might result. The patient whose behavior is unconsciously motivated might interpret the pastor's putting his arm around her as a gesture that he is seriously and intimately interested in her. The result of this might be that she would withdraw and accuse the pastor of improper advances, or proceed to think that he wants to become involved with her further. In either case, the pastor is in for difficulty because he did not monitor his countertransference sufficiently to see both his own unresolved needs and the immature style his parishioner was displaying.

Consultation with a Colleague. One of the easiest and most rewarding ways of dealing with the countertransference is to consult with one's colleagues. They are often able to shed new light on a case because of their distance from it. Presenting case material to a colleague helps to get additional data on the flow of the therapy and shows where the pastoral counselor's involvement in it is problematic. In presenting a case for review, the following minimal elements are necessary: case history; transcript of one or two recent sessions; review of personal feelings and questions about the patient with illustrations of what the therapist believes is producing them. In the event one colleague isn't of help, seeking the input of another senior colleague or supervisor is usually in order.

To seek such assistance takes a degree of courage and humility. Yet, in doing this the counselor is merely modeling the courage patients are being asked to have—i.e., to be open to the views and insights of others so it is possible to understand one's own personality and its ramifications more clearly. This point cannot be emphasized enough.

Reanalysis. In some cases, all of the preventive methods and interventions do not seem to help. In such an instance, possibly entry or reentry into a personal psychotherapy is indicated. Sexual involvement with a patient or extreme feelings of depression or anger which cannot be worked through by other methods would indicate that there is a conflict which needs to be examined and dealt with in a direct manner.

When problems arise which are resistant to any kind of normal intervention some counselors unfortunately do not have the courage to ask for help from a colleague or to enter into a personal therapy; instead they build up a new so-called "therapeutic philosophy" based on their defenses. So, rather than trying to see why it is that they are acting-out their impulses to make love or be angry at certain patients, they develop a type of "treatment" (love therapy? confrontation treatment?) which incorporates their sexual and aggressive infantile impulses and actions. This is sad and unfortunately occurs more often than one would like to think possible.

Link of Countertransference with Burnout. A good deal of attention has been given to dealing with countertransference so it does not reach the proportion where it interferes with the counselor's work with the *patient/client*. However, there are extreme problems which can result for the counselor as well if countertransference is not noticed in time and curbed. This is clearly presented by Chessic (1974, pp. 166, 167) in his discussion of Wile's (1972) comments on the dire results possible with prolonged unanalyzed countertransference.

> The therapist must systematically struggle within himself to understand and master the forces of countertransference structure, which always interfere with his correct understanding and interpretations to the patient.
> . . . In every psychotherapy the therapist "learns" from his patients. He expands his boundaries of human understanding, increases his maturity, and achieves further ego integration. Conversely, unanalyzed negative countertransference experiences over a prolonged period of time can produce what Wile (1972) calls "therapeutic discouragement," an irrational pessimism regarding his therapeutic work and his personal life. This leads to premature termination of therapy cases, and even to the abandonment of the profession itself, the susceptibility to new fads and short-cut active techniques, or an irrational overoptimism and overconfidence in one's powers of healing. Perhaps worst of all, "Deprived of his sense of purpose and value in what he is doing, the therapist may turn to his patient for compensatory reassurance and affirmation."

In the above quote, we see how countertransference and burnout are connected. If one is constantly trying to gratify childhood needs by letting primitive conflicts and inadequacies rule unchecked and unnoticed, the helper will either end up burnt out and want to leave the field, or will act out in a potentially harmful, exploitive way to the patient. This point is helpful to keep in mind in looking at burnout in terms of the person involved in ministry and pastoral care, for it helps to tie together both the topics of countertransference and burnout, thus providing a common ground from which to work when examining both issues.

Burnout

Some people see the concept of burnout as being unnecessary since the same material (i.e., symptoms and signs) are covered when talking about problems that are already defined in the literature. So, when referring to the signs of burnout and the interventions needed to prevent or lessen its symptoms, some say that it is confusing the issue unnecessarily because we are really talking about symptoms and signs similar to those encountered by therapists when they are experiencing stress, depression and undetected countertransference. Be this as it may, the term is still seen as being helpful here. If for nothing else, it makes it legitimate for counselors to experience such negative feelings. Moreover, it provides an integrated way to look at the emotional stress and depression that human services workers and other invested people commonly experience to some degree in their work.

Gill (1980, p. 21) in an article on burnout in the ministry wryly notes that "helping people can be extremely hazardous to your physical and mental health." When Gill (1980, pp. 24, 25) goes on to indicate which religious are likely to experience burnout, it sounds as if he is certainly talking about (among others) the pastoral counselor:

Judging from the research done in recent years, along with clinical experience, it appears that those who fall into the following categories are generally the most vulnerable: (1) those who work exclusively with distressed persons; (2) those who work intensively with demanding people who feel entitled to assistance in solving their personal and social problems; (3) those who are charged with the responsibility for too many individuals; (4) those who feel strongly motivated to work with people but who are prevented from doing so by too many administrative paper work tasks; (5) those who have an inordinate need to save people from their undesirable situations but find the task impossible; (6) those who are very perfectionist and thereby invite failure; (7) those who feel guilty about their own human needs (which, if met, would enable them to serve others with stamina, endurance and emotional equanimity); (8) those who are too idealistic in their aims; (9) those whose personality is such that they need to champion underdogs; (10) those who cannot tolerate variety, novelty, or diversion in their work life; and (11) those who lack criteria for measuring the success of their undertakings but who experience an intense need to know that they are doing a good job.

In reviewing his list, seeing the role again that countertransference plays in burnout is easy. With a distortion of one's actual role, potential impact, and actual abilities, a pastoral counselor can set himself up for burnout. Likewise when one is not aware of underlying needs and conflicts, being thrust in the direction of overcommitment and resultant physical and mental exhaustion is easy.

In one of the first book-length treatments of burnout among people in the human services, Edelwich and Brodsky (1980, p. 14) define the term as a "progressive loss of idealism, energy, and purpose experienced by people in the helping professions." They and authors like Freudenberger (1980), Malasch (1980), Gill (1980) and others follow this definition or one similar to it and indicate various causes, warning signs, and levels of development of burnout.

Causes, Levels, Signs, and Interventions. Most authors have developed their own unique list of burnout causes. There is much overlap though, and all of them seem to point to the problem as being a *lack* which produces frustration. It can be a deficiency of such things as: education, opportunity, free time, ability, chance to ventilate, institutional power, variety, meaningful tasks, criteria to measure impact, coping mechanisms, staff harmony, professional and personal recognition, insight into one's motivations, balance in one's schedule, and emotional distance from the client population.

Since the factors on the above list are present to some degree in every human services setting, the potential for burnout is always present. When it reaches the point where it becomes destructive, such statements (by pastoral psychotherapists and counselors) can be heard as: "I wish she wouldn't show up to see me today. I'm fed up with her constant demands. So, she's divorced and having problems with her six children; what does she expect me to do anyway?" "If I see one more person who says he is lonely I'm going to scream. Why don't they just go out and shake the bushes and meet someone?" "Another group of cases today. The same old problems with new faces. I could care less." "What's the sense in my helping them? Nothing ever comes of it. I work hard and the rest of the people involved mess it up." "This is ridiculous. I'm way over my head. I don't know what I'm doing, and there's nowhere to turn for some guidance. What a fake I am. How come I don't have anyone to turn to for help?" Frus-

---

Figure 1

Level 1—Daily Burnout:
A Sampling of Key Signs and Symptoms

Mentally fatigued at the end of a day

Feeling unappreciated, frustrated, bored, tense, or angry as a result of a contact(s) with patients, colleagues, supervisors, superiors, assistants, or other potentially significant people

Experiencing physical symptoms (i.e., headache, backache, upset stomach, etc.)

Pace of day's activities and/or requirements of present tasks seem greater than personal or professional resources available

Tasks required on job are repetitious, beyond the ability of the therapist, or require intensity on a continuous basis

tration, depression, apathy, helplessness, being overwhelmed, impatience—they all appear to some degree at each level of burnout.

There are any number of ways to break down the levels in order to understand the progression of burnout. Gill (1980, pp. 22, 23) does it in the following way: "The first level is characterized by signs (capable of being observed) and symptoms (subjectively experienced) that are relatively mild, short in duration, and occur only occasionally. . . . The second level is reached when signs and symptoms have become more stable, last longer, and are tougher to get rid of. . . . The third is experienced when signs and symptoms have become chronic and a physical and psychological illness has developed."

The above commonsense breakdown is very much in line with the medical model and there is some overlap between levels. While they could be applied to any physical or psychological constellation of symptoms and signs, they provide a reasonable way of delineating a breakdown of the burnout syndrome. The third level is self-explanatory. And in line with what is known about serious prolonged countertransference from earlier in this chapter, the signs, symptoms, and treatment are obvious.

If a counselor is experiencing a life crisis and undergoing notable ongoing psychosomatic problems, then it means that preventive measures and self-administered treatments have failed. Psychological and medical assistance is necessary. This may mean entering or re-entering psychotherapy and obtaining, as advised by the therapist, medical help if neces-

Figure 2

Level 1—Daily Burnout:
Steps for Dealing with "Daily Burnout"

---

1. Correcting one's cognitive errors so there is a greater recognition when we are exaggerating or personalizing situations in an inappropriate, negative way ("The patient canceled his appointment; I guess he didn't want to see me because I'm not doing a very good job and he didn't like me")

2. Having a variety of activities in one's daily schedule

3. Getting sufficient rest

4. Faithfully incorporating meditation time into our daily schedule

5. Interacting on a regular basis with supportive friends

6. Being assertive

7. Getting proper nourishment and exercise

8. Being aware of the general principles set forth in the professional and self-help literature on stress management (Schafer, 1978; Selye, 1976; Speilberger and Sarason, 1975, 1977; Sarason and Speilberger, 1975, 1976)

sary. Once this third level has been reached, the burnout is severe and remediation of the problem will likely take a good deal of time and effort.

And so, to avoid reaching level three becomes imperative. To accomplish this, one should be attuned to burnout as it is experienced in Level 1 (see Figure 1) and in its more extreme forms in Level 2. Level 1 can be aptly termed "Daily Burnout." Everyone experiences a little bit of burnout each day. In most instances dealing with it is possible by taking some or all of the following steps (see Figure 2).

In Level 2 (see Figure 3), where the burnout problem has become more severe and intractable to brief interventions, a more profound effort is necessary. Central to such actions is a willingness to reorient priorities and take risks with one's style of dealing with the world, which for some reason is not working optimally.

To accomplish this, frequently one's colleagues, spiritual director, and psychological mentor need to become involved. Their support and insight for dealing with the distress being felt is needed. The uncomfortable steps taken to unlock oneself from social problems and the temptation to deal with them in a single unproductive way (repetition compulsion) re-

---

Figure 3

Level 2—Minor Stress Becomes Distress:
Some Major Signs and Symptoms

Idealism and enthusiasm about being a pastoral counselor waning; disillusionment about counseling and being a counselor surfacing on a regular basis

Experiencing a general loss of interest in the mental health field for a period of a month or longer

Pervading feeling of boredom, stagnation, apathy, and frustration

Being ruled by schedule; seeing more and more patients; being no longer attuned to them; viewing them impersonally and without thought

Losing criteria with which to judge the effectiveness of work coupled with lack of belief in appropriateness of one's approach

Inability to get refreshed by the other elements in one's life

A loss of interest in professional resources (i.e., books, conferences, innovations, etc.) in the fields of psychology and theology

Intermittent lengthy (week or more) periods of irritation, depression, and stress which do not seem to lift even with some effort to correct the apparent causes

quires all of the guidance and support one can obtain. In many cases, this also requires a break from work for a vacation or retreat in order to distance oneself from the work for a time so that revitalization and reorientation can occur.

Everyone experiences Level 1 burnout; most pastoral counselors experience Level 2, and some of us, unfortunately, experience Level 3. This reality indicates why counselors should do all in their power to prevent self-ignorance from replacing self-awareness. Looking at and utilizing personal strengths, readings, experiences, mentors, and interpersonal support groups is essential. Also, riding the inevitable small waves of countertransference and burnout so that they don't turn into an emotional tidal wave is an effort that needs daily repetition.

The literature on burnout, stress and countertransference also implies something else important, namely, that everyone can learn and benefit even from serious problems in living *if there is a willingness to turn to others for help.* It is this last lesson that sorrowfully some mental health and religious professionals don't learn. And it is at this juncture that they either give up and despair, or bring on great denial which leads to the exploitation of others.

Bibliography

Chessick, R. *Technique and Practice of Intensive Psychotherapy.* New York: Aronson, 1974.

Edelwich, J. and Brodsky, A. *Burnout: Stages of Disillusionment in the Helping Professions.* New York: Human Sciences Press, 1980.

Ehrenberg, O. and Ehrenberg, E.M. *The Psychotherapy Maze.* New York: Holt, Rinehart, and Winston, 1977.

Fenichel, O. *The Psychoanalytic Theory of Neurosis.* New York: Norton, 1945.

Freud, S. and Pfister, O. *Psychoanalysis and Faith: The Letters of Sigmund Freud and Oskar Pfister.* H. Meng and E.L. Freud, editors, New York: Basic Books, 1963.

Freudenberger, H. *Burnout.* New York: Anchor Books/Doubleday, 1980.

Fromm-Reichmann, F. *Principles of Intensive Psychotherapy.* Chicago: University of Chicago Press, 1950.

Gill, J. "Burnout: A Growing Threat in the Ministry." *Human Development*, 1 (2), Summer 1980, 21–27.

Glasser, W. *Reality Therapy.* New York: Harper & Row, 1965.

Kovel, J. *A Complete Guide to Therapy.* New York: Pantheon Books, 1976.

Langs, R. *The Technique of Psychoanalytic Psychotherapy.* Volume II. New York: Aronson, 1974.

Lee, R.R. *Clergy and Clients: The Practice of Pastoral Psychotherapy.* New York: Seabury, 1980.

Maslach, C. "Burned-Out," *Human Behavior*, September 1976.

Menninger, K. *Theory of Psychoanalytic Technique.* New York: Basic Books, 1958.

Mishara, B.L. and Patterson, R.D. *Consumer's Guide to Mental Health.* New York: Times Books, 1977.

Natale, S. *Pastoral Counseling: Reflections and Concerns.* New York: Paulist Press, 1977.

Oates, W.E. *Pastoral Counseling.* Philadelphia: Westminster, 1974.

Park, C.C. and Shapiro, L.N. *You Are Not Alone.* Boston: Little-Brown, 1976.

Pattison, E. "Transference and Countertransference in Pastoral Care." *The Journal of Pastoral Care*, 19, Winter 1965, 193–202.

Racker, H. *Transference and Countertransference.* New York: International Universities Press, 1968.

Ruesh, J. *Therapeutic Communication*. New York: Norton, 1961.

Sarason, I. and Speilberger, C. (eds.). *Stress and Anxiety Vols. II and III.* New York: Wiley, 1975, 1976.

Schafer, W. *Stress, Distress, and Growth*. Davis, California: Responsible Action, 1978.

Selye, H. *The Stress of Life* (revised edition). New York: McGraw-Hill, 1976.

Speilberger, C. and Sarason, I. (eds.). *Stress and Anxiety Vols. I and IV.* 1975, 1977.

Tarachow, S. *An Introduction to Psychotherapy*. New York: International Universities Press, 1963.

Tauber, E.S. "Exploring the Therapeutic Use of Countertransference Data." *Psychiatry*, 17: 331–336, 1954.

Wicks, R. *Christian Introspection: Self-Ministry Through Self-Understanding*. New York: Crossroad Book, 1983.

Wicks, R. *Helping Others: Ways of Listening, Sharing and Counseling*. New York: Gardner Press, 1982.

Wile, D. "Negative Countertransference and Therapist Discouragement." *International Journal of Psychoanalytic Psychotherapy*, 1 (2), Summer 1980, 21–27.

Richard D. Parsons

The Counseling Relationship

Counseling and the therapeutic encounter have long been a focus of dramatic representation and extended discussion. No longer viewed as the superfluous, whimsical, indulgence of the rich, counseling is often presented as a deeply mystifying and magical process. Those who espouse such a position often suggest that counseling is an art, not a science, a special talent rather than a set of learnable skills—a process which is beyond the comprehension of most uninitiated individuals. While I would certainly agree that the intensity of the human relationship found within an effective counseling session, along with the richness and value of each human as revealed through such an interaction, is both "magical" and "mystical," the process of counseling is neither mystifying nor incomprehensible.

Leona Tyler defined counseling as a "helping process the aim of which is not to change the person but to enable him to utilize the resources he now has for coping with life. The outcome we would then expect from counseling is that the client do something, take some constructive action on his own behalf" (1961, p. 2). When placed within the specific parameters of pastoral counseling this process not only attempts to help persons to help themselves through a growing understanding of their inner conflicts (Hiltner, 1981) but does so with an openness to the role God plays within their life and a receptiveness to the role that grace can play within this relationship.

Albeit a very special type of relationship, pastoral counseling is *first and foremost* exactly that—a relationship. This point needs to be highlighted, since many neophyte pastoral counselors rush into "doing" and "problem solving" with their clients without fully appreciating the essentialness of the relationship to the "helping process." Therapy is *realized* in the counseling relationship and would not systematically occur outside of that context (Thurer and Hursh, 1981, p. 62). The quality of the counseling relationship is, therefore, the keystone to the helping process and thus needs to be of primary concern to all pastoral counselors.

As with any relationship, the nature and character of the counseling relationship will be dependent upon the unique personal characteristics of those involved, (i.e., the counselor and the client), the motive(s) for being involved (i.e., the specific problem under discussion), and their shared history (i.e., level or stage of counseling). Therefore, no two counseling relationships will be exactly alike, just as no two individuals are exactly alike. The counseling process defies definitive characterization or cookbook formula presentation. This does not mean, however, that effective counseling relationships do not share certain common, "core" ingredients. Researchers from varied theoretical and philosophical backgrounds have attempted to define the specific component parts and phases of a *quality counseling relationship* (e.g., Aronoff and Lesse, 1976; Frank, 1961; Nicholi, 1978; Strupp, 1978). These efforts have failed to provide general agreement regarding the "specific" ingredients of an effective relationship but have consistently supported the value of *the relationship* to the eventual therapeutic outcome, regardless of therapeutic modality or orientation.

Opponents of Behavioral Therapy, for example, have long argued against the impersonal nature of this mechanistic approach to counseling (Wilson and Evans, 1970). Contrary to this stereotype, behaviorists have long recognized the value of a good therapeutic relationship (Wolpe, 1958) and have even begun to identify the essential elements of such an effective relationship (Gelder, Marks and Wolff, 1966; Goldstein, 1973; Gurman, 1970; Prochaska, 1979). While no one behavioral perspective has emerged in regard to the defining qualities of effective counseling, the importance of the interpersonal relationship has been consistently supported.

From the behavioral perspective, a good counseling relationship is a *pre-condition* to therapeutic movement. This point is contrasted with the Psychodynamic orientation (Freud, 1935) and the Client-Centered Perspective (Rogers, 1957) which view the relationship as the *sine qua non* of therapy (Thurer and Hursh, 1981). The psychodynamic point of view emphasizes the anonymous, non-committal, non-judgmental nature of the therapist (Blanck, 1976). While stressing the importance of ambiguity and neutrality in the relationship, the psychodynamic perspective similarly recognizes the importance of empathy and warmth to the establishment of a therapeutic alliance. In contrast with this "neutrality" position, the Client-Centered orientation argues for the sufficiency of the interpersonal qualities of warmth, genuineness and empathy for therapeutic movement (Rogers, 1957; Carkhuff and Berenson, 1977; Truax and Carkhuff, 1965).

Thus, while disagreement and divergency abound, certain generalizations regarding the nature of the counseling relationship can be extracted from the previous efforts and are presented here in terms of three dynamic stages: (1) *Coming Together* (the Therapeutic Alliance), (2) *Ex-*

ploring Together (Reconnaissance), and (3) *Working Together* (Intervention).

It must be noted that presenting the counseling relationship in terms of clearly delineated stages and "ingredients," while proving efficient in terms of this discussion, does injustice to the "dynamic" nature of the counseling relationship and may mislead some readers to assume that counseling proceeds in rigid, stereotypical and somewhat static steps. This is not the case! Pastoral counseling is an active, viable, human encounter which will proceed back and forth across each of the stages as dictated by the special needs of the counselor and client.

Stage I: Coming Together
—Therapeutic Alliance

Counseling places the client in a new, somewhat unique social encounter. As with all social relationships, individuals entering counseling do so with a degree of anxiety surrounding (1) the level and types of demands they may experience, (2) the expectations they have for the counselor or the counselor may have for them, and, finally, (3) the set of rules to be used as guides for defining appropriate and inappropriate ways to behave within the relationship (i.e., norms).

As pastoral counselors eager to assist another individual with their current problem, we are often tempted to rush into a relationship with ready solutions. During the initial time of Coming Together, the primary job of the counselor is to facilitate the development of a "working," "caring" relationship. As such, the counselor needs to attend to the above concerns and help the client to reduce any anxieties about *this* relationship and begin to establish those conditions which will nurture the development of a Therapeutic Alliance.

Reducing Needless Anxiety. Quite often clients enter the counseling setting feeling as if they *should not* be there or that they *should be* ashamed of needing some assistance. As Sullivan originally noted: ". . . all people are taught that they ought not to need help, so that they are ashamed of needing it, or feel that they are foolish to seek it or expect it (Sullivan, 1954, p. 37).

The greeting and initial "hello" may often seem to be a trivial concern to those interested in the very serious and important business of "helping" but it is an important procedure and may in fact be the foundation upon which the relationship will develop. The impressions formed during these early stages can prove significant in establishing the expectations that this relationship is to be a positive, growth-producing experience. It is these positive expectations which will not only provide the client with a sense of hope and desire for continuation, but in fact may play the essential role to the therapeutic movement. The arousal of just "hope" and positive expectations may be at the core of therapeutic change (Frank, Hoehn-Saric, Imber, Liberman, and Stone, 1978) and has been termed by Arnold Lazarus (1976) as the "essential aspect of the artistry of effective . . . counseling" (p. 47). Thus the initial greeting and warm, friendly, hello are far from trivial concerns.

The effective pastoral counselor can assist the client over the initial concerns about this new and perhaps scary encounter, by greeting him or her warmly, in conversational tone and proceeding with social conversation around appropriate non-threatening information (i.e., the weather, the directions, etc.). Following this initial icebreaker, the counselor needs to provide the client with some clear guidelines as to what to expect within the counseling. The client needs to be informed about such matters as length of time for each session, frequency of contact, confidentiality, fees, and types of issues to be discussed. This latter point often has special significance within the pastoral counseling relationship since the client may assume that a number of topics such as homosexuality, suicide, alcoholism, incest, etc. are taboo and should not be discussed with a *pastoral* counselor.

In addition to these practical matters the counselor may also have to correct the client's misinformation regarding the counseling process or the counselor's abilities (e.g., "Can counselors read minds?" "Put me in a spell?" etc.). Such detailing will not only reduce some of the client's anxieties which emerge from misinformation (e.g., "He'll know all of my inner secrets," "Maybe she'll make me do and say things I don't want to," and "How do I know he won't tell my spouse/boss/pastor?" etc.) but will also provide the client with a sense of direction and structure.

Once the stage has been defined and the basic "conditions" of counseling have been outlined, the counselor needs to provide the client with the sense that a meaningful, working relationship is possible in this particular situation. The counselor can foster this attitude within the client by exhibiting those interpersonal traits and characteristics which demonstrate that they reflect a warm, accepting, understanding individual who has both the desire and competence to assist the client in the development or rediscovery of their problem solving skills.

Facilitating an Alliance. An effective therapeutic alliance between the pastoral counselor and the client requires that the client feel that he or she is sincerely accepted and accurately understood (Wicks and Parsons, 1984). Aronoff and Lesse (1976) found that successful counselors, regardless of their therapeutic orientation, exhibited similar interpersonal traits. According to Aronoff and Lesse (1976) such success requires that the counselor (1) provide a relaxed sanctuary, (2) engender in the client or patient a trust and confidence in the therapist's competence, and (3) demonstrate interest and understanding of the client and his or her concerns.

A number of practitioners and researchers have attempted to identify those counselor qualities or behaviors which provide for the creation of such facilitative conditions. As early as 1951, Fiedler noted that the most successful therapist demonstrates:

1. greater ability to understand the feeling(s) of the patient;
2. greater security in the therapeutic situation;
3. greater capacity to show warmth without being overly involved with the patient.

Rogers expanded upon this earlier work and identified what he felt to be the *necessary conditions* of a facilitative relationship. Accordingly, Rogers suggested that a counselor must (1) be congruent or integrated in the relations (i.e., *genuine*), (2) experience an *empathic understanding* of the client, (3) be capable of *communicating this understanding* to the client, (4) experience a warm, positive *accepting attitude* toward the client, and (5) possess *unconditional positive regard* (i.e., non-judgmental) for the client (Rogers, 1951). Rogers' early presentations have been tested and refined by a number of authors, and one presentation concluded that the primary ingredients of therapeutic aura include offering understanding, respect, interest, encouragement, acceptance and forgiveness (Strupp, 1978). It may be suggested, therefore, that effective pastoral counselors will be those who give witness to the basic, intrinsic value of the person by way of their own manifestation of a warm, accepting, genuine, and respectful attitude for the client.

Researchers have been able to operationally define these core conditions and counselor qualities and have demonstrated that counselors can be trained to develop these attitudes and behaviors needed to facilitate the counseling relationship (e.g., Berenson and Carkhuff, 1967; Carkhuff and Berenson, 1977; Truax and Carkhuff, 1965). Because of these findings and the apparent importance of these *core conditions* or counselor qualities (i.e., acceptance, warmth and genuineness), they are discussed in some detail.

Acceptance. If counseling is to prove effective there must be a climate of mutual acceptance. Such acceptance requires that we refuse to exercise control over the client or even demand mentally that the client conform to our expectations. Under such a condition of acceptance, the counselor will not attempt to impose roles or norms of behavior on the clients but will let the clients be who they are.

Counselors seeking to establish such acceptance must lay aside both formal status and informal social roles which may interfere with an open relationship between them and their clients. A facilitative counselor should be guided by the "here and now" of the interaction rather than being controlled by "a priori" role expectations. Roles such as that of male-female, young-old, and helper-helpee may set stringent demands on each participant and thus interfere with the honesty of the relationship. This may be especially important within pastoral counseling wherein roles such as pastor, lector, confessor, and spiritual director may interfere with the desired role of pastoral counselor. A client "confessing" weaknesses to a confessor expects absolution—and thus may block or undermine attempts at therapeutic intervention. Similarly, the counselor operating as confessor may be more interested in providing absolution than insight.

Acceptance does not imply absolute, wholesale approval. Such wholesale acceptance or approval of another is often a way of expressing radical non-involvement or non-concern (Egan, 1977). If I really care for you, then I will extend myself in hopes of educating, motivating or encouraging you to grow. However, even when the counselor has intentions of changing the client, true acceptance demands that he or she must actively allow clients the freedom not to change, if that be their desire. Therefore, even when the counselor knows that the recommendations are excellent, he or she must avoid the temptation to demand or expect implementation.

In attempting to maintain such acceptance, I have found it helpful to remember that it is not from the pastoral counselor that such acceptance ultimately comes but from God. By the virtue of creation, the client *is* acceptable. Therefore, the acceptance of the person, as self, by God must inevitably assure the less consequential acceptance in the therapeutic process by the pastoral counselor (Natale, 1977).

Even when such acceptance is experienced by the counselor it does little to facilitate the therapeutic alliance if it is not conveyed to the client. Too often we as pastoral counselors assume that the clients *know* that we accept them. Such an assumption can interfere with the development of an accepting relationship. Therefore, rather than simply assume that such acceptance is understood, the counselor should manifest that acceptance by (1) actively encouraging the client to express the ways in which they are different both professionally, philosophically and personally, and (2) showing care, respect, and concern for the client and the client's problem.

Non-Possessive Warmth and Respect. In addition to feeling accepted, the client needs to feel "prized" and valued. To respect others requires that we truly appreciate them and value them, because they are human beings.

Unconditional, non-possessive warmth reflects the counselor's deep non-evaluative respect for the thoughts, feelings, wishes and potential of the client as a free and responsible individual. Such non-possessive warmth and respect for the client are not only important for successful counseling but lie as a cornerstone of Christian heritage. "Prizing" another is a reflection of our belief that the client is created in the image and likeness of God, endowed with natural gifts of intelligence and freedom, in varying degrees of development (Tyrell, 1982, p. 117).

To imply that one holds unconditional positive regard for another does not imply unconditional approval of all of that person's behavior, for just as Christ could love the sinner while hating the sin, we must learn to clearly distinguish our evaluation of a person's behavior from the existential love we hold for that person. This principle is essential to effective counseling. However, we must realize and accept the limitations of our own humanity, for unlike Christ many of us find it hard to keep an unconditional, non-possessive warmth for particular clients. While aspiring toward "prizing" all clients, it is helpful for each and every one of us to know our own limitations and call upon other professionals for our own support, both in the form of consultation and referral of our client and in professional development for ourselves.

Pastoral counselors can begin to monitor their own ability to communicate this unconditional, non-possessive warmth for a client by considering each of the following:

1. Was I "attending"? Is there evidence that I was actively and accurately listening?

2. Did I actively encourage the client to contribute? to provide his or her own unique insight?

3. Did I verbally state or behaviorally demonstrate the belief that the client is competent and can take care of himself or herself?

4. Did I appear to enter the relationship assuming the "good will" of the client?

5. Did I demonstrate appropriate warmth, closeness, feeling within the relationship?

6. Did I give evidence of spending time and energy to truly understand the client and his or her problem?

7. Did I employ descriptive language as opposed to judgmental, evaluative language?

8. Did I reflect the love and forgiveness God holds for each of us?

Genuineness. Often neophyte counselors, in their eagerness to "do it correctly," appear to "put on" care and concern, as one might put on a role in a play. All of the previous discussion of facilitative conditions is for nought if the counselor is not first and foremost authentic and genuine in the relationship. Berenson and Carkhuff (1967) have suggested that "the base for the entire helping process is the establishment of a genuine relationship between the helper and helpee" (Berenson and Carkhuff, 1967, p. 11).

Attaining and maintaining such genuineness is not an easy process. As social beings we have been trained to enter most formally defined relationships, such as counseling, from the perspective of acting according to prescribed or expected roles. Genuineness is role free and involves responding authentically to the client in both a negative and positive manner (Carkhuff, 1969). Authenticity or genuineness within counseling is achieved only when the counselor is free of roles and rigid formulas.

A counselor who is genuine, is open, as opposed to defensive, is real as opposed to phony. The counselor who is genuine acts in an integrated, authentic fashion. Further, the counselor must remain non-defensive while avoiding a retreat into the facade of a professional role. For the counselor seeking to be genuine, one of the main ingredients is to be congruent in words, expression, tone, actions and feelings. Expressing and admitting discomfort or even disappointment and discouragement when they are experienced would be more facilitative than attempting to always present a positive, encouraged, relaxed image when such is not the case. In order to avoid the entrapment of role playing and scripting (doing it the way the "book says"), pastoral counselors need to monitor their relationships and their own behavior exhibited within the relationship. Counselors need to look for evidence of genuineness in their own interactive style. Genuineness is manifested by the following (Egan, 1976):

1. *Role Freeness.* The counselor doesn't hide behind titles, labels, degrees, or roles, and resists using labels as justification or disguises for manipulating the client.

2. *Spontaneity.* While being tactful and considerate the counselor does not appear to be constantly weighing what he or she says, as if in a pre-planned, manipulative exchange. The counselor appears to be reactive to the moment rather than pre-planned and rigid in his or her response patterns. Although there may be instances when the

counselor chooses freely not to express feelings during the interaction, such a decision would be made in light of an active awareness of these feelings.

3. *Non-Defensiveness*. When questioned by the client, or criticized, the counselor demonstrates accurate empathic listening and a willingness to consider the client's point. The counselor does not retreat or counter-attack when challenged by the client.

4. *Congruency*. The counselor appears to be consistent in expressing his or her thoughts, feelings and behaviors. There do not appear to be dis-crepancies between what he or she thinks or feels and what he or she ac-tually does or says.

5. *Openness*. The counselor demonstrates a capability of self-disclo-sure and mutual sharing within the context of the relationship.

Stage II: Exploring Together—Reconnaissance

Once the client's initial anxieties have been reduced and the coun-selor has given evidence of *genuine acceptance* of and *unconditional pos-itive regard* for the client, the process of problem and resource identification needs to begin. While clients need to "know" they are val-uable and valued, they often seek direction and guidance from the coun-selor in hopes of developing or rediscovering their own skills and abilities for coping with specific life problems and concerns. The second major stage in the counseling relationship is that of Exploring Together or Re-connaissance. During this stage the counselor needs to provide clients with the opportunity to talk, to ventilate and to begin to define their cur-rent concern as well as the resources available to them for problem reso-lution. The primary focus for the pastoral counselor throughout this stage is to listen and understand. All too often, however, pastoral counselors, in their eagerness and concern to "help the client," "jump into" problem re-solving without properly understanding both the nature of the problem and the extent of resources available to the client. Pastoral counselors need to be first and foremost good, facilitative, and accurate message receivers.

This phase of the relationship is characterized by the counselor's and client's mutual exploration of the manifestations, circumstances and his-tory of the current problem, and the counselor's surveying of the personal and extrapersonal resources available to the client for problem resolution. Throughout this phase the counselor needs to (1) be able to assist the client in his or her own ventilation and personal disclosure, (2) accurately understand the information presented, and (3) actively reflect that understanding to the client in hopes of providing the client with increased clarity about the nature of the problem and the potential for its resolution.

Facilitating Disclosure. Many counselor-trainees perceive the counseling interview as an opportunity for friendly sharing and mere "chitchat." Those of us involved in the counseling process can attest to the fact that it is far from idle conversation. Rather, counseling is a very intense and often exhausting series of purposeful communicational exchanges.

Since the focus at this stage of the relationship is on reconnaissance of both the problem and the potential resources available for its resolution, the counselor needs to encourage the client to "open up" and "disclose" relevant personal information. One way in which the counselor can encourage and facilitate such disclosure is through his or her employment of proper *attending and questioning skills.*

Attending. Attending, or "being with" another, requires both a physical stance or position and a psychological orientation. Gerard Egan (1977) discussed the importance of body orientation in setting the physical stage for attending. He suggests that proper attending behavior may be characterized as being face-to-face, straight body orientation, openness in body posture, a comfortable, slight forward lean to the body, and maintenance of eye contact. Support for the effectiveness of Egan's SOLER (straight, open, lean, eye contact, relaxed) attending posture is abundant. Many authors (e.g., Argyle, 1967; Mehrabian, 1967; Reece and Whitman, 1962; Steinzor, 1950) have demonstrated the increased potential for communicating and the perception of increased warmth when the communicator uses this posture.

It is essential, however, to note that the purpose of the SOLER position is twofold. First, this posture places the counselor in a body orientation which facilitates reception by "opening" the counselor to a number of channels for information reception and narrowing the band of potential noise and interference. Second, SOLER allows the counselor to convey (via body language) that he or she is attending to the client and thus encourages the client to disclose relevant information. In order to attain such a positive effect, the position assumed and the degree to which each component of the SOLER orientation is utilized must be dictated by the personal style of the counselor. That is, while it is effective to have spontaneous, relaxed and frequent eye contact, staring may not only be perceived as threatening but also act as a major source of distraction to the client (Parsons and Meyers, 1984).

In addition to using body position as a form of attending, the counselor needs to use psychological attending skills. The counselor must be efficient in placing himself or herself in a position of psychological readiness to receive information accurately and be able to communicate this state of readiness to the client.

Many of us, as children, were schooled in the notion that when others speak we should be polite "good" listeners who are quiet, non-interruptive and docile. As such we learn to "listen" with half an ear. During most day-to-day conversations, we may find ourselves daydreaming, or drifting from the conversation. Further, during such interchanges we may find that we are spending more time evaluating the person's statements or jumping to conclusions about where he or she is going with a point rather than staying actively engaged in receiving the information and understanding it as it is intended.

Effective listening is not a passive process. One cannot simply sit back and passively record the messages sent. Effective reception requires the counselor to psychologically reach out, beyond personal distraction, boredom, pre-occupation and bias and enter into the clients' phenomenal field in order to experience their world as they do and their messages as they are fully intended. Such reception is far from a passive process and requires the skills of active empathic listening.

One technique which will not only assist counselors to assume such an active posture, and thus increase the accuracy of their reception, but will also encourage client disclosure, is the use of minimal encouragers (Ivey, 1971). Minimal encouragers are brief utterances or expressions (verbal and non-verbal) which indicate continuing interest in the client's statement. The use of an appropriate "Oh?", "So?", "Then?", "And . . . ", "Uhm" or "Uh-huh" along with the repetition of one or two of the client's key words and a nod of the head will often help to convey the fact that the counselor is actively engaged in this exchange and is "with" the client.

Questioning. Often the counselor desires not only to convey "with-it-ness" to the client but also to help the client clarify the current situation. The appropriate use of *open questions* will be effective in accomplishing these goals. Special emphasis is given to the *appropriate use* of questions because the unskillful use of questions places the client in a position of feeling interrogated or challenged and in turn may result in justifying, explaining and excusing or some other form of defending by the client.

Questions asked in a manner that invites the client to expand and elaborate will prove extremely useful in clarifying one's understanding of the client. Open questions encourage the client to expand on the "how" or "what" of issues as opposed to closed questions which can be answered with a simple yes or no, or factual response. Open questions not only allow the client to give direction to the session (e.g., "What would you like to discuss today?") but also prove facilitative in having the client focus or expand on an issue as in "How does that make you feel?" (focusing on feeling) or "Would you tell me a little more about this?" (focus on content). While providing for increased depth or expanse on a topic, open questions do so without increasing the client's anxieties or feelings of being interrogated.

Facilitating Understanding. In addition to expressing a fundamental acceptance and prizing of the client, the pastoral counselor must be able to be sensitive to the subtle feelings being expressed and be able to communicate that understanding to the client. In order to fully understand the client's experiences, feelings and concerns, counselors must be able to step from behind their own frame of reference and enter the client's world and perspective through their use of *empathic, active, listening.* Interestingly, such understanding and ability to place oneself in the "other's" shoes has been exemplified by Christ himself. As Paul noted in Philippians (2:6-7): "Though he was in the form of God, he did not deem equality with God something to be grasped at. Rather, he emptied himself and took the form of a slave, being born in the likeness of man." Entering the world and sharing the debasement of the human experience provided Christ-the-man with the perspective to fully understand and communicate that understanding of the human condition. It is in one's own emptying of self that the counselor may begin to understand the world and dilemma of the client.

Active listening is a total listening. It is a reception of all of the cues (verbal and non-verbal) which are being sent from the client, from the environment, and from within oneself. These signals are then accurately identified in order to focus on the intended message. Active empathic listening demands that the counselor stop talking internally (i.e., psychologically) and quiet the voice inside which argues mentally, passes judgment and races to conclusions or points of rebuttal. It requires us to concentrate not only on what is being said but how it is said and to check our reception for its accuracy. Although it sounds simple, in practice it is quite difficult.

In addition to insuring the counselor's own understanding of the clients' disclosures, it is equally important that the clients themselves gain in clarity and insight about the problem under discussion and the resources available to them. Most people are not fully aware of how strongly or uniquely they feel about particular matters, even though they may express their opinions openly. The counselor thus seeks to increase the clients' awareness of their own personal attitudes and their potential impact on their behavior. Through the counselor's accurate reflection of his or her own understanding of the clients' condition back to the clients, they themselves begin to better understand their own feelings about certain things.

Accurate Empathy. Increasing the client's own personal insight and clarity regarding the current situation may be facilitated by the counselor's appropriate use of advanced accurate empathy. According to Carkhuff (1969) there are two levels of accurate empathy. The first, primary level accurate empathy, requires that the counselor reflect what is *explicitly* presented by the client. That is, rather than attempting to dig down and interrupt or draw conclusions based on implication or supposition, the counselor assimilates the information being presented by the client and re-flects that understanding. For example:

Client: "Boy, when she does that it makes me furious. I hate being stood up."
Counselor: "Having someone stand you up appears to really make you angry."

Quite often, clients find that "hearing" and "seeing" what they say or do as reflected from the counselor provides them with a more objective perspective and increased clarity about their current state.

Advanced accurate empathy is the second level of accurate empathy. Advanced accurate empathy attempts to get at not only what is *explicitly* expressed, but also what is *implied.* The counselor in an attempt to "com-pletely" understand that which is being presented will assimilate all of the information about the client and reflect the entirety of this information to the client. Thus, the counselor will reflect what is being presented by the client in light of *how* it is said (using tone of voice, body language as cues) and *what else* has been said (developmental and historical context). We may then see the previous client's statement reflected somewhat differ-ently:

Client: "Boy, when she does that it makes me furious (client frown-ing). I hate being stood up (voice tapering off)."
Counselor: "I know you said it makes you furious to be stood up, but your frown and softened voice almost suggest that it is hurt and sadness you feel more than anger."

It must be highlighted that such advanced empathy is not a matter of mind-reading or blind guess, but rather comes as a natural outgrowth of "truly being with the client" and seeing the world through his or her eyes. Needless to say if such a technique is used too early in the relationship it may elevate the client's initial anxieties about the counselor's ability to read minds. However, when used appropriately such advanced empathy not only provides clients with a sense that the counselor is really with them but often provides them with an insight and clarity about their problems or their resources which they did not previously possess.

Stage III: Acting Together— Intervention

Once the counseling relationship has been established as being a warm, caring, supportive encounter and the specific client concerns and problems are clearly understood by both participants, the counseling moves into a stage of action or intervention. Regardless of whether we call this stage Acting Together, Intervention, Remediation, Education, or simply Problem Solving, it is the point in the relationship in which the counselor and the client need to begin to identify potential strategies for problem resolution and alternatives to coping and adjusting. Such strategies need to be feasible given the client's style and resources. It is this demand of feasibility that requires that all such strategies develop from a *mutual* exchange and sense of Acting Together.

The somewhat narrow focus of the current chapter prevents an elaborate discussion of the varied "problem solving" techniques employed in counseling. The interested reader is encouraged to pursue in-depth study of intervention techniques discussed throughout the remainder of the book. The focus within the current chapter is on the *process* of such "problem solving" rather than the specific content. Therefore, it is sufficient for the purpose of this chapter to note that the process of "Acting Together" requires that the relationship move through the *planning, implementing*, and *evaluating* of an intervention. Further, it needs to be emphasized that throughout each of these stages, the focus needs to be on mutual involvement. The hope of the counselor is to not only assist clients with this or that specific problem but to aid clients in developing a more efficient coping style and to sharpen their own problem solving and life adjustment mechanisms so that potential future problems can be avoided. As such, concerns for making the planning, implementing and evaluating a *joint* effort of both the client and counselor are of prime importance.

Planning. Engaging in this "helping" intervention process is quite often the major "pay off" for the pastoral counselor. We must remind ourselves, however, that the purpose of our counseling is to assist clients with their needs and not simply to satisfy our own need to be a "helper." Quite often the "most appropriate" intervention plan is to seek professional assistance through referral.

As counselors, we must be aware of our limited skills and expertise and learn to recognize those clients and client-problems for which we are ill-equipped to intervene. If special, professional aid appears necessary, the development of a plan for contracting with such assistance becomes the major focus for the client and the pastoral counselor during this phase of intervention.

Although I am suggesting that we always consider referral as an appropriate strategy, I am not implying that the pastoral counselor should always refer. The decision to refer a client to another professional is a difficult and complex one. The bonding which results from working with clients on their problem and resource identification often makes referral a difficult task. If, however, we are cognizant of our mission (i.e., to assist the client) then referral will not only be possible but also a desirable strategy for helping the client. Whom and when to refer are questions which demand a personal response. There are no simple formulas. As a general rule, however, I might suggest that referral is appropriate whenever the client's demands exceed your own personal-professional resources. Thus when the client's problem is extremely severe or long-standing, or when the intervention clearly demands specialized skills or extended, lengthy contact, then one might seek referral for professional assistance.

As with any "intervention plan," referral should be done in collaboration with the client. Thus not only must the pastoral counselor recognize when to seek professional assistance, but he or she must also be able to convey the value of such assistance to the client. A client hearing that referral is being considered may react with anxiety ("Oh no, now what?"); anger ("After all we've been through, you're going to dump me") or depression ("I'm hopeless—nobody can help"). Such negative reactions need to be addressed and confronted by the counselor. Such clients need (1) to be assured that they (or their condition) are not hopeless, but that this is the logical, efficient course of treatment, (2) to accept that we are not dumping them, but rather seeking assistance for our own efforts, and (3) to understand exactly what referral will involve so that their anxieties may be reduced.

The client needs to be provided with complete, detailed information about the type of professionals being considered, their speciality and the connection between this speciality and the client's problem. Providing such detailed information, requires that the counselor be familiar with the various types of professionals available in their area and the various "specialities" and treatment regimens employed. Further, the counselor needs a basic understanding of the value of each treatment modality or speciality for each of the problems under consideration. The readings listed in the reference section of this chapter along with the information provided throughout this text should assist the pastoral counselor with the afore-mentioned concerns. In addition, it is suggested that the interested reader review *Counseling Strategies and Intervention Techniques for the Human Services* (Wicks and Parsons, 1984), *Clinical Practice of Psychology* (Walker, 1981) and *Clinical Information for Pastoral Counseling* (Mc-Lemore, 1978) for additional guidelines and contact the local Mental Health and Mental Retardation Association for a listing of services available in one's particular area.

Once the client understands and accepts the rationale and process of referral, the counselor can begin the process of contracting for professional assistance. During these early stages of the referral the pastoral counselor plays an essential role for both the client and the consultant. The client, still somewhat anxious about this new relationship, is in need of the counselor's support. Similarly, the professional to whom the referral is made can benefit from the insights and experiences of the counselor. Thus the counselor should have the client give permission to release information to the professional. This information, detailing the counselor's experience and observations with the client, will facilitate the professional's development of an intervention strategy for the client.

When referral is not deemed needed, then the process of intervention planning becomes the primary concern and responsibility of the pastoral counselor. The pastoral counselor who successfully reaches this stage in the relationship is often all too willing to *tell* the client what to do. If the goal of counseling is twofold—in that we are attempting to provide a problem solution while at the same time assisting clients to redevelop their problem solving capabilities—then we must refrain from offering "ready-made" solutions. The goals during this stage of counseling are (1) to help clients in their efforts to get in touch with their own problem solving resources, (2) to develop those skills and talents which may be essential to problem solving and which are not currently within the clients' repertoire, and (3) to move clients toward increased self-confidence and independence.

Often, in the later stages of the planning, the client may exhibit increased anxiety. It has been my experience that such anxiety stems from the client's concern over potential failure and the implications that such failure may have for the relationship. It is not unusual for clients who are anxious and concerned about attempting the plan to believe that, should the plan fail or their implementation be less than totally successful, then they may make the counselor angry. This anxiety about eliciting negative feelings from the counselor may interfere with clients' ability and willingness to attempt the intervention strategy and may act as a self-fulfilling prophecy dictating the failure they had predicted. Under these conditions, the counselor should emphasize the tentative, provisional nature of the solution, and convey to the clients that while each of the strategies discussed may appear to be potentially successful, one will only know once they have been tried and evaluated.

Placing the initial attempts within an "experimental," "pilot testing" framework can reduce much of the anxiety surrounding the "do-or-die" nature of the implementation. I have found that emphasizing the "experimental," "educative nature" of these early attempts at intervention helps clients to become much less anxious about potential failure. These clients are also better able to both accept failure and analyze it in order to better understand what correction needs to take place.

Implementing. Once a number of potential problem solving strategies have been outlined the client will be called to action. A number of caveats appear appropriate, however.

Typically, counselors and clients alike are eager to try their new skills and strategies and to begin to "resolve" problems. One's eagerness and excitement, while not being squelched, may need to be tempered. Clients should be encouraged to try and test new waters tentatively, knowing that they are *capable* of responding to roadblocks and problems they may find in the implementation of the plan.

Since it is rare that clients' initial efforts are perfectly satisfying, the counselor must be alert to support them throughout their attempts and help them maintain a realistic yet hopeful view.

One procedure I have found useful in assisting clients to maintain such a "hopeful" attitude is for the counselor to shape or design the implementation process into small units or steps. Introducing the strategy in small doses can insure the clients' successes which are needed as continual encouragement for their later attempts at "experimenting" with the intervention. Thus, for example, when working with clients who are interested in developing assertiveness skills, it will prove more productive to have them first employ such assertive skills within social settings which are supportive and non-threatening and only later, gradually, move to more resistant and aggressive encounters. Similarly, for depressive clients whose insecurity and poor self-esteem leads them to predict failure in all they will attempt, it will be more productive to have them begin with small challenges/tasks (e.g., dress up and go to the mall) as opposed to those requiring more exhaustive effort (e.g., planning a major vacation in Europe).

Evaluating. Once the plan has been implemented, clients are encouraged to assess both their own performance and the effectiveness of the intervention plan. Such reflection and assessment is viewed as an essential procedure for the (1) "fine tuning" of this particular strategy and (2) the development and maintenance of the clients' ongoing adaption and problem solving skills.

When it is clear that clients are well prepared to deal effectively with the original presenting complaint, the counselor needs to assist them in evaluating the counseling relationship and prepare for termination.

The thought of terminating the counseling relationship often evokes strong, ambivalent feelings within both the counselor and the client. Knowing that we have grown and benefited from the encounter is pleasing, and we are often eager to leave and test our new skills. But just as that newly hatched starling eagerly anticipates with perhaps excitement and some apprehension its first solo flight, clients are often unsure of their own ability to continue to cope successfully on their own and are tempted to seek continued comfort in the security of the counseling relationship. Terminating the relationship is essential if clients are ever to feel truly competent and independent.

Important as termination is, we must be sensitive to the clients' anxiety about such termination. Quite often clients will deny the inevitable termination, refusing to speak about it or consider it along with the counselor. Clients may become angry and resentful, feeling abandoned. Some clients may even become saddened as if falling into a state of mourning. To some extent these are all understandable and appropriate responses to the sense of loss being experienced by the clients. The counselor while being sensitive to these feelings needs to assist clients in freeing themselves from these negative concerns and move toward the enjoyment of the "growth" they have achieved and the independence which is now theirs.

In order to assist a client and facilitate the process of termination, the counselor should review with the client the history they have shared together. Discussing the presenting complaints, the procedures and processes used in counseling and the insights gained will help the client reach some sense of closure about what has preceded. In addition such a review will reinforce both the insights and skills learned, as well as the client's own sense of competence.

Following such a review and summarization clients are encouraged to discuss their own "felt need" for continued contact. If both the counselor and the client can mutually agree that additional counseling is not needed at this point, the counselor should explain to the client that he or she will be available should additional questions and concerns arise. After this open invitation for renewal of professional contact, the counselor needs to conclude the contract with the appropriate farewells.

Concluding Thoughts

The counseling relationship and therapeutic process is first and foremost an interpersonal, dynamic process. The nature and direction of the process is clearly influenced by the training, skills, and attitude of the counselor. As such it is imperative that as counselors we do not blindly enter the relationship, simply "hoping" that our good intentions will suffice. In addition to good intention we need skill—skill to guide us with our listening, our questioning and most certainly our problem resolving. The intent of the current chapter was to provide the reader with an introduction to the type of factors operative within the counseling relationship, in the hope of stimulating the readers' interest in further reading and development of their own counseling skills.

While the hope was to demystify the counseling process, the intent was not to reduce the "wonder" of such a human encounter to statistics, procedures or stages. As pastoral counselors we must always be amazed by the beauty and magic of the helping relationship. The "science" of counseling has taken great pains to identify, describe and test the various essential and sufficient conditions of successful counseling. It is important that we become aware of, and trained in, these facilitative conditions and skills. It is also essential that we keep in mind the reality that "stages," "steps" and "processes" are man-made models and explanations. God does not always act according to our models and prediction. Thus while attempting to demystify the relationship, I must concur with Gerald May and suggest that the effective pastoral counselor will be one who not only is the master of the science of counseling but who also is willing "to be surprised by grace" (May 1982, p. 20).

Bibliography

Argyle, M. *The Psychology of Interpersonal Behavior.* Baltimore: Penguin, 1967.

Aronoff, M.S. and Lesse, S. "Principles of Psychotherapy." In B. Wolman (ed.), *The Therapist's Handbook.* New York: Van Nostrand, 1976.

Berenson, B.G. and Carkhuff, R.R. *Source of Gain in Counseling and Psychotherapy.* New York: Holt, Rinehart & Winston, 1967.

Blanck, G. "Psychoanalytic Technique." In B. Wolman (ed.), *The Therapist's Handbook.* New York: Van Nostrand, 1976.

Carkhuff, R.R. *Helping and Human Relations. Volumes 1 and 2.* New York: Holt, Rinehart & Winston, 1969.

Carkhuff, R.R. and Berenson, B.G. *Beyond Counseling and Therapy.* New York: Holt, Rinehart and Winston, 1977.

Egan, G. *The Skilled Helper.* Monterey: Brooks/Cole Publishing Co., 1976.

Egan, G. *You and Me.* Monterey: Brooks/Cole Publishing Co., 1977.

Fiedler, F. "Factor Analyses of Psychoanalytic, Non-Directive and Adlerian Therapeutic Relationships." *Journal of Consulting Psychology,* 1951, *15*, 32-38.

Frank. J.D. *Persuasion and Healing.* Baltimore: Johns Hopkins Press, 1961.

Frank, J.D., Hoehn-Saric, R., Imber, S.D., Liberman, B.L., and Stone, A.R. *Effective Ingredients of Successful Psychotherapy.* New York: Brunner/Mazel, 1978.

Freud, S. *A General Introduction to Psychoanalysis.* New York: Liveright, 1935.

Gelder, M.G., Marks, I.M., and Wolff, H.N. "Desensitization and Psychotherapy in the Treatment of Phobic States. *British Journal of Psychiatry,* 1967, *113*, 53-75.

Goldstein, A.P. *Structured Learning Therapy.* New York: Pergamon Press, 1973.

Gurman, A. "The Patient's Perception of the Therapeutic Relationship." In A. Gurman and A. Razin (eds.), *Effective Psychotherapy: A Handbook of Research.* New York: Pergamon Press, 1970.

Hiltner, S. *Pastoral Counseling.* Nashville: Abingdon, 1981.

Ivey, A. *Microcounseling: Innovation in Interviewing Training.* Springfield, Ill.: Charles C. Thomas, 1971.

Lazarus, A.A. (ed.). *Multimodal Behavior Therapy.* New York: Springer, 1976.

May, G.D. *Care of Mind/Care of Spirit.* San Francisco: Harper & Row, 1982.

McLemore, C.W. *Clinical Information for Pastoral Counseling.* Grand Rapids: Eerdmans, 1978.

Mehrabian, A. "Orientation Behaviors and Non-Verbal Attitude Communication." *Journal of Communication,* 1967, *17*, 324-332.

Natale, S.M. *Pastoral Counseling.* New York: Paulist Press, 1977.

Nicholi, A.M. "The Therapist-Patient Relationship." In A.M. Nicholi (ed.), *The Harvard Guide to Modern Psychiatry.* Cambridge: Belknap Press, 1978.

Parsons, R.D. and Meyers, J. *Developing Consultation Skills.* San Francisco: Jossey-Bass, 1984.

Prochaska, J.O. *Systems of Psychotherapy: A Transtheoretical Analysis.* Homewood, Ill.: Dorsey Press, 1979.

Rogers, C.R. *Client-Centered Therapy.* Boston: Houghton Mifflin, 1951.

Rogers, C.R. "The Necessary and Sufficient Conditions of Therapeutic Personality Change." *Journal of Consulting Psychology,* 1957, *21,* 95-103.

Reese, E.M. and Whitman, R.N. "Expressive Movements, Warmth and Verbal Reinforcement." *Journal of Abnormal and Social Psychology,* 1962, *64,* 234-236.

Stenzor, B. "The Spatial Factor in Face to Face Discussion Groups. *Journal of Abnormal and Social Psychology,* 1950, *45,* 552-555.

Strupp, H.H. "Psychology Research and Practice: An Overview." In S.L. Garfield and A.E. Bergin (eds.), *Handbook of Psychotherapy and Behavior Change: An Empirical Analysis.* New York: Wiley, 1978.

Sullivan, H.S. *The Psychiatric Interview.* New York: W.W. Norton & Co., 1954.

Thurer, S. and Hursh, N.C. "Characteristics of the Therapeutic Relationship." In C.E. Walker, *Clinical Practice of Psychology.* New York: Pergamon Press, 1981.

Truax, C.B. and Carkhuff, R.R. "The Experimental Manipulation of Therapeutic Conditions." *Journal of Consulting Psychology,* 1965, *29,* 119-124.

Tyler, L.E. *The Work of the Counselor.* New York: Appleton-Century-Crofts, 1961.

Tyrrell, B.J. *Christotherapy II.* New York: Paulist Press, 1982.

Walker, C.E. *Clinical Practice of Psychology.* New York: Pergamon Press, 1981.

Wicks, R.J. and Parsons, R.D. *Counseling Strategies and Intervention Techniques for the Human Services,* 2nd ed. New York: Longman, Inc., 1984.

Wilson, G.T. and Evans, I.M. "The Therapist-Client Relationship in Behavior Therapy." In A. Gurman and A. Razin (eds.), *Effective Psychotherapy: A Handbook of Research.* New York: Pergamon Press, 1970.

Wolpe, J. *Psychotherapy by Reciprocal Inhibition.* Stanford: Stanford University Press, 1958.

Edgar Draper, M.D.
Bevan Steadman, M.D.

Assessment in Pastoral Care

Principles of Assessment

Lawyers, clergy, physicians, teachers, psychologists, social workers and all those whose "objects of attention" are primarily people learn to assay, evaluate, diagnose and assess their objects or fail themselves professionally. They would also fail their prized objects of service, be they clients, patients, parishioners, students or counselees. By the time one has become a client, patient, student, or counselee, good or bad judgments, decisions, diagnoses, and functional contracts have been enacted by the professional and his or her client.

For pastors, pastoral counselors, chaplains and mental health clergy this diagnostic work is both excitingly critical and at the same time largely unexamined. It prompted one of us in the 1960's to feature concepts of assessment in a book on psychiatry and pastoral care that were expressed primarily in the basic section of that work, entitled "Pastoral Diagnosis." (We recommend this reference, both as an initial comprehensive effort to understand pastoral diagnosis and assessment and as the locus for innovative additions and utilizations by others.) In this book processes of evaluation are seen as being necessarily followed by "Pastoral Treatment" and finally "Religion as a Human Resource" (Draper, 1968).

Today we use religious ideas and behaviors to diagnose psychological/spiritual problems, religious history to understand personal history and religious developmental steps to document developmental assay of adults and children.

Given this, we will therefore seek to fulfill two objectives in this chapter: (1) add new historical developments influencing the diagnostic or assessment arena of pastoral care, and (2) elaborate on foci of assessment which are new, or have not received, in our opinion, sufficient attention, or which offer special promise for the future.

118

Historical Developments

As Dr. C. Knight Aldrich, former chairman of psychiatry at the University of Chicago, pointed out in the 1950's and 1960's, psychiatric social workers and clergymen—especially the pastoral counselor—have much in common, both professionally and as willing targets for teaching by psychiatrists, especially those psychodynamic psychiatrists interested in teaching psychotherapy. In those days, psychiatry prided itself as the queen of the clinical sciences. Most psychiatrists then were psychodynamic in orientation; most training centers of worth prized psychotherapy and were dominated by psychoanalytic therapists, psychoanalysts or psychoanalytic theory. The romance between psychodynamic psychiatry, social work, pastors and pastoral counselors was intense, exciting and productive for many years. Although not over, these relationships have changed.

For multiple reasons, psychiatry has changed since the 1950's in practice and in its training direction from a psychotherapeutic speciality toward a "remedicalized" specialty, a favorite term of American Psychiatric Association leadership (Sabshin, 1977). There are a number of factors which have brought a new eclecticism to training centers for psychiatry; they include: the impacts of psychopharmacology (neuroleptic drugs) in the 1950's, community and social psychiatry of the 1960's (following the dictum of St. James: "Be ye *doers* of the word and not hearers only"), and decreased federal support to psychiatric education with greater emphasis in training on consultation to other physicians, decreased resident applications to psychiatry, diminished third party payments especially for psychotherapy, mushrooming of private psychiatric hospitals and hospital chains, and the development of competing theoretical systems including behaviorism in the 1970's.

Thus, many currently emerging graduates of psychiatric residencies do not carry the same dynamic psychotherapeutic zeal of their predecessors in the 1940's and 1950's when the pastoral care movement was beginning. In those days pastors, chaplains, social workers, pastoral counselors and many psychologists were being supervised and trained as willing students and supervisees. Today, treatment by psychotherapy, (whatever its monicker, whether called "pastoral counseling," "case work," "marital counseling") continues to be of value, interest and daily practice. Nevertheless, it is being increasingly examined for effectiveness, including time and cost effectiveness.

In those early days of the pastoral care movement, "the organically oriented," "biological" psychiatrist was not sought out any more than any other physician because what he taught, or was interested in, was not of professional use to "clinical" pastors. The early leadership of pastoral care found psychodynamic psychiatrists encouraging and eager to teach. That leadership launched the pastoral care movement toward enough success to develop its own systems of training, to place departments of pastoral care or their equivalents in all "forward-looking" seminaries, to create a bank of clinically oriented chaplains for general and psychiatric hospital services, and as "side effect," to offer new professional identifications as "therapists." Some were viewed and viewed themselves as "overtrained" or as casualties of "overskill." Many left the ranks of the clergy partly because there simply were not enough positions in seminaries or in churches or chaplaincies for many of this new generation of liberal clinical clergy.

Notice that word "clinical" seeps in as an adjective before clergy, chaplains, ministers. Clinical refers to the diagnosis and treatment of persons (healing care) and does not imply a theory or method of cure. For professionals, including clergy, who are serious about themselves as "clinicians" the informed clinicians (family physicians, social workers, psychologists, chaplains, pastors or therapists of whatever theoretical belief system) are obliged to (1) make a diagnosis in their own theoretical formulation before treatment, (2) know those vectors of diagnosis available at their own level of decision making and discrimination, and (3) refer, if they find themselves over their treatment or diagnostic heads.

One historical impact of these developments means that pastors, chaplains, pastoral counselors, must now work at finding psychiatrists interested in them as "clinicians" or even as pastors concerned about the spiritual/psychological care of parishioners, or as clergymen with potent tools to help others. Another impact is that a sophisticated community mental health clinician, who knows how helpful pastors or pastoral counselors can be, is now prone to seek out the assistance and support of pastors for *their* counseling skills. Some of these clinical administrators, especially directors of mental health centers, view psychiatrists as "script writers," legally necessary physicians, more than as skilled psychotherapists; unfortunately, this is sometimes an accurate perception!

Another impact is that clinical clergy now turn to other professionals for training or collaboration, instead of their old allies (psychodynamic psychiatrists), especially if those professionals attribute value to psychotherapy whatever its methods, e.g., the behavioral schools of psychotherapy. Another impact is the likely decline of the thrust of the pastoral care movement in numbers and possibly in "esprit," since the movement has been so closely tied to psychodynamic psychiatry. Seminaries', churches' and hospitals' concerns with obtaining "clinically trained" clergymen will be influenced by psychiatry's new faces, priorities and functions.

One sign of the times is that the Committee on Religion in the American Psychiatric Association, of which one of the authors of this paper (E. Draper) is chairman, recently appealed to the APA, at large, to request the Joint Commission on Accreditation of Hospitals (JCAH) *not* to discard their own previously established standards regarding the job descriptions, qualifications, and performance of chaplains in American hospitals. These standards were an important and hard-won achievement of the pastoral care movement and seemed to be a reflection of enlightenment by hospitals and JCAH. How did our committee learn this JCAH intent? Through our own liaison member to the American Health Clergy, Dr. Clark Aist. We should add that few hospitals, few medical centers and few M.D.'s find the JCAH a *highly* useful standard-bearer for truly good clinical care of patients. But, "It's all we got." As such, however, its cavalier decision to remove hard-won standards for clinically trained chaplains is not just a reflection of JCAH, but also a reflection of the times. Chances are good that if our A.P.A. Committee on Religion was less sophisticated, negatively biased against religion, or theoretically biological, our successful efforts to reverse JCAH's intent to remove clinical standards for chaplains would never have occurred.

Things have changed since the birthing days of mental health clergy. They will continue changing. The issues related to greater sophistication in assessment, diagnosis and assay (or whatever term is used that means evaluation of persons by clergy) will eventually be decided over the long haul by "organized" religion, by our professional clinicians of whatever ilk, and by the clinical/psychological standards the public wishes for its clergy. Even though we can't speak for any of the above named groups, we *can* outline, in the light of these historical developments, some aspects of evaluation that are likely to remain important in "pastoral diagnosis."

Psychodynamic Legacies

If we don't know where we've come from, we have great difficulty in knowing where we are going. The legacies of the psychodynamic movement to pastoral assessment and pastoral care movement are so multiple and monumental that we can do little more than acknowledge those contributions in wholesale fashion. For instance, the analogy used in my (E. Draper) chapter on "Pastoral Diagnosis" owes much to the psychodynamic mode of diagnostic thinking. The analogy described a farmer who needs to know his soil (culture), climate (family influences), seed (genes, stock), growth processes (development), plant composition (personality/character), strengths and weaknesses of the plant (the self's strengths, weaknesses, signs and symptoms), if he is to assess (diagnose) conditions and if he is to provide for the harvest of a successful crop (effective solution of "therapy").

There are also special assessment tools, such as the ability to listen intuitively with the "third ear" (Theodore Reik), the understanding of the need to drape the professional with the antique robes of past parental figures (transference), the calibrated use of one's own reactions to others that leads to or confirms assessment accuracy, the search for the "straw that broke the camel's back" (precipitant event that sets off symptom formation), the spotting of the disabling behavioral patterns or repetitious failures, and, finally, a system for unraveling the mysteries of the peculiar motive and the strange act (unconscious, unintended, unwitting messages). All these and many more are products of the psychodynamic movement and related theories and practices (ego psychology, psychology of the self, existential psychology, etc.).

In psychodynamic psychology, too, tools were provided to understand the multiple psychological functions of religion which our study, "The Diagnostic Value of Religious Ideation" (Draper, 1965), has demonstrated. Although this study was done on fifty random psychiatric in- and out-patients, it has been successfully replicated on "normals," including divinity students, psychiatric residents and children. This study has established that an individual's belief or theoretical system, his religious ideas, behaviors, expressions, ethic and religious history are as useful pieces of data to understanding (diagnosing) him as any other data! This study (and others' creative utilizations or corollaries of this study) is still being used for teaching diagnostic principles to pastors and chaplains and for understanding parishioners who still like to talk in the language of religion.

The "latent language" of religion matches other "royal roads" from dreams to projective tests in understanding (diagnosing) individuals psychiatrically/psychologically/spiritually. Skillful users of their "third ears" in the religious framework of evaluation will be able to recognize well-known psychological signs or symptoms *or* psychological strengths in their patients', clients' or parishioners' communications. The greater the clinical skill and internal freedom from religious/theoretical bias, the more accurate the assessment (diagnosis).

Goals for Clinical Training

Effective "clinical training" for clergy ought to provide multiple capabilities. One, it should permit recognition of psychosis that is masquerading in religious trappings. As examiners of the American Board of Psychiatry and Neurology, we regularly have the opportunity and privilege to examine physicians, who are board eligible in psychiatry. These physicians, who are seeking to become certified as board psychiatrists, have had at least four years of psychiatry and medicine after their medical degrees. When their "Boards" are passed, they are entitled fairly to the term "Board certified" as specialists in psychiatry.

At one recent oral examination (which requires previous written examination passage for eligibility) a video-tape of a patient was shown. The patient called himself "Jesus Christ, Superstar" and dressed and acted the part with some success. To the examiners and to those perceptive candidates viewing the film, there was no doubt that "Jesus Christ, Superstar" was psychotic, and most probably suffering from paranoid schizophrenia. However, among those who failed that portion of the exam, the patient was perceived as "very religious," or they noted, "Jesus Christ Superstar? I never heard of him," and/or said "He was an excellent actor" (those answers were but symbolic representatives of other fairly glaring inabilities that were found by examiners) whereas candidate psychiatrists who passed had little trouble immediately recognizing the patient's degree of illness and were not thrown by the "religious trappings" of the patient's pathology.

Two, training should help identify "religiosity," "religious" hallucinations, "scrupulosity," and "miracles" as non-supernatural. Three, the well trained should recognize magic, exorcism, voodoo, poltergeist, "advertised" E.S.P., living reincarnations (including double personalities), talking with the dead (even in the dying) as deliria (acute brain syndrome), primitive psychological regressions, defenses or cures of a terrestrial nature. Four, training should add perspective and differential diagnostic acumen to the assay of "religious conversion," "religious experience," "spells," fugues and dream states. Five, the trained clinician will allow parishioners flights into health, by whatever means effected, including by TV evangelists. Six, training should help one recognize that most espousers of the "power of positive thinking" are themselves depressed. Seven, it should provide a framework for character of personality assay that would, for example, "separate the men from the boys," "the women from the girls," the smooth sociopath from the socially skilled, the quiet schizoid from the inhibited reticent, the affectively bland schizophrenic from the frozen obsessive, the dull (deficient) from the dull (boring intelligent). Eight, training enables one to pinpoint the source of a parishioner's tears, whether generated from grief, allergy, depression (overt or masked), joy, anger, empathy, pleasure, foreign body (e.g., contacts), hysteria, tearduct obstruction, emotional ability, or chronic sentimentality. Nine, the well trained will recognize that certain psychotic symptoms (craziness) may be caused by delirium (acute brain syndrome) or other toxic conditions and may need the immediate consultation of a skilled physician. For example, visual hallucinations of bugs, vermin, animals, bizarre creatures are more likely to be secondary to brain insult or toxic states than to functional psychosis (e.g., schizophrenia). Ten, training should help one assay, with some clinical skill, suicidal risk, but a pastor should *never*, however advanced his clinical training, decide without consultation with a competent psychiatrist that "this one's just a gesture." Physicians, in general, or general physicians do not do too well on this same issue, either. Nor does the computer analyst clinician who trusts statistics. Psychiatrists *ought* to be able to perform this evaluation or consultation more effectively than other specialists. My own barometric reading (Draper, 1976) fingers psychological pain as the primary focus for judging suicidal risk. The bottom line is: when no relief to his suffering, whether physical or mental (usually the latter), is visualized or fantasized, and no light at the end of the tunnel is seen, the serious suicidal risk turns to anesthesia as his only release. This state of reality distortion can be considered a *passing* psychotic state because reality perceptions, e.g., that others *do* care, are muted or obliterated. It is, also, a *transient* state which is amenable to help. A few "paradoxical" observations about suicide: (a) fortunately, most depressed people do not commit suicide, nor do the sickest of patients, e.g., hebephrenic schizophrenics except by accident; (b) even the terminally ill rarely kill themselves although newly diagnosed or chronic illness may be a precipitant; (c) homicidal people are good candidates for suicide; (d) many successful suicides have never sought help nor have been considered by others as "sick" although some "announce" their intentions without being heard; (e) most suicides are preventable if properly diagnosed and treated; (f) religious belief or denomination does not determine suicidal morbidity or mortality rates. (If the only thing keeping a person from suicide is "I'm Catholic and killing myself condemns me to hell," get him to a competent professional quickly.) Further, if suicide *fulfills* certain strongly held religious beliefs, the danger is enlarged, as with a person who believes that death will bring reunion with the one "already over there."

Eleven, training can alert the clinical pastor to another paradox: the undiagnosed physically ill person will often think he has new emotional problems and the emotionally ill will often think he is afflicted with physical disease—*both* trying to account for their symptoms by denial. Twelve, a solid foundation of training should prompt the assessor to the fact that one of the most common causes for memory and concentration loss, or headache or constipation or malaise or fatigue or sleep disturbance or undereating (overeating) or addictions or feeling bad or failures is depression, a treatable syndrome. Thirteen, training skills should permit the perception of "who's the patient?" and recognize that family relationships, such as portrayed in Alice Walker's *The Color Purple,* do different things to children and adults than the influences of families that are less prone to incest, abuse, psychological slavery or ambition, shorn of people value.

Fourteen, a training background should introduce clergy to aspects of the psychopharmacological world. Fortunately or unfortunately, pharmaceutical houses are now much more intensely interested in "detailing" (selling, advertising their products) to all physicians, including psychiatrists. Anxiolitic, antidepressant, anti-psychotic drugs are now prescribed at top volume of *all* drugs prescribed. The *undesired* side-effects of these drugs can be (a) danger to life, (b) crippling, (c) disabling, and (d) bothersome to the patient enough to make compliance a recognized problem. Do we think everybody (patients, physicians, laymen, pastors), ought to know about these side-effects? Yes!!! (Note: We omitted lawyers.) Drug-induced (iatrogenic, if you will) parkinsonism, tardive dyskinesia, the "shakes," paradoxical psychosis, suicidal risk, addiction, neuro-muscular-disorders, etc., are all new "diagnostic" possibilities with our "curatives," not to mention the simple derivative side-effects, like dry mouth, sunburn, constipation, or more usual drug problems like allergic reactions or overdose. (Some of the neuroleptics are *especially* deadly in overdose.)

Fifteen, training also ought to alert pastors to other iatrogenic-induced illnesses or pharmacological agents that produce symptoms that can be recognized, such as from the anti-hypertensive drugs, so commonly dispensed. We are against hypertension. It can be a killer. "Essential" hypertension (unknown reasons for high blood pressure) seems to be associated with aging, obesity, alcoholism, stress, type-A personalities, salt retention, etc. Its pharmacologic *treatment,* unfortunately, is also *commonly* associated with mental and physical depression. This terrible side-effect is so common that the first question we have learned to ask our patients and to teach our medical students and residents in psychiatry when a patient presents with depression is, "What medications are you taking?" Physicians were alerted more than twenty years ago to the fact that rawulfia drugs can lower blood pressure (and *cause* depression). We, however, have only recently learned that all *major* anti-hypertensive drugs, even those without rawulfia, *also* can cause or precipitate depressions. It is also newly being appreciated that even the "minor" antihypertensive drugs, namely, diuretics and potassium-retaining drugs, also precipitate or aggravate depressions in vulnerable patients. Finally, appropriate pharmaceutical agents are marvelous when and if they are correctly applied, and the side-effects are negligible. But, if prescribed incorrectly in quantity (dosage) or quality (correctness), they are deadly, poisonous substances. *Pastors ought to know these things!*

Sixteen, training should familiarize clergy with the "other" drugs that too often cause great difficulty, especially "with youth." Above we have cited problems caused by "clean" (legal, prescribed, counter) drugs. "Street" drugs deserve at least enough attention by pastors to arm them with diagnostic thoughts about these potential killers, psychosis inducers, and addictive substances. Wishes to stamp out illicit use of drugs and addictions to marijuana, cocaine, heroin, morphine derivitives, LSD, "uppers," "downers," "smoothers" (tranquillizers), tobacco, alcohol, caffeine, are useful desires of a society, let alone clergy. Also, effecting treatment for these street drug abuses is totally rational. But wishes to stamp out the users can be the sad consequence of invoking a "treatment" regime before diagnosis has been established. The basic question is "Why is this child or youth on drugs?" (My focus here on drugs and youth is for affective, not statistical emphasis since most drug abuse is not, in volume, the primary problem of teenagers. Drug abuse, whether with street drugs or with accumulating arsenals of "medicines" by the elderly, starts at any age.)

Finally, training can sensitize the pastor to differential diagnostic possibilities with the aging parishioner, including the "senile" patient. Much could be written about the aging patient and the importance of accurate diagnosis, including the necessity of the usual diagnostic process. Unfortunately the aging patient has drawn relatively little research attention. He has also drawn so little clinical attention as to make it necessary for medical educators to induce physicians-in-training to carry out their usually meticulous diagnostic processes with the elderly. The much too common assumption, by physicians, is that aging is an illness itself: that all senile-like behavior, including memory loss, disorientation, apathy, is caused by "cerebral arteriosclerosis" or "senility." This is incorrect! If our society has been guilty of "warehousing" the mentally ill, we are now no less indicted by "warehousing" the elderly. "Warehousing" pre-empts cures or amelioration of treatable conditions, e.g., pseudodementia (depression in an older person), by eliminating diagnostic processes. (For an ethical and economic examination of the "treatment" of the elderly, see Dr. Theodore R. Reiff's article, "It Can Happen Here" [as it happened there in Nazi Germany].)

It is certainly possible, and might feel justifiably comprehensive, to describe something like twenty or even fifty clinical diagnostic goals for the "clinically trained" clergy. However, since diagnosis is a *process* that has a beginning, and it ends *only* with assay of whatever treatment is applied, we will trail off, like renditions of rock 'n roll, with seventeen such goals.

We would like to note that the diagnostic process in psychiatry and in pastoral care *is* a process and still is *in* process. In the 1940's and 1950's and 1960's, in graduate and undergraduate education in psychiatry, the diagnostic process was *perhaps* overfocused toward psychological assessment, psychological theory, psychological applications, psychological technique and treatment by psychological therapies. A famous analyst teacher, Dr. Michael Balint, led a regular and controversial case-conference at the University of Cincinnati, Department of Psychiatry, in the 1950's. At one such meeting, a competent resident and colleague presented a case during the course of which the young psychiatrist noted that the patient called attention to a small mass in the patient's thyroid region, inferring a request for the physician to examine it. To this, Dr. Balint blurted out, "Did you interpret it?" The resident's reply, "No, I examined it," precipitated peppered discussion the rest of the session (and more). Dr. Balint's point and the young psychiatrist's response give hint of the dialectic that demands diagnostic and treatment perspectives that range broadly and still command depths and precision in assessing the mind, body, soul, spirit—a person.

Because we grew up in an earlier era when Benny Goodman and Glenn Miller ended their pieces with definite percussive conclusions, this chapter would not be complete without mentioning that there are now excellent psychiatry texts that can be helpful references (Kolb, 1977; Goodman, 1984). The American Psychiatric Association has relatively recently published the *Diagnostic and Statistical Manual III* (American Psychiatric Association, 1980) in large and small paperback, which outlines psychiatric diagnosis from A to Z. As noted above, however, diagnosis is a process, so that already there are redactions, rethinking, restudy, and regroupings that harbinger the future entrance of DSM IV.

Finally, most of our medical students, plagued by inundation of memory challenges, find associational methods to help their recall. For example, freshmen (M-1's) learn a jingle verse which begins "*On Old Olympus' Towering, Top—.*" Recalling this twelve worded statement allows the student to use the first letter of each word as a recall stimulus to remember the twelve cranial nerves. "O" stands for Olfactory, "O" for Optic, "O" for Ocularmotor, "T" for Trochlear, "T" for Trigeminal, etc.

The mental status examination is both a portion of the diagnostic process and a method for documentation of a patient's psychological functioning. It forms a similar core of examination and recording for psychiatrists as the review of symptoms and the orderly elements of the physical examination do for the internist. To assist the attention of the medical students, especially, and to give them a handle for recall of all primary elements of the mental status, we introduce them to a certain Mr. J-I-M M-O-T-S-I-G-A. "He" helps the student recall Judgment, Insight, Mood,

Memory, Orientation, Thought processes and content, Speech, Intelligence, General appearance and behavior and Affect, when assessing a patient. The clergyman, including the clinically trained, may not find JIM MOTSIGA necessary to recall the salient factors of the mental status exam, but *some* kind of framework for his diagnostic process and its documentation would probably be helpful.

While we have suggested one such model, it should be stated that many others are currently operative. For example two of the present co-editors have suggested a "BASIC" approach to mental status interviewing (Wicks & Parsons, 1984). These authors note that a mental status interview is designed so as to acquire data essential for the basic understanding of the clients' current situation—their *basic* resources, *basic* style and coping method. The authors use BASIC as a mnemonic device for the types of information sought. That is, in each such interview, the interviewer needs to pay close attention to the client's Behavior and physical appearance, Affect and emotional state, Sensorium or information reflecting the functioning of the client's central nervous system, Intellectual functioning, and Cognitive Processes.

Items to be considered for each of the listed domains have been highlighted by Wicks and Parsons (1984) and are presented, in part, below.

Behavior and General Appearance. The interviewer needs to develop a clear picture of the client's general style and manner. As such, information is recorded which reflects the client's demographic characteristics, such as name, age, address, marital status and description of physical characteristics (e.g., height, weight, posture, obvious physical disabilities, etc.). In addition to such demographics, the interviewer should take note of the client's body motion, gate, unusual movements, tics, expressive mannerisms, both verbal (e.g. "ooops," "you know," "ah . . .") and non-verbal (tongue protrusion, lip smacking, blinking, etc.).

Affect and Emotional State. The client's expression of emotion and their awareness of their own emotional state are important areas of focus during such a mental status examination. Identifying any incongruency between the client's self-identified feelings and the interviewer's impressions should be noted, as should any abrupt changes or inappropriateness of the affect expressed (i.e., in terms of degree or kind).

Sensorium and Functioning of the Central Nervous System. Throughout the mental status examination the interviewer should be alert to record evidence of impaired general alertness or consciousness, orientation, memory and concentration. Such impairments may be suggestive of neurological or organic involvement in the presenting complaint. Wicks and Parsons (1984) suggest that interviewers should be attentive to any inconsistency or fluctuations in the client's ability to be responsive and alert throughout the interview. As previously suggested, the interviewer needs to evaluate whether the client is oriented to person (his own name), time (hour, day, month, year) and place (being interviewed by . . .).

In addition to such general orientation, the client's short and long term memory needs to be assessed either through formal testing (e.g., Wechsler scales, Memory for Designs test, etc.) or by having the client repeat digits or phrases posed by the examiner.

Intellectual Function. Insight and Fund of General Information. A number of standardized intelligence tests could be used to tap such general intellectual functioning. When such standardized tests are not available or practical, the interviewer notes vocabulary for intelligence assay and could pose general questions of geographic orientation (e.g., Where is Brazil?) or common cultural concerns (e.g. How many senators are there? or How far is it from New York to Los Angeles?").

The last area of focus in such a "BASIC" interview is the client's *Cognitive Processes.* Taking note of the client's form, speed and content of expressed thoughts will provide the interviewer with insight into the client's cognitive abilities and judgment. Being sensitive to the speed with which the client can make decisions, resolve problems and use conventional, logical means for such resolution will provide the interviewer with invaluable information regarding the client's ability to function. By attending to such "processes" the interviewer can assess the degree to which the client's thoughts are "reality" based, or represent delusional or hallucinatory responses.

In addition, all too often, in our eagerness to resolve problems, we fail to fully appreciate the "place" the presenting complaint has in the overall pattern of the client's life. An historical interview can provide the counselor with the needed information to fully comprehend the etiology, duration, severity of the presenting problem and the client's "natural" resources for problem resolution.

It is important that we establish the client's current concern (i.e., presenting complaint) while at the same time seeking to identify the client's level of awareness about the nature, course and impact of the current presenting problem. In addition to obtaining a detailed description of the presenting complaint, it is helpful for the interviewer to place this complaint within the psychological history of the client. Gathering information regarding previous psychological problems and types of treatment experienced is not only important for determining the severity and diagnosis of the problem but may also provide insight into the client's expectations about "counseling" and the forms of treatment to be used. The counselor should ask the client to sign "release of information" forms, allowing the counselor to acquire records on such previous counseling and, where indicated, medical records. Such records might provide the needed elements for the counselor's understanding of the nature of the client's presenting complaint.

The client's current level of functioning and presenting complaint needs to be reviewed within the light of the family history and current environment. Tracing the client's family history will aid in the determination of the time and conditions surrounding the initial onset of the problem and may provide insight into the significant factors (e.g., genetic, family role models, current work or family climate) which might play a role in the etiology or maintenance of the current condition.

Finally, the evaluative interview, skillfully done, will usually in its *natural* process evoke essentials of the mental status for "JIM MOTSIGA" or for "BASIC" *without* recourse to unnatural questioning, e.g., "What day is it?" or "Who's President?"

Freud's diagnostic curiosity prompted him to jump to conclusions but rarely. In one of his earliest contributions, "Analysis of a Phobia in a Five-Year-Old Boy" he requested, "For the present we will suspend our judgment and give our impartial attention to everything there is to observe" (Freud, 1955, p. 23). In conclusion then, if a person in ministry is to make a pastoral diagnosis with sophistication, he will have worked out his own process of assay including a "spiritual status" that pre-empts a reflex grasp for a "treatment" action to solve an undiagnosed problem—fitting for the "medicine man," questionable for the clergy.

Bibliography

American Psychiatric Association. *Diagnostic and Statistical Manual of Mental Disorders* (3rd ed.). Washington, D.C.: 1980.

Draper, E. *Psychiatry and Pastoral Care*. Englewood Cliffs: Prentice-Hall, Inc., 1965 (reprinted in paperback, Fortress Press, 1968).

Draper, E., Meyer, G., Parzen, Z., and Samuelson, G. "On the Diagnostic Value of Religious Ideation." *Archives of General Psychiatry*. September 1965, *Vol. 13*, pp. 202-207.

Draper, E. "A Developmental Theory of Suicide." *Comprehensive Psychiatry, Vol. 17*, No. 1, January/February, 1976, pp. 63-80.

Freud, S. "Analysis of a Phobia in a Five-Year-Old Boy," *Standard Edition of the Complete Psychological Works of Sigmund Freud*, Vol. X. London: Hogarth Press, 1955, p. 23.

Goodwin, D., & Guze, S. *Psychiatric Diagnosis* (3rd ed.). New York: Oxford, 1984.

Kolb, L. *Modern Clinical Psychiatry*. Philadelphia: W.B. Saunders, 1977.

Reiff, T. "It Can Happen Here." *Journal of the American Medical Association, Vol. 239*, No. 26, pp. 2761-2762.

Sabshin, M. "On Remedicalization and Holism." *Psychiatry in Psychosomatics Vol. 18:* No. 4, October 1977, pp. 7-8.

Wicks, R. and Parsons, R. *Counseling Strategies and Intervention Techniques for the Human Services* (2nd ed.). New York: Longmann, 1984.

David K. Switzer

Crisis Intervention
and Problem Solving

A rising young executive, extremely competent in his work, called his minister about 9:00 A.M. and asked for an appointment that very day. The minister agreed to see him at 4:00 that afternoon at the church. When Mr. S came in, the minister noted that he seemed not to be his usual smiling, friendly, lively self. They sat down. Mr. S speaks slowly, softly.

> Mr. S: I need help.
> Minister: You look and sound troubled.
> S: I just feel terrible. I can't do anything.
> M: What are these terrible feelings?
> S: I'm so depressed. I haven't even been to work for three days. I can't force myself to do anything.
> M: Your feelings must be unbelievably strong, because you're usually on the go all the time.
> S: Yeah, that's why I can't understand it. I've never felt anything this bad before. I can't go on like this.
> M: You sound desperate.
> S: Yeah, I am. It seems so hopeless.

If you were that minister, what would you do at this time? Does S need to go to a psychiatrist? How can you make that determination?

The Minister as a Counselor

This opening exchange between a minister and a parishioner, while sounding as if the problem is quite severe, is still fairly typical of the many times that people call upon ministers for help when they feel bad, are not functioning well, do not know what to do in a particular situation. Ministers, on the other hand, *do* need to know what to do, since people continue to call or come by or such a situation is discovered during a home visit or a conversation in the hallway of the church. We cannot avoid our responsibility for pastoral counseling.

The parish minister is in a unique position both to be sought out by and to discover troubled persons by virtue of his or her visibility in the congregation and community, ready availability in terms of location and having the tradition of "being there for people," pastoral initiative, flexibility of procedure, prior relationships with many persons, and the particular meaning ("symbol power") he or she has for many persons (Switzer, 1974, pp. 20-28, 65-68).

As a result, the minister is called upon to be a counselor to members of the parish and to numerous other people in the community. Most of the instances involved are of a crisis-nature. I know of no data which indicates the precise percentage, but my own experience and conversations with clergy lead me to guess that it might well be eighty to ninety percent of their pastoral counseling.

In order to know what to do in any situation of distress which a person begins to share with us, regardless of the specific description of the problem which they first present, we need to be able to make a diagnosis. Whether we think of ourselves as diagnosticians or not, we evaluate people all the time. Just as with counseling, it is not a matter of doing it or not, but how self-consciously and effectively we do it. Pruyser (1976) has called ministers to task for not taking the evaluation process seriously and especially tending to ignore theological diagnosis, an area in which ministers should be specialists. Without ignoring his essential point of the value of theological diagnosis, it is also absolutely necessary, because of the ways we are called upon to try to help people, that we be able in every first conversation with a person in distress, or certainly no later than the second, to determine whether this person is or is not in crisis, and, if so, in what kind of crisis. It is also critical that the minister be sensitive to clues which may indicate suicidal thoughts and skilled in assessing lethality potential, topics beyond the scope of this paper (see Pretzel, 1972). S's minister needs to make this judgment before any other decisions can be made about the most appropriate helping procedure to follow. If S is in a situational crisis, his minister may be the most effective counselor for him, first, because a relationship of trust is already established, second, because the minister is the one to whom S has already chosen to go and the counseling process has already begun and is "immediate," and third, because the procedures themselves are within the capabilities of most ministers.

At this introductory point in the counseling session, then, the minister has three responsibilities: (1) not to panic in the face of the hopelessness and desperation being expressed by S, (2) to help him explore his present feelings more fully, and (3) to begin to look for any clues which might signal that S is in a crisis.

What Is a Crisis?

Naturally, the discussion of the minister's procedures cannot continue any further without a precise definition of crisis. If we do not know what we are looking for, it will be only very coincidental if we find it. Confusion is compounded because the word crisis has been in use for a long time in everyday language as well as in psychiatric literature. It has been applied to many different social situations and human conditions. Therefore, there is a tendency to apply it to almost any set of conditions which seem to be problematic in any way. This does not help us.

Even in psychiatric literature, there has been very little consensus as to the meaning. Articles and book chapter titles which contain the word may be referring to a psychotic episode. Or, overlapping with this, it may mean a psychiatric emergency, the very first handling of a person who seems to be becoming psychotic, suicidal, or homicidal. The word may refer to a developmental or accidental (situational) crisis.

A systematic classification has been made by Baldwin (1978, pp. 538-51). The need for the six distinctions which he makes is the practical goal of making the interventions which have the highest probability of being helpful. It would be useful for any helping person to study this categorization carefully. However, this chapter is going to deal exclusively with the reactions which he calls "sudden traumatic stress," referred to in this chapter as situational crises. A brief review of the history of the contemporary definition and forms of intervention in this type of crisis can be found in Switzer (1974, pp. 39-45) and Whitlock (1978, pp. 10-13). The minister is required to respond to many such instances, can learn very readily to identify them, and can learn to assist persons to a rapid successful resolution of them in a high percentage of the cases. The procedures to be stressed here apply to this type of crisis and this type only!

Situational crisis theory is based upon the need of an individual for the maintenance of self-identity, self-esteem, a sense of self-coherence, ego-integrity. There is the assumption that there are a number of physical, psychosocial, and sociocultural needs that, when adequately met, contribute to such a sense of one's self. The sudden cutting off of the expected meeting of these needs from the potential sources of supply triggers anxiety, the awareness of threat to one's self (that is, to one's self-identity, self-esteem, etc.), and produces a series of adaptational struggles in order to preserve one's self as the self has grown accustomed to knowing itself (Caplan, 1964, pp. 31-33).

Merely to experience anxiety, of course, is not to be in crisis. Most people are confronted with events almost daily that pose threats of a certain degree, but also most people have learned methods of coping with these, either tolerating a modest level of anxiety for a brief period of time, finding a way to change the situation itself, or reducing the anxiety internally without changing the situation. These are the sorts of adjustments which all of us make day to day without giving all that much thought to it. But certain events, because of their radical newness in our lives, or because of their particular similarities to earlier situations which have produced great internal conflict or disruption and which have not been adequately resolved, produce a much greater sense of threat than we ordinarily experience. In the latter case the painful affect of the earlier experience may be triggered in the present but without the earlier event coming into consciousness (Lukton, 1982, p. 283).

It is important to remember that the crisis is within the person and not inherently within the event itself. Although there are events that we usually expect to have a very potent negative emotional impact upon a person (the death of a person deeply loved, a divorce suddenly announced by the other partner, the loss of a long-term meaningful job, etc.), the truly significant source of emotional impact is the interpretation of the meaning of the event for the person experiencing it (Hoffman and Remmel, 1975, p. 260). An event which some people might pass over lightly or which some people might even celebrate, another person, because of her or his unique early life experiences, level of self-esteem, pattern of meaningful relationships, or present vulnerability due to other present situational factors, might interpret as being extremely threatening. Crisis counselors need to be alert so that they are not misled by their own appraisal of the so-called "objective" seriousness of the event.

Although there are many similarities between persons, it is essential that the pastor always look for the uniqueness of each person's response. Not only does each person have his or her own interpretation of the event, each person also has an assessment of his or her own capacity to deal with this degree of threat at this particular time. Halpern (1977, p. 343) refers to Lazarus' description in making this same point. Something happens. The person makes a primary appraisal (interpretation, attribution) in terms of threat versus non-threat. Then, if it is judged to be a threat, a secondary appraisal is made of one's own present available resources to cope with it.

So there is a complex interaction between the event, the particular interpretation the person makes of the event in the light of her or his unique history and present set of circumstances, and her or his self-appraisal in terms of capacity to cope effectively with this degree of threat within a learned expected period of time.

It may sound reductionistic to say with Strickler and LaSor that "in each crisis situation . . . there is a predominant loss or threat of loss with respect to one or another of (certain major needs: for self-esteem, for sexual role mastery, or for nurturing)" (1970, p. 302). At this point in my own experience, however, I am inclined to agree with them. Obvious losses, such as a person by death or divorce, a job, income, a home, etc., very clearly trigger either immediate or anticipated internal losses related to self-image. Yet there are other events that not only may seem neutral, but may even look like gain to other persons. Yet these may be experienced as a loss of one or more of the needs referred to by the particular individual involved. If a person has been working for a company for several years, has gained some promotions, strives for another, attains it, and then within a few days is quite depressed, how do we explain that? Look for the immediate and real or the anticipated or even the symbolic loss. It can usually be identified.

Perlman has referred to three levels of coping: the unconscious (ego defense mechanisms), the pre-conscious (almost automatic responses to stress which can quickly be brought into consciousness) and the conscious (behaviors of which we are quite aware and which we can use selectively) (1975, pp. 213-225).

When we are confronted with a radically new event or one which triggers earlier unresolved anxiety, often our conscious and pre-conscious behaviors are not effective in changing the situation or reducing our anxiety. The unconscious mechanisms are then activated and begin to function in a rigid, compulsive manner. What has happened is that the conscious and pre-conscious responses which are a part of what Perlman refers to as a person's *mastery* of one's self and one's social environment give way to the responses of *self-protection*, which in their inflexible extreme themselves become disruptive of the person's life. What Perlman has described is the deterioration of our usual level of adjustment as we feel increasingly confused and helpless and anxious and our behavior seems now to be unpredictable and erratic. The intense emotion of crisis interferes with the usual patterns of clear thinking and problem-solving and a person is no longer in conscious touch with her or his strengths. As a person now begins a process of trial and error behavior, some behavior or combination of behaviors may begin to be effective in reducing the anxiety and the person returns to the pre-event level of functioning. If, however, no behavior seems to produce the desired results of reducing the anxiety, that feeling continues to escalate into panic and increasing helplessness, and a person may give up, feel hopeless. Hooker (1976, pp. 194-98) has applied theories of learned helplessness in psychiatric depression to the very rapidly stimulated feelings of helplessness in situational crisis.

The descriptive language used here I hope has made clear that anyone may have a crisis, and in fact all persons do. No one is so "healthy" (strong, flexible, wise, high self-esteem, having social supports, etc.) that he or she is not faced with events in life which are radically disruptive. Obviously, some people may be vulnerable to fewer types of events than others and may respond more constructively and more quickly, have more resources in their personal environment, and move through their crises more quickly than others, but no person is immune.

The behavior of crisis may look like any one or a combination of the behaviors of any form of emotional or behavioral disorder, from mild to extreme: confusion, lack of attention, the inability to do one's work effectively, mild to extreme depression, constant anxiety or anxiety attacks, irritability, withdrawal, loss of interest in sex or eating, sleep disturbances, or even the very extreme behaviors which we would ordinarily attribute to psychosis. However, the behavior of crisis is not psychopathology as such. It is more properly to be thought of as the disturbed behavior of a transient state, having both potential danger and potential opportunity. Because of the intolerable confusion and the intensity of emotional pain and the often erratic behavior a person is in a very labile state, which lasts at times only a few hours or days, usually contained within a six week period, give or take a week or two.

It is important to note here that there are certain major situational life crises whose *normal* course of resolution may well take one to two or more years. This is the case in grief which is the result of a death of a person with whom one has been closely related emotionally (Parkes, 1970, p. 464) or the loss of a person by divorce (Weiss, p. 236).

The situational crisis as such does not begin with the event itself or the first interpretation that it is a threat, but with the experience that one's usual means of dealing with anxiety are not effective and with the rapidly increasing sense of helplessness that results.

Having discussed the definition and dynamics of a situational crisis in detail, we are ready to proceed with the case with which we began. Even though S is depressed and sounds hopeless and desperate, it would be premature at this point for the minister to refer him to someone else, because the minister must first determine whether it is a crisis or not.

The Crisis Counseling Process

Numerous clinicians have described the process of crisis counseling and have organized it into stages and/or steps. These have considerable similarities with each other, and after having read a number of these and having learned from my own experience, I see no reason to change the basic, simple, yet complete outline of the process as I have earlier presented it (Switzer, 1974, p. 79; used by permission):

Contact	Focus	Cope
1. Establish the relationship.	5. Explore the present situation.	7. Inventory problem-solving resources.
2. Identify the presenting problem and the precipitating event.	6. Identify the threat.	8. Assist in decision making.
3. Assist catharsis.		9. Emphasize relationships with others.
4. Build hopeful expectation.		10. Summarize new learning.

(Another very helpful outline of the helping process, detailing the counselor's cognitive and affective tasks in each of four stages, has been developed by Baldwin, 1979, p. 49.)

Contact. Contact, of course, has already begun: the prior relationship between S and the minister, the telephone call for an appointment, and the first few exchanges reported at the beginning of this chapter. In much of the crisis counseling a minister does there is already some relationship established with the person, although all ministers have persons whom they do not know come to them for help. In either instance, the beginning point may well be the same. "What feelings were you having that led you to call (or come by)?" There can be a number of variations on this opening, but it is important that somehow the minister communicate that he or she is interested in exploring feelings and is concerned about the particular intensity of the feelings that led the person to seek help now rather than sooner or later or which has led that person to respond to the minister's initiative.

The conversation is then stimulated merely by the minister's accurate communication of empathy and open end questions inviting more detail. This process leads to the establishing of an increasingly effective working relationship, with the minister's realizing that the person's pain and fear and regression to earlier levels of dependency lead more quickly to that person's fuller self-exploration and emotional expression. At the same time, catharsis, the identification and expression of feelings, is taking place and at least some amount of information is given concerning the presenting problem and sometimes even about the precipitating event itself. So 1 through 3 in the outline of the process are really describing three aspects of the same interpersonal event.

As a person's feelings are identified and expressed, if it is a crisis, there is the tendency for the person to experience a lessening of the anxiety, a raising of the depression as the sense of hopelessness decreases, and, therefore, the coming into more effective functioning of the person's thinking processes. In addition, in such an exploration, persons often give information that is needed to determine whether they are in crisis or not. That determination is usually possible in the very first conversation.

S continues to talk about how he has become increasingly immobilized. He feels exhausted all of the time. Every movement is an effort. Not only has he called in sick to work for three consecutive days, he has not gone out of his apartment at all. He is single and has not prepared any meals for himself and has eaten only very little. In response to the critical question of what led him to come see the minister when he did, he states that he believes something terrible is wrong with him and that he has gotten very frightened.

In the exploration of his present feelings and the reason he came to see the minister, S did not give the minister the information needed to judge whether he was in crisis or not. According to the definition of a *situational* crisis, it is essential to know whether there has been a recent and therefore a relatively rapid onset of the distressing feelings and dysfunctional behavior, whether the person's condition has been getting worse, and whether there was some specific event which preceded the change in feelings and behavior by a few hours or days.

> M: You've really been suffering a lot, but I'm not sure when it all began.
> S: Oh, I don't know.
> M: You mentioned not having gone to work for three days. That would have been Tuesday. Were you aware of feeling bad before that morning?
> S: Oh yes. Sure.
> M: How long would you say?
> S: Several days.
> M: I wonder if you could tell me when you first became aware of any changes.
> S: I'm not sure.
> M: Well, were you feeling pretty low over the weekend?
> S: Not really. *(pause)* Well, I wasn't feeling on top of things. I remember feeling awful at work Monday. I couldn't concentrate.

Couldn't get anything done. Something was just filling me up and choking me.

M: So it really got a lot worse on Monday, but you weren't feeling as good as usual over the weekend. What about Thursday or Friday? Did you notice any difference at all?

S: This is so hard. Is it that important? I just hurt so much right now.

M: I know you do. Everything seems like such a strain, but pinning it down might be the first step in getting better. What about Thursday or Friday?

S: I guess I really began to notice it during the day Friday. I began to be just exhausted during the early afternoon, as I remember, and had trouble doing things. And I didn't want to talk with anyone. I remember that.

M: So you clearly noticed a change on Friday. Did anything out of the ordinary happen that morning?

S: Not that I recall.

M: What about Thursday or in the few days before that?

S: Well, yes, now that you ask, but I got that taken care of all right.

M: Tell me about it.

At this point, S begins to recount a period of upset at the office that took place over a couple of weeks. Some important papers disappeared out of an adjoining work team's office. They had to do with a project that S was assigned to from his section, so from time to time he had to go over and consult with members of the other team. The rumor began in the other section after the disappearance of the papers that S himself had taken them. There could have been some advantages to him to have them. One person went to S's supervisor and told her S was responsible. Ms. E, the supervisor, asked S about it. S told her that he had not seen the papers nor had he handled anything at all in that office. She seemed to be convinced that he was telling the truth. S had had a good working relationship with Ms. E, and when she seemed to believe him he thought that the issue was closed.

Later, however, the supervisor from the other section talked to Ms. E about it and said that he was going to report it to the division manager, which he did. The division manager then called S in, told him of the accusation, and said unless it could be cleared up, S's job was in danger. Obviously, S became anxious. The manager reported that he had talked with Ms. E and the other supervisor and that he did not understand Ms. E as particularly supporting S on that occasion. Later that day, Thursday, the papers were found misfiled in the other section. The division manager called S directly and told him about it, apologized sincerely about the accusations and the stress that he had been forced to experience, and told him not to worry about his job. Once again, S thought that the matter had been settled.

The next day was Friday, and he began to feel bad during the day.

What is the minister to do with this information?

If S had been feeling depressed for two months, or even if the symptomatic behavior were of recent onset but no precipitating event could be found, it would not be a situational crisis. You will note how the minister went about trying to pinpoint as closely as possible the exact time of the first noticeable change. It is critical to determine as precisely as possible the starting point for the search for the precipitating event. The persistence which this minister demonstrated is not always necessary, but frequently it is, and, in fact, the search for the time the change began and for the precipitating event may sometimes take much longer. At this point we must be thorough. We must do all that is possible to discover the precipitating event, because if we are not able to do so, the person is probably not in a situational crisis and therefore some of the specific procedures which are so effective in a situational crisis will lead only to frustration and failure when applied to other instances of emotional disturbance. A number of important guidelines relating to the identification of the precipitating event are given by Kardiner (1975, pp. 4-13).

The presenting problem is not necessarily the first problem the person talks about in the conversation. Many times it is. But often enough a person may fairly consciously begin with a peripheral issue in order to test the counselor's ability to listen non-judgmentally and to respond empathically, or a person will begin with behaviors related to the central problem but will first mention only certain ones of the symptoms and not the most potent ones merely because of his or her own anxiety and confusion.

S has described the presenting problem very clearly, but what is the precipitating event? Parts of the story point to events which would be emotionally upsetting to many people, but it also sounds as if it has a satisfactory ending. S is absolved of blame; the division manager personally apologizes; his job is not in jeopardy. What has he lost?

M: It sounds as if things came out all right, yet the next day at work you began to feel bad and have felt increasingly worse ever since.

S: Yes. *(pause)*. . . . Maybe all that didn't have anything to do with the way I feel.

M: Possibly, but it is curious that after several days of pressure and anxiety and the apparent resolution you have felt worse than you did while it was going on.

S: Yeah. I sure was upset all right.

M: What were you feeling during that time?

S: I was afraid for a while that I was going to lose my job.

M: Real anxiety! You didn't know what was going to happen.

S: Yeah.

M: Are you aware of any other feelings that you had along with the anxiety?

S: *(Pause. Seems to be thinking.)* What do you mean?

M: Well, you were anxious about your job, as almost anyone would be, but what about the *reason* that you might lose it. After all, it wasn't your fault.

S: Yeah. *(pause)* I guess I was hurt that they didn't trust me.

M: They?

S: Whoever those people were that blamed me.

M: You were hurt, but how did you feel about *them*?

S: Well, I didn't like it.

M: You didn't like their blaming you, and you were hurt, and so how do you feel about them?

S: Irritated, I guess.

M: You guess?

S: I'm irritated.

M: They didn't trust you. They blamed you and reported you, and you might have lost your job. And you're just irritated?

S: *(a slight smile)* It's really hard for me to say that I'm mad.

M: How *do* you feel?

S: Mad. Damn mad!

M: Are you aware of being mad at anyone else?

S: No. I don't know. I guess not. Why?

M: How do you feel about Ms. E?

S: We've always had a good working relationship. She's helped me a lot.

M: You always counted on her.

S: Yeah, I really did.

M: And how did you experience her role in all this trouble at the office?

S: *(Pause)* Mixed, I guess. She believed me when I told her I had nothing to do with it, but . . . *(pause)*.

M: And then?

S: She didn't stand up for me, or at least that's what the manager told me. If she believed me, she could have said so. After all, she has a lot of influence there.

M: And so you feel . . . ?

S: I guess I'm really hurt by that. *(he flushes)*

M: And?

S: And what?

M: Any other feelings?

S: *(pause)* No, not that I'm aware of.

M: Well, you trusted her. You counted on her. And yet when you were accused of something you didn't do and your job was in danger, your information is that she didn't stand up for you. You were hurt, and a lot of people get mad at those who hurt them.

S: That's awfully hard for me to do.

M: To get mad?

S: Yes. *(pause)* Especially when it's someone like that.

M: What do you mean, "like that"?

S: It's a number of things. I like her. She's helped me. *(pause)* She's the boss.

M: So you find it hard to be aware of being mad at just about anybody, but when it's a pretty close relationship and if you need that person in some way, that's a lot harder.

S: Yeah. That's about it.

M: You had a real good relationship with her, but it sounds as if you're really not sure about it anymore.

S: Yeah.

M: How do you feel toward her now?

S: I don't know. Kind of sad, I guess. And kind of mad that she didn't support me any better than she did. She let me down. *(long pause)* I sure do feel uneasy about what I've just said. It feels as though I'm a bad person or something, as though I'm going to be punished for saying what I have about her. *(pause)* I guess I feel sort of relieved, too.

M: You've had a good relationship with her; you've experienced it as close. But it's as if she's betrayed you, as though you've lost this relationship, and you *are* sad, but you're also very mad.

In this exchange, the minister has helped S to identify and express some feelings about the situation which S had not previously been aware of, thus facilitating catharsis. This was done in the midst of the process of identifying the precipitating event. By determining the exact time when S was first aware of the change in his feelings, the minister was able to use that as a starting point for searching for the precipitating event, in this case, the loss of an important relationship (Ms. E) as he had known it before. This is the type of event which can be seen as logically connected with S's particular feelings and experiences: beginning to feel the difference *at work*, feeling depressed (in this case, a combination of hurt, sadness, and repressed anger), feeling worse *at work* on Monday, and then feeling so bad that he did not go to work for the next three days.

Even in the process up to this point, the stimulation of hope was going on, even though hope was never discussed. First, S had been feeling more and more helpless and had obviously been isolating himself. He broke through his own sense of helplessness by calling his minister, dressing, and going to the appointment. He *did* something. The minister, through the accurate communication of empathy, very quickly established a closer, deeper relationship with S, thus breaking down the isolation and enabling S to explore the situation and his feelings. With the identification and expression of his feelings, the sense of inner pressure began to diminish, and he could then begin to think about himself and his situation more clearly. The anger could be consciously experienced as energy, in contrast to his experiencing himself as powerless and without energy when his anger was repressed. The downward spiral in which S had found himself had been interrupted and he now is becoming aware of movement in the opposite direction. He can actually notice the difference. He has some hope. It is possible, though not always essential at this point, to stimulate hope even further in something like the following way. The helping person might ask someone like S at this point, "Now that you've clarified how you feel toward some of the others at the office, especially how you see the relationship between you and Ms. E disrupted in this way, do you see any connection between all of this and the way you've been feeling and acting?"

Some persons will be able to make several or even all of the connections very well: the sadness over a perceived loss of relationship, the sense of helplessness and fatigue and depression related to repressed anger, the feelings about Ms. E and his feeling worse at work and not even wanting to go to the office. The crisis counselor will need to help other people by being more concrete with questions or statements: "Since so much hurt and anger are connected with your work, I wonder if you can understand why you might not want to go back into that situation." In whatever way, the counselor and the person in crisis need to put together a sensible connection between the elements of the precipitating event and the particular feelings and behaviors of the crisis.

Once this is done, the person sees that his or her symptoms have an understandable meaning. This tends to reduce the fear that many people experience when their behavior changes and they do not know the reason. In the absence of a clear knowledge of the reason, they attribute their changes to some very frightening source (Skilbeck, 1974, pp. 371-75). But when the symptoms are connected with the concrete event that has taken place, understanding comes, and hope is increased. The person's thinking becomes clearer and there is the experience of beginning to participate in his or her own recovery.

The minister can say something like, "Even though you've been feeling terrible for several days and were somewhat immobilized, together we've been able to discover the reason for it. My experience is that in situations like this, people begin to improve very quickly. You've already begun to feel different during this time together today, and I believe that you'll continue to do better."

In a situational crisis as it has been defined here, when the precipitating event has been identified, when the person has not been in crisis for too long, and when the person has made the connection between the precipitating event and the way he or she has been feeling and behaving, the counselor can make such a statement with considerable confidence. In turn, such a statement made by the person who has been successfully involved in the helping process to this point can increase the other person's hope and confidence.

However, it is very irresponsible to make such a prediction of rapid improvement without the prerequisites just specified. If it is not a situational crisis, such rapid positive change frequently does not take place, and the counselor's "hopeful" statement will lead in a short time to extreme frustration and can very well have the impact of disrupting the therapeutic relationship. If in doubt, do not say it. If it turns out to be a situational crisis, the person will get better during the course of the helping process anyway.

The first session between S and his minister was coming to an end. Certain very important first session goals had been accomplished: the establishment of a working relationship, the communication by the minister of his understanding of the feelings of distress which S had been experiencing, catharsis by S, the clarification of the presenting problem and precipitating event, and S's beginning to have some hope.

For a number of reasons it is useful for the minister to build on what he has just indicated about the short term nature of the disturbance and make very specific with S that they will be working together no more than five or six weeks, perhaps fewer, and that at least in the first two or three weeks it will be more effective if they get together twice a week. The minister will emphasize the importance during this time of focusing only on this present problem as the way of best helping S and that if other issues arise they will need to put them aside for later consideration.

Because it is always the growth oriented counselor's responsibility to communicate that the whole process is a collaborative task, the minister will ask if S understands what is being suggested, if he has any questions about the reasons for these guidelines, and finally ask for his agreement.

When this is done, the minister will then affirm his commitment to S, clarify that the sessions are confidential, and say something about their shared responsibility for the process. This is referred to by Nelson and Mowry (1976, pp. 37-44), Baldwin (1979, p. 49) and others as "contracting."

S and his minister set their next meeting for three days later. The spacing of sessions every two, three, or four days contributes to the more rapid reduction of the symptoms of crisis because of the fact that crisis is such a short, intensely emotional transitional phase. In addition, the minister called S the next night just to see how he was doing. S had gone to work that day. He said that it had been quite a strain and that he felt extremely fatigued. He had tended to avoid Ms. E and had felt very controlled and awkward the few times he was around her. However, he felt better about himself for having gone to work, and even though fatigued felt no sense of hopelessness or desperation.

Focus. The second session began with a review of how S was feeling and what he had done in the intervening days and then of what they had gone over together in the first session. Then they moved on into Stage II in the process. In this particular case, it was a coincidence that the second session and Stage II began at the same time, although such a coincidence is not entirely unusual.

Stage II involves a detailed exploration of the present situation, present situation being defined as that time period between the precipitating event and this very moment, with perhaps a few occasional elements from the past which are determined to be directly related to this present reaction. The exploration is carried out in order to identify the particular nature and intensity of the perceived threat. There are three critical points which must be connected to form a triangle of meaning, essential to rapid and constructive resolution of the crisis. The question to be answered is: "Why is it that *this particular event* has had the power to produce in *this particular person* at *this particular time* the intensity of threat that leads the person to respond with the *particular feelings and behavior* of *this* crisis?"

Important in this process is a procedure referred to as focusing. Focusing is based on the need in crisis counseling to deal only with matters which chronologically and/or dynamically have to do with *this* crisis. No matter how important (or interesting) a particular past or present problem or relationship may sound to the helping person, it is properly pursued only after it can be determined that it has some relationship with this present crisis. The person who is in crisis, of course, has a complex history and present, and a number of problematic elements may be revealed in the midst of this crisis and the helping process. Each time the person raises something from the past or some other present problem, the counselor very persistently says something like, "I wonder if you're beginning to tell me about (this past event, this present problem in a relationship) because you see it as somehow related to this present situation." The crisis counselor directs any and all material which the person talks about through a narrow channel. The channel is defined by the relevance of any issue to the presenting problem. Time cannot be wasted talking about other issues in the midst of the crisis. Efforts must be focused on the most rapid reduction of the present disturbing feelings and behavior. Pursuing matters irrelevant to the crisis will slow down or even block crisis resolution and could even lead to longer term distress on the part of the person.

In this detailed exploration stage, it was discovered that S had broken his engagement just a few months ago. He had noticed that the young woman did not seem to be quite as available to him in terms of amount of time as she had earlier in their relationship. He interpreted her behavior as her loss of interest in the relationship. She had told him of the increased demands of her work, but with his own long-standing lack of self-esteem, he persisted in his own interpretation. So without talking with her about it in any detail, he took the initiative to break the engagement. He missed her companionship and emotional support a great deal, but handled his feelings of anger, anxiety, and loneliness by plunging even more deeply into his work. Now it was his sense of the lack of support by yet another woman, his supervisor *at work*, coming at a time of increased vulnerability, robbing him of his work as a way of coping with the loss of his fiancée, that produced the powerful reactions of this crisis. The results of this detailed exploration did, in fact, reveal the intensity of the threat stimulated by this particular event at this particular time with this particular person. In the discussion about the connection between the precipitating event, the interpretation of the threat, and the specific feelings and behavior, the young man began to understand very clearly what was happening to him.

Coping (Problem Solving). They had a few minutes left before time was up in the second session, so the minister raised the question with S if he could identify at this point any resources that could help him change anything about the present situation. This type of question initiates the final stage of crisis counseling, that of coping, or problem solving.

What internal and external resources does a person have? What about friends and family members? Are there other professionals, agencies or institutions which could meet particular needs of the person? Does the person have a vital religious faith to draw on or seeds of faith that can be stimulated? Is there some appropriate group within a congregation that would be supportive? Are there other appropriate community groups in which to participate? How has the person solved problems in the past?

Because of the importance of this last question, this is probably the first time in the process that the counselor would deliberately ask about the past. "Have you ever had an experience like this before?" "Have you ever felt this way before?" First, if the person has had similar experiences and feelings before, remembering them may lead to added insight into the present reaction. Second, as the person is encouraged to remember how the earlier crisis was resolved, solutions that were effective then might be adapted to the situation now. If the person has already attempted something which worked earlier but has not now, it is often enlightening to explore the possible reasons for this failure. Finally, a review of past problematic situations may sometimes be an additional stimulation of hope as the person realizes that he or she has come through such times before and might make it through this one also.

The inventory of problem solving resources is a necessary prelude to active problem solving itself. It should be clear by now that crisis counseling is not just sitting around talking about feelings or indulging in deciphering mental puzzles, and then dropping the whole matter. Rather, it is an action oriented process. The purpose is to assist the person in taking whatever action that is possible to try to change the situation and his or her way of interpreting what is going on. The crisis situation is viewed as a complex problem with many facets which needs to be solved. A person, after the greatest intensity of anxiety and/or depression is reduced and the reason for his or her own specific reaction is understood, always needs then to reassess his or her own ability to solve the problems related to this situation. It is absolutely amazing how the most intelligent people can overlook the simplest courses of action in the midst of the confusion produced by the intense emotions of crisis. These feelings act as blinders, resulting in the very narrowest tunnel vision through which we view ourselves and the external world. With the reduced intensity of the affect, we are now free to discuss from a more realistic perspective what to do.

Steps 8 and 9 in the outline of the procedure are really not separate steps but are listed that way merely to call attention to the overarching importance of relationships with other persons as a major area to give attention to in problem solving. Disrupted personal relationships (or the perceived disruption of them) are either the direct stimulus or are among the exacerbating dynamics in a large percentage of crises. Therefore, doing something about one's relationships only makes sense in terms of crisis resolution. Even in those few instances where relationships are not involved in the production of the crisis, a person may find some of the support and guidance that he or she needs in relation with some significant person or group.

Steps 8 and 9 may actually be broken down into another set of steps:
1. The setting of goals.
2. The evaluation of alternatives for action.
3. Decision making.
4. Acting.
5. Evaluating the results of the actions taken.
6. On the basis of the evaluation, continuing on one's chosen course or going through steps 2-5 of this part of the procedure once again.

The first principle is that the only goals to be discussed are those related to this present crisis. The procedure of focusing comes into play once again. The person is asked in some form, "What do you want to accomplish at this time?" Most people's response is very much in line with the primary purpose of crisis intervention, and they do not have to read a book to find out about it. "I want to feel better." "I want to be able to function better." "I'd like to have a good relationship with him or her again." The return of persons to their former level of functioning is the primary and first level goal of crisis counseling. In fact, however, truly successful resolution usually leads to a somewhat higher level of human living in the sense that persons have some additional insights about themselves and their effect on others and how they are affected by other persons and events. They often develop some additional sensitivity to others, discover ways of identifying potential crises earlier than they have this present one, and are aware of new behaviors of how to nip it in the bud. In addition, for some people, it is a time of growth in faith and the minister naturally wants to be attentive to this possibility.

Sometimes a person may propose a goal that is somehow related to the crisis, but which is not at the heart of it. The counselor would appropriately affirm the legitimacy of the goal but also would exercise discipline in helping the other person evaluate the relevance of the achievement of that goal to the reduction of the symptoms of this particular crisis. For example, if S had stated, "I'd like to have my fiancée back," that goal would need to be discussed in terms of whether it would be of immediate help in working out the present crisis. Realistically, even though very important in S's life, that goal would probably be placed chronologically after the resolution of *this* crisis has progressed further than it has at this time.

General goals need to be put into operational (or behavioral) terms. If they are not, we are handicapped in discussing the specific behaviors to attempt in order to reach the goal.

As an example, let's look at the latter part of the third session between S and his minister.

S: I'd like to feel better.

M: Well, as a matter of fact, it's pretty obvious that you're already feeling somewhat better and are working a bit more effectively in the last week. What do you think you need to do at this time to improve even more?

S: I'm still awfully uncomfortable at the office. I feel a lot of pressure there. I'm very self-conscious.

M: What do you see as the source of those feelings?

S: Mainly my relationship with Ms. E.

M: You still don't know where you stand with her, what's really going on with her in relation to you.

S: Right.

What has been clarified here is that "feeling better" as a goal has been made more specific by identifying that a lot of the bad feelings are at the office and that their source is the uncertain relationship with Ms. E. Therefore, in order to achieve a *general* goal of feeling better, the *operational* or *specific* goal is that of the clarification of the relationship with Ms. E.

M: What can you do about that?

S: Well, *(chuckles)* the obvious thing is to talk with her.

M: That makes sense.

S: I'm sort of scared about approaching her, though.

M: Are you aware of what it is you are afraid of?

S: *(pause)* Several things, I guess. First, she's the boss. I've always had a hard time with people who were over me in any way. Another part of it is that I'm afraid of what she'll say. I guess those are connected, but they're not quite the same thing.

M: What's the worst thing she could say to you?

S: "I really don't support you. I have doubts about you."

M: And what if she said that?

S: I'd feel awful.

M: And what else?

S: What do you mean?

M: Is there anything else that could happen after she says that and you feel bad?

S: *(slight smile)* Well, I could tell her that that makes me feel bad. That's what I've been trying to learn to do here, isn't it?

M: *(smiles)* Yes.

S: And then, I guess, we'd have the opportunity to try to work it out.

M: That's the point, isn't it? She either has confidence in you or she doesn't, and right now you don't know which, and, not knowing which, you don't know what to do. If you talk to her and she affirms you, then that's fine. You'd feel better. But if she doesn't have confidence in you, you'll find it out. You'll feel bad, and you'll tell her so. Then, it sounds as if you're saying that you might raise with her the issue of how you might work it out. If it got to that point, we don't know for sure how it would turn out, but you would have done all you could do to change things.

The making of goals more and more concrete, or behavioral, in nature begins to blur any sharp distinction between the statement of the goal and the behavior by which it is to be achieved since there is a short direct line between them. This is not always the case, of course, and even when it is, second and even third action alternatives need to be discussed. For example, the fact that we make the major step of talking with someone about an issue or relationship does not guarantee that the person will respond the way we would like. The counselor's task is to help the person take what has been determined to be a reasonable action but also assist the person in being realistic about the uncertainty of the outcome. In the midst of this discussion is the counselor's reassurance that if this particular action does not seem to turn out constructively, they are still going to be having another appointment shortly after that and that additional alternatives can be discussed.

In this process, the helping person's responsibility is to continue to lead the person in crisis to assume the responsibility for thinking of every possible course of action which might relate to any of the concrete goals that have been set. The person is encouraged to say whatever pops into mind without any censorship whatsoever. Evaluation will take place later. Then, after the person has done his or her best to list all of the possible courses of action, the counselor may think of still others. At that point, the counselor lays these out for consideration also. It takes some amount of sensitivity and skill to do this without communicating to the person who still may be feeling somewhat shaky and dependent that, "O.K., I've heard yours; now here are mine, the better ones." Rather, forms of speech which continue to emphasize the collaborative nature of the process must be used.

"If I've got it right, you've mentioned the following three possibilities. (state them) I wonder if you might also have thought of (state the additional ones)."

Wait for the person's response. Then,

"I wonder if you would be willing to take a look at these alongside of the ones that you've mentioned."

Then the counselor and the other person begin to play the game of "What if." What if you were to do this? How would you feel about it? How do you think he or she would respond? What would you do then? What do you think the results would be? How do you see this as helping you achieve your goals?

Each alternative is reviewed thoroughly, with the counselor helping the other person think about the relevance, timing, and consequences of each. Not to do anything is, of course, always one alternative, but it needs to be openly discussed like any other alternative and its consequences have to be investigated just as thoroughly.

After each alternative has been reviewed in this manner, the person is asked what he or she is going to do first. The decision may be based upon what can be done most easily and/or most quickly, which has the best assessed possibility of positive outcome, which is most central to this particular crisis, which remains after others are eliminated as unfeasible, or some combination of these.

Although the counselor has been very active in the process up to this point, the person must always understand that it is his or her decision. The counselor always participates in the discussion concerning the listing and concretizing of goals and the assessing of courses of action, but the particular person himself or herself must do the choosing. It may sound too coy, but something more or less like the following may often be necessary.

The person in crisis asks, "What do you think about my doing this?"

The counselor responds, "What do *you* think about it?"

Once the person has made the decision, the counselor affirms the person in it and promises that they will talk about how it went the next time they get together or even suggests that the person call as soon as the action has been taken. The only time that I personally do *not* affirm the decision is when it is for suicide, murder or other physical attack, other crime, or some precipitous action like leaving home or quitting a good job before any other alternative has been attempted. I state the reason that I do not affirm the decision, share whatever combination of my values, my personal feelings and my personal experience has led me to judge the probable consequences to be, and then invite the person back to the drawing board.

Even if the person decides to do something very simple and which the counselor believes may not do much to change the situation, such a decision can still be affirmed because at least the person will be doing something rather than nothing. Any act, unless it has drastic negative consequences, can have the positive effect of putting the person back in touch with his or her initiative taking potential which had been lost in the sense of helplessness that has characterized the crisis.

Once the person has carried through with the particular action agreed upon, there is the opportunity for review. What was it like for you? What happened? How did the other person respond? How did you feel then? Can you point to specific results at this time? If it did not seem to work, can we pinpoint possible reasons for that? Do you need to do something else now or do you need just to wait a bit longer to see what the results of the first action might be? Is there anything you need to do to follow up on this particular course of action?

Once the review, evaluation, and any further planning has been done with regard to the action already taken, the minister and person in crisis are ready to look at some of the other courses of action previously talked about but postponed, and any new alternatives which have come to mind in the meantime.

By this time in the crisis counseling process, usually no more than six or seven sessions spanning three or four weeks, most or all of the symptoms of crisis will have disappeared, and one or the other of the persons involved will initiate a discussion of termination. If the crisis seems to be almost resolved, but the other person has not mentioned it, it is helpful for the counselor to do so. If the person is progressing well, this can be an additional occasion of the counselor's affirming that person's capacity to handle the rest of the crisis related issues himself or herself.

To complete the crisis counseling process, the persons involved engage in a review of what has taken place, the changes that have come about, the new learning that has occurred, and how the person might utilize all of this experience in the future. Such a discussion will help the person continue to strengthen his or her present coping resources and organize the various aspects of this present crisis and the counseling sessions so that the positive values are internalized. In addition, the final discussion calls attention to any of the longer standing problems that might have come up during the sessions, but which were not pursued because they were not central to resolving this crisis. Some disposition needs to be made of these. Does the person want to work on one or more of them at all? If so, does he or she want to begin immediately? Are they problems with which the minister has the training and time to help? If not, does the person need help in finding another professional?

Finally the counselor serves as a model, if needed, of a person who can initiate and carry through a conversation which deals with their relationship with one another, what these sessions together have meant to each of them, and how they feel toward one another and about concluding these sessions.

This crisis counseling process with S was concluded after five sessions covering a three week period. He talked with Ms. E, who indicated that she appreciated his initiative in wanting to clarify their relationship since she valued it also and had not realized that he had felt hurt and angry toward her. She also stated that she valued him and his work in that company. Even though she had believed him when he said that he had not taken the papers, when asked in the meeting with the other supervisor and the manager if there were any sort of concrete evidence which she had that would exonerate him, she realistically had to reply in the negative. That is what had come back to S as her not supporting him.

S was still angry at the unknown carriers of the rumors in the other section, but he had expressed this anger to the minister and then to Ms. E in the conversation with her. There was not anything else for him to do about it. In the fifth session, he said that he thought things were going well and that he did not believe that he and the minister needed to work on the crisis any longer. After a quick review, the minister agreed and they moved on into the appropriate review.

One insight that S had gained had the effect of causing him additional pain. He saw the irrationality of the way he had broken his engagement and very much wanted to try to re-establish that relationship. He asked if he could talk with the minister specifically about that in a future session and whether, if necessary, he and the woman could come in together. The minister judged that to be appropriate. They agreed that S would call her, share with her, to the extent that she was willing to listen, his pain, what he had learned about himself, his regret about the pain which she had felt, and say that he would like to get together with her. S realized the risk. She could very clearly reject him. But he decided that it was worth it.

He and the minister agreed on a session to be held after S had contacted his ex-fiancée in order to review what had happened and take a look at what else might need to be done. The minister was also open to their coming together to see him to discuss their relationship.

Additional Procedural and Counselor Issues

Premature Termination. As the process seems to be moving toward a successful ending, the counselor must pay attention to two extremes of behavior. The first of these is the person who says at the end of a session that things are going well and that there is no reason to come back.

Anyone who has ever done any counseling has noticed occasional behaviors by people which are on two extremes of a continuum. First, there are those people who say at the end of a particular session that things are going well, and that since they are, there is no reason to come back. "Thanks a lot and goodbye." With the former, if in fact the counselor agrees that things are going well, he or she will need to hold the person for a few more minutes in order to suggest at least one more session in order for them to do the type of concluding summary described above. Very frequently those who want to announce a conclusion right at the end of a session and then leave are those who wish to avoid the intimacy of a more complete and meaningful leave-taking.

Dependence. The second extreme of behavior are those who do not seem to want to stop at all—ever. They flatter the counselor. They keep raising additional problems with which they need help and, of course, no one can help them but you.

Such situations, and every minister knows them, call for some additional discussion here. Traditional therapists who have not had the opportunity to learn situational crisis theory, and who have not had experience in crisis counseling, often raise the question of the dependence of the person upon the counselor. These therapists are aware of the intensity of the feelings a person may have, the regression that is taking place and therefore the person's being in a state of heightened dependence. With the counselor's taking such an active role in the helping process, with the person's being highly suggestible, does not this combination produce an increased dependence that is extemely difficult to resolve?

The answer is, "No!"

In the first place, the ongoing process of crisis counseling itself, admittedly beginning with "an intense, regressively-tinged, dependent, and positive relationship" (Flegenheimer, 1978, p. 348), very quickly produces the conditions which lead to a diminishing of the intensity of the anxiety and feelings of helplessness and thus a reversal of the regression and of the dependence produced *by the crisis*. The counselor has effectively used the dependence to facilitate the rapid movement into self-exploration and the expression of feelings. Also inherent in the crisis counseling process is the emphasis throughout that it is a collaborative relationship, and that the person is going to be taking responsibility for his or her decisions and their consequences. When the person in crisis expresses magical expectations of the helper, the helper injects in a very straightforward way the pertinent realities of the helper's own role and capacities. One of the most important helper skills is that of taking the very active role required but at the same time following Flegenheimer's principle that the counselor also will do "the *least* amount of therapeutic activity and intervention that will enable the patient to do the necessary work" (1978, p. 350). Murray has proposed a provocative analogy when he speaks of "the therapist as a transitional object . . . a secure anchor point that allows the individual a certain control at times of regression, and safeguards his newly won autonomy and growth" (1974, pp. 123, 125). The particular combination of reality and illusion which create the child's image of the transitional object is similar to the way in which a person in crisis relates to the counselor. Reality will come to dominance when the regression is turned around and the counselor, like the transitional object, will be given up.

However, remember that we have indicated that *anyone* may have a crisis. Thus it is not surprising that some people who come to see us in crisis are characterologically highly dependent people. Now things get more complicated in a hurry, because we are dealing with a situation in which the minister may observe the most intense symptoms of the crisis diminishing or even disappearing but the person *not* growing less dependent. Some of the first clues may very well come at the point of the decision-making and action phase. There is more of a struggle in getting the person to decide. The person really wants us to say what is best for him or her to do. At this point, still resisting the pressure to make the other person's decision for him or her, the minister becomes aware that there probably is going to be a termination problem.

Sometimes the problem in discontinuing the crisis counseling sessions is in us and in our own need to be needed. In this case, ministers often continue to see persons, but with ill-defined goals and usually with no observable positive outcome and with increasing frustration and lack of knowledge as to how to get out of it (Baldwin, 1977, pp. 667-668).

When a person wants to continue even after the crisis is apparently resolved, the most effective action is to take seriously and to raise with the person openly the terms of the original contract, the agreement to see the person through this crisis for a specified approximate period of time and an approximate number of sessions. The minister reminds the person of the agreement, affirms his or her caring and desire to be helpful to the person, indicates that if the person does want to work on some longer term problematic areas this is something that the minister is not in a position to do. If the person does not know another counselor, the minister will be happy to make some recommendations, and will, of course, if the person is a parishioner, continue to function in a supportive role as that person's pastor. Then the minister seeks to engage the person in a review of the crisis, the counseling process, and a discussion of the meaning of this mutual relationship to both of them as described above. If the person is a basically dependent person and does want to continue a counseling relationship with the minister, but the minister has been firm in concluding the sessions as we have just discussed, the person may very well be hurt and angry. The review and summary as it would ordinarily take place in a concluding session might be very difficult since the person will be resisting. If the minister can help the person articulate that hurt and anger, the minister would be playing a very constructive role in the person's life.

Failure To Identify the Precipitating Event. If the precipitating event seems to have been identified early in the process, but, after three or four sessions, the intensity of the symptoms have not significantly diminished, one of two possible situations may prevail.

First, the actual precipitating event may not have been identified and the consensual formulation of the problem will then be flawed. The situation needs to be discussed candidly with the person as together they move back into the investigation of the period of time immediately prior to the onset of the experience of crisis in order to attempt to discover the actual precipitating event. If successful, and a satisfactory connection between event, interpretation, threat, and behavior can be made, then the symptoms of the crisis will diminish rapidly.

However, if this procedure is not successful, even though the person may be in a genuine situational crisis, the nature of the precipitating event is such that it has aroused an overt expression of a long-standing psychopathology whose unconscious roots have never been resolved.

Yet another possibility may be that if no precipitating event at all has been found. Occasionally an inexperienced crisis counselor will attempt to force a focus on some external event anyway. This can be a serious mistake. If there is not a clearly identifiable event which can logically in the minds of the participants be related to the onset of the particular symptoms, then there is probably no situational crisis. Most ministers would find themselves in over their heads in attempting to be the primary counselor for such a person, because "the very earliest evidence of an impending psychotic decompensation may be occurring" (Kardiner, 1975, p. 7). The minister's most helpful course of action at this time is to assist the person to get to a psychotherapeutic professional for evaluation and treatment.

Accumulation of Events. If there appears to be an accumulation of events over a longer period of time, the highest probability for effective intervention under most circumstances is to start with the last event first, treat it as *the* precipitating event, and then if necessary move on to the next event before that, and so on. Most frequently, the successful resolution of the *last* event of the series will in fact reduce or extinguish the symptoms of crisis. Occasionally two recent events, separated from one another by only a short period of time and both also logically linked with the particular feelings and behaviors of crisis, may be dealt with as a single, though more complex, event.

Counselor Role and Attributes. The person who wishes to do effective crisis counseling must, of course, have the same personal characteristics, knowledge, and skills for any other form of counseling. This section is hardly the place to go into great detail, but certainly it is important to mention the capacity to be able to enter into a highly charged emotional relationship very rapidly. People in crisis come at a point of intense emotion. Anyone who recoils from strong fear, anger, sadness, depression, confusion, dependence, will be handicapped as a helper in time of crisis.

It has been made clear throughout this chapter that the counselor in this process plays a very active role. No one puts it more strongly than does Kardiner when he speaks of the negative, obstructive impact of passivity on the part of the crisis counselor (1975, p. 8). (See also Rusk and Gerner, 1972, p. 882.) Baldwin discusses the need for crisis counselors in training to learn to be direct (1977, p.667). And Wolberg emphasizes the counselor's need for flexibility in both personality and approach, for spontaneity and creativity, the ability to move in quickly in relationship, and for the initiative to take action in mobilizing help (1972, p. 1269).

The danger in all of this is that the activity and directness may be expressed in ways which communicate paternalism or authoritarianism, which are directive in the sense of suggesting that the counselor will do for the person what that person must do for himself or herself. The delicate balance of being direct without being directive, of being active without being authoritarian, of being one upon whom the other can be temporarily dependent while still seeking to nourish an egalitarian relationship requires attention on the part of the counselor both to his or her own personality and to particular skills of intervention.

Other Helping Procedures

It has been impossible within the space limitations of this chapter to present adequately a number of other issues concerning crisis intervention. This concluding section can be only a listing of some of the very important ones, a very brief comment on only a few of those, and a pointing to sources of fuller discussion. In an earlier work I spoke of the value in crisis intervention of visiting in the home and with other members of the family, drawing additional people from the person's social network into discussion and supportive action, of flexibility concerning the frequency and length of counseling sessions, of the use of the telephone, of referral or transferral, of follow-up, and of the use of crisis groups (Switzer, 1974, pp. 102-35).

Additional work has been done on a number of these. Several writers have stressed the value of the utilization by the person in crisis of his or her natural social network. Lukton, for example, has stated: "Typically . . .

people in trouble turn to natural networks before they seek out mutual aid groups or professional help. Usually, it is only when natural helping systems have failed to avert or resolve a crisis that professionals are asked to intervene" (1982, p. 284). This is a particularly interesting statement for ministers to consider, because, in fact, the minister is a significant part of the *natural* network for some fair number of people, and, therefore, talking with a minister is a very *natural* thing for a person to do. On the other hand, a minister is outside of that natural network for many people. So when they go to a minister in times of distress, they are going to a professional person. Elaborations of the value of the social network to persons in crisis are made by Attneave (1979), Puryear (1979), and Walker (1977).

In addition to calling together the family of the person in crisis as a part of the plan to aid that individual, increasing attention has been given to family crisis intervention *as such*. It is obvious not only that when one person in a family is experiencing a crisis the whole family in some sense is involved in it, but that some events directly affect a whole family and therefore the whole family is in crisis. Concepts of family crisis and means of working with those families have been discussed by Doyle and Dorlac (1978), Puryear (1979), and Umana *et al.* (1980).

Fairly often it is appropriate to refer or transfer the person in crisis to an institution, agency, program, or another professional, either as an adjunct supportive to the counseling we are doing or, because of a number of possible reasons, for someone else to become the primary crisis counselor. The term transferral is distinguished from the word referral and refers to the particular procedure used in occasions of extremely severe crisis. The crisis counselor does not merely recommend that the person see someone else, but also takes whatever steps are necessary to get the person to the proper place. The counselor does not relinquish primary responsibility with a person until the other professional or agency clearly assumes it. Whenever we plan to refer or transfer, our procedure with the other person must take into consideration that referral or transferral itself is usually experienced as an additional crisis. The person has the tendency, especially in an already vulnerable condition, to interpret it as rejection and as the problem's being worse than he or she had originally thought. In addition, for many people seeing a minister, it means a sudden change in social role identity from parishioner, neighbor, friend to an agency *client* or doctor or hospital *patient*. There is a discontinuity between the roles, they are not prepared for the unexpected change and they usually have ambivalent feelings toward the new role. It is possible for the crisis counselor to use his or her awareness of crisis theory and procedures to focus on the referral or transferral as a new precipitating event, anticipate the potential threats to the person, and move on to discuss openly the variety of issues involved, including what it means to this present helping relationship (Wolkon, 1974, pp. 367-68).

The parish minister is in a unique position in church and community to serve as a helper to persons in crisis, functioning to reduce human distress, prevent more serious disorder, and contribute to their growth, including the possibility of growth in faith. Understanding the details of situational crisis theory and procedures presented in this chapter can be a contribution to the minister's effectiveness in these situations. Nothing, however, can take the place of training workshops and doing counseling under supervision. It is hoped that the readers of this material will search out training opportunities for themselves.

Bibliography

Attneave, C.L. "Therapeutic Effectiveness of Social Network Interventions Compared to Groups of 'Intimate Strangers' " *Group Psychotherapy, Psychodrama and Sociometry*, 1979, 32, 173-177.

Baldwin, B.A. "Crisis Intervention in Professional Practice: Implications for Clinical Training." *American Journal of Orthopsychiatry*, 1977, 47, 659-670.

Baldwin, B.A. "A Paradigm for the Classification of Emotional Crises." *American Journal of Orthopsychiatry*, 1978, 48, 538-551.

Caplan, G. *Principles of Preventive Psychiatry*. New York: Basic Books, 1964.

Doyle, A.M. and Dorlac, C. "Treating Chronic Crisis Bearers and Their Families." *Journal of Marriage and Family Counseling*, 1978, 4, 37-42.

Flegenheimer, W.V. "The Patient-Therapist Relationship in Crisis Intervention." *Journal of Clinical Psychiatry*, 1978, 39, 348-350.

Halpern, H.A. "Crisis Intervention: A Definitional Study." *Community Mental Health Journal*, 1973, 9, 342-349.

Hoffman, D.L. and Remmel, M.D. "Discovering the Precipitant in Crisis Intervention." *Social Casework*, 1975, 56, 259-267.

Hooker, C.E. "Learned Helplessness." *Social Work*, 1976, 21, 194-198.

Kardiner, S.H. "A Methodological Approach to Crisis Therapy." *American Journal of Psychotherapy*, 1975, 29, 4-13.

Lukton, R.C. "Myths and Realities of Crisis Intervention." *Social Casework*, 1982, 63, 276-285.

Murray, M.E. "The Therapist as Transitional Object." *American Journal of Psychoanalysis*, 1974, 34, 123-127.

Nelson, Z.P. and Mowry, D.C. "Contracting in Crisis Intervention," *Community Mental Health Journal*, 1976, 12, 37-44.

Parkes, C.M. "The First Year of Bereavement." *Psychiatry*, 1970, 33, 444-467.

Perlman, H.H. "In Quest of Coping." *Social Casework*, 1975, 57, 213-225.

Pretzel, P. *Understanding and Counseling the Suicidal Person*. Nashville: Abingdon, 1972.

Pruyser, P. *The Minister as Diagnostician*. Philadelphia: Westminster, 1976.

Puryear, D. *Helping People in Crisis*. San Francisco: Jossey-Bass, 1979.

Rusk, T.N. and Gerner, R.H. "A Study of the Process of Brief Psychotherapy." *American Journal of Psychiatry*, 1972, 128, 882-886.

Skilbeck, W.M. "Attributional Changes and Crisis Intervention." *Psychotherapy: Theory, Research, and Practice*, 1974, 11, 371-375.

Strickler, M. and LaSor, B. "The Concept of Loss in Crisis Intervention." *Mental Hygiene*, 1970, 54, 301-305.

Switzer, D.K. *The Minister as Crisis Counselor*. Nashville: Abingdon, 1974.

Umana, R.F., Gross S.J., and McConville, M.T. *Crisis in the Family*. New York: Gardner, 1980.

Walker, K.N., McBride, A., and Vachon, M.L.S. "Social Support Networks and the Crisis of Bereavement." *Social Science and Medicine*, 1977, 11, 35-41.

Weiss, R.S. *Marital Separation*. New York: Basic Books, 1975.

Whitlock, G.E. *Understanding and Coping with Real-Life Crises*. Monterey, California: Brooks/Cole, 1978.

Wolberg, L. "Psychiatric Technics in Crisis Therapy." *New York State Journal of Medicine*, 1972 (Part 3), 1266-1269.

Wolkon, G.H. "Changing Roles: Crises in the Continuum of Care in the Community." *Psychotherapy: Theory, Research, and Practice*, 1974, 11, 367-370.

Sr. Madonna Marie Cunningham, O.S.F.

Consultation, Collaboration and Referral

Introduction

In the last twenty years, the field of community mental health has developed a growing body of knowledge about the processes defined as consultation, collaboration and referral. The emergence of these cooperative processes among professionals working in specialized disciplines has created new interesting models which as yet have not undergone the rigors of strong empirical investigation. They have, however, become widely used techniques among many in the helping professions.

The purpose of this discussion is to identify concepts and processes of consultation, collaboration and referral which can be helpful to the pastoral counselor. The discussion assumes that the spiritual and psychological healing ministry of the pastoral counselor, by its very nature, identifies itself with the broader body of professions which make up the mental health community. The presentation is limited to a pragmatic application of selected schemas directed to help the pastoral counselor function more effectively with other helping professions in the broader healing ministry.

Consultation

The practice of consultation draws the pastoral counselor into the mental health arena along with other care-givers such as social workers, psychologists, psychiatrists, educators and spiritual directors. Consultation has been defined by Meyers, Parsons and Martin (1979) as "a technique that, at a minimum, always has the following six characteristics: (1) it is a helping or problem-solving process; (2) it occurs between a professional help-giver and a help-seeker who has responsibility for the welfare of another person; (3) it is a voluntary relationship; (4) the help-giver and help-seeker share in solving the problem; (5) the goal is to help solve a current work problem of the help-seeker; and (6) the help-seeker profits from the relationship in such a way that future problems may be handled more sensitively and skillfully" (p. 4). Consultation provides a method for the mental health professional to assist another worker to function more effectively with a counselee or a group. It is based on an egalitarian relationship, with the person seeking consultation retaining responsibility for the person he or she is trying to assist. (Macht, 1978).

The use of consultation by the pastoral counselor broadens the effectiveness of the counselor well beyond one's original training and strength. Numerous situations arise in the course of a pastoral counselor's ministry where assistance to the counselee would be enhanced if consultation were sought by the counselor. Macht (1978) categorizes four main types of consultation: client-centered case consultation, consultee-centered case consultation, program-centered administrative consultation, and consultee-centered administrative consultation. The first two types can be particularly helpful to the pastoral counselor.

Client-Centered Case Consultation. This approach derives from the pastoral counselor's desire for assistance from a specialist. The specialist actually assesses the counselee in order to assist the counselor to find the most effective way to help the counselee.

Frances is an assistant pastor and pastoral counselor at St. Matthew's Church. Joan, a thirty-two year old mother, came to see her very distressed over her growing incompetencies as a mother and wife. She was feeling depressed and tired, often having to rest in the mid-afternoon. She found it difficult to handle her two small children, and now her husband was constantly irritated over her slowness and awkwardness. Frances noticed that Jean's movements were not smooth and that she seemed to have difficulty in focusing her eyes. Frances suspected some neurological problems, but was in need of a consultation with a medical doctor. She recommended an evaluation either by Joan's family doctor or by a neurologist, so it could be determined if Joan was having any physical problems. Because Joan had no family doctor, she and her husband agreed to have the evaluation by the neurologist Frances contacted. The clinical assessment by the neurologist revealed that Joan was in the beginning stages of multiple sclerosis. Frances now redirected her counseling to help Joan and her family get in touch with their spiritual and psychological resources to deal with the traumatic effects of the progressive disease.

This client-centered consultation, which involved a direct neurological assessment of the counselee by a specialist, enabled the counselor to identify the problem clearly so that she could help more effectively.

Rather than deal directly with the presenting problems Joan brought to the initial session, counseling was now directed to coping with the effects of this progressively disabling disease.

Consultee-Centered Case Consultation. In this form of consultation, the pastoral counselor needs the assistance in order to function with a counselee more effectively. Now the consultant's job is to assess the counselor's difficulty, not the counselee's problem. The difficulty may arise from lack of knowledge, skill, confidence, objectivity, or from interpersonal difficulties which impede effective counseling (Macht, 1978).

Our pastoral counselor, Frances, finds that Joan and her husband now trust her and desire to continue to see her regularly until they learn to cope with the severe crisis in their lives. They are both religious and seek to find ways of coping which are consistent with their belief in God's intimate role in their lives. Frances also believes that she can be of help to this couple as they journey through this crisis. She also is aware that she knows very little about the psychological effects of multiple sclerosis on the person and her family.

Frances seeks a second kind of consultation, this time for herself. She contacts a clinical psychologist with whom she has worked professionally in the past. They assess the problem together and identify a mutually agreeable plan for Frances' education and extended consultation over the course of Joan's counseling. For Frances the consultation results in greater knowledge of the psychological components of multiple sclerosis and in stronger skills as she counsels Joan and her husband.

All counselors are vulnerable to a loss of objectivity due to their own personality or unconscious dynamics. This may occur when the presenting problems of the counselee trigger unresolved conflicts in the counselor's own life, or when characteristics of the counselee are repulsive to the counselor. One way of handling this difficulty is by a kind of consultation described by Caplan (1970) as "theme interference reduction." The difficulty within the counselor is not explored, but the consultant helps the counselor find positive alternatives to his or her pre-conceived negative notions about the counselee. The interfering negative theme is thus reduced and the counselor can begin to allow for more positive outcomes in the counselee. If the pastoral counselor does not provide for such consultation, poor outcomes may be inevitable for the counselee when the interfering block in the counselor remains inoperative.

Collaboration

Another concept which draws the pastoral counselor into the broader system of community mental health is that of collaboration. Macht (1978) clarifies the technique of collaboration as follows: "In collaboration, whether work is focused on a client or on the development and operation of a program, two or more people work together to solve a common problem and share responsibility for the process and outcome. They may, as the result of discussion and joint planning, arrive at joint decisions and carry out action together—in marked contrast to consultation, where the consultant acts only as an advisor and the consultee alone carries out the action" (p. 637). Such collaboration may occur in any setting in which the pastoral counselor shares responsibility with other professionals.

Thomas is a pastoral counselor in a large metropolitan hospital. He has been involved with a number of other staff in the care of a fifty year old married male patient named Mark. Mark suffers from chronic obstructive lung disease and has been on a respirator in the hospital for a year. He has developed a fear of death, severe depression and compulsive masturbation. The staff social worker is helping the wife find solutions to the heavy financial burdens of a long hospitalization. The physician is a lung specialist, very concerned about the physical implications of Mark's emotional state. The nurse is monitoring the quality of care being given to a patient who is viewed by the nursing staff as very troublesome. The psychiatrist is focusing on relief from the depression and compulsive masturbation. Tom is working with both Mark and his wife in helping him to deal with his feelings about death as well as the psychological dynamics which are thwarting his progress. The team meets regularly to chart Tom's progress and to plan jointly for his care. All share responsibility for the process and the outcomes. The pastoral counselor is an important part of the collaborative effort, for often Mark will share with the pastoral counselor more than with the other professionals.

According to Macht (1978), another technique similar to collaboration is coordination. "In coordination, two or more people providing services to a client or program inform each other of their activities and attempt to synchronize their actions and develop ways of preventing unconstructive overlap, duplication, or counterproductive action as they work to provide separate but relative services" (p. 237). When a person approaches a pastoral counselor for on-going assistance, the counselor should ask if the individual is under the care of any other professional. If so, permission from the counselee should be secured to contact the other professional to coordinate their services.

Helen is a forty-five year old career woman who contacted a pastoral counselor in her parish for spiritual direction. She has felt the desire for a deeper spirituality in her life, following several years of mid-life turmoil. She is being drawn to make an extended spiritual retreat in place of a vacation in the summer. The counselor, through the initial interview, discovered that Helen has been seeing a psychologist for over a year for the treatment of extended depression. Helen gave the counselor permission to talk with the psychologist. The psychologist did not recommend the extended retreat at the time suggested, for he judged that a long period of introspection would be counterproductive to his therapy plan. The pastoral counselor and psychologist synchronized their services to Helen, well aware of the action plan of the other as they worked separately for the spiritual and psychological growth of their counselee. Helen was healthy enough the following year to enjoy the retreat she so desired.

Such functions as collaboration and coordination are necessary and enhancing to the important work of supporting the total growth of the person. It is crucial that the pastoral counselor understand the importance of his or her contribution to the wholeness of the services rendered by the mental health team, because of the uniqueness of the spiritual and psychological ministry the pastoral person can provide.

Pastoral counselors can collaborate with other care-givers not only in crisis intervention or counseling to restore stability, but also in the development of preventive programs. Church groups, schools, civic groups, businesses and corporations constantly are in search of mental health teams who can present preventive programs on a wide range of topics in order to promote overall good health and prevent the development of serious problems. Most of these programs lack integration of the spiritual/religious aspects of wholeness, mainly because the professionals offering them have no background in religion or spirituality to bring to the presentations. The pastoral counselor with a strong background in religion and psychology can fill the gap and add an important element to preventive programs. Inclusion of the pastoral counselor in these programs will not take place, however, until the counselor personally perceives the importance of his or her own contributions and can convince others that the programs are incomplete without the unique gifts the pastoral counselor can bring to preventive programs.

Referral

Pastoral counseling, psychological counseling and psychotherapy are by their very nature vital parts of the healing ministry of the Church. A concerned Christian companion who refers a hurting person to a pastoral counselor shares in the ministry of healing to which all Christians are called (Kane, 1982). A pastoral counselor who refers a counselee to a spiritual director, psychologist, psychiatrist or medical doctor for more specialized care extends the effectiveness of his or her own ministry of healing. The process of referral, therefore, is an important part of the healing experience of the individual seeking wholeness and is important to the effectiveness of the pastoral counselor.

Self-Referred Counselees. Often the pastoral counselor is the first professional to whom a person experiencing difficulties is referred. A large number of these people are self-referred. Self-referred counselees usually are self-motivated and relatively clear about the sources of difficulty in their lives. When John, who values his marriage, comes to the pastoral counselor because his wife has threatened to leave him, the counselor is clear about the immediate cause of John's distress. Open communication, which is the essence of counseling, is present because John desires to improve the deteriorating relationship he has with his wife. His self-motivation will help him through the tough part of counseling which will require a commitment to change some of the present behaviors destroying his marriage. Open communication and desire to change are two important elements of counseling usually present in self-referred counselees.

Other-Referred Counselees. Counselees referred by others, however, frequently present certain difficulties in the initial sessions of counseling. Beth Ann is the fifteen year old only daughter of Vivian, a widow of three years. Beth Ann has become "unmanageable," according to her mother. She talks back to her mother and teacher, skips classes in school, spends long hours away from home and refuses to attend church services. Vivian's relationship with Beth Ann has deteriorated rapidly over the last year. Vivian has insisted that Beth Ann seek help from the pastoral counselor of their parish.

Beth Ann came to the first session hostile, withdrawn and resistant. She did not consider her behavior any different from that of her friends and felt that her mother was the one who needed help. In the interview, she initiated no information voluntarily, and gave monosyllabic answers to all questions asked of her.

Dealing with an other-referred counselee such as Beth Ann can be difficult. Resistance must be reduced in order to define the difficulties, establish strategies and fully engage the counselee in the process of change. Some pastoral counselors attempt to open communications with a series of questions: "How old are you?" "What grade are you in?" The problem with this method is that it sets up the counselor as an interrogator and the counselee as a one-word responder. Trust in a counseling relationship is established most easily through honesty. Open and honest communication by the counselor establishes for the counselee expectations and ground rules. Candid confrontation also allows the counselee the options of disagreeing with what has been observed (Delaney and Eisenberg, 1972). The pastoral counselor, responding to Beth Ann's initial resistance, confronted her with an honest statement: "Your mother describes your behavior at home and at school as irresponsible and hostile. It might be worthwhile if you and I could talk about it." Beth Ann immediately burst into an angry tirade about her mother's controlling influence over her since her father's death, and so the work of counseling began. With most resisting other-referred counselees, honest confrontation has a favorable effect.

Pastoral Counselor as Referring Agent. The pastoral counselor, as a minister of healing, also is an important referral agent to other helping professionals. Although professionally trained pastoral counselors are geared to work with the normal spiritual and psychological concerns of the whole person, individuals needing more specialized assistance will seek out the pastoral counselor. In these cases, the pastoral counselor is obligated to recognize his or her limitations and to refer the counselee to an appropriate specialist.

In order for the referral process to be truly an extension of the healing ministry of Christ, the pastoral counselor must make sound professional judgments regarding the nature of the needs of the counselee, the counselor's own limitations in diagnoses and counseling, and identification of the professional who can best serve the counselee.

Martin, a deacon in the Church, approached a pastoral counselor specifically for assistance in deepening his personal relationship with God. It became evident in the early sessions that this young man had such uncontrolled anger toward authority that it was blocking any healthy understanding of God. The pastoral counselor, trained primarily in a strong theological tradition, recognized the intrapsychic forces within Martin, but he could not help the young man respond to God or to the usual means of dealing with anger. The counselor judged that the emotional conditions warranted the services of a psychologist or a psychiatrist. Referral was appropriate for the emotional and spiritual health of Martin.

Another young man, Lee, sought out another pastoral counselor and also stated his desires for a closer relationship with God. The first several sessions revealed that Lee had a rich spiritual life and was being called to an even deeper mystical union with his God. The counselor recognized that Lee needed far more expert assistance than he was capable of giving. The counselor's training had been strongly psychological and focused on average faith struggles and spiritual development. Lee required someone more skilled in spiritual direction to accompany him along his intense spiritual journey. Referral was made to a trained spiritual director.

The issue in referral is not to draw distinct lines between pastoral counseling, spiritual direction and psychotherapy. There are some important areas where spiritual direction, pastoral counseling and psychotherapy overlap or appear to conflict (Leech, 1977). The critical issue is the clear definition of the person's problem and the identification of the individual who can best assist that person's movement toward wholeness. Pastoral counseling training programs vary in their content: some are clearly theological in emphasis; others have strong spiritual direction components; still others draw heavily on psychology and counseling skills. The individual pastoral counselor must recognize where his or her strengths end and where referral is the best action to assist the counselee.

The pastoral counselor working with Beth Ann eventully involved Beth Ann's mother in the sessions. Much of Beth Ann's acting out was reaction to Vivian's possessiveness following the death of her husband. The counselor was working well with Beth Ann, but eventually referred the mother to a psychiatrist from whom she received the help she needed in working through the loneliness and fear she experienced following her husband's death.

Referral Network. The American Personnel and Guidance Association's Code of Ethics states that it is incumbent upon the counselor to be knowledgeable about referral resources so that a satisfactory referral can be initiated (Nugent, 1981). In the event the counselee declines the suggested referral, the counselor is not obligated any further. This ethical principle is as relevant for pastoral counselors as it is guidance counselors.

A competent pastoral counselor builds a referral system branching through the surrounding geographic area. The system includes community mental health agencies, psychologists, psychiatrists, social workers, spiritual directors, physicians and clinics. Referrals to other professionals should be compatible with the financial means of the persons referred. Once the referral network is identified, the counselor should meet with the various mental health specialists. The purpose of these meetings is threefold: to insure the professionalism of the other specialists, especially concerning religious issues of the counselees to be referred; to establish good working relationships with the various specialists in the area; to develop a mutually acceptable manner of handling referrals. Once the referral network is in place, the pastoral counselor will discover that his or her own effectiveness has been enhanced significantly.

Conclusion

The place of the pastoral counselor as part of the community mental health team has not received the attention it deserves. Where this has been recognized, such as in prisons and in hospitals, the role of the pastoral counselor is defined as solely religious. Yet, in practice, pastoral counselors have been as successful as other counselors in dealing with such problems as alcoholism, family relationships, interpersonal and job-related problems. Pastoral counselors, however, have not made active attempts to be a significant part of a social agency team. Where consultation, collaboration and referrals have taken place, usually it has been when a pastoral counselor in a church setting has needed assistance or has been sought as a consultant. Hiltner (1976) holds that with the recent development of the fluid-role approach among professionals in community mental health centers, the pastoral counselor has a legitimate place on the team. The fluid-role mental health team provides services to counselees, not by professional titles of the staff such as psychiatrists, psychologists, or social workers, but by who best can carry out counseling with a particular person. A pastoral counselor, who is an expert in spirituality and has sound knowledge of human personality and strong counseling methods, has a distinct contribution to make to a community mental health team. If this were recognized, the pastoral counselor would then be sought for consultation, collaboration and referral more frequently than occurs at the present time. No longer would we look suspiciously at "secularized mental health," but would find ourselves enriching significantly the delivery of community mental health.

Bibliography

Caplan, G. *The Theory and Practice of Mental Health Consultation.* New York: Basic Books, 1970.

Delaney, D.J. and Eisenberg, S. *The Counseling Process.* Chicago: Rand-McNally College Publishing Company, 1972.

Hiltner, S. *Pastoral Counseling.* Nashville: Abingdon, 1976.

Kane, T.A. "Ecclesial Leadership, Pastoral Care and Psychological Referral." *Sisters Today,* 1982, 54, 158-162.

Leech, K. *Soul Friend: The Practice of Christian Spirituality.* San Francisco: Harper & Row, 1977.

Macht, L.B. "Community Psychiatry." In M. Nicholi, Jr. (ed.), *The Harvard Guide to Modern Psychiatry.* Cambridge: Belknap Press of Harvard University Press, 1978.

Meyers, J., Parsons, R.D. and Martin, R. *Mental Health Consultation in the Schools.* San Francisco: Jossey-Bass, 1979.

Nugent, F.A. *Professional Counseling.* Monterey: Brooks/Cole Publishing Company, 1981.

Richard Osmer
James W. Fowler

Childhood and Adolescence—
A Faith Development Perspective

This essay will approach childhood and adolescence from a Faith Development perspective. Unlike other psychological approaches which are widely used in the field of Pastoral Care and Counseling, this theoretical framework will focus upon the importance of understanding normal patterns of human development in assessing both typical and pathological problems during these stages of life. Moreover, it will examine the role of faith in human development, leading it to raise questions about definitions of normalcy and human maturity which are inevitably presupposed by developmental theories. The essay will be divided into four parts: (1) Prelude to Practice: The Background of Faith Development Theory; (2) Childhood and Adolescence in the Faith Development Perspective; (3) The Concept "Crisis" in the Structural Developmental Tradition; (4) Crises of Childhood and Adolescence in the Faith Development Perspective.

1. Prelude to Practice:
The Background of Faith Development Theory

Faith Development Theory affords a perspective on human development and crisis that is different than those which are widely used in pastoral care and counseling. Rather than drawing on psychoanalysis, humanistic psychology, or behaviorism, it brings together two central traditions: the structural developmental tradition of psychology and the hermeneutic tradition of philosophy and theology. This opening section will explicate central concepts of each of these traditions, allowing us to grasp how they are brought together in Faith Development Theory. It is extremely important that practitioners of care and nurture in the church do not simply take over psychological theories that are fashionable or seem immediately useful without examining underlying philosophical and theological questions. It is the purpose of this section to point to these issues as they appear in Faith Development Theory. We will examine first the structural developmental tradition and, then, the hermeneutic tradition.

Faith Development Theory stands in a close relationship to the structural developmental tradition of psychology. With roots in the thought of George Herbert Mead (1934), John Dewey (1916), James Mark Baldwin (1906), and Heinz Werner (1948), the structural developmental approach was given its most influential formulation by Jean Piaget (1952, 1969). Piaget never thought of himself as a psychologist per se but as a person who was interested in epistemology, that branch of philosophy which studies how persons know.

The theory which Piaget's lifelong research spawned has been given a variety of names: genetic epistemology, cognitive development, and a constructive developmental approach, to name but a few. For the purposes of this article, we will refer to both Piaget's theory and the growing body of theory and research which he engendered as the structural developmental school of psychology (Piaget, 1970). There are two central ideas implied in this title. The first of these focuses on the "structuring" activity of the knowing self, the second on Piaget's understanding of development. Let us begin with the former.

As a result of research on children and adolescents, Piaget came to believe that humans are engaged in an active process by which they form and shape in significant ways the world around them. The philosopher Immanuel Kant first drew attention in modern thought to the fact that persons do not apprehend the world around them by making a copy of it. Rather, they use certain *a priori* categories, such as time, space, causality and numbers, to organize their experience. Broadly speaking, Piaget adds to the Kantian position a genetic or developmental perspective. Piaget revolutionized Kant's basic insight by demonstrating that there is a developmental history to the process of acquiring such basic cognitive constructs as the categories of space, time, and causality. Our construal of our experienced-world is an active process carried out by patterned operations of knowing.

When we refer to Piaget's theory as a *structural* developmental approach, we are drawing attention, first of all, to his concern with those internal processes by which persons structure—give form and shape—to their experience. Piaget offers us several important concepts by which to understand how this structuring process takes place. In any theory that takes seriously the human contribution to the structuring of experience, the question arises: How much of external reality is a product of the human imagination and how much of it is a result of the sheer givenness of the outer world or environment? Piaget attempts to take into account the contributions of both the inner and outer worlds in his account of human knowing. All humans, he believes, engage in a process of equilibration.

By the concept "equilibration," Piaget means that our structuring of the world is a dynamic, interactional process. He offers two additional concepts by which to describe this process, assimilation and accommodation. By "assimilation," he means the process by which sense objects in the external world are shaped to fit the internal categories that a person already possesses. A two year old, for example, has learned that her dog is named Lady and points at every picture of a dog and says, "Lady." The external world is forced to conform to structures of meaning which she already possesses. By "accommodation," Piaget means the stretching of a person's inner structures of meaning better to take into account some feature of the external world. As she grows, the two year old will learn that the term "dog" is a more inclusive category than "Lady" and takes into account a wide variety of dogs with very different names. Her structures of knowing will have accommodated to the external world.

Equilibration is the ongoing, dynamic interplay of assimilation and accommodation. At any given time, persons bring certain pre-existent patterns of knowing to their interaction with the external world, patterns which are more or less adequate to grasp that world. At times, these patterns will remain relatively stable. They are in a state of equilibrium. At other times, particularly times of growth, they will undergo alteration. The process of equilibration is the most basic dynamic of development in Piaget's theory. As humans interact with the world, they inevitably come into contact with objects, events, or persons which do not fit in easily with the structures of knowing that they already possess. They can resist the intrusion of such novelty and strangeness or they can alter their way of making sense out of the world. It is the willingness to accommodate to the new that is the basic dynamic of development in Piaget's theory. Persons develop as they expand their structures of knowing in ways that more adequately take into account new features of reality. This brings us to the second, central dimension of his theory which we will explicate, his understanding of *development*. What does the structural developmental tradition mean by development? Why and how do people develop?

The concept of development in the structural developmental tradition has, in large part, been taken over from the field of biology. While it may be applied by analogy to physical systems and systems of ideas, development, most basically, is associated with the organization of living structures and life processes. It is based on an open-systems model of evolutionary biology in which the important unit of study is not the organism alone or the environment alone but the exchange of information between them.

Typically, discussions of development include the following concerns: (1) an understanding of the organism as a living system; (2) time; (3) movement over time toward an increasing complexity of organization; (4) a hierarchy by which the various parts or functions of adaptation are seen as part of larger wholes; (5) an end-state of organization which is maintained with some stability and self-regulation (Harris, 1957). The dominant "root metaphor" informing development in this sense is that of organic life adapting to its environment.

The central focus of the structural developmental tradition, however, has been on alterations in persons' internal structures of knowing which govern their adaptation. It has attempted to chart the process of development by positing a series of stages involving shifts in the patterns or operations of knowing. A stage represents a typical, almost rule-like, way of organizing some form of experience. In one of Piaget's stages, for example (concrete operations), children are able to reason about concrete objects, persons, and events, organizing them into systems of classification and patterns of causality. They can bring this style of reasoning to any number of areas. To say that they are in the stage of concrete operations is to say that they will typically use this style of reasoning in structuring their experience.

The structural developmental approach views stages as existing in an invariant, sequential pattern. Persons do not skip from stage to stage in a kind of random, hit-or-miss fashion. Rather, the movement from one stage to another involves development in the process of equilibration described earlier. Typically, development to a higher stage is described as involving the differentiation and integration of increasingly complex elements. This refers to the fact that a higher stage is able to understand new domains of reality in a more nuanced and complex fashion, even as these domains are placed in a more sophisticated relationship to one another.

Within the structural developmental tradition, a number of different domains have been studied. Piaget concentrated his attention on the development of perception and logical thinking (Piaget and Inhelder, 1958). Building on Piaget, Kohlberg has focused on persons' ability to reason about situations of moral conflict (1976). Selman has examined persons' perspective-taking ability, the capacity to view experience from another individual's or group's vantage point (1980). Kegan has described the human personality as a whole as a process by which the self is reconstituted as it moves through a series of different subject-object relations (1982). Loevinger has described the human ego as a meaning-making process in similar terms (1976). Throughout the different domains which are studied by the various theories in the structural developmental tradition, childhood and adolescence have typically been described as involving movement through four stages, initially noted by Piaget: Infancy (birth to 2); Early Childhood (2–3 to 5–7); Childhood (5–7 to 12–14); Adolescence (12–14 to later teens). Since Faith Development Theory incorporates many of the domains studied by other structural developmentalists, explicitly using Piaget, Kohlberg, and Selman as aspects of its description of human development, we will use our presentation of the stages of Faith Development Theory to characterize the stages of childhood and adolescence which are broadly accepted by the structural developmental tradition as a whole.

One of the important questions debated among structural developmentalists involves the status of stage descriptions in their theories, especially Piaget's use of mathematical and logical models to understand human cognition. Kegan, for example, believes that the fundamental fact of human life is the ongoing, dynamic *process* of meaning-making and that stage descriptions must remain subordinate to this primary reality. Stages capture this process in a moment of relative equilibrium (an "evolutionary truce") and are, at best, useful models which help us understand, only partially, a more complex and dynamic process. Piaget, on the other hand, posited a strong isomorphism between the models of logic and the actual functioning of human reason, leading him to claim that the stage descriptions which he offered actually expressed the rules governing human operations of knowing. Faith Development Theory offers a unique answer to these questions which lead it beyond the philosophical structuralism on which Piaget's work is based. In both its view of the status of stage-descriptions and its understanding of the human, it draws on the hermeneutic tradition of philosophy and theology. Of particular importance in this regard is the work of H. Richard Niebuhr (1941, 1963).

Hermeneutic theory was originally associated with the art and science of the interpretation of biblical and classical texts. With the advent of modern historical awareness, dogmatic, typological, and literal interpretations of the Bible became problematical. Certain questions came to the fore. How can a document which was written in a different language and relying on very different cultural-religious categories have meaning for the present situation? How can understanding be achieved? The Protestant theologian, Friedrich Schleiermacher, was one of the first persons to address these questions, attempting to formulate a general theory of hermeneutics that was designed to be applicable to every expression of language, oral and written (1977). His ground-breaking work was followed by that of his biographer, Wilhelm Dilthey, who made hermeneutics the heart of the human sciences, which were described as concerned with *understanding*, as opposed to the natural sciences, which were concerned with *explanation* (1922). In nineteenth century sociology, Max Weber (1922) and Ernest Troeltsch (1911) drew upon these insights in recognizing the importance of the interpretive dimensions of social activity. In twentieth century philosophy, Martin Heidegger (1962) and his pupil, Hans Georg Gadamer (1960), went even further in this direction by claiming that understanding is a fundamental constituent of human existence. All persons are involved in a process by which they construct a *world*, a comprehensive understanding of life in which they order the various activities and possibilities of existence. Understanding in this sense is broader than knowing, even as it is conceptualized in the structural developmental tradition. It has to do with the most fundamental and comprehensive patterns of the imagination and the affections which constitute a person's world. Successive differentiations of the subject and object, as described by Piaget, take place within this broader context of meaning. It is precisely this most fundamental sense of world that Faith Development Theory attempts to examine.

The thought of H. Richard Niebuhr has been of particular importance for Faith Development Theory in this regard (1941, 1963). Central to Niebuhr's theological reflection was the hermeneutic insight that all forms of human knowing, including theology, are most basically matters of interpretation. That is, both our everyday human interactions and our more systematic attempts to know the world rest on basic images and symbolic patterns by which we interpret our experience. In his descriptions of revelation and the moral life, Niebuhr gave particular attention to three items that are present in this activity of interpretation: (1) fundamental narratives which allow human experience to be organized into a story form; (2) centers of value to which persons give their trust and loyalty and which have an ordering impact on their pattern of life; (3) the affections, those enduring and characteristic emotional dispositions which are shaped by both the important narratives and centers of value which order persons' lives.

While Faith Development Theory is clearly indebted to the structural developmental tradition and we will continue to refer to it as a part of that psychological tradition throughout this essay, it is crucial to grasp that in central ways it is more fundamentally grounded in the hermeneutical theology of H. Richard Niebuhr. Its central focus is epistemological in only the broadest sense and is best described as focusing on the activity of human understanding by which experience is ordered into a world organized around certain master stories and centers of value which profoundly shape the human affections. From a Faith Development perspective, such is the activity of faith. It is a universal activity, an ontological constituent of human existence. Hence at a later point in this essay, when we describe various crises of faith, it should be clear why such crises are so disruptive: the person's world is at stake. Moreover, the goal of development within such a perspective is not merely a more adequate and complex differentiation of the self and other but involves the attempt to grasp more fully the meaning of the whole of life. Such understanding involves human cognition to be sure. But, more basically, it involves a broader form of reason, what Niebuhr calls the "reasons of the heart," those fundamental constructs of the human imagination which give meaning to life. The activity of faith in this sense involves those tradition-bearing communities which give humans a sense of the whole and special moments of disclosure by which new possibilities of self-world understanding are given.

2. Childhood and Adolescence in Faith Development Theory

In this section, we will describe the stages of Faith most typical of persons from infancy to adolescence. It is important to see these four stages in relation to the later three stages most typical of adulthood. For those we refer you to the senior author's previous extensive writings on stages of faith (1978, 1980, 1981, 1984).

PRIMAL FAITH: We start as infants, you and I. Someone picks us up, wipes off our afterbirth, and provides a nipple with breast or bottle, and we are launched as human beings. Prior to the event of birth itself, we have enjoyed one of the most remarkable of symbiotic relationships. Somatically, we likely have already derived from our life n the womb some sense of whether the world that welcomes us has meaning and purpose, and whether it intended and rejoices in our presence, or whether we come as intruders. Birth itself is a trauma. Students of the birth process tell us that even in the twenty minute passage through the birth canal in a normal birth, we nearly smother. There is a threat of negation in our emergence into life. We are bruised and squeezed into life; we gasp our way into community.

During the first year the mutual tasks of baby and caring others involve bonding and attachment, and the generation of a trusting give and take. Such a wondrous process! The baby's early efforts at relating and making self at home have the effect, when things go well, of recruiting tenderness and mobilizing energetic care. In the mutuality of need and the need to be needed the baby forms a rudimentary but deep sense of the rhythms of intimacy and of the texture of its environment. Without a reflexive sense of selfhood yet, it nonetheless—in the undifferentiated state which Ulrich Neisser calls the "ecological self"—begins to wrap the coils of centration around primal images of the felt goodness and badness of *self-world*. Basic trust versus a sense of basic mistrust, Erik Erikson named it.

The struggle is for some balance of trust in the worth and irreplaceability of the self, and in the reliability of the environment made up of those in whose eyes and under whose care the mirrored self has begun to gather. Paul Tillich called our inevitable sense of vulnerability to dropping out of being "ontological anxiety"—the anxiety that comes with being, and with the threat of non-being. Primal faith arises in the roots of confidence that find soil in the ecology of relations, of care, and of shared meanings that welcome a child, and offset our profound primal vulnerability.

The first symbols of faith are likely to take primitive form in the baby's hard won memories of maternal and paternal presence. As dependable realities which go away, but can be trusted to return, our primary caregivers constitute our first experiences of superordinate power, wisdom, and our dependence. These primal others doubtless are present, in their mixtures of rigidity and grace, of arbitrary harshness and nurturing love, in the images of God which take more or less conscious form by our fourth or fifth years.

INTUITIVE-PROJECTIVE FAITH: About age two a revolution begins to happen for the child. Language emerges to mediate relations to the world and others in new ways. Important preparation for this emergence has gone on in the interchanges between the child and those providing primary care, where—as video-tapes of mother-child interactions show—each is teaching the other to talk. The mothers' imitations of the facial expressions and vocal experiments of their babies seem to provide a crucial mirror—both visually and vocally. And as the child matches sounds and objects he or she gains new leverage in communication and in the interpretation of the world. Language makes possible a qualitatively new reflectiveness on the environment, and a qualitatively new reflexiveness with regard to the self.

The child, now able to walk freely and question everything, daily encounters novelties and newness. Whether we remember the vividness of our daily (and nightly) delights and terrors at three, four, and five, or whether we have access to it only by observing others now in childhood, we know that the active, inquiring mind of the child will never again be so fresh and free of pre-formed constructions. Perception, feelings, and imaginative fantasy make up the child's principal ways of knowing—and transforming—his or her experiences. The ordering tendencies of logical operations will come later. For now, stimulated by experience and by stories and symbols and examples, children form deep and long-lasting images that hold together their worlds of meaning and wonder.

While the following statement would never be said this way by a child, this effort to synthesize some of the feelings and imagery of Intuitive-Projective faith is suggestive:

> I feel as though I am the center of the world. Everything important to me is there because of me, to be for me. When we travel at night the moon follows just our car. Flowers are there to smell with, and stars are there to fly to.

> Sometimes I have scary dreams at night. They are right there in my room. If you were in the room with me you could see them too. Sometimes during the daytime I think about things like those in my dreams. Sometimes they make me scared.

> I wonder sometimes where heaven is, and what being dead means. If it is like a monster taking people away, or if it hurts, or if mommy and daddy will be with me. What happened to our pet bird the neighbor's cat got?

> My friend told me that the devil will come up out of a hole in the ground and get me if I'm not careful, so now I won't play in the backyard by myself.

> I think about God a lot. I think God must be like the air—everywhere. Can God see me? Will God help keep our house from fire? Is Granddad with God? Where's that?

Here we see the Intuitive-Projective child's awakening to the mystery of death. We see the awakening to a world of reality beyond, around, and penetrating the everyday. We see lively imagination grasping the world, endeavoring to give it unity and sense. The preschool child who has access to the symbols, stories, and shared liturgical life of a religious tradition awakens to an expanded horizon meanings. Though such symbols, in their archetypal power, can be misused (i.e., the devil imagery), they also enrich the child's stores of meaning and can provide powerful identifications and aspirations, as well as sources of guidance and reassurance.

MYTHIC-LITERAL FAITH: At about the time a child starts to school (six or seven, give or take a year), we see the beginnings of a new stage. Part of the groundwork for this revolution in knowing and valuing relates to the development of what Piaget called "concrete operational thinking." Stable categories of space, time, and causality make the child's constructions of experience much less dependent on feeling and fantasy. Now able to reverse processes of thought and to coordinate more than one feature of a situation at a time, the world becomes more linear, orderly, and predictable. Children in this stage routinely take the perspectives of others on matters of mutual interest, and recognize others' perspectives as different from their own. This means that they can tell stories with new accuracy and richness. It also means that they can develop a strong sense of fairness based on reciprocity (this means elevating the associations of reward for doing good and punishment for doing bad to the level of cosmic principle) in their thinking about right and wrong, good and evil.

Faith becomes a matter of reliance on the stories, rules, and implicit values of the family's community of meanings. Where the family (or its substitute) is related to a larger community of shared traditions and meanings, faith involves valuing the stories, practices, and beliefs of that tradition. *Narrative* or story is the important idea here. With the abilities to take the perspectives of others, and with a much improved grasp of causal relations and consequences, narrative seems to be the favored and most powerful way of gathering and expressing personal and shared meanings. Knowing the stories of "our people" becomes an important index of identification and of evaluation of self and others and their groups. The ability to create classes based on distinguishing characteristics of objects or groups makes these kinds of identifications (and exclusions) important matters in this stage.

The following composite passage suggests some flavor of how the Mythic-Literal child typically describes self and faith:

> You asked me who I am: I'll tell you. I am Robert Kelleher, the son of Tom and Diane, and the brother of Kristen and Kevin. Do you want me to tell you about all my grandparents and cousins too? No? Well . . . uh, I'm a member of Mrs. Cates' fourth grade class at Hawthorne School . . . uh, and I am the third best soccer player in my grade, after Donald Pruitt and Teddy Jackson. Oh yes, uh, I go to Christ the King parish. My scout troop meets there—it's Troop 27, Cub Scouts, that is. Well, that's about it.

> Yes, I believe in God. What is God like? Hmn . . . Well, I guess God is like Jesus, sort of . . . . We believe that God is, like, in three parts, Father, Son, and um . . . Spirit—*Holy* Spirit. But I picture God mostly as Jesus. But sometimes I sort of think of God as an old man, and sort of like a judge or ruler. . . . Yes, God made us and loves us, and wants us to love each other. I think the worst thing God doesn't like is all the nuclear bombs. I would like to tell all the presidents of the world, "Don't use those bombs.

Let us grow up. Let the earth, the grass and all the animals continue to live."

The most important thing is not to tell lies and stick up for your friends if they need help. Like when my best friend, Roger, got into trouble last week. The teacher who monitors the hall thought that . . . well, you see, this locker got broken into and some stuff was stolen from it, and, uh, the hall-teacher thought she saw Roger taking some stuff from the broken locker, and he *did* have a "Walk-Man" just like the one that was stolen, so the principal called him in because they thought Roger did it. Roger didn't deserve that! Well, I went straight to the principal and told him it was not Roger, that he already had a Walk-Man that he got for his birthday, and besides that, Roger would never steal anything. The principal really listened to me, and he and the teacher apologized to Roger.

In these statements we hear something of the concreteness and literalness of this boy's appropriation of his community's beliefs. We also see that he does not construct his sense of himself, or of others, in terms of personality or inner feelings and reflectiveness. Persons are defined by their affiliations and their actions. He speaks to us from the midst of the flowing stream of his life, without stepping out onto the bank to reflect on its overall direction or meanings. He does not yet have a "story of his stories." His poignant statement about the threat of nuclear warfare *is powerfully typical* of our interviews with children in this stage.

We do, from time to time, encounter adults whose ways of structuring their faith have features very similar to Robert's. A substantial number of adolescents share his way of constructing their images of self, others, and ultimate environment. From this stage on, we are dealing with ways of being in faith that *can* typify adults as well as the age groups where they most typically have their rise.

SYNTHETIC-CONVENTIONAL FAITH: We come now to a stage that typically begins to emerge in early adolescence. Before we discuss its particular features it may be helpful to inject a few observations about the phenomenon of stage transition. It would be a mistake to think of the movement from one faith stage to another on the analogy of climbing stairs or ascending a ladder. This for two reasons: (1) it necessarily locks us into a kind of "higher"-"lower" mentality in thinking about the stages, when the real issue has to do with a successive progression of more complex, differentiated, and comprehensive modes of knowing and valuing; (2) the stair or ladder analogy, further, might lead one to think of transition as a matter of the self clambering from one level or rung to another, essentially unchanged. Faith stage transitions represent significant alterations in the structures of one's knowing and valuing. In the process of transition we have the feeling, as one character in the film "Green Pastures" put it, "Everything nailed down is coming loose." Because of new operations and comprehensiveness in our knowing and valuing, both our previous knowledge and values, and our very ways of verifying and justifying our perspectives, our values and actions undergo change and must be reworked. Our very life-meanings are at stake in faith stage transitions. In relation to the transition we are just considering—from the Mythic Literal to the Synthetic-Conventional stage—let me share an example. We have interviewed a number of what we have come to call "eleven year old atheists." These young people, almost on the cusp between concrete operational thinking and formal operational thinking (a Piagetian term we will examine more fully in a moment), begin to experience the breakdown of the moral principle of reciprocity which they frequently have used to compose their images of God. They have found, by observation and experience, that either God is powerless with regard to punishing evil people and rewarding the good, or God is (as one morally sensitive girl put it), "asleep." The God, therefore, who is constructed on the basis of moral reciprocity effectively dies, and must be replaced. Such an experience involves, to a greater or lesser degree, coming to terms with feelings of anguish, struggle, and possibly guilt and grief. This is the stuff of which faith stage transitions are made.

Now to Synthetic-Conventional faith. Key to our understanding of the structure and dynamics of this stage is an appreciation for a revolution that adolescence typically brings in cognitive development. In formal operational thinking the mind takes wings. No longer is it limited to the mental manipulation of concrete objects or representations and of observable processes. Now thinking begins to construct all sorts of ideal possibilities and hypothetical considerations. Faced with the challenge of developing the perfect mousetrap, the formal operational mind doesn't limit itself to modifying and perfecting the type of mousetraps it has seen, but starts with the fundamental problem of disposing of a household pest and imagines a great variety of ways the problem might be solved. Imagination, one writer has said, is intelligence at play. Formal operational thinking makes possible the generation and use of abstract concepts and ideals. It makes it possible to think in terms of systems. And it enables us to construct the perspectives of others on ourselves—to see ourselves as others see us. Part of the confusion and difficulty of adolescence can be traced to the new self-consciousness I have summed up with the following couplet:

I see you seeing me . . .
I see the me I think you see . . .

And its reciprocal:

You see you according to me . . .
You see the you you think I see . . .

Putting these two together as elements of consciousness (which takes a period of several months, at least) results in what students of perspective taking have called "mutual interpersonal perspective taking." This emergence accounts for the "self-consciousness" of adolescence. It accounts for the rather sudden new depth of awareness and interest in the interiority (emotions, personality patterns, ideas, thoughts, and experiences) of persons—others and oneself. It makes for a newly "personal" young man or woman.

"Synthetic," as we use the term here, does not mean "artificial." Rather it means pulling together and drawing disparate elements into a unity, a synthesis. In the name of this stage the drawing together in question is twofold: Due to the rich new possibilities of interpersonal perspective taking, the young person now has available a variety of relationships or mirrorings of the self. In every significant face-to-face relation, he or she has access to someone's construction of the self he or she is becoming. Like distorting mirrors in an amusement park fun-house, the images of self which one discerns that others have constructed do not necessarily fit together. Nor are they necessarily congruent with one's own felt images of self. St. Augustine, writing about his own adolescent experience with this, said, "And I became a problem to myself." Synthesis in the first instance, then, means a drawing together, an integration into one, of that viable sense of unity in selfhood we have come to call "identity."

The other aspect of synthesis crucial to the forming of the Synthetic-Conventional stage has to do with the drawing together of one's stories, values, and beliefs into a supportive and orienting unity. In this stage a person struggles with composing a "story of my stories"—a sense of the meaning of life generally, and of the meaning and purpose of his or her life in particular. Our research suggests that this involves a process of drawing together into an original unity a selection of the values, beliefs, and orienting convictions made available for two important reasons: (1) It is a synthesis of belief and value elements which are derived from one's significant others. The elements themselves, then, are conventional, although they may be formed into a novel, individual configuration. (2) It is a synthesis of belief and value which has, in this stage, a largely "tacit" (as opposed to *explicit*) character. By this we mean that the beliefs, values, and stories which compose a person's faith outlook, and support his or her emerging identity, are not yet objectified for critical reflection by that person. The synthesis is supportive and sustaining; it is deeply felt and strongly held; but it has not yet become an object of (self) critical reflection and inquiry. In this stage one is *embedded* in his or her faith outlook, and one's identity is derived from membership in a circle of face-to-face relations.

Consider the following composite statement from a fifteen year old girl:

> My life is so full of people! And it seems as though all of them want something special from me. Start with my best friend: she wants me to spend at least an hour a day on the telephone with her. She would like it if we sat together in all our classes and ate lunch together everyday. Her parents are moving toward a divorce, she doesn't have a boy friend, and all her other brothers and sisters have left home. But that's just the beginning. There's Sam. He's *my* boy friend. He's a year older than I. *He* wants me to spend all my time between classes and at lunch with him. And then he wants to bring me home from school everyday and talk on the phone every night. We fight a lot—not about your usual thing—who's jealous of whom, etc.—but about beliefs and values. He tries, but he comes from a family where male chauvinism reigns supreme. He is the last child—and the first son—and he has always been spoiled terribly. Then he has this romantic nonsense about chivalry and male honor and superiority. We argue and debate and even shout at each other on the phone.
>
> Then there's my parents. Since my older sister went off to college we have been very close. I know that they have high expectations of me. Even though they don't say too much about it directly, they always ask questions like "How was your day? . . . How did your test go? . . . How are things with Sam? . . ." and so on. They don't mean it to be pressure, but it makes me feel that there are a lot of demands on me.
>
> Then there are my teachers, my friends at church, my flute teacher, my grandparents, and my sister. All of them, in one way or another, want a piece of me, or symbolize some set of demands I make on myself. And yet, I wonder if any of them really know *me*?

I don't think any of them know, really, about my relationship to God. I don't think of God as an old man or even a person anymore. Instead, I have this deep feeling that God is a kind of friend, a presence that loves me, cares for me, and *really* knows me. God knows me—my present me, and my future me—even better than I know myself. When I wake up early in the mornings—4 A.M. most mornings—to study, in the loneliness and tiredness there is God. When I feel on the outs with my parents, or Sam, or my friends, there is God. When I feel that I will *never* be good enough in math and chemistry to get into veterinarian school, there is God.

I don't speak of God as "he" any more. In the Apostles' Creed I say "Maker" instead of "Father." But other than that, I think my church's teachings about God are true and good—especially my teacher Mr. Martin. He knows so much, and has so much enthusiasm, and makes it all so clear. I just wish my church lived up to all it knows!

It is important to recognize that many persons equilibrate more or less permanently in the Synthetic-Conventional stage. The world-view and sense of self synthesized in this stage, and the authorities who confirm one's values and beliefs, are internalized, and the person moves on through the life cycle with a set of tacitly held, strongly felt, but largely unexamined beliefs and values.[1]

3. The Concept "Crisis" in the Structural Developmental Tradition

Faith Development Theory and the structural developmental tradition afford a unique perspective by which to understand the vicissitudes of childhood and adolescence. In our discussion of the different types of crises which characterize childhood and adolescence, we will draw on the structural developmental tradition as a whole and, then, in the final portion of this essay illustrate each type of crisis in depth from a Faith Development perspective. The structural developmental tradition offers persons who are involved in the nurture and care of children and adolescents four categories by which to understand the different types of crises which may appear: (1) developmental crisis; (2) situational crisis; (3) crisis of social pathology; (4) crisis of vocational inadequacy. In this section of our essay, we will examine each of these understandings of crisis.

1. Developmental Crisis

As we have seen, the structural developmental tradition views children and adolescents as passing through a developmental sequence in which they structure their life's experience in qualitatively different ways at different stages. Piaget's initial research into the stages of reasoning has reverberated outward and been related to major changes in the young person's personality. The adolescent, for example, who is able to use abstract reasoning, now also possesses the ability to construct hypothetical, ideal alternatives to the present world. Ideal parents are compared to real parents; a new social order, to the present one. Hence, the hypercritical and judgmental tendency of many adolescents. Within this broad understanding of how persons grow, the structural developmental tradition typically views a developmental crisis in a twofold fashion: (a) as those common stresses and problems that are related to stage change, and (b) those limitations-tendencies which are a product of a particular stage's way of structuring life.

If parents, priests, or teachers understand the various difficulties and changes of children and youth from a developmental perspective, then they will be able to do three things. First, they will be able to recognize as *normal* certain features of behavior that often pose difficulty for those who work and live most closely with a child or youth. Certain stresses and turmoil are an inevitable part of all growth. It is quite helpful for parents to know, for instance, that the difficulties which their child or adolescent is experiencing are normal and not a sign of pathology.

The second thing which an understanding of normal developmental crises affords is a perspective in which to locate the nature and source of the crisis. A child, for example, who has given up a quasi-magical, fantasy-filled understanding of God, formed during the stage of Intuitive-Projective faith, may experience a real crisis of faith as he or she begins to take account of the "real" world, operating according to laws of cause and effect. Does God have any place in the real world or is God just a figment of the childish imagination, like Santa Claus and ghosts? A developmental perspective allows persons to anticipate such problems and form a clearer idea of what actually is involved in the crisis at hand.

Moreover, a structural developmental perspective not only affords a clearer sense of the "normalcy" of a developmental crisis and a clearer definition of what is going on, but it also offers concrete, practical strategies by which to respond to the crisis at hand. Lickona offers a distinction between "horizontal" and "vertical" development which is helpful in describing the different modes of response to a developmental crisis (1983). The latter refers to the shift from one stage to another. The former refers to an extension of already-achieved, structural capacities to new areas of experience. Each of these affords a somewhat different strategy for persons who are involved with children and youth. If the developmental crisis at hand is a vertical one, then strategies to aid stage transition are appropriate. For example, the shift from an idiosyncratic, fantasy-filled view of God in the Intuitive Projective faith to one that has a place in the "real" world and is more in line with the representations of a particular religious community in Mythic Literal faith can be helped by parents who make a point of telling the child during this period of life the various ways that God is a part of their world. Parents can pray with their child in a manner that does not invoke the logic of magic, but begins to open up ways of viewing God's activity in the world that respects the laws of nature.

Kegan, in particular, has drawn attention to the difficult nature of stage transition (1982). As he points out, a shift from one stage to another represents a reconstitution of the self and its relation to the world. New understandings of both must come into being.

Horizontal development, on the other hand, calls for strategies which help a child extend a stage or an inadequately-achieved stage to deal with a wider range of life experiences. For example, a child who possesses reasoning ability to follow rules and take on certain roles within structured game situations (concrete operations) might consistently attempt to cheat in his or her game-playing with a neighbor child who is at a lower stage. A parent might appeal to the child's basic sense of moral reciprocity by encouraging him or her to imagine what it would be like if the friend constantly broke the rules? What would happen to the game? How would he or she feel if an older child did that sort of thing to him or her? This would afford the child the opportunity to use already-achieved structural competencies in a concrete situation and would increase the possibility of their spontaneous use by the child in similar, future situations.

In summary, the structural developmental tradition offers an understanding of a developmental crisis calling attention to both typical periods of stress and strain that are related to stage change and the typical limitations of a given stage. It offers a "map" by which persons charged with the care and nurture of children and adolescents can understand, anticipate, accept, and work with persons who are part of an ongoing developmental process. Development in this tradition involves fundamental shifts in the ways that persons construct life. Normal amounts of difficulty for the developing person and those with whom he or she is in close contact are to be expected.

2. *Situational Crisis*

Unlike a developmental crisis, a situational crisis is not related directly to the shifts or limitations of a person's internal developmental processes. A situational crisis is related to disruptive events and/or relationships which impinge upon the child and adolescent from external sources. Here we have in mind such things as the death of a parent, the need for surgery, a divorce, destructive familial relations, a move to a new city, or any event which threatens the child's or adolescent's well-being.

Situational crises cover a wide range in degree of severity. A life-threatening illness is obviously a greater situational stress than entering a new school. Those who are involved in the nurture and care of children and adolescents must assess the impact of such events in light of their severity and the developmental competencies of the person being affected. Certain situational crises can be anticipated and planned for. A parent's return to work and the consequent placement of a young child or infant in day care is more stressful at certain periods of development than at others. For example, just as an infant begins to give signs of an internalized representation of his or her primary care-taker, often referred to as "stranger anxiety," is not an opportune time for day care to begin. To the extent that it is possible, situational crises should be planned in ways that take into account the needs and ability to cope of the child or adolescent put under stress.

It is obvious, however, that many situational crises cannot be planned. It is their sudden and unexpected quality or their length of duration that makes them so traumatic. An awareness of developmental theory can help in only a limited fashion in the face of much human suffering. Nothing can bring back a parent who has died in an automobile accident. The negative impact of parent-child incest cannot be easily or quickly removed. What the structural developmental perspective can do, however, is two basic things.

First, it can afford those dealing with children in the midst of situational crises a better understanding of *whom* they are attempting to aid, such that assistance can be offered in a developmentally appropriate manner. A conversation full of abstract concepts about the afterlife, for example, is of no use to a five year old whose parents have just died. But knowing that a child at this stage understands cause and effect relations very poorly and frequently uses magical, fantasy-filled reasoning in understanding why things happen does provide insight into why a child would blame himself or herself when a parent dies or gets a divorce. It also points in the direction of appropriate modes of response.

The second contribution of this approach in the face of a situational crisis is an understanding of the impact of such a crisis on a child's or adolescent's long-term development, especially if the crisis is a severe one. There is much evidence, for example, that major surgery often retards the normal rate of development among infants and very young children. Language acquisition may lag behind expected rates. It is important for persons who are involved in the nurture and care of children and adolescents to have some idea of the long-range impact of crisis events upon the development of these persons. Typically, a slower rate of development that is due to a situational stress is not irreversible and is not a signal of pathology.

However, there are instances in which a situational crisis can affect a child or youth in ways that are detrimental to the entire course of his or her development. In such a situation, negative events or relationships have consistently inhibited normal development over a long period of time. In the face of such circumstances, persons often exhibit a kind of developmental "splitting" in which certain portions of their personality continue to grow and others do not. Such persons may be able to reason at a fairly advanced level under optimum conditions, for example, but consistently demonstrate egocentric behavior in their relations with others.

From a structural developmental perspective, such pathology is not simply a matter of the repetition of unconscious conflicts, as in psychoanalysis, or the result of inadequate or poor conditioning, as in behavior modification. It is due to a breakdown in the normal processes of development by which persons restructure their world and their participation in it in ways that are consistent with advancing age and social expectations. In other words, pathology is the inability to develop in ways that are consistent with the possibilities afforded by physiological maturation, cognitive potential, and social expectations. It is not pathological for a four year old to engage in impulsive behavior that disregards the needs of others. The child is egocentric at this stage. It is pathological, however, for this sort of behavior to be present in a teenager on a regular basis. Stealing, lying, and acts of violence with no regard for others are evidence of a cognitive and moral self-centeredness that is not appropriate to this age of life. Rather than viewing such sociopathic behavior as the result of an inadequately-formed superego or an "acting out" of unconscious conflicts with internalized parental figures, a structural developmental perspective would understand it as the result of arrested or "split" development. The teenager is structuring his or her world and responding to it in ways that are appropriate to early childhood. Kegan has undertaken major theoretical work in the area of clinical practice and is in the process of extending the structural developmental tradition in this field (1982).

In summary, a situational crisis refers to the disruptive effects of events and relationships that are not specifically related to the developmental process. The structural developmental tradition recognizes these crises as potentially retarding a child's or adolescent's development in either short-term, reversible ways or in a more serious "splitting" of developmental functions that is pathological. Persons offering care or nuture to children and adolescents in the midst of a situational crisis are encouraged to attempt to understand the developmental level of those whom they are assisting and to assess the possible impact of the crisis on long-term developmental processes.

3. The Crisis of Social Pathology

The first two categories of crisis which we have discussed have primarily stayed on the individual level. The structural developmental tradition, however, does more than offer a map and timetable of predictable developmental crises and a way of understanding the impact of situational stress on individual development. It offers a critique of social patterns and norms which impact the development of children and adolescents in major ways. Hence, it suggests an understanding of children and adolescents in terms of the category, social pathology, something that is often overlooked in strictly psychological approaches and clinical practices.

Children and adolescents are not the only ones who fail to adapt to the external world, but the external world fails to adapt to them. All too frequently it offers them an ecology of growth that systematically neglects, distorts, or suppresses their needs and abilities as developing human beings. In a very real sense, this category of the crisis of social pathology overlaps with the one that follows, an inadequate view of the human vocation. More than any other psychological approach, the structural developmental tradition has articulated clearly an end-point of human development, an image of what humans might become and be. In the present category of crisis, we are examining ways that a given social-economic system negatively impacts human development in a widespread, typical fashion. At least some of the children and adolescents who end up in the principal's office or on drugs or even in jail are victims as much as they are social misfits who are immature developmentally.

The category of the crisis of social pathology refers to a society's failure to take seriously the *readiness* of children and adolescents in the developmental process. It can do this in one of two ways: (1) by forcing certain cultural information or expectations upon children and adolescents which they are not ready to assimilate meaningfully or which force them to develop prematurely; (2) by failing to meet a child's or adolescent's emerging competencies with appropriate social support and responsibility. Both of these lead to individual developmental difficulties. It is essential that persons involved in the nurture and care of children and adolescents understand these difficulties, not simply as personal failures, but as symptoms of an underlying social malaise for which the child or adolescent has little responsibility. All too frequently, therapeutic and educational communities have focused their attention only upon the individual person who is experiencing or causing difficulty without attending to the very real, systemic dimensions of developmental failure.

The readiness concept, thus, points to two dimensions of social crisis: (1) the failure to recognize the developmental limitations of children and adolescents at given stages; (2) the failure to match and support emerging developmental competencies. The first of these social failures in contemporary American society has been powerfully articulated by David Elkind in his understanding of how our society "hurries" children to grow in ways that are not appropriate to their level of developmental readiness (1981). He identifies three areas which, all too often, foster a social climate that is not developmentally appropriate: the media, parenting, and the schools. Television and movies, for example, enable children to have access to information about such things as violence and sex for which they have neither the cognitive-emotional maturity, nor the experience to deal with. The pressures of single parenting and two-career families can place demands upon the child or adolescent which are often inappropriate. A young child might be forced to adapt to multiple day-care settings in a single day or come home to an empty house after school or take on certain responsibilities like cooking and baby-sitting for which he or she is not yet prepared. Moreover, frequently children are made confidants and emotional supporters of parents in ways that force them beyond their capacities and dilute their sense of being able to depend on adults. Elkind identifies a variety of ways that our present school systems do not adequately honor the developmental readiness of their students, gearing education to standardized tests which leave no room for the "late bloomer" and encouraging the swift development of cognitively-oriented reading skills to the exclusion of social interaction competencies.

In a slightly different direction, Egan (1979) and Lickona (1983) have emphasized the need for children and adolescents to fully realize the potential of a given stage before they are encouraged to move to the next one. We have already drawn attention to Lickona's understanding of horizontal development in this regard in which he suggests ways that parents and teachers can encourage children and adolescents to extend the abilities of their highest stage to new areas of life. Egan goes one step further and calls attention to the developmental deficit which can take place if children and adolescents are rushed through a stage and are not allowed to take advantage of its full potential. This is something which Faith Development Theory has also drawn attention to. For example, if a child is not allowed to playfully form the highly idiosyncratic and fantasy-filled images of God, characteristic of the Intuitive Projective stage, but is forced prematurely to conform to the roles and understandings of a particular religious group, then he or she will be robbed of one of the most important ways that religion becomes meaningful and a motivational basis can be laid for the later exploration of mature forms of faith.

The first line of social criticism offered by the structural developmental tradition calls into question the various ways that a given social order refuses to honor the developmental limitations of children and adolescents. Judged by this sort of standard, it is ironic that the modern West can be seen as falling behind more traditional and "primitive" cultures in many respects, which seemingly allow development to occur at more appropriate rates. As was mentioned earlier, the concept of readiness, as we are using it here, draws attention to a second form of social pathology which creates a crisis for the healthy development of children and adolescents. This is the failure by society to meet and support emerging developmental competencies. In discussing this form of social pathology, we must especially focus our attention on those segments of the population which experience the negative effects of racism, sexism, and other forms of social oppression.

Urie Bronfenbrenner was one of the first people to seriously investigate the ecology of human development. His work has been extended in important ways by developmentalists who have studied the negative impact of ecologies of oppression (1979). Spencer has made particularly important strides in this direction in her studies of the impact of racism on minority children (1981, 1982a, 1982b, 1983, in press: 1984, 1985). Calling into question the psychoanalytic approach to this issue, which has typically portrayed the victims of racism as internalizing the negative images of self provided by the dominant culture and engaging in self-hatred, Spencer has focused her attention on the all-important role of the nurturing environment on the development of minority children. Her research has demonstrated that institutions, like the family and church, and the presence of visible black leadership in the political and business communities can "screen out" the negative impact of racism on the child's self-image in significant ways. But when adolescent competencies emerge and the minority youth is able to take into account wider social spheres and project possible personal futures, he or she all too frequently experiences no social support for these dreams and aspirations. The readiness for new social roles and forms of identity is not matched by the availability of resources and life chances in a racist society. In many instances, a normal developmental trajectory is derailed.

In a similar fashion, Gilligan has recently called attention to the impact of a male-dominated culture on the development of girls and women (1982). When the values and norms of a culture are centered predominantly on the experience of male development, it not only encourages girls and women to evaulate their own experience negatively, but also fails to recognize and support an important, alternate pattern of human development. The social pathology of sexism is so all-pervasive as to be almost invisible. It seriously impairs the development of the full range of human competencies in both men and women. Much of Gilligan's critique to the present has focused on Kohlberg's understanding of moral development which places a high value on the process of individuation and the ability to reason in an abstract, principled fashion about moral rights and responsibilities in situations of social conflict. The development of girls and women, Gilligan contends, moves along a different trajectory, one in which development toward greater complexity of relationship and interdependence is highly valued.

Gilligan thus raises important issues about the nature of sex role stereotypes and the extent to which they foster the full range of human development. She has also raised significant questions about developmental theory itself, asking what constitutes a fully adequate understanding of the human vocation, the final category of developmental crisis which we will examine. Before turning to this topic, however, let us summarize the crisis of social pathology.

By this category, we mean those widespread and long-lasting social structures which negatively impact the development of children and youth. We have identified two basic ways in which this is done, both of which have to do with a social system's failure to honor the readiness of the developing young person. Children and adolescents are placed in crisis when the systems by which they are nurtured in early life do not respect the limitations of their developmental capacities, placing great stress on their ability to adapt. They also experience crisis, however hidden and all-pervasive, when the social systems which shape their patterns of growth do not acknowledge newly emerging developmental potentials with sufficient social support. Both of these trajectories lead to a crisis of social pathology in which individual difficulties of development are not the result of inherent deficiencies but are directly related to failures in the child's or adolescent's social milieu.

4. The Crisis of Vocational Inadequacy

The category of the crisis of vocational inadequacy draws attention to the ethical issues which are inevitably present in all scientific inquiry, especially inquiry involving human beings and having practical implications. We are using vocation in a broad sense, referring to those normative definitions of what it means to be a human being and to pursue the Good. A recognition of the vocational issues in psychological theory is of the utmost importance, especially when children and adolescents are involved. Our discussion will follow two lines: (1) the need for criteria other than empirical adequacy in the evaluation of psychological theories in general and development theories in particular; (2) the need for and usefulness of developmental theories in the discernment of the modal level of development fostered by a given community.

A. Models of Development and Ethical Adequacy

Our discussion of Gilligan's work under the category of the crisis of social pathology raised an issue that is central to all developmental theory, although it is not always directly addressed by developmentalists themselves. Who or what decides what constitutes development? From the perspective of women's experience, Gilligan has raised serious questions about typical emphases in developmental theory on individuation and increased rational autonomy. Faith Development Theory directly raises the question of the adequacy of theories of human becoming in offering a framework that places at its apex a universalizing form of faith. There are many complex issues inherent in these concerns, issues which can only be touched on briefly in this essay.

There are very real differences between various representatives of the structural developmental tradition, as the recent discussion between Gilligan and Kohlberg has made clear. What is particularly important about the emerging discussion is how it draws attention to the relationship between science and ethics. If it could be proved empirically that Gillligan is correct in her assessment of a developmental trajectory that has been left out of the Kohlbergian approach, the question as to its preferability would still be left up in the air. How shall we decide between the various understandings of human development which are available? This raises important issues about the relationship between philosophy and science.

Developmental theories are no different than other psychological theories in this regard. Indeed, the question we are addressing must be raised about all scientific theories, especially those which are influential in the human sphere. Can scientific findings be evaluated solely on the basis of empirical reliability or is there an inextricable philosophical and even theological dimension to such evaluations? In our view the latter is the case. As it is widely recognized, many scientists no longer make the claims to truth offered by the old-style empiricism. Rather, recent work by Thomas Kuhn (1962), Max Black (1962), Stephen Pepper (1942), Mary Hesse (1954), Ian Barbour (1974), and others have drawn attention to the role of the human imagination in scientific research. All empirical research involves the use of certain models which structure the nature of the problems to be pursued, the technologies used, what constitutes reliable evidence, and other fundamental assumptions. A new awareness has emerged that the findings produced by scientific inquiry may be true, in the sense of empirically verifiable, and at the same time be predetermined in range and nature by their relation to initial concepts and models.

Developmental theory is no different in this regard. As was pointed out in our initial section of this essay, the root metaphor of the structural developmental tradition is borrowed from the field of biology: organicism. In its model of the self, the organism is portrayed as in an interactive relationship with its surroundings in which it plays an active role in structuring its various adaptive responses. How are we to judge the adequacy of such an understanding of human beings? Certainly, a model's ability to handle a wide range of empirically-derived observations is one criterion of adequacy. But of equal importance is an assessment of the models of the self presupposed by various psychological theories from the perspective of philosophy and theology. To put the matter rather simply, persons who are involved in the nurture and care of children should not be reticent to subject the various models of childhood and adolescence offered them by a particular psychological theory to evaluation from the perspectives offered by other disciplines of a more explicitly normative nature. There is a very real sense in which the most basic and important concepts of any systematic attempt to understanding and practice are derived from the interaction and mutual influence of a number of fields.

In the field of developmental theory, we suggest the concept of vocation as particularly fruitful in helping persons assess the adequacy of developmental theories from philosophical and theological perspectives. What is the view of the human vocation that a particular developmental theory offers? It is our view that some sort of vocational concept is implicitly at work in every developmental theory for two basic reasons: (1) the *selectivity* of a given developmental theory in its focus on only certain domains or qualities which are seen as possessing a developmental character; (2) the *normative* dimension inherent in any concept of development. We will briefly explicate why we believe this to be the case.

In our initial discussion of the concept of development as it is used in the structural developmental tradition, we drew attention to the fact that this concept typically refers to greater complexity in the internal organization of an organism's adaptive capacities. Inevitably, such a view entails both an understanding of the capacities with which an organism is genetically-potentiated and an understanding of the end-point toward which development moves. Indeed, by definition, development means the movement from the organism's initial state at birth to a higher level of organizational complexity. To chart such movement, developmental theory must do two things: (1) it must *select* those capacities or functions of the organism which have a developmental character; (2) it must define clearly the highest level of organizational complexity toward which development moves. To state the matter simply, a developmental theory must ask: What does the organism come with, where is it going, and how does it get there? Developmental theories thus are inevitably selective and normative in their approach. Only certain capacities are viewed as possessing a developmental character; higher levels of development are posited.

It might be argued that while developmental theories are normative in the sense that we have just described them, they are not normative in an ethical or vocational sense. A higher stage of reasoning does not necessarily mean that it is a better stage, philosophically or ethically. We would agree with this contention and point to the fact that both the ethical and practical adequacy of a developmental theory must be argued on grounds that are not totally immanent to the theory itself. The ability to engage in universal perspective taking, for example, does not, in and of itself, say anything about how such a capacity will be used. However, developmental theories inevitably move beyond the realm of pure theory and enter into therapeutic and educational forms of practice. At this point, it becomes clear that what seems merely descriptive has prescriptive dimensions which must be carefully assessed.

Faith Development Theory is normative not only in the sense of describing a course of human development, but also, within proper limits, in a prescriptive sense. It charts a course of human development in which persons move toward an increasingly universal faith stance. While resisting an understanding of the stages of faith as a kind of step ladder which children should be hurried up as quickly as possible, for the reasons mentioned in our discussion of the crisis of social pathology, it does appeal to the theological concept of the kingdom of God as the grounds for its understanding of the human vocation. For this reason, it stands between a purely descriptive understanding of development and full-scale theological or philosophical analysis of the human self. In working with children and adolescents it offers a means by which to assess their current level of development and the normative trajectory along which they might continue to develop. Hence, it raises the question of the impact of therapeutic, educational, and religious communities on the development of children and adolescents, which is the second level of analysis of the crisis of vocational inadequacy.

B. *Community Modal Levels of Development*

Certain theoretical perspectives in the structural development tradition have attempted to bring their empirical-but-normative perspective to bear on the way that particular communities impact the development of the children and adolescents whom they influence. In Faith Development Theory, we refer to this in terms of the *modal level* of a given community, that is, the average expectable level of development which a community assumes. This also raises the question of vocational adequacy in that a community can be assessed as impeding or encouraging a person to develop toward a particular goal of human maturity.

In Moral and Faith Development Theories, this sort of analysis is a particularly important tool by which to analyze and critique a group's socialization practices. Since we will deal with this approach from a Faith Development perspective in the following section, we will focus on Kohlberg's theory for the present. A variety of persons who are working out of Kohlberg's theory of moral development have attempted to describe the "moral atmosphere" of schools and families. Blatt and Kohlberg initially came to the conclusion that moral learning is not something that is best taught discursively but is the result of the richness of "role-taking" opportunities afforded by a given community (1973). An atmosphere that is conducive to moral development is one in which persons are provided with rich and variegated opportunities to take into account the vantage point of persons other than themselves and to reason about moral conflicts in such a way as to better take into account the needs of others.

Both teachers and parents can do a number of things in their relationship with children and adolescents which makes for a richer moral atmosphere. In their styles of discipline, for example, they can give reasons for their decisions, instead of arbitrarily demanding blind obedience, thereby stimulating the moral reasoning of children and adolescents. They can provide opportunities for democratic forms of family and school decision-making. Lickona calls this the "fairness" approach to family conflict, an approach in which children, youth, and parents strive to achieve mutual understanding and cooperative problem resolution (1983). This teaches children and youth to reason morally by encouraging them to think of others' needs besides their own and by providing them with opportunities to practice the skills of conflict-resolution: expressing a viewpoint, listening to another person, and finding a common middle ground.

In a similar fashion, Kohlberg's theory has been used in the attempt to create the sort of atomosphere in an alternate high school in Cambridge, Massachusetts that would encourage moral development (Wasserman, 1978). The accent was on the formation of a participatory democracy in which persons are actively involved in a group decision-making process which provides them with real-life opportunities to reason about situations of moral conflict and to be exposed to more adequate levels of moral reasoning. The opposite side of this issue has been studied in Kohlberg's work in assessing the impact of a prison system on its inmates. Not surprisingly, he found the operative structures of the prison to be operating at a Stage 2 level of moral development, in which persons are rewarded for making trade-offs with one another. Such a form of community life simply reinforced a low level of moral reasoning among its inmates and actually seemed to have a negative impact in terms of rehabilitation.

Such studies are indicative of the various ways that a community can be examined in terms of its impact on the development of its members. This is a crucial issue for those working with children and adolescents. They must especially be sensitive to the level of vocational analysis, both of particular developmental theories and the modal level of actual communities, grappling with their own understanding of what it is to be a mature human being and the shape of the human calling. They can be certain that some such understanding is already operative in both the theories they use and the practices which they undertake.

4. Crises of Childhood and Adolescence in the Faith Development Perspective

In this section, we will examine several cases from a Faith Development perspective, illustrating each of the crises which has just been discussed. By necessity, our presentation of each case will be brief but, hopefully, suggestive of possible uses of Faith Development Theory in the face of actual situations of nurture and care with children and adolescents.

1. Developmental Crisis

Charlie is a sixth grader whose parents approached the minister of education with a concern. Charlie had recently begun to ask them questions about God, sharing with them that he no longer felt as close to God anymore. He then refused to talk about the subject with them at all, claiming that he was no longer worried about things. His parents were not severely alarmed but wondered if something had happened in Sunday school or in the Sunday evening youth meetings in which Charlie participates on a regular basis. Since the minister of education led the Sunday evening meetings for Charlie's age group and had a good relationship with him, the parents asked him if he would listen for clues as to what was going on. As a sixth grader, Charlie would shortly be going through confirmation classes. The minister of education typically did a modified Faith Development interview of every confirmation class and decided to use this interview to see if he could gain better insight into what was going on with Charlie. That way the boy would not be singled out from the others but would have a chance to share his difficulties in a context that all his friends were also experiencing.

During the interview, it did become clear that Charlie was experiencing a crisis of sorts. His childhood faith was beginning to fall apart. He had always been interested in talking seriously about God and the Bible. His father had almost gone into the ministry, and Charlie had mentioned in passing several times that he might be the one in the family who ended up pursuing that vocation. But now he was beginning to experience difficulty for the first time in his elementary years. His Mythic Literal understanding of God's activity in the world was now breaking down in the face of a newly emerging recognition of the seeming incompatibility of the findings of science and his own religious beliefs. The following portions of this interview bring out his concern in relation to the issue of the origin of the world.

> Minister: Suppose a person was to come from another planet and did not know anything about God. What would you tell that person?
>
> Charlie: I'd tell them that he was the creator and everything. He created the universe and all that. And I'd probably show them the Bible.
>
> M: Do you think that everyone believes those sorts of things?
>
> C: No, not everybody believes that God created the world. Sometimes I wonder if even I believe it. We've been studying evolution in school, and I can't understand how what we're studying there and what my Sunday school teachers say to me about Adam and Eve can really be true.
>
> M: Do you worry about that?
>
> C: Sometimes. I'm afraid if I don't believe then the Spirit of the Lord won't be with me anymore.

At various points in the interview, Charlie gave indications of a predominantly Mythic Literal faith stance. After he spontaneously brought up the topic of heaven and was asked to describe it, for example, he responded by saying, "I think it's way, way out in space . . . circling all the galaxies and all that." Likewise, hell was described as being "in the middle of the earth and they say it's just fire." His symbolic funtioning is still quite literal and one-dimensional. Heaven and hell are real places with certain tangible characteristics.

However, Charlie's Mythic Literal faith is beginning to face a real crisis. Increasingly, he is not willing to compartmentalize the literal beliefs of his faith and the seemingly contradictory beliefs of science. He is beginning to give evidence of his ability to reason abstractly, allowing him to stand outside of both sets of stories and engage in the risky business of comparing and contrasting them. The story of Adam and Eve as real people who were created a long time ago to tend a garden which really existed was now being challenged by alternate versions of the beginning of the world that portrayed humans as evolving over a long period of time.

It is important to see how serious a crisis this was for a young boy like Charlie who dreamed of being a minister someday and took his religious beliefs very seriously. His Mythic Literal faith was literally beginning to crumble, with deep emotional consequences. His parents were concerned enough to seek help. We gain some insight into how traumatic this was for Charlie in other portions of the interview. In his initial reference to the disconcerting effect of his taking seriously the stories of evolution, Charlie made reference to his fear that the "spirit of the Lord" would no longer be with him. This proved to be a recurrent theme in the interview. When asked what sorts of things make him feel bad, Charlie replied, "When I've disappointed God. When I do things or say things or think things that I shouldn't." The interview continued:

> M: What happens when we really disappoint him?
> C: He takes his spirit out of you.
> M: Has that ever happened to you?
> C: Yeah.
> M: When does it happen?
> C: Different times. There's this song that we're singing in choir. It's a beautiful song. It's weird. It makes me sort of, my eyes start watering and all . . . I feel really empty. It's called "Here Am I, Send Me," and it's just like asking God to send me into his hands or something.
> M: I wonder why that makes you feel empty.
> C: It makes me feel as though he's left me . . . as though I'm not as close to God as I used to be. I don't know if he's going to send me. I don't know what I think about him anymore.

There are many ways that we could interpret what is going on with Charlie. A person who is theologically conservative, for example, might see this as one more instance of how our secular, humanistic society corrupts the faith of our innocent youth with its teachings about evolution. A psychoanalyst might view Charlie's disconcerting relations with God as an initial sign of the onset of the second individuation process in adolescence in which he must rework his relationship with his inner parental figures. From a Faith Development perspective, however, we would contend that an important part of what is going on with Charlie is a normal developmental crisis of faith. It cannot be reduced solely to the psychological process of individuation, although it certainly enters into the picture on one level. Nor is his exposure to the insights of contemporary culture and the inner turmoil which it engenders necessarily demonic.

Charlie is experiencing the beginning of a shift in the way he structures and relates to his centers of value and meaning. The loss of the images and understandings of intimacy which had held his world together throughout the Mythic Literal stage are now beginning to fall apart. In his own way, Charlie is experiencing the void. It is fairly normal for persons during this period of early adolescence to undergo the sort of crisis of faith which Charlie is experiencing. Mythic Literal religious beliefs and some form of modern thought come into conscious conflict, forcing an incipient form of demythologizing to take place. The Genesis stories, for example, can no longer be taken at face value. Nor is heaven a tangible place "up there" in the sky.

Indeed, in Charlie's case it is the deep level of personal religious commitment which makes this crisis so intense for him. Those young people who have not formed a strong Mythic Literal understanding of God will not have as much to lose, if anything, when they begin to face in a more mature fashion a scientific world view. But there is also the risk that with no real images and beliefs of transcendence such people will merely conform to the given social order, possessing no leverage on the taken-for-granted world. There is clear evidence that Charlie, at this point, has a strong motivation to work through the crisis that is confronting him, *if* his newly emerging developmental readiness for more mature forms of faith is met by a religious community that will help him appropriate the meaning of God the creator in a way that moves him beyond the choice between a Mythic Literal faith and the findings of modern science.

2. Situational Crisis

Julie is a four year old whose mother was recently killed in an automobile accident. An only child, Julie had been extremely close to her mother and now lives along with her father in a predominantly rural area. Their family has participated in a small United Methodist church since Julie could remember, where her mother had sung in the choir. The following is part of a longer conversation between the minister of that church and Julie which took place several months after the mother's death. The minister had made a concerted effort to visit Julie and her father on a regular basis following the car accident. Julie had come to look forward to the visits, for the minister would often go with her to the family room where they would sit on the floor and build things with small wooden blocks while talking. During one of these visits, Julie spontaneously brought up the question:

Julie: Why did God take away my mommy to heaven?

Minister: That's a hard one to answer, Julie. When your mommy was hurt so badly in the car accident she was in a lot of pain. Maybe God did not want her to hurt so much, so he took her to be with him in heaven.

J: But why did God make that man run into my mommy's car?

M: I guess I don't think that God made that happen, Julie. Sometimes things happen that God doesn't do. I think he probably felt very sad when your mommy was hurt.

J: When Tabby died (the family cat) mommy said that God took her to heaven? Didn't he take mommy away too? I want her back. Why doesn't God bring her back?

Anyone who has experienced such a conversation with a child knows the limits of language. It is difficult to care for a bereaved adult, but trying to comfort a child and help her make some kind of sense of her mother's death seems almost impossible. After all, what answer is there to give? What can we say to any person who has experienced first-hand the absurdity of suffering? Even a four year old, however, is trying to compose the events which have transpired into some sort of meaningful pattern. While there is no logical answer to the question of suffering, religious traditions have always attempted to assist persons by offering them ways of expressing their grief and helping them to an affirmation of the meaningfulness of life because of its grounding in something or someone who lies beyond even death itself.

Faith Development Theory does not, in and of itself, provide an answer to the questions which arise in the face of death. Every religious tradition will have its own way of responding to such a crisis. What Faith Development Theory can offer is a perspective within which to understand persons who are facing a crisis of meaning because of events which have punctured their taken-for-granted world. In Julie's case she has experienced one of the severest situational crises which a young child can encounter: the death of a parent. The fact that she is struggling to make some kind of sense out of the event is evident in the portion of the conversation recorded above. *She* initiates the question about why God took her mother. In addition to the terrible emotions that Julie feels—loneliness, anger, guilt, sadness—there is a cognitive component of her suffering. The world no longer makes sense: why did God take away my mommy?

Julie's faith is solidly Intuitive-Projective. Her understanding of God does not distinguish between fact and fantasy. God took away Tabby; God took away mommy; God could bring her back; God caused the other driver to run into her mother. It is impossible to appeal to any sense of causality in this stage of faith which might help Julie separate God's activity in the world from the ongoing flow of events. Her imagination is not yet bound by reason in sorting out why things happen. But still her young mind stretches outward to find some sort of meaning.

Persons in the Intuitive stage like Julie are forming vague, internal representations of life's meaning and purpose; they are composing *images* of ultimacy. The central, all-important force in a child's initial formation of faith images is those adult figures who are closest to him or her. For Julie, her mother both mediated cultural and religious understandings of God to her and was her god in terms of emotional attachment. Those earliest images of God which Julie was beginning to form were being constructed in interaction with the religious contents offered by her church, but given real meaning through her conversations with her mother. It is her mother's explanation of what happened when Tabby died that Julie recalls. Undoubtedly, the explanation was originally comforting to her; God had taken Tabby to be with him. But now she wonders why God has taken away her mother. As yet, Julie's God representation is a fragile construction which rests on the support of significant others who embody, if only partially, the characteristics of God which she is beginning to form.

A psychological approach is apt to overlook the faith crisis which Julie is experiencing. Even if she had not verbalized such a concern as directly as she was able to do in the above conversation, she would have been facing, on some level, a crisis of meaning. All too frequently, those who are involved in the care and nurture of children and adolescents do not take seriously enough the dimension of faith in their attempts to assist them in the midst of situational crises. Concern is focused on the management of household and babysitting tasks, such as who will feed the children and take care of them after school. Crises of meaning are usually associated with the bereaved adult. How many ministers and priests even attempt pastoral care to a bereaved child? Julie was, however, experiencing a crisis of faith. Whether she had been able to verbalize it or not, she was struggling to make some sort of sense out of the events which she had experienced. What kind of world is it in which my mommy is so swiftly and brutally taken away? Is it a world where love is too risky? Is it a world where nurturing persons will always let you down?

The answer to these questions will not be played out on an intellectual level at this stage, but on the level of images, images with deep emotional valence, images by which Julie will form an incipient sense of who she is and what she can expect from life. In the face of such a situation, providing a child with religious answers is not enough. Nor is it enough to assume that somehow, mysteriously, she will make her way through this crisis of faith as she works through her grief. Something more serious is at stake here: the fact that the very person who was most "god" to Julie, who most consistently modeled qualities of God for her and mediated the contents of her religious tradition, is now gone. Will Julie's emotional and cognitive relationship with God die along with her mother? Or will God become a kind of maternal figure who represents the possibility of a continued relationship with her dead mother?

There is no way of predicting what will happen to such a girl. At the very least, however, Julie's father and other persons who are close to her, especially her minister, can recognize the fact that she is going to have to struggle on some level with this issue at various points in her life. The fact that she is willing to use religious language, even at age four, is a strong indication that she will struggle to make sense of her mother's death in terms of how she understands God.

It is not uncommon for ministers to undertake pastoral counseling with persons who experience a crisis of meaning later in life that is ultimately related to faith images that were formed during childhood in the face of some situational stress and which have not been re-elaborated in light of further developmental potential. Hidden questions and hurts re-emerge with a power that surprises the person involved. From a Faith Development perspective, there is no need to wait until a person reaches a crisis in adult life before real progress can be made in helping him or her come to grips, in a developmentally-appropriate way, with early situational trauma. As early as Harry Stack Sullivan (1953), certain schools of psychiatry recognized that early situational stress or relational deprivation can be offset in significant ways by relationships which emerge in later stages of development.

At Julie's stage of life, there is little doubt that no one can take her mother's place. However, her cognitive and emotional understanding of this event can be influenced by the entry of new nurturing figures into her life. Her father, for example, can begin to develop a new closeness in his relationship with her. Other adults can begin to cultivate a special friendship with her. The fact that the minister has actively sought Julie out, has been willing to play on her level, and is open to her religious questions without trying to force her to accept some sort of doctrinal or biblical answer that is beyond her ability to really grasp bodes well for his ability to be of help to Julie. As important as any words that might be spoken is the relationship of trust and special interest which will give Julie some sense that tragic events are not the last word in life. The goal is not to move her beyond her confused understanding of how God was involved in her mother's death, as fantasy-filled as it is. This is merely an indication of her stage of faith. The goal is to provide her with new relationships of trust and care which can continue to embody, as well as verbalize, the fact that death is not the final victor.

3. *The Crises of Social Pathology and Inadequate Vocation*

In this final section, we will examine jointly the crises of social pathology and inadequate vocation by focusing on the issue of nuclear awareness. We will examine the recent research that has begun to emerge on the impact of nuclear awareness on children and adolescents and raise certain issues from a Faith Development perspective about how the modal level of development of a given community determines in significant ways persons' ability to come to grips with this threatening issue.

Over the last three years, persons associated with The Center for Faith Development have undertaken a number of Faith Development interviews with children in the fifth and sixth grades who are about to enter confirmation class. Many of these individual interviews have been followed by group interviews of a particular class in which many of the same questions are talked about by the group as a whole. Consistently, in both the individual and group settings, children have spontaneously responded to the question "What causes you to be afraid?" by expressing fear of a nuclear disaster. In one group interview, the entire group grew quiet as an exceptionally articulate sixth grader said, "We go on making plans about getting married and dreaming about what we are going to be when we grow up, but I think all of us wonder, really wonder, if we ever will grow up. My mom and dad don't like nuclear weapons, but they don't know what to do about it. None of my teachers at school do either. What are we supposed to think when even you grown-ups don't seem to know what to do? Sometimes I wonder if you even really care."

There is not much real research on the psychosocial impact of nuclear awareness. The research that is available corroborates our growing suspicion that our children and adolescents are aware of the escalating threat of nuclear warfare and that they are deeply and constantly disturbed by it. Too often, adults seriously underestimate the depth and scope of the impact of the nuclear threat on young people, perhaps reflecting their own adult narcotization towards this issue. From a Faith Development perspective, the effect of nuclear awareness is particularly damaging to our children's and adolescents' ability to envision the future with confidence, to trust the adult generation, and, most basically, to form a sense of a meaningful life.

One of the most important bodies of research on the effects of nuclear awareness on children and adolescents has been undertaken by William Beardslee and John Mack, two psychiatrists at Harvard Medical School (1982). One of the major findings of the interviews conducted by these two men centers on the sense of hoplessness which nuclear awareness engenders. An awareness of the overwhelming destructiveness of nuclear war both for those destroyed immediately and for survivors, coupled with a widespread belief that such a disaster will very likely occur in their lifetime, has made many children and adolescents pessimistic in their assessment of the possibilities of the human future. One of the most disturbing pieces of information offered by these two men is the evidence that since their research began in 1978, there has been a widening and deepening of children's fear, and a consistent movement downward in the age span of children who are aware of and frightened about these developments. Very young children, frequently under eight, know about the threat, the fear, and the danger of nuclear disaster.

What sort of impact will this have on their development? With little longitudinal evidence available, we can only hazard a guess on the basis of the developmental difficulties which we have observed. Much of the impact of the nuclear issue is at a subliminal level. That is, it operates as an ever-present undercurrent which influences development from beyond the reaches of immediate consciousness. In Faith Development Theory, we have come to acknowledge the significance of the many important ways that the "taken-for-granted" world structures our centers of value and meaning. Sex role stereotypes, for example, are not transmitted primarily through direct, verbal communication but are passed from one generation to another by the way that children see their parents divide up the household tasks and the various emotional and work roles which each plays. This is what makes the attempt to break such patterns so difficult. They are a part of the "taken-for-granted-world" which must be explicitly raised into consciousness before its effects can be altered.

Nuclear awareness operates at this same level. While children and adolescents can articulate, if asked, the various negative feelings which they associate with a potential nuclear war, most of the time this threat exerts its deadening influence from beyond the reaches of consciousness. In our earlier discussion of the crisis of social pathology, we drew attention to the concept, "readiness," and how a society can systematically thwart or ignore the developmental limitations or potentials of children and adolescents. The nuclear threat does this in several significant ways.

During the Mythic-Literal stage children are struggling to form an initial sense of identity in the midst of a world that is no longer the product of their imagination. They have to deal with a "real" world that has a certain order and lawfulness about it. One of the most significant ways of achieving a feeling of security and new sense of identity in the face of a world "out there" is through an identification with the heroic figures of stories. Such stories are often provided them by their religious communities. Heroic figures, who face and conquer the challenges of the real world, serve as models for children in this stage as they attempt to form inner ideals of who or what they might be in a world that is not of their making.

Nuclear awareness deals the Mythic-Literal child a double blow. Not only is the real world with which he or she must come to grips so frightening as to be beyond any meaningful comprehension, but it also offers a real life challenge for which there are no meaningful stories. Who can imagine a heroic conquest of a nuclear disaster? Even elementary students are aware of what happens to survivors. As one of Beardslee and Mack's subjects replied: "No, even if we weren't killed, we'd all have cancer in thirty years, and our kids would be mutants, not to forget what the land would be like." The nuclear threat is of such cataclysmic proportions that it virtually robs Mythic-Literal children of heroic models which can embody those qualities of personhood transcending such a threat. Perhaps the only meaningful stories which we can offer are those which portray persons who do not lose courage in the face of overwhelming odds, like David facing Goliath, persons who will march forth in the face of impossible odds to do all that they can to alter the present situation.

Synthetic-Conventional adolescents also are impacted by the nuclear threat. One of the most important dimensions of faith during this stage of life is the formation of a sense of oneself and the possible futures which one may pursue within a larger framework of life's meaning and purpose. As we saw earlier, a racist society can rob a minority adolescent of the sort of hope that undergirds such newly emerging aspirations. The nuclear threat can have this impact on all adolescents.

Again, we must draw attention to the subterranean nature of its influence. It is not as if adolescents spend all of their time explicitly worrying about the threat of a nuclear war. They continue to date, play football, study, and make plans for the future. But looming above all of these activities is the threat that at any time it may all come to an end. For many adolescents, there is a kind of unspoken belief that it will come to an end before they have a chance to fulfill all of their life's potential. As one adolescent said in a conversation with her father about the future: "I'm glad we live in this city. You know why? I've learned in school that there are eight ICBMs trained on this city, and that when the war comes, we will be instantly vaporized instead of having to deal with fallout and radiation and burying all of the other dead." When asked if she really thought this would happen, she replied: "I think it will happen before I get out of high school."

Some social commentators have said that we live in an apocalyptic age. That is one way of expressing the underlying sense of foreboding that pervades the struggle by children and adolescents to name the threat which constantly looms on their horizon. It is truly a crisis of social pathology. For individuals to seek escape from the nuclear threat is to hide from reality; for them to take it into themselves with no transcendent grounds for hope is to be overwhelmed. Is it possible for religious communities to offer images of the human vocation that avoid either of these extremes? Is it possible to name directly and to face that threat which constantly lurks on the edge of consciousness without losing hope or succumbing to cynical despair?

There are no easy answers to such questions. But we must evaluate our religious, educational, and political communities to see if they are helping our children and adolescents in the face of such an overwhelming threat. We are convinced that the concept of vocational adequacy can prove helpful in this regard, drawing attention to the images of human maturity which are operative in a given community. Closely related is the concept of modal level in the Faith Development perspective which attempts to assess the average expectable level of development of a group. A recent conversation with a young teenager who attends a very conservative church brings home the relevance of these ideas:

> Did you see "The Day After"?
> No. I think it's stupid to watch those kinds of programs.
> Why do you say that?
> Well, if the Lord is going to take us all, he's going to take us all. Nothing we can do about it.
> Don't you think we should try to do everything we can to end the threat of nuclear war?
> My preacher says that all that matters is that a person accept Jesus as the Lord and Savior. Then you don't have to be afraid of even a nuclear war.

While the Center for Faith Development is only beginning to undertake research on the concept of community modal level, it has done enough to offer the hypothesis that the following factors are of great importance in the developmental level of religious communities: styles of leadership and authority, contents of religious beliefs, inclusion of a pluralism of viewpoints, and regular opportunities to reflect upon communal norms and practices. In the conversation recounted above, each of the religious factors is present in a negative fashion, functioning to protect the young woman from the threat of a nuclear disaster. Religious authority is lodged totally in external figures; the group participants are sheltered from understandings of life that are different than their own, focusing entirely on an understanding of Jesus as a kind of parental figure who will magically take care of the "saved"; moreover, the participants are encouraged to resist all opportunities to reflect on the group's beliefs and practices in light of contemporary issues. While the effect on the young woman is to insulate her from the anxiety of nuclear awareness, the vision of the human vocation is inadequate from a Faith Development perspective.

More than any single issue the nuclear threat brings to consciousness the reality that we can no longer afford to live in a world of tribal gods, a world in which each community clings to its own practices and beliefs as if they stood at the center of the universe. We must discover a way to move in and through our particular faiths to the universal which lies beyond every finite comprehension. Our visions of vocational adequacy must not be limited to narrow understandings of health or successful living but must take clear cognizance of the threatened world in which we live. To develop truly and faithfully in such a world is finally to discover that which is the secret ground uniting us all.

Note

1. This description of Faith stages is from the senior author's forthcoming book, *Becoming Adult, Becoming Christian*, Harper and Row, 1984, and is reprinted by permission of Harper and Row.

Bibliography

Baldwin, James Mark. *Social and Ethical Interpretations in Mental Development.* New York: Macmillan, 1906.
Barbour, Ian. *Myths, Models and Paradigms: A Comparative Study of Science and Religion.* New York: Harper & Row, 1974.
Beardslee, William and Mack, John. "The Impact on Children and Ado-

lescents of Nuclear Developments," in *Psychological Aspects of Nuclear Developments*," in a task force report of the American Psychiatric Association, No. 20. Washington, D.C.: The American Psychiatric Association, 1982.

Black, Max. *Models and Metaphors*. Ithaca: Cornell University Press, 1962.

Blatt, Moshe and Kohlberg, Lawrence. "Effects of Classroom Discussion upon Children's Level of Moral Judgment," in *Recent Research in Moral Development*, ed. Kohlberg. New York: Holt, Rinehart & Winston, 1973.

Bronfenbrenner, Urie. *The Ecology of Human Development*. Cambridge: Harvard University Press, 1979.

Dewey, John, *Democracy and Education*. New York: The Free Press, 1916.

Dilthey, Wilhelm. *Gesammelte Schriften*, 17 vols, 1914–1974; vols 1–12, Stuttgart: B.G. Teubner & Göttingen: Vandenhoeck & Ruprecht; vols 13–17, Göttingen: Vandenhoeck & Ruprecht.

Egan, Kieran. *Educational Development*. New York: Oxford University Press, 1979.

Elkind, David. *Children and Adolescents*. New York: Oxford University Press, 1974.

———. *The Hurried Child*. Reading, Mass: Addison-Wesley, 1981.

Fowler, James W. *Becoming Adult, Becoming Christian*. New York: Harper & Row, 1984.

———. "Faith and the Structuring of Meaning" in *Toward Moral and Religious Maturity* (ed. Fowler). Morristown, N.J.: Silver Burdett, 1980.

Fowler, James W. (with Sam Keen). *Life-Maps: Conversations on the Journey of Faith*. Waco, Texas: Word Books, 1978.

———. *Stages of Faith: The Psychology of Human Development and the Search for Meaning*. New York: Harper & Row, 1981.

Gadamer, Hans-Georg. *Wahrheit und Methode*. Tübingen: J.C.B. Mohr, 1960.

Gallie, W.B. "Essentially Contested Concepts," in *Proceedings of the Aristotelian Society*, 56, 1955–6.

Gilligan, Carol. *In a Different Voice*. Cambridge: Harvard University Press, 1982.

Harris, Dale. *The Concept of Development*. Minneapolis: The University of Minnesota Press, 1957.

Heidegger, Martin. *Being and Time*. New York: Harper & Row, 1962.

Hesse, Mary. *Science and the Human Imagination: Aspects of the History and Logic of Physical Science*. London: SCM Press, 1954.

Kegan, Robert. *The Evolving Self—Problem and Process in Human Development.* Cambridge: Harvard University Press, 1982.

Kohlberg, Lawrence. *Collected Papers on Moral Development.* Cambridge: Center for Moral Education, 1976.

Kuhn, Thomas. *The Structure of Scientific Revolutions.* Chicago: The University of Chicago Press, 1962.

Lickona, Thomas. *Raising Good Children.* New York: Bantam Books, 1983.

Loevinger, Jane. *Ego Development: Conceptions and Theories.* San Francisco: Jossey-Bass Publishers, 1976.

Mead, George Herbert. *Mind, Self, and Society.* Chicago: University of Chicago Press, 1934.

Niebuhr, H. Richard. *The Meaning of Revelation.* New York: Macmillan, 1963.

————. *The Responsible Self.* New York: Harper & Row, 1941.

Pepper, Stephen. *World Hypotheses.* Berkeley: University of California Press, 1942.

Piaget, Jean and Inhelder, Barbel. *The Growth of Logical Thinking from Childhood to Adolescence.* New York: Basic Books, 1958.

Piaget, Jean. *The Origins of Intelligence in Children.* New York: International Universities Press, 1952. Originally published in 1936.

————. *The Psychology of the Child.* New York: Harper Torchbooks, 1969.

————. *Structuralism.* New York: Basic Books, 1970. Originally published in 1968.

Schleiermacher, F.D.E. *Hermeneutics: The Hand-Written Fragments.* Missoula, Mont.: Scholars Press, 1977.

Selman, Robert. *The Growth of Interpersonal Understanding: Developmental and Clinical Analyses.* New York: Academic Press, 1980.

Spencer, Margaret B. "Black Children's Race Awareness, Racial Attitudes and Self-Concept: A Reinterpretation," in *Journal of Child Psychology and Psychiatry.* In press.

————. "Children's Cultural Values and Parental Child Rearing Strategies" in *Developmental Review,* Vol. 4, 1983.

————. "Differential Effects of Expressive and Receptive Language Use on the Inference Task Performance of Middle- and Lower-Income Children," in *Journal of Black Psychology,* Vol. 10, No. 2, Feb. 1984.

————. "Personal and Group Identity of Black Children: An Alternative Synthesis," in *Genetic Psychology Monographs.* Provincetown, Mass.: The Journal Press, 1982.

————. "Preschool Children's Social Cognition and Cultural Cognition: A Cognitive Developmental Interpretation of Race Dissonance Findings," in *The Journal of Psychology*. Provincetown, Mass.: The Journal Press, 1982.

————. *Social and Affective Development of Black Children: New Beginnings*. New York; Earlbaum, in press for 1985.

Sullivan, Harry Stack. *The Interpersonal Theory of Psychiatry*. New York: W.W. Norton and Company, 1953.

Tracy, David. *The Analogical Imagination*. New York: Crossroad Publishing Company, 1981.

————. *Blessed Rage for Order*. New York: Seabury Press, 1975.

Troeltsch, Ernst. *The Social Teaching of the Christian Church*, Vols I & II, 1911. English edition, New York: Harper & Brothers, 1960.

Wasserman, Elsa. "Implementing Kohlberg's 'Just Community Concept' in an Alternative High School," *Readings in Moral Education*, ed. Peter Scharf. Minneapolis: Winston Press, 1978.

Weber, Max. "Religions-soziologie" in *Wirtschaft und Gesellschaft*, Tübingen: J.C.B. Mohr, 1922.

Werner, Heinz. *Comparative Psychology of Mental Development*. Chicago: Follett, 1948.

Donald Capps

Pastoral Counseling for Middle Adults: A Levinsonian Perspective

It is widely recognized that the pastoral counseling movement of the 1950's and 1960's was heavily influenced by the client-centered or Rogerian approach to psychotherapy. It is also generally recognized that Rogerian therapy has been especially attractive to adults in their twenties and thirties. Most of the clients discussed in books by Rogers and his associates are young adults experiencing the usual difficulties of young adulthood, e.g., gaining independence from parents and in-laws, adjusting to married life, struggling with career choices, coping with graduate school, achieving greater competence in parental responsibilities to young children. This orientation of client-centered therapy to the young adult fit especially well with the growth of suburban churches in the 1950's and 1960's because churches in suburbia had a disproportionate number of young adults among their membership. Client-centered pastoral counseling, with its emphasis on the concerns of young adults and its "non-directive" style, was quite compatible with suburban church life.

However, in the late 1960's and 1970's, the growth rate of suburban churches among mainline Protestant denominations slowed, and the membership of existing suburban churches became (like the suburban areas themselves) more middle-aged. In this new social context, client-centered pastoral counseling lost much of its previous influence and prestige. To be sure, the client-centered approach to pastoral counseling has not been repudiated. Many of the central tenets of client-centered therapy are so fundamental to pastoral counseling that one doubts it will ever be repudiated in total. On the other hand, the personality theory which underlies client-centered therapy, a theory based on the concept of the "fully-functioning personality," is clearly oriented toward the aspirations and concerns of young adults.[1] It is becoming increasingly clear that this personality theory does not provide an adequate theoretical basis for pastoral counseling that aims to be sensitive to the concerns and aspirations of middle adults. I believe that such developmental theorists as Eric Erickson, Robert Jay Lifton and Daniel Levinson provide concepts about the personality and its formation which are especially useful for undergirding pastoral counseling of middle adults.

In this essay, I focus on the work of Daniel Levinson, showing how his theory of adult development may ground the pastoral counseling of middle adults. As my discussion proceeds, it will become evident that I continue to support the central therapeutic objectives of the client-centered approach, but I locate these objectives within Levinson's developmental theory and not Rogers' own personality theory. I would also want to emphasize that Levinson is just one of three major developmental theorists (the others being Erickson and Lifton) whose work provides a grounding for the pastoral counseling of middle adults. Thus, while this essay makes a case for Levinson's theory as a foundation for pastoral counseling of middle adults, I do not mean to suggest that his is the only or even necessarily the most important theory in this regard. What I would argue is that the appearance of his theory was especially timely, because it coincided with the shifting emphasis in American church life, especially among mainline Protestant churches, from the concerns of young adults ("How can I become a more self-directed person?") to the concerns of middle adults ("How can I become a more integrated or "whole" person?").

My discussion in this essay will take the following form. First, I will provide a general overview of Levinson's theory of adult development. Next, I will focus on his mid-life polarities, which are the key elements of his concept of the "mid-life transition," and will illustrate their diagnostic usefulness through brief vignettes selected from actual pastoral care and counseling cases. Then, I will use these case analyses to address the question of the goals of pastoral counseling; here I will discuss Rogers' view that a major therapeutic objective of counseling is the restructuring of clients' perceptions (of self, world and other persons). In my judgment, Levinson's theory of adult development, especially his approach to the mid-life transition, provides a more illuminating basis for understanding such perceptual restructurings than does Rogers' own theory of the fully-functioning personality. Finally, in a somewhat wide-ranging concluding section, I develop the argument that in counseling which is self-consciously pastoral, one objective of this restructuring of perceptions is increased self-awareness in terms of three self-metaphors which are grounded in the Judaeo-Christian tradition. I suggest that these self-metaphors, which I call the responsible, believable and accessible selves, stand in fundamental opposition to the narcissistic personality, which is generally regarded as the dominant cultural personality of our time. Levinson says that one of the major developmental tasks of young adulthood is the forming of a Dream.

I contend that the Dream of young adults is inherently narcissistic, and that a major goal of pastoral counseling with middle adults is to facilitate their desire to replace the Dream of their young adulthood with a Vision more appropriate to the "transformed" narcissism of middle adulthood (Kohut, 1978).

Levinson's Theory of Adult Development

Let us begin, then, with Levinson's theory of adult development as formulated in *The Seasons of a Man's Life* (1978). As we do so, it needs to be noted at the very outset that his theory is based on studies of males. I cannot go into the reasons Levinson offers for this exclusive focus on men, nor is it possible to assess the adequacy of these reasons. This would call for a much more extensive discussion than space allows. Suffice it to say that while his theory may not be applicable in all respects to women, I will be centering to a considerable extent on his mid-life polarities, which in my judgment are most certainly applicable to women.

Levinson and his associates divide the life cycle into four *eras* of roughly twenty-five years duration each: the era of childhood and adolescense spanning the years from birth to age 22; the era of early adulthood (age 18 to 45); the era of middle adulthood (age 40 to 65); and the era of late adulthood (age 60 to 85). In each case, there is an overlapping period of five years marking the transition from one era to the next.

Levinson has little to say about the childhood and adolescence era. His comments about the late adulthood era (age 60 to 85) are also very sketchy. He does, however, provide detailed analyses of the young or early adult era and the middle adult era. While my major concern in this essay is the pastoral care and counseling of middle adults, we need briefly to consider Levinson's handling of early adulthood since this sets the context for middle adulthood. In fact, because Levinson sees early adulthood continuing through one's late thirties and even into the early forties, much of what he says about the later stages of early adulthood has very direct relevance to the pastoral counseling of middle adults. In his schema, middle adulthood comes into its own around age 45, but many adults perceive themselves to be middle adults in their later thirties. So we should recognize the relevance of Levinson's views on early adulthood for pastoral care and counseling of middle adults.

Early Adult Era

Levinson divides the early adult era into two major phases. There is the *novice phase* from age 17 to 33 when the first adult life structure is being formed. Then there is the *settling down phase* from age 33 to 40 when the early adult structure is completed. These two phases are, in turn, subdivided into stages. The novice phase consists of three stages of roughly equal duration. These include the *early adult transition* stage from age 17 to 22, the *entering the adult world* stage from age 22 to 28, and the *age thirty transition* stage from age 28 to 33. Since the early adult transition stage between ages 17 and 22 mainly involves the termination of the life structure formed during childhood and adolescence, the most important stage in the formation of an adult life structure is the second stage from age 22 to 28 when the individual begins to take a place in the adult world. During these six years, the individual works on the major developmental tasks of the novice phase. There are four such tasks, including forming an occupation, forming a marriage and family, forming a mentor relationship, and forming the Dream.

Space does not allow me to discuss these developmental tasks in any detail. However, as my earlier comment on the Dream indicates, this particular developmental task is central to my argument, so a word about it is clearly in order. Noting that this feature of young adulthood is rarely considered in academic research, Levinson suggests that the Dream is a complex mixture of reality and illusion: "It has the quality of a vision, an imagined possibility that generates excitement and vitality. At the start it is poorly articulated and only tenuously connected to reality" (91). It may, for example, have strong mythical or even magical overtones as one dreams of being a great hero in one's chosen profession. It is also likely to have a strong element of destiny and thus of unquestioned legitimacy. The young man who betrays his Dream will suffer the consequences later. But, in any case, during the first years of middle adulthood individuals "have to reappraise the magical aspects of the Dream and modify its place in their middle adult lives" (92). Levinson calls this subsequent reducing of the Dream down to size a process of "de-illusionment." As I will indicate later, such reappraisal of the Dream is a central, perhaps *the* central focus of pastoral counseling for middle adulthood.

Work on these four developmental tasks continues through the novice phase (i.e., to about age 33). The *entering the adult world* stage from age 22 to 28 is the period when the real formation of occupation, marriage, mentor relationship and Dream takes place. Then, the *age thirty transition* stage from age 28 to 33 is used to address the flaws that have become evident in the life structure as formed thus far. This age thirty transition can be quite difficult because a person by this time is usually too committed to the life structure being formed to turn back, but many unclarities remain as to what this life structure entails for the future.

As the novice phase comes to an end at age 33, the effects of the developmental work accomplished during this phase are strikingly apparent as what the individual has become at age 33 is compared with the life structure at 17 or even 22. As Levinson points out, in the period between age 17 and 22, "a man's life is still strongly rooted in the family of origin and the pre-adult world; the process of separation is just getting underway. He has a Dream, incoate or differentiated, and diverse hopes, fears, fantasies, plans for the future" (111). By the time he reaches the end of the novice phase at age 33, a qualitatively new structure, quite different from the life structure formed in childhood and adolescence, has emerged: "By this time he almost certainly has a wife and family—perhaps is even divorced and remarried—and his sense of what it means to be a husband and father has altered dramatically" (111). Also, "The character of his occupational life is taking a new shape. Even if his present occupation is the one he had helped form, it contains possibilities and limitations he did not imagine in the Early Adult Transition. In most cases, the occupation is different in crucial ways from his earlier expectations" (111).

Once the basic life structure of early adulthood is formed in the novice phase, the remaining years of the early adult era (the *settling down phase* from 33–40) are spent either in refining and solidifying this structure or in attempts to create a more satisfactory structure. This process, which Levinson also calls "becoming one's own man," involves two major tasks. The first is to establish a place in society. This is a time when an individual's life is anchored more firmly in family, occupation and community. The second involves working toward advancement. This entails building a better life, using and improving one's skills, becoming more creative, and contributing to society and being affirmed by it. In one sense, these two tasks are antithetical. To the extent that an individual wants roots and stability, there must be a willingness to moderate the upward striving. Conversely, the person who wants desperately to make a mark in this world may be reluctant to place great value on stability, such as making strong commitments to family solidarity or home town loyalties.

Levinson identifies five typical sequences within the settling down phase from age 33 to 40. Each sequence deals in a different way with the life structure that was formed during the middle to late twenties and modified in the *age thirty transition*. Each reflects a unique pattern of dealing with the two major tasks of finding a place in society and working toward advancement. They include (1) advancement within a stable life structure; (2) serious failure or decline within a stable life structure; (3) breaking out—trying for a new structure; (4) advancement which itself produces a change in life structure; and (5) unstable life structure. Space constraints do not allow us to describe, much less explore any of these sequences in any depth. But it can readily be seen that Levinson is here trying to identify the *range* of possible patterns a person's life structure may follow in the mid-to-late thirties. In Levinson's own study of forty men, thirty had stable life structures (sequences 1 and 2), while ten had changing or unstable structures (sequences 3, 4 and 5). Just over half were in the "normative" sequence of *advancing within a stable structure*. There were relatively few men (five) in the *breaking out* pattern. This suggests that the vast majority of men in Levinson's study were attempting to work within the life structure formed in their twenties. Quite evidently, maintaining continuity in the life process is very important to persons in the mid-to-late thirties. In fact, the need for continuity may be one of the strongest motivations they have for sustaining the commitments of their middle twenties.

Middle Adult Era

After the relative stability of the settling down phase, which brings the early adult era to its culmination, there is a roughly five year transition phase (from age 40 to 45) to the *middle adult era*. As Levinson puts it: "In a stable period the major tasks are to build a life structure and enhance one's life within it. In a transitional period one must terminate the existing structure, explore possibilities (in self and world) out of which new choices can be formed and make the initial choices that provide the basis for a new structure" (331). This transition between age 40 and 45 marks a "developmental crisis." The word *crisis* suggests that the changes occurring in this period are comparable in their intensity and disruptiveness to the "identity crisis" in mid-adolescence (Erickson, 1968). In Levinson's theory, this mid-life transition is structurally comparable to the transition from adolescence to adulthood between ages 17 and 22. Both mark the termination of one twenty year life structure and the beginning of another. We will be focusing here on the mid-life polarities that emerge in this transition period in one's early forties. But before I discuss them, we need to flesh out very briefly Levinson's stages in middle adulthood.

After the *mid-life transition* period of roughly five years, the next five years from 45 to 50 mark the entrance into middle adulthood, and are comparable to the *entering the adult world* stage (age 22 to 28) in the early adult life structure. The following five years from age 50 to 55 make the *age fifty transition* and are comparable to the *age thirty* transition in the early adult structure. The years from 55 to 60 complete the middle adult era. Levinson's discussion of the three stages following the very crucial mid-life transition consists mainly of comments on the life decisions some of his subjects made as their mid-life transitions came to an end. Thus these stages are mainly based on his surmise that the middle adult era has a structure similar to the young adult era, with alternating stages of transition and stability. However, there are no further conceptual formulations for these three stages between age 45 and 60, not even an attempt to provide them with descriptive names. Thus, in exploring the value of Levinson's theory for undergirding pastoral counseling of middle adults, I will focus on the *mid-life transition* and, more specifically, on his view that this transitional period introduces a process of *individuation* involving four major polarities. His focus here on individuation, and his formulation of the four polarities in the individuation process, justifies my claim that Levinson provides a conceptual basis for pastoral counseling of middle adults based on a particular understanding of the personality. By formulating the individuation process in terms of polarities, his view of personality and its development in mid-life clearly reflects what we earlier claimed the major developmental concern of middle adults to be, namely, a concern for personal integration, but not at the expense of, rather, in service to, a more fully differentiated personality.

Following C.G. Jung, Levinson belives that the *mid-life transition* is a key period in the developmental process of individuation. This process, which begins in infancy, involves recognizing the boundaries between self and world, and clarifying one's attachment to the world. Levinson suggests that the early adult transition from age 17 to 22 is an early but very key period in this individuation process because this period marks the loosening of the individual's ties to the pre-adult world and pre-adult self. However, he also claims that individuation does not increase all that much between the individual's middle twenties and late thirties because there is considerable preoccupation during these years with the more external tasks associated with finding a niche in the world and advancing toward one's goals. Hence, after the early adult transition, the next major stage in the individuation process is the mid-life transition between ages 40 and 45. During this transitional period, the individual is engaged in redefining the boundaries between self and world, and in reconstituting the attachment to the world.

Levinson discusses this mid-life individuation process in terms of four polarities: young/old, destruction/creation, attachment/separateness, and masculine/feminine. He views the young/old polarity as the major one and gives considerably more attention to it. I will discuss these polarities in some detail because they constitute the basis for my contention that Levinson's theory has value for the pastoral care and counseling of middle adults. I would also reemphasize that I consider these polarities to be equally salient for women as for men.

The Young/Old Polarity. In depiciting the young/old polarity, Levinson identifies its three most prominent themes: (1) the integration of the *young* and the *old* dimensions of the self; (2) the sense of mortality and wish for immortality; and (3) the question of one's legacy to future generations.

Regarding the integration of the young and old dimensions of the self, Levinson points out that each stage of life requires an integration of the young and the old appropriate to that stage. But the mid-life transition is a special case because, for the first time in one's life, a person is as old as he or she is young. This fact is reflected in the change in "generational status" that occurs at age 40. Between ages 30 and 45, an individual is part of the *initiation* generation. During the mid-life transition, there is a move into the *dominant* generation, and by the mid-forties a person is clearly a generation removed from those who are involved in the settling down process of their thirties. Given this shift in status, an individual needs to achieve a new balance of the young and the old selves. This means that his or her early adult conceptions of what is *young* and what is *old* will no longer do. In early adulthood, we tend to view youth as possibility and potential, while middle adults experience the *young* in themselves as energy and openness. Likewise, young adults may conceive the *old* as rigidity and decline, whereas middle adults experience it as stability and structure. Levinson contends that middle adulthood should therefore be a time of optimal young/old balance because, in this era, individuals can have a "firmer structure" with which to use their considerable energy, imagination and capacity for change: "Middle adulthood is, in this sense, the center of the life cycle" (213).

A second theme in the young/old polarity is the sense of mortality and wish for immortality. It may appear odd that a person who is only at the midpoint in life would become anxious about matters of personal mortality. But Levinson found this was in fact the case with the vast majority of his subjects. He attributes this concern for personal mortality to a number of factors. One is the perception of decline in certain physical abilities (e.g., the inability to run as fast or lift as much) or perceptible changes in physical appearance (e.g., hair loss and weight gain). Another factor is a decline in certain mental capacities, such as difficulty in remembering details and in learning masses of specific information. A third factor is the experience of the mortality and suffering of others. An individual's parents, now in their sixties, seventies or even eighties, are more likely to have recently died or be facing problems of retirement, physical disability and dependency on others. Also, a person has more contact with persons who are dying, or becoming seriously ill, or experiencing other kinds of tragedy (including divorce, depression, job failure, alcoholism and drug abuse, and intergenerational conflicts within the nuclear or extended family). A fourth factor is the psychological letdown that follows the striving in one's thirties:

"Even if he has accomplished a great deal and is on the path to greater attainment, his basic orientation toward success and failure normally begins to change. It is no longer crucial to climb another rung on the ladder" (214). A fifth factor is the wish for immortality. This wish is present at every stage of the life cycle, but it becomes an especially important factor in the mid-life transition because individuals' awareness of their mortality and that of others is so acute. There are two sides to this collision between the wish for immortality and the sense of one's own mortality. One is the concern with personal survival after death, a concern that arises as an individual experiences some decline in physical and mental ability. The other is a concern with the meaning of one's life, especially its value for oneself and the human community. Even if we do not feel that our life has actually been wasted, we typically feel at this period in life that it does not have enough "accrued value." Our achievements seem rather modest and even inconsequential when viewed in the light of our original Dream.

The third theme in the young/old polarity, our legacy to future generations, is directly related to the mortality theme. As Levinson points out, a person's legacy, including material possessions, creative products, enterprises and influence on others, "defines to a large degree the ultimate value of his life—and his claim on immortality" (218). Typically, middle adults become very protective of this legacy. They look after their material holdings, lash out against critics of their work, and maintain close oversight of their teenage and young adult offspring (e.g., encouraging them to make the "right" friendships and marry the "right" person). While protective of this legacy, however, middle adults also recognize that to hoard this legacy is not only to lose it but also to stagnate as a person. So they seek ways to expend it, channeling it toward the needs of future generations. They make contributions to institutions that will survive long after their own careers are over, they seek ways to make their creative work available to larger numbers of persons, and they enlarge the legacy itself. Of course, some middle adults come to the conclusion that building a legacy is no longer worth the trouble. The author of the biblical Book of Ecclesiastes, for example, concludes that he has been building a legacy that will be inherited by a younger generation who are likely to treat it with disdain. While such extreme cynicism is relatively rare, the middle forties generally involve reassessment of the very meaning and value of one's personal legacy. As Levinson puts it: "In every era, a man normally has the need and the capability to generate a legacy. But in the Mid-Life Transition the meaning of legacy deepens and the task of building a legacy acquires its greatest developmental significance. As we learn better how to foster development in adulthood, 'creating a legacy' will become an increasingly important part of middle adulthood" (221).

The Destruction/Creation Polarity. Levinson observes that no one can reach forty without some experience of human destructiveness. Other persons have damaged our self-esteem, hindered our advancement, and erected barriers against our effort to achieve important personal goals. And we have all done the same to others. In the individuation process in mid-life, a person becomes more deeply aware of the place of destruction in his or her life. This means gaining a better understanding of our grievances against others for the harm they have done, and coming to terms with our guilt and remorse for the harm we have done to others. It also means recognizing that our creativity, whether in the form of products, relationships, imaginative acts or social enterprises, does not occur *in spite of* our destructiveness but by means of a deeper understanding of it. Such understanding, though, cannot be achieved only through conscious reflection: "The main learning goes on within the fabric of one's life. During the Mid-Life Transition, we often learn by going through intense periods of suffering, confusion, rage against others and ourselves, grief over lost opportunities and lost parts of the self" (225). Destructiveness is inherent in all human life, but it is during the mid-life transition that an individual begins to recognize how central it is to the individuation process itself. Destruction is involved in the separation of the self from other selves and in the differentiation within the self.

The Attachment/Separateness Polarity. In the early adult era, we tend to emphasize attachment at the expense of separateness. Middle adulthood requires a more equal balance of the two. During the mid-life transition, we are less likely to be exclusively engaged in the external world and to be moving toward more serious engagement with ourselves. We draw more on our inner resources and are less dependent on external stimulation. We are more trusting of our own perceptions and less reliant on the opinions of others. One major effect of this greater balance of attachment and separateness is what Levinson calls "detribalization." That is, a person "becomes more critical of the tribe—the particular groups, institutions and traditions that have the greatest significance for him, the social matrix to which he is attached. He is less dependent upon tribal rewards, more questioning of tribal values, more able to look at life from a universalistic perspective" (242). This does not mean a rejection of one's own tradition and background. In fact, individuals who felt cheated by the "tribe" in early adulthood may come to a more benign view of it in the mid-life transition. Rather, it means that individuals' attachment to the world is more inclusive, less concerned with the need to assert the superiority and maintain the separateness of their own social and occupational groups.

Levinson relates these changes in the attachment/separateness polarity to the individual's Dream. In early adulthood, we have an intense desire to realize our Dream. As we enter middle adulthood, some of these desires fade away, while those that remain are realized more fully. Levinson sees this as an opportunity to become a wiser person: "He can develop greater wisdom if he is less focused upon the acquisition of specific skills, knowledge and rewards" (242). In this way, the de-illusionment a person experiences in relation to the Dream is rechanneled into a newly developed wisdom, especially about the world of human relationships and aspirations. Later, we will locate this shift from dream to wisdom within the Judaeo-Christian framework, and will see how it is implicated in the movement from "pure" to "transformed" narcissism.

The Masculine/Feminine Polarity. I have questions about Levinson's use of the terms "masculine" and "feminine" to describe this polarity. No doubt, David Bakan's (1966) terms "agency" and "communion" would capture the meaning of this polarity just as well, and without the connotation that certain personality traits are gender specific. In any event, Levinson says that in the mid-life transition the male adult is more accepting of his "feminine" side. Conversely, we would assume that the female adult is more accepting of her "masculine" side. The middle adult is also more suspicious of traditional sexual stereotypes (masculine toughness vs. feminine vulnerability, masculine ambition vs. feminine concern for stability and security, masculine power vs. feminine weakness, and masculine rationality vs. feminine emotionality). These stereotypes continue to have great force in contemporary society, and they are important to many young adult males. But middle adults who are honest with themselves (admittedly, a very large qualification) perceive that these stereotypes are increasingly irrelevant to their understanding of who they are. Even men and women who continue to give them lip service realize that they no longer carry much existential weight or are clearly dysfunctional for themselves. On the one hand, middle adult males are more accepting of their own vulnerability, weakness, need for security and capacity for deep emotion. On the other hand, they are increasingly ambivalent if not disdainful toward the need for toughness, ambition, power and rationality. In short, the middle adult male and, we assume, the female as well, achieve a more even balance between the "masculine" and "feminine" sides of their personalities.

Levinson's mid-life polarities could be discussed in much greater detail. But enough has been said about them to capture their basic thrust. I now want to proceed to their diagnostic use in pastoral care and counseling.

Mid-Life Polarities as Diagnostic Guidelines

In recent years, much attention has been given in pastoral counseling theory to the importance of diagnosis. It figures prominently in Howard Clinebell's basic text (1984) and is especially highlighted in Paul W. Pruyser's *The Minister as Diagnostician* (1976). Pruyser recommends the use of six theological themes (providence, faith, grace, repentence, communion, vocation and awareness of the holy) as "guideposts" for the pastoral counselor's "diagnostic thinking and as ordering principles for the observations he makes" (96). In my book *Pastoral Counseling and Preaching* (1980) I have adapted six types of theological diagnosis employed in preaching for use in the pastoral care and counseling setting, viewing these types as diagnostic strategies for counseling. In my more recent book, *Pastoral Hermeneutics* (1984), I have proposed that diagnosis is the middle stage in an interpretive process that moves from identifying the *dynamics* of the situation, to *diagnosis* (both theological and psychological), to the experience of *disclosure*. There are obvious parallels between this hermeneutical model and what I will have to say later about the restructuring of perceptions.

As we now begin to explore the applicability of Levinson's theory of adult development to pastoral counseling, I propose that his mid-life polarities are a potentially valuable diagnostic resource for pastoral care and counseling of middle adults. To illustrate their diagnostic value, I have chosen four pastoral care and counseling cases, each reflective of one of the four polarities.[2] In keeping with Levinson's focus on middle adult males, these pastoral cases involve men who are in or near the mid-life transition. While the four polarities are also relevant for young adults and may be diagnostically useful in pastoral counseling with persons in their twenties and early thirties, I incline to the view that they are most appropriately used with persons (women as well as men) who are at least in their late thirties (Levinson's *settling down* stage). They fill essentially the same need in the pastoral care and counseling of middle adults that Rogers' characteristics of the fully functioning self have filled in the pastoral care and counseling of young adults.

The Case of Carl Johnson: Young/Old Polarity

As indicated above, the young/old polarity includes three major themes: the integration of the *young* and *old* dimensions of the self, the sense of mortality and wish for immortality, and the question of one's legacy. The following case involves all three. Carl Johnson is a forty year old government employee. The following is a portion of an informal pastoral counseling session after a board of elders meeting at a local church. Carl Johnson, a member of the board, asked the pastor if he had a few moments to talk. As the conversation developed, Carl indicated that he has begun to question whether he has gotten as much out of his life and career as he could have.

Carl:

I don't think I ever knew what I was supposed to do in college. I never knew what it was all about. So I never felt I had any purpose or goal, but I always said a person ought to have. I've wondered if other people were doing better in this regard than I am.

Pastor:

You have not been able to see clearly where you are going, and you wonder if other people have the same difficulty.

Carl:

Yeah. It bothers me. I'm a religious person and I feel I've goofed. I've been sort of buried in the ground—this troubles me very much—because I feel that one is accountable for what he is given, and I've squandered mine. Not in riotous living, darn it, just in no living at all. I feel that God is lawful, and I wonder, is it too late to do something now? Have I reached the point of no return?

Pastor:

You fear you have passed up all your opportunities and maybe your present torment is in some sense a judgment of God on you?

Carl:

Sure. But I couldn't have taken hold any earlier because I didn't know what I was supposed to do! Maybe the trouble with me is that I'm in a hurry, and God is not. I'm like Moses in the desert. He took forty years to wander around. I guess he was just waiting for all the old "moss-backs" to die off, so he could do something for his people.

Pastor:

You see the strategy in his "sojourn in the desert."

Carl:

Yeah.

Pastor:

But, you wonder whether you are even now being rather impatient. As you reflect on your own behavior, you see that you have been rather ambitious and impatient with yourself for not getting there.

Carl:

Well, I guess my impatience has been with God, too, for not showing me the way, if I may be as bold as to say so.

Here, Carl is reassessing his life to date, realizing that he is no longer young and sensing that he has not really "lived" up to this point in his life. If he were a young adult, the counselor might focus on his sense of being without any clear direction. But, now, in middle adulthood, he describes his lack of direction as a "structural flaw" in the life he formed during his early to late twenties. Now his concerns are focused on his sense that he has squandered his life, that his legacy to date lacks much accrued value. As he looks to the future, he realizes that there are more years of waiting ahead of him before he will have his chance to make something of his life. Specifically, in terms of his occupation, he will have to wait until the "old moss-backs" retire before he will have a position of some stature or influence. Presumably, his chosen occupation exacerbates this typical "waiting game." No doubt, his reference to Moses wandering in the desert reflects an underlying concern that he may never reach any significant goals in life.

Thus, in terms of the major themes of the young/old polarity, Carl Johnson is greatly concerned about his legacy ("I feel that one is accountable for what he is given, and I've squandered mine"), is much aware of his mortality and the fact that his life is already half over ("Have I reached the point of no return?"), and is having considerable difficulty integrating the *young* and *old* dimensions of the self as he sees the structural flaws in his young adulthood but does not yet see a way to overcome them ("So I never felt I had any purpose or goal").

There is also a religious dimension to Carl Johnson's struggles with the young/old polarity. His discovery that he has reached middle age and has little to show for it causes him to question the guidance, or lack of it, he received during his earlier years. He feels that God could have provided clearer guidance during the crucial formative years of his young adulthood so that now he would have a clearer vision of what direction his life ought to take. Perhaps he lacked a mentor in young adulthood who might have served as a surrogate for God in providing guidance, someone to instill confidence that the choices he was making in his early adulthood were promising and sound. In any event, his tone is accusatory. He is now less impatient with himself than with God, whom he perceives as having failed to show him the way he was to go so that he might have made something significant out of his life. Even now, he feels that God is unsympathetic with his impatience, that God is in favor of his resigning himself to his present fate or simply waiting patiently for something better. At the same time, the fact that he has initiated this conversation with his pastor indicates that he is aware the life structure formed in his twenties has run its course and he now has an opportunity to form a new life structure more congruent with his current aspirations. Much like adolescence, middle adulthood offers the opportunity to perceive oneself and one's life course in a significantly new way. By diagnosing Carl Johnson in terms of the various themes of the young/old polarity, the pastor is in the position to help Carl form a new life structure commensurate with middle adulthood, and Carl's perception that he is in danger of "squandering" the second half of his life as he has squandered the first.

The Case of Frank Larson:
The Destructive/Creative Polarity

As we have seen, the middle adult becomes more deeply aware of the role that destructiveness is playing in his or her life. The following pastoral counseling case involves a parishioner, Frank Larson, who gained significant insight into the psychodynamic causes of his destructiveness. Frank is a salesman for a manufacturing firm. One evening he phoned his pastor and asked to see him immediately. The pastor told him that he was just leaving for a ministers' conference but would be back the following evening: "Is it an emergency?" Frank said it was not exactly an emergency, and then related to the pastor how that afternoon he had "taken a swing" at one of the sales managers and had to be restrained by the man: "It's getting embarrassing. I seem to be letting go more than I used to, and it scares me. I have an uncontrollable temper, but until recently I've been able to keep it in check. I don't know what I'm going to do. I'm sure I'll get fired. Can I talk to you when you get back?"

During their first counseling session, Frank Larson expressed surprise that his employer had not fired him, then went on to talk about his inability to control his temper. He said he was not only jeopardizing his work, he was also alienating his wife, who had been able to tolerate his outbursts up to now but was getting extremely impatient with his hostile behavior toward their thirteen year old son. He admitted that his attitude toward his son was poor, and that he was hurting himself at work but contended that there was no way he could change. He asked the pastor for an interpretation of his problem and for an immediate solution. When the pastor resisted this request, pointing out that it was not his way to try to give people a ready-made solution to their problems, Frank got angry and remarked, "I never did like smug preachers." He stood up and stormed out of the office.

The following day Frank called the pastor and apologized for his outburst, and requested another appointment. This session enabled Frank to gain significant insight into the roots of his destructive behavior, with the important breakthrough coming near the end of the hour.

Frank:
There was this manual arts teacher I had in high school. For some reason he didn't like me. This guy, he joined in when the other guys razzed me, and I just took it. Boy, I hated his guts! But I never did say anything to him, or to anybody for that matter. I don't think I have ever got that thing out of my system. Anybody starts razzing me—I see red! I got to thinking this week, I've been taking it out on the wrong people ever since.

Pastor:
You're seeing that you have probably never really dealt with that situation.

Frank:
Yeah, but the other day, I went to this sales manager I was telling you about and told him I was sorry about what happened, that I'd been pretty touchy lately. He said he didn't hold it against me, to forget it and be friends, that I was a good man and he didn't want to lose me from the force—he hadn't meant to push me either. I can't ever remember doing anything like that before, I mean, trying to be friends with somebody I thought needed a punch in the nose.

Pastor:
This is a new way of dealing with the same kind of situation you experienced in high school.

Frank:
Yeah, and my wife has noticed the difference in me. She said last night, "Whatever is happening to you, I like it." I guess what really made it tough for me was that I never had a chance to tell that teacher how I felt about him. When I found out he was killed in Vietnam, I hate to say it, but I was almost glad. I know it isn't right to feel that way—now, I think I am mostly sorry for him, but I've been all mixed up about it.

Pastor:
You've been ashamed of hating him, but frustrated that you weren't able to let him know how you felt.

Frank:
Exactly. It's ridiculous I have kept this thing buried for so long. It's sure helping to face up to it, which I have been avoiding all these years. I was too ashamed even to tell my wife about that thing. I thought, "Well, that's just kid stuff. I've outgrown that." I'll admit it has flashed back a few times, but I just sort of dismissed it from my mind. I guess I was more affected by it than I thought.

Pastor:
Apparently you are quite aware of how this pattern has been working in you.

Frank:
Yeah, I've been kicking him in the rear end all along.

In this case of Frank Larson, we see a destructiveness toward others that is also having a destructive effect on Frank's own life. Through the stimulus of pastoral counseling, Frank gains the insight that his destructive attitudes and behavior can be traced to his high school days when he was the victim of a teacher's ridicule. Now, years later, essentially the same dynamic situation has occurred, this time involving one of his supervisors who had apparently joined in with the other salesmen in "razzing" Frank. But this time the situation ended quite differently because Frank was able to "own" his destructive tendencies and no longer dismiss them as irrelevant or untypical of him. The result was a creative handling of the problem. His apology not only elicited an apology from the sales manager, but also a clear vote of confidence in Frank. Not incidentally, he followed the same course after his outburst against the pastor. He apologized, his apology was accepted, and the counseling process got back on track again. Evidently, Frank was able to come to terms with his destructive behavior when he was able to find a certain justification for it in his past history. This also enabled him to recognize that he was taking his anger out on the wrong individuals. His real contention was with the high school teacher who held him up to ridicule and shame, and thus inflicted a severe injury on his positive self-perception.

Obviously, the destructiveness Frank Larson exhibited here is not unique to middle adults. Such angry outbursts are common among men and women of all ages. What is perhaps distinctive about the middle adult's handling of such destructiveness as part of one's personality. To me, the critical insight in this case was not Frank's discernment that his destructive tendencies can be traced back to his altercation with a high school teacher, but Frank's readiness without any prodding from the counselor to accept the fact that he does in fact have destructive tendencies. He readily acknowledges that his destructiveness was essentially unprovoked, that it was basically prompted by changes going on inside him rather than by the external environment. Here, then, we have a clear case of a middle adult recognizing that he has destructive tendencies and not trying to minimize their influence in his life.

The Case of Don Benson:
Attachment/Separateness Polarity

As indicated earlier, Levinson believes that the middle adult is becoming a more "separate" person but not at the expense of becoming isolated. This separateness, in fact, enables individuals to become both more and differently attached to the world around them. In the following case of Don Benson, we have a middle adult male who is having difficulty separating himself from his daughter's problems and taking a more detached view of his paternal responsibilities. But circumstances are making it difficult for him to maintain his customary involvement in his daughter's life, and are challenging him to separate himself from her and, in so doing, to establish their relationship on a new and more mutually satisfying basis. The situation is a hospital visit paid by the pastor to a faithful parishioner who is convalescing from surgery. The pastor asked Don Benson how he was feeling, and then suddenly noticed Don's twenty-one year old daughter Melanie sitting beside the bed. She seemed very dejected. With prodding from her father, she proceeded to tell the pastor what the two of them had just been discussing. She was having misgivings about her approaching marriage to Ted in three weeks. This will be her second marriage; her previous marriage ended in divorce. She insists that she had had no trouble or arguments with Ted, that it's simply a matter of having serious doubts as to whether she should marry him. She concluded, "I just want to get away from all this. I don't want to get married."

Don:
Melanie, you made one mistake. Why didn't you think of all this before you announced your engagement? You know your mother and I are going to be hurt terribly by this fooling around of yours, and I sure would think you had hurt us enough. Haven't we been through enough already trying to straighten out your first marriage?

Melanie:

All you say is true, and Ted and I have tried to consider all these things carefully, and I was trying to do all I could to do my share so you and mother would not have any more heartache and embarrassment.

Don:

I told her, Reverend, her mother and I are plenty upset that she carries on this way. She's old enough. She should have outgrown this flightiness and remember what we've been through.

Melanie:

Well, you and mother don't want me to make another mistake, do you? Can't I make either of you understand that for some reason I don't even understand myself, I don't want to go through with this marriage? Have you got to insist that I do?

Don:

Why didn't you think about this before you went ahead and sent out all your announcements? What are people going to think?

At this point, there was a knock on the door and one of Melanie's women friends came in. They left together.

Pastor:

Don, would you mind telling me why Melanie divorced her first husband? This might have something to do with her problem just now.

Don:

I don't mind telling you. He was a pervert. We were sick when we found it out, which we didn't for a long time. Melanie had insisted that she be married against our wishes, and she hated to tell us. In fact, she told her sister first and her sister told us. Believe me, when I found it out I sure sent him on his way. Had I known sooner, I would not have insisted that Melanie stay with him as long as her mother and I insisted.

This case illustrates the attachment/separateness polarity. Strongly influenced by "tribal" thinking, in which his grown daughter's actions reflect on him as a parent, Don Benson has been unable to let Melanie make her own decisions and lead her own life. He feels he must be intensely involved in her life, directing the course of her life as he did earlier, when he first repelled her efforts to leave her husband and then, on learning that he was homosexual, taking personal responsibility for expelling him from his daughter's life. Don's personal involvement in the lastest crisis involving Melanie is so strong that he senses there may be a direct connection between his current hospitalization and Melanie's problems. As he put it later in the pastoral visit: "Reverend, she's old enough to stop this wishy-washying about. The whole mess is just killing her mother. In fact I am sure part of my trouble is worrying about her and her fooling around this way."

Indeed, she *is* old enough to be making her own decisions without such close parental supervision or interference. Certainly Melanie's problems have caused her parents much pain and anguish. By the same token, Don's approach to her problems only isolates the persons involved in the situation from one another, so there is no real sense that they are *sharing* one another's pain. As a middle adult, Don is facing the challenge of finding ways to separate himself from his daughter's difficulties, not as a way to become more isolated from her but to begin to relate to her in a less paternalistic and "tribal" fashion. His question "What will people think?" indicates that he is very concerned about how his daughter's problems reflect on the family in general, and him in particular. Don needs to become less concerned about how the family looks in the eyes of others, to transcend much of his tribal perspective on life and begin to see Melanie less as a daughter who needs his protection and more as a young woman who is trying to find her direction in life. Undoubtedly, Melanie's problems also reflect negatively on Don's Dream. To the extent that being an effective parent was a part of this Dream (and there is no reason to believe from the case materials provided that he ever took his parental responsibilities lightly), Melanie's marital problems must surely threaten his Dream. By the same token, this latest crisis offers an excellent opportunity for Don to rechannel the de-illusionment he is experiencing now into a new form of wisdom. New visions arise out of broken dreams. Don's physical disability, together with his sense that "the whole mess is just killing her mother," suggests that they are ready to relinquish certain aspects of their Dream as young and hopeful parents, and to replace these with a *shared vision* (Erikson, 1977).

The Case of Bill Harris:
The Masculine/Feminine Polarity

Levinson sees middle adults becoming more open to that "side" of themselves which they have previously left undeveloped because they considered it inappropriate to their identities as men or women. This is the challenge that is now confronting Bill Harris, who has been dominating and overpowering his wife and children. For the first fifteen years of his marriage, Bill's wife Arlene accepted his domineering ways. But when they both reached forty, she decided that she could no longer tolerate him and threatened to file for divorce. When he came to the stark realization that she really meant it, Bill called their pastor and asked him for an appointment with the two of them.

Bill:
Yesterday she filed for divorce. I don't want it. I want her. She says she doesn't love me, but I don't believe this. We've been married fifteen years. People don't stay married that long if there isn't something there. I don't understand her attitude. I've been a responsible husband and father all along. What am I doing that's wrong?

Arlene:
It's not that you do anything. There just isn't anything there. I can't say anything without his twisting it all around. He's so hard on our daughter. He makes her feel this high.

Bill:
Somebody's got to discipline the girl! You don't! You'd just let her run wild.

Pastor:
You feel she's too permissive with your daughter?

Bill:
Well, wouldn't you want to know where your daughter is at all times—especially with all that's going on in our city streets?

Pastor:
You mean you are justified in feeling the way you do?

Bill:
You're just like my wife. You keep trying to put it back on me. I wish you would tell me what she really expects of me. She won't even tell me what she doesn't like about me.

The pastor proceeded to point out that Arlene appears to be tired of being continually squelched. Significantly, Bill accepts this judgment and asks whether it would help their marriage if he tried to change this. But

Arlene is unconvinced that Bill really wants to change. Moreover, she confesses that she is simply tired of the fighting:

Arlene:
You're more clever with words and arguments than I am, and you know it. So what are we trying to prove, that you are always right? I just can't live with this kind of tension all the time.

Bill:
Of course I am not always right—that's absurd! But I try to be responsible. I don't drink and carouse around.

Arlene:
Yes, you are "Mr. Pure and Right."

Given his aggressive and domineering orientation to life, and his refusal until now to recognize that this is a serious problem, Bill Harris has constructed his life according to a stereotypically masculine self-image. But Bill is now faced with the necessity to develop the more receptive side of his personality, to tone down his masculine aggressiveness, and to begin to listen—really listen—to others' expressions of anguish and hurt. In the beginning moments of the pastoral counseling session, he tried to defend himself on the grounds that, after all, he is a responsible husband and father. But it was precisely this type of defense that reflected his inability to hear what others were saying to him. What Arlene wanted from him was an acceptance of his personal weaknesses (witness her withering comment, "Yes, you are 'Mr. Pure and Right' "), and a new or renewed capacity to open himself up to her on a more authentic emotional level. It is not that he fails to express his emotions, but that the emotions he is able to express (i.e., his domineering attitude) reflect a limited range of emotions, and destructive ones at that.

Bill appears to subscribe to the cultural stereotypes of masculine and feminine traits, seeming to believe that aggression and control are masculine traits while submission is a feminine trait. To the extent that he operates on this perception, he is unwilling or unable to develop the other side of his personality: the capacity for nurturance as opposed to dominance ("He's so hard on our daughter"), the ability to listen to others ("I can't say anything without his twisting it all around"), and the capacity to use restraint in a constructive way (i.e., fewer responses that begin like this: "Of course I'm not always right—that's absurd!"). Bill even seems to believe that change itself is a feminine trait, something to be despised as a sign of weakness. He wants to keep his marriage exactly as it was fifteen years ago (when Arlene was his "girl") and cannot believe that if she loved him at that time, she could not love him now. He says he is now willing to change, but Arlene is justifiably suspicious of his motives for saying this (he does not want to lose control of her), and his expressed willingness to change contains the proviso that he will do so if others (his wife, his pastor) tell him what he needs to change. Arlene's reluctance to do so presumably grows out of previous experience when her suggestions were met by counter-arguments, many of which were undoubtedly irrelevant to the issue at hand ("I don't drink and carouse around"). Significantly, the wife of Frank Larson, the salesman who got into a fight with his sales manager, viewed her husband's capacity to change as a very positive sign. Bill Harris has not yet reached the point where change for him is positive. For him, it remains a feminine trait.

The foregoing all-too-brief analyses of pastoral care and counseling traits prompt an important observation. While we have identified a specific mid-life polarity in each case, other mid-life polarities were certainly operative in each. For example, the primary polarity in the case of Don Benson was, as I have suggested, the attachment/separateness polarity. But the masculine/feminine polarity is also important here as Don confronts the fact that his efforts to control his daughter's life are proving ineffective. The complaints that Bill Harris lodges against him (e.g., he is domineering, he does not take time to listen) could also apply to Don Benson. Similarly, while Frank Larson is the most obvious example of a man struggling with his destructiveness (i.e., physically attacking his supervisor), each of the other men reflect the destructive/creative polarity. Carl Johnson recognizes that he has been self-destructive through his lack of self-direction, while Don Benson and Frank Larson have been very destructive in their relations with other family members. Also, while Carl Johnson is the most obviously concerned with mortality and legacy issues, all four men are having difficulty adjusting to the realization that they are now as old as they are young, and none of the four is finding it possible to grow older gracefully. (The exception may be Frank Larson who, as indicated above, appears willing and able to change.) Thus, from a diagnostic point of view, the mid-life polarities are usually interrelated, and the pastor should therefore avoid a simplisitc diagnostic assessment based on a single mid-life polarity. In most cases, there will be a dominant mid-life polarity and a second polarity that is only a slightly less influential factor in the individual's mid-life transition.

Next, we take up the implications of these case studies for the goals of pastoral counseling with middle adults.

Perceptual Restructuring in Pastoral Counseling

In my last introductory comments, I suggested that the primary goal
of pastoral counseling with middle adults is to foster the restructuring of
their perceptions of themselves, of other persons, and of the world around
them. All four men in the cases we have just reviewed are in the process
of such perceptual restructuring, though some are resisting this more than
others. For an individual approaching middle adulthood, this restructuring of their perceptions of themselves, others and the world is comparable
to the perceptual reorganization that occurs in adolescence, as the perceptual frameworks formed in childhood are replaced with wholly new perceptions of self, others and world. Both are periods of crisis in which a new
orientation to life is being formed. In our role as pastors, we are privileged
to participate in a small but significant way in the restructuring of a person's perceptual set toward his or her life. To illustrate this concept of perceptual restructuring, and to make a case for its relevance to pastoral
counseling of middle adults, I would like to cite a case from Carl R. Rogers'
early essay on perceptual reorganization in client-centered counseling
(1951).[3]

Rogers' Case of Mr. W.

From a psychiatric point of view, Mr. W. was "deeply paranoid," with
an extreme suspiciousness of his wife when he entered therapy. But he
gradually relinquished his original perception of his wife as a wicked,
scheming, adulterous person. Midway through the counseling process, he
began to see her as "a devoted wife who had been driven into sexual mis-
behavior by his own accusations growing out of his own fears regarding his
sexual adequacy." While this was a major shift in his perceptions of his
wife, it reflected only a partial perceptual reorganization. He still believed
she was unfaithful to him. But still later in therapy, "he had a dramatic experience—whether a dream or a type of conversion could scarcely be determined from his description—in which the whole Gestalt of his
perceptions came to be viewed in a new fashion, much as the Gestalt figure
in a textbook is first viewed as an ascending staircase, and now is seen de-
scending." This dramatic experience enabled him to relinquish his perception of her as an unfaithful wife.

The following excerpt from the counseling transcript indicates that
this experience triggered a profound perceptual reorganization:

Mr. W.:
I had a funny experience last night that sort of turned my mind inside out.
(*He goes on to describe the strange quality of this dreamlike experience.*)

This business about my wife and Jim—that sort of blots out somehow. I can't quite straighten it out. I would like to be sure. I thought it all over. I *could* be mistaken. I thought, too, about my wife. I put a lot of different little things together, and I realize that I might be mistaken.

Counselor:
It made you feel that your suspicions might not be correct.

Mr. W.:
That's it. I'm reasonably sure that she was right. The sudden point in this dream, or whatever it was, was this thing about my wife. I see that I'm the one at fault there.

Rogers comments: "Here the perception has completed a full about-face. The perception of his wife as a shameless, deceitful, adulterous person has shifted completely to a perception of her as an individual devoted to him and not involved in any deceitfulness or sexual misconduct." Along with this change in his perception of his wife, Mr. W. experienced a new perception of himself which he had previously tried to avoid. Rogers continues, "Concurrently, the perception of himself as a righteous and aggrieved husband has changed to a picture of himself as having felt sexually inadequate, and as having imagined his wife's unfaithfulness."

Explaining this perceptual reorganization, Rogers stresses the importance of the therapeutic relationship itself in making this possible. Mr. W. was accepted as he was, with all his paranoid tendencies, and through the security this acceptance provided, he was able to risk new perceptions of himself and his wife. In a real sense, his paranoia went unsupported in his immediate therapeutic experience, and this encouraged perceptual changes that more accurately reflected the reality of his situation.

Rogers stresses the fact that such perceptual reorganizations result in greater *personal stability*: "Where the client does face more of the totality of his experience and where he adequately differentiates and symbolizes this experience, then as the new self-structure is organized it becomes firmer, more clearly defined, a steadier, more stable guide to behavior." At the same time, there is less *perceptual rigidity*: "A change in the manner of perceiving also comes about. Because there is less defensiveness, there is less perceptual rigidity. Sensory evidence can be more readily admitted to awareness. It can be interpreted and perceived in a greater variety of ways and with a greater degree of differentiation." Thus, the new self engages the world with greater confidence: "There are fewer experiences perceived as vaguely threatening. There is, consequently, much less anxiety. There is a less insistent need for closure and more tolerance of ambiguity. Thus, there is both a greater tentativeness and a greater assurance in the perceptions of the individual at the end of therapy.

In Mr. W.'s case, greater personal stability and less perceptual rigidity provided the foundation for other positive self-perceptions as the therapeutic process continued. But the important perceptual reversal had already occurred, and Rogers is right to wonder whether Mr. W.'s experience was "a type of conversion." Or, to put it differently, are "conversions" largely a matter of perceptual reorganization?

The perceptual reorganization that Rogers identifies here is an appropriate goal of pastoral counseling for persons of any age. I have argued elsewhere (1981) that the restructuring of perceptions is a major component of pastoral marriage counseling. Since troubled marriages are not the special province of middle adults, it would be foolish to contend that the goal of perceptual restructuring is limited to counseling with middle adults. Yet, I *would* want to claim that, for middle adults, perceptual restructuring is the central goal of counseling with middle adults regardless of what the presenting problems or difficulties may be. This is not necessarily the case with the pastoral counseling of young adults. In fact, it is worth noting that Rogers himself, in his later writings, gave less attention to the goal of perceptual reorganization. This may have been due in part to the fact that, in his counseling with young adults, the goal of perceptual restructuring was less important than the goal of becoming "fully functioning." As Rogers' characteristics of the fully functioning personality reveal, the key to becoming fully functioning is to increase one's capacity to assume direction for one's life. Middle adults are less concerned about how to become more self-directed and much more concerned with how to become a more "whole" person and how to perceive the world more "wholly" (or "fully"). This necessarily entails perceiving oneself and one's world in new and unaccustomed ways.

Three Self-Metaphors

The goal of perceptual restructuring is not peculiar to *pastoral* counseling. Perceptual restructuring is a psychological process that, in and of itself, may have little to do with the *religious life* (here understood as life interpreted by the Judaeo-Christian tradition). However, perceptual restructuring can be religiously informed and, when it is so, the counseling that issues from this religious understanding may be deemed to be genuinely pastoral. The question is how the goal of perceptual restructuring is to be religiously understood. This is a question that invites many different answers. I could not begin to identify them all, much less discuss them in any detail. But one answer that especially commends itself to me is that a religiously grounded view of perceptual restructuring in counseling will have considerable self-consciousness about the ultimate goals or purposes of perceptual restructuring, with such goals or purposes clearly informed by the Judaeo-Christian tradition. It will not specify these goals in moralistic or legalistic terms, but will instead want to set forth a vision of the Judaeo-Christian self. I suggest that this Judaeo-Christian self is a complex of self-metaphors, among which the most central are the *responsible self*, *believable self* and *accessible self.*[4]

I have explored these self-metaphors in some depth elsewhere (Capps, 1984). For our purposes here, a very brief summary of the major identifying features of each metaphor will have to suffice. The *responsible self* is one who is faithful to his or her life's vocation, who is responsive to God's leading ("response-able"), and who manifests this responsiveness by being an agent of reconciliation toward others. The *believable self* is one who seeks congruity between one's personal sense of identity and the social roles he or she adopts, who discerns the hand of God in ordinary human events, and who acts truthfully in relations with others. The *accessible self* is one who is making new self-discoveries, who is profoundly aware of his or her dependence on other selves (including God), and who is concerned to find ways to become more emotionally accessible to other persons.

I view these as *metaphors,* not concepts or even images of the self, because they function as metaphors in the lives of religious persons (i.e., persons whose lives are interpreted by the Judaeo-Christian tradition). A metaphor establishes a likeness between two objects (*"life* is a *bowl of cherries"*) but the metaphor works precisely because the two objects are also *unlike* one another (i.e., there are times when life strikes us as a bowl of cherries but other times when it decidely does not: "Life is the pits."). The responsible, believable and accessible selves function metaphorically in pastoral counseling (as in the religious life generally) because, as we grow in likeness to them, we also become more deeply aware of being unlike them—of being irresponsible, unbelievable and inaccessible. Thus, by introducing here the notion of self-metaphor, we are able to understand perceptual restructuring from a Judaeo-Christian point of view. And, by insisting on a plurality of such metaphors, we do not limit the goal of perceptual restructuring to a narrow vision of the religious life. Indeed, as we saw in Rogers' case of Mr. W., one effect of counseling in which perceptual restructuring occurs is a change in the perceptual process itself toward less rigidity and greater differentiation.

By and large, the men discussed in the previous cases had oriented their lives prior to the mid-life transition toward the metaphor of the responsible self. Bill Harris referred to himself specifically as having been "a responsible husband and father all along." Don Benson and Carl Johnson also suggest, in a more indirect fashion, that they have tried to be responsible in their work and family life. If Carl has squandered his life, it has not been in "riotous living, darn it." And Frank Larson has actually taken steps, through insights gained into his destructive tendencies, to become a more responsible self. On the other hand, each of the four men is now being challenged to become a more believable self, a more accessible self, or both. Melanie Benson wants her father to become more emotionally accessible to her. Arlene Harris appears to want Bill to become more accessible, though she has virtually given up expecting it, and believes his offer to change is essentially unbelievable. But Frank Larson seems genuinely to want to become a more believable self, more authentic in his dealings with work associates and his family. Undergirding this movement toward a more believable self is a new perception of what it means to be a responsible self (i.e., accepting personal responsibility for his destructiveness) and a move toward greater accessibility, especially to himself (i.e., through new insight into the psychodynamic roots of his destructiveness). Carl Johnson is also painfully becoming more accessible to himself, recognizing his feelings of impotence, anger and resentment. Thus, in all four cases, the counselees' claim to be a responsible husband, father or employee has begun to ring hollow—even to themselves. They now recognize that there is more to life than being a responsible self and that, indeed, to be a genuinely responsible self in middle adulthood entails growth toward becoming a more believable and accessible self as well.

Moreover, their original claim to being responsible selves was generally voiced in a self-righteous, self-justifying manner. The rather unconvincing nature of their claim to being responsible selves seems to suggest that these men were basically narcissistic personalities who tended "to cultivate a protective shallowness in emotional relations" (Lasch, 1979: 81). Their claim to being responsible selves was actually a kind of pseudo-insight into their own personalities. Unlike our description of the responsible self, these men were unable to "respond" to others. They were essentially "unresponsive." As various interpreters of narcissistic personality of our times point out, the narcissist wants to be able to manipulate personal relationships, to control them and make them serve his own ends. Due to narcissistic injury suffered earlier in life (e.g., the riducule Frank Larson suffered at the hands of a high school teacher), the narcissistic personality has great difficulty "responding" to others in anything other than a defensive, self-protective manner.

The self-metaphors that I have proposed are able to address the claim that the narcissist is the dominant personality type of our times. I propose these self-metaphors, however, not to indict the narcissistic personality but to provide for a *perceptual restructuring* of the narcissistic personality itself. Each of these metaphors addresses a prominent characteristic of the narcissistic personality. As we have seen, the responsible self addresses the narcissist's inability to respond to the legitimate claims of others because he is preoccupied with his own self-image. In like fashion, the believable self addresses the narcissist's tendency to manipulate the impressions he makes on others (inauthenticity), and the accessible self addresses the narcissist's sense of inner emptiness or void, the shallow emotional life of the narcissist in which he is neither dependent on others or open to being depended upon. The goal of pastoral care and counseling with these men would be to enable them to become more truly responsible, believable and accessible selves.

But how is this possible? As Heinz Kohut points out (1978), it does little good for the counselor to try to "heal" the narcissist by replacing self-love with object-love, for the narcissist lacks the capacity to make such a transfer. Moral exhortation is not the answer. What is required is a fundamental reorientation of the personality through the kind of perceptual restructuring we saw in Rogers' case of Mr. W. From the religious perspective represented here (i.e., the Judaeo-Christian tradition), this can only be realized by replacing oneself as the center of one's existence with God, who is the Eternal Self (Erikson, 1968: 220-21). This is the necessary perceptual restructuring that needs to occur before a transfer from self-love to object love can become a realistic goal. As indicated in my brief comments on the identifying features of the three self-metaphors, growth in human relatedness in each case is mediated through growth relatedness to God. The perceptual restructuring that is involved here is a perception of oneself as *symbolic* of the Eternal Self, formed in the image of God. This means that the ultimate ground of the three self-metaphors is God, who is the utimately Responsible, Believable and Accessible Self.[5] It is not that one understands these self-metaphors as human projections onto God (the projection theory is itself inherently narcissistic), for then the human self remains the center of existence, and the narcissistic personality is at best reformed but not fundamentally changed in its orientation to life. Rather, these three metaphors are understood as integral to the divine Self, and thus an individual's growth in likeness to these metaphors is growth in likeness to God.

This suggests that, in response to Rogers' question regarding Mr. W.'s perceptual restructuring—was it a dream or a type of conversion?—we may say that it was indeed a *type* of conversion. However, we might refine this use of religious language for interpreting perceptual restructurings in pastoral care and counseling by differentiating *illumination* (often rendered "insight" in pastoral counseling literature), *transformation*, and *conversion*. I would suggest that counselees who experience growth in terms of their already central self-metaphor (whether responsible, believable or accessible) find pastoral counseling an *illuminating experience*. For counselees who experience a significant shift from one central metaphor to another (e.g., from a predominantly responsible to predominately accessible self), pastoral counseling is a *transforming experience*. For counselees who experience a radical change from being irresponsible to responsible, unbelievable to believable, or inaccessible to accessible, pastoral counseling is itself a *conversion experience*. Thus, insofar as pastoral counseling involves the restructuring of perceptions toward these self-metaphors, such pastoral counseling is a form of religious experience.

To the other half of Rogers' question—was Mr. W.'s experience a dream?—here again religious language enables us to make an important distinction between *dreams* and *visions*. In my judgment, the Dream of young adulthood is essentially narcissistic. As we saw in our earlier discussion, the Dream gives legitimacy to a young man's pursuit of his personal destiny, providing cultural and even moral approval for his perception that the dreams of the significant others in his life must be conformed to his Dream or relinquished. Biblical precedent for this construal of the Dream is provided by Joseph (Gen 37-48) whose career is noteworthy precisely because the primary narcissism of his young adulthood was later transformed through his growth into a genuinely responsible as well as believable and accessible self.

As we have seen, the transition to middle adulthood is a period of *de-illusionment* when the illusory and magical features of the Dream are subjected to reappraisal. The process here is a perceptual restructuring in which the Dream of young adulthood is replaced by the Vision of middle adulthood. This Vision is not based on the desire for self-direction but by aspirations for personal growth in ways our three self-metaphors attempt to articulate. We envision here significant growth in all three dimensions of the religious life, and thus a movement toward self-integration through increased differentiation. A biblical illustration of this person of Vision is Paul, whose letters give strong testimony to the rich complexity and yet essential unity of the responsible-believable-accessible self.

Conclusion

Pastoral counseling is just one among many resources provided by our religious tradition to enable us to become more responsible, believable and accessible selves. It takes its place alongside worship, sacraments, preaching, Bible reading, prayer and service as resources available to us to grow into likeness to the eternal Self. But pastoral counseling is an especially valuable resource for those, like Carl Johnson, who have begun to question whether God is indeed responsible, believable or accessible to them. As Levinson puts it, there are many men who feel they were cheated or "done in" by the tribe during early adulthood, and who are now in middle adulthood going through a stormy period when, like Job, they rage against the tribal God (242). For such persons, men or women, pastoral counseling can be the occasion in which they have experience of God as responsible, believable, or accessible to them. With this experience they may also perceive that they are free to grow into likeness to God. Then, out of the dissolution of the Dream of early adulthood will emerge a new Vision appropriate to middle adulthood. If the Dream of early adulthood is grounded in the desire for self-direction, the Vision of middle adulthood is the freedom to grow into likeness to God. If the legitimate goal of pastoral counseling of early adults is to help them gain a clearer perception of themselves, the equally legitimate goal of pastoral counseling of middle adults is to free them to mirror the life of God.

Notes

[1] These include (1) moving away from facades, "oughts," meeting expectations, and pleasing others; and (2) moving toward self-direction, being process and complexity, openness to experience, acceptance of others, and trust of self (Rogers, 1961).

[2] Cases 1, 2 and 4 are adapted from Colston (1969). Case 3 is adapted from Cryer and Vayhinger (1962).

[3] I discussed this case in Capps (1981).

[4] I develop the biblical foundations for these three self-metaphors in Capps (1984).

[5] While this conclusion is based on biblical portrayals of God, the Christian trinitarian formulation may also provide support for it.

Bibliography

Bakan, D. *The Duality of Human Existence.* Chicago: Rand McNally, 1966.

Capps, D. *Biblical Approaches to Pastoral Counseling.* Philadelphia: The Westminster Press, 1981.

Capps, D. *Pastoral Counseling and Preaching.* Philadelphia: The Westminster Press, 1980.

Capps, D. *Pastoral Care and Hermeneutics*. Philadelphia: Fortress Press, 1984.

Clinebell, H. *Basic Types of Pastoral Care and Counseling*, rev. ed. Nashville: Abingdon Press, 1984.

Colston, L. *Judgment in Pastoral Counseling*. Nashville: Abingdon Press, 1969.

Cryer, N.S. and J.M. Vayhinger (eds.). *Casebook in Pastoral Counseling*. Nashville: Abingdon Press, 1962.

Erikson, E. *Identity: Youth and Crisis*. New York: W.W. Norton, 1968.

Erikson, E. *Toys and Reasons*. New York: W.W. Norton, 1968.

Kohut, H. "Forms and Transformations of Narcissism." In P.H. Ornstein (ed.), *The Search for the Self: Selected Writings of Heinz Kohut, 1950–1978*, Vol. 1. New York: International Universities Press, 1978.

Lasch, C. *The Culture of Narcissism*. New York: Warner Books, 1979.

Levinson, D. *et al. The Seasons of a Man's Life*. New York: Alfred A. Knopf, 1978.

Pruyser, P. *The Minister as Diagnostician*. Philadelphia: The Westminster Press, 1976.

Rogers, C. *On Becoming a Person*. Boston: Houghton Mifflin, 1961.

Rogers, C. "Perceptual Reorganization in Client-Centered Therapy." In R.R. Blake and G.V. Ramsey (eds.), *Perception: An Approach to Personality*. New York: Ronald Press, 1951.

James N. Lapsley

Pastoral Care and Counseling of the Aging

Diversity is the most accurate word by which to characterize persons over 65 or 70 years of age in this longest of all life's "stages." If it is, indeed, a stage, it is not only the last but may be as long as 30 years or more, which is one of the reasons for diversity within it. Another factor is the sheer numbers of persons over 65. We are increasingly aware of this now, and some projections put this group at 25% of the total population of the United States by the year 2025 (Butler, 1977). The fact that all these persons have done more living than others, allowing more time for differences to develop, also contributes to their diversity, as does the diversity of settings within which the pastoral care giver finds them—their own homes, those of their families, rest homes, nursing homes, hospitals, and rehabilitation centers.

These opening comments about diversity seem necessary because of the still powerful stereotypes about the aging prevalent in our society, even though many readers know that these have been challenged. We have tended to view the aging as physically ill, mentally dull or worse, emotionally flat and withdrawn from other persons. Some aging persons do more or less fit these dismal descriptions, but others, probably a considerable majority, do not. Recently completed research has exploded the myth of the inevitable decline of mental powers of the aging. Some intelligence factors—those called "crystallized intelligence" by the researchers, may actually increase into the ninth decade of life. These factors include the ability to make judgments on the basis of accumulated information, range of "world knowledge, and fluency and richness of communication." "Fluid intelligence," or the abilities related to perceive the relationships among abstractions, as in mathematics and physics, or in chess, does seem to decline with aging. To be sure, the continued development of "crystallized intelligence" among the elderly is thought to depend upon education and a developed intellectual life before 65, as well as flexibility of personality (New York Times, 1984). Nevertheless, human mental capability in advanced years is now well established, as is artistic capability, as a retrospective exhibit of Picasso's paintings during the last ten years before his death at age 91 well attested in 1984.

It is worth noting that diversity among the aging accounts in part for our perplexity about what to call these people. (Our difficulties with a name for those in this age group is also due in part to the pejorative stereotyping which tends to contaminate all names.) Some persons over 65 find "Golden Age Club" attractive or at least not offensive, but for others this name is an ill fitting euphemism. "Senior citizen" has a ring of privilege and dignity for many, but connotes being over the hill for others, and some organizations have dropped the word "senior" in favor of "adult." "Gray Panthers" represents an attack on the injustices of the treatment of older persons in our society as those involved in that organization view it, but some others feel that it suggests more predatory aggression than they can be comfortable with. The term "aging" which has been adopted in this chapter also has its problems—all persons are aging, not only those over 65. But it is the term in most general use, and does suggest a central fact in the lives of those in this age group without denoting that the aging process has come to an end, as does "aged." By whatever name we call them it is important for us to remember that some members of this large group of human beings, only about 5% of whom live in nursing homes or similar institutions, will not feel included under our verbal umbrella.

In a book devoted to pastoral counseling it seems necessary to try to clarify a bit how that term is understood in this chapter. Pastoral care is the larger term for the church's reaching out toward the personal and spiritual needs of persons through its representatives, and pastoral counseling a somewhat narrower term denoting a process of helping based on an understanding or "contract" involving both parties about what is being attempted in ongoing conversations. Pastoral counseling is, thus, but one form of pastoral care, and most pastoral work with the aging is of the more general kind, including seemingly rather casual conversations, rather than contractual pastoral counseling, although that, too, has its place. We shall be discussing both pastoral care and pastoral counseling in this chapter.

I. Some "Basics" of Pastoral Care with the Aging

Here I shall present some "basics" of the pastoral care of the aging. These are neither all basic principles of what to do, nor are they merely some basic ideas about the aging to keep in mind. Some are more nearly one of these and some more nearly the other, but as a whole they are, perhaps, best thought of as areas of special awareness of some characteristics of aging that are particularly relevant to pastoral care. In order to provide a concrete vehicle for this discussion, and some illustration of the concerns within it, the following report of a seminarian in conversation with a nursing home resident is presented in part:

Helen is 78 years old and lives in a nursing home near the church where I do my field work and where I visit occasionally as a part of my work.

She has been at the home a little over a year, and seems quite happy with it. Her husband died some fifteen years ago, and she has lived alone and with various children. She has had several heart attacks, including one three weeks ago. She is of Slovak descent, the child of immigrants, and her husband was Italian. She is Roman Catholic. She has four living children (see H5), all of whom visit her from time to time. She lives on Social Security and Medicaid.

Helen was dressed quite attractively, and obviously takes care of her appearance. She had been told by a supervisor that I was a seminary student learning to be a minister. She seemed to approach the interview as something of a social occasion. She had good posture, perfect hearing, clear eyes, and quick responses. I do not always enjoy being with old people, but she was pleasant to be with.

The supervisor brought Helen into the lobby of the nursing home and introduced us.

Helen 1: It's good to meet you.
Student 1: Yes, it's good to meet you. Could we sit down right over here? I hope you don't mind my taking you away from bingo?
  H2: Oh no!(*laughs*) I'm sick of that, anyway. I play all the time. Bingo is nothing compared to a conversation. (*We sit down.*) So you're studying to be a minister?
  S2: Yes, I'm a student at Princeton Seminary, and I work at the Baptist church down the road.
  H3: I'm Catholic, actually, but I accept all religions. I go to the Protestant services, the Catholic services, sometimes even the Jewish services. They've all become so much alike recently, I don't see much difference. We all worship the same God—don't you think so?
  S3: Yes, I do. Is there a priest who comes to see you regularly?

H4: Well, there is a priest who does services but I don't see him much. If you want to know the truth, I don't think he does as much as he should. He doesn't visit much.

S4: Do you have any family in this area?

H5: (*This question apparently pushed a button and she launched into a description of her family: "Dr. T—," the college dean, her oldest daughter; Angela, the mother of three teenagers with whom Helen lived for over a year before coming to the nursing home; Sister Catherine, a nun who lives in a nearby convent; and a son, a businessman who at one time was studying to be a Jesuit priest.*) My husband died fifteen years ago. We were just sitting watching TV and he got up to go to bed and when I came in he was gone. He was a good man, but he didn't leave me anything. We started from nothing and we never owned a house or a car or anything. Can you imagine living all those years and never having a house?

S5: It must have been a terrible loss for you.

H6: Of course it was. It broke my heart and even now I wish he was here. I think when my back is sore, if he were here he could give me a back rub. But I always thought he died for a reason. You know I lost two of my children. That was harder.

S6: I didn't know that. I'm sorry to hear it.

H7: (*She mentioned the death of a son several years ago, but I cannot recall any of the details.*) And two years ago I lost a daughter, of cancer. That was hard, but she had such a good spirit. I never worried because she was such a good girl. It was for a reason. Sometimes I think it was because of her husband. He is a good man and comes to visit me, but so much trouble for her, drinking and having problems—I think maybe God wanted to spare her from any more of that trouble.

S7: It must have been rough on you to lose your daughter.

H8: Yes it was, but I always thought it was for a reason. I used to live with her, but then I had to move in with my daughter Angela. I was there for a year, but I was too much of a burden. An old lady just can't live in a home with three teenagers. And I would hear her on the telephone, when neighbors would invite her out—she would say, "I'd love to go, but I can't because I have to stay with mother." That wasn't fair to her. And it was too much for her to raise those kids—and she doesn't raise them right; you wouldn't believe the things they do nowadays. I never interfered, I just kept quiet, but I don't know what happened. We raised our children strict. —Anyway, she couldn't raise those kids and take care of an old lady. I was ready to leave.

S8: So you wanted to move here?

H9: Yes, it just didn't work out at Angela's. Here there are always nurses in case something happens, like a heart attack. I've had six of them, you know. I asked the doctor if I was a cat with nine lives. I had a couple of attacks at Angela's and it was a lot of trouble for them. I just got over one three weeks ago.

S9: That must have been scary for you.

H10: At the moment it was, but I'm not afraid to die. I believe that when I die it will be for a reason. I'm 78. I've had a full life. I believe God must want me here for a reason. I try to help people around here and love them. There are so many sad people who can't get around or talk or nobody visits them. They appreciate it so much when somebody loves them. I'm a very touching person. I hold their hands or hug them and they just smile. Or some people don't speak English and I translate into Slovak or Polish. One of the nurses said they should give me a white coat, I do so much work around here.

S10: (*joking*) Do you want them to put you on the staff?

H11: (*seriously*) Oh, no! I don't want any money or anything. I don't ask for anything, I just want to love people. (*Here she describes various crafts projects she had made for party favors and decorations, and how much they were appreciated.*)

S11: Well, it sounds to me like you're really useful around here, probably more useful than you were back at your daughter's.

H12: Heavens, yes, I wasn't any use at all back there. They wouldn't let me do anything.

S12: But you feel as though here you have a reason for living.

H13: Yes. I'm happy here. I don't complain. Some people complain, but to tell you the truth, they're just big babies. They expect too much. I don't cause anybody any trouble and I'm always cheerful. (*Here she folds her arms and sits back.*) Well, that's enough about me. I talk too much about myself. I know you have some things you want to talk to me about. Just what did you want to ask me?

1. There are several motifs occuring in this segment which are of importance. The first one that I shall note is that the seminarian is at some points, notably at S 5, S 7, S 9, and S 12, trying to convey to Helen that *he understands something of how she felt in the past about her losses or how she is now feeling in the present about her current situation* (s12). This attempt to convey empathy or understanding, of course, is not unique as a principle of the pastoral care of the aging, but is a cardinal general principle of all pastoral care, and is so recognized by virtually all in the field. Although few would now hold, as once was held by many, that it is a suf-

ficient principle, most still hold it to be a necessary one. In current par-
lance this attempt to convey understanding is often termed "listening," or
"reflective listening." Without denying the importance of listening in this
complex interpersonal process, it is an inadequate term to convey the central thing involved—a certain kind of responding based upon listening, observing, and sometimes also on tactile and olfactory sensing of the other
person. The term "empathic understanding" is probably the best we can
do, in spite of the difficulties involved in defining precisely what is meant
by empathy—a "feeling into" the life of the other and conveying that, without necessarily experiencing the same complex of affect and cognition
which the other does experience. Feeling the same, or nearly the same,
sort of emotion as the other, we call sympathy, a feeling *with* the other.

Our point here is that the aging need empathic understanding as
much as others, perhaps more, for often their emotional life is not as
sharply defined as once it was, and empathy helps to awaken it. In the
case, Helen is in basic touch with her emotions, and so this latter function
of awakening is not prominent. Only at S 12 does the student focus directly
on her feeling in the present, which we may call her sense of self worth,
even though that is not mentioned as such in the case. In the other instances noted he is responding to what she must have felt in the past—her
grief at the various losses of family members, and her fear for loss of her
own life through heart failure (S 9). Responses to feelings from the past do
not have the same character as those to present emotions and thoughts,
but they do have the effect of enabling the person to continue to recount
events in the past, some of which may have been, or may still be, painful,
since she knows that she is being heard, and to some extent understood.
As Helen's response in H 13 shows, attempts at understanding, even if
they are not completely correct or as accurate as they might be, have the
effect of enabling a person to say more about what is on her mind—in this
case to contrast her own attitude with that of some others in the nursing
home. As a person feels better and better understood, and hence affirmed
as a person, the more she will be able to clarify her own thoughts and feelings in many instances. Not all responses need be of this kind, but many
should be, especially in the initial phases of a conversation.

2. A second "basic" of pastoral care with the aging is the importance
of memories. This importance is clearly well represented in the segment
of "Helen." Her memories are about her family. Some of them still have
painful associations—the losses of her husband and two of her six children,
even though she now seems to have "accepted" the losses. But other memories are more positive, of her son the college dean, of her daughter the
nun, of her son the businessman, and, perhaps more ambivalently, of her
oldest daughter, Angela, with whom she lived before coming to the nurs-

ing home, all of whom come to visit her. The seminarian is responsive to the pain-laden memories, so we have more detail about them, but the positive memories of the four living children and their reinforcement of these through visits are very important for Helen's sense of identity and self worth. In a production oriented society they may be partly the "products" she has offered to the culture, but this is only speculation, as we do not know her inmost motives. Clearly they are important as persons to whom she has given love, and from whom she now receives.

Memories do not have just one function for the aging but several. Some do seem to live only in the past through them, as the stereotype suggests. But many, like Helen, use memories to try to live in the present. Memories remind the person of who she has been, both in mourning and celebration, and thus of her present identity as a person with these participatory links through the past to the present world. Pastoral care and counseling with the aging depends in large measure on how sensitively the care-giver responds to memories. As already noted, the care-giver in this case was rather one-sided in his response to memories, focusing more on the negative ones than on the positive ones. If he had been more responsive to Helen's feelings of pride and love for her family the interview would have gone somewhat differently and perhaps better for Helen, even though our impressions about her might have been changed a little.

Reminiscence sometimes takes the form of repeated stories in which events which have happened long ago are recounted, often with very little, if any, change in the content. These stories, which seem to the listener to have an almost audio tape-like character, as if they are segments of linked experiences which have been somehow separated from other memory tracks, are not recounted by all the aging, but they appear frequently enough to constitute something of a special question for the care-giver. How shall he or she respond to them? I think that the answer to this question depends on a number of factors, and I shall discuss these in the next section, "Special Issues," even though I do not by any means have all the answers. Here I simply underline the general principle of paying close attention to memories and responding to them.

3. A third "basic" of pastoral care of aging visible to some extent in the segment of "Helen" that we have been examining is a responsibility to be clear about who the care-giver is and how he or she perceives the purpose and process of the conversation. This need for self-definition and structure is, to be sure, not restricted to the pastoral care of the aging, but it is of particular importance with the elderly. They do not always see and hear well, and even if they do, strangers may initially seem to them to be persons whom they may have known and not seen for a while. Sometimes this is quite conscious, in other instances it may be beneath the surface of

consciousness but nevertheless playing a role in their responses to the care-giver. The seminarian did clearly identify himself at S 2, but he did not offer a structuring response in this segment, which in fact ends with a request from Helen that he do so. We shall see how he tried to structure the conversation in the next segment. It would have been clearer for Helen if he had done so earlier. Sometimes it is necessary to repeat and amplify one's self-identification, including offering some personal response to the care-receiver's communication. In this way the care-giver comes alive as a real person for the aging, an important factor in their pastoral care. They need to know "who" is present with them, if they are to know that the person cares.

S13: (*I am a little thrown off balance by this shift, since I don't know what the supervisor has told her about my interests.*) Well—I'll just be straightforward with you. I'm taking a course in seminary on how to minister to people who have had deaths in their family. I was wondering if we could talk about your feelings, and your experiences of death.

H14: (*leans forward, quite animated*) I'll tell you what I think. You should always say, "It's for a reason." That's the important thing. If you know that God has taken the person for a reason, then you can take anything. When my daughter died it was hard but I said "It's for a reason." That's what a minister should say to people. That's what they need to hear. Don't you think that's right?

S14: Yes, I believe that God is in control, ultimately, but I also think it's important for people to be able to express and accept their feelings of pain and loss.

H15: God knows, I've felt pain. I've had my share of troubles. My heart has been broken over and over. But even so I believe that God doesn't take someone without a reason. I don't have any reason to be afraid, because my conscience is clear. That's another thing you should tell people, to pray. If they have any sins they should confess them—I don't mean to a priest or to anyone else, just to God. Sometimes at night I go into the therapy room, which is empty, and just tell God that I spoke harshly with someone or had some mean thoughts and then I feel better. If people are afraid to die, it's because they are afraid of God because they have done something they are guilty about, even if it was a long time ago. They should just pray.

S15: You mean they are afraid that God will punish them?

H16: Yes, because they haven't asked God to forgive them.

S16: You don't think that some people are just afraid of the process of dying, afraid of the pain and the unknown?

H17: No, I don't think so. I don't know anyone in this place who is afraid of dying itself. We're ready to die. It's only the bad people who are afraid of what comes after. Look at me: I'm 78. I may live another year or two; I may go tomorrow. I have more family and friends who are dead than are alive. I'm ready to go be with them up there. At least I think they're up there. My husband was a good man, he never ran around or anything; my children were all good children. It will be good to be with them. Don't you think so?

S17: Yes. I think it will be different from life before, but I believe we will be together.

H18: Well, what else would you like to know?

S18: Uh—you seem to have accepted the deaths of your family members very well. But did you feel that way at the time?

H19: It broke my heart but I still accepted it. After all, it's just part of life. We all have to go sometime, right?

S19: Sure. There's not much we can do about it. Let me ask you this: When your husband died, how long did it take you to get over it?

H20: Oh, years. Years. It took me two years to come out of the daze. I still miss him. But I think it was for a reason and God knows the reason. Maybe if he had lived it would have been worse.

S20: So you really believe God is in control of the whole situation?

H21: Oh, yes. And he only does what is good for us. He is all love and he knows what is best. He is so forgiving because his heart is so much bigger than ours. He knows everything and still he loves us and takes us for a reason. And he has let me live for a reason, so that I can do good around here.

S21: Well, from what you've told me it sounds as though you're doing a lot of good.

H22: (*Here she went into another catalogue of her good deeds and told how well liked she is. Several staff persons passed by and exchanged greetings. Our conversation rambled on for a while and I looked at the clock on the wall.*)

S22: We've been talking for quite a long time.

H23: Yes, I suppose it's long enough. Did I tell you what you wanted to know? Do I get an "A"?

S23: Oh, yes, you get an A + ! I didn't have anything particular in mind. I just wanted to talk about your feelings.

H24: I've certainly talked enough. Will you tell the supervisor that I was good or will you tell her that I was a little boring?

S24: Don't worry. I'll tell her that you were very helpful. I'm not here to evaluate you. I just wanted to talk.

H25: Listen. (*She reaches over and takes my hand.*) You're going to be a very good minister. I'm sure you won't have any trouble with dying people. Just tell them to pray and it's for a reason. You are the right kind of person for a minister and you won't have any trouble. (*She lets go of my hand.*) You see, here I go getting lovey again. I'm a very loving person.

S25: Yes, I can see that. I don't mind at all. (*I take her hand.*)

H26: Come on, I'll take you to see Mrs. Rail (*the supervisor*).

4. A fourth "basic" in the pastoral care of the aging is the question of the future and the care-receiver's response to it. In making this point I am not asserting that the past and the present may not also be problems, but they are not necessarily so. For the aging the future is, of course, a special issue because beyond the near term it may not be there, and before too long it will not. This fact virtually removes one of the most widespread psychological devices by means of which adult human beings cope—that of delaying gratification beyond the present, or at least hoping or wishing that things will get better. It makes many kinds of planning problematical at best, even though some persons, including those who are thought to be dying, continue to do it as a means of coping. This problematic is not, of course, nearly as large a factor in the lives of many in their sixties and seventies, but in time it becomes a factor for all.

Helen's approach to the problematic of the future is twofold. On the one hand she has a clearly developed personal eschatology of life beyond the grave evident at H 15 and H 17, and we shall examine this more closely in discussing the next "basic"—that of spiritual needs. On the other hand she has perhaps even more significantly learned to make the present serve also as a future. She gets a great deal of gratification from her role as helper in the nursing home as is clear from H 10 and H 22. Apparently the supervisor and other nurses value her contributions: "One of the nurses said they should give me a white coat, I do so much work around here." This emphasis on the present is undergirded by her strong sense of God's purpose for her life: "I believe God must want me here for a reason." To be sure, it seems that Helen has probably always lived by giving love, and also that she hoped for a return in the present. But now the present has to carry also the load of meaning she might formerly have invested in the future. Now the future is envisaged as a reunion in heaven with her family—a future toward which she does not have to strive.

Yet the future is still "there" for Helen. For some others who have accepted the limitations of their lives its absence may be accepted. Rosalie

Otters-Hollander, commenting on "Mrs. Smith," 87 years old, whom she has interviewed for a thesis on aging and the local church, wrote:

> Mrs. Smith lives in the present and feels that she does not have much of a future because of her age. She does not think about dying because "I don't think I am the age I am. I just don't think about age. I know I'm getting older but I just keep going." Mrs. Smith, though, also feels that ". . . he's (God) left me here for a certain purpose, that I'm hanging around here for some reason (laughs)."[1]

Not all of the aging have come to terms with the problem of the future as well as Helen and Mrs. Smith apparently have done. Pat Kalish, postulating that attitudes toward life and death are related, found in a study of 214 men and 354 women in small towns that 33% feared death but little and valued their lives both past and present (we might place Helen and Mrs. Smith in this group), 26% felt that their lives were a failure and feared death, 22% feared death as a threat to unfulfilled ambition, and 19% tended to accept death as a welcomed end to a disappointing life (Keith, 1981). This study shows us something of the diversity on this important dimension of the lives of the elderly, even though other ways of approaching the question might well yield somewhat different results.

The pastoral care-giver needs to be alert for signals that provide clues to the shape of concern about the future and how the person is responding to that concern. Although the aging cannot simply be exhorted to accept the limitations of future that their time of life imposes any more than they can be exhorted to accept most other troublesome aspects of their lives, the sensitive care-giver can often assist persons in their struggle to a better vision of the future and the present. Not all are struggling, however, as Kalish's study indicates. Some have resigned to death rather than accept its meaning and have given up the struggle (the last 19% of the study), and no pastoral purpose is served by trying to insist that they struggle. Pastoral care for them is supportive in character.

5. *Spiritual Needs and Religious Resources.* In referring to spiritual needs as a fifth "basic" of the pastoral care of the aging, I am admittedly muddying the waters, for in a quite fundamental sense we have been discussing spiritual needs all along. Broadly understood, spirit touches and permeates all of human life. It is not a special segment of the person that is immaterial or necessarily more permanent. Spirit at its root means "life or breath," and it has been shown to defy precise definition. For our purposes it may be taken to mean the intensity and direction of human life in three vectors (denoting magnitude and direction of energy flow) toward

other persons, toward self, and toward a vocation or purpose in living. Sometimes religion, as we in the Western world understand that term, is important to the aging person in one or more of these vectors, and sometimes not, although most older persons regard themselves as being religious in some sense (Hammond, 1981). Trying to determine precisely in what sense or senses the aging are religious has proved to be a difficult task for sociologists of religion and final answers have eluded them. Two broad trends are discernible, however. As persons move into their seventies church attendance decreases (here a number of "external" factors such as health and transportation problems probably play large roles), and personal religion as exemplified by private prayer and the reading of the Bible and other religious works increases. Phillip E. Hammond has rightly cautioned us that these findings do not tell us whether an increase in personal religion is characteristic of aging as such or simply of this generation of the elderly (Hammond, 1981). Nevertheless, in general terms the aging today are far more interested in religion as a personal resource than are other age groups.

Helen is obviously a good example of this general finding. She gives every evidence of sincerely believing that God has brought about her severe losses for a reason, that he has a purpose for her now, and that her death will come when he providentially ordains it (H 10, H 14, H 17). Only the guilty are afraid to die in her view (H 15). The seminarian is somewhat taken aback by this outpouring of seemingly unassailable faith and he questions her about it closely at S 15, S 16 and S 20. To his credit he sees that, whatever he may think of her theology, it is of great importance to her, and he ceased his implied challenges to it.

Many care-givers to the aging (as well as to others) have found themselves in similar situations in the sense that the theology held by the aging person, and sometimes attitudes of prejudice and even hostility which seem closely related to it, clash with their own views or perhaps unarticulated assumptions. There is general agreement that the integrity of the care-giver does not demand that his or her views simply be imposed upon the aging care-receiver. Indeed, in most instances they cannot be. Persuasion also has severe limitations since it may impinge directly on the integrity of the care-receiver, thus doing more harm than good even if successful.

Sometimes people ask the care-giver direct theological questions which are difficult to answer. "Why doesn't God heal me?" and "Why have I lived so long when all my family and friends are gone?" are questions in varying forms often heard from the aging. It is important for the care-giver to have thought through such questions, but *not* in order to supply the *correct* answer in most situations. Such an answer does not really do justice to the concerns of the questioner, which flow from unique concerns and attitudes, as well as those common to all humanity. Rather, the care-giver, without withholding relevant information about the question, does better to try to help the person refocus the question through understanding and linking the question to personal concerns, thus providing assistance in working out a view that has integrity for the person. The cry of anguish in such questions as those mentioned is evident, and response must be made to the cry, though without ignoring the theological language in which the question is framed.

Returning now to the case of Helen, we need to note that not all of her spiritual concerns are focused on the future or the past. Her sense of dignity, or self-worth, is greatly enhanced by her feeling that she is contributing in the present to the life of those in the nursing home. This need to give as well as receive is not labeled "spiritual" in the case, but it is no less so for not being thus named. She has indicated that she is there for a purpose, so her giving has theological roots. Even if this were not so, it would still be in the service of spirit, for without a sense of dignity she could not be a full participant in the future, either. We may wonder whether there may be some overcompensation in her concern that the supervisor get a good report on her conversation, and that she get an "A" from the seminarian (H 23), and we may wonder if her theology is too pat. From some theoretical viewpoints she is still struggling and has not reached an ideal plateau of complete acceptance. But relative to that of many others, her struggle is a very successful one.

6. *"Reritualization" and Other Contextual Factors.* Here we note that the pastoral care and counseling of the aging does not take place in a vacuum, a point so obvious that it could be saved to last in this sequence, but which must not be overlooked. There are many of these of importance, such as money and housing, which may affect pastoral care, but which may be little affected by it. There are at least two areas in which pastoral care may affect these factors. One of these is what Erik Erikson has termed "reritualization." In its most basic sense the term "ritualization" for Erikson means ". . . a certain kind of informal and yet prescribed interplay between persons who repeat it at meaningful intervals and in recurring contexts" (1982, p. 43). Reritualization, then, refers to the new patterns of relationships which the aging need to establish both with their peers in age and with those in later generations. Erikson regards these as being of far more than "social" significance, since they are needed to provide some central meaning for the life of the aging: ". . . a more meaningful interplay between beginning and end as well as some finite sense of summary and, possibly, a more active anticipation of dying" (1982, p. 43). Pastoral care-givers can help to awaken motivation for participation in such patterns of

relationships and help the aging to make the necessary connections. Many church-related programs provide these opportunities, ranging from bus trips for the elderly to discussions with junior high students, who seem to relate well with the aging.

A second area in which pastoral care-givers can often help, though not always, is the relationship that the aging have with their children and other family members. Contrary to our stereotype, families do not, as a whole, neglect their aging parents and often go to great and sometimes inappropriate lengths in their efforts to care for them (Shanas, 1981). Complications in these relationships do, however, often arise due to communication difficulties and the long history of the relationships involved. Sometimes the care-giver can become a direct link between generations, and in some cases referral for family counseling may be appropriate. More often the care-giver can help by facilitating understanding by the aging of the efforts made by families, and by helping the aging to communicate to their families their own needs and wishes as clearly as possible. Admittedly, care-givers do not always have confidence in the families and their motives, but in many cases some reconciliation can be effected.

II
Special Issues

Now some special issues in the pastoral care and counseling of the aging which involve only some of this diverse population will be discussed. Those selected are thought to arise rather frequently in pastoral work with the elderly, and to be of considerable importance, though they are not the only ones.

1. *Illness*. The crisis of illness is, of course, not restricted to the elderly, but they are, as a group, more likely to suffer from illness than are others. Pastoral work with hospitalized persons is the focus of a later chapter of this volume, and I shall not discuss it as such. But hospitalization does often affect the aging more intensely than it does other groups, especially those who are living in their own homes or with their families. They are removed from their familiar environment and those with whom they are accustomed to relate. The prospect of permanent disability or of death frequently looms. Loneliness is intensified or becomes a fear in the hospital. The aging often worry a great deal about the cost of hospitalization—in many instances with good reason. Some of these are visible in the following sequence between a chaplain and an 80-year-old woman, even though they are not all being felt acutely:

Mrs. S. is a woman of eighty years. She was alone in a two-bed room. She was dressed in a hospital gown and there was paraphernalia extending from under her right hip and leg. She spoke softly and with a slight accent. During the entire interview she played with a cross around her neck.

C: Hello, Mrs. S., I'm Jean Jones, a chaplain.

P: Hello.

C: I can see you have just come into the hospital.

P: Yes. My leg is bad. The doctor had to scrape away the brown skin. Then he put salt water on it. Oh, that hurt. But he said that would dry up the spot. They will have to operate and replace the skin.

C: It sounds as though you're really having a bad time with that leg.

P: Yes. My daughter is very nervous. She brought me here today. She was worried. She has just come to live with me. (*My son lives on the other side.*) She thought I ought to be in the hospital.

C: She was very concerned about you.

P: Yes. This is the best place to be. I've been here before.

C: This is not new to you then.

P: No. I've been in the hospital several times, for high blood pressure, sugar, and four weeks for a heart attack.

C: You have had more than your share of problems.

P: Yes, well I'm old. I'm eighty years old. I guess you have problems then.

C: It seems likely that you have more problems as you grow older. Eighty years is a long time to live.

P: Uh huh. My husband was eighty-five. We had our fiftieth anniversary and several more years.

C: That's wonderful! That's a record not too many people achieve.

P: Yes. These are my rings. (*two gold bands, one of which is broken*) He's been gone five years.

C: You must miss him very much.

P: I do. My daughters are very good to me. My twins are fifty-seven now. (*extended conversation about her family*)

C: Your family is very important to you, isn't it?

P: Yes. (*beaming*)

C: They must be a comfort to you at a time like this.

P: Yes. I don't want to have this operation I'm a little scared.

C: It is scary to think about an operation.

P: Yes. My family is a big help. They are very good.

C: They'll be a help to you when you have surgery, but you still must be worried about the operation.

P: Yes. (*holding on to her cross*)

C: That's a lovely cross—very unusual.

P: Thank you. It's an Orthodox cross. We go to a beautiful Orthodox church in the city.

C: Your faith is important too.

P: Yes, yes it is. I'm glad you came.

C: I'm glad I came, too. I'd like to come again tomorrow. (*Mrs. S's eyelids are closing involuntarily*)

P: Yes. It's nice to see someone when you're alone.

C: Would you like to have a prayer before I go?

P: Oh yes. I would like that.

C: Most Gracious Heavenly Father, we thank you for being our God. We thank you for your promise never to leave us or forsake us. Father, you know our needs before we ever speak. You know how Mrs. S. has suffered with this leg. You know how anxious she feels about the surgery. We pray you will give her strength and courage to face what she must. We pray you will grant her your peace which is beyond our understanding. Thank you, Lord, for Mrs. S's long and happy marriage, and the family which is so dear. Watch over them while they are apart. In Jesus' name we pray. Amen.

The chaplain offered a lot of understanding in this sequence, perhaps overly accenting the positive in Mrs. S.'s responses, but basically staying close to "where she is." The chaplain's prayer is appropriately supportive while acknowledging the anxiety felt by Mrs. S. We may note that this free prayer seems to have been effective, even though it had to reach across Christian traditions from Protestantism to Orthodoxy. The importance of the love and support of Mrs. S.'s family is highlighted in this interview, even as the fear of surgery and its aftermath remains. For those hospitalized without such support, the chaplain's care is all the more needed.

One of the most crucial questions for those who care for the elderly who are ill is the distinction that needs to be made between organic impairment of the brain and nervous system and the person's reaction to various kinds of stress with depression, anxiety and confusion. As Robert N. Butler, whose work has done much to make us aware of this problem, has pointed out, such stress often includes such long-standing stressors as the perception on the part of the public that the aging are "only senile," and the ravages of unresolved grief, but it also includes sudden shifts in the environment, such as hospitalization (Butler, 1977). If, for instance, the hospitalization is the result of a fall, an all too frequent traumatic experience of the aging and one which often involves a blow to the head, a temporary confusion may result. Such temporary confusion may be mistaken for irreversible organic damage and the person treated accordingly.

Although pastoral care-givers are not, obviously, equipped to make these diagnostic distinctions on their own, they need to be aware of these possibilities and alert for signs that confusion may be temporary. Also, they are in a good position to prevent confusion in some cases by helping the person who has been hospitalized as a result of a fall or other accident to re-establish contact with reality through recounting the events of the trauma with an understanding person. The general point here is that once a mental or emotional problem begins to be regarded as organic and irreversible, the more it tends to become that—even though the basis may remain only functional. Many of the elderly suffer from problems properly associated with mental, rather than physical, illness, especially depression, and need to be treated with a full range of medical remedies, as well as with appropriate pastoral care, an idea only now beginning to take hold.

To be sure, numbers of the aging do suffer from irreversible organic brain and neurological problems—at least they are irreversible according to the current state of medical knowledge. More understanding of and differentiation among the types of these difficulties is occurring now, however, because of increasingly sensitive scanning devices. Alzheimer's Disease, which formerly was thought to be due to "hardening of the arteries," was found in the 1970's to be due to the deterioration of certain kinds of brain cells, distinguishing it from other forms of irreversible organic problems. It may well be that improved treatment will follow from this improved understanding in the future, but for now pastoral care follows other helping modalities in offering support and reassurance. Traditional religious resources, though not unimportant in other pastoral care ministries to the elderly, are often particularly significant for this group. Bible reading and free prayer are the mainstays of most Protestant traditions, while Holy Communion and Anointing have great meaning for many Catholics. I may add that these are emphases and not exclusive kinds of ministry. Blending traditional ministries is often a good prescription for the aging, as Helen's experience suggests! (H 3)

2. *Pastoral Counseling.* Understood as a sustained attempt on the part of a representative care-giver to offer an attempt at better understanding and amelioration of a relatively specific difficulty, as sketched earlier in this chapter, pastoral counseling is sometimes appropriate for the aging. The general goal of such counseling is the attainment of the most traditional of all virtues of the elderly—*wisdom.* Erikson has furnished us an enriched perspective on wisdom by linking it to his emphasis on ritualization, which I have discussed. "What is the last ritualization built into the style of old age? I think it is *philo-sophical*: for in maintaining some order and meaning in this dis-integration of body and mind, it can also advocate a durable hope in wisdom" (Erikson, 1982, p. 64). This order and meaning must include also a coherent vision of the world—past, present, and fu-

ture, which can be shared with following generations. Pastoral counseling is for those struggling toward wisdom, or to recover widsom which may have been partially lost due to a crisis of some kind. Not all the aging are struggling; some have "given up," or have been forced to abandon the struggle by organic impairment or repeated stresses spanning a lifetime. But for some, the attainment of wisdom is possible with appropriate help. I note that, lest wisdom sound too intellectual a note, it must include a sense of connection between body and mind, as Erikson has emphasized. Integrity is another word to describe it.

What are some of the indications for pastoral counseling, then, as we keep this broad goal in mind? (1) *Loss or losses.* Losses in old age are often but the latest in a long series, many of which have been confronted, and at least in basic ways, worked through. But a particular loss may be felt as somehow particularly significant, whether it is diminished eyesight resulting in loss of driving privileges, loss of a pet, or loss of a long beloved spouse. Such losses threaten to destroy the integrity the person has achieved, and can be more devastating, even, than grief and loss earlier in life, and despair, a temptation pervading the organism itself, often looms. Pastoral counseling is useful as a supportive relationship allowing the grief to be ventilated, sources of strength, both religious and non-religious to be identified and tapped, and some vision of the future upon which hope depends restored. Counseling is not appropriate in every case of loss; sometimes devastation is too great for the sufferer to make use of it, and sometimes occasional pastoral care is sufficient. But for those genuinely struggling to regain a center for their lives, it is optimal pastoral help.

(2) A second indication for pastoral counseling is "unfinished business." Erikson has recognized that the aging sometimes search the past for solutions to present developmental conflicts in a discussion about psychotherapy (1982, p. 63), and we may note that such searches are also appropriate for pastoral counseling. The stories told by the aging are always more than mere "reminiscence." Sometimes they are accounts which show the continuity and meaning of their lives, but sometimes they also conceal, at least in part, clues to unresolved conflicts in the past. They are "screen memories" which portray events in such a way that true sources of psychic pain to which they may be related are hidden. Particularly is this apt to be true of repetitive, tape-like stories, which seem to be unwound again and again, although they may be "plugged into" different aspects of psychic life.

Crude attempts to break these codes are obviously not in order. Indeed, probing them at all is a task for experienced pastoral counselors, for the fragile integrity of the person can be at risk. Nevertheless, some of the aging are ready to probe the past in search of authenticity in the present.

Heije Faber, in his *Striking Sails*, has interpreted Erikson's "integrity" in terms of acceptance at the end of life—an acceptance which reaches both backward and forward to the future (1984, p. 118). For many, acceptance means releasing the self from conflicted situations in the past so that the future may be faced with hope.

(3) *Decision Making.* The aging frequently face difficult decisions and have trouble in making them, especially if they are alone. Decisions involving moving their living arrangements are particularly difficult to make, for example. Counseling with the elderly about decisions is essentially the same as counseling with members of other age groups about similar problems. The counselor needs to use a lot of understanding, or reflective listening, clarification and support in decision making process. The counselor's own values and judgment inevitably play a role in this process as well, so the counselor needs to be as aware as possible of what these may be, and what their sources may be. These values may or may not be verbalized in the counseling, but if they are communicated, they should be stated in such a way as to make clear that they are the counselor's values and judgment, and not demands made by church, family, or God.

If the families of the elderly are involved in decision making, the caregiver will need to be in touch with them, if possible. Their point of view is of obvious importance, and their presence shifts the dynamic from individual counseling to a kind of "shuttle diplomacy," in which the care-giver tries to understand the differing points of view, if they exist, and to mediate a resolution that all members can live with comfortably. Sometimes this is not possible, of course, and the counselor's values come directly into focus in helping him or her decide what is the most responsible course to take.

3. *Support Systems.* The systems of financial, interpersonal, and institutional support which the aging require for support is not always an issue with which the care-giver must deal, as these are in place for many of the elderly. But when these are lacking or threatened they cannot be ignored, for personal contact with a care-giver is only one element in care needed by the aging. In my view the care giver does have a responsibility to try to mobilize these services on behalf of those who need them— whether they are in the realm of what the churches can provide, as modeled, for instance by The Shepherd's Center in Kansas City, Missouri, or in the realm of social and public services. For some care-givers this concern will extend to political lobbying and marching in picket lines on behalf of the rights of the aging, and for all it means considered attention to and a willingness to take initiative about matters pertaining to the context in which the aging are living, as well as to the persons with whom they have a direct relationship.

4. *Boredom.* Many who have tried to offer help to the aging have felt themselves bored by them, especially those of more advanced years who are given to much repetition of the same stories or who seem to be responsive to nothing that the care-giver says. We may recall that "Helen" anxiously inquired of the seminarian whether she was boring him (H24), for that would be a bad grade for her with the supervising nurse!

What we experience as boredom is not a completely understood phenomenon. We experience the environment as lacking in interest for us, and in cases of prolonged confinement or the monotony of a long sea voyage, it may well be. But in other circumstances boredom is actually a psychic defense against an experience that is even less wanted. When some of us are confronted with the apparent disintegration of some members of the aging population, our own anxiety is aroused, for we know that we, too, shall someday grow old and die. In other instances boredom may be a symptom of countertransference—feelings about others, usually our parents, projected onto the person we are seeking to help. These anxieties may be manifested in other ways of course, but boredom seems to be a particularly widespread defense against it, for, after all, "everyone knows" that the elderly are uninteresting. Only the developed self-awareness of the care-giver can answer the question about whether this is the significance of his or her boredom—a self-awareness that usually requires the help of others to develop.

In other instances boredom may be due to our actually finding the aging to be uninteresting—they do not somehow fit the specifications of what an interesting human being is like. In these cases we need to become more imaginative in our approach. Sometimes we need to ask what the meaning of the repetitive "tapes" may be, and perhaps to do some gentle probing about them. In other instances we need to accept the "childlikeness" of the very old person and approach him or her in a basically non-verbal way, emphasizing activities or "rituals," as Erikson would have it. Physical touching and hugging may be important, and doing things such as group singing of old favorites can still reach the heart of many older persons. These are but examples of some elements in approaches to the elderly who are boring. Using imagination in the context and with the particular person is the key.

III
Conclusion

I shall not provide here a complete summary of all that I have tried to say in this chapter. The diversity of the aging population again needs emphasizing, so that we do not have a "standard" approach to the aging in pastoral care, even though in this chapter I have stressed certain basic elements in our approach.

More than a generation ago Paul B. Maves and J. Lennart Cederleaf published the results of a pioneering and comprehensive study to which they devoted two years of intensive work—*Older People and the Church* (1949). Although now obviously dated in some respects, their study contains many of the same ideas touched in this chapter. In spite of our increasing sensitivity to the aging population, our knowledge has not increased proportionately regarding ways of helping them. We have learned some things about memory and its possible uses in the present with the aging; we have a rather larger vocabulary to discuss the problems of aging, thanks in large measure to Erikson. But much more needs to be known and new approaches developed as our general knowledge about the aging process increases. It is my hope that readers of this volume will be active participants in this process of pilgrimage with the aging.

Note

1. Quotes taken from Rosalie Otters-Hollander, "A Theology of Aging with Implications for the Local Church" (unpublished thesis: Princeton Theological Seminary), p. 154.

Bibliography

Butler, Robert N. *Why Survive? Being Old in America.* New York: Harper and Row, 1977, p. xi.

Erikson, Erik H. *The Life Cycle Completed.* New York: W.W. Norton, 1982, p. 43.

Faber, Heije. *Striking Sails: A Pastoral-Psychological View of Growing Older in Society,* tr. Kenneth R. Mitchell. Nashville: Abingdon Press, 1984, p. 118.

Hammond, Phillip E. "Aging and the Ministry," in Carol LeFevre and Perry LeFevre, eds., *Aging and the Human Spirit.* Chicago: Exploration Press, 1981, p. 145.

Keith, Pat M. "Life Changes and Perceptions of Life and Death Among Older Men and Women," in Carol LeFevre and Perry LeFevre, eds., *Aging and the Human Spirit.* Chicago: Exploration Press, 1981, pp. 197-205.

Maves, Paul B. and J. Lennart Cedarleaf. *Older People and the Church.*
    New York: Abingdon-Cokesbury, 1949.
The New York Times, February 21, 1984, p. C-1.
Shanas, Ethel. "Social Myth as Hypothesis: The Case of the Family Rela-
    tions of Old People," in Carol LeFevre and Perry LeFevre, eds., *Ag-
    ing and the Human Spirit.* Chicago: Exploration Press, 1981.

Loy O. Bascue
Roy Lewis

Marital and Family Therapy Skills for Pastoral Therapists

As American society settles into the final quarter of the twentieth century, it is ever more apparent that marriage and family relationships are experiencing considerable transition. The transition is emerging from, or perhaps in concert with, such factors as increasing economic pressure, changing roles and expectations of women, and escalating ambiguity of personal and social values. The influence of both the current economic condition and also the changing roles of women is perhaps best reflected by the fact that 52% of all adult women are now employed and, in fact, over two-thirds of all women between the ages of twenty and forty-five work outside the home (Robey, 1983). The impact of changing values is evident by the fact that over 50% of all marriages currently end in divorce (Francke, 1980). In fact, the importance of these factors upon family life led Robey (1983) to conclude that the American family "looks radically different than it used to, with later first marriages, fewer children, and more divorces than in the past" (p. 2).

In addition to all the likelihood that families are changing because of these current pressures, there are a variety of other issues that have always had the potential to stress the texture of the American family life. For example, individuals and families have always had to face the psychological, physical, and social difficulties of illnesses, accidents, and death and they have had to occasionally come to terms with the painful consequences of natural disasters such as floods or fires. Moreover, for some families, there are both psychological and social adjustments that accompany such decisions as to adopt children, relocate geographically, or return to school for further education.

Of course it is against the stress of these issues that families struggle to maintain both equilibrium and also develop a gratifying and rewarding atmosphere in which to live. An additional dilemma for family members is where to turn when they need or want help in their struggles.

The Pastoral Therapist

The pastoral therapist is in a unique position to respond to the myriad of problems associated with marriage and family life. In fact, they are frequently sought out to help with such problems. In a 1976 survey, for example, it was found that 39% of a large sample of adults reported they turned first to clergy for help with problems and 59% did so for conflicts they believed were related to marriage or family life (Veroff, Douvan & Kulka, 1976). Thus, there is some reason to believe that pastoral therapists will be among the first professionals sought for help by people and, moreover, that the majority of problems presented to them will be marital and family difficulties.

It is with this perspective, then, that this paper is presented. First, that people in marriage and family relationships face considerable pressure in their struggles for growth and happiness and, second, that it is not uncommon for people contending with their problems to seek help from clergy, including pastoral therapists. Given this view, it is the purpose of this paper to provide an initial foundation in the specialty of marital and family therapy so that pastoral therapists will have both a sufficient background about treatment alternatives available for clients they serve and also so that they will have basic information necessary for evaluating their own individual training needs in the area of marital and family therapy.

An Overview of Marital and Family Therapy

Broderick and Schrader (1981) have provided an excellent overview of both the history and current professional status of marital and family therapy. A review of their article, as well as material from other sources (Olson, 1970; Madanes and Haley, 1977), leads to three general perspectives potentially useful to pastoral therapists who are attempting to evaluate the importance of marital and family therapy.

The first perspective useful to pastoral therapists is that while marital and family therapy appears to be emerging as a unified treatment specialty, it is both historically and currently most appropriately thought of as an amalgam of several distinct treatment and research areas. While all the areas might fit under the general rubric of marital and family therapy, each one has distinctive historical roots, requires unique skills, and proposes special training requirements. For example, Broderick and Schrader

(1981) report that marital therapy actually began as the field of marriage counseling. They indicate that the American Association of Marriage Counselors was founded in 1945, but it was not until 1970 that the name was modified to include family counselors. Moreover, it was not until 1978 that the organization's name was changed to the American Association of Marriage and Family Therapy.

Thus, prior to this recent synthesis of the two areas, marital therapy was at least somewhat distinct from family therapy which, in turn, had its own history and developmental benchmarks. Sex therapy, with the specific purpose of evaluating and treating sexual dysfunction, can also be viewed as a distinct professional sphere, as can the areas of parent training (Levant, 1983a), marriage enrichment (Levant, 1983b), and divorce therapy (Kaslow, 1981), although each area might also be considered a facet of marital and family therapy.

For pastoral therapists, recognizing the historical diversity and current breadth of this seemingly unified specialty is important so that they both are aware of the variety of specialized services and also can understand that each area has its own purposes, skills, and perhaps training guidelines. Hopefully, this perspective will influence the therapist's appreciation of the need to make appropriate client referrals and the complexity of training possibilities available in marital and family treatment.

The second perspective evident from the history of marital and family therapy is that it is a multi-disciplinary specialty with important historical and current contributions from many professional disciplines, including, among others, a variety of religious professionals. For example, the Reverend Otis R. Rice was among the committee members of the 1948 group which first established standards for marriage counselors (Broderick and Schrader, 1981). More recently, of course, both the programs of Marriage Enrichment and Marriage Encounter grew directly out of the efforts of lay and professional church workers concerned about promoting positive family life, with Marriage Enrichment having developed out of weekend retreats for Quakers (Mace and Mace, 1975) and Marriage Encounter having grown out of family work in the Catholic Church (Bosco, 1973).

Thus, the religious community has made important and enduring contributions to the specialty of marital and family therapy. Pastoral therapists have every right to expect to continue building upon this foundation created by other religious workers. Moreover, because of these past contributions, pastoral therapists need not view marital and family therapy as an unapproachable specialty belonging to other professional disciplines. The specialty belongs as much to the religious community as to any other professional group.

The third perspective growing out of the history of marital and family treatment which is relevant to pastoral therapists is the recognition that, like individual and group therapy, marital and family therapy is made up of a variety of specific systems or schools of treatment. Just as there are, for example, psychoanalytic, behavioral, and interpersonal theories of individual and group therapy, there are a variety of systems operative in marital and family therapy. This means, of course, that pastoral therapists will need to identify treatment systems compatible with their own personal values and beliefs about people. Just as individual and group methods reflect beliefs about people and how to help them change, the various marital and family systems also reflect differing values about people, what factors influence their growth, and what activities or techniques will help them change.

Systems of Marital and Family Therapy

As just stated, there are a variety of theories of marital and family therapy. It is not the purpose of this paper to enumerate and review all those theories, since excellent reviews already exist (Madanes and Haley, 1977; Paolino and McCrady, 1978; Gruman and Kniskern, 1981). However, in order to provide an initial impression for pastoral therapists about the variety of approaches, this section will provide a selective account of some of the major themes developed by the various schools of marital and family therapy.

Psychoanalytic Themes. Some marital and family therapists approach treatment from a psychoanalytic viewpoint. Generally these therapists focus on the individual psychodynamics of family members and are concerned both with how unconscious wishes and fantasies influence family interpersonal relations and also how family interaction influences individual psychodynamics (Skynner and Skynner, 1979). Moreover, they are likely to view marital and family conflicts as reflecting the attempts of individual family members to come to terms with their own unconscious wishes and needs. In turn, changes in family relations are likely to reflect changes in individual attempts to gratify personal needs and desires.

Intergenerational Themes. Some therapists are concerned about the influence of family generations upon succeeding generations, including the influence of past generations upon the behavior of individual family members. Of course, intergenerational theorists might also be concerned about the interpersonal interaction of current family members, but they are likely to believe that the behavior of past generations (grandparents, aunts and uncles) has influenced the structure and interaction within a given nuclear family, including the development of current family problems. As Boszormenyi-Nagy and Ulrich (1981) state, for example:

At any point in time, at least three generations overlap. Even if the grandparents are absent or dead, their influence continues. Psychological, transactional, and ethical aspects lose crucial meanings if they are not seen in this perspective (p. 162).

Often theorists using this approach stress the importance of family members in treatment contacting members of their extended family and attempting to assess the impact of past generations upon current conflicts. From this view, treatment success is seen as the ability of current family members to differentiate from past generations and function as a family autonomously in response to existing family needs and problems (Bowen, 1971).

Communication Themes. There are some therapists who apply principles of communication theory to nuclear family interaction, with the goal of improving member communication in order to promote effective problem solving and interpersonal conflict resolution. Communication theorists attend to both verbal and non-verbal modes of communication and try to understand patterns of family interaction, norms of behavior, and the expression of individual values as these elements are expressed in communication (Satir, 1967). In addition to helping family members improve communication, therapists might also teach individuals how to evaluate effective communication themselves so that improvement continues after treatment.

Structural Themes. Structural therapists are concerned about the social organization of marital and family units. In therapy these therapists often attempt to point out this structure to family members and often even attempt to change the existing structure. The underlying assumption is that by identifying and changing the physical structure, the psychological relations among members will also change. Thus, for example, structural therapists might suggest in therapy sessions who sits next to whom or suggest changes in the content or direction of conversation as methods of influencing the relation of one family member to another (Aponte, 1974).

Behavioral Themes. Behavioral family theorists are concerned about changing specific manifest behaviors of individual family members. Generally, behavioral models view problems of family members from the point of view of social learning theory, which means they believe that behavior changes in response to the rewards provided. In turn, the behavior of one family member is viewed as resulting from the rewards provided by other members, although environmental forces both within and outside the family are also believed to shape and encourage behavior. In essence, family problems can result either from rewarding the behavior of one family member that does not promote the satisfaction of other family members or from failing to reward behavior that does promote satisfaction (Graziano, 1983). Therefore, in treatment behavioral therapists attempt to identify individual or interactional problems within the marriage or family unit, develop methods to reduce reinforcers of problem behaviors, and encourage the reinforcement of positive behaviors.

Overall, even from this brief account, it should be obvious that there is considerable richness of values and diversity of treatment strategies within the scope of marital and family therapy. However, transcending this diversity are two contributions that warrant special attention by pastoral therapists since the contributions might easily influence how all therapists investigate and treat client problems, regardless of their interest in marriage or family therapy. The first contribution is the belief that the family unit is an organized social and psychological system with operational principles that can be understood and influenced, and the second contribution is that conjoint sessions are a valuable tool for both identifying and treating psycho-social problems.

The development of the concept of the family system is probably the single most important contribution to the specialty of marital and family therapy. As described above, theorists offer a variety of alternative models for understanding family conflict and treatment. Yet what transcends most of these theories is the assumption that the couple or family itself represents a psycho-social system. Moreover, the system and the way it operates is thought to account for many of the conflicts of family members. In turn, conflicts can be understood, and their resolution influenced, by examining the system and the rules by which it operates.

In essence, the system perspective represents a conceptual shift (Kerr, 1981) from the paradigm that problems are conflicts of single individuals to the belief that problems result from the emotional forces within the family unit and the principles that govern its operation. Systems theorists view the family as a gestalt and attempt to identify the patterns, norms, and values with the hope of influencing those factors to improve the functioning of the system and its members.

The second contribution of marital and family therapy is the utility of conjoint treatment sessions. Conjoint sessions can be defined as the simultaneous treatment of more than one family member by one or more therapist. Thus, for example, a therapist might treat a couple together or two co-therapists might see a couple together for evaluation. Conjoint sessions, however, imply more than simply seeing a couple together. For some therapists conjoint sessions might include children (Aponte, 1974) and for intergenerational theorists might include members of the extended family (Framo, 1976).

To reiterate, for pastoral therapists the important aspect of both the systems perspective and the technique of conjoint sessions is that they both provide a resource for understanding client problems, gathering information about those difficulties, and ultimately treating them. Both contributions offer therapists new options for interpreting behavior and, potentially, for helping people change.

In addition to the many theories of marital and family therapy, there are a variety of other service areas which can also be considered a part of the specialty. What follows is a summary of four of those areas potentially important to pastoral therapists.

Sex Therapy. Sex therapy can be defined as an activity or set of activities designed to treat sexual dysfunction, with the general goal of increasing an individual's pleasure from sexual activity. There are a variety of sexual disorders which might lead a pastoral therapist to consider this form of treatment for clients. An introductory review of major sexual disorders and their signs and symptoms is available in the *Diagnostic and Statistical Manual of Mental Disorders* (American Psychiatric Association, 1980). Modern sex therapy treatment techniques seem to be, at least to a great extent, an outgrowth of the work of Masters and Johnson (1970). While there are other forms of treatment for sexual problems, the work of Masters and Johnson seems to have been the forerunner of the direct, behaviorally-oriented approach which currently appears to be the dominant model for treatment. This behaviorally-oriented treatment technique is usually brief, with specific treatment goals, and therapists are usually verbally active with their clients. Treatment might include both individual and conjoint sessions, involve homework assignments such as completing suggested practice sexual experiences, or incorporate values clarification exercises into treatment sessions. Therapists might also show films or encourage sense-awareness activities as part of treatment.

Overall, recent publications which review the current standing of sex therapy (LoPiccolo and LoPiccolo, 1978) provide some guidelines which might be helpful to all pastoral therapists. First, current writing confirms the importance of obtaining a sexual history from every client to rule out sexual dysfunction or aid in determining if a reported sexual disorder is physical, psychological, or social in origin, and, second, the literature underscores the importance of medical consultation in the assessment of sexual complaints.

Parent Training. Parent training is a method for improving parenting skills and can be used either as a treatment for families in which the child has an identified problem or as a method of enhancing parenting in families without problems. Of course the three models of parent training reviewed herein are by no means the only alternatives, but they do serve to illustrate for pastoral therapists the range of options available. For example, one method of parent training, designed as family treatment, is filial therapy (Guerney, 1964). Filial therapy is designed for parents of children under ten years of age and is frequently used to treat mild-to-severe emotional and behavioral problems of the children, including such problems as aggressive behavior, phobias, and problematic anxiety. The therapy uses parent training groups which focus upon both didactic and experiential activities and teaches parents a method of non-punitive interaction with their children which is designed to improve parents' capacities to identify their children's feelings, accept those feelings, and reflect back to the children that the feelings are understood and accepted. This focus on communication skills is presumed to enhance the quality of the general parent-child relationship as well as aid in reducing specific problems.

Another training model used for treatment of children's problems is behavioral parent training. In contrast to the relationship and communication skills enhancement orientation of filial therapy, behavioral training uses principles of social learning to increase parenting skills. Behavorial methods are often used in response to families in which the children are experiencing severe disorders such as mental retardation, brain damage, or autism (Graziano, 1983). Through such programs, parents are taught skills to promote their children's self-care activities, personal hygiene, or language and social skills. While there are a variety of behavioral methods, most use group and individual training sessions in which parents are taught to reformulate problems into specific behaviors that make up the child's difficulty and then identify factors which encourage or reinforce each behavior. Parents are then taught to use both verbal and behavioral activities designed to reward more positive behavior.

A parent training program which is more appropriately thought of as an enhancement rather than a treatment program is Parent Effectiveness Training (Gordon, 1970). Usually organized as eight three-hour sessions of both didactic and experiential activities, Parent Effectiveness Training aids parents in developing listening skills, stresses the accepting personal responsibility for one's own feelings, and develops mutually acceptable solutions to problems, all in a family atmosphere of acceptance and empathy of family members for one another.

Marital Enhancement Programs. Programs designed to improve the quality of relationships are termed enhancement or enrichment programs. They are generally recommended for relationships which might be impaired, but not dysfunctional. The programs usually involve a time-limited, structured format, designed to teach participants skills for improving their relationship. Two examples of such programs have already been mentioned: Marriage Enrichment and Marriage Encounter. These two represent national efforts at relationship building and, therefore, have the advantage of providing practiced techniques provided through networks of local training centers. For pastoral therapists, they have the added advantage of having their roots in organized religious settings and, as a consequence, might be readily adapted to a local church or pastoral counseling center.

In addition to these two organized programs, there are other techniques for relationship enhancement which offer therapists the flexibility of designing their own programs for specific client needs or even incorporating them into ongoing marital or family therapy relationships. While these techniques will only be identified here, detailed reviews are available from the sources listed for the techniques that can provide information about organizing and implementing each activity. Specifically, the guidelines of fair fighting developed by Bach (Bach and Wyden, 1969) provide a method of conflict resolution in a relationship which permits the expression of anger so as not to be destructive to the marriage. Communication skills training (Miller, Wackman, and Nunnally, 1983) has also been applied to couples and is a method of teaching personal self-awareness, verbal expression, and feedback skills as a way of helping couples more effectively communicate with one another. Finally, structured assertiveness training can be used to help people verbally express themselves to a partner in order to clarify guidelines and limits of acceptable behavior and protect one's self-interest in a relationship (Lehman-Olson, 1976).

Divorce Therapy. It is as important for pastoral therapists to be aware of the therapeutic needs of individuals who separate and divorce as it is for them to recognize the needs of people trying to preserve and enhance their relationships. Two areas of particular concern for pastoral therapists are, first, the importance of recognizing that for many people divorce has religious meaning and implications for which pastoral therapists might be uniquely suited to respond and, second, the need for pastoral therapists to be sensitive to their own values and beliefs about divorce precisely because they are religious as well as mental health professionals.

In this context, Kaslow's (1981) eloquent statement provides an important view about the potential meaning of divorce:

> Although I do not equate divorce with dysfunction, it does appear that the decision to divorce is an attempt to extricate oneself from a trying, conflicted or unsatisfying relationship. It may well be a flight toward health—a seeking to escape from a living arrangement that has ceased to be tolerable and fulfilling (p. 663).

Clinical reports suggest that while a variety of therapeutic methods can be used to help adults and children facing the prospect of divorce, conjoint sessions can be of particular benefit in the midst of marital conflict as people assess the decision to separate and divorce (Whitaker and Miller, 1969). Conjoint sessions, including sessions with children, and individual sessions are helpful to people as they face the prospect of divorce itself and the loss which can accompany separation, single-parenting, and independent living (Kaslow, 1981). Moreover, peer groups can be useful during the post-divorce phase to provide social support when individuals come to terms with life-style changes associated with defining new relations with their children, deciding about appropriate social and sexual behavior, and making financial and vocational adjustments.

Conclusion

Historically, a pastoral therapist has been defined as a pastor who provides psychotherapy. In turn, the term pastor has meant a professional minister, a person called by God and set apart by their congregation to be God's ambassador to prepare the way for salvation. Moreover, this view of a pastor has been associated with the concept of a shepherd, one who helps others help themselves by providing an environment for growth, health, and salvation (Hiltner, 1959).

We are convinced, however, that the concept of pastoral has a deeper meaning than that of ordained clergy. Pastoral also refers to people especially trained and uniquely sensitive to the domain of religious-value-meaning systems of human nature. For us, it follows that pastoral therapy is that discipline which synthesizes special training, sensitivity and commitment to understand this religious-value-meaning dimension of people with training, sensitivity, and commitment to provide mental health services and psychotherapy. In fact, it is this willingness and ability to deal with the religious-value-meaning dimension of the human condition that makes the pastoral therapist a unique professional.

Thus, the pastoral therapist brings to marital and family therapy a special perspective not available from other professionals. The purpose of this paper has been to help the pastoral therapist obtain an initial foundation in the specialty of marital and family therapy with the underlying expectation that both the content and references of the paper would serve as a starting point for evaluating the need for further skill. At the same time, we hope that our presentation has helped the pastoral therapist recognize and value the important perspective that the profession alone brings to the specialty of marital and family therapy.

Bibliography

American Psychiatric Association. *Diagnostic and Statistical Manual of Mental Disorders* (3rd ed.). Washington, D.C.: 1980.

Aponte, H. "Organizing Treatment Around the Family's Problems and Their Structural Bases." *Psychiatric Quarterly*, 1974, 8–12.

Bach, G. and Wyden, T. *The Intimate Enemy: How To Fight Fair in Love and Marriage*. New York: W. Morrow & Co., 1969.

Bosco, A. *Marriage Encounter: The Rediscovery of Love*. St. Meinard: Abbey Press, 1973.

Boszormenyi-Nagy, I. and Ulrich, D. "Contextual Family Therapy." In A. Gurman and D. Kniskern (eds.), *Handbook of Family Therapy*. New York: Brunner/Mazel, Inc., 1981.

Bowen, M. "Family Therapy and Family Group Therapy." In H. Kaplan & B. Sadock (eds.), *Comprehensive Group Psychotherapy*. Baltimore: Williams & Wilkins, 1971.

Broderick, C. and Schrader, S. "The History of Professional Marriage and Family Therapy." In A. Gurman and D. Kniskern (eds.), *Handbook of Family Therapy*. New York: Brunner/Mazel, Inc., 1981.

Framo, J. "Family of Origin as a Therapeutic Resource for Adults in Marital and Family Therapy: You Can and Should Go Home Again." *Family Process*, 1976, 15, 193–210.

Francke, L. "The Children of Divorce." *Newsweek*, 1980, February 11, 58–63.

Gordon, T. *P.E.T.: Parent Effectiveness Training*. New York: Wyden, 1970.

Graziano, A. "Behavioral Approaches to Child and Family Systems." *The Counseling Psychologist*, 1983, 11, 47–56.

Gruman, A. and Kniskern, D. (eds.). *Handbook of Family Therapy*. New York: Brunner/Mazel, Inc., 1981.

Guerney, B., Jr. "Filial Therapy: Description and Rationale." *Journal of Consulting Psychology*, 1964, 28, 304–310.

Hiltner, S. *Pastoral Counseling*. New York: Abington Press, 1959.

Kaslow, F. "Divorce and Divorce Therapy." In A. Gurman and D. Kniskern (eds.), *Handbook of Family Therapy*. New York: Brunner/Mazel, Inc., 1981.

Kerr, M. "Family Systems Theory and Therapy." In A. Gurman and D. Kniskern (eds.), *Handbook of Family Therapy*. New York: Brunner/Mazel, Inc., 1981.

Lehman-Olson, D. "Assertiveness Training: Theoretical and Clinical Implications." In D. Olson (ed.), *Treating Relationships*. Lake Hills: Graphic Publishing, 1976.

Levant, R. "Toward a Counseling Psychology of the Family: Psychological-Educational and Skills-Training Programs for Treatment, Prevention, and Development." *The Counseling Psychologist*, 1983a, 11, 5–27.

Levant, R. "Client-Centered Skills-Training Programs for the Family: A Review of the Literature." *The Counseling Psychologist*, 1983b, 11, 29–46.

LoPiccolo, J. and LoPiccolo, L. (eds.). *Handbook of Sex Therapy*. New York: Plenum, 1978.

Mace, D. and Mace, V. "Marriage Enrichment-Wave of the Future?" *The Family Coordinator*, 1975, 24, 131–135.

Madanes, C. and Haley, J. "Dimensions of Family Therapy." *Journal of Nervous and Mental Disease*, 1977, 165, 88–98.

Masters, W. and Johnson, V. *Human Sexual Response*. Boston: Little, Brown, 1970.

Miller, S., Wackman, D., and Nunnally, E. "Couple Communication: Equiping Couples To Be Their Own Best Problem Solvers." *The Counseling Psychologist*, 1983, 11, 73–77.

Olson, D. "Marital and Family Therapy: Integrative Review and Critique." *Journal of Marriage and the Family*, 1970, 32, 501–538.

Paolino, T. and McCrady, B. (eds.). *Marriage and Marital Therapy: Psychoanalytic, Behavioral, and Systems Theory Perspectives*. New York: Brunner/Mazel, Inc., 1978.

Robey, B. "Five Myths." *American Demographics*, 1983, 5, 2, 4.

Satir, V. *Conjoint Family Therapy: A Guide to Theory and Technique* (rev. ed.). Palo Alto: Science & Behavior Books, 1967.

Skynner, A. and Skynner, P. "An Open-Systems Approach to Teaching Family Therapy." *Journal of Marital and Family Therapy*, 1979, 5, 5–16.

Veroff, J., Douvan, E., and Kulka, R. *Americans View Their Mental Health*. Ann Arbor: University of Michigan Survey Research Center, 1976.

Whitaker, C. and Miller, M. "A Re-Evaluation of 'Psychiatric Help' When Divorce Impends." *American Journal of Psychiatry*, 1969, 126, 57–64.

Emma J. Justes

Women

Introduction

The majority of persons who seek and receive pastoral counseling are female. This remains true regardless of geographical or denominational setting. Yet it has been only in recent years that the issue of the pastoral counseling of women has become a matter of any concern. The growing number of female colleagues within the ranks of pastoral counselors and ordained clergy and the impact of the Women's Movement have been influential factors in raising this concern. Pastoral counselors and pastors are dealing with the impact that sex defined roles and changes in these roles due to growing consciousness (both female and male) have had on individuals, marriages and families. The impact of growing awareness and role changes has affected pastors and pastoral counselors personally as well as professionally.

Women seeking pastoral counseling today pose some particular new problems for the pastoral conselor. (1) New psychological perspectives and emerging feminist and liberation theologies raise questions about long-standing theory and practice in pastoral counseling. (2) If pastoral counselors are not aware of the nature and effect of sex defined roles as well as the changes that are taking place, women's experiences may be seen as problematic rather than as occasions for growth. (3) Recognition of the realities of incest and other violence toward women—long clouded by psychological theories—has begun to enter the picture for the pastoral counselor. (4) Good skills in pastoral counseling alone are not sufficient for good pastoral counseling of women.

New problems also can be seen as offering positive potential. These particular problems related to the pastoral counseling of women offer opportunities for growth and development in pastoral counseling and in the individual pastoral counselor. Most of the preparation and training that pastoral counselors have received has not dealt adequately, if at all, with the specific problems related to counseling women. Dealing positively with particular problem areas related to counseling women cannot help but also improve the pastoral counseling of men. One cannot hold limiting attitudes and expectations about women without also holding other similarly limiting attitudes and expectations about men. At the heart of concern regarding the pastoral counseling of women is the definition and assignment of roles and behaviors according to one's sex. Sex-role definitions and assignments have influenced psychology and theology. Sex defined roles affect pastoral counseling as they remain effective components in the attitudes and expectations of pastoral counselors.

Two essential factors must be mentioned before proceeding to deal further with the pastoral counseling of women. First, it is not constructive to refer to one another as members of the "opposite sex." Abundant research has demonstrated that we are not truly "opposite" as female and male. We are much more alike than we are different. Seeing ourselves as *opposite* only provides fuel for seeing ourselves *in opposition*. It seems quite sufficient to use the phrase "the other-sex" wherever one feels the need for expressing "the opposite sex." The referent would be just as clear. Second, in dealing with the pastoral counseling of women we are dealing with issues of sexism. Sexism cannot be addressed adequately if it remains in isolation from racism. Theologian James Cone (*My Soul Looks Back*, p. 115) has stated this reality effectively: "Racism, classism, sexism, and imperialism are interconnected, and none can be correctly understood and eventually defeated without simultaneous attention to the others."

Re-Examination of the Bases for Pastoral Counseling. Pastoral counseling is rooted in both psychological theory and theological tradition and reflection—however varied the balance between these two sources may be. Both of these fields have been shaped and defined from male perspectives. The view of woman in each has been reflective of a male point of view. Definitions of female by theology and psychology have reflected the female defined according to the male. Both fields have exerted powerful influence on the shaping of women in terms of women's self-understanding and self-image as well as in terms of the theoretical perspective on woman. Thus, the images of humanity that have informed pastoral counseling have been limited by the one-sided perspective offered from a male-only point of view. If this one-sided perspective truly has limited these foundations on which pastoral counseling rests, then the changes in our understanding and practice of pastoral counseling could be profound.

Counselors have been moving toward a willingness to admit and confront the fact that counseling and psychology do not emerge and exist as value free. And theologians have become more willing to recognize that theological reflection is not culture free. Acknowledgement of these factors enables us to reconsider and re-evaluate our roots of pastoral counseling in order to move toward more constructive theory and more effective practice in pastoral counseling. Pretense of being value-free in regard to women and ignoring the value-laden nature of role perceptions prohibit such movement. If I hold as true that woman's role is in the home, this is a value and it will be conveyed in the ways in which I respond to counselees. Awareness that this is a value I hold and that such values do sneak into counseling will help me be alert to its impact on those I counsel. I also must put such values to the test of examining them in light of my theology with the factor in mind that *pastoral* counseling carries the implied values of religious tradition. The parishioner does not expect me to be value-free.

Both theology and psychology have defined female as different, as "other," and have built traditions and theories that proceed to ignore that difference. To truly understand the difference we must begin to hear about humanity from a female perspective. When we do more fully comprehend our difference as female and male, then we can take the differences into account in the shaping of theological traditions and psychological theories.

Some Theological Considerations

Theology has not provided a consistently constructive base on which to develop the pastoral counseling of women. Some theological traditions hold that woman's "secondary nature" was determined by her being created second (Gen 2:21–23). Some hold Eve (and proceed from her to all who are female) as responsible for the fall of "man" (1 Tim 2:11–15). Some base sex-role definitions on the order of creation (Gen 2:21–23), woman's "helpmate" status (Gen 2:18) and on the curse that follows the fall (Gen 3:16–17). Some support biblical injunctions that require women to submit to their husbands as "head over them as Christ is head of the Church" (1 Cor 11:3; Eph 5:22–24). Even some who would not feel bound by this scripture raise the concern that *someone* has to make the final decision when there is disagreement. Some would carry from scripture a sense of woman as the "property" of man (Ex 20:17; 21:7; Eph 5:22–24). Differences in roles assigned to females and males find grounding in scripture and in theological interpretations of scripture.

These interpretations have affected the pastoral counseling of women whether they have been used intentionally for a counseling base or not. Prior to the influence such interpretations can have on the theory and practice of pastoral counseling lies their influence on the attitudes and expectations held by the pastor or pastoral counselor. The effects of these interpretations emerge across a wide range of theological orientations.

The passages of scripture mentioned above have had some force in determining women's roles. They have also contributed to the perception of female as understood to be "different from" and "other than" male. Roles and identity are shaped in relation to this status of "different" and "other" in relation to man.

In contrast to that which would define female by its differentness we discover Paul's declaration in Galatians 3:28. Paul proclaims an alternative perception of differentness and an alternative vision for humanity. It is *not* a vision that eliminates differences but a vision that sees Christianity as embracing differences. Here difference does not divide but participates in unity.

While theology has emphasized an understanding of female as different from male this differentness has been ignored in areas in which other matters are being emphasized. Valerie Saiving Goldstein published an article in 1969 that helps point out this inattention to difference. She discussed theological emphases placed on the sin of pride which ignore that woman's experiences of self-abnegation may lend her more to sin in ways better described as "sloth." A person caught in self-abnegating patterns and subordinate self-perception does not get that self into perspective with theology that emphasizes sin as pride. Here we have one example in which difference emphasized elsewhere is ignored in regard to women's tendencies toward sin differing from those of men.

Alternatively, a theological base for pastoral counseling might take into account other emphases in text and interpretation. Paul suggests such an alternative interpretation in regard to the order of creation. In 1 Corinthians 11, Paul is considering this order and adds the parenthetical reflection: "For man was not made from woman, but woman from man. Neither was man created for woman, but woman for man . . . Nevertheless, in the Lord woman is not independent of man nor man of woman: for as woman was made of man, so man is now born of woman. And all things are from God." Paul questions whether the order established in creation was intended to be an order for all time and seems to answer that question in the negative (1 Cor 11:8–9, 11–12).

The fall might be better understood not as a condition that is *intended* for us, but rather as a condition from which we have been redeemed by Christ. What does our redemption mean when we affirm the fallen condition of humanity as establishing a pattern that is supported by the church?

A view of humanity might be based on an injunction from Jesus:

> You know that the rulers of the Gentiles lord it over them, and
> their great men exercise authority over them. It shall not be so

among you; but whoever would be great among you must be your
servant . . . (Mt 20:25–26).

How do we proceed in our interpretation of New Treatment passages that
affirm a male-female hierarchy in light of these words of Jesus?

Finally, there is an alternative available to us regarding how we can
assign roles—other than according to sex. 1 Corinthians 12:4–11 and 27–
31 offer the possibility and the vision of seeing roles as resulting from gifts
of the spirit bestowed within the community. The vision does *not* establish
a hierarchy of gifts but affirms the functioning of a multiplicity of gifts as
that which enables the body as a whole to be effective.

Such shifts in theological interpretation could offer pastoral counselors changes in theory and practice and challenge counselors to shifts in attitudes and expectations regarding female and male roles. An affirmation
of the distribution of gifts by the Spirit and not according to sex might call
on the pastoral counselor to play a role in enabling persons in the discernment of their gifts rather than assisting persons to adjust to roles pre-de-
termined according to sex.

Spiritual and religious issues are at the heart of struggles and special
needs for women who seek pastoral counseling. In part this is due to traditional theological perspectives outlined above. Theology's role in shaping woman has resulted in the Church's role in *depressing* women
(Stoudenmire: 1976) as well as in *oppressing* women. And the pastoral
counselor stands in the role of authority and resource to appropriately
meet both depression and oppression with new interpretation and new
life. Such movement on the part of pastoral counselors requires personal
attitude change as well as increased professional awareness.

Psychological Roots Reconsidered

Pastoral counselors claim a wide variety of influences from the field of
psychology—psychoanalytic and ego-psychology to Transactional Analysis
and family therapy movements. In every instance these psychological
roots have been "man-made." Our theories have come from male perspectives in psychology. These male perspectives have understood the female in terms of being "not male." Women have been understood in terms
of the ways they differ from men and not in their own right.

To illustrate this point Freud's concept of "penis envy" offers a vivid
example. From Freud's perspective as a male it would seem as though the
female would find her lack of a penis to be rather life-determining. Freud
thought the female would understand herself in terms of her lack of a penis

and her behavior would be affected by this understanding. This is a vision of female from a male perspective. Karen Horney began to offer the suggestion that the female might form her self-understanding around her own anatomy rather than around that of the male (1926).

Women in recent years have begun to challenge psychological theories with new research and from a different perspective. Judith Bardwick, Jean Baker Miller and more recently Nancy Chodorow and Carol Gilligan are making contributions to psychology that push pastoral counseling theory to take their perspectives and their research into account as formative for pastoral counseling. The often quoted Broverman study (1970) illustrates the impact of sex-defined role expectations and attitudes on counselors' perceptions of individuals. In this study both female and male counselors and therapists were asked to describe healthy adult, healthy male and healthy female. Descriptive terms assigned to the healthy adult and healthy male were similar and included independence and assertiveness. Terms assigned to the healthy female included dependence and submission. The healthy female would be more emotional and less aggressive. The choice for the female is to be either adult or female. Being healthy adult she appears to be an unhealthy (or immature) female.

Women creating alternative psychological theories are taking the impact of socialization as female or male seriously. Research reveals the differences in our socialization almost from the *moment of birth* (Lips and Colwill: 1978). The pastoral counselor has not escaped this socialization and should remain open to new theories and research done by women. For the most part we have not hesitated to claim and affirm pastoral counseling roots in psychology. The changes in psychological theory being initiated by women will be far-reaching. If so for psychology, then also for pastoral counseling.

One way in which the impact of these new perspectives on psychology can be avoided is if the pastoral counselor's theological bases stand in contradiction to the theories. Change has to be admitted in both areas both psychological theory and theological position.

Sex-Defined Roles: Limitations and Change

Every society assigns some roles to persons according to sex. Different societies make different sex role assignments. What is considered a male role in one society may be considered a female role in another. Female-assigned roles in one society may differ from those in other societies. Sex-defined roles are not cross-culturally consistent (Mead: 1949). Sex-defined roles also change over a period of time within the same society: They also vary according to class, economic status and race within a particular society. "Leisure class" women of the late nineteenth century filled roles defined by their perceived "delicacy." "Working class" women, however, were seen as capable of filling roles requiring hard physical labor. Physiological, psychological and theological bases have been claimed to support the determination of roles according to sex. What the pastoral counselor holds to be true about these bases for the maintenance of sex-defined roles will influence her or his effectiveness in pastoral counseling.

Physiologically, sex-defined roles have been based on the fact that only women can bear and give birth to children and lactate. These physiological facts have contributed to an expansion of sex-defined roles that makes women the primary care-givers for children. Fatherhood has not carried the same expectations regarding primary care-giving. The father role has been interpreted as being that of providing the often somewhat removed financial support of the family. Economic and sociological realities have made it necessary for some women to supplement the financial support from the father role with work outside the home. These realities have made it necessary for other women to become the sole support of their families. At the same time the basic roles of "mothering" have remained in the hands of the women—cooking, cleaning, child care. Why women are more physiologically or psychologically equipped for cleaning has not been made evident.

Sex-defined roles function in many cases to define characteristics of persons as well as the roles they fill. Females expected to be the primary care-givers for children reliant on financial and physical support of males are encouraged to develop nurturant and dependent characteristics (Chodorow: 1978). Males, expected to be providers, learn to be assertive and independent—skills needed "out there in the business world." The effect of such "channeling" of the development of characteristics has is to limit, according to sex, what human characteristics one learns to express. Individuals have amply demonstrated that males can be nurturant and females can be aggressive. Each of us, regardless of our sexual identity, possesses potential for the development of a whole range of human characteristics. To encourage the development of some characteristics and discourage the development of others because of a person's sexual identity is to deny the development of the full range of human potential within individuals and within society.

Struggles with Change

Women and men are struggling with change regarding sex-defined roles. Some people plunge ahead eager to enter new territory that has opened up with changes taking place. Others long to make changes and feel unable to or restricted from such change. Some resist change feeling that what *is* is right. And still others remain oblivious to changes that are occurring. Those who resist or deny changes are still being affected by change. All of the dimensions of these struggles are dramatically affecting individuals, marriages, families and churches.

Women who become aware of how they have been objects of discrimination and oppression respond with various degrees of anger. Expression of anger has been considered incompatible with "femininity" and when evident has been dismissed with responses that turn the woman's anger aside: "How cute you are when you're angry!" Women of the women's liberation or feminist movement have been labeled as "masculine" at least in part due to their expressions of anger. Societal response to the expression of anger by women indicates the importance of understanding the process through which some women go. Increased awareness on the part of women often leads to a realization that one's humanity has been diminished by the effects of stereotyping and discrimination. Anger is an appropriate response to that which is experienced as injustice. When discrimination and stereotyping appear as injustice rather than as the expected order of things, the result is anger.

There can be any number of ways to understand and describe the movement of women through an increased awareness. Some elements remain common for many women. That anger follows awareness when awareness reveals injustice should not be surprising. Experience of pain and struggle with change follow growing awareness. Just as anger is not easy for many of us to face, pastoral counselors also may find dealing with pain and change difficult. Change will affect others, family and congregation, friends and community. The pastor or pastoral counselor may be well aware of the potentially far-reaching impact of newly opened eyes. Any urge to protect the individual or the wider community from this impact only serves to stifle the growth inherent. Even though pastoral counselors see their work as enabling growth, the work can falter when the parishioner/counselee threatens to grow *beyond* the pastor's/counselor's vision.

The pastoral counselor's range of vision may become limiting in another way. Faced with a woman's increased awareness the pastoral counselor's vision may include an image of her family becoming broken by divorce. The pastor senses that her husband would never consider "letting her work" and himself sharing in the housework. Or a woman's new realization that she does not have to tolerate physical abuse may mean she leaves the husband who periodically beats her. The counselor also may have an image of the man whose own potential would be far outstripped by the newly aware wife once she begins to "move." In any of these situations the marriage and family relationships are likely to begin to falter. Faltering does not mean failing. To falter does not mean to fail. Faltering *does* carry the danger of falling and failing. It also carries potential for new configurations within family and community. When a woman's new awareness is dealt with by a pastoral counselor whose vision does not include the possibilities that new configurations (relationships) offer, her new awareness may not be given full rein. Her possibilities for growth, her potential for contributions may not be realized.

The pastoral counselor's ability and willingness to see and accept a wide variety of role functioning for women and for men will in part determine how the woman's new awareness is met, how her growth is enabled.

Women who are not experiencing discrimination against themselves or expressing desire for change still face struggles with change going on around them. Some women hear the voice of women's liberation as negating their lives as wives, mothers and homemakers. The voice these women hear is affecting them. They feel they must voice their opposition and begin to kick against the changes others strive for. Change affects those who kick against it, if only in its causing them to kick. What is the role of the pastoral counselor with women facing this kind of struggle? Dealing with this woman's anger and resentment is as valid as dealing with the anger and resentment of a woman who has recognized her experience of oppression.

Women of color may express resistance to matters of women's liberation. This cannot be understood as reflecting their lack of experiences of the oppression of sexism, but must be seen within the context of their experience of racism. For some the struggle with pervasive racism must take precedence over struggles as women who face additional discrimination because of their sex. The differences in the struggles for white women and for women of color must be seen. While white women frequently struggle to move *into* the work force outside the home, black women have seldom had the opportunity to be homemakers in their own homes without also laboring in the work force outside their homes. The goals of these racially different women as they struggle for wholeness and liberation may be very different goals. (Joseph: 1981).

Continuing Limitations of Sex-Defined Roles. Even while we experience tremendous repercussions of change that has been and is taking place in the redefining of sex roles, there is much that remains bound by traditional sex-defined role patterns. The implications such patterns carry are not evident without intentional consideration.

Sex-defined roles influence areas of stress and create particular problems for women. Theology and psychology support sex roles that have been defined and upheld by society. Roles are given different values and these values affect the self-worth of persons who see themselves as confined to particular roles and who are convinced of the role value. Low self-esteem, negative self-image and lack of identity are results for women who experience being confined to roles that are not valued (Friedan: 1963).

Economic Issues. Sex-role stereotyping contributes to the growth of a phenomenon known as "the feminization of poverty." Women and their dependent children make up the majority of the nation's poor. The gap between the poverty of women with dependent children and the poverty of males is increasing rapidly (Ehrenreich and Stallard: 1982). The continuing assumption that the man is the support of the family encourages disparity in wages in which women receive an average of only forty-six cents to each dollar a man receives (Gwartney-Gibbs: 1984). Work defined as "women's work" pays less than comparable work that is seen as "man's work." Women's work is valued less whether the woman is in a job defined as "women's work" or in a job considered "men's work." When women fill positions that are traditionally "men's work" they are paid less than men at the same level. When women do "men's work" they are paid less than men doing the same work. Salaries for pastors have not been an exception.

While the assumption that men provide primary support for women and children prevails, the numbers of women who are heads of households with dependent children are increasing. These working women are paid as though they *don't* have to live on what they earn. The situation for women of color is even worse.

For women who are employed outside the home either by necessity or by choice the expectations are that they continue to perform homemaking roles while they also function in full-time employment outside of the home. Performing well in all that is required in these roles is stress-producing. Couples with or without children in which both adults are employed often maintain the expectation that the woman will carry the burden of responsibility for homemaking chores (Blumstein and Schwartz: 1983). Even when the man "helps out around the house" it is often understood as just that—he is helping her with *her* work. He is being benevolent when both parties feel that the work is really hers to do. When both understand that half of the responsibility is his, the perspective on the work changes.

Identity Issues. Traditionally, women have withheld the shaping of their identities until they have found (or been found by) the men who become their husbands. This has been understood as a legitimate part of female development and identity formation (Erikson: 1968). The typical American practice of women taking the family names of their husbands when they marry is symbolic of this perception of female identity. While some males are raised to fill particular roles as farmer, minister, lawyer, for example, some females have been raised to become *wives* of farmers, ministers or lawyers. Few females have been raised to be farmers, ministers or lawyers themselves. Female identity has been understood as derivative and secondary. Women have been known by the men to whom they are primarily related—as wife, as daughter or even as secretary. Derivative identity leads to particular stresses with which women find themselves coping.

A woman whose primary identity has been as "wife of" and who fills the traditional role of support to her husband and his work finds life transitions can bear particular problems. When a woman whose identity was bound up in her husband and his work is widowed, who is she? After his death she can claim identity as "widow of" and even take up and fill the position his death left vacant. She remains derivative even in his absence. An alternative for her might be to begin to define herself, to establish her identity apart from what she has derived from him. There is not much societal support for such an exploration on her part. Her route, in either case even with the burden of her loss, is probably easier than that of the woman in late middle or old age who is divorced by the husband from whom she has derived identity and role as well as financial support. The widow may be left with pension, social security and insurance policies. The divorcee may be left with none of these.

"Gray Divorcee" is a phrase being used to describe the woman over 60 years of age who is being divorced by her husband. The *New York Times Magazine* in December 1982 reported on experiences of the increasing numbers of women who fall into this category. The divorces are initiated by husbands and leave women whose roles have been derivative and home-bound without marketable skills or work experience. With these over-60 women the problem is magnified by their lack of support systems. The void created by children who have left home is compounded by the loss of the abandoning husband. The woman who has not had children may face this loss as an even greater trauma. What does she have "to show" for those many years of marriage and devotion? A life lived in dependence without the development of marketable skills creates an overwhelming dilemma for a woman who may be left without an income. Derivative and dependent existence not only precludes skill development but also creates low self-esteem. Forced to be on her own the woman is not only left without skills but also lacks ego strength and confidence required to develop a new life and face new endeavors.

Women whose entire sense of identity is grounded in their homemaking and mothering roles face life crises in the loss of these roles. Being mother as definition of one's self and identity faces limitations when one can no longer reproduce or take care of children. The onset of menopause, the necessity for a hysterectomy or the realization of the "empty nest" circumstance may bring home the limitations inherent in an identity grounded in motherhood. Who is this woman when she is no longer able to function as mother? Who is she to herself? Who is she in the community?

Body Issues. Women also have been encourage to find their value and identity as women in their bodies—physical beauty and breast size being manifestations of this in addition to ability to reproduce. A woman whose identity and self-worth hinge on her physical attractiveness (according to predominant cultural norms) is likely to arrive at a point in life at which she experiences some loss of attractiveness. She may experience this as a loss of worth and loss of identity as a woman. The very beautiful film stars who spend their latter years in seclusion may be symbolic of this experience for women. Woman is defined by society as youthfully attractive. Mastectomy and hysterectomy may be experienced as primary assaults on a woman's identity when her identity is connected with breasts or with being mother (whether potential or actual). A woman who is unable to bear children may face similar identity or self-worth issues when being mother is felt to be essential. Over the past four decades the image of the ideal female body has steadily lost weight—almost ten pounds per decade. The ideal Marilyn Monroe figure is no longer in style and would be considered today to be a "fuller figure." Women experience great pressure to conform to the current ideal. Body image demands go with role assignments. Dieting is a major preoccupation for women. Women feeling valued for their appearance are vulnerable to low self-esteem when they do not meet the demands of "the image."

This preoccupation with being thin contributes to the growth in the numbers of females who are suffering from anorexia nervosa and bulimia. The adolescent and pre-adolescent female feels the pressure to be thin most keenly. Victims of anorexia nervosa pursue a route of self-starvation that is sometimes fatal. Many victims live with this problem for years—sometimes maintaining very minimal body weight, ceasing to have menstrual cycles and halting physical development. Far from being lethargic, the anorexic is frequently hyperactive. Anorexia is often coupled with bulimia—gorging followed with forced vomiting—and other means that quickly rid the body of food before calories and nutrients are absorbed. Therapists who have studied and worked with anorexics are aware of some family patterns that seem to contribute to the onset and continuation of this disorder. I would emphasize that dynamics within society that demand of women a particular body size and type and confine women to particular roles also contribute to these eating disorders. The anorexic who is pre-adolescent is sometimes trying very hard not to develop into a woman

(Chernin: 1981). What is she trying to avoid? What does she know about being a woman that urges her to resist her own development toward maturity?

Violence Against Women

Violent acts against women are manifestations of sex-defined roles and their accompanying attitudes. Forms that this violence takes include rape, battering and incest. Many churches and pastoral counselors seldom deal with these forms of violence. We have denied the existence and extent of these kinds of violence. Women have been the victims of these violent acts and also victims of our denial that they occur and victims of blame that they cause these acts. We are reluctant to believe that these forms of violence span every economic, social, educational and racial barrier. They are not perpetrated exclusively by uneducated lower class males. The perpetrators are often upstanding and respected citizens who are fervent in their religious beliefs. The victims are not seductive youth and sleazy women, but include very small children and old women. The myths around these crimes of violence shape attitudes and expectations that may be expressed in pastoral counseling responses.

How the act is understood and interpreted by the pastoral counselor will influence the effectiveness of the counseling that is offered for the victim or for the perpetrator. A traditional psychoanalytic approach to the female who claims to be a victim of incest would see her experience as fantasy rather than as reality (Masson: 1984). She would be helped to see why she needed to create that fantasy. She would not be helped to cope with the destructive impact of this particular violence on her—emotionally or physically. Other attitudes would hold the woman as being to blame for the violence to her that has occurred. The woman's own initial reaction to violence toward her is to blame herself for the incident. She immediately thinks, "What did I do to provoke him?" The pastoral counselor's approach can alleviate this blame or reinforce it.

A Pastoral Situation. One pastor reported a conversation with a young woman in his congregation. His report emphasized how beautiful the woman is and the fact that he, the pastor, did not know her husband. He noticed the bruises on her face, but waited for her to mention them. This exchange occurred several minutes into the conversation.

Carol: My husband did this to me. I thought I might as well tell you.
Pastor: He hit you pretty hard!
Carol: Yes, he did. It still hurts a lot. And it's the last time he'll do that!

Pastor: You know, Carol, I have known you a long time, but I don't know
         your husband well. Do you love him?
Carol: I don't know right now.
Pastor: Does he love you? Why did he hit you? Is he jealous of you?

As the conversation proceeded it seemed like the provocation for the beat-
ing had indeed been the husband's feeling jealous because his wife came
home from work late and had been talking with some male co-workers.
The pastor discussed the situation:

> When she came to see me I thought she might have been to
> blame for her husband's striking her. So I asked, "Why did he hit
> you? Is he jealous of you? I can see why a man could be jealous
> of a wife who is that beautiful."

The pastor seemed satisfied that his suspicion about the jealousy of the
husband was proven to be correct. Carol was encouraged to work harder
within the marriage and not give her husband any cause for jealousy.

The pastor in this situation presents an illustration of a societally
borne attitude about women being to blame for violence done to them.
This attitude enabled the pastor to deal with the surface problem and avoid
deeper troubles in the relationship or in the husband. The solution arrived
at with this pastor's help encourages Carol to feel responsible for what her
husband does to her. It forces Carol to try very hard not to "create" jealousy in her husband. She is left with the responsibility for keeping him safe
from these feelings.

It is also important to note that in this incident the pastor waits for
Carol to mention what has happened even though her bruises are quite evident. In doing this he demonstrates the unwillingness of the church to acknowledge violence toward women. Avoidance of "interfering" may take
more priority than the welfare of the woman.

When the pastor initiated a meeting with Carol's husband, he reported that the husband was a very likeable man and also very handsome,
demonstrating that the men who do such violence are not stereotypical
brutes. Would this perception of the husband further support blaming
Carol?

Marie Marshall Fortune's book on sexual violence (1983) marks a
growing awareness of sexual violence against women. Her discussion that
defines "consenting adults" enables the reader to distinguish between sexual activity and sexual violence. The latter part of her book is directed toward pastors and pastoral counselors who are in the position to respond to
such violence. Pornography and sexual harassment are other forms of vi-

olence against women that need to be interpreted accurately by the pastoral counselor.

Sex-defined roles and attitudes maintain that women are subordinate to men and should be submissive. They include images of the manipulative or nagging wife, the provocative whore, and the castrating bitch, all daughters of the evil that Eve brought into Adam's life. Violence against such images seems justified or at least understandable. At the other extreme we have the idealized daughters of Mary—virginal and pure. If a woman cannot measure up to this latter image, violence toward her is to be anticipated. These images are extreme, but are a part of woman's self-perception and society's messages to her.

Skills in Pastoral Counseling

Good skills in pastoral counseling alone are not sufficient for good pastoral counseling of women. There is a particular necessity for dealing with one's attitudes and expectations regarding female and male differences, roles and relationships for pastoral counseling to be most effective. The pastoral counselor (either male or female) has been influenced by stereotyped role definitions, attitudes and expectations communicated by the predominant culture. These attitudes and expectations form impediments to effective pastoral counseling. In order to diminish these limitations on counseling it is necessary for pastoral counselors to experience what might be called "consciousness raising." Awareness of the ways that fixed role expectations influence interpretations and responses requires new consciousness of the expectations and attitudes one holds.

Stereotypical Attitudes in Counseling. Dorothy was a timid 23 year old who had recently left her husband Joe after only a year of marriage. Her history included a life of domination by her mother who still called her every day, and inability to take over management of her own life. She had taken the step to leave Joe and was struggling with a decision about divorce or returning to work out a better relationship with him. Dorothy was full of fears and resentments, afraid of living fully and resenting that she had not been able to do so. She had found little support and encouragement in her life and had taken few steps on her own. She visited a pastoral counselor not certain about what she wanted from counseling but needing help in finding direction in her life. After a few moments during which she described her present situation, the pastoral counselor asked how she felt about her situation:

D. I'm—I guess—I'm feeling very bad.

P. You're feeling very badly about it.

D. And I don't want it to be a—don't want to be a failure at the marriage and—I don't—and—I'd rather us be, you know, together. I don't—I just can't live with him.

P. You left him, that's what I understand. Well, you feel bad, uh—uh——and did I catch you saying that you felt you had failed, or you don't want to feel that you've failed?

D. Well, I guess both things. And I feel as though I have—I—I mean I always thought that—I—when I got married it was going to be forever and *(pause)* . . .

P. Yes?

D. . . . that's the way it was supposed to be and that's the way it would be for me.

P. How do you feel towards him now?

D. *(pause)* Well, I guess—I just—you know really—still love him but I can't live with him.

P. Would you care to tell me why?

D. Ah—because he doesn't care about me.

P. Ummmm, you don't feel that he loves you?

D. No. I don't think he ever did.

P. Well, then you pulled out of the relationship to protect something. What was it you wanted to protect?

D. *(pause)* I guess—ah—it got so I didn't know what—what—anything was true—what—was true about anything but it was. I would think things were one way and he would say, "No they are another way," and so I didn't even know what I was feeling about anything.

P. Well, how were you reacting to his attitudes toward you as a person?

D. Well, I guess I would cry a lot and then sometimes I'd get angry. It was very—it make me very—you know—very unhappy. It made me feel bad about myself.

P. Were you able to sit down and talk to him about what he was doing to you?

D. I tried to and then he would say, "No, that's not right."

P. In other words, your judgments about his attitude toward you were not right. Which would mean then, I would suppose, that he would recognize he really loves you. You were feeling neglected by him but he's saying, "No, you're wrong." So what does that mean? What is he saying?

D. Well, that sounds as though he does.

P. It would *seem* so. Now, did you ever ask him what his reactions are to your attitudes? You've told him what your attitudes are and what your attitudes are to his reactions. Have you ever asked him how he's reacting to you?

D. Yes. But he won't say anything about it.

Dorothy continued to explain that Joe was that way while they dated, but she expected him to change with marriage. She described how she had tried to work on the marriage and felt there was nothing more she could do to make it better. She exhibited great ambivalence because she also expressed desire for the marriage to work. They continued:

P. . . . When you came to see me, did you come with the hope that maybe I'd help find some way for you to get back together?

D. Uh huh.

P. You did. So you didn't just come to get some things off your chest?

D. No.

P. You really want to do some hard thinking about how to rebuild this marriage. How long have you been married?

D. Oh, it's only been about a year.

P. You think that you've given enough time to really develop as a relationship?

D. Well, it seems as though it was just getting worse.

P. Getting worse—you sat down together but not any progress was made with that. Do you feel that you have in any way contributed to the problems?

D. Well, I think that he wasn't satisfied with what I would do. You know, he wasn't satisfied. He was always complaining about what I was doing—the way I did things. So I guess that I *(unclear)* was contributing.

When the pastoral counselor was asked about his interpretation of Dorothy's situation he responded:

P. Well, I think—I think she acted just in the typically *inarticulate* and *dumb* way that many wives do who are—ah—who are lousing up their marriage. I think that if the facts were known—ah—the young man is filled with all kinds of resentment because—ah—things are not in good order when he comes home and—ah—expresses his resentment by throwing his stuff around and he can't—ah—feel gracious and cordial in relation to his wife so he doesn't say anything. And the possibilities are that if she could—ah—shape up and really fulfill his expectancies which don't sound like—ah—too great—and it would really sweeten him up and their marriage could get going again.

He saw Dorothy as insensitive in not recognizing what might be producing Joe's attitude. The pastoral counselor added that he saw Dorothy as a "slob" and a type that he had "run into before."

The attitude of this counselor toward Dorothy expressed blame and contempt toward her. He saw her as the one who was to blame for the difficulties in the marriage relationship. It was a matter of her more effectively performing roles expected of one who is female. If she filled her role better Joe would be more amenable and the marriage would work.

The counselor who is not bound by stereotyped expectations would be able to help Dorothy work toward taking charge of her own life whether this would turn out to be within or outside of the marriage. The counselor might become aware of dimensions of Dorothy's ambivalence toward her marriage and her relationship with Joe and enable her to explore these and evaluate them to aid her in making future decisions. Her struggle to acknowledge and express her feeling would be part of the agenda. Dorothy might be encouraged to invite Joe to be a part of the counseling so that clarity in their communications could be facilitated by the counselor. The denigrating, negative attitude toward Dorothy would not be likely to appear in the absence of stereotypical sex-role assumptions. The primary goal for Dorothy might not be that she continue in the marriage, but that she be able to break patterns of dependency and come to be in charge of her own life; not that she live irresponsibly in relationships with others, but that she live with some responsibility for herself and her decisions, having awareness of her feelings and assurance of her self-worth. What a different outcome for Dorothy would result from work with a pastoral counselor who would not hold her bound to a stereotype of what woman should be!

Changing Attitudes. Attitude change can be initiated by experiences that raise one's consciousness. Purposefully allowing oneself to be exposed to attitudes that are different and reading books such as those included among the resources mentioned here are routes to new consciousness. Bringing one's theology to bear on culturally endorsed attitudes may also shed new light on previously held attitudes. Theological positions of some pastoral counselors also need to be encountered with the heart of the Gospel message. A strong base for doing pastoral counseling of women should be grounded in one's theology.

The Pastor's Sexuality

The sexuality of the pastoral counselor is an issue in the counseling of women. Historically most pastoral counselors have been male and their counselees have been female. The issue of the pastoral counselor's sexuality is not confined to this configuration of male counselor-female counselee. Sexuality is present in every human relationship (Nelson: 1978).

Sexuality is a particular issue in pastoral counseling relationships. The focus for discussion here will be the relationship between male counselors and female counselees.

Pastoral counseling takes place within a context that both emphasizes and denies sexuality. Advertisement as we know it would cease to exist if the element of sexuality were removed. At the same time the church tends toward positions that deny the existence of sexuality or that see it alternately as "dirty" or as "sacred" dependent entirely upon the circumstances. We are expected to know all about sex while programs of sex education for children and youth are hotly debated. The state of our relationships to sexuality is confusing at best.

Needy and vulnerable counselees find pastoral counselors to be a source of strength and nourishment. Vulnerable people can be particularly attractive to those who are alert in responding to all who are in need. Women who seek pastoral counseling at times of need may experience feelings of loneliness and needs for affirmation, human warmth and closeness as well as need for understanding and guidance. The combined roles of counselor and pastor enhance the perception of the pastoral counselor as a safe person with whom vulnerability can be expressed. The safety factor may exist only in the perception and mind of the counselee if the pastoral counselor has not dealt with his or her stance on sexual behavior between pastoral counselor and counselee. Sexual activity between pastoral counselor and counselee, between pastor who counsels and parishioner is not a matter of mutually consenting adults (Fortune: 1983). The counselor is in a position of power in relation to the needing counselee. There cannot be a matter of free choice under such circumstances. Explicit sexual "acting out" cannot be seen as either theologically admissible or psychologically therapeutic. It is most fundamentally destructive. Human warmth and caring, closeness and touch are legitimate parts of pastoral counseling. To avoid expression of warmth or any physical touch is not an answer that creates safety. The answer lies in clarity about oneself in the professional role of pastor/counselor. The answer lies in keeping the welfare of the counselee as primary and one's personal needs as appropriately met elsewhere.

The Value of the Pastoral Counselor. Many of the issues which are of particular relevance for women are issues that have roots in matters of faith and spiritual growth. Sex-defined role perceptions that are foundational to many of the problems discussed here are not strictly cultural, social or psychological but have deep roots in our understanding of our faith and some of the teachings of the church. Theologians and other pastors have found biblical roots for male dominance of women and women's submission to men.

For a woman whose faith is of deep significance to her, the dimension added to counseling done with a pastoral counselor will have great importance. Matters of identity and self-worth are not solely matters of psychological importance but also carry significant spiritual dimensions. Pastoral counseling can provide the occasion for women to re-examine their faith and for engaging in spiritual growth. Women may be encouraged to develop more fully and utilize their gifts. Pastoral counseling may be the forum for the voice of God's grace to be heard by women who have experienced long standing low self-esteem. The church has been a force in discouraging women from expressing anger. Again the pastoral counselor has the opportunity to offer a counter-force as women's feelings are heard and accepted.

Pastoral counselors who find that they are unable to travel the route of hearing women's anger, of exploring with women the painful depths of experiences of incest and rape, or enabling women to break free from cultural stereotypes that define their existence, should not be doing pastoral counseling with women. Buried scars of experiences of incest, for example, are not readily brought forth by some women. The task requires ability to perceive the pain of the victim's willingness to admit its source and avoid blaming her. Pastoral counseling with women requires that the counselor become aware of attitudes and expectations held by society and individuals—especially her or his own attitudes and expectations. Pastoral counseling with women requires that culturally defined stereotypes be questioned and challenged and that new images of women be allowed to blossom.

Bibliography

Armstrong, L. *Kiss Daddy Goodnight*. New York: Simon and Schuster, 1978.

Bardwick, J. *Psychology of Women*. New York: Harper, 1971.

Blumstein, P. and P. Schwartz. *American Couples: Money, Work, Sex*. New York: Morrow, 1983.

Brady, K. *Father's Days*. New York: Seaview, 1979.

Broverman, I. and D. Broverman, et al. "Sex-Role Stereotypes and Clinical Judgments of Mental Health." *Journal of Consulting and Clinical Psychology*, 1970, 1-7.

Brownmiller, S. *Against Our Will: Men, Women and Rape*. New York: Bantam, 1975.

Chernin, K. *The Obsession: Reflections on the Tyranny of Slenderness*. New York: Harper, 1981.

Chodorow, N. *The Reproduction of Mothering*. Berkeley: University of California Press, 1978.

Cone, J. *My Soul Looks Back*. Nashville: Abingdon, 1982.

Ehrenrich, B. and K. Stallard. "The Nouveau Poor." *Ms.*, 1982, 21.

Erikson, E. *Identity: Youth and Crisis*. New York: Harper, 1976.

Fortune, M.M. *Sexual Violence, The Unmentionable Sin: An Ethical and Pastoral Perspective*. New York: Pilgrim, 1983.

Friedan, B. *The Feminine Mystique*. New York: Dell, 1963.

Gilligan, C. *In a Different Voice: Psychological Theory and Women's Development*. Cambridge: Harvard University Press, 1982.

Goldstein, V.S. "The Human Situations: A Feminine View." *The Journal of Religion*, 1960, 40, 100-112.

Gwartney-Gibbs. "Mid-Revolutionary Mores." *Ms.*, 1984, 12.

Horney, K. *Feminine Psychology*. New York: Norton, 1967.

Lips, H. and N.L. Colwill. *The Psychology of Sex Differences*. Englewood Cliffs: Prentice-Hall, 1978.

Joseph, G. and J. Lewis. *Common Differences: Conflicts in Black and White Feminist Perspectives*. New York: Doubleday, 1981.

Masson, J.M. *The Assault on Truth: Freud's Suppression of the Seduction Theory*. New York: Farrar, Straus and Giroux, 1984.

Mead, M. *Male and Female: A Study of the Sexes in a Changing World*. New York: Dell, 1949.

Miller, J.B. *Toward a New Psychology of Women*. Boston: Beacon, 1976.

Nelson, J. *Embodiment: An Approach to Sexuality and Christian Theology*. Minneapolis: Augsburg, 1978.

Olsen, R. *Changing Male Roles in Today's World*. Valley Forge: Judson, 1982.

Pearce, D. and H. McAdoo. "Women & Children Alone and in Poverty." National Advisory Council on Economic Opportunity, Washington, D.C., 1981.

Plaskow, J. *Sex, Sin and Grace: Women's Experience and the Theologies of Reinhold Niebuhr and Paul Tillich*. Washington, D.C.: University Press of America, 1980.

Ruether, R. *Sexism and God Talk: Toward a Feminist Theology*. Boston: Beacon, 1983.

Schaef, A.W. *Women's Reality*. Minneapolis: Winston, 1981.

Stoudenmire, J. "The Role of Religion in the Depressed Housewife." *Journal of Religion and Health*, 1976, 15, 62-67.

Task Force on Sex Bias and Sex Role Stereotyping in Psychotherapeutic Practice. "Guidelines for Therapy with Women." *American Psychologist*, 1978, 1122-23.

Trible, P. *God and the Rhetoric of Sexuality*. Philadelphia: Fortress, 1978.

Walker, A. *The Color Purple*. New York: Pocket Books, 1982.

Walker, L. *The Battered Woman*. New York: Harper, 1979.

Edward P. Wimberly

Minorities

Counseling and therapy within the American context have been described as culturally bound. In fact, counseling and therapy have been labeled as white middle-class professions that have served directly and indirectly to acculturate or assimilate persons from varied cultural backgrounds into a specific picture of mental health and wholeness without considering the unique cultural heritage of minority persons (Sue, 1981). Cultural boundness refers to values, theories, and practices rooted in and reflective of dominant American culture. Groups of persons whose historical, racial, and cultural backgrounds are different from dominant culture may experience counseling and therapy as culturally oppressive. Because of this oppression experienced in many minority persons, it is important for counseling and therapy to become cross-culturally conscious of the divergent minority groups and subcultures that exist in America. In addition to this, counseling and therapy also will have to become aware of their own culture and class-bound values and the verbal and non-verbal issues involved in counseling minorities.

Many efforts have been made by the counseling and therapy professions to address the culture and class-bound nature of their professions. This is also true of pastoral counseling. A major effort toward becoming cross-culturally sensitive took place in San Francisco in the summer of 1983 at the international Congress of Pastoral Counseling. This meeting discussed cross-cultural and international issues in pastoral counseling. This chapter is designed to continue this effort started in pastoral counseling in San Francisco with regard to cross-cultural sensitivity. This effort will focus on the cultural, racial, and historical factors that often cause problems to pastoral counselors, who have been trained in counseling and therapy models of dominant culture, when they confront counselees from minority groups.

The particular approaches employed in this discussion are the cultural variant model of conceptualizing cultural uniqueness of minority groups and the growth-wholeness practical model of pastoral counseling. These theoretical and practical perspectives will be applied primarily to Afro-Americans though a briefer treatment of other minority groups will also be included. The basic assumption is that the cultural variant model and the growth-wholeness counseling perspectives are applicable in general to all minority groups discussed in this chapter.

Definition of Minority

The term minority within the American context has been used to describe unmeltables in Anglo-American culture (Ethnic Minorities In The United Methodist Church, 1976). Anglo-American usually refers to white Americans of non-Spanish descent and includes northern and southern Europeans. Anglos represent the majority culture making up wider society in America. Unmeltables are primarily non-white populations whose racial characteristics have enabled them to be easily distinguishable from dominant Anglo-culture. These non-white populations include Afro-Americans, Hispanic Americans, native Americans (American Indians), and Asian Americans. Significant numbers of Near Eastern immigrants are in America, but the discussion here will concern the four primary ethnic minorities mentioned above.

Racial differences not only distinguish primary minorities in America. Language difficulties, cultural ancestry, historical-political considerations, and in some cases surnames also serve as distinguishing elements of minority groups in America. Some minority groups cling to their cultural identity, customs, and folkways while others have been forced to modify their traditional heritages because of policy and discrimination in wider society. Moreover, the Americanization process—a process in which minority groups adopt the values, lifestyles, and culture of dominant society—has not been completed among minority groups and will probably be slowed because of racial pride and emphasis on cultural pluralism. This means that the cultural heritages out of which minorities come will have to be addressed by wider society and by pastoral counseling.

Prior to giving detailed analysis of Afro-American cultural heritage it is important to examine the other three minority groups mentioned. Primary attention will be given to census data and to unique cultural heritage factors.

Hispanic Americans are distinguished primarily by the Spanish language, Spanish surnames and ancestry, and home origins in Mexico, Puerto Rico, Cuba, and Central and South America. In 1978 7.2 million Mexican Americans were in the United States (Cortes, 1980). This is by far the largest Hispanic group with the total number of Hispanics ranging from 11.2 to 17.5 million including illegal residents. As a group, Hispanics are undereducated, are overrepresented in occupations that are low paying and menial, and have high rates of unemployment when compared to the general population (Ruiz, 1981).

Hispanics are predominantly urban dwellers. Mexican Americans live primarily in the southwest; Puerto Ricans reside mostly in New York State and Connecticut, and Cubans are mostly found in Florida.

From a cultural heritage point of view Hispanics have a culture ancestry of rigid sex-role distinctions and an extended family tradition where kinfolk interact with one another across generations. There are also a rich Spanish language, religious traditions, food customs, and home medical remedies. The cultural ancestry and contemporary adherence to these traditions are distinct enough from Anglo culture to call attention to the need for culturally specific and relevant models of counseling and therapy. However, since Hispanics differ in the degree of adherence to tradition and assimilation into Anglo culture, great care is needed in choosing the correct treatment approaches with individuals and families of Spanish descent.

Hispanics who are Spanish dominant in their culture would need a bicultural approach or a Spanish culture specific program of counseling including the use of the Spanish language and family network strengths. Those Hispanic Americans who have assimilated into Anglo culture could respond favorably to treatment programs practiced in general by the majority of counselors and therapists in Anglo culture.

Native Americans or the American Indians are an important ethnic minority group which should be included in our discussion of minorities. Native Americans are perhaps the most consistently exploited and oppressed minority in America from a cultural standpoint. Very little attitudinal behavioral respect has been shown for native American culture by wider American society historically. Moreover, the exploitive oppressive outlook toward native American culture continues today through the activity of white professionals including counselors (Richardson, 1981).

The exploitation of native Americans over the years can be envisaged by examining the state of residence of many native Americans today. The 1970 census indicates that there were 800,000 native Americans (Spicer, 1980). Approximately 700,000 live west of the Mississippi River equally divided among the states of Oklahoma, Arizona, and California. States east of the Mississippi, excluding Michigan and Wisconsin, had approximately 120,000 or the remaining native American population. The lower numbers east of the Mississippi reflect decimation caused by European-introduced diseases brought by the colonists, warfare, massacres, and forced migration via government policy.

Culturally, many stereotypical notions of American Indians exist through the media which influence how professionals behave toward native Americans. For example, native Americans were not nomadic hunters or fishermen as popular notions would have it. Rather they were permanent settlers in villages and communities where they farmed and fished. Their community life was well organized around social, political, and agricultural models reflecting a rich and distinctive cultural ancestry of languages, religion, music and dance expression, tribal ritual, and ornamental dress. A rich variety of social customs existed among the different tribes in diverse geographical locations. While distinct cultural ancestry and native languages existed, forced assimilation through education has eventuated in a mix of dominant culture with native American culture. Indeed, culturally specific and relevant models of counseling could be helpful.

Economically, educationally, and occupationally native Americans are the most oppressed minority in America. This is an often ignored fact.

Asian Americans, like the native Americans and Hispanics, have a rich cultural ancestry. This minority group is composed of Chinese, Japanese, and Korean Americans. In 1970 there were 440,000 Chinese Americans (Lai, 1980), 600,000 Japanese Americans (Kitano, 1980), and 300,000 Korean Americans (Kim, 1980). Chinese Americans came to America soon after Europeans settled in the New World and were servants of Spaniards who settled in Mexico. In the eighteenth and nineteenth centuries many Chinese Americans settled on the West Coast because of American trade with China. American trade with Japan brought Japanese persons to America as early as the nineteenth century. Koreans also came to America as early as the nineteenth century, but the majority of them came after the Korean War in the 1950's.

Asian Americans have a cultural ancestry including language, social and family organization and customs, and complex religious heritages. The family values of loyalty and responsibility in the Asian American background are often in conflict with the value of individualism held by Anglo-oriented counseling and therapy models. Indeed, awareness of the cultural ancestry of Asian Americans by pastoral counselors is essential.

Not all minorities have assimilated completely into dominant American culture. In fact, biculturalarity exists in many minority groups in America in that there has been a wedding of distinct ancestral values, customs, and traditions with those of dominant American culture. Pastoral counselors must be aware of this biculturalarity and employ appropriate counseling and therapy models that take into consideration this cultural variance. Thus, knowledge of cultural heritages that are wedded to and are divergent from dominant American culture is an important aspect and prerequisite to counseling with the culturally different.

Afro-Americans

The writer of this chapter is an Afro-American who has become aware of the bicultural approach to counseling minorities because of his involvement with counseling black Americans. In this section an in-depth examination of the cultural heritage of black or Afro-Americans will be presented. This examination will present a conceptual paradigm that will illustrate the depth of cultural analysis needed when attempting to gain a cognitive grasp of the cultural uniqueness of minority clients when doing pastoral counseling with them. Such knowledge can be learned from cross-cultural literature and from minority clients through showing interest in cultural material when it arises in counseling.

Sensitivity of Afro-Americans to their cultural uniqueness emerged because of negative theories toward them existing in behavioral science literature. A black identity and consciousness emerged in the 1960's and 1970's through which black people sought to affirm their self-worth as whole persons in the face of negative stereotypes, racial and oppressive policies, and denied economic opportunities. Part of the efforts of black professionals and academicians has been to help black persons to reinterpret their personal and corporate identity and history in ways that affirm black pigmentation and their cultural heritage.

Also included in this reinterpretation has been an effort to help black folk accept the historical importance of black families and extended families. In addition there have been efforts to help black people to reject uncritical assimilation into white middle-class values at the expense of black folkways. Black professionals and academicians also challenged the research done by white scholars that portrayed black people as pathological living in disrupted families and communities. In short, black consciousness was an attempt to affirm the positive aspects of black life and living that had been ignored by wider society. The result of this effort to affirm the positives by black academicians and behavioral scientists has been the development of a perspective called the cultural variant model.

The cultural variant model recognizes the differences that exist between black culture and wider culture and how the cultural divergence influences individual, family, and group behavior of minority persons. This model seeks to explain individual and corporate behavior and life from within the black community context (Allen, 1978). This model counteracts the cultural deviant and pathological models that exist and describe black culture as an inferior divergence from white middle-class culture.

Moreover, the cultural variant model enables researchers to explore the normal majority of black persons and their family and community strengths rather than the convenient problem populations such as mental patients, prisoners, and welfare clients. Thus, the focus of researchers from the cultural variant model has been on the black family and extended family, male and female relationships, and values that undergird the health and growth of black persons.

What follows is an examination of the strengths of black people from the perspective of the cultural variant model. However, some statistics and vital descriptive data are essential prior to the discussion of the strengths of the black community and the implications of these strengths for pastoral counseling.

Black persons have been 12% of the American population since 1890. In 1970 there were 24 million Afro-Americans (Holt, 1980). West Africa was the origin of Afro-Americans who came to America with the original explorers and the first settlers. Afro-Americans came as bond servants from places in Africa we now call Angola, Southern Nigeria, Ghana, Senegal, Gambia, Sierra Leone, Benia, and Mozambique (Holt, 1980).

Culturally, Afro-Americans inherited diverse social systems, African dialects, and religions. However, the cultural diversity was undergirded by a common world view based on kinship ties, economic organization, and the nature of the physical and spiritual world. The corporate identity of persons, the social-wholistic contextual nature of persons, cooperation with the rhythm of nature, interaction between the here-and-now world with the spiritual realm, a present-time orientation, and the importance of the extended family were important distinctive values inherited from Africa. These cultural inherited values are reflected today among the majority of black people and have been integrated in a bicultural manner with the dominant culture. Thus, there is a significant bicultural orientation among many Afro-Americans.

Although racism and oppression of black Americans had existed historically and exists contemporarily also, the remarkable strengths of black culture to enable black people to transcend oppression and to grow with dignity in spite of racism have often been overlooked. The capacity to transcend and to live with dignity has been attributed to the African heritage of kinship ties undergirded by a spiritual world view. The historical strength producing kinship ties can be envisaged in the black family, in the black extended family, and in black male and female roles.

Recent research on the black family between 1750 and 1925 (Gutman, 1976) reveals the presence of stable dual-headed households in slavery and after slavery. Moreover, this research also reveals that husbands and wives as parents were central figures in the rearing of their children. Such households made up about 80% of the total population in southern and northern black communities during this period.

This internal dynamics facilitating the stability in black families during this period included cumulative slave experience which fashioned rules of conduct for life within the black community. Such rules included commitment to long-lasting marriages and kinship naming practices that reflected strong kinship ties. Many examples of marriages lasting more than 50 years during slavery were found by Gutman (1976). He also pointed to the record concerning the efforts of separated black families to reunite after emancipation from slavery. Moreover, examples exist of freedmen returning to slave states risking capture in order to free members of their own families who were still in slavery. Family loyalty and family commitment were the norms rather than the exceptions for the black families during the 1750–1925 period.

Following 1925 the black family began to suffer breakups. These laid the foundation for pathological models of research on the black family that have emerged since 1925. Single-parent families headed by females increased in the period after 1925. Absentee fathers also began to increase during this time. However, the breakup of the black family was reflective of a more general technological and industrial impact affecting the American family in general. It did not reflect inherent pathology within the black family itself. The breakup of black families came when families in general were under a great siege. Kinship loyalties and strong extended families are not valued in technological society as a rule.

The strengths of the black family reported during 1750–1925 have been traced to African ancestral emphasis on kinship ties (Gutman, 1976). The extended family was central to black life during this period of history and is central today (Martin and Martin, 1978). The black extended family has been a multigenerational, interdependent kinship system having rules of obligation, organized around a household, but extending across geographical lines (Martin and Martin, 1978). In the black extended family there is a built-in mutual aid system for the maintenance of the whole extended network financially and emotionally. Moreover, single parent families fit well within the extended family network which points to the fact that the single parent, black female-headed household is not cut off and vulnerable. The fact that the black extended family rallies around extended family members during crisis periods is a central strength of the black family.

There is also a subextended family within the black extended family (Martin and Martin, 1981). A subextended family is similar to the nuclear family in that it is composed of the husband, wife, and children. However, the difference between it and the nuclear family is that the subextended family is not cut off from relatives in the extended family. The subextended family envisages itself as part of the extended family and maintains close emotional ties with the extended family. Along with the single parent family the subextended family receives the mutual support of the extended family.

Other patterns exist which reinforce mutuality within black families. One such pattern is the egalitarian allocation of roles in black families that enables them to be more adaptive toward economic limitations placed on black males in a racist society (Allen, 1978). Because black women have traditionally had a role in employment outside the home, researchers have mislabeled this fact as a matriarchal and dysfunctional pattern in black families. That is, black women have been compared to their white counterparts who traditionally were housewives. However, black women working outside the home is not a sign of dysfunctionality or of a matriarchal pattern. Rather, it points to a cultural pattern of egalitarianism where black men and women have traditionally pulled together in order to enable the family to survive. This mutuality in black male and female relationships is supported by research that reveals that black men are more supportive of their wives' working than are white men (Allen, 1978). Also there is mutuality in sharing household chores, child rearing, and decision making.

Correlative to the egalitarian pattern is a pattern of flexibility in the assignment of roles within the black family (Allen, 1978). The emphasis is on function within black families rather than on structure, and roles are assigned so that the family survives.

There is also research that indicates that role stereotyping in black families is less severe than in wider society. Black children are raised androgynously by black parents. That is, black males and females are socialized into a synthesis of same sex-role characteristics. Aggressiveness, independence, nurturance, and emotional expressiveness are social expectations for both black male and female children.

While not all black families are egalitarian with mutual and androgynous roles, it is important for pastoral counseling to be aware of the cultural divergence existing in black families. More precisely, pastoral counseling needs to be aware of the inherent strengths of black families so that these strengths can be drawn on in the process of counseling. Extended family values, egalitarian values, and androgynous values are strengths. However, these values may clash with the nuclear family, male hierarchical, and individual values of wider society. Yet, the pastoral counselor needs to be value free enough to employ black family strengths in helping to resolve counseling problems.

In addition to paying close attention to the strengths of black families, the pastoral counselor needs to become familiar with the cultural specific patterns that directly influence pastoral counseling with black people.

These concerns include cultural specific traits such as non-verbal communication, people oriented values, views of responsibility and locus of control, and attitudes toward the profession of counseling in itself.

With regard to non-verbal communication behavior, black culture tends to be a high-context culture (Smith, 1981). In contrast to low-context cultures which place a greater reliance on the verbal part of the message, high-context cultures emphasize non-verbal aspects of communication. Black grass-roots culture, in contrast to the black middle-class and white culture, is considerably more oriented toward non-verbal communication. The non-verbal communication has to do with culturally learned cues of sending and receiving messages and patterns of eye contact. It has been pointed out that black people are keen in their ability to read non-verbal cues of both white and black people (Smith, 1981). Also it is not necessary for black people to look you in the eye at all times when communicating. Also many black persons do not nod their heads or make little noises to show the other person that they are listening. (Often white counselors interpret some of these non-verbal styles of communicating as lack of interest and fear.)

High-context cultures tend also to emphasize group identification as opposed to low-context cultures that are more individually oriented (Smith, 1982). This is related to the kinship cultural orientation discussed earlier. Thus, black people tend to be more people-oriented than thing-oriented. Service vocations are emphasized over thing-oriented technological vocations, for example. Concern and service to family and community are central and are viewed as a natural part of life rather than as a burden.

Another important factor specific to the counseling context is that black people tend to be more relationally oriented than analytically oriented in cognitive style (Hale, 1982). In the analytical mode abstraction is emphasized and logic is organized in a linear way. That is, time is a continuum and authority and responsibility are hierarchical. Black people, in general, tend to be meaning-oriented, global and whole-picture focused, and not geared to the analysis of parts. They infer conclusions from relationships more than deriving knowledge from abstract thought. Emotional involvement and participation, immediate responses and action are more important ways of learning than abstract concepts. In short, black persons, as a general rule, tend to be gestalt learners.

The gestalt relational-cognitive style and non-verbal orientation of black people mean that pastoral counseling needs to be more participatory and action-oriented when working with black persons. High verbal, non-participatory, passive, and interpretive models of therapy may not be culturally specific enough for many black counselees. However, such a conclusion may reflect the needs of white counselees also, but who tolerate more cognitive approaches to counseling in order to get the help they need.

Other important issues for pastoral counseling with black persons are the concern for locus of control and locus of responsibility. Locus of control relates to cultural world views where a person envisages his or her life as controlled internally by one's own values and choices or externally controlled by outside influences (Sue, 1981). Locus of responsibility refers to where a person places the blame or responsibility for what has happened to him or her (Sue, 1981). Counseling and therapy as professions tend to emphasize the internal locus of control and personal responsibility for individual behavior. However, the reality of racism and oppression with regard to black people tends to coerce them into envisioning themselves as pawns of fate. Pastoral counselors need to be sensitive to this external orientation in order to help the black person to focus on the goal of establishing realistic internal control in one's life and to take realistic responsible steps toward resolving wider community-lined problems affecting his or her life without the counselor's denying the validity of external problems.

Attitudes exist in the black community that may not facilitate the use of many models of counseling and therapy (Smith, 1981). For example, discussing family matters with outsiders is often considered a violation of family ethics. Personal problems are often carried to kinship members and especially to the mother. Moreover, a general feeling exists that it is in church where one's deepest thoughts and emotional stresses should be addressed. Other attitudes hindering the use of counseling include not seeing the value of childhood experiences as the cause of poor mental health, viewing mental health/illness as environmentally determined, and the rejection of the intrapsychic model of counseling and therapy (Smith, 1981). Often the role of the counselor is viewed as alien, and many do not see how counseling can help the fight for survival. Counselees want specific advice on matters and tend to see white counselors as irrelevant to black contexts because of the menacing social and economic problems that black people face.

The final counseling concern for this section has to do with the issues of transference and countertransference. For some white counselors, black counselees stir up unconscious feelings that must be addressed in the counselor's personal supervision and therapy (Wimberly, 1976).

On the other hand, black clients may consciously or unconsciously subject white counselors to a series of racial tests to ascertain whether or not the pastoral counselor is racially prejudiced. It is important that racial issues be confronted early in the initial counseling in facilitative ways so that the way becomes clear for helping the client with his problem. Overreacting or underreacting (countertransference) by the pastoral counselor to the tests of the black client (transference) is not facilitative to the counseling process. Rather, the white pastoral counselor should address racial concerns in ways that the counselor's competence for handling the presenting problem is demonstrated. The counselor should take the racial suspiciousness of the client as a serious concern that needs to be treated with exploration. The attitude often communicates to the client openness on the part of the counselor, and counseling can begin after the rapport is established.

This section on Afro-Americans has presented some basic cultural issues unique to Afro-Americans that are essential to know and understand when counseling with black minority persons. Attention to cultural biases of the counselor and unique cultural facets of black culture can improve the ability of the pastoral counselor to be facilitative and effective in helping black persons and their families to grow.

The Growth Model of Pastoral Counseling

The previous section focused on the unique cultural orientation of Afro-Americans which seemed to come into conflict with commonly held assumptions undergirding many models of counseling and therapy practices in wider culture. For example, extended family values, the values of androgyny and egalitarianism, non-verbal communication styles, active and participatory involvement, relational cognitive styles, external locus of control and responsibility, the need for concrete advice, and the rejection of intrapsychic models of counseling and therapy all seem to suggest that counseling and therapy models that emphasize individualism, abstract verbal behavior, intrapsychic interpretation, and one-to-one counseling are at variance with some segments of Afro-American culture. What this variance means is that an alternative model of counseling and therapy is needed—one that can utilize the strengths of Afro-American culture. Such a model is the growth counseling model (Clinebell, 1979, 1981).

The growth counseling model is a human wholeness approach to the helping process developed in the theorizing and practice of pastoral counselor Howard Clinebell. Its basic goal is to facilitate the maximum development of a person's full possibilities at each stage of the life cycle in ways that enable the growth of others and contributes as well to the development of society. It is growth-oriented in that it draws on whatever methods and resources are necessary to liberate blocked growth. It draws on resources in traditional and contemporary psychotherapies and growth-oriented psychologies and relates them with the growth-wholeness resources of the Hebrew Christian tradition. Moreover, it draws eclectically from a variety of behavioral-science therapeutic models for its growth-wholeness orientation including the resources from the human-wholeness movement, relational systems and radical therapies, and spiritual growth models. It emphasizes growth-health-systems values in contrast to individualistic, hierarchical, pathological, and medical orientations. It seeks to focus on a person's strengths rather than on weaknesses. Finally, the social network is utilized whenever possible to facilitate growth.

The value of the growth counseling model for counseling black people and the culturally different needs some exploration at the risk of redundancy. Its emphasis on the inherent strengths of persons, the importance of the natural social network of systems for healing, the constructive aspects of behavior, and the facilitative role of the community, education, and action/participation methodologies and therapies enables the growth model of pastoral counseling to address the needs of many minority persons and their families. Its rejection of hierarchical and power models of the client/counselor relationship makes it possible for the counselor to learn from the culturally different client. Moreover, growth counseling also recognizes the impact of injustice and negative social forces on personality development and takes seriously a person's struggle with injustice. The model, when applied appropriately, has the potential for affirming the role of the unique cultural resources of African Americans for growth and wholeness.

In addition to the philosophical orientation of the growth model, which is foundational for pastoral counseling with minorities, there are key skills, processes, and issues which must accompany the application of the growth model. The specific skills of empathy, immediacy, self-disclosure, respect and challenging seem to be central. Ability to address issues of victimization attitudes emerging in transference is crucial, and the ability of the pastoral counselor to spend time educating the counselee and his or her family concerning the counseling process is key. These skills, processes, and issues need further exploration.

Empathy is an effort to be present and to give attention to the specific meaning world view of the person seeking counseling. A world view generally consists of ideas, attitudes, and feelings that inform the counselee's behavior whether that behavior is functional or dysfunctional. Seeking to understand the world view surrounding the presenting problem of the counselee helps to create an environment of care and acceptance that is essential for a successful counseling process. Such skills as being interested in what the client is saying, attending and listening posture, exploratory responses to the counselee's utterances and brief facilitative statements summarizing the world view help to build an empathic environment.

Immediacy refers to the capacity of the pastoral counselor to address the dynamics taking place between the pastoral counselor and the client when it occurs in concrete counseling situations. Usually immediacy is discussed within the counseling relationship when it arises in connection with the presenting problem. For example, the client may respond to the pastoral counselor as if the pastoral counselor represented a significant other from the counselee's past. Treating the counselor as if he or she is a significant person in the client's past is called transference, and addressing the transference when it occurs is called immediacy.

Often the counselee from a minority group will bring into the counseling relationship concerns that relate to the counselee's interaction with the majority group which need to be addressed if counseling is to progress. Addressing such issues is particularly crucial in the first stages of counseling when the counselee is testing the openness of pastoral counselor to minority group concerns. The skills of immediacy, where the concern of the counselee/counselor relationship are addressed, is important in the testing period. It facilitates a working relationship. Also disclosing one's own struggle with majority-minority group concerns in ways that convey openness and desire for learning from the client about his or her world view can be helpful in facilitating the counseling relationship. Self-disclosure can help facilitate immediacy.

Respect is another core ingredient which is an attitudinal skill usually related to accepting the counselee as a person of worth who has the right to make the major decisions concerning his or her life. Respect for the minority client is usually developed through how the pastoral counselor is empathic and responds to the racial and cultural issues when they implicitly or explicitly arise. Also respect is established when a working contract or agreement is made between the client and pastoral counselor. A contract is a firm but flexible agreement between the pastoral counselor and client concerning the goals and responsibilities of each participant in the counseling relationship. It includes the steps and responsibilities the client will exercise in resolving the presenting problem and the steps the pastoral counselor will take in helping the client to resolve the presenting problem.

With a contract defined, the hope is that the pastoral counselor will avoid the kind of paternalism that ignores the client's own strengths and capacities for resolving his or her problem. To take away the client's right to resolve his or her problem is to show a lack of respect. To allow the client to give the decision-making possibilities to the pastoral counselor is also a demonstration of lack of respect to the client. The role of the pastoral counselor with minorities is to help the minority person exercise whatever degree of decision-making capacity the person has over his or her life.

After a working relationship has been established between the counselee and the pastoral counselor, dysfunctional patterns of behavior that do not contribute to the resolving of the presenting problem can be challenged. Challenging is a counseling skill that gently brings to the client's attention ideas, attitudes, and behavioral patterns that prevent the client(s) from achieving stated goals or resolving the presenting problem. Dysfunctional ideas and behavior on the part of the counselee presuppose that a contract concerning the presenting problem has been reached. To challenge an idea or behavior without having a firm contract is to show disrespect for the client, and it allows for the introduction of culturally biased values by the pastoral counselor. However, if a firm contract is established, then the pastoral counselor can facilitatively introduce responses that challenge non-productive attitudes and behaviors related to the resolution of the presenting problem.

One general pattern I have noticed when working with minority clients is a victimization attitude. Victimization is adopting the attitude of a helpless, dependent victim in the face of real or imagined suffering at the hands of others. Acknowledging the reality of minority group victimization at the hands of wider society's attitudes and practices is important and should not be denied when the minority person raises such issues. However, the victimization attitude used to escape exercising what limited control that one has over his or her life in the oppression should be called to the attention of the minority counselee. Indeed, empathy is needed, but this empathy needs to help the person exercise the decisions needed so that the person does not see himself or herself as a helpless victim. Often the victim may try to get the pastoral counselor to treat him or her as a helpless victim, but to respond to the client as a helpless victim, by not enabling the person to do what he or she can, is to respond out of the needs of the pastoral counselor (countertransference) rather than to respond to the needs of the client. The key to helping the minority client face the victimization issue is the helping of the client to develop or formulate an action plan for resolving the presenting problem. It is important for the pastoral counselor to help the client explore what is possible in terms of action even in the most difficult circumstances.

The final consideration for pastoral counseling with the minority client is the need to educate the client concerning the process of pastoral counseling. It can be assumed that the culture from which the minority client comes will not have prepared the client for understanding the counseling process as white middle-class culture has prepared its cultural adherents. Therefore, the pastoral counselor needs to take time to explain how the process of pastoral counseling works when the opportunity arises. This should be done very early in the counseling process. For example, I point out early that the initial phase of counseling involves the exploration of the problem and that I need all the relevant information that can be given. Second, I point out that the problem needs to be understood in as broad a context as possible. That is, I introduce a variety of ways of understanding the problem so that the client(s) can grasp a picture of the problem as a whole. Third, I point to the need to set goals outlining the steps needed for the client to resolve the presenting problem once it has been understood. Such a three step explanation alerts the client(s) to what to expect in the actual counseling as well as to know what their role will be in the counseling process itself.

Case Study

This chapter will conclude with a brief case study illustrating selected aspects of the preceding discussion of pastoral counseling with minorities. The specific case to be presented is of an upper-middle-class black family functioning as an extended family. Specific concerns to be raised include a family systems therapy approach to pastoral counseling, the integration of a black male into a central role within the family, and the counseling skills needed to carry out a counseling process with a family. The case study is designed to illustrate the practical nature of the discussion of the cultural variance and growth counseling approach to pastoral counseling with minorities.

The Johnson family is composed of the husband-father, David, who is 33; a wife-mother Martha, age 32; a son, James, age 3; and a brother-brother-in law, John, age 15. John is Martha's brother. Parents of Martha and John are named Maurice and Janice Smith. Maurice is 59 and is a successful dentist, and Janice is a housewife and is 55 years old. Maurice and Janice have another son in addition to John who attends college in a fashionable eastern school. David works for a computer company and his wife Martha is a housewife.

The presenting problem emerged when David and Martha came for counseling complaining that John, the 15-year-old brother of Martha, was disruptive, unruly, and prevented them from giving attention to their own 3-year-old son. As the problem was explored through the counseling skills of empathy, it was revealed that the brother John was sent to David and Martha's home because Martha's parents were having marital problems. Janice, John's mother, felt that John would be better off living with his sister in a southern city. Janice decided that John would be sent south without the consent of her husband Maurice or of her daughter Martha. Martha and her father accepted the decision passively.

After the first session with David and Martha, John was asked to accompany David and Martha to counseling. All three persons came to the second session and the problem exploration and clarification phase of counseling continued. John revealed his resentment at being forced out of his family of origin in the north. He described his dislocation as being dumped. He indicated that his disruptive behavior was an attempt to get his sister and brother-in-law to send him back home to live with his parents. He also indicated that he desired to have a closer relationship with his father.

Following the third session with David, Martha, and John a relationship of rapport had been established with each person individually so that new perspectives or enlarged ways of looking at the problem could be introduced. David and Martha had perceived the problem to be theirs rather than belonging to Janice and Maurice. The idea that they had let someone else's problem become their own exclusively was introduced by the pastoral counselor for exploration of the counselees. During the session they explored how they let this happen and began to consider the new perspective as their own. After they embraced the new perspective, the pastoral counselor suggested that they invite Janice and Maurice to come south to meet as an intergenerational extended family network to decide what would be done about the problem. Both Janice and Maurice came to the fourth and fifth sessions.

At the fourth and fifth sessions Maurice's concern for his son surfaced, and he expressed real hurt that he had been left out of the decision-making with regard to both of his sons. He also regretted that he had allowed his dental practice to take him away from his family. He resolved to become more involved with his sons and to become more active in the decision-making in the home. He said right there in the fifth session that his son John would be going home with his parents even though the marital problem had not been resolved. Janice resisted Maurice's new-found involvement in the matter with John, but she relented when she saw that John was happy. Janice and Maurice resolved to go to marital counseling when they returned north.

Although this was a black middle-class family, certain cultural dynamics were apparent. There was the extended family network where certain family obligations were expected. The daughter was expected to help out the parents in crisis situations. Second, the father experienced his exclusion from the home as abnormal, and this reflects the egalitarian orientation of black folk toward rearing children. Given the family network and the egalitarian orientations, the pastoral counselor utilized a family system therapy-growth-problem-solving orientation to help resolve the family's problem. The phases of problem exploration, clarification of the problem, introducing new perspectives on the problem, and formulating and taking action to resolve the problem were the phases of counseling. During these phases many core counseling skills were used in carrying out the counseling. Specifically, the skill of challenging was the most obvious in the case although many others were used. Challenging took place when new perspectives were introduced through which a new understanding of the problem emerged. Based on this new understanding an action plan was developed designed to use the whole family resources in resolving the problem.

By way of conclusion, it is important not to assume that all minority clients have to be forced into a cultural specific model of pastoral counseling. Indeed, each case should be treated uniquely, because there is great variety within minority groups. However, when certain culture specific characteristics appear, the culture specific model should be employed where appropriate.

Bibliography

Allen, W.R. "The Search for Applicable Theories of Black Family Life." *Journal of Marriage and the Family,* February 1978, 117–129.

Banks, W.M. "The Social Context and Empirical Foundation of Research on Black Clients." In R.L. Jones (ed.), *Black Psychology.* New York: Harper and Row, 1980.

Clinebell, H. *Contemporary Growth Therapies: Resources For Actualizing Human Wholeness.* Nashville: Abingdon Press, 1981.

———. *Growth Counseling.* Nashville: Abingdon Press, 1979.

Cortes, C.E. "Mexicans." In S. Thermstrom (ed.), *Harvard Encyclopedia of American Ethnic Groups.* Cambridge: Belknap Press, 1980.

Ethnic Minorities in the United Methodist Church. Nashville: Discipleship Press, 1976.

Fitzpatrick, J.P. "Puerto Ricans." In S. Thermstrom (ed.), *Harvard Encyclopedia of American Ethnic Groups.* Cambridge: Belknap Press, 1980.

Gutman, H.G. *The Black Family in Slavery and Freedom 1750–1925.* New York: Vintage. 1976.

Hale, J. *Black Children: Their Roots, Culture, and Learning Styles.* Provo: Bringham Young University Press, 1982.

Henderson, G. *Understanding and Counseling Ethnic Minorities.* Springfield: Charles C. Thomas, 1979.

Holt, T.C. "Afro-American." In S. Thermstrom (ed.), *Harvard Encyclopedia of American Ethnic Groups.* Cambridge: Belknap Press, 1980.

Kim, H. "Koreans." In S. Thermstrom (ed.), *Harvard Encyclopedia of American Ethnic Groups*. Cambridge: Belknap Press, 1980.

Kitano H.H.L. "Japanese." In S. Thermstrom (ed.), *Harvard Encyclopedia of American Ethnic Groups*. Cambridge: Belknap Press, 1980.

Lai, H.M. "Chinese." In S. Thermstrom (ed.), *Harvard Encyclopedia of American Ethnic Groups*. Cambridge: Belknap Press, 1980.

Martin, E.P. and Martin, J.M. *The Black Extended Family*. New York: University of Chicago Press, 1978.

Richardson, E.H. "Cultural and Historical Perspectives in Counseling American Indians." In D.W. Sue (ed.), *Counseling the Culturally Different: Theory and Practice*. New York: John Wiley & Sons, 1981.

Ruiz, R.A. "Cultural and Historical Perspectives in Counseling Hispanics." In D.W. Sue (ed.), *Counseling the Culturally Different: Theory and Practice*. New York: John Wiley & Sons, 1981.

Smith, E.J. "Cultural and Historical Perspectives in Counseling Blacks." In D.W. Sue (ed.), *Counseling the Culturally Different: Theory and Practice*. New York: John Wiley & Sons, 1981.

Spicer, E.H. "American Indians." In S. Thermstrom (ed.), *Harvard Encyclopedia of Ethnic Groups*. Cambridge: Belknap Press, 1980.

Sue, D.W. (ed.). *Counseling the Culturally Different: Theory and Practice*. New York: John Wiley & Sons, 1981.

Wimberly, E. "Pastoral Counseling and the Black Perspective." *The Journal of Pastoral Care*. December 1976, 264–272.

Lowell G. Colston

The Handicapped

What are some of the guiding principles in doing pastoral care with handicapped persons? The first will be called "advocacy." I use the term advocacy in preference to other words because it more nearly describes what I assume to be the primary task of those who would presume to be helpful to people who are disabled. The word "advocate" literally means "to call out" which fittingly indicates what is essential to what is required in pastoral care, that is: to "call out" the real potential of the disabled person—in other words, to challenge him to become whatever is possible for him to become.

One way to describe this process is to say that we are helping the handicapped person to help himself. Usually the disabled person desires to be as independent as he can be. He earnestly wishes to operate as best he can in the "mainstream" of life. He knows that everyone has certain handicaps regardless of how nearly normal he seems to be. The handicaps of some people are more obvious than those of others. To be pitied, ignored, avoided, catered to, or in any other way singled out for special treatment in either a condescending or patronizing way can be deeply distressing to a disabled person who primarily wishes to live with, and make the best of, his handicap rather than to be forced to be aware of it continually.

Another meaning of the term "advocate" is "one who walks along with" or one who accompanies the other on his "pilgrimage" through life. It refers to one giving support to another not out of his own safety, but out of his willingness to experience what the other experiences. The advocate is one who "stands by the other" in the sense of taking the other's suffering upon himself. Jesus Christ is the model of this kind of advocacy. No less is required of one who would presume to offer pastoral care to handicapped persons.

What I have said about advocacy implies a set of attitudes and behaviors which are appropriate to fulfill the meaning of the word. Specific reference needs to be made to the behaviors which flow from basic attitudes.

Also, one changes his attitudes in relation to disabled persons the more he actually experiences such persons. Consequently, we will deal throughout this chapter with the theme of hope for the handicapped as provided by the community of people who support them. We will do this by discussing specific attitudes and behaviors which may be regarded as conducive to "calling out" the real potential of the disabled.

Most of the handicapped persons with whom I am acquainted desire to live a fulfilled life within the limits of their possibilities. They wish to be regarded as persons first, and then consider what is possible for them under the conditions of their disability. The special considerations they want have to do with structural planning in architecture and other areas of their environment that will facilitate their functioning in the "mainstream" of life. They wish to have equal opportunities with other people and not face discrimination in employment or in other areas of life.

The basic dilemma of handicapped people was very aptly set forth in a moving address by Dr. William Martin Smith, retiring president of the Pension Fund of the Christian Churches (Disciples of Christ) at the General Assembly Ministers' Breakfast, in San Antonio, Texas, September 1983. His question, which served as the provocative theme of his address, was: "What do we do with what we have left, when everything else is gone?" This is a fundamental question all people face at some time in their lives, especially if they live to old age. It is a perennial question for the disabled person.

How one answers this question is determinative to the hope in his existence. One may excuse himself from participation in anything on the grounds of his disability. On the other hand he may carry out his life in bitterness and resentment, continually spewing out his anger at his disability, making himself and those around him miserable. Or he may actualize his potential to the fullest and find fulfillment in his life. What one does in this regard reflects the power and love of the supportive community in which he lives as well as his basic regard for himself.

In a parable (Lk 21:1–4) regarding a widow depositing a few coins in the treasury, Jesus was reported to have said that she was more blessed than those who had given out of their abundance. "I tell you this," he said, "this poor widow has given more than any of them, for those others who have given had more than enough, but she, with less than enough, has given all she had to live on."

The implications of this parable for disabled persons is clear. Many times they give the last ounce of their effort to be and do in ways that seem extremely meager in comparison to those who are full-bodied and with an abundance of energy.

Jesus was rightly saying, "Properly assess the relative value of your gifts and continue to give what you are able to give and what you are prompted to give. You will be richly blessed for that."

Hope for the handicapped, then, is engendered by the wise, sensitive, intelligent, and spiritually discerning efforts of those offering pastoral support and encouragement to such disabled persons. This is done best, as I am declaring here, in a spirit of advocacy.

Advocacy is manifest initially in the act of entering into the phenomenology of the other person. In other words, it means as fully as possible to take on the sufferings, the pain, the anxieties, the joys, the desires, and the whole range of experience of that person. That is not easy to do. One risks increasing one's own pain, suffering, and anxiety often to the point of intolerability.

However, a prerequisite to doing effective pastoral care with a disabled person is to see the disability as *he* sees it. I do the person considerable injustice if I simply assume that he sees his own situation the way I see it. I cannot be supportive if I do not view his handicap as much through his eyes as is possible for me. Such sharing of the inner core of experiencing is the first order of business in extending pastoral care.

I may assume that he is bothered by things that actually do not faze him; conversely I may not be aware of things that bother him very much. In short, I must be concerned about this particular individual's specific experience of the handicap in its particular meaning for him.

Certainly advocacy cannot be relevant if it is not based upon some diagnostic information. Having a general knowledge of the struggles of the paraplegic, the quadriplegic, the sight and hearing impaired, the neurologically impaired or deficient, and others as they seek to be self-sustaining and productive as possible, is important to intelligent preparation for pastoral care with such persons.

Advocacy is in direct relation to the hope of the handicapped for being in the "mainstream" of life. Thus, the second guiding principle has to do with the engendering of hope.

I will discuss hope for the handicapped under three categories of analysis: (1) the hope which adheres to technological advances, especially contributions of medical science to our health and welfare; (2) the hope which is inherent in interpersonal relationships in the support communities such as churches and synagogues which sustain us; (3) the hope which permeates all of life, which I am calling the hope of ontological acceptance based upon love which is at the center of reality itself. I will share how the pastor can be supportive of each of these factors.

The two former dimensions of hope are rooted in the ontological character of love, which I will spell out in the concluding section of my remarks. Love is not a vague, esoteric something, but is at the very heart of hope for us all. It concerns a basic orientation to life which critically affects all we say and do in relation to each other. I will also spell out specific ways this becomes manifest in our behavior.

Methodologically speaking, I find that I am continually struggling to maintain a dialectical tension between psychology and theology. The two people who have influenced me most in the effort to do this are Abraham Maslow and Paul Tillich. You will see evidence of the thought of both theorists in what I am about to say. I believe that Tillich spelled out some of the assumptions which Maslow simply makes about the nature of reality.

Maslow schematizes his theory as follows:

Enhance the dangers   Enhance the attractions
Safety ←——————————→ Person ←——————————→ Growth
Minimize the attractions   Minimize the dangers

"Healthy growth (is) a never ending series of free choice situations, confronting each individual at every point throughout his life, in which he must choose between the delights of safety and growth, dependence and independence, regression and progression, immaturity and maturity. . . . We grow forward when the delights of growth and anxieties of safety are greater than the anxieties of growth and the delights of safety" (Maslow, 1962, pp. 44–45).

Tillich, on the other hand, says the growth pull is toward unity with the ground of our being. His view is relationship oriented—no matter what happens we are assured of God's love for us, and that sustains our hope (Tillich, 1963, p. 20).

Essential to any discussion of "hope" is a consideration of the term from the point of view of semantics. Hope, as defined by Webster's Dictionary, is "a feeling that what is wanted will happen; desire accompanied by expectation." The apostle Paul explains "hope" theologically: "Now hope that is seen is not hope. For who hopes for what he sees? But if we hope for what we do not see, we wait for it with patience" (Rom 8:24b–25). Thus hope in Paul's view means waiting for "what we do not see" with patience. This statement is based on assumptions about "hope" which Paul made earlier in his Letter to the Romans.

Thus, hope has been variously defined as desire with expectations and waiting with patience. Those who provide the care for persons participate in that hope as much as the people they serve. It is in this common expectation "and destiny" that we are united in a common bond of human striving and hopefulness. It is important to recognize this fact as a priori ground for all of our being.

For this reason, technological developments are a source of hope for us. We know that as technology breaks through the barriers of ignorance which prevent us from offering hope to people who are afflicted, we can then enable them to experience what they desire to have happen.

In my own case, I suffered kidney failure and was on hemodialysis for a period of eight years. Sometime during the early phase of my treatment, I became quite discouraged at being tied to a kidney machine day in, day out, week in, week out. Several complications developed during my early years of attempting to adapt to dialysis. My calcium level became alarmingly high. My physician deemed it necessary to remove my para-thyroid glands to cut down the calcium level. Although it proved not to be, this development seemed life-threatening to me. I worried about what the phenomenon really meant for days. I struggled through the healing process and the post-operative consequences for several weeks in discouragement and despair. Then I began to rally my strength and feel better.

Later I developed a serious prostate infection which persisted. Seemingly I could not overcome it. Hence, it became necessary to do a surgical procedure for scraping the prostate glands so they would heal properly. This was an agonizing experience. The whole situation was complicated by my need for a powerful antibiotic which temporarily affected my mental capacities so that I began hallucinating. Eventually, I came through this experience as well. My point is, however, that no one seemed willing to be with me in the extremities of this experience. Oh, how I needed someone! Of course, my wife was supporting me as much as she could. But she also experienced some panic during this time.

A few months after this treatment, I was back on the routine of dialysis on the kidney machine and returned to my teaching duties. However, I was in what may possibly be described as a "blue funk" by which I mean I was resenting the treatment process and was depressed much of the time. In fact, during that period of time, I went to my doctor and asked him to give the dialysis personnel permission to let air come back into my body and end my existence on the spot. He questioned me, but did not condemn me.

I went home and discussed my feelings with my wife. She became quite angry. She reminded me sharply of her need for me. "I took training so I could run you on the machine. That was not easy for me. I have been frightened from the beginning that I would do something unintentional and let air get into you. After all that worry and anxiety, you want them to let air into you? You have a family. Consider us. You are not about to do something stupid like that. I will not have it."

Her confrontation, which I have not fully reproduced here, was long and hard and shocked me out of my depression. So, I accepted the fact that

I was probably to spend the rest of my life on a kidney machine and became willing not to hasten my demise.

That decision was providential, because not long after I saw an article about peritoneal dialysis in *Time* magazine. I was greatly cheered and encouraged by the assurances that it was being developed as an alternative to the kidney machine. The procedure had been perfected, especially by the development of the Tenkhoff catheter, which greatly reduced the incidence of peritonitis in dialysis patients who had been equipped with it.

I immediately talked with my doctor about changing to peritoneal dialysis. He not only said it was possible, but also began to initiate steps to convert me to that procedure before I left his office—that very day. (This is what I like about him. He will do what I ask him to do immediately.) He arranged for me to have the surgery that would equip me with the Tenkhoff catheter and explained how the transformation would take place.

I have now been on continuous ambulatory peritoneal dialysis (CAPD, as it is abbreviated) since that time. It has improved my general physical condition immensely. It feels more natural to me for my own body to do the work of dialysis. The general lift it has given my spirit is hard to describe.

All of what I have just said illustrates how technological developments have given me a new lease on life. My times of despair have given way to new hope. Naturally, I hope that eventually even more promising technical advances can enhance my hope for the future. I realize now how much I needed to share the despair I was facing with someone who could understand and accept it.

The fact remains, I have a chronic kidney disease and neither CAPD nor anything else will change that. However, the hope for a relatively healthy existence, in spite of that fact, remains strong within me.

Still another manifestation of advocacy is in interpersonal relationships within the context of the supportive community. Hope is generated in anyone who realizes that other people care about him and will rally to his needs when he becomes afflicted.

Basic to the support community is an attitude which ought to be central to all of life: I care enough for you to challenge you to become whatever it is possible for you to become. The theologian Paul Tillich has said that "the actualization of potential is a structural condition of all beings" (Tillich, 1963, p. 30). He applies this notion especially to human life.

I regard my essential task in the various groups I serve to "call out the potential person" in the individuals present. Sometimes this is painful both for them and for me, but no less is required if persons are to realize their potentials as human beings.

Such confrontation is different from efforts to manipulate and control. It is based on a primary faith in the capacity of the person to be as self-directing as he possibly can be. Therefore, the primary attitude from which I approach these persons is essentially love, which certainly includes the belief in the person's capacity for actualizing his own potential.

In the following paragraphs, I will explicate the principles which I deem best to implement the ministry of advocacy based on love for handicapped people. I am indebted to Charlotte Epstein for the framework of this presentation. Although she was writing expressly for nurses in her book *Learning To Care for the Aged,* what she says is just as appropriate to learning to care for the disabled, and can be equally applicable to those persons doing pastoral work with handicapped people.

Advocacy is characteristically evidenced in an ambience of relaxed use of time. Despite my beginning statement of hope brought about through confrontation, this is done in an atmosphere of relaxation and freedom. I do not push the person to deal immediately with his deepest feelings.

It is extremely important to me to take time to listen to the other person. It increases self-esteem when someone "pays attention to him." That helps the person value himself, which is important to his self-regard.

Relaxed use of time is not keeping someone waiting for a long time. After waiting an hour or so, it is disconcerting to say the least to have a doctor spend fifteen minutes with me only half listening to my cursory questions. But that's just one example of how one may not take time for people in the busy schedules we keep.

A physician may excuse himself for keeping a person waiting for inordinate periods of time, then limiting that person to a few moments of consultation, but that seems inexcusable for a clergy person. Yet, I have been aware of ministers who have not spent sufficient time with any of their parishioners to really know them. Such clergy persons rarely spend the time necessary to know, even in a cursory way, what the disabled person is experiencing. Basically, the handicapped person does not expect to have more time than anyone else, but he expects at least as much.

The highest compliment one can give another person is expressed in willingness to give some uninterrupted, undiverted time to him. Doing so is evidence that we value that person. Such realization is at the basis of hope. To know one is valued and appreciated enhances one's self-esteem considerably.

A corollary to providing an ambience of relaxed time is a concern for the expectations and anxieties of the other person. It is important to establish that there are no taboo feelings or thoughts.

The person may regard his feelings or thoughts as silly or inconsequential, not worthy to put on busy people around them. Sometimes people around them *do* give such signals, i.e., they do not wish to be bothered by foolish worries. Or they do not take the anxieties seriously. Thus the negative feelings may remain unexpressed. Often the person feels hurt by the realization that no one wants to hear about his worst fears or anxieties, so he is left along with them. Often nagged by needless worry over concerns that may be misplaced or grossly in error, people may remain silent when they need to speak. Just a word or two from someone could relieve him of hours of misery.

One woman patient expressed it this way: "You know, when I've been waiting for a long time to see a doctor, I begin to wonder about all the other people on his mind, and all their ailments. I can't help feeling that I'd better not take up too much of his time with my little aches and pains. Then, after I leave, I'm sorry that I didn't mention this or that, and it bothers me until my next visit."

I have heard similar remarks from people regarding clergy persons: "I wouldn't take my deepest doubts and worries to my minister; he's too busy or he probably would not approve anyway."

The principle operating here is: Tell the person how much time you are allotting to him; have it in your own mind that it is his time; be fully present and available to him during that time; be patient in listening to his expectations and anxieties because dealing with these are just as important to the total healing process as any of the other things you do for him.

Another effector of hope is in the encouragement of the person to put into words whatever questions he has. It is not enough just to hear what he is anxious about; the next step is to give the person an opportunity to verbalize questions which may be on his mind. It is true that some people seem to have an unending supply of questions to keep one occupied ad nauseum. However, if the person feels constrained to respond only minimally to those who seek to help him, then he is usually left with many unanswered questions that add unnecessarily to his pain.

Still another action on the part of those of us who form the supportive community around the person is some conscious and obvious effort to see him as a whole person.

Actually, I prefer the term "centered person" to whole person. It is as we regard and respect the "core" or "center" of another person that we fulfill the responsibilities of a moral life. We actually know that fact deep within ourselves, but we are often so blindly self-centered that we do not act in terms of what we know. True self-fulfillment comes as we develop our appreciation of the "centeredness" of the other person. He does not then become a thing or an object for our manipulation or control, but a person in his own right.

Fortunately, my own doctor will take the time to discuss other things about my life, work, and interests other than just my medical problems. I have the feeling he is concerned about me as a whole person and he leads me to believe that. I know he is exceptionally busy and cares for a number of patients, but I have the feeling that my time with him is *my* time.

While he is working with me, he is continually asking me questions about what I am doing and commenting on the answers I give. I have the feeling that I can discuss anything with him and I feel that he respects my knowledge as well.

We feel free to discuss movies we have seen, or a play, or a music concert, or a best selling novel, or even politics where our differences are often greatly pronounced.

Regard for me as a whole person enhances my hopefulness that I will be accepted no matter what and assures me that I am respected as a person with a "center" to my existence.

Another action which communicates advocacy is the interaction we have with friends, relatives, or family who surround the person in his daily life. The person cannot really be understood apart from the immediate context of his life.

Family attitudes contribute immeasurably to spiritual welfare of its individual members. If, in the case of a dying patient, the family begins their grief work before the death occurs, the patient may feel that they have taken leave of him and basically left him "to go it alone." This is a subtle means of undercutting the patient's hope.

Dealing with the fears and anxieties of family members is as important as dealing directly with the disabled person. Hope increases proportionately with the degree of support to the person offered by members of his family.

It is not enough just to deal with attitudes of the person or members of his family, we need to institute a process of informal education, clearing up misconceptions by explaining processes which affect the person and are critical to his growth and understanding. Of course, again, there is much technological information often too technical for the person to understand, but some explanation, in his own terms, can be given of what is happening to him. An example of how critical this can be is given in the following account of my own experience.

I was being x-rayed for the purpose of determining my kidney function. Dyes were being inserted into my veins and their progression through my bloodstream was timed and pictures taken at intervals. I heard the technicians discussing the procedures and heard one of them say to the other: "Obviously there is quite a bit of necrotic tissue in the kidneys. There is not enough tissue left for proper filtration." When I heard these words, my heart sank. This was my first awareness of the realization that I was dying. In fact, much of the tissue in my kidneys was already dead. I assumed with great despair that I was soon to follow. I had understood just enough of what they were saying to get the message.

The old saying, "A little knowledge is a dangerous thing," was working to my distinct disadvantage in this situation. I was completely depressed by what I understood and would not be reassured to any degree until I talked with my doctor. Better preparation for that experience would probably have helped me. I am not sure at this point. However, I was not told what to expect and actually learned it in a very painful manner.

Developing the skill of translating technical knowledge into common understanding is a difficult but significant task. There is never a situation that is completely hopeless, and being able to underscore the degree of hope in it is a talent that is to be used and cherished.

Very important in the process of engendering hope is learning to read the context of each person's life which is the community that nourished and supports that life.

No one can really know a person—his needs, expectations, anxieties, and so on—without knowing the community in which he lives. "No generalizations gleaned from lectures and textbooks can substitute for the living unfoldment of events, the everyday evidences of attitudes, and the immediate effect of behaviors that every community uniquely presents" (Epstein, 1977, p. 134).

Within the past few years, I have required my students to diagram the network of relationships which critically affect the person's feelings, thoughts and behaviors. Who are the people who influence him? Somewhat, or a whole lot? Of whom is he most aware as he lives his life in the community and why? To whom does he turn when he needs help? When he wishes to share confidences? And so on.

Friendships range from casual contacts, to close friends, to the people with whom we are intimate. All of these dimensions are needed for a full life. Hope is enhanced by the degree of our participation in the lives of other people.

Intimate relationships are the most risky. We not only give people the power to fulfill us but also to hurt us if they are so inclined. The problem involved in the inevitable ultimate separation from the intimate other deters many people from becoming involved in intimate relationships at all.

However, the price of "playing it safe," so to speak, is missing the fulfillment one experiences in the truly intimate relationship in which deep caring is present.

Interpersonal participation and fulfillment is a very important dimension of hope. The challenge and support in it keeps us alive and growing, enhances the interest and vitality in all of life, and establishes the quality of the whole of our lives.

A form of advocacy which has social, economic, and political implications for the handicapped has an analogy in concern for the aging and is termed "senior advocacy." Similarly, I am referring to this dimension as "disability advocacy." It implies the need for handicapped people to rally around their own cause for just treatment in the various arenas of life and for clergy persons to support them in that cause. Among the issues involved are: accessibility of public places to handicapped persons, including offices, restrooms, and other such facilities, and whatever measures will increase mobility, feasibility, or any other concerns which enhance possibilities for disabled persons to be a significant part of the "mainstream" of life.

New structural forms for facilitating the ebb and flow of daily life should be designed to include the disabled person in that flow of life. Reserved parking spaces and ramps are already being designated as being expressly for the handicapped. However, much is yet to be done to facilitate the lives and increase the potential contributions of disabled persons to the society of which they are a part.

Basic to all that I have said thus far is my assumption about the ontological character of hope, which will be the concluding section of my remarks.

Hope is generated by faith. Faith is based on love. We have faith that love is in the very nature of reality itself. We get manifestations of that love through the community which nourishes and supports us. In theological terms, this is called grace—the gift of love which has no expectations for return. It is freely given as an act of faith in us and hope for us.

In the First Epistle of John, the ontological character is simply stated: "So we know and believe the love God has for us. God is love, and he who abides in love abides in God, and God abides in him" (1 Jn 4:16).

In a comprehensive discussion of hope, the apostle Paul puts the whole matter in a context of faith. "Therefore since we are justified by faith, we have peace with God, through our Lord Jesus Christ. Through him we have obtained access to this grace in which we stand and we rejoice in our *hope* of sharing the glory of God."

He is saying, of course, that our hope comes from the "grace in which we stand" to which we have access through faith. "More than that," Paul continues, "we rejoice in our sufferings."

Having spoken of joy and hope in the same breath, Paul recalls his sufferings and those of others and feels challenged. The challenge is that far from being destroyed by these experiences, his *hope* has been strengthened. I can identify with Paul considerably in this regard. I discovered that I was greatly challenged by the sufferings in my illness. I doubt if I would have dealt as realistically with the fact of my own mortality had I not had these experiences. Why did it take that to sharpen my awareness? I was forced to deal immediately with the possibility of my own death.

Paul went on, "Suffering produces endurance, and endurance produces character, and character produces hope." Sufferings result in *disciplined endurance*. Literally, suffering "hardens us up" for life, which is what the word "endurance" means. We are no longer "soft," easily hurt, seeking to avoid pain at all costs even to the detriment of our own growth through the realization of our possibilities.

One of the parables attributed to Jesus was that regarding the pearl of great value to which he refers in the gospel of Matthew (Mt 13:45–46). Although the parable clearly serves as an analogy to the kingdom of heaven, I have taken the liberty of seeing it also as a symbolic reference to the human soul. Thus the human soul is like the pearl of great value.

A few years ago, I visited the Sea World attraction in San Diego, California. I was fascinated by the pearl diving concession operated primarily by people of Japanese descent. I watched with wonder as the skilled young ladies were diving to retrieve oysters from the bottom of a large pool which could be viewed in its entirety through a large display window. I purchased one of the oysters which was duly cracked open to reveal a shiny small pearl snuggled down in one corner of the shell.

I took the pearl into my own fingers, slowly turning it around. In the brief moment of my perusal, the thought flashed through my mind, "It is amazing how this pearl came to be."

I reflected upon the fact that this intentionally cultured pearl had gone through a "painful" process. At some time, someone had inserted a piece of grit (probably a tiny bit of sand) into the oyster shell. Thereupon the organism went about its wondrous work of fashioning a pearl to protect its delicate meat from the irritation that the grit produced.

I thought, "How like the human soul!" When irritations and frustrations of life threaten its sensitive tissues, it spins an encasement around itself that often is a thing of beauty to behold. However, the analogy breaks down at the point of the imperviousness of the case. Usually in the human soul the whole being takes on more beauty in the midst of the suffering it endures, but it is more open to transactions with its environment as a result of those sufferings.

Nevertheless, the human soul which moves through sufferings may become like the pearl of great value. The "buyer who is looking for fine pearls," when he finds one of great value, invests all that he is and has in order to possess it. Likewise, when people see the beauty of the spirit and courage in people who have faced suffering and adversity triumphantly, they usually want to possess it for themselves.

The experience of enduring hardship cheerfully and patiently tests and hardens character. Character is seen in the willingness to take risks and withstand hurts when a greater fulfillment is possible for having done so.

This character makes possible a more vigorous hope than we might otherwise have had. In my own case, having gone through the suffering made me more sensitive and useful to other people in their sufferings. I wrote several of my best books while I was on the kidney machine. Now that I am on peritoneal dialysis, I am more inspired to write and to share what I have learned with other people.

It is impossible to say that Paul intended to imply that character is the source of that hope. The source is clearly the point at which Paul began his statement, i.e. *the source is clearly the grace in which we stand.* We hope to receive the glory of God, Paul states, because we have already begun to receive the *love* of God. We know that by experiencing it through those who love and care for us. That is the power in our lives, Paul said elsewhere, and that power is the true source of our salvation.

Hope is thus more than mere hopefulness (in the sense of some kind of expectation of what may happen in the future); it is a *living reality,* already beginning to be realized in our midst.

Our hope of sharing the glory of God, then, is the realization of our true life in which God who has made us is no longer hopelessly beyond our reach, but is very much with us in our joy and in our pain.

With Paul, *we rejoice because of our sufferings. We do not rejoice in our sufferings.* In a basically hostile or apathetic environment, hardship would break our spirits. It would be insupportable if we felt that determining forces were antagonistic, at worst, or even indifferent, at least, to us.

We need not consider the limits merely of our own human capacity. In Christ, we see what God has done for man—to redeem the life of the individual; to transform the nature of his society; to open up limitless possibilities for him. This is always true no matter what happens to us. It is our task to find the key to those possibilities. In his death camp experience, Viktor Frankl discovered that even when he was stripped of everything he valued, he still had the realities of the love of those who cared for him to sustain him (Frankl, 1963). It is in the realization of this reality which always keeps hope alive within us—the realization that "nothing can separate us from the love of God."

Now we return to the agonizing question with which we began this chapter: "What do we do with what we have left, when everything else is gone?" The answer is: "We do the very best we can with what we have, knowing that we are supported by the unfailing love of God."

As the apostle Paul has put it: "For I am persuaded that neither death, nor life, nor angels, nor principalities, nor things present, nor things to come, nor powers, nor height, nor depth, nor anything else in all creation, will be able to separate us from the love of God in Christ Jesus our Lord" (Rom 8:38).

Hope flows from our essential feeling that God will never abandon us or that nothing in this world can separate us from the love of God. All of us are held together by this faith and we minister to each other in terms of that faith.

Bibliography

Epstein, Charlotte. *Learning To Care for the Aged.* Reston, Virginia: Reston Publishing Co., Inc., 1977, p. 134.

Frankl, Viktor. *Man's Search For Meaning.* Boston: Beacon Press, 1963.

Maslow, Abraham. *Toward a Psychology of Being.* Princeton: D. Van Nostrand, Inc., 1962, pp. 44, 45.

Tillich, Paul. "The Multidimensional Unity of Life," Part IV, Life in The Spirit, Vol. III, *Systematic Theology.* Chicago: The University of Chicago Press, 1963, p. 20.

Ralph L. Underwood

Pastoral Counseling
in the Parish Setting

The purpose of this chapter is to identify key ways in which the parish setting gives shape and direction to pastoral counseling. In part any kind of
counseling is a function of its setting. To what extent and in what ways does
the parish setting influence and determine the nature of pastoral counseling? In the process of exploring this question both the promise and some
of the problems of parish pastoral counseling will be examined. The thesis
is that the parish setting gives shape and direction to pastoral counseling
by virtue of its distinctive embodiment of the meaning of community of
faith.

Of almost 500,000 clergy in the United States, more than 300,000
serve in congregations. A survey published in 1978 reports that 98 percent
of the pastors polled felt that counseling was an integral aspect of their total
ministry. The same survey suggested that a larger portion of their working
time was devoted to counseling than had been the case ten years prior to
the survey (Baldwin, 1978). It is estimated that 10 percent of clergy in the
United States have received some systematic, clinical supervision of their
pastoral care and counseling. This means that the clergy in parish locations
represent the largest number of persons in the helping professions who
have some clinical training and who are readily available in communities
to assist persons in their troubles and questions (Jackson, 1978). Most of
the professional help that is available to persons in their daily living comes
from clergy, and most pastoral counseling is provided by clergy in the parish setting.

To explore the parish setting as a factor in pastoral counseling, this
study will first establish some working definitions along with distinguishing features of the parish setting.

What Is Parish Pastoral Counseling?

The *Encyclopedic Dictionary of Religion* offers four definitions of the term "parish": (1) a subdivision of a diocese, typically with its own building under the guidance of a rector, priest, or pastor who is charged with the care of souls, (2) any local church or congregation, including its activities, (3) the collective of members of a parish, and (4) the charge of a pastor (Meager, 1978). For our purposes these refer to two basic understandings: a territorial meaning in which all persons within a designated geographical area are viewed as members of one universal church, and a gathering and covenanting of God's people in a congregation. The latter understanding has prevailed in the Protestant definition, and the former, while prominent in Roman Catholic thought, is not as significant as it once was. The notion of parish as any charge of a pastor extends the meaning beyond its common neighborhood connotations. Thus a clergy person's "personal parish" might be one's charge in the military chaplaincy. The focus in this chapter is on the parish setting as a geographical area or a congregation.

The pastor is one who cares as a shepherd cares for the sheep. In relation to the parish setting, the pastor is one who is ordained and either appointed or called to care as one who represents Christ's ministry in the world and in the church. Consequently, the pastor represents the church's ministry in the world as well. The term "pastoral" then refers to one who represents Christ and the church and who is expected to care and counsel in that spirit. Ordinarily such persons are ordained to the ministry of word and sacrament, but in many church traditions its meaning is extended to include lay persons when they occupy a symbolic role. Even so, the term "pastoral" does not refer as such to the calling of all Christians and is not intended as a synonym for the term "Christian." Accordingly, counseling is "pastoral" when it is conducted by one who symbolizes the ministry of Christ and the Church, is called to care in a manner that vitally communicates the spirit of the Gospel, and has authority and competence to teach the Christian way. Consequently pastoral counseling is counseling that symbolically, dynamically, and verbally brings Christ to people.

Finally, some distinction is to be made between care and counseling, so that pastoral counseling is understood in the context of pastoral care. For our purposes here pastoral care refers to the work of the representative ministry as it brings Christ to persons and celebrates the presence of Christ among persons in interpersonal gatherings, such as small groups and individual conversations. Within this personal dimension of ministry, counseling refers to those pastoral conversations which take place when people acknowledge a need for healing, sustaining, guiding, or reconciling. Consequently, pastoral counseling is the consultation required when people's need is addressed, whether that need be for help in time of brokenness, adversity, decision, or alienation.

In short, as understood here parish pastoral counseling is personal consultation with individuals or small groups, in which persons who represent Christ and the ministry of the church and who serve in the context of the life of a Christian congregation seek to help those whose celebration and conduct of life can in principle be engaged in dialogue with the Christian gospel.

With this working definition in mind, let us proceed to analyze the ways in which the parish setting gives distinctive life and form to pastoral counseling. In our time pastoral counseling occurs in many settings and has integrity in various places, yet these settings make for important differences. Currently, the question of setting has to be framed in a paradoxical manner. Traditionally, most pastoral counseling has taken place in the parish context, and actually this remains true today. Even so, in much of the Western world ministers in parish settings evaluate their own pastoral counseling by reference to their colleagues in special ministries. This means that pastoral counseling in non-parish contexts, especially in the pastoral counseling center, functions as the paradigm, and pastoral counseling in the parish setting is understood as a variation that appropriates and approximates the wisdom and standards of pastoral counseling as a special ministry usually developed in settings beyond the parish church. Certainly, parish clergy can learn much from their colleagues in particular counseling ministries, most of whom have had more clinically supervised training, yet such appropriation needs to be sensitive to the requirements of the parish context. At the same time, given the integrity of pastoral counseling, pastoral counselors in non-parish settings can enrich their own ministry by careful attention to the dimensions of pastoral counseling that are strongest in the parish church and that can be creatively adapted to non-parish contexts.

In the parish context, pastoral counseling is structured in various ways. Most frequently, the pastor or pastors in a parish serve as generalists who in the course of their overall ministry give counsel to parishioners. Such counsel is a mixture of informal comments and formal consultations. A growing number of parishes have an associate pastor or pastors who have advanced training and devote most of their time to pastoral care and counseling. Though they specialize in pastoral care and counseling they regularly participate in the worship, teaching, and other dimensions of parish life. Finally, a significant number of parishes sponsor and house a pastoral counseling center. While located in the parish, the extent to which the pastoral counseling offered in such centers is shaped and directed by the parish context varies according to involvement of the parish counselors in parish life. If the counselors do not lead in worship at the church, teach, or participate in activities other than counseling at the center, the parish setting is likely to have limited bearing on their counseling ministry. In actuality, there are varied arrangements which structure the relationship between a pastoral counseling center located in a church building and the total life of the church. Consequently, generalization is difficult. The discussion that follows highlights features of parish life that influence pastoral counseling when pastors, whether generalists or specialists, are involved with more than counseling per se in parish life.

The analysis of the parish setting will focus on its major features, and with respect to each distinctive feature both the promise and problems presented to the ministry of pastoral counseling will be discussed. Finally, in each area practical guidelines for parish pastoral counseling will be identified. No feature is exclusively characteristic of the parish context, and therefore is relevant to other settings. Yet each feature is so thoroughly characteristic of the parish context that it is both readily associated with this setting and is a key to the significance of the parish setting. Accordingly, the question to be addressed is not how the parish setting influences the pastoral counseling specialist alone. Rather, the question is how the parish setting gives shape to all pastoral counseling within its context.

The Community of Faith as a Center of Worship

The first feature of the parish setting is that it is an institution whose primary reason for existence is corporate worship. The praise of God and celebration of the gospel form and bind the community. All are invited to participate in this central purpose regardless of their circumstances, whether troubled or not, in every season of their lives. Certainly, pastoral counseling in other settings also is linked to corporate worship. In most hospital settings, for example, chaplains conduct worship for personnel and patients, and this is as vital a dimension of their ministry as is their counseling. Even so, corporate worship is not the primary reason for the existence of the institution in which they serve, and so the question arises: What difference, if any, does this make?

When persons comes to parish clergy for counseling they are keenly aware that these pastors are overseers who regularly lead the congregation in worship and exercise much practical leadership in its organizational and instructional life. Parishioners who are active participants see their pastors repeatedly as they preach, pray and administer the sacraments. Typically non-active persons who come for help have these associations in their minds. The parish context undergirds people's awareness that the pastor represents life's sacred dimension and the call to worship. The parish pastor is one who takes worship seriously and serves the people of God in their worship life. Symbolically pastors stand for the spiritual values of transcendence and grace. When they come to ministers for reasons other than convenience, people implicitly acknowledge a quest for reality and meaning that is beyond their own grasp and control. Ordinarily, this is true for all pastoral counselors, whatever the setting. Nonetheless, the primacy of worship in the parish sets the stage whereby this connection is strengthened.

The context of a community of worship underscores the availability of the means of grace. This context affirms the awesome truth that our identity is God-given and cannot be reduced to our personal achievements or troubles at certain times in our lives. Unfortunately, accomplishments and troubles often are allowed to constitute a profane identity. That is, people come to identify themselves with their achievements or their problems. An example is the person whose self-orientation is expressed in these words: "I am a person who has anxiety attacks." The grace of God in Christ cuts across such self-preoccupation and redeems us from this kind of profanity. The community of worship beckons people to come to be released from the dominating power of such self-understanding.Often coming to the pastor is part of people's response to this invitation. Whether consciously or not they are beginning to make the journey of seeing themselves and their life in a new light. The corporate and liturgical affirmation of the transcendent and gracious meaning that undergirds our lives is one source of what has come to be a common understanding about the parish setting: it has great potential with respect to "preventive mental health" (Clinebell, 1973). This is not to suggest that mental health and salvation are identical. Nor is it the case that all instances of mental illness entail profane identities. Even so, the emphasis on worship in parish life has potential to undergird the trust in God's grace which redeems from profane identities and thereby strengthens people in every season of life.

The promise of pastoral counseling in the parish setting, then, is first of all a promise that derives from the vigorous affirmation of the transcendent grace of God in Christ in the context of a community of worship. This same promise extends to pastoral counseling in other contexts insofar as connections to worship or equivalent affirmations of the divine dimension in our lives are evident.

Let us examine two consequences of this promise. One has to do with the integration of the means of grace with principles of counseling. Pastoral counselors have been trained to observe the general principles of counseling as they inform various helping professions. The sacraments are part of the office of the pastor, and other means of grace such as prayer and

Scripture are key resources in pastoral work. Since they are such an integral aspect of the pastor's work in the parish setting, the pastor can readily explore how to integrate the means of grace with valid principles of counseling. When and how can prayer, for example, help persons be engaged in counseling and not serve as a pious escape from self-confrontation? Or when can prayer open persons to a genuine hearing of the word of grace in their lives? Let us examine a pastoral conversation. A parishioner had been counseling with her pastor and for the first time had requested prayer. Though she had identified at least initially some of her concerns about her relationship to her daughter and son-in-law, the pastor responded to her request by asking for her help in creating the prayer. He asked her to reflect on what she would like to be included in the prayer. After a pause she said, "It's hardest to not intervene, but that's what I want. I need to know that God is with me when I feel helpless." When the pastor prayed he included this request, and then they both joined in the Lord's Prayer. In light of the counseling principles of helping persons explore their own experience and of being responsible for their own perspectives, the pastor invited the parishioner to participate in the process of developing self-awareness before God. In addition, it should be noted that inclusion of the Lord's Prayer also invited her participation on a mutual basis and gave expression to their identification with the whole people of God. Since in the parish context pastors are expected to make use of the means of grace in their ministry and since they are committed to principles of good counseling, the parish context affords plentiful opportunity to explore their integration.

By virtue of the variety of ways in which it calls on pastors to demonstrate genuine caring, the parish context underscores the meaning of authenticity. Genuine caring is a mark of one who is struck by the holy. As one who leads worship and is the shepherd, the pastor is expected to be one who really cares. As a symbol of this expectation, in the parish setting counseling ordinarily is provided without fee for service. In part this is made possible because in the context of worship the people of God give of their means and provide an adequate standard of living for the pastor. No material personal gain is at stake in providing counseling. More importantly, the parish context helps to enhance the meaning of genuineness as applied to counseling. Not only is personal genuineness appropriate, it is critical in the life and ministry of the pastor. The spontaneity and responsiveness that characterize authentic caring are more to the point of people's expectations than are the more technical aspects of professional competency in counseling, significant as the latter may be. The parish setting provides multiple tests of the pastor's authenticity. Their spiritual and personal sensitivity are challenged in the sanctuary, the board room, the pastoral study, the hospital room, the home, the parking lot, and wherever counsel is sought. Probably no context for pastoral counseling entails the actual diversity of setting that comes with parish ministry. Whereas the pastoral counselor in a counseling center almost always sees people in the counseling room, the parish pastor counsels virtually everywhere! Consequently, the pastor's genuineness in caring is developed through extensive and varied exposure to environments, not all of which are readily controlled. In the parish context the focus on authenticity as a sign of true love clarifies that our ultimate hope is in God. Such an emphasis does not detract from the requirements of professional accountability. In fact, this focus strengthens the motivation for such competence.

Along with the promise of the parish as a community of worship arise particular problems. Given the role of the pastor in corporate worship and general oversight in the life of the congregation, the time devoted to pastoral counseling, however significant, is limited. Given such limits, the parish pastor cannot develop a degree of competence in some technical aspects of counseling which matches that of pastoral colleagues in other settings, even when the levels of formal education and supervision in counseling are comparable. One consequence of the time limitation is the guideline that the parish pastor should not engage in long-term counseling with parishioners. To do so runs the risk of neglect of other pastoral duties. Of course the prohibition applies to formal counseling in which the pastor meets at least weekly over an extended time with parishioners, say three months or more. In no way does this guideline inhibit the development of long-term relationships that involve occasional, short-term pastoral consultation. Nor does this rule of thumb imply that all of the pastor's counseling need be informal. How much a pastor engages in formal counseling that is scheduled by regular appointment depends on one's training, style, and circumstances. In the parish setting pastoral priorities often dictate referral of parishioners to pastoral counselors in other settings or to others in the helping professions. Such referral, however, is an act of ministry. As representative of the community of faith the pastor maintains supportive contact with these parishioners so long as doing so does not interfere with the counseling process.

Paradoxical as it may be, a problem in parish pastoral counseling is that people will act inauthentically precisely by using their piety as a cover for unacceptable realities in themselves. The paradox lies in the fact that the parish setting tests pastoral authenticity to the limit and true worship is marked by genuine poverty of spirit in contrast to pretense, yet people convince themselves that they cannot tell all to a pastor. Of course, the tendency to idealize the self and to present to others a good image of the self, even one that is too good to be true, is encountered commonly in all counseling regardless of setting. Nonetheless, commonplace distortions of the meaning of worship and the significance of the worshiping community make this an acute problem area in the parish context. Pastors can handle such problems by resisting ploys to idealize and, where necessary, referring persons who need distance from their unbalanced religious expectations to therapists in secular settings.

As a center of worship the parish setting nourishes a sense of the sacred in others and self. Representing this community and the sacred dimension of life, the pastor participates in the counseling process in ways that help persons to be authentically open to the reality of God in their lives. For the parish pastor, the counseling process is a moment in a larger drama about the glory of God and the human good.

A Community of Inquiry

The parish that gathers to worship is also a community of inquiry. Faith seeks understanding. The pastor who leads the people in their worship is also one who engages them in the venture of learning. Parish life is marked by attention to the learning of faith. James Gustafson (1970) has interpreted the life of the church as a community of moral discourse, and Don Browning (1976) has analyzed the implications of this model of the church for pastoral care. According to Browning, the ethical inquiry organized and fostered in the life of the congregation forms a context that makes the acceptance experienced in pastoral counseling meaningful and effective. He also argues that pastoral counselors need to take the moral task and the work of ethical inquiry more seriously than they have done. Often the moral tradition of the church has been viewed as a problem in counseling, especially in the case of those who are oppressed by a severe conscience and those who avoid depth encounter with life by obsessively concentrating on minor moral concerns. On the other hand, a growing concern with a narcissistic orientation which has emerged in our culture suggests that a community of moral discourse is often the best context in which pastoral counseling can be pursued.

The life of a parish characteristically includes educational programs that promote understanding and debate. While other institutions also incorporate this feature, such as Sunday Schools for patients, they borrow this feature from the parish and often are not able to develop its promise to the same extent that marks parish life. Ordinarily one expects the parish to be a place of spiritual and moral inquiry; one hopes that other institutions also have a significant place for this endeavor. Certainly, in addition to educational programs for patients non-parish institutions promote ethical inquiry, especially among their professional staff, who make decisions that entail moral considerations.

The constructive power of moral guidelines for the welfare of the individual has been overlooked and the parish context promises to develop this source for all pastoral counseling. In the church moral and practical wisdom flow from the springs of faith, particularly from the celebration of the presence of God re-enacted in corporate worship. The grounding of the ethical life in the reality of grace is fundamental to the formation of a parish context that has redemptive potential. Otherwise, moral demands or ideals oppress the individual spirit and distort personal appropriation of faith. At the same time, given the qualities of genuine caring, respect and acceptance, ethical confrontation has significance as an integral aspect of pastoral counseling. The parish context facilitates such confrontation because people hear the word of grace and are in the process of learning its moral implications. By virtue of this context moral confrontation in the right spirit is expected and acknowledged as a need by parishioners. Personal consultations with the pastor often are true inquiries into the moral dilemmas people face. The approach that fits the context is that of mutual exploration or open inquiry, not dogmatic prescription. It is the third use of the Law (Calvin, 1960) and not the others that belongs to pastoral counseling. The didactic moment in pastoral counseling is not a matter of correct filling in of blanks. It is open dialogue.

All this implies that as a general rule, pastors may offer interpretations of the faith for discussion in the same manner that other counselors, according to the general principles of counseling, offer interpretations to their clients. For pastors, however, these are not primarily psychological interpretations. They proffer for individual consideration some of the wisdom that Christian understanding brings to life. Pastoral counseling should not be reduced to teaching any more than it should be seen as nothing but preaching to the individual. Even so, there are significant moments for teaching and moral inquiry in pastoral counseling. Such moments occur with timely spontaneity because they are consistent with the parish context as a community of faithful inquiry. The differences between corporate, including classroom, settings and individual settings are crucial. Far greater sensitivity to the requirements of respect is needed in interpersonal conversations than in public proclamations. If the requirements for respect are significant and demanding in public proclamations and communication, such requirements are even more complicated in individual settings. Accordingly in the counseling process, a teaching moment typically comes after support and empathy have enabled the pastor to enter into the parishioner's dilemmas, and in essence is an invitation for the parishioner to join the pastor in listening respectfully to what Christian tradition says. Though the pastor is expected to be resourceful in explaining Christian tradition, the counseling situation calls for an atmosphere of mutual exploration. Therefore, pastors should observe appropriate tentativeness.

Most often didactic moments in counseling help parishioners in two ways: to make informed choices and to consolidate personal gains. The first function helps to provide persons with resources for their decision-making. Limited information-sharing can enrich the ethical considerations that are appropriate to making a decision. Often parishioners grow in appreciation for the decisions they face when they realize that Church teachings, while suggestive, do not tell what the decision should be. For example, a woman who has been physically abused by her alcoholic husband and who has separated from him is in conversation with her pastor regarding the prospects of reconciliation with her husband. Though the pastor cannot provide her with a pat formula by which she will know when they are ready to try living together again, the pastor can note some of the wisdom of the Scriptures and the experience of the church which point to signs in the experience and behavior of both the woman and her husband which give evidence of genuine and enduring reconciliation.

A second function interpretation is to help consolidate gains. With this significance in mind, it is important that pastors not interpret prematurely. For the couple just discussed, quick talk of reconciliation and forgiveness might have encouraged idealistic and inauthentic compliance. On the other hand, after genuine struggle about working out their relationship, a pastor can say, "For me what you're experiencing now is called forgiveness and reconciliation. You're feeling it now and you will continue to encounter this experience in the days ahead." This naming of experience, or pointing out what the pastor sees to be happening in the lives of parishioners, raises their consciousness and helps to confirm their experiences.

Interpretation is especially useful with the religiously minded. Pastors have ample opportunity to explore people's references to biblical stories. People identify with Job, the psalmist, Jacob, David, or Ruth. Pastors can help them to articulate the relation between the larger story of God's relation with his people and their own personal histories. At times pastors must counter misunderstandings and misapplications, for people will use theological ideas inaccurately and destructively.

Generally, pastors are caring people who demonstrate much of their love and concern by way of teaching (Nehl, 1979). In their educative role pastors find an effective vehicle of caring for people. Ours is a time when many people need this kind of care, for their development has lacked clear moral guidance and example. The reverse side of this promise in the pastor's role is the tendency, inevitably present, to rely too heavily on the didactic moment in counseling. While there is a vital place for sharing the wisdom of Christian tradition with people, counseling necessarily entails dynamic, interpersonal encounter. Overreliance on didactic dimensions may signal avoidance of interpersonal dynamics. Therefore, especially in the parish setting pastors need to hold onto the corrective insight that learning the correct ideas is not the goal of counseling and is not a substitute for re-experiencing oneself in relation to God and others. A more literate Christian is not necessarily one who hears the word of God afresh. The classroom is not the model for pastoral counseling. The goal is not literacy but communicating Christ to people.

Because the parish is a community of inquiry where people have access to learning opportunities, teaching can be kept to a minimum in personal and small group counseling. On the other hand, counseling provides the occasion for persons to be engaged in mutual inquiry in a way that personalizes the wisdom of Christian faith. As a community of inquiry, the parish setting helps parishioners and pastors to re-examine the Christian story in relation to personal histories and encounters so that both pastors and people are learners in the counseling process.

The Parish and the Formation of Primary Relationships

Most parishes are located in neighborhoods where people reside. On the other hand, most pastoral counseling centers serve an entire metropolitan area or rural county. Pastoral counseling in institutions such as hospitals and prisons relates to people in time-limited residencies, either volitional or required, that typically are not designed for the formation of primary relationships as are residential areas with intergenerational families and activities.

No doubt this factor of being located in neighborhoods where people have their homes is not as significant as it once was. In a less mobile time, this location in communities where people lived had a more telling logic. In part the justification for special ministries has been based on the changes in life-style that disclose the shifts of human energies into vocations and voluntary associations or interest groups. People in urban neighborhoods do not know each other as well as used to be the case. An individual's closest friends often are not in his neighborhood. Given such developments, it is understandable that one might question the value of pastoral counseling in parishes. Yet the significance of the home or household cannot be dismissed facilly. Note how people resent intrusion into the home. The home remains a center of the inviolability of the person. Perhaps more than ever before inviting another into one's home is a special act of friendship. In any case the tradition whereby the pastor is welcome in the home in the sense that pastors may take initiative to contact people and get to know people in their homes is distinctive. Such initiative is suspect in all professions sustained by a fee for service structure, and when pastors collect fees for their counseling they sacrifice much of this tradition of trust. Community psychology, nursing, and other community services have adapted themselves well to this approach to helping, but no profession enjoys the privileges, trust, and responsibility that characterize pastoral ministry in this respect. Such initiative provides an unusual degree of flexibility in pastoral counseling. By taking initiative pastors stimulate the minimally motivated and encourage the passive. They can provide helpful follow-up care and counseling and make available minimal yet critical support for persons with whom they have counseled. The privilege of initiative fosters an informality that enables pastors to express genuine care.

Such promise in parish pastoral counseling is not without its pitfalls. At times the difference between taking initiative with a person and assuming responsibility for the person when responsibility should be left with the person is not always clear or is not clearly maintained. Some persons want to rely on others' initiative. Taking initiative is a sacred trust and not a license for fulfilling pastors' control needs. Finally, exercising initiative is sound only when ministers are committed to maintain respect for people's freedom (Oglesby, 1980). The boldness of taking initiative is to be balanced by the courage and grace to acknowledge the right of people to refuse help without apology and to maintain distance when they so choose. Another problem often encountered in parish counseling is confidentiality. In the confessional the expectations are clear enough. On the other hand, there is a strong tendency in parish life to share information, and pastors as well as others may miscalculate the true requirements of a situation. On the whole it is better to err on the side of keeping confidence even when it turns out not to be expected than to err on the side of sharing non-confessional information about parishioners and their situations.

To the extent that they function in the context of family life, parishes can serve as communities of faithful response in the midst of the formation of primary relationships. Though urban neighborhoods often do not facilitate the development of close adult relationships, family life still provides the context whereby primary relationships are first formed. Pastoral counseling frequently involves marital and family counseling, including guidance for the generative role of parents. Also, in neighborhoods churches facilitate the development of meaningful adult relationships that otherwise would not be developed.

Does this context offer promise for pastoral counseling? Marriage and family enrichment groups cluster couples and families in small groups committed to sharing and learning together for a limited time. Parishes or clusters of parishes, as institutions which serve the intergenerational family, frequently sponsor these groups (Sawin, 1982). Consider further the readiness with which a variety of support groups are formed in parishes. While a significant number of these groups originate in the life and fellowship of the congregation, frequently outside self-help groups find the church to be a cooperative partner who provides space and referral. Consequently, the pastor serves in a context of a community in which numerous supportive and even confrontational small groups are available as a network of concern and help for persons who struggle with stress or who face key crises in their lives. Not only is this a convenience for pastors in their counseling, but also it provides a context that helps persons readily to integrate personal, social, and spiritual needs and aspirations.

In the course of analyzing the meaning of context, Seward Hiltner and Lowell Colston (1961) note that pastoral counseling "is a matter of creating, out of a previous general pastor-parishioner relationship, a special and temporary helping relationship—and with the recognition that, upon conclusion of the special and temporary relationship, the general relationship will be resumed." In the parish setting this shift in relationship occurs with great regularity. In contrast, in most pastoral counseling centers no such shift occurs, since the relationship is limited to counseling. In numerous institutional settings, this shift in relationship is also an important factor in the pastoral counseling that is provided.

One important consequence of this feature of parish pastoral counseling is that pastors know their people in their daily lives and observe how they behave in various roles and places. This knowing in the course of daily life exposes pastors to some realities that might remain hidden if these persons were known only in terms of their behavior during counseling sessions. Of course, their immediate interactions in counseling conversations indicate much of their personalities and characterological qualities. Even so, this picture is greatly enriched and expanded for the caring and observant pastor in the parish setting. This broader knowledge of the person is especially helpful in the process of discerning personality disorders.

A constant problem in parish pastoral counseling has to do with transference and countertransference. As a context where primary relationships are formed, parish life fosters transference and countertransference in interpersonal relationships. People readily apply to pastors deep, irrational feelings that are energized by their own formation of primary relationships in childhood. This becomes a special problem for pastors who tend to take personally the attitudes that others adopt toward them. The parish context is one that expects pastors to be involved and warm in their response to people. It will not do for pastors to remain objective or always to conceal their personal reactions to people's dilemmas. Usually pastors can be responsive and personal in their counseling and also maintain sufficient objectivity. At times, however, they cannot. In additional situations, parishioners' troubles are of such a nature that, whether they want it or not, they need the distance and discipline of therapy in a context more isolated than parish pastoral counseling can afford. In no counseling situation should the pastor's own emotional needs be served at the sacrifice of service to the parishioners' needs. Seward Hiltner (1977) places intimacy and distance on a continuum and points out how different situations in the parish setting, including pastoral counseling, call for a relationship that lies at various points along this continuum.

Parishes are places where both superficial and life-transforming relationships are formed. In the parish setting pastoral counseling has potential for rich and varied social support, which can lessen dependency on counseling and the pastor. For some persons, the need they seek to fulfill calls for more than the development of relationships, vital as that need is. For them the meaningful life entails self-investment in the right action. When counseling with these persons especially, the parish as a community of service is a resource for pastor and parishioners.

A Community of Service

One dimension of counseling is the acquiring of insights that help one to come to terms with one's limits. Other insights can help persons to envision broader horizons for their lives. To be added to the significance of insights, however, is the significance of action in relation to pastoral counseling. The modern emphasis on insight has contributed much to the welfare of the individual, yet the importance of behavioral change and its relation to insight has not received adequate attention in insight-oriented counseling theories. The assumption has been that if insight is authentic, action will follow. Not all insights call for action, but many do and parishioners may fail to act on significant insights. The Christian vision of service especially as it is embodied in parish life can help people to capitalize on their insights in terms of action. The Christian understanding of service gives salience to action. Moreover, it holds out the hope that in action people can share suffering and share faith. Christians are called to care for and serve one another, and to reach out in caring ways to serve others. Faith without works is dead (Jas 2:17).

Accordingly, the orientation toward service and service opportunities is another promise of the parish setting that affects pastoral counseling. To the extent that counseling is directed toward action, the parish setting provides an atmosphere of activity and service to others, not to mention actual opportunities to put one's energy and talent to work. Accordingly, pastors can readily invite people to consolidate the insights gained in counseling by implementing new changes in behavior suggested by their personal learning. When persons are grateful for the growth they have experienced in counseling, they may want to express their appreciation in the form of some service. Or, at a deeper level, their insights may have reoriented them so that they are free to find rich meaning in service to others. Of course, pastors should avoid imposing any service expectations on parishioners. Furthermore, pastors need to be alert for the tendency of some, out of enthusiasm, to overextend themselves.

Another problem in connection with this feature of parish counseling arises out of people's and pastors' tendencies to settle for quick insights and fail to adopt a life posture of deep listening to God, self and others. Decisions to act need not be hurried in most situations. In fact, some persons would profit greatly if they were taught how to take more time with many of their decisions and, as appropriate, to let decisions be tentative. However brief, follow-up consultations with persons who have been in counseling can help them to continue to listen and reflect on the changes in attitude and action they have initiated. A parishioner who had come to terms with some of his guilt in relation to a tragic suicide in his family began to work with youth in the church. He discovered that he could not handle all the feelings that arose when a teenage youth expressed depression, and so he looked for another meaningful avenue of service in the church. Had he not been listening while doing he might have buried unresolved problems in himself and been ineffective with those he wanted to help. Pastors have the role of being listeners and helping people listen to themselves, even as they take action and endeavor to serve. This parishioner's pastor had raised the question of what effect depression in youth would have. Consequently, a seed had been planted and the parishioner cautioned against assuming that his growth had resolved all limitations.

Because pastors minister in communities of service, they are able to help people where appropriate to develop counseling insights in the form of constructive service. Typically, such endeavors involve working with other people and entail a system of accountability that can strengthen the social and moral capacities of parishioners. In helping people find avenues of self-giving pastors can help them to listen so that they have hope of engaging in genuine service, not mere busyness. Pastors can help people to find meaningful avenues of service and can support people in their efforts to grow and know the grace of God as they share faith and suffering with others.

Conclusion

This study has emphasized the significance of the parish as a context for pastoral counseling. The parish is a larger context or system in which the counseling process has meaning. In the parish setting pastoral counseling is part of the total work of the ordained ministry and part of the ministry of the church. In turn it is true that the parish is part of a larger whole, the universal ministry of God's people. The parish is one concrete expression of the Christian meaning of community. The kind of community the parish can be and is to be establishes a framework for the meaning of pastoral counseling in the parish setting and the role of the pastoral counselor in this setting. Consequently, the analysis undertaken in this chapter has highlighted the significance of the parish as a community for the pastoral counseling process. The parish community structures, channels, and nurtures particular dimensions of belonging to a community: (1) celebrating a common faith in worship; (2) seeking to understand faith, interpreting its message for coming generations, and exploring mutually the guidance it offers for contemporary life; (3) developing relationships that can sustain and transform the person; and (4) calling to serve God and people in sharing personal faith and suffering. These dimensions of parish life suggest particular areas of promise and distinctive problems for pastoral counseling. While these themes are suggestive, not nearly enough is known of the manner in which the parish context affects pastoral counseling. Careful research, both conceptual and empirical, is needed.

The modern parish is a community that has been influenced by various developments from without, including developments in pastoral counseling in non-parish contexts. The pastoral counseling speciality as it has grown in institutions and counseling centers has contributed much to the awareness of techniques in counseling, the role of interpersonal communication skills, and the psychological resources that can be of help to pastors and pastoral counselors. All these have influenced pastoral counseling in the parish context. In the other direction the parish context not only gives direction to pastoral counseling in that setting, but also is modifying pastoral counseling in other settings. The professional leadership of the church has seen a period of high appreciation for the psychological disciplines, in which theologians and counselors have sought to listen to the knowledge and wisdom ensconced in the psychological tradition. Currently, pastoral counselors more and more are examining the bearing that Christian tradition has on their ministry, and this change of focus has brought these counselors into more serious conversation with their colleagues in the parish context. Pastoral counselors in both parish and nonparish settings now are engaged in study of the significance of worship, the means of grace, spiritual direction, ethics, small groups, and participation in meaningful action as these relate to the counseling process.

Bibliography

Baldwin, J.W. "A Survey of Pastoral Counseling in the Evangelical Free Church of America: Training, Attitudes and Practice." Unpublished master's thesis, Trinity Evangelical Divinity School, 1978.

Browning, D.S. *The Moral Context of Pastoral Care*. Philadelphia: Westminster, 1976.

Calvin, J. *Institutes of the Christian Religion*. J.T. McNeill, ed. Philadelphia: Westminster, 1960 (2.7.12).

Clinebell, H.J., Jr., ed. *Community Mental Health*. Nashville: Abingdon, 1970; and Whitlock, G.E. *Preventive Psychology and the Church*. Philadelphia: Westminster, 1973.

Gustafson, J. *The Church as Moral Decision Maker*. Philadelphia: Pilgrim Press, 1970.

Hiltner, S. and Colston, L.G. *The Context of Pastoral Counseling*. Nashville: Abingdon, 1961, p. 30.

Hiltner, S. "Optimal Intimacy/Distance in the Church," *Pastoral Psychology* 26 (Spring 1977), pp. 178–186.

Jackson, E.N. *Parish Counseling*. New York: Jason Aronson, 1975.

Meagher, P.K., *et al.*, eds. See "Parish," *Encyclopedic Dictionary of Religion*. Washington, D.C.: Corpus Publications, 1979. 3:2675–2676.

Nehl, L.G. "Nurturing and Mythus Bearing in Clergy Work Motivation," *Journal of Religion and Health*, 1979, 18:29–37.

Oglesby, W.B., Jr. *Biblical Themes for Pastoral Care*. Nashville: Abingdon, 1980, especially pp. 45–77.

Sawin, M.M., ed. *Hope for Families*. New York: Sadlier, 1982.

Gerald Fath, O.P.

Pastoral Counseling
in the Hospital Setting

Pastoral counseling in the hospital provides one of the richest settings for enabling people to transcend the apparent meaninglessness of suffering and reach a deeper level of self-acceptance in relation to others and their God. Nowhere else does the drama of life and death unfold and confront people with the serious question about the purpose of life. People from all walks of life, the rich and poor, young and old, believers and doubters, all share in this question and have the opportunity of opting for growth or abandoning themselves to a life of emptiness and pain.

Because of the urgency and circumstances presented, the pastoral counselor is called upon to perform an extraordinary ministry that cannot be tied down to the traditional norms of counseling. Establishing rapport, trust and confidence necessarily need to happen within the very first moments of contact. The luxury of time, setting and circumstances are not often a part of pastoral counseling in the hospital and thereby necessitates a unique sensitivity on the part of the counselor to intuit and assess each person individually.

Life and death are the two extremes that are commonplace within the hospital setting. Between these two focal points there is also much that deserves the sophisticated examination of one engaged in pastoral counseling. For example, suffering, pain, loss, grief, joy, loneliness and emptiness are but a few of the emotions that prevail in the hospital. The profound bonding between nature and grace is constantly questioned within the reality of life and fused with the need for redemption. People in crisis search for a meaning to their suffering. If there is no purpose, then a bleak acceptance of fate allows for the insignificant passing of life. However, if there is some meaning found, new life occurs in depth yielding purpose and healing that transcends the otherwise meaningless journey through earthly existence.

In this chapter, I will focus attention not only on the patient, but also the family. Too often, concern is marshaled around the patient with the primary goal of physical healing. But what happens to the family during this ordeal? Are there ways in which the family is contributing to the illness? How can each become an effective agent in the healing process? Are there healings that need to take place within and between family members? These and other questions will be addressed in this chapter.

Finally, consideration will be given to those committed to the healing profession. For some, the medical world is merely a lucrative form of employment. But for the vast majority, there is a desire on the part of these professional men and women to be a significant part of the healing process on a very human, compassionate level. Because the demands of this commitment are so great, some, unfortunately, have moved from compassionate caring to a functional fulfillment of a job description.

In my experience within the hospital, some doctors, nurses and other health care professionals have taken refuge in the science of medicine and repressed the power of their human ability to care because the pain within themselves in risking on a personal level became so overwhelming that distance and isolation were the only answers. How tragic that no one was there to heal the healer and touch the giftedness of the one who serves!

During and since my years in the hospital setting, I have continued to reflect on how my health care colleagues have ministered to me and helped me to understand the value of this kind of care. Hopefully, some of this combined wisdom will unfold as I try to discuss the role of the pastoral counselor. Far from being a "how to" description, this chapter is designed to heighten one's awareness of the multi-faceted opportunities found within those suffering people of God, to integrate one's personal reflective life in a way to bring a sense of hope, purpose and meaning to those we are called to serve. First, then, let us turn our attention to the patient.

The Patient

For the most part, people who enter the hospital do not consciously choose to become subjected to the multiple testings, complicated procedures and perhaps surgical interventions. I say "consciously" because there is evidence that between 75 and 85 percent of all illness is psychosomatic in origin. For example, if one were to look closely into the circumstances immediately surrounding the onset of the common cold or the flu, doubtless there would be significant stress that disposed a body toward illness. Being exhausted, constantly working, poor sleeping, no exercise and an unbalanced diet are all factors that reduce a person's ability to fight off disease. The question then that needs to be asked is why a person is in this state of exhaustion and disposed toward illness.

When other more serious illnesses are contracted or experienced, an inquiry into these predispositions can be very helpful. Significant stress-filled experiences such as the loss of a loved one through death, divorce, separation, termination of relationship, moving, being fired, etc., may be contributing to the illness. As a counselor, I would often ask patients about these and other life events that had taken place prior to their illness. The significant time frame is within 6 to 12 months before their symptoms appeared. Often within the sacrament of reconciliation, people might mention some unresolved conflicts. Here the pastoral counselor has the opportunity to help patients deal with these problems that have added to and perhaps have significantly contributed to their sickness.

Too often, people retain a paralyzing amount of guilt for being themselves. Many, for example, repress their angry feelings, believing that the expression of these would be wrong, un-Christian and socially unacceptable. Being angry, like any other emotion, is God-given and, therefore, good if used in a creative manner. Unfortunately, rage has generally been the manifestation of anger and to this extent becomes destructive. Role models for the destructive use of anger far outweigh the creative utilization of anger. Anger when turned inward becomes depression and, clinically, is one of the two most prominent issues presented in a therapeutic setting. The sensitive pastoral counselor needs to be constantly aware of repressed anger when counseling patients.

Another therapeutic issue which typically affects medical pathology is sexuality. Society identifies closeness with genital intimacy when, in reality, genitality is only one form of expression in a well-integrated relationship. Moreover, a disembodied understanding of spirituality in the past has reinforced guilt reactions to sexuality and has failed to encourage a more wholistic and healthy approach to life, loving, intimacy and sexuality. These two issues, then, need to be carefully considered as possible stress factors in helping patients deal with illness.

Beyond these issues, there are a myriad of experiences and conflicts that may be intensifying a patient's pain. For instance, questions concerning the meaning of life, worth as a parent or spouse, death, and saying goodbye to loved ones are but a few. The pastoral counselor is given the unique opportunity of combining the best therapeutic skills with a pastoral presence to enable people to be themselves and express hidden questions and fears. If we look at the scriptures and the role of Christ as counselor, he encouraged people to be themselves and speak authentically from the depths of their being. His presence alone touched and cured many. The pastoral counselor, because of his own spiritual journey, knowledge and objectivity, has the same opportunities.

Jesus, as counselor, healed the depths of a person's being so that whatever enslaved that person might be set free for new life. The role of pastoral counselor needs to reflect this same healing presence. The best gift one can give is to live the good news in a way that will reaffirm people and help to set them free from unwarranted guilt and fear.

In order to view the patient in a more wholistic way, it is important to incorporate the family within the context of hospitalization. Let us now focus in upon the family as a significant factor in illness and healing.

The Family

The parameters of the pastoral counselor in a hospital setting need to include the patient's family. Family members share deeply in the patient's illness, and their reactions, in turn, influence the way that the patient handles the illness.

It is important to note here that in using the word "family" and "family member," I am consciously aware that there are other relationships emerging in our society that cannot be considered "family." Some examples of this may be the divorced or separated, the elderly with no family members, those separated by geography, people living together without formalized marriage commitment, etc. I bring this up for several reasons because the pastoral counselor must see these circumstances as opportunities for intervention. Unresolved guilt may be just one facet of this, commitment another. Lack of societal acceptance of those living together may ostracize an individual from being close to a loved one in time of need. Here the pastoral counselor must be particularly aware of his unique and important presence to the patient, family and the staff.

Hospitalization, regardless of its severity, conjures up many feelings. Irrespective of the projected length of stay, it is as if the world stops and both patient and family pause to take inventory about the past, present and future. Countless stories about simple operations that have led to crisis lend themselves to pre-existing fears.

The crisis of illness in a person's life can serve as a beneficial time for the whole family to appraise their life together or a time dominated by fear and isolation. Too often, productivity and earning money have become the hallmark of success. The fact that 80 percent of men claim that they do not have any intimacy in their lives necessarily causes one to question the real meaning of life. Hospitalization may draw this question into a painful awareness. Women, on the other hand, seem to have more intimacy due to the fact that they are able to risk more of their feelings. However, instead of yielding a rich harvest, too often the pain of rejection surfaces and, if unresolved, adds more suffering to an already complicated life.

The question in point is one of intimacy. The high divorce rates as well as the increasing members of the lonely and brokenhearted should center the focus of attention for the pastoral counselor while working in the hospital setting. Family members have endless moments of waiting outside surgical units and endless hours of anticipation in secluded areas near the intensive care units. Questions about the meaning of life and death are prominent. Guilt regarding commitment often surfaces. Anger toward an apparently distant God is another issue. Alienated family members that reappear in the midst of a crisis are but a few highly emotionally charged issues that present themselves to family members during this critical time.

Here, the role of the pastoral counselor may be that of a reconciler. Attempting to bring a ragged past into a realistic and acceptable present could be a primary goal. Perfect answers are seldom found to problems that have existed over the period of many years. Compassionate solutions, however, are possible. The family member needs to attempt finding some acceptable answers to the meaning of his or her life in relation to the patient. These realistic answers must take into consideration the specific individuality of all persons involved.

I bring this up because the process of self-identity is a difficult task since the influence of society tends to discriminate against a self-definition. Individual, personal uniqueness creatively formed into the image and likeness of God is too often overshadowed by fleeting role definitions rendered by an insecure society. It would seem that here the pastoral counselor's presence as reconciler is crucial. Issues such as the fear of closeness, arrested psychosexual development and a poor self-image are but a few examples that could be addressed and considered significant at the time of hospitalization. Too often, failures in friendship are defined in terms of sinfulness and add to the brokenness of both patient and family members alike. Self-forgiveness and redemption seem far from being real entities that can serve as powerful healing agents.

With regard to sinfulness and forgiveness, people are expert in itemizing their faults and sinfulness. It is not uncommon for a family member to consider hospitalization a result of sinful behavior both for themselves and the patient. Some even take the opportunity of confessing their sins to a priest or counselor. Forgiveness is given by the shaman, but the crucial point is whether or not the person forgives himself. Too often, the burden of one's sinful, broken condition is shackled to their bodies. This type of enslavement limits the horizons of the individual and relegates him to a self-made hell.

Pastoral counselors have the unique opportunity of offering an atmosphere for reconciliation on the level of self-forgiveness. The results of this conversion experience are self-acceptance, an ability to feel the powerfulness of redemption and the freedom to transcend oneself.

Being in the hospital setting certainly challenges the traditional role of the pastoral counselor. The time frame for establishing rapport is severely limited. I believe that all the interior functions of the counselor, i.e., the intellect, sensitiveness, feelings and intuition, need to be marshaled together in order to make up for what is lacking in the more ideal clinical settings. What has been discussed in term of crisis intervention with the possibility of death certainly taxes the creativity of the pastoral counselor. But let us turn our attention to the other side of this, to survival with the same mandate to utilize the personal resources of the counselor.

The unwritten rule that hospital visitations are to "make the patient feel better" is laudable on one hand but deceptive on the other. Too often, family members attempt to instill a false sense of security and that "everything is going to be okay." This masquerades the truth and severely inhibits the potentiality for meaningful communication. In fact, this is like a game and both the patient and the family members know it. The real winner is the one who can break the rules and begin conversing on a deep, interpersonal level.

The problem is that we have very few role models to tell us how to communicate in this way. The voyeurism that encourages the production of more soap operas cannot provide the real-life script for conversation between two people. The correct words and the right lines are present deep within a person's gut. Trusting in this well-spring of interior wealth is the issue at point. Risking is the bottom line.

The pastoral counselor, when working with a family member or the patient, may indeed surface many issues and concerns by enunciating the "unspeakable" feelings. Things that too often are said only at the funeral home, when it is too late, are best said face to face. Feelings of love, affirmation, fear and grief are concrete examples that need encouragement to be said openly. The counselor must try to support family members in their willingness to communicate from the depths of their being for the future of survival, too. The guts that it takes in view of death to speak the truth is one thing and even more important in view of survival.

Highly emotional issues like loneliness and isolation are feelings that severely limit the healing process. In fact, the failure to effectively communicate these may be the reason why one is in the hospital in the first place. The role of the pastoral counselor is one that attempts to bridge the gap between an isolated existence and a meaningful life. Commitment by way of marriage is no more a guarantee for a meaningful life than ordination to the priesthood, or the conferral of a medical degree. Loving and being loved are the most innate desires of every created person, and the realization of this need, in a concrete way, requires much hard work on a daily basis demanding the ability to risk.

Pastoral counselors have the unique opportunity of modeling this fundamental human desire not only by their academic background but even more importantly by their personal integration of life's experiences. Clinical skills combined with a commitment to spiritual values provide the milieu for grappling with the mysteries of life and death. Moreover, these two components offer an ability to transcend the inconsistencies of life and find meaning beyond the self and in God.

The possibilities of the pastoral counselors with families go beyond the imagination. Instead of sickness or death being a stumbling block, the pastoral counselor may bring light to this apparently meaningless situation. Health for many is seen as a given, and a feeling of entitlement to this state of being may seem to prevail. Some even regard being good and being healthy as an unwritten insurance policy. Pain is too often viewed negatively. Our society perpetuates this myth by emphasizing youth, beauty, and countless remedies to avoid suffering. Escaping the reality of life through drugs is but another way of attempting to hide the facts of life.

The truth is that we are brought into existence to eventually die and, in the meantime, whatever years are granted to us, attempt to grapple with the mystery of our creation in relationship to a God, others and ourselves. Suffering is a significant part of this journey. The God whom we Christians worship created us for life in abundance, not just for the other side of the grave, but in this life, too.

Pastoral counselors are pivotal in helping family members, especially in the midst of suffering, to come to grips with truth, meaning and purpose. The moment is explosive and the possibilities for growth and self-acceptance limitless.

The final consideration in this chapter is the staff. Their influence within the healing process of both patient and family is vitally important. The pastoral counselor's presence to medical personnel rises to new levels when considering a ministry to healing the healers.

The Staff

Patients and families constantly pass through the hospital doors, but the core of the health care facility is the staff. Continually immersed in a sea of human suffering, people committed to the healing profession are vulnerable to multiple emotional and spiritual reactions to their work and therefore need to be of prime concern to the pastoral counselor.

In my experiences with men and women preparing for medical

school, a nursing career, or some other related technical aspect of the healing profession, I have been inspired by their desire to serve others. Initially, there is a sense of dedication and commitment to be with human beings in pain and in need of healing. As their education and clinical experiences progress, the constant battle between the ideal and the reality of the health care profession emerges. Some have, unfortunately, left the health care field because of an apparent irreconcilable struggle between the ideal and the real; others, because of their interior strengths, have managed to overcome the barriers that could have dissuaded them in their career choice, and still others have just endured for less than altruistic reasons.

A career in the health care field is long and arduous. Acceptance into medical school is fierce. Moreover, the nursing profession demands long hours, multiple work schedules and generally a minimal pay. It is no wonder that nursing schools are closing and enrollment is down. With the lack of skilled nurses the workload even becomes more overwhelming and less inviting. An introverted society has much difficulty in encouraging self-lessness. Therefore, the once sought after and prestigious choice of a nursing degree has fallen on very difficult times.

Academic excellence and vigorous competition in both medical and nursing schools have produced some extremely well-trained scientists. However, it is not uncommon for some students to break in the midst of their training. The significant factor to remember from a therapeutic standpoint is the fact that when a rugged individualism is fostered and perhaps even the belief in the invincibleness and Godlike qualities of medical professionals are engendered early on in one's training, loneliness and isolation result.

It seems to me that the medical professional has changed emphasis from the art of healing to the science of healing. In effect, sophisticated procedures and complicated tests have distanced health care professionals from the patient and the healing touch of life has been replaced by a pill or some cold, stainless steel object. When this separation between the healer and the healed occurs, a vital part of humanity is sacrificed.

There are many reasons that could be theorized about this distancing, but, for practical purposes, let me propose just one. Doctors and health care professionals occupy a very prestigious and unique place in our society. In fact, the key to life and death often rests upon skills and knowledge of a doctor. In a society where suffering must be avoided at all costs, anyone offering an escape from this pain is to be revered. Some have entered the medical world with the high intentions of service and healing. In fact, some have even become overly inflated with their profession and, when confronted with the fact that they are not invincible, cannot save humanity from pain and death, a certain disillusionment can take place.

It is here that these medical people stand at the crossroads of their personal and professional lives and the pastoral counselor emerges as an individual to help confront these issues. Enabling health care professionals to arrive at a realistic involvement with patients and families and an acceptance of their human condition becomes a key therapeutic issue that must surface in order for a personal and professional self identity to evolve.

In order to substantiate the enormity of the struggle between the professional and personal lives of doctors, let us focus our attention on the fact that there are higher than average rates of suicide, alcohol and drug addiction, and divorce among doctors. Perhaps the resolution of self-identity questions, in some cases, were never asked. Self-inflicted isolation often prevented necessary intervention. Nursing professionals, too, are more prone to these destructive elements. It seems as if the risks of being human and fully alive are too costly a price to pay which, unfortunately, results in a cold and aloof health care professional.

I might also add that some of the most "earthy" jokes and stories that I have heard have been told to me by people in the healing profession. I mention this not as a criticism, but rather as an observation that this detached attitude may result from the constant bombardment of apparently meaningless tragedies. Health care professionals may become dulled to this pain and, as a way of survival, insulate themselves from their deepest feelings. This facade offers a bold front but continues to isolate them from others, as well as themselves, while underneath there is a cry for closeness.

Oftentimes, I would be called to different sections of the hospital when conflicts arose between physicians, head nurses and staff. One particular meeting deserves mention and, indeed, summarizes a most important point.

The intensive care nursing unit had been undergoing a rapid turnover of personnel. Absenteeism was a daily occurrence; short tempers and bitter words were becoming common place. Other "little things" were being overlooked, such as coffee break messes, unanswered phone calls, etc. Factions and divisions were emerging within an otherwise outstanding, well-qualified staff. Doctors, too, became overly demanding, short fused, and even more absent and hard to reach than usual.

When called to "arbitrate" this problem, I felt like an early Christian martyr being cast into a den of lions. The staff was able to enunciate their grievances against each other. After a sufficient amount of time, I began asking about the patients who had been admitted to the unit. The inventory began with Ricky, the seven-year-old child still in a coma after an automobile accident; Sara, the thirty-one-year-old wife and mother of two small children who shot herself and the life support systems had been shut off; the "everyone's" grandfather who, just before being moved out of the unit, suffered a cardiac arrest and died.

The list could go on, but the trauma of so many tragedies had taken its toll on the staff. Fortunately, I had known most all these people and began expressing my feelings of sadness, loss, grief and even my anger at God for allowing such atrocities to happen. One by one, the real feelings of helplessness, sadness, loss and other emotions began surfacing. The scapegoat had served its purpose; now the real issues were on the front line and the process of healing for the staff began.

Countless other hours have been spent in my office with many health care professionals who struggle daily with the conflictual tension between the professional stance and the personal involvement. The balance between these two elements is a battle that is waged constantly. When it isn't, a part of a person has become terminal.

This type of disillusionment is a common therapeutic issue that is grist for the mill. Health care professionals are constantly subjected to the "injustices of life." This influence can jade their self-perception and have a significant influence upon one's personal life as well as one's professional commitment.

The question becomes: Who heals the healer? It is here that the role of the pastoral counselor surfaces as one not with the answers, but another struggling pilgrim who at least has the boldness to focus on the dilemma.

Health care professionals are not exempt from the search for meaning in life, suffering and death. Because of the intensity of their commitment, these emerge more acutely and with more intensity. Americans in general have attempted to find quick and easy answers to the complexities of life. Idol worship of wealth, position, psychology, sects of various sorts, etc., have all risen and tumbled down. The restless search for meaning continues to surface.

Meaning, purpose and a commitment for life must transcend the self. Suffering, in particular, has no meaning or purpose in and of itself. What one does with pain reveals a person's make-up. To turn in upon oneself and give up is an escape into a meaningless, empty hell. As tragic as this may seem, too many people do choose this. But, on the other hand, others can and do choose to transcend the moment of pain, not escape from it, reassess their lives and commitment to others and to themselves. This is where redemption takes place. This is where the role of the pastoral counselor is most strongly needed to be an enabler and trusted companion on the journey to Emmaus.

The pastoral counselor's role in the health care setting goes beyond the imagination. The constant confrontation with life, death, grief, joy, separation, loss, etc., provides ample opportunities for sharing a compassionate presence to those in dire need, whether they be patients, family members or staff.

Pastoral counselors share in the same highs and lows of our counterparts in health care. Just as we share the glory, the destructive disillusionment that can take place within the health care professional can also devastate us. It seems to me that the role of the pastoral counselor is one of witnessing the values of life in a transcendent manner. By attempting to balance one's personal and professional life with a sound spirituality and a commitment to healthy living, our presence can be healing on all levels of human life. Moreover, with this commitment to spiritual values, to oneself and others, our therapeutic interventions, no matter how confrontative, will come across as a healing touch of affirmation to those in pain and free those enslaved to the meaningless bondage of suffering.

Carole A. Rayburn

Prison

Prison is more than the stone or brick walls, the bars and cells, and the isolation which constitutes a part of the special deprivation of incarceration. More than the physical environment marking the special bleakness of prison, the very idea of prison is depressing. It is that personal freedom is taken away from individuals by impersonal legal authorities when court systems mete out punishment to those convicted of criminal behavior. The insecurity, hopelessness and helplessness, shame, feelings of degradation and failure, family disruption, loss of choice and of privacy, and need to survive somehow under the most trying of circumstances make up part of the picture of imprisonment.

Savitz (1973) has suggested that the criminal justice system is discriminatory for blacks, and blacks seem to believe that this is so. Some researchers such as Sattler (1973) have pointed out that black psychotherapy patients who are seen by white therapists may have such resentment and suspiciousness toward the therapists as to seriously interfere with treatment. This may be accentuated in prison settings, where the nameless, faceless authority figures in society who are seen as the punishing agents are also usually envisioned as powerful whites.

While there is a tendancy for young adult offenders to be anxious, depressive, and acquiescent when reacting to interpersonal stress, racial differences have been found in prison populations. When Perry and Hokanson (1977) studied black and white inmates with black and white experimenters, they found significantly more frequent acquiescence and fewer reports of anger, as well as less frequent intropunitiveness for blacks. The black prisoners were quite vulnerable to the acquiescent "helplessness" syndrome.

Besides blacks and other racial minorities, there is another special group to be considered within the prison setting: women. Velimesis (1981) noted that judicial selection in sentencing, the negative effects of prison control methods, and inadequate medical services may well lead to the depression, suicide, and drug problems of women in prison.

360

In an interesting study of female and male prisoners (Joesting, Jones, and Joesting, 1975), it was found that females had significantly higher intelligence scores and higher MMPI scores on Prison Adjustment, on the Lie scale, and on K (defensiveness against personality weakness) than the males. The women were more likely to act in hostile ways as a response to prison stress and confinement, to show dominant, impulsive, self-seeking, and deceitful behavior, and to express their innocence when accused of wrongdoing. The men were higher on all other MMPI scales: they more often tended to avoid conflicts by escaping or attempting to escape from prison, more usually displayed lack of confidence in decision-making and much submissiveness, made efforts to avoid difficulties rather than face unpleasantness, resisted authority more and were indifferent to the distresses of others, thought they were at the mercy of their feelings and impulses, and were more physically aggressive. Further, the men tended to be more preoccupied with physical symptoms in the absence of physical problems, to be more pessimistic and depressed, to avoid responsibilities and solve difficulties through physical symptoms, to show less ability to benefit from negative experiences, to have more delusional beliefs, obsessive-compulsiveness, abnormal fears, and trouble concentrating, and to be more apathetic, cold, and indifferent and introverted. Thus, the men appeared to be more emotionally disturbed. It was suggested that emotionally disturbed women may be sent to mental hospitals or they may be protected by their families. Society may see it more appropriate to send emotionally disturbed men to prison, considering these men as more responsible for their acts. However, women may be committed to mental hospitals, implying that females should be healed rather than punished as are incarcerated males.

Crastnopol (1982) has suggested that women offenders show disturbances in mother-daughter relationships, with problems in separation-individuation. Those in a symbiotic relationship with their mothers saw themselves as depleted, weak, or empty when they needed to function independently. Women who were in a countersymbiotic relationship with their mothers thought of themselves as bad, mean, or otherwise self-worthless. Two main groups were found: women whose mothers died when the women were young (usually leading to feeling of abandonment by an idealized good mother) and those whose mothers had severely rejected them (these women felt cast aside by cruel, non-ideal mothers). Attention to the expression of emotion of these women, as to the shame, guilt, rebellion, confusion, and emptiness that they may feel, is necessary in working meaningfully with them. Developing an atmosphere of acceptance in which they may grow more trusting and have less fear of further abandonment and rejection will be invaluable in establishing a good counseling relationship.

The Role of the Pastoral Counselor
in the Prison Setting

Several studies (Dittes, 1962; Virkler, 1979, 1980) have stressed that most pastors do not think that they are adequately prepared in the area of counseling. Ministers have indicated a need for having more counseling courses in their seminary training, some reporting in Virkler's (1979) survey that they had had no seminary courses in counseling (27% indicated this), or only two courses (27%), or two or less counseling courses (60%). This study also showed that often pastors were hesitant in expressing their own anger or sadness to those whom they counseled, and the pastors did not wish to physically display feelings of concern or warmth (e.g., occasionally holding a hand, patting a back, giving a hug). Nor did pastors tend to make referrals readily to other mental health professionals.

In another study of pastor facilitativeness, Virkler (1980) tape-recorded ten minute counseling modules conducted by randomly selected Protestant ministers. The ministers' responses were then rated for levels of empathy, respect, concreteness, and genuineness. The ministers were found to function below minimally facilitative levels, particularly on their conveyance of warmth, empathy, and acceptance. Conservative ministers were even less facilitative than the more liberal ones. Maturation and experience did not prove to increase facilitativeness: courses in pastoral counseling increased facilitativeness only a little and the completion of the general seminary curriculum made no difference at all. It was concluded that there are differences between counseling process and counseling content, with no amount of theological content being able to engender process skills that help ease the situation in the struggles of life.

What does this sense of inadequacy in pastoral counseling mean for the pastor working in a prison setting? An incarcerated population, perhaps more than any other except that found in a mental institution, places great demands and expectations on the training, sensitivity, maturity, and humility of the staff serving it. Some appreciation of the various diagnostic categories of problems experienced by imprisoned individuals, their particular stresses and defense mechanisms, and their often low frustration-tolerance is vital in doing meaningful work with them.

Here, more than in any other setting, adapting a humble stance and a non-judgmental attitude is extremely important. For some prisoners, the loss of freedom and family disruption accompanying their conviction and incarceration, plus any shame and sense of failure in life, are almost unbearable and overwhelming. Many may initially perceive pastoral counselors and chaplains within the prison setting as painful reminders of what they have done and what the costs of such behavior have been to them and their families. They are likely to deny their guilt to themselves and to others. When they are able and willing to admit their involvement in criminal activity and its associated emotional and spiritual problems, it is most likely going to be in an atmosphere of trust and warmth in which they sense a genuine caring for themselves as human beings. Some may see themselves as having been looked upon as mere entities in a cold, indifferent society which places tangible evidences of success—money, education, good jobs—at the top of its list. Now they have the glaringly devastating facts of their failure to achieve success, of their being outwitted by what they may view as a cruel and non-caring society, of hurling themselves into troubles with the law and the bleakness of prison existence. Depression becomes a daily reality.

Cooper (1974) spoke of depression as a rather quiescent state in which there is a characteristic sinking into non-activity. Marked by apathy and disinterest in the pleasures of life, depression may be most effectively dealt with by the individual flowing with the emotion, that is, by not denying or giving in to the depression. Suicide may become a real danger whenever the depression is less passive and the prisoner sees this as a way to express the sorrow. Too, the self-inflicted injuries and the fighting which occur in prison may be the manner in which the inmate resists boredom, monotony, and sadness.

Ministering to depressed individuals has been discussed by Smith (1972) and Andreasen (1972). The prisoner may verbalize some pain at having lost faith in God, as Smith pointed out. Then the pastor can be of help in getting people to look beyond the depressed state to discover what faith can bring about: persistence in the hope of spiritual rebirth after a spiritual death. The pastoral counselor may effect a "family absolution," reconciling the individual to his or her family and helping all of them to understand the meaning of the depression. If the pastor is able to bring about a supportive gathering of a spiritual community around the prisoner, the church or other religious establishment becomes a healing and inspirational reality as well as a resource in times of need.

Andreasen reminded us that pastoral counselors need to maintain the long-held perception of guilt as useful and helpful at times. He viewed guilt as having regenerative vitality which was capable of producing disturbed moods that result in behavioral changes. While some guilt is unrealistic and comes from a punitive and very sensitive conscience, he noted that this is not always the case. Further, he categorizes four groups of depressive content: worthlessness and non-specific guilt, isolation from God or meaning, predominant sinfulness, and worthlessness derived from particular sins or crimes. He suggested that treatment of the anxiety over the emptiness or meaninglessness be effected through assertive behavioral therapy.

While arguments such as Andreasen proposes may be helpful in the general stresses presented by life, once again caution must be urged in dealing with guilt and shame. It is one thing for the guilt to emerge spontaneously from the inmate, and another for the individual to sense that the pastor is judging her or him for past crimes/sins. Yet, the pastoral counselor can be the attendant midwife in the spiritual rebirth which occurs once guilt for wrongdoing is admitted, fully experienced, and resolved spiritually as well as emotionally.

Because individuals with personality disorders and personality trait disturbances and similar problems have often been over-represented in prison populations and because these persons often do not seem to benefit from experience but constantly disregard social customs, there has been a tendency to believe that they do not have a conscience. Professionals and non-professionals alike have usually assumed that such people commit crimes with little or no concern for the well-being of others and without thought of taking responsibility morally for their wrongdoing. Yet, what often passes for lack of conscience may be defensiveness to avoid blame rather than actual disavowing or denial of blame. Many individuals whom I have treated in similar settings have felt so mistreated by life itself that they refused to admit blame for infringing on someone else's life-space. Once in a group therapy session, a delinquent gave as his reason for snatching other adolescents' money in front of grocery stores the fact that that had been done repeatedly to him and he was "just evening the score." He knew that his behavior was wrong and he did feel bad at some deep level for the individual whom he stole from, but he allowed his anger and resentment for similar treatment at the hands of others to cover up his sorrow for the wrongdoing.

In a study of the moral judgment of prisoners in a maximum security correctional facility (Griffore and Samuels, 1978), the prisoners showed "principled" moral reasoning not different from that found in those in non-incarcerated settings. The prisoners were basically oriented toward law and order morality (i.e., in support of absolute authority), the morality of "being good" (living up to the expectations of others), and the support of relative rules, democracy, and the "social contract." It was concluded that the criminal behavior of the prisoners was not necessarily inconsistent with their conventional moral judgment orientation. Moral judgment is a necessary but not sufficient condition for mature moral behavior. Immature moral action involves weak ego strength. Individuals can have a strong conscience, and they can still commit crimes and other wrongs.

The pastoral counselor will do well to think of the hardened criminal as having a very vulnerable soft-spot deeply felt—and feared—somewhere in his or her psyche and spirit. It is this awareness to the vulnerabilities and the sensitivities of prisoners which serves as a constant reminder to the pastoral counselor that such persons are wayward humans, such as others functioning outside prison walls and even as themselves. Perhaps more than anything else, it is this search for the good in others, especially prisoners, which connects with the human and God-seeking element in us all, that makes for effective pastoral counseling in prison settings.

However, the felt vulnerability experienced by most prisoners is part of a lifelong pattern and is deeply ingrained into their psychosocial personalities. They both fear and defend against the threat imposed by such vulnerability. They have in some very real sense perceived themselves to be victims of society or in-groups for so long that they lose patience with the means at their disposal to achieve their desired ends. So, while there is indeed good in them, they may have given up long ago on faith in the good of others and in an abstract good which will win them their fair share of rewards in life. This is much of the basis for their depression, and the more they are frustrated in the unrewarding nature of their efforts, the more they become resentful and depressed. Some may be plagued with morbid ideas all of their lives. One delinquent whom I saw in psychotherapy for several years while he was institutionalized, for instance, had recurring thoughts of holding up a bank and being killed by gunshot when he was 18 (luckily, he was able to work through this frightening fantasy, and it did not become a reality).

Pastoral counseling in prisons often involves Bible study. Phillipy (1983) suggested that, for religious conversion to really bring about a change in behavior, prisoners need to integrate their newly acquired religious beliefs into their personalities. The Bible study program in this instance worked on themes such as money, anger, and trust, and it focused on behavioral elements of learning. Ways of integrating the content of religious faith into daily behavior were stressed. Further, the use of religious language to change thoughts and feelings, and the concept of "repentance" as "change of mind" is employed to introduce the program. Hearing and doing Jesus' words is seen as leading to the most appropriate and effective actions for the individuals. Biblical passages such as Matthew 7:24, "Every one then who hears these words of mine and does them will be like a wise man who built his house upon the rock," are used in a behavioral modification program, with its token system. This helps prisoners to learn to broaden their options and to trust the trustworthy. While this program was built upon cognitive restructuring and rational-emotive therapy, the pastoral counselor could well adopt it as a sensitive and effective means with which to reach prisoners spiritually and emotionally. It would be applying biblical object lessons to practical, everyday life, and this would have immediate use and rehabilitative value to inmates. It is just such connections to actual problem-solving that will serve to reinforce the biblical information and spiritual pathways in the mainstream of the individuals' lives.

One area of sensitivity concerns racial awareness, with appreciation of various cultures of individuals seen in pastoral counseling. Lattimore (1982) cogently argued that pastoral counseling with blacks requires cultural adaptations at many important junctures. Probably in few other situations is this as true as in working with blacks in prison, especially in pastoral counseling. For the most pertinent pastoral counseling with blacks in a prison setting, the counselor needs to understand the positive contributions of blacks' group-identity, family life, work orientation, and improvision as a way of life. Blacks have a need for group solidarity and cohesion. They need to know that being black has a positive value, that blacks have made great contributions to society, and that white persons understand these facts. Too often, whites have been presumptuous in attempting to get blacks to "adjust" to the value system of the white culture. Not only has this been insulting to blacks and pompous of whites, but it has usually missed the mark in not giving due credit to the black value structure.

The pastoral counselor, working with blacks who are in prison, is confronted with individuals who may see themselves as the flotsam and jetsam of society: they have not only had an uphill battle as minority group members but have also lost in the effort to "even the score" through a "successful" criminal career. Unless those working with these individuals can help them to understand the validity of racial pride for their minority group, as well as at least an existential understanding of these prisoners' involvement in criminal activity, the necessary rapport for successful pastoral counseling will most likely not occur.

Much of the time, misunderstandings between racial groups is not so much due to racial as to social class differences. For instance, when the socioeconomic and ethnic variables in the concept formation of late childhood were studied, it was found that children from the same socioeconomic backgrounds (based on the Roe job classifications of the head-of-household) thought alike, regardless of whether they were white or black. All of the children were of average intelligence (Rayburn, 1969). While classism is no better an excuse for discrimination of a group of individuals than is racism or sexism, it does help to explain some of the lack of empathy and confounding of errors in one group failing to relate adequately to another.

The religious experiences which those in prison have had in their early years may involve a high level of conformity to parental expectations rather than deep personal religious conviction. They may have spent a childhood with half a day Sundays in church, only to go into a delinquent existence in late childhood and adolescence. While it is not impossible for those from poor and minority families to hold onto the concept of personal sacrifice often spoken of in the Bible, it is understandable if the message gets turned around in the individuals efforts toward acquisition of some material wealth, albeit through unlawful means in some cases. Too, the pastoral counselor must be aware that not only the individual may have formed certain ideas about the unfairness that often exists in the distribution of wealth in society, but whole neighborhoods and communities may have those values as well. This makes counseling with the family of those in prison especially relevant: they too need help in being more effective in dealing with authorities in their environment. Sometimes the parents of those who have been sent to prison had very limited and unhappy childhoods themselves. They may have been single parents with very limited finances and job opportunities who, in effect, remained in an extended state of immaturity while perhaps emotionally depending upon their children for support. Thus, the child who got involved in illegal activities may have been a victim of a lost childhood, expected by parents to grow up too soon and too completely.

Getting individuals in touch with this missing stage of childhood by pastoral counseling is important to spiritual development. Passages of scripture about understanding the kingdom of heaven as would an innocent and perceptive child would be appropriate. Those in prison have spent much of their lives building thick walls of defensiveness around themselves, often fearing censure if they appear the least bit immature or unsophisticated. Much can be excused by their friends and relatives, they think, if only they maintain a "cool" facade and do not become easily shaken. There is much underlying frustration and anger for the pastoral counselor to uncover and to help the inmate to deal with spiritually.

Perhaps the best way to effect this is through analyzing the ways that frustrations have occurred and, in a non-threatening and non-judgmental manner, to deal with the human elements in desiring certain pleasures in life. If the problems presented by the inmate involve sexual behavior, the pastoral counselor needs to be aware of his or her attitudes about sexuality. As Virkler (1979) pointed out, there should be further study of pastors' attitudes toward sexual behavior and issues. Instead of casting aspersions upon the lawbreaker for poor judgment or a sinful nature, the persons who would work with those in prison would do well to recognize there may have been a paucity of material goods or of desirable and pleasurable experiences which the inmate has attempted to acquire later in life. Once this is appreciated, the unlawful behavior may be understood—though perhaps not easily forgiven—as an exaggeration of a more appropriate need to satisfy a normal desire. Of course, it is conceivable that, in some cases, individuals may have been led to expect that society owed them satisfaction in whatever they desired; these persons would not have sufficiently developed a separation of ego-boundaries between what is theirs and what belongs to others. Pastoral counseling with them might deal with treating others as they themselves would like to be treated and considering long-range goals, as in the rewards of the kingdom. It is not complete abstention in all things now, but moderation in all instances for greatest happiness which probably would be most convincing to them.

Some interesting considerations were raised in a study by Keltner, Marshall, and Marshall (1981). Investigating assertiveness in prison inmates, they evaluated over- and under-assertiveness through measures of behavior (role-playing) and self-report. Hypothesizing that there were at least three dimensions of assertiveness, they noted assertiveness that is behavioral (what persons actually do), intention (what they say that they will do), or knowledge (what persons say that they should do). Felt social fear was also evaluated. In general, the inmates tended to be under-assertive, especially on the behavioral measure. Thus, the common perception of prisoners being dangerously aggressive was questioned and found to be inaccurate. Little evidence was found to support the idea that social fear is the basis for under-assertiveness. Prisoners were slightly more under- than over-assertive, particularly on the behavioral dimension (what they do). The researchers noted that prisoners have had a very limited range of adaptive responses to difficulties in life, hindering their informed options and engendering a battle between individual and social norms of society as a whole. Many who are convicted of crimes and go to prison have come from quite impoverished situations which do not provide much opportunity to acquire an adequate range of skills that they would need for social transactions. It was suggested that social skills training would be appropriate treatment, even more than intervention aimed at reducing anxiety. The best treatment most likely would combine training in social skills and desensitization in correcting erroneous social responses.

Such a lack of adequate socialization may be evidenced at an early age. When I worked at a center for adjudicated juvenile delinquents, I witnessed that there were great discrepancies in the areas of competency of juvenile (adolescent) delinquents in the institution. On a summer outing to a local beach, the adolescents were observed to shy away from some of the planned activities which the mainly white staff thought that they would enjoy: bicycle riding and tennis. Upon further study of the situation, it was discovered that most of the adolescents did not own a bicycle nor had they counted tennis matches in their repertoire of sports activities. This is a rather simple and concrete example of possible differences between the counselor and the counselee, stressing the necessity to forego seeing the person in prison as having experienced all that the counselor has known in the absence of checking out the presuppositions with the individual.

A paper by Goldman (1976) gives special incentive to female pastoral counselors to work in prison settings. She spoke of the female psychologist in an all-male correctional institution. Such a woman staff member would provide a contrast to the previous life experience of the prisoner: she would be a constant presence who is not rejecting of the prisoner and toward whom the prisoner can direct both positive and negative feelings. In the continuous role model of good and bad object fused into the single woman, she gives prisoners the chance to gain ego strength when they learn to resolve the good-bad splitting.

The woman who is a pastoral counselor may encounter three main problems in a prison setting. First, if she is white and is serving a basically black prison population, she may have to be especially sensitive to racial and cultural variances. Second, because she is a female, she may well have to overcome the prejudices against women in society in general and against her in a prison setting in specific. For instance, she may need to establish her authority or equality in holding her own in the interpersonal relationship of the pastoral counseling situation. Her religious humility must not be mistaken for any supposed gender weakness on the part of women. Third, the female pastoral counselor must overcome the prejudices against women religious leaders which is still prevalent in our society (Rayburn, 1981a). As with her male counterpart, she needs to be taken seriously as a pastoral counselor and to be nurturing and sensitive in her offer of spiritual help. Too, she can show the nurturing side of her womanhood within the religious leadership role, without necessarily suggesting that religion and spirituality is only a feminine type of enterprise (in the sense of the worst kinds of stereotypes, with regard to gender, such as "sissy" or weak, or frivolous and impractical, or illogical). Of course, she most likely will not infer any of these traditional misconceptions. However, they may be in the mind of the inmates whom she seeks to help in pastoral counseling, and part of her task may be to deal with the imbedded prejudicial messages that they have about women and religion.

Women who are pastoral counselors in prison settings may also serve as role models of the self-sufficient and centered woman to women in prison, who see themselves often as super-losers in life. In a society which is struggling to become more egalitarian, giving equal opportunities to its women as well as to its men, such female pastors can act as facilitators for women prisoners in using non-sexist language in general and non-sexist concepts concerning the language of religion in specific (Rayburn, 1984; The United Presbyterian Church in the U.S.A., 1979). Coursework in assertiveness training, as well as psychology of women courses, will prove to be invaluable to women and men working with women in prison. Many women who are in prison are black and from low socio-economic backgrounds: they feel a sense of impotence from their being relegated to second-class citizenship on two levels in society, and they usually become more open to the benefits of pastoral counseling when such phrases as "children of God" or "people of God"replace the far less inclusive "sons of God" or "men of God" (Rayburn, 1985).

Less passive-aggressive behavior and more realized sense of personal freedom and self-actualization will be possible when potent and devout women of the Bible are held up to them as role models: Ruth, Deborah, Leah, Rachel, Miriam, Vashti, Esther, Anna, Mary Magdalene, Christ's mother Mary, Mary of Bethany, Dorcas, Lydia, Priscilla, Junia, and many others. Unless the women of scripture and their times can be brought up-to-date and made relevant to our day, little will seem important in their example. An example such as Mary Magdalene presents an opportunity to speak of redemption from sinful living, as does the thief on the cross. Many women of today are not satisfied with male models of biblical times, and they are not apologetic about wanting to gain independence from patriarchal systems of all kinds. All of this does not mean that they are not reachable by pastoral counseling techniques, but they must be approached on their level: an egalitarian striving in reaching out in faith to God from a position of strength as well as humility. This does imply that women in prison will necessarily want to see themselves as strong in terms of divine strength, but equal in human strength (at least moral and emotional, as well as spiritual), to men.

Women inmates have special problems: often the prison is set up to meet needs of men in prison; staff of correctional institutions may have traditional, sexist ways of relating to females; females may be looked upon as either tough and undesirable or as mere sexual objects who are otherwise of little worth in society. Women personnel on prison staffs may come into contention with female prisoners because they do not like their authority questioned. Women in prison who have been drug users, however, especially those who may have been rebelling against mothers and fathers, society in general, males, and certainly parent-surrogates, do not tolerate very domineering people, even the kind of personnel often found in correctional facilities (Rayburn, 1975). Usually they can respect authority best when they have a sense of having some power themselves. If they can learn a sense of this potence in the potential they can fulfill, given to them by a loving and kind Creator, they will see relevance in pastoral counseling.

Before I went to a theological seminary to get my Master of Divinity degree, I worked as a clinical psychologist at a center for adjudicated delinquent children and adolescents. The youths' struggles to find answers to their religious difficulties through religious explanations impressed me. This happened just often enough to convince me that a more holistic approach to helping them was needed. Sometimes, during an individual or a group psychotherapy session, adolescents would ask for further explanation of biblical passages or stories that they had heard from the chaplains on staff or the church volunteers who visited the institution weekly. Often the most burning questions on their young and ever-probing minds were what the nature of sin was, how sin originally started, whether God knew or cared about their sins and salvation, and whether they could still hope to get to heaven (Rayburn, 1981b).

The main assurance that such adolescents seemed to want was that they too were children of God, despite their sins/unlawful activities. They needed to know that they were not ready for assignment to the trash-heap of life. Those who had been charged with violence against females (rape, mugging women and robbing them) were especially appreciative of understanding and forgiveness from female staff. Women who are pastoral counselors can not only bring delinquents and prisoners a first-hand experience of strong, centered women but can offer them appropriate forgiveness for their transgressions against women. It is sometimes because of the very often assumed weakness of females—weakness despised by males who have viewed themselves as less than strong (especially the minorities and economically depressed)—that these males take advantage of females. The females seem to be easy preys to them, and they become scapegoated as victims in many cases.

Prisoners have often given up hope and faith in themselves, so they have the greatest difficulty in believing that anyone else could hold out much hope for them. As a religious psychotherapist, I held onto a faith in the goodness of all people, hoping to tap this good by the use of human skills in combination with a deep belief in the God who moves mountains and saves individuals who become victims of temptations. In any event, those who committed crimes usually did not appear to be without guilt and remorse, once the surface of the tough-guy facade was penetrated by the techniques of psychotherapy. Psychologist or pastoral counselor, the rough exterior which has been built up after years of defensive survival tactics must be excoriated to reveal the more vulnerable and caring interior of the person. It is that layer, less defensive and open to help from the outside, which holds out hope of change and of reflection on other options of behavior.

When inmates ask for spiritual guidance, they are often experiencing a breakthrough in their veneer of nonchalance. They are rendering themselves vulnerable, opening up the possibility of being touched spiritually by another human being and admitting to the power of a supreme being outside themselves. Since the whole topic of powerfulness has been such a sensitive one for them, this seeking is of no little importance and significance.

When delinquents asked me questions concerning religion and theology, I usually referred them to the clergypersons on the staff. However, many of these individuals in psychotherapeutic treatment did not see the clergy on a regular basis or did not want to discuss even religious problems and questions with them unless they had established previous rapport. Often the institutionalized persons viewed religious or spiritual elements as an extension of other areas of their lives. They did not separate the theological into another area which required another type of specialist. As a sort of expedient measure, they sometimes asked for this kind of help from their therapists. Denial of this aid by a trusted therapist could well have been seen as a betrayal. The situation presents a psychotherapist with a highly charged predicament. Conversely, the pastoral counselor might also be concerned with crossing professional lines and venturing into areas of emotional difficulties in which he or she was not trained.

Yet, helping inmates to sort out their religious thoughts, along with their emotions and behavior, leads to the greatest progress in their overall amelioration. A collaboration between clergypersons and psychologists would be highly beneficial, then, to prisoners. Thus, while the more basic aspects of religion would be referred by psychologists to the clergy, some initial discussion of the individual's beliefs, whether religious or philosophical, could logically begin in psychotherapy. The pastoral counselor may be the first to uncover some important matter that is causing the individual to have emotional difficulties, and this would be passed on to the psychologist. When full cooperation between clergy and psychology staff exists and is maintained, with trust extended from both sides, the real beneficiaries are the prisoners served by the two specialists.

Certainly, one of the most vital areas for the pastoral counselor is draining off some of the intropunitive thoughts and behavior of the prisoner. The abundant depression engendered by prison life itself, in addition to the ideas of one's having been a loser before the incarceration, must be dissipated to a large extent if the prisoner is not to become suicidal. The pastoral counselor helps to instill hope into the situation, through awareness that God cares, God saves, and that only God gives life and therefore should alone be responsible for taking it away. The belief in a better day, hope for the new dawning of redemption, is essential to overcoming the gloominess of lives often lived in deprivation and continued dreariness encountered in prison. Often the sensitive pastoral counselor can truly make the difference between life and death to the prisoner.

A word of caution must be given, however. Prisons rarely have enough staff on board, and some lack sufficient training to cope with the myriad problems confronting them. Assessing the number of psychologists and psychiatrists electing to go into delinquency and prison settings, the researcher will find it perhaps not too surprising that this is the lowest number possible for all different settings chosen. Prison is simply not an attractive place for most professionals to work. The financial, emotional, and physical rewards are minimal for most people wanting to help those committed to prison. However, for the pastoral counselor who would work in a prison environment, the rewards of the spirit are plentiful. Perhaps no place else are religious concerns as important to any potential change in life-style. Certainly, no other population is as despised by society, suffering from feelings of failure, self-worthlessness, and often hopelessness, as that of the prisoner. The pastoral counselor may, in the final analysis, be the strongest thread to connect the prisoner with the mainstream of society and its life. The lifeline to centering the prisoner may be supplied by the pastoral counselor, or at least by the team efforts of the pastoral counselor and the psychologist.

Pastoral counselors would do well to remember that, while the psychologist can aid the prisoner to resolve emotional problems and get the individual back into society again, functioning adequately and believing in himself or herself, pastoral counseling can deal best with questions of morality, guilt, shame, and repentance. That will be invaluable in the ex-prisoner's deciding issues of right and wrong that will keep him or her outside of dreary prison walls and functioning as a productive citizen and self-actualizing individual.

Due to the tremendous challenge presented by prisoners, pastoral counselors must realize that not all can be reached soon or adequately enough to always see the results heading in a positive direction. Yet the seeds of faith may be planted and the harvest may come only much later. If one small nugget of hope may be passed along to one who has little or no hope, the true gem of faith will shine forth brightly in the life of the prisoner later. When another human being believes in the prisoner, one who is a professed believer in God, forgiveness and salvation become a living reality. It is then that the prisoner can learn to believe in self and in that power outside the self which is God. True healing can then be effectuated and perpetuated by God, through pastoral counseling by the caring and sensitive pastoral counselor.

Bibliography

Andreasen, N.J. "The Role of Religion in Depression," *Journal of Religion and Health*, 1972. 11 (2), pp. 153–166.

Cooper, H.H.A. "The All–Pervading Depression and Violence of Prison Life," *International Journal of Offender Therapy*, 1974, 18 (3), pp. 217–226.

Crastnopol, M.G. "Disturbances in the Mother-Daughter Relationships of Women Offenders," *Counseling and Values*, 1982, 26 (3), pp. 172–179.

Dittes, J.E. "Research on Clergymen: Factors Influencing Decisions for Religious Service and Effectiveness in the Vocation," *Religious Education*, 1962, 17, pp. 141–165.

Goldman, J.G. "The Female Psychologist in an All-Male Correctional Institution in Philadelphia," *International Journal of Offender Therapy and Comparative Criminology*, 1976, 20 (3), pp. 221–224.

Griffore, R.J. and Samuels, D.D. "Moral Judgments of Residents of Maximum Security Correctional Facility," *Journal of Psychology*, 1978, 100 (1), pp. 3–7.

Joesting, J., Jones, N., and Joesting, R. "Male and Female Inmates' Differences on MMPI Scales and Revised Beta IQ," *Psychological Reports*, 1975, 37 (2), pp. 471–474.

Keltner, A.A., Marshall, P., and Marshall, W.L. "The Description of Assertiveness in a Prison Population," *Corrective and Social Psychiatry and the Journal of Behavior Technology, Methods, and Therapy*, 1981, 27 (1), pp. 41–47.

Lattimore, V.L. "The Positive Contribution of Black Cultural Values to Pastoral Counseling," *Journal of Pastoral Care*, 1982, 36 (2), pp. 105–117.

Perry, A.M. and Hokanson, J.E. "Race Factors in Responses to Interpersonal Stress among Young Adult Offenders," *Criminal Justice and Behavior*, 1977, 4 (1), pp. 45–61.

Phillipy, D.A. "Hearing and Doing the Word: An Integrated-Approach to Bible Study in a Maximum Security Prison," *Journal of Pastoral Care*, 1983, 37 (1), pp. 13–21.

Rayburn, C.A. "Promoting Equality for Women Seminarians," *Counseling and Values*, 1985, (Spring), 29 (3).

Rayburn, C.A. "Impact of Nonsexist Language and Guidelines for Women in Religion," *Journal of Pastoral Counseling*, 1985, 20(1).

Rayburn, C.A. "Socioeconomic and Ethnic Variables in Concept Formation of Late Childhood," *Dissertation Abstracts*, 1969, 31/01-A, p. 468.

Rayburn, C.A. "Some Reflections of a Female Seminarian: Woman, Whither Goest Thou?" *Journal of Pastoral Counseling*, 1981a, 16 (2), pp. 61–65.

Rayburn, C.A. "Wilderness Wanderings," *The Other Side of the Couch: What Therapists Believe*, E. Mark Stern (ed.). New York: Pilgrim Press, 1981b, 153–164.

Rayburn, C.A. "Young Students of Crime," *Drugs, Alcohol, and Women: A National Forum Source Book*, Muriel Nellis (ed.). Washington, D.C.: 1975, pp. 98–99.

Sattler, J.M. "Racial Experimenter Effects," *Comparative Studies of Blacks and Whites in the United States*, K.S. Miller and R.M. Dreger (eds.). New York: Seminar Press, 1973.

Savitz, L.D. "Black Crime," *Comparative Studies of Blacks and Whites in the United States*, K.S. Miller and R.M. Dreger (eds.). New York: Seminar Press, 1973.

Smith, W.A. "Ministering to the Depressed Person," *Journal of Pastoral Care*, 1972, 26 (1), pp. 15–25.

The United Presbyterian Church in the U.S.A. *The Power of Language among the People of God and the Language about God "Opening the Door": A Resource Document*. New York: Advisory Council on Discipleship and Worship, 1979.

Velimesis, M.L. "Sex Roles and Mental Health of Women in Prison," *Professional Psychology*, 1981, 12 (1), pp. 128–135.

Virkler, H.A. "Counseling Demands, Procedures, and Preparation of Parish Ministers: A Descriptive Study," *Journal of Psychology and Theology*, 1979, 7 (4), pp. 271–280.

Virkler, H.A. "The Facilitativeness of Parish Ministers: A Descriptive Study," *Journal of Psychology and Theology*, 1980, 8 (2), pp. 140–146.

Samuel M. Natale

Pastoral Counseling in an Industrial and Corporate Setting

Introduction

Industrial and corporate life has become the backbone of our national activity. The reality is that all of us in one way or another find ourselves involved in corporate life and living. Much of our day is determined by the structures of the corporations in which we live and everything from our sense of self-worth to our "buying power" seems directly related to our ability to interphase with corporations which employ us. This might not be the ideal situation for which the more humanistically oriented among us had hoped, but it is a reality—and one which informs much of our lives.

There seems to have been a natural separation between religion and industrial life—one deeply ingrained in us by the fallacious assumption that somehow these two *necessary* aspects of human living were mutually opposed. Religion spoke of one side of us (transcendence, the search for meaning, humanism, etc.) while industry spoke only to our need to succeed, become powerful, develop skills, etc. This dichotomy goes back to the ancient Greeks (and before) but has come under increasing fire over the recent decade. Individuals have begun expressing their desire to *integrate* the various aspects of their lives so that *who* they are and *what* they do can be more closely allied.

This state of affairs has set the stage for a new phenomenon—counseling in industry and, most recently, pastoral counseling of a very specific kind employed with business people in their own work setting.

I. Life in Business

A. Success and Achievement: The Rewards and Penalties

One major area of concern in industry is the search for personal values, the cornerstone of success and achievement. One might well ask what types of values successful individuals adhere to, and just how one learns and reinforces these values. Further, where are these values learned, and what type of environmment breeds achievement?

The first matter with which one must concern oneself is what individuals in industry think and feel successful accomplishment involves, whether it be taking over a smaller corporation, making a profit, etc. Certainly, when one discusses success in business today, one must realize and admit that there is a pervasive tendency to regard success in economic terms, high earnings, and substantial position. Many people, however, also equate success with stability and responsibility (Natale, 1983a). *Achievement* in business, like success, is customarily defined in terms of monetary rewards, and it is in the marketplace where successful business people are most likely to be distinguished from the less successful ones by their self-set motives and goals, e.g., desire for money, prestige, and power.

Many individuals are distinguished by their willingness to pay the price of achievement and success: isolation and job insecurity.

However, a new theme is emerging among younger people in business; they appear to measure success in terms of job satisfaction *and* more meaningful work, instead of purely monetary terms. Many people today describe success as something that reflects goals and aspirations which have very little to do with one's career advancemment. Therefore, the nature of one's job and commitments becomes more important than security or pay (Natale, 1983b).

It is clear that business people in general regard success highly and expend considerable effort in pursuing it and in adopting values which help to attain success. However, these same individuals are also dissatisfied with the current state of affairs and are clearly searching for more and how this "more" can be developed. It is the direct concern of pastoral counselors to help individuals develop and search for the components of this "more" in their lives. For there is increasing empirical evidence that the burnout and stress which seems epidemic and characterizes such a large segment of the population is, in fact, largely derived from a moral conflict between what one values and what one does. The single-minded preoccupation with getting ahead and "making one's mark" has led to an inevitable downward spiral which seems inescapable. Before we begin addressing the possible interventions of a pastoral counselor, it would be useful to turn our attention to a reconsideration of the kinds of stressors that one in industry faces.

B. Burnout and Stress

One natural result of any single-minded concern with achievement and monetary success is personal burnout and stress. Therefore, let us consider this topic of personal stress and burnout, in addition to pastoral approaches one can take to alleviate the pressure of professional burnout, a major problem and concern in industry (Natale, 1983c).

Of course, stress, whether psychological or physical, becomes a real problem only when an individual's ability to cope with stress is impaired. For example, there are numerous variables which are involved in an individual's ability to cope with a given environment, especially in the business world. Change itself may well be the most significant change that modern people face, especially in the business and industry environment. Such topics as titles, departments, and divisions are created and dismantled at an alarming rate.

Work overload is another obvious factor which contributes to the business person's stressful world, and this is usually the first factor mentioned in relation to the work environment. One would think that a method of dealing with this problem of work overload would be simply to give the individual less to do. However, too little stress can be a stress itself as the body and brain must have sufficient stimulation to function properly. So, an individual must seek a *balance* which can be achieved only through active control of one's life.

Lack of control, whether it is actual or perceived, is an important stress factor, and stress itself is a type of cycle. Excessive stress leads to physical and psychological weaknesses of differing degrees (leading to burnout). An afflicted individual will simply become ever more vulnerable to future stress, and the cycle ultimately will become a spiral with the passage of time as each successive encounter debilitates the individual unless the situation is remedied.

On the job in business and industry is an excellent place to perceive emotional or psychological disturbances, and since such a significant amount of one's life is spent in the workplace, personal and performance disturbances are their most obvious here. Therefore, this would appear to be the most obvious area in which to suggest remedying these disturbances. Events of burnout and stress will ordinarily reveal themselves as *anxiety* and *depression*, the twin siblings of burnout and stress.

Burnout itself suggests a waning vitality, a fire diminishing. The burnout process usually involves levels or stages, and the process itself usually accelerates almost imperceptibly and can be intercepted, reversed, and perhaps prevented. Clearly, it can be experienced by anyone.

Basically, there are three distinct levels in the burnout process with respect to severity and duration. The first stage of burnout is characterized by observable signs and relatively mild symptoms which might occur only occasionally. One attains the second burnout level when the signs and symptoms are more stable, last longer, and are more difficult to extinguish. The third level, and obviously the most extreme one, is experienced when signs and symptoms are more chronic and a definite physical or psychological illness has occurred (e.g., hypertension or some manifest form of it) (Maslach, 1978).

It is at this latter point or stage that immediate medical and/or psychological intervention is required. It is at this point that the pastoral counselor may enter with sensible questions to address the problem of personal achievement and success. If the pastoral counselor is able to sustain the creative tension between personal achievement-success and profit-making concern, some considerable progress can be made. The pastoral counselor offers a particularly attractive combination of skills which make him particularly competent in this area where the exploration of values and a concern with transcendence is the condition of possibility for remediation of the burnout and stress. Pastoral counselors must, of course, be highly credentialed as counselor/psychologists but their affinity and expertise in areas traditionally touching on the search for meaning, ultimate goals, integration, and comfort with the interaction between social, behavioral, and religious goals enables them to aid the individual in their personal search for integration. It is increasingly clear that any full integration must, of its very nature, involve psychological, economic, career, *and* spiritual concerns.

Clearly, the cost of business can be measured in terms of a person's physical, emotional, and spiritual life. Therefore, before one considers the various ways in which burnout can be dealt with remedially or preventively, one would do well to review some of the signs and symptoms which clinical experience and research have discovered to characterize the process. These symptoms, such as difficulty in decision making, guilt feelings about work performance, preoccupation with problems, etc., should provide the educator with a departure point, as well as enable the teacher to predict any behavioral changes *as a result* of specific interventions.

Once a worker's degree of burnout has become severe, the problem clearly requires treatment. Therefore, whether one's symptoms are basically physical or emotional, professional help is expedient, and with the appropriate care, from a physician, psychiatrist, or psychologist, restoration to reasonably good mental or physical health can be attained. Any restorative efforts can attain a balance again but cannot sustain it unless there is a *remedial educational component.* A value remedy is absolutely essential in the case of a value disease (burnout/stress), and from the very specific elements of disturbed behaviors, the teacher assists individuals in painting a portrait of the world picture which they seek. One presumes that there is a correlation between behavior and goals, and at the junctures where the goals are not in tandem with behaviors, the pastoral counselor has a point of natural intervention.

Overall, positive recognition of a person's value, cooperative/communal growth, and liberation form the cornerstone of any effective intervention in handling stress and burnout and are the foundation of traditional ethical wisdom. After all, who is better equipped to address the reality of community salvation, liberation, and personal dignity than the serious pastoral counselor who is involved in implementing wisdom in terms that are sufficient and vital to our contemporary situation?

II. Distinctions Between Counseling, Spiritual Development, and Therapy

The spread of interest in pastoral counseling and pastoral clinical training has triggered a revival of the healing dimension in pastoral care. Indeed, the growth of the pastoral counseling movement was a significant feature of American church life in the 1950's and 1960's. The growth of the pastoral counseling movement existed in marked contrast to another significant growth in pastoral practice, that of the managerial and consultancy models of ministry.

What then is counseling, one might well ask? The word, though it is now employed in areas totally foreign to the Christian church, owes its origin to the Judaeo-Christian tradition. The word itself is derived from the same source as consul, conciliate, consult, and suggests an interchange, a two-way process. As a general rule, counseling is more restricted to *specific crises* than is, for example, the more long-term work of psychotherapy. While the concept of pastoral counseling is quite close to that of psychotherapy, pastoral care, and social casework, there are important areas of demarcation. For example, the psychotherapist may be involved for years with a patient, and unlike the pastoral counselor he is often not involved with the patient's life situation and family background. The work of pastoral care is sometimes distinguished from that of counseling by the fact that it involves drawing more on one's spiritual resources (Lake, 1967).

Most important, the counseling movement has been the "I-Thou" relationship, the person-to-person encounter, and the concern with personal change, and it is this emphasis which has led to frequent comparisons with the Christian ministry. The counseling movement appears to be very close indeed to Christian spirituality, and the counselor appears to have stepped into the breach created by religion's decline. In counseling one sees the usage of concepts such as love, self-respect, and maturity; many writers on pastoral counseling also utilize these concepts, and it is quite common to find Christians working in this field who emphasize the virtues of non-direction, personal wholeness, integration, authenticity, etc.

Since the formative work of Carl Rogers and others, there has been much stress placed on "unqualified acceptance" and "full mutuality" in the therapeutic relationship. However, in recent years a different emphasis has evolved: one which depends on confrontation, conflict, and the acceptance of personal responsibility. Also, in recent years there has been more of an emphasis on the group as the locus of counseling and of therapy. There is also now an extensive industry of counseling courses and programs, and many clergy members have examined these disciplines as ways of finding help and support in their ministries. Therefore, can we then see in the pastoral counseling movement a contemporary form of spiritual direction? Is pastoral counseling the form, or one form, which direction and maybe confession should take in the twentieth-century church?

There are some important differences between the pastoral counseling movement and the tradition of spiritual direction; it is most important to recognize these. First, the pastoral counselor's concern has tended to be with states of emotional distress; pastoral care in the Christian understanding is not restricted to the troubled or distressed or to crisis points in life. Second, the counseling movement has been clinic-based or office-based rather than church-based or community-based. It has therefore lacked the continuous involvement with people in their homes and families which is so essential to pastoral care. Third, the movement has tended to focus excessively on individuals' problems, a fault which it has shared with social work and with the church at various stages of its history.

In recent years there has also been a great deal of attention paid within all therapeutic schools to the issues of spirituality and spiritual values. Despite substantial differences between C. G. Jung and R. D. Laing, both placed great stress on the importance of recovering spiritual life. In the 1930's Jung claimed that many of his cases were suffering not from any common identifiable neurosis but from senseless and empty lives. Many psychotherapists argue today that the aim of psychotherapy is to *heal* the soul, while religion's aim is to *save* the soul. Psychological health is thus a necessary side-effect of religion; therefore, today among analysts there is more concern with the areas of value and meaning.

However, the analyst's relationship to his patient is of an essentially different character from that of the priest to his parish or community. The analyst will be less concerned than the counselor with the patient's life situation, his family background, and the social problems which face him.

Rather, his role is to explore the inner world of the unconscious forces, feelings, expectations and fantasies. The priest, however, cannot ignore the unconscious, and spiritual direction cannot be totally separate from a search for psychological health.

Another therapist who places great emphasis on spirituality is the Persian analyst, Reza Arasteh, who combines analytic and mystical approaches in this concept of "final integration." Arasteh stresses that integration is not the curing of neurosis by an adaptation to society, but is the psyche's maturing on a transcultural level.

The topic of sexuality is also important in this discussion. The spiritual director, of course, is concerned with union with God, and this union process demands a profound degree of self-knowledge and maturity. Since a person is a sexual being, this involves the acceptance of one's sexuality and integrating sexuality with the rest of life. This integration is one of religion's central purposes; therefore, there is an insistence in the spiritual tradition that the guide should be someone who is experienced in the passions. Religion and sex are inextricably linked, and certainly an honest facing of human sexuality is vital to spirituality. When this latter does not occur, spirituality becomes twisted and unbalanced.

Therefore, one of the most vital tasks for contemporary spirituality is to learn from and work through sexuality's contemporary insights and understandings; much of a spiritual director's time may be taken up with this. Sexuality must be redeemed from its detractors, and this integration of sexuality and of the physical aspects of being human is therefore of the greatest spiritual importance and one of true religion's essential functions. Clearly, spirituality and sexuality are inseparable, and the sexually immature person cannot bypass the quest for sexual integrity in the search for spirituality.[1]

A final point in this section of the discussion is that priests, therapists, and other members of the "healing professions" need to create supportive teams with an area in order to fulfill their roles more effectively. Any interdisciplinary discussion and sharing of ideas and problems are always valuable; the achieving of wholeness involves medical, psychological, and spiritual needs. The establishing of such groups for mutual consultation and support could well lead into a study of wider issues in medicine and theology and could well illuminate the understanding and practice of both disciplines. It is the continued professionalization of pastoral counseling with its emphasis on the tension implicit in most living that is in large part responsible for the increasing willingness of corporations to encourage counselors with a pastoral orientation to become members of their personnel/hospital, etc. staffs. It is crucial here to note that few if any reasonable organizations would seek to hire sectarian proselytizers whose purpose is to "win converts." This has never been the goal of pastoral counselors, however; the exploration of personal values and a concern with moral and religious beliefs has always been a central concern and an appropriate arena of intervention.

III. Emphasis on Counseling Stages

The central idea behind the client-centered approach is that any individual's potential tends to be released in a relationship in which one person experiences and communicates his or her own reality, caring, and non-judgmental understanding. The uniqueness of this approach lies in its being oriented to the relationship process, rather than to the symptoms or their cure, and in drawing its hypotheses from the raw data of therapeutic and other relationships. The term "client" rather than patient indicates that this is indeed not a manipulative or medically prescriptive model.

Therapeutic success depends primarily not on a therapist's technical training or skills but *on the presence of certain attitudes in a therapist.* Three attitudes especially appear to be most important for therapy's success: (1) the genuineness or congruence of the therapist, (2) the therapist's complete acceptance of or unconditional positive regard for his client, and (3) the therapist's sensitive and accurately empathic understanding of the client.[2]

When therapy conditions are present, a process of therapeutic change is put in motion, and one may broadly describe this process as the client's reciprocation of the therapist's attitudes. Gradually, as the client discovers someone is listening to him, he becomes more able to listen to communications from inside himself. Gradually, the client also becomes able to listen to inner feelings and moves toward a greater congruence towards self-expression. The client is now free to change and grow in directions that are natural to a maturing person.

As in most counseling situations, there occurs a standard continuum of process that can be divided into *seven* stages (as detailed in *Modern Synopsis of Comprehensive Textbook of Psychiatry/II*—Second Edition). Let's apply these steps to pastoral counseling in industry. In the first stage the client is so remote from the immediate experiencing going on within himself that he is unaware of it, and there is no awareness of any desire to change or grow. In this state the person exists in a certain world of fixed constructs and communicates only by externals. This is the usual situation which the pastoral counselor encounters when first meeting with an individual. The person presents himself as "overly tired" or stressed but is basically unaware of any need to change his life. He neatly separates his home life from his work life and these two components from his moral and/ or religious beliefs. Such an individual knows he is feeling poorly but lacks any sense of insight. In fact, if the counselor were inexperienced and would even suggest a value conflict, the employee would probably never return to a consultation. The person lives in his own world of "goals," "target dates," and "objectives," all nicely scheduled. He keeps running and begins to realize that no matter how fast he runs, he will always be behind. Work assumes more time; family recedes; concern with transcendence and religion becomes cynically assumed to be irrelevant and/or insignificant to the matter at hand. It will be the challenge of the pastoral counselor to explore the individual's life experiences in such a way as to help the individual experience the discrepancy which emerges when individuals emphasize one or another aspect of their lives to the exclusion of others.

In the second stage the client or person is able to express himself on topics not concerned with self and about problems which are perceived as external. Feelings are occasionally described as unknown or as past objects. This often expresses itself as complaints about "the boss," work load and continual demands.

If in step two a client experiences himself as being fully received as he is, a loosening process begins to develop which leads to step three. Freer expression about self as an object develops, and even self-related experiences are described as objects. In addition there is now much expression about feelings and personal meanings that are now present.

In step four, feelings are described as objects in the present, and occasionally feelings are even expressed in the present. Experiencing is less remote and may occasionally occur with little postponement, and there is also a loosening of the way experience is construed. The client should begin to develop a sense of self-responsibility for problems. In any type of therapy, much of the actual therapy takes place or exists at about the stage 4 level. At this level the client is exploring and is beginning to sense himself as a feeling and experiencing creature who is frightened and disorganized by elements dimly sensed or occasionally blurted out. It is in this stage that the pastoral counselor really "gets to work." That is to say, the individual begins to express his self-doubt, confusion, and uncertainty about the life he is living, the commitments he has made, and, most importantly, about the personal hierarchy he has *created for himself*. This, in industry, is the essential point of intervention, for it is here that the pastoral counselor must enter to enable the individual to experience the necessity of recreating a hierarchy of goals and achievements. For the individual this *must* involve some level of career, economic, and spiritual concern. It is absurd (and ineffective) to suggest that an individual who is searching for a new self should throw off the shackles of his oppression and go off to some retreat where he will continue to develop as a "beautiful person." The pastoral counselor has, regrettably, been associated on occasion with such soft thinking. It is necessary for the counselor to help the individual explore the reality that while he may need to realign his goals and aspirations, most individuals struggle with blending (or trying to blend) the necessity of a productive career, positive self-concept, and a concern with others that can be described as nothing else other than religiosity.

When stage five has developed, the client feels quite secure in the therapeutic relationship and much less frightened by the discoveries in himself, and now feelings are expressed freely as existing in the present. Personal feelings or meanings previously denied are now close to being fully experienced—frequently with fear, distrust, or amazement. The client desires to own his feelings and also to be *the real person*. Further, the therapist should now be able to recognize the client's recognition of and facing of the disparities between the self previously built up and the actual experiencing. The client now should be more fluid than in stages one and two and is much nearer to being an organic, visceral being—something which is always in process. The client also should now be more aware of self and begin to sense that truly *emerging* self.

The sixth stage of the therapeutic process is perhaps the most distinctive and often the most dramatic, and its most compelling element may be the full and accepted experiencing of feelings which were previously denied to one's awareness. In this stage there exists no longer any particular awareness of self as an object; indeed, the self *is* now the experiencing, the ongoing process which is changing from moment to moment. The constructs by which the client has been living can now be seen for what they are—construings that have taken place in him. This is the stage during which the individual is becoming freer to explore what his real values are. Individuals begin to be able to explore the prices which they have to pay for the things they desire. Individuals begin to experience the discrepancy between "doing well" and "doing good." In short, this is the time when individuals are able to evaluate their personal situation more honestly. They find themselves beginning to be concerned about their generativity. The office at the top is not seen as the only affirmation, and individuals begin to expand their horizons to include family success, caring, and empathy as well as economic affirmation. Ironically, those individuals who develop the most successful career patterns seem also to have a hierarchy of values which leaves plenty of room for the affective, behavioral, and cognitive as well as overarching spiritual values.

In this sixth stage, individuals begin to reorganize their goals in living and begin taking those tentative—and frightening—steps toward establishing a corrective in their lives. Religious and moral values are *explicitly* raised and discussed. Ethical decision making becomes a concern and social responsibility begins to loom largely in their consciousness.

The final stage, seven, is a trend or goal rather than something which is fully achieved. In this stage the client or person no longer fears experiencing feelings with any immediacy or richness of detail. This occurs not only in therapy, but also in outside relationships. This welling up of experiencing in the moment constitutes a referral point by which the person is able to know who he is and accepts himself, trusting in his own organismic process. Each experience determines its own meaning and is not interpreted in terms of a past structure. The self is the subjective awareness which the client is experiencing.

Experiencing simply is the process that includes all that is going on within the envelope of the organism that is available to awareness. When an experience has been denied to awareness because it is inconsistent with the self-concept, it may, in therapy, come into awareness with a rush.

Now, for any therapeutic change to occur, some conditions must be present. First, the client must experience at least a vague incongruence which causes anxiety in him. Second, the therapist must be genuine or real in the relationship—picture of self and the way he communicates immediate experiencing. Third, the therapist must experience a caring or accepting attitude toward the client and must also have a sensitive understanding of a client's internal and external reality which the client perceives. Finally, the client perceives to some degree the reality, caring, and understanding of the therapist; this perception is usually partially based on a therapist's words.

When these latter conditions do exist and continue, a set process is set in motion. The client feels increasingly freer to express feelings and personal meanings via verbal and motor channels. The client should also be able to differentiate more accurately feelings and perceptions and their objects, whether others or self. Further, the client comes to experience *fully*, in awareness, any discrepancies and lives feelings and meanings that have previously been denied to awareness. Finally, the client's concept of self should ultimately become more congruent with the immediate experiencings and also become more fluid and changing. Increasing congruence between self and experiencing usually is synonymous with improved psychological adjustment.

Therefore, certain, clear changes should result for the client in becoming more effective in meeting and coping with life's problems and in handling relationships. For example, there should be an accompanying relaxation of tension, physiological and psychological tensions, and also a reduction of the anxiety level and a clearer sense of goals. Furthermore, the client should become more confident and self-directing, as well as more mature, more within his own control, and better related to others.

Overall, client-centered theories and methods have been employed in a wide variety of settings that bear really no resemblance to the formal therapy situation. Whether a group of people convene because they are experiencing serious problems, as in group therapy, or get together to enrich and enhance their personal development, as in the encounter group, a client-centered approach has been discovered to be directly applicable. The frontier of its application remains industry.

Clearly, the basic concepts, theory and methods of client-centered approach have basic relevance to industry. For example in a number of corporations changes have been based on the client-centered pastoral counseling approach with overall favorable results seen in promoting self-directed change. Too, the encounter group plays a part in affecting change in management's attitudes. Pastoral counseling has also had a wide and quite positive reception by a great number of professional groups in addition to therapists, such as business executives, marriage counselors, etc. And it has been employed effectively in any number of widely disparate cultural settings, e.g., France, Belgium, Italy, Japan, Northern Ireland. The pastoral counseling approach remains a possibly potent intervention technique for aiding individuals redevelop their personal lifestyles—and their corporations.

Notes

1. This argument is developed directly from Kenneth Leach, *Soul Friend*, Harper & Row, 1980. pp. 113–115.

2. For further elaboration of this point see R. Parsons, "Counseling Relationship," in R. Wicks, R. Parsons, and D. Capps, *Clinical Handbook of Pastoral Counseling*, Paulist Press, 1985.

Bibliography

Lake, Frank. "The Place of Counseling in the Church," *The Times*, August 19, 1967.

Maslach, Christina. "Burned Out," *Human Behavior*, September 1978.

Natale, Samuel M. "Success in Industry: Personality Considerations," *Thrust: Journal of Employment and Training Professionals*, Winter/Spring 1983a.

Natale, Samuel M. *Ethics and Morals in Business*, Birmingham: Religious Education Press, 1983b.

Natale, Samuel M. "Endless Corridors: The Stress of Organizational and Industrial Life," *Thought*, Volume 43, No. 230, September 1983c.

Sharon Parks

Pastoral Counseling
and the University

My first semester was really a lonely time and I remember lots of long walks and lots of tears, and I pretty much decided that if I couldn't find the answers I was looking for, if I couldn't find a purpose for living, I might as well quit living. And if [the college] wasn't going to help me in that, that I was going to give up.

This experience was shared by a college senior, reflecting on her first year in higher education. But the questions of purpose, identity, meaning, and ultimate concern—the issues of faith—again and again confront each of the persons who participate in the institutions of higher learning, whether they be students, staff, faculty, or administrators. The pastoral counselor is one who responds to this on-going motion in the life of faith. Because the university is a context in which religious faith and belief inevitably undergoes examination and perhaps transformation, it is particularly important that the pastoral counselor be able to perceive faith not as a discrete, isolated aspect of life, nor as always manifest in explicit religious terms, but as recognized in its most generic and profound sense.

For faith may be thought of as the on-going weaving of the fabric of life-giving form, order, pattern, cohesion, and holding power to the disparate elements of existence. Faith embraces and relativizes each element of our experience. Faith forms our conviction of the character of reality, our sense of what is ultimately true and trustworthy; and it may, therefore, be expressed in both religious and secular forms. Faith is both grounding and dynamic. Faith is an activity in which all human beings are engaged.

As such, faith is not merely a matter of intellectual assent to dogmatic propositions, though matters of faith are matters of the mind and its formulations of truth; neither is faith merely a matter of church membership

388

or other religious affiliation, though faith has everything to do with connection, community, communion; neither is faith only a matter of feeling, though the affections and passions of the human spirit manifest the power of faithful being; neither is faith simply a matter of the formulation of a positive vision for human life, though the possibility of hope and affirmation of the good is integral to the experience of religious faith. The issues of the true and the false, power and powerlessness, alienation and belonging, hope and despair, good and evil, passion and emptiness, stand at the core of human experience and create the dialectic of faith. Faith is the activity of spirit; and it is, perhaps in a particular way, the activity of the academy of higher learning. For the academy of higher learning has a particular capacity to evoke the push and pull of this dialectic.

The academy of higher learning takes many forms: two year community colleges, four year colleges, institutes, professional schools, and universities. These may be public or private, religiously affiliated or otherwise particularly defined by heritage, competence, reputation, and/or constituency. For the purpose of our reflection here, we will assume the context of the university, the form which has the capacity, more than any other, to embrace the fullest range of the experience of higher education. The aspect of this experience most important to us from the perspective of pastoral counseling is that the vocation of the academy serves, for good or ill, the on-going formulation and reformulation of faith.

For whether the university is primarily defined by its research activity, its teaching activity, its liberalizing purpose, or its preparing of persons for professions, the university intends that the meaning-making of persons will be transformed. If persons come in search of knowledge and enter into study and research, inevitably the search for understanding requires not only additions to previously held knowledge, but the dissolution of earlier assumptions in the light of new insight. If a person comes to the university simply because social class and general aptitude make it both expected and possible and thereby submits himself or herself to the teaching-learning process, it is the hope of the faculty that the encounter with the university environment will, nevertheless, stimulate reflection and change, even if it was not sought in a self-conscious fashion. If one enters the university for professional preparation and/or the expectation of attendant economic security, presumably the purpose of the university is to expand one's concept of the profession itself, orient one to its values and commitments, and enable one to acquire the skills necessary to its function. It is difficult to undergo any of these processes (much less all, as is typically the case) without setting at risk one's sense of truth, purpose, and being.

The university is, therefore, an environment with power to transform not only one's sense of truth, but also one's sense of self. Personality is formed not simply by some unfolding process from within, but rather in the interaction between the self and environment. The values, social norms, and structures of the environment are powerful shapers of personality.

Thus it is significant that the university is for many something of what Erving Goffman describes as a "total institution" (1961, pp. 5–6 & 12):

> A basic social arrangement in modern society is that the individual tends to sleep, play, and work in different places, with different co-participants, under different authorities, and without an over-all rational plan. The central feature of total institutions can be described as a breakdown of the barriers ordinarily separating the three spheres of life. First, all aspects of life are conducted in the same place and under the same single authority. Second, each phase of the member's daily activity is carried on in the immediate company of a large batch of others, all of whom are treated alike and required to do the same thing together. Third, all phases of the day's activities are tightly scheduled, with one activity leading at a prearranged time into the next, the whole sequence of activities being imposed from above by a system of explicit formal rulings and a body of officials. Finally, the various enforced acitivites are brought together into a single rational plan purportedly designed to fulfill the official aims of the institution. . . .
>
> The total institution is a social hybrid, part residential community, part formal organization; therein lies its special sociological interest. . . . In our society they are the forcing homes for changing persons; each is a natural experiment on what can be done to the self.

Goffman explicitly exempts educational establishments from his definition, but designates them as examples of institutions, which while not fully representing the dynamics he describes, do in their provision for eating and recreation facilities approach the condition he describes. And since his key criterion is "the handling of many human needs by the bureaucratic organization of whole blocks of people," and since even faculty and administrators are in many places affected by a variety of housing, day care, health care, parking, and other policies determined by university administration, the power of the environment and its encompassing tendencies becomes obvious. The university has a significant degree of power to "provide something of a world" for its members.

Psychologies of many traditions increasingly recognize the power of the interaction between self and world. A central dynamic of this interaction is located in what we may call two great yearnings—the desire to belong and the desire to be distinct. Human beings seem to yearn at once to be included, to feel a sense of connection with others, to be in communion, but also to express a conviction of one's own particularity, strength, and competence—to distinguish oneself. The self in relation to other seeks a balance of agency and communion (Bakan, 1966), and we do not seem to have a sense of well-being except when there is a sense of this balance. The self in the context of the university, therefore, experiences a great irony. One comes to a university in some sense to distinguish oneself (from family, within a profession, within a culture); and yet one needs so much to belong, to fit, to feel connected with this new environment—this world— which is powerful precisely in its capacity to confer both distinction and belonging.

These dynamics of distinction and belonging are closely related in the university to issues of competence and failure. Often a person has come to the university on the assumption that one is (or should be) "a promising person." The expectation is that one will (and must) do well. But it is also assumed that the university will test that expectation. Evaluation (of both students and faculty) in the forms of exams, grading, recommendations, appointment and promotion procedures places the majority of individuals within the university perpetually "on trial." Even tenured faculty feel the implicit pressure to build and maintain reputations as scholars and teachers. Thus whether one is a first year student preparing for exams or a faculty member preparing a paper for the academic guild, the question of one's competence and the possibility of failure are immediate.

It is also the case that the university has the responsibility to teach critical reflection, the capacity to stand apart from one's world, to objectify and to analyze. The cultivation of this capacity may enhance one's sense of power and competence to act, but it may also facilitate a recognition of the complexity and power of destructive dynamics and eventuate in a sense of powerlessness, cynicism and even despair.

Thus it is that the university is an environment with a particular power to heighten the tensions between truth and untruth, belonging and exclusion, competence and failure, hope and cynicism or despair. And it is in the midst of these tensions that one may seek or be found by a pastoral counselor. A pastoral counselor, in the broadest sense, is anyone who serves as a helpful companion to another's meaning-making, including ultimate meaning or faith, making accessible the resources of a faith tradition. The pastoral counselor may be a student, a member of the staff (maintenance, secretarial, or other), a professor, an administrator, and/or a chaplain, rabbi, priest or campus minister. It is also the case that the one who experiences these tensions may be anyone in the university environment. And it may, therefore, be useful to focus on each of the sub-populations within the university in terms of their experience of these tensions.

Undergraduate Students: While the question of truth and untruth are not peculiar to undergraduate students, we may see something of the experience of the undergraduate student by focusing on this tension. We are helped by the work of William Perry who has studied the journey of undergraduate students in relation to knowing. He has elaborated a series of nine positions or forms through which students may move in their ongoing composition of truth. What is important for our purposes here is the broad outline of his descriptive scheme. We may thereby recognize students as moving from a dualistic and authoritarian mode of knowing, through unqualified relativism,[1] toward commitment in relativism. This means, simply, that there is a time when one perceives the world as composed of truth and untruth, good and evil, we and they. Further, one's trusting of what is true or untrue is determined by trust in a gestalt of assumed authority—usually a configuration of family, educational, religious, and other cultural authorities constituted by individuals, communities, media, etc.

However, as Perry's study shows, in the course of a good liberal arts education, if not before, and/or in the context of contradiction between assumed truth and experience, a student begins to wonder how the prevailing authorities know what they know. For example, one begins to notice conflicting opinions between authoritative professors; or for the first time one shares a social context with persons from different backgrounds who were "they" but become "we." It may occur as one finds oneself participating in behaviors by which "I" no longer recognize myself as "me." What is true and untrue, right or wrong becomes a matter of wonder, questioning, doubt and perhaps even a source of distress. This dissonance tends to be resolved by the composing of a sense of unqualified relativism—a stance from which one may simply rest with the difficult "truth" that all knowledge is relative, and therefore since we cannot know any absolute truth, one perspective is as valuable as another, and morality is a matter of personal preference.

Some persons live out the whole of their adult lives in a mode of meaning-making which is essentially that of unqualified relativism. However, in the university one is typically required to explicate and substantiate each point of view. One discovers that within a relativistic world some points of view are more plausible than others; points of view may be appropriately qualified within a relativized world (Perry's position 5). Yet when many positions are plausible there is no place for the self. And in ongoing intellectual reflection on lived experience the student begins to look for a place to stand—a position of commitment within relativism. Commitment in an uncertain world is an act of faith.

For the undergraduate student this epistemological journey is rarely an exclusively cognitive matter. One's whole being is engaged; for truth and untruth is sorted out in the context of one's relationship with the new environment as a whole, and in particular with roommates, romantic partners, professors, coaches, teammates, lab partners, and the folk back home. Matters of truth become in part matters of "with whose truth shall I be joined." For the locus of authority is not yet located within the self, but rather oscillates between multiple and conflicting authorities "out there" and an emerging but still fragile authority within (Fowler, 1978; Parks, 1980). Accordingly, for the undergraduate the pastoral counselor may play a crucial role as a place of support and committed value.

When undergraduate students are engaged in this recomposing of truth, as described above, self, world, and "God" are being redefined. Faith—one's sense of ultimate meaning, one's sense of power, belonging, and hope—is being reconstituted. This may be an exhilarating, terrifying, bewildering, liberating, confusing enterprise. It is inevitably a matter of highs, lows, and plateaus. The issues of faith may coalesce in matters of sexuality, vocational choice, conflict with parents or other authority, fear of failure, intellectual intrigue or doubt, socio-political concerns, rejection in primary relationships, low self-esteem, drug use, etc. In any case, if one is to undergo the relinquishment of truth as one has known it, one must have the support of a "holding environment" which sustains the person while the self comes apart in order to come together again (Winnicott, 1965; Kegan, 1982). This is particularly the case if one is to let go of truth at the level of transcendent faith—the whole of one's knowing.

There is a sense in which the recognition of this need for a "holding environment" has been institutionalized for much of undergraduate life. Though recent efforts to reform the inappropriate features of "in loco parentis" have also sometimes obscured the legitimate needs and dependencies of undergraduates, universities generally do give special attention to undergraduate living environments (providing counselors/advisors and group activities which sponsor shared exploration), and some faculty design undergraduate courses with particular attention to the needs of undergraduate education. Yet the adequacy of such attempts is dependent upon the capacity of the environment "to create a space where obedience to truth is practiced" (Palmer, 1983, p. 69). This means, in part, the offering of a particular receptiveness to truth that is both continuous and discontinuous with the past history of the self.

For example, when a person comes to the university there is often a strong sense of "nobody here knows me."[2] This is both an opportunity and a danger. The exploration of new frontiers of thought, feeling, and behavior may be possible in the emancipation from previous social norms; yet in the absence of the familiar bonds of affection and accountability one also may feel "at sea," uneasy, and anxious, and dwell in a sense of "I don't know me here either." The counselor who can recognize the significance of the context, culture, and meanings from which one has come offers a space where the truth of the self one-has-been may be in conversation with this new environment and the self one-may-become. Finding such a counselor is often particularly difficult for women, persons from ethnic minorities, persons from other countries, and those who have known meaningful religious faith. In the new environment of the university, the absence of familiar language and life style may be disorienting and render impossible a sense of the continuity of self and world. It is not surprising that first and second year students are most apt to seek out religious affiliation in a local congregation—seeking the familiarity of a place that sounds like home, that sounds like "me."

On the other hand, if the university pastor or rabbi sounds exclusively like the home and me I was before I came here, as the learning-socialization process of the university continues, the new self I am becoming no longer feels at home in the once familiar environment. Juniors and seniors may be seen less frequently in local religious congregations. Thus the effective pastoral counselor provides space where obedience to the truth that is former and the truth that is new can be in conversation and perhaps communion. It is in such space that the most adequate truth, the most profound integrity of identity, and the deepest conviction of faith as both dynamic and grounding may be forged.

Some students may negotiate this reformulation in the context of their own religious heritage. Others are drawn toward a tradition different than their own by the very attraction of its discontinuity with the familiar, as they seek to differentiate and to test the powers and limits of their heritage. In this case, participation in some religious tradition represents a continuity of the self in relation to the Holy, the Sacred, God. However, if one has a religious heritage and can find no context where the continuous and discontinuous in one's relation to the Ultimate may each find expression, then one is vulnerable to "retreat," or a preservation of earlier truth, which Perry describes as the "active denial of the potential of legitimacy in otherness"—a denial of a larger or more adequate truth (Perry, 1968, p. 262). Alternatively, the affirmation of the new "other" may occur at the cost of the bifurcation of the self.

These vulnerabilities are vividly illustrated in the life story portrayed in the film, "Running Brave," in which Billy Mills, a native American, leaves the reservation to go to the university. He experiences the demeaning insults of a racist culture. But as an outstanding runner he succeeds in creating a place and a self in the university context. Eventually in his alienation from his native American community and thus from himself, his success in running becomes empty, and he attempts to escape his new self and world and return to the reservation, his people, and their ceremonies. For a time he suffers the frustration of fitting and not fitting in both "worlds." Then through conversation with his sister/pastoral counselor, he is able to join the self he was and the strength, pain, and dreams of his people with a sense of vocation and purpose in his new self and world. A grounded identity and renewal of passion takes form. He returns to running both for his people and for the value of the self he is becoming, and later becomes an Olympic gold medalist. He only narrowly escapes the fate of his boyhood friend, who, caught between ethnic values and mainstream culture, dies in fear, despair, and alcoholic stupor.

The pastoral counselor (professor, department secretary, coach, dean, chaplain), who creates a space where obedience to the dynamic truth of one's selves, worlds, and God or gods may be practiced, serves the formation of faith.

Graduate Students: Graduate student experience also manifests the dialectic of faith, particularly as expressed in the concerns of power and powerlessness or competence and failure.

Graduate students are typically in their twenties or thirties (though some, particularly women, may be in their forties or older). Study in developmental psychology is contributing to a growing awareness that a new era is emerging in the human life cycle, and this age group is most apt to represent this developmental place. I wish to speak of this era as young adulthood, distinguishing it from both adolescence and full adulthood (Parks, 1980). Persons in this period generally have accomplished the tasks of differentiation from family, graduation from college, and perhaps marriage and parenthood. Nevertheless, the educational needs of a post-industrial culture require them to maintain an apprentice status in relation to the adult world of work (Keniston, 1960). Thus graduate students find themselves at once "grown up" and "still in preparation."

As a consequence, there is a fundamental "in-betweenness," ambivalence, or dividedness which the graduate student may experience. This ambivalence seems to be composed of both the outer reality of still being in studies, and an inner reality. It is rather arbitrary to assume that the completion of undergraduate work at the age of twenty-two coincides with the emergence of a fully equilibrated or centered adult self. Indeed, the post-adolescent period of young adulthood extends to the ages of twenty-six or thirty, or even later. During this period the adult self is coming into being in self-conscious form and the locus of authority is moving from without to within. However, there is still an appropriate dependence upon authority "out there" which one self-consciously chooses because that authority addresses and beckons the integrity of the emerging self. This is the time in which a mentor, sponsor, guru, or guide serves a critical function. The graduate student may appropriately seek a guide, typically and most satisfyingly a professor in one's field of study, who offers sponsorship into one's own profession. But what is yearned for is not simply the sponsorship of mind and technical skill narrowly conceived. What is desired (and appropriately so) is sponsorship in the on-going composing of the adult self—attention to the full integrating pattern of one's emerging vocation, life style, relationships, commitments, competence and meaning. The young adult graduate student is inevitably recomposing his or her most fundamental sense of self and world, and tacitly or explicitly choosing the God or gods one will serve. The graduate student (as well as the undergraduate) is recomposing faith. When a pastoral counselor is in meaningful relationship with persons in the process of this transition, the counseling relationship may partake in the mentor-mentee relationship, serving as a guide-companion (one who knows something of the path) in the on-going journey toward mature adult faith.

Thus the graduate student continues the process of formation begun in the undergraduate years. However, while much attention and study has been given to the dynamics of the undergraduate experience, so that academic curricula, student development programs, and campus ministries have become in many places quite sophisticated in their capacity to respond to undergraduate concerns, much less attention is given to the quality of the graduate school experience (apart from the academic program narrowly conceived), with the possible exception of some intentional cultivation of colleagueship within some graduate departments.

This neglect stems, in part, from the fact that graduate students are less apt to live on campus, and from the assumption that graduate students are "adult." It is also the case that the wider culture as well as the academy is more willing to grant to the undergraduate a moratorium from matters too serious and to provide resources, if necessary, for the purposes of growing up. However, while graduate school is one of the few places of refuge for one not yet ready to participate in full adult commitments (and may intensify rather than diminish the stresses inherent in accomplishing the tasks of young adulthood), it is presumed that the graduate student is more mature and has made a commitment toward a particular vocational direction. There is disappointment when graduate students seem ambivalent or can't "get their act together."

In the absence of a context which will encourage and inform an ongoing quest for a truly fitting identity and vocational commitment, the graduate student is vulnerable to either a premature commitment denying attention to some aspect of the self (talent, interest, feeling, fear, hope), or to a floundering which results from being essentially disconnected from any particular professor, department, or field of study—typically the only sources of sponsorship. At the graduate level, commitment precedes sponsorship. There is little access to sponsorship prior to commitment to particular studies. There is little sponsorship for the renegotiation of vocational commitment. Accordingly, the pastoral counselor who can provide space for the exploration of ambiguity and frustration, and who can address and beckon the potential power and competence that is yet unformed, may be of particular importance in the graduate school context.

When the choice of graduate studies does represent a commitment to an intellectual focus and/or a vocational direction, the graduate student is in a position to test his or her own strength and competence. However, the university is a problematic context for this task. On one hand, the student attempts to cultivate and to speak in his or her own voice—and indeed must do so in order to succeed in graduate school. On the other hand, the student is asked to listen to the voices of others and, indeed, to learn their voice first almost as one's own (you begin to footnote every thought) and then to continue to give power to those voices as dialogical partners (a scholar knows the field). Composing the relationship between one's own voice and the voice of others is particularly frustrating or bewildering when the emerging self, which is needing to risk asserting its strength, is also dependent upon the confirmation of authoritative and valued others. The consequence is a vulnerability to arrested development or the diminishment of self, intensified in the university context by one's dependence upon the political and affectional power of professors and others who control access to fellowships, research appointments, exams, dissertation approval, and recommendations.

Thus the graduate student may seek out the pastoral counselor feeling keenly the seesaw motion of power and powerlessness, competence and failure. "Presenting problems" may range from the decision to live in the dorms or in an apartment, the frustrations of needing financial resources to support an adult life style (wanting an apartment of one's own) while only having the earning power of a student ("living in the dorm would be cheaper, but I can't do that anymore"); the situation of being dependent upon private (often family) or public financial aid when the culture perceives financial independence as a mark of adulthood; the haunting dilemma of wondering if the field one has chosen has the same appeal after several years of investment in a program as it did when one began; the conflict between the long-range values of scholarship and the values of immediate socio-political involvement; the depression of "writer's block" or dissertation isolation; failure in exams; the desire and/or pressure to create a quality of personal and family life when the university implicitly still assumes a monastic model; the prolonging of graduate studies because one does not yet feel competent to assume full adult responsibilities; or the frustration of feeling a readiness to do creative and significant work of one's own while having still to meet the requirements of others to secure the credentials one needs. This last frustration may be felt particularly intensely by the older graduate student who may be a peer with faculty in terms of age and many dimensions of experience and competence, but it may also be very painfully experienced by the student who feels the pressure to compromise his or her intellectual and moral integrity to "get through."

Thus a poignant reality of graduate experience is that one feels ready to make a contribution to the world and needs to test one's competency to do so, but does not receive a clear and consistent confirmation that one is, in fact, competent enough. This is in part due to the on-going process of learning—each new insight leads to a new horizon of yet-to-be-mastered material and questions; one oscillates between the roles of expert and neophyte. The seesaw is also powered by the absence of access to positions of real power. Indeed, one may desire to shape the policies of the world immediately at hand—a social issue and/or some aspect of the university world itself. One may have considerable insight into both problems and solutions. Yet one does not yet have access to the positions of power and influence that would test and confirm one's inner sense of competence. A sense of frustration, failure or temporizing may prevail, unless the environment serves as a mentor, inviting, supporting, guiding the potential adult competence into being.

Graduate studies may be infantilizing or empowering; and because the dynamics of appropriate dependence and emerging strength are both real, graduate school will typically be experienced as both. Therefore, as the graduate student desires both to distinguish himself or herself and to belong, and continues the process of dialogue between the self one was and the self one is becoming, it is a most fitting gift of sponsorship when the professor-counselor-mentor creates a space where not only obedience to truth, but also one's expression of that truth (power and voice) may be practiced. (This may mean offering access not only to a counseling conversation, but also to the lectern, the committee room, the lunch with visiting research colleagues.)

This dialectic between dependence and strength is vital to faith formation, for a robust faith is dependent, in part, upon a sense of connection with or participation in the power of life itself. Thus the pastoral counselor who self-consciously assists in the moral inquiry of the community of faith will want to be alert to the power of the graduate school experience to enlarge or diminish the strength of the self and to shape the moral response of that strength.

Staff: Staff represent those persons who support the educational enterprise in direct services, but whose responsibilities do not require them to participate directly in the formal teaching-learning-research process. These persons may be in secretarial, maintenance, or administrative assistant roles. They are integral to the "world" of the university which cannot function without them. But they are uniquely vulnerable to the tensions of alienation and belonging in relationship to that world.

Earlier we recognized that a conviction of belonging, participation, and connection is integral to the formation of adequate meaning. However, the university is an institution, the value structure of which is dominated by the competence and power to shape realms of knowledge and the social arrangements that control that knowledge. This power and competence is symbolized by a hierarchy of academic degrees. These degrees are appropriately and inappropriately correlated with intelligence, effectiveness, and quality of contribution to the world. Staff who do not directly participate in this ladder structure of value (and especially those who do not hold a doctorate) are embedded in an environment in which the value norms at best bypass, at worst negatively address them.

This is particularly difficult for secretaries and administrators without faculty rank, e.g., placement officers, nurses, and business, registrar, admissions, and public relations personnel. These persons may, in fact, have baccalaureate and master's degrees and be required to exercise an intelligence as sophisticated in their area of expertise as that of the faculty in theirs. But as they are in a service role, they are vulnerable to the subtle and not so subtle forms of discrimination and invisibility that service personnel throughout our culture experience.

For maintenance personnel these issues, though they may be as keenly felt, may take essentially the same forms as class discrimination throughout the culture and may not function in forms particular to the university. But for secretaries and others the issues may be quite particular. The reference point of value for the carpenter in the university may not be the senior faculty, but a master builder. However, a secretary may be working in the university precisely for the benefits of reduced tuition and participation in the value ladder of knowledge (and its socio-cultural benefits). Also a faculty or student spouse may share in the values of the university and its social world. But each of these may experience feeling both inside and outside the circle of "real belonging." This is made more complicated when there is a consciousness that one's being outside has been conditioned by race, class, or gender—and further complicated when one is valued as a secretary because of particular competencies in language, efficiency, experience, and commitment.[3]

The consequence is that the task of achieving a healthy measure of self-esteem and satisfaction in one's work is very difficult. It is not easy to maintain a clear sense of identity and dignity. Because one is both "inside and outside" at the same time, one's feelings are not consistent, and one may feel alternately outraged and then guilty for feeling outraged. One may simply come to feel "down" most of the time, indifferent to one's work, or recognize an on-going low grade frustration. Or one may feel a sense of choice and serve loyally—even putting in extra hours—only to be confronted from time to time with a deep sense that one is not regarded and appreciated as one who is essential to the life and purposes of the university.

It is here that we begin to see the importance of the pastoral counselor's awareness, not simply of individuals and the inner dynamics of their psychology, but also the social-political context in which they dwell. Private hurts are public pain. These issues are matters of the quality of the public, collective life of the university. The pastoral counselor may be in a position, not only to assist individuals in sorting out the dynamics and choices of their particular situation, but also to participate in the university's on-going examination of its own practice of moral truth. This is to suggest a perspective from which one recognizes that not only are individuals engaged in the on-going transformation of meaning, but that the university as an institution is also engaged in the composing of collective meaning.

I am reminded of a college chaplain who reported formally to the president of the institution each year. On one such occasion she said simply, "It is my perception that this particular department (which she named) is a source of an inordinate amount of pain in this institution." There was no further conversation between them, but in the following year, dramatic and healing changes were made in that area of institutional life. Sometimes, of course, such a response is not appropriate, or matters are far more intractable, and the pastoral counselor must also be an educator, enabling others to come to see vividly the distortion and oppression that is invisible because it is considered normal within the traditions of the university.

Faculty and Administration: The faculty and administration may be perceived as having "arrived" or arriving on the value ladder of the university. Members of the faculty are all assumed to have achieved some equilibrated sense of adulthood and to exercise real power and influence. Faculty credentials entitle one to full participation in the circle of university belonging, and persons at the highest administrative levels typically hold the same rank as senior faculty, share in its benefits, and in some instances the administrative role confers additional status and power. However, it is the possible gap between these perceptions and actual experience that render faculty and administrators vulnerable to the tension between hope and despair.

When one has worked for a number of years in order to arrive at a certain goal, it is particularly discouraging when one's expectations are not actually realized. It is difficult when the result of one's research is not as significant as had been hoped. It is discouraging when there is no funding for a project or no publisher for a study. Competence in scholarship does not insure competence in teaching and vice versa—hence one may feel caught in a dilemma between developing one's weaker side or focusing on one's preferred mode. The disappearance of mobility for most faculty in higher education may lead to despairing stagnation. Junior faculty may feel that "the next rung on the ladder" looks very much like the powerlessness of graduate school. Senior faculty may feel that there is too little of consequence resulting from years of institutional investment (committees). One may feel that one's professional achievement is drained empty of meaning and satisfaction because the cost to one's personal life has been too high.

Indeed, the university is a context in which the artificial split between personal and professional life may be felt particularly keenly. One may be engaged in teaching values one feels unable to live out in one's own life. One may feel that the university is so professionally and cognitively oriented that though personal and affective elements condition the quality of intellectual work, they have little recognized place in university life. One may perceive so little hope for the integration of career and personal values that one feels powerless to create and to shape a style of life expressive of one's deepest integrity. The pastoral counselor who creates a space where personal and professional concerns may be in conversation provides a service essential to the university.

The tension between personal integrity and professional commitments may be intensified if the university is not, in fact, one's world, but was chosen as a means of service to the larger society. For one may be discouraged by the ambiguity inherent in the life of an institution in which education toward truth is conditioned by public policy, private economic interests, and a prevailing cultural ethos. Thus the critical awareness which the student-now-faculty-member has perhaps mastered very well may enhance one's confidence in the value of the university and one's own work in it, but critical awareness of the embeddedness of the university in the self-conserving interests of culture can also blunt the conscience and render cynical the desire to see clearly, to make a contribution to one's culture, to search for an understanding of truth worthy of the best impulses of the human soul.

This despair may be further confounded by an even deeper malaise arising from the less articulated intuition that all institutions now partake in a cultural historical paradigmatic shift which the university participates in but seems only occasionally able to lead.

In this climate colleagueship may seem to give way to competition, and self-investment may seem to be replaced by self-interest. In such a climate the pastoral counselor cannnot offer mere platitudes of hope. If a hope vital enough to transcend the "realistic" if discouraging appraisals of the intellectual community is to take form, a faith of only the most sturdy and worthy sort must be woven. The pastoral counselor (and faith community) who would effectively serve the university must create a space where an informed, robust, and prophetic moral imagination may be practiced. The university yearns for this sort of credible moral leadership; for its passion for truth can only be renewed when rooted in moral vision.

Don Browning has observed that on the whole, "moral inquiry is not the major goal of the university as it exists today. More frequently the intention of rendering visible the way things *are*, rather than how they *should* be, constitutes the major preoccupation of the university" (Browning, 1976, pp. 104–105). However, the separation of the questions of the true and the good into separate domains becomes increasingly untenable as such issues as genetic engineering and government funding confront the university. And, indeed, it has been implicit throughout our reflection here that the pastoral counselor does not represent moral neutrality in the sense of either indifference or unqualified relativisim. Nor does the pastoral counselor who effectively serves the university represent mere moralism in the sense of uncritical affirmation of moral/theological dogma. Rather, as Don Browning has suggested, the pastoral counselor serves a process of moral inquiry, and brings particular resources to that inquiry; for the pastoral counselor is oriented to a religio-cultural vision of value, the consequence of the on-going moral inquiry of the faith community—a process in which the university is an increasingly significant partner. This is to say that the pastoral counselor creates a space in which the quest for truth may have access to religion in terms of its capacity "to make, modify, and remake a moral world" (Browning, 1976, p. 90).

As such, religion is a critical resource for the university. Yet it is not unusual, in the context of higher education and the pluralistic, rapidly changing world that it represents, for persons to feel that intellectual integrity demands that religious experience and convictions must be left behind. This is not the case when religious practice demonstrates its capacity to critically create the positive meanings which orient commitment to truth. If the pastoral counselor mediates access to this sort of religious vision, members of the university may participate in symbol and myth adequate to empower their collective vocation.

Such moral inquiry oriented to a religio-cultural vision of the kingdom or commonwealth of God marked by inclusion, justice and love would call for a re-examination of the hierarchical character of the university and a reordering of the division of persons into the separate domains of concern reflected in our discussion here. For students (undergraduate and graduate), staff (maintenance, seretarial, and other), faculty (junior and senior), and administrators (lower and higher) all participate in the weaving or formulation and reformulation of the fabric of life and in each dimension of the dialectic of faith. Undergraduates are not alone in their struggle to recompose truth; graduate students suffer the tension of power and powerlessness precisely because it is a tension shared with other members of the university; staff may experience particularly, but not exclusively, the anxiety of exclusion; and faculty and administrators feel the most intense despair when conscious of the hopelessness of others. The pastoral counselor and the community of faith have an opportunity to provide a space where forms of common life may be created in which each member of the university may experience recognition of the integrity of their particularity—but so as to simultaneously manifest the interdependence the university is.

The pastoral counselor who would serve the university will also attend to the power of ritual. The meanings woven in the dialectic of faith are formed most efficiently by words but most profoundly by ritual (Langer, 1942). Whether for the celebration of collective or personal affirmations, or for the acknowledgment of individual pain or shared grief, there is no substitute for ritual—even among cognitive and word-oriented folk. Indeed, fitting and meaningful ritual has the power to *affect* us, to move us into new truth, and to awaken us from empty exercise into a fuller understanding.

The university may be served by access to the ritual traditions of established religious communities, but there is also a place for rituals responsive to the particular needs of the university. The importance of the latter is illustrated by Don Shockley, chaplain of Emory University, and his response to the medical school. He has recognized that medical students working with cadavers undergo the extraordinary experience of having bodies brought to them to be cut up for the sake of learning. Students typically may cope with whatever feelings they have by "objectifying" the bodies with which they work. Therefore, he has worked with faculty and students to create a ritual to bring appropriate closure to this experience.

A ritual of "reflection in gratitude" has been designed to restore the human dimension that has been distanced in order to do the work.

By means of such ritual imagination we may be enabled to cross boundaries which distort and limit truth; by the means of ritual we may live into more adequate ways of knowing; ritual may serve to create a holding environment, enabling new meaning and faith to find form.

In summary, the pastoral counselor who would effectively serve the university in its vocation of transformation toward truth will combine religious commitment, psycho-social understanding, and clinical skill so as to create a space where the dynamic truth of the self may evolve, where the voice of emerging competence may speak, where alienation may be transformed into communion, where an informed hope may overcome despair, and where moral passion and vision may thrive.

Notes

1. Perry uses the term "multiplicity." However, the term "unqualified relativism" better communicates the meaning he intends. See G. Rupp, *Beyond Existentialism and Zen: Religion in a Pluralistic World.* New York: Oxford University Press, 1979.

2. For insight into these dynamics I am indebted to Ann Fleck Henderson, former Associate Director of the Bureau of Study Counsel, Harvard University.

3. For insight into these conditions I am indebted to Dorothy M. Lewis, Financial and Business Officer (and a staff supervisor), The Divinity School, Harvard University.

Bibliography

Bakan, D. *The Duality of Human Existence.* Chicago: Rand McNally, 1966.

Browning, D. *The Moral Context of Pastoral Care.* Philadelphia: The Westminster Press, 1976.

Fowler, J.W. *Stages in Faith: The Psychology of Human Development and the Quest for Meaning.* San Francisco: Harper and Row, 1981.

Fowler, J. and Keen, S. *Life Maps: Conversations on the Journey of Faith.* Waco: Word Books, 1978.

Goffman, E. *Asylums: Essays on the Social Situation of Mental Patients and Other Inmates.* Garden City: Doubleday Anchor Books, 1961.

Kegan, R. "There the Dance Is: Religious Dimensions of a Developmental

Framework," *Toward Moral and Religious Maturity*, J.W. Fowler and A. Vergote, eds. Morristown: Silver Burdett Company, 1980.

————. *The Evolving Self: Problem and Process in Human Development.* Cambridge: Harvard University Press, 1982.

Keniston, K. *Youth and Dissent: The Rise of a New Opposition.* New York: Harcourt Brace Jovanovich, 1960.

Langer, S. *Philosophy in a New Key: A Study in the Symbolism of Reason, Rite, and Art.* Cambridge: Harvard University Press, 1942.

Niebuhr, R. *Experiential Religion.* San Francisco: Harper and Row, 1972.

Palmer, P. *To Know as We Are Known: A Spirituality of Education.* San Francisco: Harper and Row, 1983.

Parks, S.L. "Faith Development and Imagination in the Context of Higher Education," Th.D. diss., Harvard University, 1980.

Perry, W.G. *Intellectual and Ethical Development in the College Years: A Scheme.* New York: Holt, Rinehart, and Winston, 1968.

Rankin, R., ed. *The Recovery of Spirit in Higher Education.* New York: The Seabury Press, 1980.

Smith, W.C. *Faith and Belief.* Princeton: Princeton University Press, 1979.

Winnicott, D.W. *The Maturational Processes and the Facilitating Environment.* New York: International Universities Press, 1965.

F. Clark Power

The Role of the Pastoral Counselor in the Primary and Secondary School

You shall love Yahweh your God with all your heart, with all your soul, and with all your strength. Let the words I urge you today be written on your heart. You shall repeat them to your children and say them over them whether at rest in your house or abroad, at your lying down or your rising (Dt 6:4–7).

Any attempt to define the role of the pastoral counselor in the school must derive that role definition from an understanding of what schooling itself is supposed to be. This is not an easy task. Schools, whether they be public or religiously affiliated, are multi-purpose institutions; and school counselors serve in a variety of capacities. As the introductory quotation from Deuteronomy indicates, throughout the Judaeo-Christian tradition the religious and moral education of the young has been one of the most sacred duties of the adult members of the community. In contemporary schools the noble duty to provide religious education must find a place along with other duties, such as a civic duty to provide citizenship education and a practical duty to provide career-oriented skills and values. Given these duties may appear at times to be widely disparate or even in conflict, it is not surprising that members of religiously oriented educational institutions engage in continuous self-examination about their religious identity, nor is it surprising that pastoral counselors in these schools engage in a similar self-examination about their unique pastoral identity.

In order to respond to the identity crisis of the religious school and the pastoral counselor I will first examine Dewey's (1933) position that socio-moral development should be the primary aim of education. I will include within that developmental aim an explicit focus on religious concepts and values. Then I will describe the implications of such a developmental perspective for the counselor, emphasizing that counselors should assume an educational role in promoting development and thereby addressing in a preventive way problems such as irresponsibility, low motivation, and discipline. Taking an educational role requires that counselors take the lead in transforming the hidden curriculum of values education in the school (the ways in which decisions are made, punishments and rewards are distributed, and relationships are formed) into an explicit program for socio-moral education, reflecting the values of justice and community. As builders of community in school, pastoral counselors are exercising the traditional ministry of establishing *koinonia* or fellowship in the Church. It is within the context of a vibrant community that pastoral counselors, working with teachers and administrators, can provide a moral and religious education which does not divorce academic learning from lived experience. Within that context also pastoral counselors can collaborate with students and staff in reaching out to care for all those in need of support and guidance.

Development as the Aim of Education

For Dewey socio-moral development was at the core of the developmental process and educators had a moral responsibility to promote that development. In confronting the tension between development and career preparation as educational ends, Dewey went so far as to claim that schools should prepare students, not simply to accommodate to the economic institutions of society, but to reform those institutions so that they could better serve human needs. This view of development as the aim of education is relevant to the question of the identity of the religious school and the pastoral counselor for three reasons. First, Dewey considered development in a most comprehensive and profound way as having to do with what he called "character" or "soul activity." Dewey's assertion that education be an integrated process which addresses students' most vital concerns is certainly shared by those in religiously oriented schools who wish to provide the best context for entertaining ultimate questions of meaning and value. Second, the priority which Dewey gave to socio-moral education is also a priority for those faithfully educating in a Judaeo-Christian tradition which inextricably links love of God with love of neighbor. Third, the notion that schools should not reflect the injustices of the existing social order but become agencies for social reform finds support in ecclesiological reflection on the Church's mission of diakonia or service. The Church and a fortiori the religious school must maintain a critical distance from society in order to act as an institution of liberation and reform.

In advocating Dewey's view of development as the aim of education I wish to give proper consideration to the responsibility of religious educators to initiate the young into their community with its specific rituals, traditions, norms and values. This sense of school as a catechumenate differs somewhat from Dewey's view that schools should promote the development of general cognitive and socio-moral competencies. Nevertheless, the emphasis given in religiously oriented schools to initiation in a particular community need not conflict with the aim of development. Educators in religiously oriented schools must be concerned with enabling students to participate in a common search for truth and moral principles in a pluralistic social context. They must also take into account the universal features of child development. Cognitive developmental research into children's theologizing (Goldman, 1964; Power and Kohlberg, 1980; Oser, 1980) indicates that children interpret religious concepts according to their stage of development. Each stage represents a distinct theo-logic, that is a logical structure for constructing theological meanings. Religious educators must then be developmental educators in leading children to a mature faith. They must also be developmentalists in the ways in which they introduce children to participate in a community of shared faith.

The Developmental Ideal and the Counselor's Reality

To suggest that the aims of education should be the development of the person and the betterment of society is to suggest an ideal which, while inspiring, nevertheless appears remote and impractical. Perhaps no one in the school experiences the contradictions involved in actual educational practice more than the counselor. Historically the school counselor's role emerged from a need to provide vocational guidance in the schools. The vocational counselor is a mediator between the institutions of school and work, helping to correlate students' aspirations and qualifications with the demands of available job positions. In this position counselors are aware of the extent to which the structures of the economy determine the structures of the school. They are also at times painfully aware of how the process of discerning a vocation, religiously viewed as a call from God, can be reduced to a matter of supply and demand in the job market. From its origins in vocational guidance, the role of the counselor has expanded to include dealing with students whose learning, social, or affective problems have interfered with their performance in school and counseling their parents and families when possible and necessary. In intervening in times of crisis and breakdown, counselors come to the realization that many of the problems which individual students manifest have their origins in the failures of the social systems of family and school.

Ironically counselors, who bear a unique responsibility for students' passage from home to society and for the social and affective dimensions of their school experience, find themselves on the periphery of the school, distant from its functioning as an educational institution. According to the developmental view, the affective and social dimensions of schooling should be at the center of the school's educational functioning, not at its boundary. Counselors should pro-act rather than react to problems in the school. This entails that counselors have a responsibility to become educators and in that role to work with teachers and administrators in constructing and implementing organizational and curricular policies which give priority to socio-moral education in a religious context.

The Meaning of Development

Before suggesting ways in which counselors can exercise their role as socio-moral educators, promoting students' development, I wish to clarify what progressive educational theorists from Dewey to Kohlberg mean by the term development. In their essay, "Development as the Aim of Education," Kohlberg and Mayer (1972) distinguish three psychologies of development: maturationist, associationist, and interactionist. According to the maturationist position, development consists of pre-patterned, internal growth. On the other hand, the associationist position describes development mechanistically as the accumulation and combination of discrete environmental inputs. The interactionist position mediates this dichotomy between innate maturation and environmentally determined learning by positing that development consists of a reorganization of psychological structures through interaction with the environment. Cognitive developmentalists, such as Piaget (1970) and Kohlberg (1976), have attempted to demonstrate that there are very basic competencies, such as logical-mathematical thinking and moral reasoning, which develop through an invarient sequence of hierarchically ordered stages. More recently cognitive developmentalists, such as Fowler (1981) and Kegan (1982), have suggested that faith and the fundamental meaning-making activity of the self also undergo development through experience.

The cognitive developmentalists argue for development as the aim of education by making a case that there is a parallelism between their psychologically defined stage sequences and philosophically defined criteria for determining the adequacy of such normative ideals as truth, justice, beauty, and happiness. This parallelism is no mere coincidence, since cognitive developmentalists construct their stage sequences with epistemological and ethical criteria in mind. By uniting psychological descriptions of development with philosophically defined standards of truth, justice, beauty, and value, cognitive developmentalists are able to forge pedagogical principles which are both rationally justifiable and empirically relevant.

The Cognitive Developmental Approach to Education

What does this research have to say to counselors about promoting development through deliberate educational intervention? At the outset I should acknowledge that many cognitive developmentalists have been rather skeptical of the contribution which formal education makes to development as distinct from skill training or the acquisition of information. They point out that developmentally significant interactions can occur in a variety of contexts outside of the school. In schools, didactic teaching practices may actually impede development by encouraging students to go to the teacher-authority for answers rather than to think for themselves.

Given that schools have at best a limited role in promoting development, research in cognitive developmental education (Elkind, 1976; Higgins, 1980) indicates planned programs can have modest success when properly conducted. Such programs mimic to a certain extent the conditions naturally occurring in informal experience which generally lead to development. That is, these programs are deliberate attempts to create in the classroom and school an artificial environment which is, in a sense, a distillation of the most developmentally stimulating features of experience. This entails an understanding of the stage of the child's cognitive functioning and a matching of the proper environmental stimuli to that stage. Cognitive developmental educators must be careful to allow children to be active in resolving the problems which are presented in the classroom and the school. Once educators have managed to create cognitive conflict they must be patient and respectful of children's efforts to reconstruct new, more adequate perspectives on their world. Having patience and respect does not mean that the cognitive developmental educator should assume a laissez-faire stance in the classroom. Rather, the developmental educator must be continuously active in structuring the proper environmental conditions.

There are at present two complementary ways in which counselors can apply the principles of cognitive developmental psychology in promoting socio-moral development in the school. The first and most widely used way is the discussion approach (Mosher and Sprinthall, 1971; Reimer, Paolito, and Hersh, 1983). In this approach students engage in a dialogue in which conflicting points of view are examined and a resolution is attempted. The dilemmas for discussion may be hypothetical or real. Counseling groups take their problems from crises arising in home and school, as Mosher and Sprinthall (1971) suggested in their proposal on psychological education. The model for leading these discussions is the Socratic one of acting as a midwife in assisting students in their labor of giving birth to new ways of meaning-making. This requires that the discussion leader carefully select and pose dilemmas, invite students to consider each other's point of view, focus and integrate the discussion, and ask searching questions.

The second and, for the counselor, the most significant application of the cognitive developmental approach to education has been to build community classrooms and schools. This involves a direct confrontation with what Jackson (1968) refers to as the "hidden curriculum." Sociologists of education from Durkheim (1961) to Bowles and Gintis (1976) have argued that one cannot adequately understand how schools function in society without attending to their processes of socialization. Because these socialization processes are so powerful and pervasive they deserve to be thought of as a curriculum of value education. As I noted earlier, counselors often deal with students whose problems are created or exacerbated by these very socialization processes. Thus counselors have a special responsibility to understand and address the effects of the hidden curriculum.

The Hidden Curriculum

What makes up the school's hidden curriculum of socialization? I suggest we look in the following areas: (1) the ways in which schools and classrooms are organized and decisions are made, (2) how discipline is administered, and (3) the extent to which students with different backgrounds are segregated into various tracks, clubs, and cliques. As I will indicate, the hidden curriculum of the school thus described may be at odds with the explicit curriculum. This is another way of saying that schools do not always put into practice what they preach.

School Organization. Let us consider why the hidden curriculum merits the counselor's attention by noting gaps between ideals and realities in the areas listed above, beginning with the organization of the school. We profess to educate the whole person. Yet we present subjects in isolated courses, taught by teachers in similarly isolated departments. In the typical elementary or high school, teachers, administrators, and counselors try to meet specific needs of students for intellectual stimulation, order, and guidance; but they often fail to communicate and coordinate their efforts. Educational specialization and bureaucratization have led to a greater diversity of curricula and services but result in a segmentation of the educational experience. It is not surprising that in such an organization students will feel estranged from each other and the adults in the school.

We may better understand the connection between the schools organization and student alienation by recalling Baker and Gump's (1964) classic study on the psychological effects of school size. They found that small schools tended to produce cohesive and challenging environments because of a favorable ratio of students to the opportunities available for participation in school activities. The large schools provided fewer opportunities for participation and, as we might expect, the academically marginal students were the ones generally excluded. An additional problem for academically marginal students in the large school is that they do not receive the kind of continuous and careful adult monitoring which has been shown to be important for their success in school (Garbarino, 1978). Many of the students who are referred to the counselor for motivational and disciplinary problems are the victims of an organizational structure which fails them in order to promote the achievement of others.

Related to the organizational structure of the school is the issue of decision-making. While we say that schools ought to prepare students to take their place as free and equal persons in society, we virtually exclude them from any meaningful participation in decision-making on the school or classroom level. Some object to involving children and adolescents in decision-making because they feel that one of the reasons why they are in school in the first place is because they are immature and lacking in the knowledge necessary for making sound decisions. They argue that we must educate them before we can give them responsibility. This assertion makes some sense to the developmentalist who would agree that students in school are not yet fully mature by developmental standards. Nevertheless, the question remains how we should educate for responsibility. If we exclude students from accepting responsibility for making decisions are we actually teaching them to be irresponsible or at the very least depriving them of the experiences which could help them to grow as responsible persons? Dewey (1933) counsels us to maintain continuity between the means and ends of education. If we are preparing students to become free and responsible participants in their faith community and democratic society, must we not introduce them to participatory decision-making while they are in school? This presents an enormous challenge to the typical hierarchical authority structure of schools which excludes not only student input into decision-making but staff input as well.

Discipline. Another related part of schooling which presents a gap between our ideals and practice is discipline. Often counselors become involved as advocates for students who are on the verge of being disciplined for some flagrant or persistent violation of the rules of the school. Frequently they find themselves caught in the middle between the demands of teachers and administrators for order and control in the school and their counseling orientation to be responsive to the particular needs of the individual student. When teachers and administrators view disciplinary problems principally in terms of behavioral management and counselors view them principally in terms of an individual's psychological well-being, two problems result. First, there is little concern for discipline as an expression of the morality of the school and a lack of attention to issues of procedural justice. Second, the disciplinary process is not designed to educate anyone except perhaps the student who is about to be punished. The other students in the school are absent from the process. They have little idea, except through rumor, just how school officials have dealt with the violation of rules. When discipline reduces to behavioral management with its norms of efficiency and control rather than the norms of justice and good pedagogy, then moral education has been compromised in a serious way.

The behavioral management approach to discipline can create as many problems as it attempts to resolve when the moral dimension of discipline is neglected. For example, let us take the problem of stealing in school. If we are simply interested in eliminating the undesirable behavior, then we may make a rule prohibiting stealing and attempt to uphold it through such strategies as policing hallways and locker rooms, installing television cameras to monitor sensitive areas, or providing heavier locks. All of these measures employ technical means of behavioral control. All of them fail to address the consciences of the students who, even if they do not steal themselves, allow stealing to go on either by ignoring it or by feeling helplessly resigned to it.

Consider the following discussion with high school sophomores about the problem of stealing in their school. The adult discussion leader has just posed a situation to the group concerning a student who stole a tape recorder, left in an unlocked locker, and later bragged about stealing it to his friends in school. The leader starts the discussion by asking if his friends should express their disapproval. Mary is the first to respond. She giggles that this has really happened and then responds, "I'd say you'd better not brag about it. You'd better shut your mouth or you'll get caught." Sally agrees, "If somebody is going to be dumb enough to bring something like that into school, they deserve to get it stolen. If you aren't together enough to lock your locker, then what can you expect? If somebody is going to steal, then more power to them. If you can get away with it, you might as well." The leader probes, "Is that what other people think—that it's O.K. if you can get away with it?" Harry retorts, "No, it doesn't make it all right to steal the thing. That's ridiculous."

In order to bring the class closer to an agreement on what students should do about the problem of stealing, the leader suggests that students make a contract in which they agree not steal. There is general laughter. Harry explains, "Sure, everybody is going to say 'I won't steal'; not to agree to that would be ridiculous." The leader, acknowledging the general disapproval of stealing, asks whether the hypothetical contract should go further and stipulate that those who have knowledge of a theft, such as the students in the above situation, should try to talk the thief into returning the stolen goods. Mary objects: "You can't put pressure on students like that." She later explains, "We are the ones who are teenagers. The teachers are grown up. They are the big people. They are supposed to control the students in the school. We are here to learn." Todd adds another idea: "You shouldn't steal. But the way society is everybody does it . . . . (Expressing disapproval) depends on a lot of things—who is whose friend. . . . It depends on what they want to do. Let them say something if they want to take the risk of losing a friend or let them say nothing." Jimmy concurs: "It's really up to the person who steals. It's really up to them."

This discussion indicates that there is a gap between the formal rule against stealing in the school and the informal norms which influence students' attitudes and behavior. While students are willing to agree that stealing is wrong, they accept it as part of life and take little offense at it. There are even points in the discussion in which students appear to be condoning stealing, as, for example, when Sally blames stealing on the carelessness of the victim. Behavioral management approaches, which stress security and deterrence, do not help students to reflect on why stealing is wrong or to feel any sense of collective responsibility for dealing with it. Instead, they appear to support the view held by several students in this discussion that the only good reason not to steal is if there is a risk of getting caught and that students should not have to face peer group opprobrium for enforcing school rules.

Counselors may feel some sympathy for Mary's position that students should not have to feel the pressure of enforcing school norms and rules. Admonishing or reporting a peer is uncomfortable and may lead to ostracism by one's peer group or even provoke a violent reprisal. It is difficult for students to feel responsible for upholding the norms and rules of their school when their peer group does not support such action. Nevertheless, is the only solution to such a difficulty to see the issue of rule enforcement as the exclusive responsibility of adults?

The issue of student responsibility cannot be properly addressed unless we understand that responsibility is to a certain extent a function of one's environment or what I will later call moral atmosphere. In a threatening environment, we react by becoming self-protective and responsible only for ourselves. In an environment characterized by a sense of trust and care, we respond by becoming self-sacrificial and responsible for the needs of others and the community. Certainly the students I have quoted find a lack of care and trust in their school. Why should they be anything but self-protective in that kind of social setting? If we go a step further and ask whether self-protectiveness is, finally, the only appropriate way to live in an unjust and uncaring world, we are asking a religious question about the trustworthiness of the ultimate environment or what we might call God or the kingdom of God. Our willingness to commit ourselves to the cause of justice and community in a world of injustice and mistrust depends upon a faith that that cause has some eternal or eschatological significance. We may not be able to achieve perfect justice or community in our schools but we share a belief that the struggle for these ends is a worthy one. Should we not find ways of allowing students to join us in that struggle?

Tracking and Integration. Let us turn to another problem presented by the hidden curriculum, the problem of formal and informal integration of students of different ability levels, family backgrounds, and ethnic and racial identifications. We like to think of our schools as giving students an equal opportunity to get a good education. We also like to think of our schools as "meeting places" in which students can learn to respect and appreciate differences while at the same time forming relationships. Often we find that our schools are not as fair and integrated as we would like and that there are specific practices which stand in the way of greater fairness and integration. One such practice is that of grouping students by ability level or tracking. An advantage to tracking is presumably that students with greater abilities will be challenged by more accelerated study, while students of lesser ability will proceed at a slower pace with less difficult subject matter. Not only does tracking seem to meet the different intellectual demands of students, it also seems to protect the self-esteem of the students of lesser ability who might suffer in a competitive classroom environment.

In spite of these expected benefits, tracking presents us with four immediate problems. First of all, are the methods and criteria used for tracking students fair and appropriate? Second, once we have tracked students, is it not difficult for students in lower tracks to advance? Third, are the students on different tracks given an education of equal value? Fourth, do not tracks constitute a barrier, segregating students on one level from those of another? The fact that there is a high correlation between tracks and socio-economic status (Rosenbaum, 1976), coupled with research indicating that tracking has a negative impact on lower track students' self-esteem, grad-uation rates, behavior in school and aspirations for higher education (Alex-ander, Cook, and Dill, 1978; Schafer and Olexa, 1971), raises the nagging question of whether tracking is not a subtle way of perpetuating the ine-quities and divisions in our society.

Another threat to educational equality and to integrated community are peer group norms which exclude students of one clique from associ-ating with students of other cliques and may determine for some students which extracurricular activities are acceptable. It is very difficult for schools to directly address this issue of informal peer group segregation. We tend to think that this is one area of student life which adults should leave alone. Nevertheless, when student cliques, clubs, and teams divide on racial and social class lines, is continued non-interference justified?

Assessing the School's Moral Atmosphere

Once counselors have become aware of the power and pervasiveness of the hidden curriculum, they must find ways of joining with teachers and administrators to bring it into harmony with explicit, justifiable educa-tional aims. This requires a renewed appreciation for the church's mission of *koinonia* or establishing fellowship and community. The first step in the exercise of *koinonia* is to become conscious of the school's culture or what we (Higgins, Power, and Kohlbert, 1984) have called the school's moral at-mosphere. The school's moral atmosphere is a product of the hidden cur-riculum. It is not an aggregate of individual student and staff beliefs and values; rather, it is a characteristic of the school society, taken as a whole. A moral atmosphere arises out of the interactions of the aggregate mem-bership of the school, as influenced by organizational structures and edu-cational practices in particular settings.

Our notion of a moral atmosphere is a dynamic one. A moral atmo-sphere can develop or decline over time. In our discussion of the hidden curriculum we have seen how certain practices (or the non-practice of non-interference) can have a negative impact on moral atmosphere. For ex-ample, if we exclude students from participating in decision-making we may encourage irresponsibility and the development of a student culture, hostile or at least indifferent to the staff culture in the school. However, if we give students a significant participatory role in making decisions which concern them, then we may draw staff and student cultures together, creating a shared sense of responsibility for the school.

A moral atmosphere, as we define it, has four dimensions: (1) how the school or classroom is valued as a group; (2) the moral stage of the norms and values which regulate interactions in the classroom and school; (3) the degree to which these norms and values are shared; (4) the extent of commitment to uphold the norms and values of the school. When we assess our first dimension, we ask whether students intrinsically value their classroom or school society as a community or whether they value their school and classroom instrumentally as a pragmatic association. In a pragmatic association individuals cooperate because it is in their self-interest to do so. In contrast, in a community individuals cooperate for altruistic, other-centered motives and values. As Macmurray (1961) notes, reflection on the desirability and possibility of community raises basic questions about what it means to be a person in relation to others and what the good of human life really is. These questions go to the heart of any religious standpoint.

Paul Tillich (1952) in his well-known ontological analysis of courage pointed out that we may characterize human existence as exhibiting an equilibrium between the polar elements of self-affirmation and participation in the community of being. At each polar element there is a danger or a threat to what it means to be a self. At the pole of self-affirmation, there is the possibility that we can become estranged, isolated egos, while at the pole of participation, there is the threat that we can become conformist members of an impersonal collective. From the perspective of psychology true personal existence demands a twofold courage: the courage to be an individual and the courage to be a part of a group. From the perspective of sociology personal existence requires a special form of association which can sustain such courage: the community. The pastoral counselor must combine the psychologist's sensitivity to individual development with a sociologist's sensitivity to group development if children and adolescents are to come to a full experience of their own personhood in relationship to others. This entails careful assessment of whether students value their school as a community or whether they value it solely for what it can provide for them as individuals.

Our next three dimensions of moral atmosphere refer explicitly to particular norms and values which, in a sense, symbolize the way in which the school as a whole is valued. Let us take the norm of trust with respect to property. Trust is a norm characteristic of a community of persons who value their relations of mutual care and sharing. If members of a school have established a norm of trust, then we might expect that they could leave their lockers unlocked without the threat of theft. As the previously cited stealing discussion indicates, trust is unlikely to take root in a school which is valued as having no more a sense of community than a department store or a subway. On the other hand, in a community we would not only expect to find a norm of trust but other norms as well, such as caring, integration, participation, publicity, collective responsibility, and attachment to community. These norms uphold the intrinsic value of community, that is they are directed toward the building of the harmony of the group as a community. They prescribe a way of relating through sharing which transcends the minimal requirements of order and respect for individual rights. For example, caring implies sharing concerns and affection; trust, sharing one's confidence and property; integration, sharing of communication between subgroups; participation, sharing time, energy, and interest; and publicity, openly sharing knowledge about matters which affect the community.

In examining the nature of shared norms in school, such as trust, integration, or peer group exclusivity, we evaluate their stage according to Kohlberg's (Kohlberg, Colby, Gibbs, Speicher-Dubin, Power, Candee, 1979) scoring system. This stage framework gives us a basis for a critical assessment of the moral adequacy of a group's shared norms and a direction for future development. This application of a structural stage framework for the assessment of group norms and values presupposes that shared norms and values are embedded in a deeper context of shared meanings. Any attempt to assess the stage of these norms and values must probe beyond a group's rules, norms, guiding ideals and values to their justification and significance.

In contrast to Kohlberg's assessment of individual moral judgment, we assess the stage of norms which are genuinely shared. The analysis of this dimension of sharedness or collectivization requires identifying the degree to which members of a group speak for the group as a whole in presenting prescriptions for group members' attitudes and actions. Our concern is determining whether, when individuals make normative statements, they are simply speaking for themselves or are speaking on behalf of a group's agreed upon norms and values. Once we know the degree to which norms are collectivized and their stage, it is important to assess the strength of these shared norms and values. We determine the strength of a norm by questioning the commitment which group members are willing to make to uphold and enforce their norms. Do group members look at their norms and values as empty ideals or do they genuinely expect each other to live up to them? Are they willing to enforce group norms by persuading and helping fellow members who violate the norms to make amends?

Building Community

With a critical awareness of a classroom's or school's moral atmosphere, teachers, administrators and counselors are better able to take steps necessary for its development. Projects in democratic moral education, led by Kohlberg (1980), Mosher (1980), and myself (Power, in press), offer some guidelines for creating more positive moral atmospheres in schools. Crucial to any effort is the division of large schools into smaller sub-units which represent the diversity of social class, ethnicity, and achievement levels in the school. These small groups make direct participatory democracy and a sense of community possible. Democracy stimulates individuals to think for themselves, engage in moral discussion, and cooperate. Democracy also helps in building of community because when group members have the responsibility for making agreements they are more likely to assume responsibility for seeing that those agreements are upheld. Furthermore democracy serves as a way of counteracting group pressure toward conformity and impersonal collectivism.

Counselors must take differences between elementary and high schools into account when considering steps to improve moral atmosphere. In elementary schools the focus of attention should be given to the moral atmosphere of classrooms because of their small size, relatively simple organizational structure, and the fact that elementary school students generally take all or most of the courses with the same teacher. Elementary school teachers can promote the development of the moral atmosphere of their classrooms through such processes as socio-moral discussions, cooperative learning, and participatory decision-making. (Lickona, 1980). Because elementary school teachers have continuous contact with their students throughout the day, they have a unique opportunity to serve as counselors to their students and to guide them through the common difficulties which they may experience.

In high schools attention should focus on the school itself, or, in the case of large schools, on the sub-units within the school. By the time students reach high school, they should be capable of interacting within a larger group with a more complex structure. Also high school students take courses with different teachers and generally spend more time than elementary school students "hanging out" in various parts of the school between classes. Promoting the moral atmosphere of the high school will require the cooperation of teachers, administrators, and counselors in creating regular opportunities for group meetings. These meetings can be used for discussion and decision-making about problems of school life and discipline. Because high school teachers do not have the continuous contact with students that elementary school teachers generally have and because there are too few high school counselors to monitor individual students on a regular basis, the role of the homeroom teacher should be re-examined. Given sufficient time for homeroom meetings and suitable training, homeroom teachers can serve as counselors, leading small group discussions, offering guidance about courses and activities, mediating conflicts, and making referrals when unusual problems arise.

In noting that elementary school and high school homeroom teachers can assist counselors in providing counseling and guidance to students, I wish to note from a developmental perspective a difference between the task of counseling and that of educating. As Kegan (1982) points out, when we counsel we are less concerned about creating the environmental conditions which stimulate development than we are with supporting students who may be overwhelmed by some crisis or developmental transition. Although counselors cannot do the work of constructing new meanings, making career decisions, and forming new relationships, they can join with students in their work, offering them companionship and assurance.

Collective Responsibility and Discipline

Educators in elementary and high schools should pay particular attention to the ways in which students are rewarded and punished. Durkheim (1973) recommended that we consider the use of collective rewards and punishments as ways of awakening in children feelings of solidarity and collective responsibility: "Nothing can draw them out of their narrow individualism as much as making them feel that the value of each is a function of the worth of all, and that our actions are at the same time causes and consequences, which transcend the sphere of our individual personalities. There is no better way of instilling the feeling that we are not self-sufficient, but a part of a whole that envelops, penetrates, and supports us" (p. 245). Durkheim's position is not merely a tactical one without a moral basis. On the contrary, his viewpoint rests on a recognition that individualistic accounts of moral responsibility cannot be exhaustive, because individuals are related to each other in society. We have seen the importance of this collective influence in our discussion of the school's moral atmosphere. Once we have become aware of its presence we should directly address it by cultivating a spirit of community with collective norms and values which reflect a commitment to justice and care.

When disciplinary problems arise, it is necessary that staff and students regard them as community concerns. As I indicated previously, a group's rules are no mere means of social control; rather, they symbolize the moral nature of the group itself. When the rules of a group fall into disrespect, the group itself is in danger. The purpose of punishing individuals who break the rules, then, must have some rehabilitative purpose for the group as well as the individual. In emphasizing the rehabilitative function of punishment for the community, I wish to take issue with approaches which treat punishment primarily as a means of retribution or deterrence. In these approaches punishment is not a means of education nor is it a means of community building. Retributive punishment tends to communicate the primitive moral view of "an eye for an eye, a tooth for a tooth," described by Kohlberg's first moral stage. Punishment as deterrence tends to communicate the instrumental moral view that what makes an act wrong is the price of getting caught, described by Kohlberg's second moral stage. In both approaches the offense and the corresponding punishment are seen individualistically without due regard for the moral atmosphere of the group.

Durkheim's symbolic view of punishment as a reaffirmation of the community's faith is an alternative which is both educative and rehabilitative. According to Durkheim, punishment should be a meaningful demonstration of the community's strength in the face of violations which demoralize members of the community and undermine their respect for its authority. How can we implement Durkheim's approach? We can begin by treating discipline as a public rather than as a private matter and by involving students in its administration. If this approach to discipline is to succeed, it is important that the staff help students to understand that breaches of discipline have consequences for the community. Students and even staff frequently overlook this. For example, students often think that the only negative consequence to missing a class is that they miss the material covered on that day. They fail to realize the negative effects of their non-participation on the spirit of the class. Staff, particularly counselors, can reinforce privatistic attitudes by focusing exclusively on consequences that cutting class will have for them as individuals (they may flunk the course, fail to graduate, not be accepted into a good college, etc.). Instead, they must appeal to students' responsibility for the sake of the class and other students in the class.

One objection that counselors frequently made to the Durkheimian approach is that the public administration of discipline, particularly by other students, may lead to the humiliation of students being disciplined. This objection has merit and can be met only in those schools and classrooms which are becoming communities with a sense of collective responsibility. When norms are violated, members of a community with a sense of collective responsibility acknowledge their own complicity. They also work together to encourage those who violated their norms to live up to them in the future. The purpose of symbolic punishments is not to help the community at the expense of the person violating the rules. It is a way of helping everyone in the community to understand and reaffirm their norms and ideals.

Conclusion

In this chapter I have urged that pastoral counselors see themselves as educators with particular responsibility for the socio-moral curriculum of the school. This emphasis on the educational role of a counselor may run counter to a more popular conception of the counselor as a psychologist, interpreting test scores, offering therapy, intervening in crises, and providing college and career guidance. My intent has not been to discount such a conception but to broaden it. Counselors with specialized training in developmental and group psychology and with acknowledged responsibility for the social welfare of students are in a privileged position to evaluate the hidden curriculum and to work to transform it. They should not allow their professional expertise to constitute a barrier between them and others, but, as I have suggested, they should train staff and students to enable them to provide counsel and guidance for those in need.

Pastoral counselors reflecting on their ministerial identity should see themselves as exercising the threefold ministry of the church: *kerygma*, *koinonia*, and *diakonia*. In terms of *kerygma* the pastoral counselor must assure that the young hear the word in ways which allows its power to transform them. They should work with teachers to achieve an integration between faith and experience. Teachers and counselors alike should present their religious tradition in ways which take into account the developmental levels of children and their most fundamental questions and longings. In terms of *koinonia*, I have stressed that the pastoral counselor has a particular responsibility to build community in the school. This demands the greatest effort. In order to build community, staff and students must address organizational structures, discipline, and tracking, aspects of schooling which often remain unexamined and require significant institutional change. Finally the pastoral counselor has a ministry of *diakonia* in reaching out to the alienated and troubled in the school and in helping the community to serve the needs of society.

Bibliography

Alexander, K.L., Cook, M., and Dill, E.L. "Curriculum Tracking and Educational Stratification: Some Further Evidence." *American Sociological Review*, 1978, pp. 43, 46–66.

Barker, R.G. and Gump, P. *Big School, Small School.* Stanford: Stanford University Press, 1964.

Bowles and Gintis. *Schooling in Capitalist America.* New York: Basic Books, 1976.

Dewey, J. *Democracy and Education.* New York: Macmillan, 1933.

Durkheim, E. *Moral Education: A Study in The Theory and Application of The Sociology of Education.* New York: Free Press, 1961.

Elkind, D. *Child Development and Education: A Piagetian Perspective.* New York: Oxford University Press, 1976.

Fowler, J. *Stages in Faith: The Psychology of Human Development and the Quest For Meaning.* New York: Harper and Row, 1981.

Garbarino, J. "The Human Ecology of School Crime." *Theoretical Perspectives on School Crime, Vol. 1.* National Council on Crime and Delinquency, Department of Health, Education, and Welfare, 1978.

Goldman, Ronald. *Religious Thinking from Childhood to Adolescence.* Atlantic Highlands: Humanities Press, 1964.

Higgins, A. "Research and Measurement Issues in Moral Education Interventions." In R. Mosher (ed.), *Moral Education: A First Generation of Research and Development.* New York: Praeger, 1980.

Higgins, A., Power, C. and Kohlberg, L. "The Relationship of Moral Atmosphere to Judgments of Responsibility." In J. Gewirtz and W. Kurtines (eds.), *Morality, Moral Development, and Moral Behavior: Basic Issues in Theory and Research.* New York: John Wiley and Sons, 1984.

Jackson, P. *Life in the Classroom.* New York: Holt, Rinehart, and Winston, 1968.

Lickona, T. "Democracy, Cooperation, and Moral Education." In J. Fowler and A. Vergote (eds.), *Toward Moral and Religious Maturity.* Morristown: Silver Burdett, 1980.

Kegan, R. *The Evolving Self.* Cambridge: Harvard University Press, 1982.

Kohlberg, L. "Moral Stages and Moralization: The Cognitive Developmental Approach." In T. Lickona (ed.), *Moral Development and Behavior: Theory, Research, and Social Issues.* New York: Rand McNally, 1976.

Kohlberg, L. "High School Democracy and Educating for a Just Society." In R. Mosher (ed.), *Moral Education: A First Generation of Research and Development.* New York: Praeger, 1980.

Kohlberg, L. and Mayer, R. "Development as the Aim of Education." *Harvard Educational Review,* 1972, 42, pp. 449–496.

Kohlberg, L., Colby, A., Gibbs, J., Speicher-Dubin, E., Power, C., and Candee, D. *Assessing Moral Stages: A Manual.* Cambridge: Center for Moral Education, 1979.

Macmurray, J. *Persons in Relation.* London: Faber and Faber, 1961.

Mosher, R. "A Democratic School: Coming of Age." In R. Mosher (ed.), *Moral Education: A First Generation of Research and Development.* New York: Praeger, 1980.

Mosher, R. and Sprinthall, N.A. "Deliberate Psychological Education." *Counseling Psychologist,* 1973, 2(4), pp. 3–82.

Oser, F. "Stages of Religious Judgment." In J. Fowler and A. Vergote (eds.), *Towards Moral and Religious Maturity.* Morristown: Silver Burdett, 1980.

Piaget, J. "Piaget's Theory." In P.H. Mussen (ed.), *Carmichael's Manual of Child Development, Vol. I.* New York: John Wiley and Sons, 1970.

Power, C. "Democratic Moral Education in the Large Public High School." In M. Berkowitz and F. Oser (eds.), *Moral Education: Theory and Application.* Hillsdale: Lawrence Erlbaum Assoc. (in press).

Power, C. and Kohlberg, L. "Religion, Morality, and Ego Development." In J. Folwer and A. Vergote (eds.), *Towards Religious and Moral Maturity.* Morristown: Silver Burdett, 1980.

Reimer, J., Paolito, D., and Hersh, R. *Promoting Moral Growth: From Piaget to Kohlberg.* New York: Longman, 1983.

Rosenbaum, J. *Making Inequality: The Hidden Curriculum of High School Tracking.* New York: Wiley, 1976.

Schafer, W. and Olexa, C. *Tracking and Opportunity.* Scranton: Chandler Publishing, 1971.

Tillich, P. *The Courage To Be.* New Haven: Yale University Press, 1952.

Brian H. Childs

Community Service Setting

The community service setting is defined in this chapter as any public service agency or institution not directly supported by any ecclesiastical body. Generally this type of setting is supported by public funding such as the United Way or local, state, or national governmental grants. While such agencies may collect fees from clients the primary support comes from public resources.

Most community services agencies are community mental health agencies often with specializations in such areas as substance abuse, mental retardation, and family services. While community service agencies can be concerned with areas related, but not directly, to mental health, such as YM and YWCA, soup kitchens, and social services clearing houses, most pastoral counselors find themselves in mental health delivery instead of these other types of agencies.

Because the pastoral counselor who works in the largely secular community service setting is accountable in his or her work to secular and often governmental authorities, as well as dependent on public funding for his or her own income, certain unique problems need to be confronted. The issue of identity must be considered. A major problem for the pastoral counselor is to maintain a pastoral or ministerial identification in a setting that does not confer on the counselor an ecclesiastical designation such as chaplain. More often than not the pastoral counselor is not hired by virtue of his or her pastoral identity in the first place but is hired by virtue of certain clinical or administrative skills not necessarily related to the person's theological education. Indeed most pastoral counselors working in the community service setting do not have "pastoral" as part of their job title. One is far more likely to have the title of counselor, case-worker, or administrator and be called Mr., Ms., or Dr. rather than Rev. or chaplain.

The issue of pastoral identity is not an issue just of self-identification but is an issue for the pastoral counselor's ecclesiastical authorities as well. As Morris Taggert has pointed out (Taggert, 1972), pastoral counseling could well be moving in the direction of being a profession within the mental health field rather than a specialized type of ministry. This certainly has been the point of view of more than just a few denominational governing bodies as these bodies chose to strike from the roles of active ministers those who had identified themselves as counselors in a secular setting rather than being directly involved with the life and work of a local parish or church sponsored institution. While this is a problem for the counselor involved with a pastoral counseling agency it certainly is a major problem for the pastoral counselor involved with the community service agency.

The remainder of this chapter will consider the problem of pastoral identity in the community service setting as being of prime importance. For this reason the various issues discussed, such as the role of the inter-disciplinary team, consultation, and supervision, to name a few, will be considered as they apply to the issue of pastoral identity, both from the subjective point of view of the counselor as well as the objective point of view of both the denominational governing bodies and the institutions and clients served.

Much of this chapter will be anecdotal in nature. The primary reason for this is that very little scholarly research has been carried out in investigating both the joys and problems of pastoral counseling in the secular community service setting. While there will be some references to work done in this general area over the past few years the majority of this chapter will be based on the author's own experience in and reflection on community service settings over the past eleven years.

Pastoral Identity and the Interdisciplinary Team

Certainly one major asset in working in a community service setting is the opportunity to work with mental health professionals from fields other than pastoral counseling. A pastoral counselor working in a community mental health setting can expect to have contact with social workers, clinical psychologists, and psychiatrists, as well as certified alcohol counselors and various paraprofessionals. Clearly, then, the opportunity to be introduced to a wide variety of resources is something to be capitalized upon. Unlike the pastoral counselor who works in a pastoral counseling agency that may only have occasional consultants from the mental health disciplines, the pastoral counselor who works in a secular agency has the opportunity to work with these mental health workers on a daily basis.

From the social worker one may learn about the social service resources in the community or at least learn how to find them. From the clinical psychologist one may learn about the value of psychological testing and when it is indicated either as a diagnostic source or even a therapeutic one. The psychiatrist is a source of medical and legal support. Of course from each of these mental health professionals one may learn about the art of therapy and counseling and benefit from a multiplicity of training backgrounds.

It is assumed too that the other members of the agency will also learn from the experiences of the pastoral counselor. In many instances, in fact, it has been my experience that a well-trained pastoral counselor has more training and supervision in psychotherapy than most other professions. This is to say that a pastoral counselor with a graduate degree in pastoral counseling beyond the basic theological degree and supervision qualifying the counselor for basic membership in the American Association of Pastoral Counselors will have more supervision in doing psychotherapy than most M.S.W. social worker graduates and M.D. psychiatrists just out of residency ("Standards for Membership," AAPC Handbook). While the pastoral counselor can learn about diagnosis, pharmacology, administration, and legal issues from other professionals, the others too can learn from the pastoral counselor on issues of clinical management and treatment.

There are real dangers for the pastoral counselor's sense of pastoral identity as he or she works in the community service setting. While there are real assets in working in an interdisciplinary setting the dangers of being swallowed up by identifying with the secular mental health professions is a common one. It is not hard to understand why this happens. More often than not the pastoral counselor is the only minister on the staff, and while there may be several social workers and psychologists who have similar training and educational backgrounds there may be little in common with the pastoral counselor. The only area that the pastoral counselor will have in common with the other professions is the one of therapeutic technique and theory. It is around this issue, then, that the pastoral counselor and the others have commonality. That is the area in which conversation can be carried out at the expense of the minister's counseling identity as pastoral. The others too begin to see the pastoral counselor as another mental health professional. It is not uncommon to hear a psychologist say in amazement about a pastoral colleague, "If someone were to observe her and me for one day, that person would only have a fifty-fifty chance of picking the one who is the psychologist and the one who is the pastoral counselor."

The same problem usually does not affect the psychiatrist in this setting. While the psychiatrist too may be the only representative of the medical profession in the setting, he or she has a special advantage in that the medical professional is usually at the top of the clinic hierarchy due to legal and social traditions. The psychiatrist is supposed to be set apart. The pastoral counselor is supposed to be part of the team, and often to be an accepted member of the team certain ministerial identities and functions have to take a back seat. Such basic and traditional pastoral functions as worship, pastoral care, and evangelism are often considered as secondary, at best, by many pastoral counselors, as demonstrated by L. Vande Creek in a statistical study (Vande Creek, 1983).

Pastoral Identity and the Consultation

The term consultant usually refers to some outside person with a particular expertise who is invited to an institution for a limited period of time. The purpose of the consultation is to allow the consultant to present his or her observations and recommendations to those in charge. The consultant never assumes ongoing responsibility for the operation of the institution or for the treatment of any client. The consultant is different from a supervisor in two most critical ways. First, the consultant, unlike the supervisor, will not necessarily have any further contact with the therapist or institution after the consultation visit. Second, the consultant's recommendations have less direct authority than a supervisor's recommendations due to the brevity of the relationship and the minimal legal and professional responsibility to the client and therapist.

Most community service agencies will, from time to time, hire outside experts to consult and lead workshops on both clinical and administrative issues. Many agencies will also hire consultants with special ability in group dynamics for the purpose of staff development. Probably the most common form of consultation is the psychiatric consultation in an agency with no full-time psychiatrist or medical person. This form of consultation may take place as often as once a week to as minimally as once a month. These consultations usually deal with issues such as medication and diagnosis.

Consultations need not be limited exclusively to outside experts. Many an enlightened administrator will also make use of in-house consultations as well as the outside expert. Such areas as staffing, diagnosis, and the location of resources outside the agency are areas of expertise often found in any staff of most community service agencies.

One form of consultation that is available to the community service agency that has a pastoral counselor on its staff is the theological or religious consultation. Unfortunately very few staffs make use of this type of consultation. As Pruyser has pointed out (Pruyser, 1971) there almost seems to be a conspiracy of silence among psychotherapists on issues of religion. The reason for this may well be because religion is a symbol for authority and power. Both clients and therapists may follow the taboo of keeping religious issues to themselves.

When religion does become an issue for a client and for a therapist the pastoral counselor can offer an invaluable service in making a theological evaluation of the ideation. As has been pointed out by Seward Hiltner (Hiltner, 1972) the theologically trained consultant may help solve what he calls the "denominational problem." This is the case where a client belongs to a religious group whose beliefs and practices are not known to the staff and may appear rather bizarre or ill when in fact it is orthodox in the client's tradition. Here the pastoral consultant armed with a theological education and practice as well as such tools as F.S. Mead's *Handbook of Denominations in the United States* becomes valuable.

Clearly the use of the pastoral counselor in the religious consultation within the community service setting will result in the deeper understanding of human behavior for those not theologically trained as well as underscore the unique abilities and education of the pastoral counselor. This will not only reinforce the pastor's own identity as a minister but will also reinforce this identity with the secular members of the staff. Of course this reinforced identity will have ever so much more power and authority if it is communicated from the existential sensitivity and experience of the pastoral counselor as well as from some rational or purely academic perspective.

Pastoral Identity and Supervision

According to Rader (Rader, 1977) supervision serves two essential functions in any mental health clinic. The first is the function of "quality control" of the services given to the client in accord with the standards of the clinic as well as certain governmental agencies. The second function is that of affording the therapist the opportunity of acquiring greater skill in the delivery of clinical services. Presumably these functions apply to the supervision of the pastoral counselor as well as any other mental health professional. Is there any difference, however, between the supervision of the pastoral counselor and the secular worker? The common sense answer to this question would be yes. Each profession does indeed have its own unique approach to supervision. The medical profession has a long tradition of clinical supervision based on the biological model which is increasingly more important in psychiatry with its concern with the biological basis of disease and the treatment of psychiatric disorders with medication. While social work and psychology may have many supervisory methods in common, in that both concern themselves with the therapeutic relationship as "talk therapy," the mode of supervision often will reflect the unique educational background of the profession. More often than not social work will concern itself with existing social and political factors that the psychologist often is just not trained to look for. The psychologist, on the other hand, may be far more interested in the psychometric aspects of treatment as well as the interpsychic. While these may be gross generalizations about the supervisory attitudes of these professions there is more than a hint of truth to each characterization. The fact that each profession (psychiatry/medicine, social work, and psychology) has its own standards for practice and its own code of ethics that is unique to the profession testifies to the particularity of its supervisory practice.

Pastoral counseling also has a unique approach to supervision, and this creates some particular problems for the pastoral counselor in the community service setting. More likely than not the pastoral counselor in the community service setting will be supervised by a member of the secular professions, and if he or she desires pastoral supervision it must be pursued on his or her own time and money. This is not to denigrate so-called secular counseling and supervision one bit. In fact The American Association of Pastoral Counselors encourages and indeed requires for membership some supervision outside the pastoral supervisory process. The issue for the pastoral counselor is the very real danger of being swallowed up by the simple fact of being outnumbered.

What is unique about pastoral counseling and by implication pastoral supervision? While there is no real consensus of an answer to this question there are several general qualities and components to pastoral counseling that point to its unique form of supervision. Certainly the most obvious requirement for a pastoral counselor is theological education and certification—that is, either ordination or, in the case of members of religious orders, sponsorship by an ecclesiastical body. Of course it must be assumed that ecclesiastical sponsorship entails the requirements of participation in the ongoing life of the church by the counselor. Pastoral counseling is a legitimate form of specialized ministry, and it is because the counselor self-consciously asserts his or her ministerial identity by participating in the life of a local congregation and in utilizing the other pastoral resources available, i.e., scripture, prayer, and the sacraments. "Ministry is validated by its representativeness as well as by its competence; and if it represents nothing that is visible, it has ceased to become a ministry of the church" (Hiltner, 1977, p. 200).

B.W. Grant and D.M. Moss (Grant and Moss, 1981) have outlined some distinctive qualities of training and supervision that underscore the difference between pastoral counseling and the secular helping professions involved in mental health. Besides a theological education that encourages us to think in terms of turning points (conversion) in human development, as well as a faith in a God of providence, the pastoral counselor brings to his or her profession a style that directly comes out of a unique clinical training experience. According to Grant and Moss most pastoral counselors received their initial training either in Clinical Pastoral Education centers or some comparable pastoral counseling training center. As anyone who has received training is such centers would attest, the method of education is one that most secular mental health professionals have not experienced. One way of describing the supervisee experience is that the student is encouraged to be both subject and observer at the same time. "The focus of supervision has been on helping candidates, who are struggling to avoid being swept away, overwhelmed, or submerged in the training experience, to consciously articulate what is happening to them as a way of becoming aware of their own processes and learning to conceptualize them while under substantial environmental stress" (Grant and Moss, pp. 240–241). The result of such supervision and training is a desire and in fact a need of the pastoral counselor to constantly monitor his or her own feelings and to conceptualize them in some coherent process. This process has been likened to a pilgrimage and is part and parcel of theological method. Supervision, then, for the pastoral counselor should be a process of linking the experiences of the counselor and the client with a theology of the corporate experience of the religious community and its ministry (Hommes, 1977). The secular mental health professions are more than likely to have a supervision process of teaching skills and techniques with little emphasis on the holistic conceptualization of the counseling and human experience.

To lose this form of supervision for the pastoral counselor in the community service setting is a critical one. Not that secular supervision is less than adequate. It just is not profession specific, that is, pastoral supervision. It is obvious that the loss of this type of supervision could put in jeopardy the pastoral identity of the counselor. Secular mental health training and supervision does not produce pastoral counselors. It produces secular mental health professionals (psychologists, social workers, or psychiatrists). One cannnot expect it to do anything else. The pastoral counselor who receives exclusively secular supervision runs the risk of falling into a secular socialization process and therefore a loss of the pastoral identity. Likewise it is difficult for the secular supervisee to feel all that comfortable with the theological or pastoral style of supervision, thereby complicating an already difficult process. This is a problem not easily solved and it takes a very dedicated and disciplined pastoral counselor to avoid the very dangerous pitfalls.

Pastoral Identity and Accountability

The issue of accountability may be the most important issue facing the pastoral counselor in terms of pastoral identity. While it is obvious that the counselor is responsible to the clientele served by following prescribed clinic procedures, obtaining supervision and review, and maintaining a professional and helpful relationship with the clients, there are other avenues of accountability that must be addressed.

To whom is the pastoral counselor serving in a secular community service setting accountable in terms of his or her specialized ministry? Surely the denominational judicatory is ultimately responsible for sponsorship for any ordained or commissioned representative of the church. While this may not necessarily be true for members of the so-called Free Churches, such as the Baptist church that has no ecclesiastical hierarchy, it certainly is true for those members of the "main line" churches and those in the Roman Catholic tradition. The real question is, however: Can the church endorse a ministry of a person when that person's employer is not self-consciously hiring him or her as a minister or pastoral counselor but rather as a psychotherapist and/or administrator? The trend in the Presbyterian Church (U.S.A.) is no—the church cannot endorse secular work as ministry in and for the church, that is, as ministry of the church. For this reason ministers not working in a local parish are required to give an accounting of their ministry on an annual basis (*The Book of Order*, 1982–1983, 42.31). Ministers have been taken off the role of presbytery because their work in private practice or in non-church agencies was not considered valid ministry in the reformed tradition. Some association with a local congregation and the opportunity to perform the sacraments and ordinances of the church are minimal requirements for continued membership in the local presbytery. It is important to note that ecclesiastical endorsement is a basic requirement for membership in the American Association of Pastoral Counselors.

Working in the community service setting also presents another accountability issue that confronts the pastoral identity of the minister/counselor. This issue is the pressure to obtain membership in secular professional organizations, some of which are also certifying organizations. It is quite understandable that a pastoral counselor would feel certain pressure to gain "peerage" with his or her secular colleagues by joining such organizations as The American Association for Marriage and Family Therapy, The American Family Therapy Association, The American Psychological Association, The National Association of Social Workers and the like. While membership in these organizations need not compromise the identity of the pastoral counselor, especially if the organization accepts them in their role as clergy, organizations that certify a profession could pose a threat to that person. The American Association for Marriage and Family Therapy, The American Psychological Association, and The Academy of Certified Social Workers are certifying organizations, and membership in such organizations could qualify the ministerial identity. The critical issue in becoming a member in such organizations is whether it becomes the primary mode of professional identity.

A closely related issue for the pastoral counselor is the acquisition of state licenses to practice as a certain kind of mental health provider. For instance, the state of New Jersey has a marriage counseling license that requires certain educational backgrounds and the passing of a written exam (N.J.S.A. 45:8B–1 ET SEQ., January 10, 1969). Section 8 of this bill clearly states that the act should not be construed as limiting the activities of other qualified professionals (such as physicians, psychologists, *and* clergy). Yet, many pastoral counselors have taken the examination and have licenses. The reasons for this are many and subtle. Surely there is a desire for recognition by secular mental health professions for much the same reason that many pastoral counselors join secular professional organizations. There is also the at times not so subtle desire of agency administrators to have bona fide licensed personnel on their staff. There is also the interest both of agencies and individuals to be eligible for third party payments that licensure could provide. Even pastoral counselors may want a piece of the national health insurance pie when that becomes a reality.

Even more threatening to the ability of the pastoral counselor to maintain the pastoral identity is the issue of licensing of pastoral counselors by the state. New Hampshire, for instance, has the bill *Licensed Pastoral Counselors Act* that forbids any pastoral counselor from presenting himself or herself as a licensed and certified pastoral counselor. In two articles published in *The Journal of Pastoral Care* (Myers, 1976 and Prest, 1976) the pros and cons of state licensure are discussed. Clearly one issue for the pastoral counselor in obtaining state licensure is monetary, that is, being able to dip into the third party payment well. The reason cannot possibly be who can control or define what is ministry, for only the church can do that. As Hiltner has said (Hiltner, 1977) having state licensure for the practice of ministry is like wearing a belt and suspenders at the same time, and that if the state can approve of a form of ministry it can also someday disapprove of it. It seems we have certain constitutional protections from that state initiative. As Florell has said: "It seems to me that we are precariously close to cutting ourselves off from the most vital resource we have, our identity as pastors. I do not feel we can serve two masters well by being pastoral counselors-psychotherapists on the one hand and psychologists, social workers, educational counselors on the other. One allegiance will suffer, and I fear the church allegiance will be the one. Unless we can be true to our faith body for the practice of ministry in a responsible fashion, we have no recourse but to become secular specialists" (Florell, 1976, p. 74).

The pastoral counselor in the generally public and secular sector of mental health practice is quite vulnerable to losing the pastoral or ministerial identity especially when it comes to professional accreditation. It seems that the best protection against losing the identity is association with a local faith community, participation in clergy organizations, and the increasing influence and guidance of ecclesiastical authorities on the work of specialized ministers. With these protections, membership in the other various professional and interest organizations would present fewer real problems.

Moral Guidance and Pastoral Identity

An interesting and critical dilemma that the pastoral counselor in the public and secular mental health area must face is the role of moral and ethical guidance in his or her practice of pastoral care and counseling. It is generally understood by most secular mental health models that the suspension of the therapist's moral and aesthetic value is essential for the therapeutic process. It is commonly believed that a therapeutic alliance is developed through the complete and unconditional regard and acceptance of the counselor toward the client. In addition, normative values have appeared to have taken a secondary role to the at times solipsistic value of the subjective "inner" person. As Grant and Moss have pointed out, (Grant and Moss, 1981), a major difference between pastoral counseling and secular counseling is that pastoral counseling is committed to radical change (conversion) and continued growth and ever changing human possibilities. "To a mature religious consciousness, the notion of people making peace comfortably with their 'sinfulness' and continuing to live in it sounds abhorrent" (Grant and Moss, 1981, pp. 239–240). Don Browning, too, has sounded the call (Browning, 1976) for pastoral counselors as well as all pastoral ministers to be aware of their roots in the Judaeo-Christian moral tradition, albeit not in a heavy-handed or oppressive way.

Unlike the person or persons seeking help from a parish clergy or from a pastoral counseling center, the person or persons seeking help from a community service agency are not expecting to be met by a religious professional. For this reason one cannot even argue that there is an assumed or implicit contract to explore moral values in the counseling process. Certainly the person who goes to the community service agency under a court order (a common occurrence) does not expect, nor should he or she be submitted to, pastoral/moral intervention. What happens then because of these cultural and social expectations of secular neutrality is that the pastoral counselor attempts to keep their religious light hidden under the basket of secular professionalism.

Probably the best way to confront this problem is to make clear in the joining process with the client the professional background of the counselor. In this way the opportunity for explicit contract making can be made and the process of pastoral counseling can proceed or a referral can be made. My own experience has been that very few people reject a pastoral counselor especially if the counselor can communicate his or her own professional competence and caring for those with which they work. As Lapsley has pointed out (Lapsley, 1983), pastoral care cannot derive its direction from some static moral or ethical norm. Pastoral care must first be able to diagnose and test the possibilities of a human life rather than rest with a normative question that often ignores those possibilities.

General Clinical Issues

Having worked in the parish, in a pastoral counseling agency, and in a theological seminary I have found some real differences in the so-called clinical style used in the community service agency from these traditional ministerial work settings. Community outreach is probably one of the more exciting elements of the community service setting. While the pastor in a local church may encourage community services the community service agency has a clear and publicly dictated mandate for such work. While working for a community based adolescent drug abuse center I found much of my counseling work being done outside the office building. Much of my work took place in the schools, on the streets, and in the county detention center. There was also an opportunity to get to know the workings of various other service organizations, both church and secular, along with police and public health agencies. The education was beyond any measurable value!

Because my contact with my clients was not exclusively in an office setting my perspective on the origin and maintenance of human problems broadened from the intrapsychic to the interpsychic and the social. In many ways because of my theological and professional training I was able to exercise one of the birthrights of the ministry: pastoral initiative. Unlike the psychiatrist, the psychologist, and the social worker (though to a lesser extent in social work) the pastor has a tradition of outreach, home visitation, and even the solicitation of services so long as it does not result in additional financial advantage.

In line with the outreach mandate of the community service agency therapeutic strategies evolved that were in many ways quite different from those most of us were originally trained to use. Systems theory and strategic interventions soon became more useful than office centered interpretations and mild behavior modification. Many of us sought out and received training in systems and structural therapy in family therapy training centers such as the Ackerman Institute in New York and the Child Guidance Clinic in Philadelphia, the latter clinic having a unique training program for "lay" therapists, i.e., community members from the inner city learning structural counseling techniques to help their neighbors. To this minister, the program was not unlike many "lay" pastoral care training workshops offered by many churches. Usually the community service setting allows for a ministry/service to a population that the private mental health practitioner and most pastoral counseling centers do not serve because this population cannot afford them and does not have insurance to pay for services.

Along with community service and new modes of learning about and treating problems the community service setting has its own unique set of irritations that have to be met. Because most service agencies are government run (city, state, or federal) the amount of bureaucratic paperwork and reporting can be oppressive. While adequate record-keeping and the accountability of time and money is essential it is not just an unfair characterization to say that many of these agencies are compelled to fill out forms and follow strict guidelines in a way that would drive all but the fanatical obsessive-compulsive to the brink of total frustration. Burn-out is a major problem.

In this chapter I have limited the definition of a community service setting as being secular in its mission, administration, and funding. There are church sponsored community service agencies, such as community-based pastoral counseling agencies, as well as denominational social service agencies such as the Salvation Army, Catholic Charities, and Lutheran Welfare. Generally the social service agencies have the pastoral person as the administrator with secular mental health professionals serving on the staff positions. The community-based pastoral counseling agencies generally will have the majority of the staff occupied by pastoral counselors. Both the social service and the pastoral counseling services depend upon church funding but generally also depend on public sources of funding such as the United Way and also revenues generated from client fees.

In actual practice the social service agency sponsored by a denomination is very similar in its workings to the secular community service agency. While the identity problems for the pastoral counselor found in the secular agency are less severe in the church agency, my own experience has been that it is just a matter of degree. The issues of pastoral practices besides pastoral care and counseling, secular professional endorsement, and licensure are quite pervasive. While the denomination will endorse a member of its clergy working in such an agency, pastoral identity still suffers, that is, unless the pastoral counselor also participates in the life of a local community of faith and maintains contact with clergy from other areas of specialization as well as from the parish.

The community-based pastoral counseling service, while affording some of the strengths of the secular community service setting, such as interdisciplinary teams, generally does not have the ability to offer the outreach of such agencies. The reason for this is financial. These agencies have to depend upon client fees to such a great extent that non-revenue-generating activities such as outreach have to be kept at a minimum. Very few pastoral counseling agencies receive enough funding from local congregations to free up the staff for work other than in-office counseling. In addition, while most of these agencies do have sliding fee scales the number of low paying clients must be kept at a level in proportion to the number of high paying clients, a tricky balance indeed. For this reason many of these agencies find themselves serving the middle class, thereby neglecting a considerable population in great need of services. In addition there is a growing trend for pastoral counseling agencies to accept third party payments for their services. This brings the most difficult question of accountability and responsibility for services to the forefront. Since most pastoral counselors are not acceptable providers according to most insurance companies, the pastoral counseling service must depend upon licensed providers, usually psychiatrists and psychologists and in some states social workers. Who, then, is the responsible agent for the service? In many instances the pastoral counselor, in order to have some sense of responsibility for signing the insurance forms and having legal authority, will apply for some form of state licensure or accreditation in a secular accrediting body. The problems of this move in terms of pastoral identity have been discussed above.

Conclusion

Pastoral care and counseling in the community service setting is one of the most challenging and exciting forms of specialized pastoral ministry. It is also a form of specialized ministry that paradoxically seems to have built into it elements that inhibit ministry through the inhibition of ministerial and pastoral identity. My own experience and my observation of the experience of others involved in such settings is that the pastoral counselor must constantly go through identity crises in terms of calling to ministry and also in terms of professional accountability. It has been my experience that most pastoral counselors in a specialized ministry in a secular community service setting eventually give up their pastoral identity, that is, if their ecclesiastical bodies don't do it for them. Those in the community based pastoral counseling agencies or denominational social service agencies seem to keep their pastoral identity longer, though the functional identity does seem to suffer. In addition to service to a local congregation the pastoral counselor who is lucky enough to work in close proximity to a seminary can also maintain service of and in the church through field work supervision. Of course continuing education should not only be clinical education but theological education such as those courses offered in most continuing education programs of many seminaries.

Bibliography

Browning, D.S., *The Moral Context of Pastoral Care*. Philadelphia: Westminster Press, 1976.

Florell, J.L., "Editorial: Licensing—Clerical or Secular?" *Journal of Pastoral Care*, June 1976, Vol. XXX, No. 2, pp. 73–74.

Grant, B.W. and Moss, D.M., "A Training Philosophy and Its Implementation," in J.C. Carr, J.E. Hinkle, and D.M. Moss (eds.), *The Organization and Administration of Pastoral Counseling Centers*. Nashville: Abingdon Press, 1981, pp. 239–254.

Hiltner, S. "Theological Consultants in Hospitals and Mental Health Centers," *American Journal of Psychiatry*, 1972, 128:8, pp. 965–969.

Hiltner, S. "Pastoral Counseling and the Church," *Journal of Pastoral Care*, September 1977, Vol. XXXI, No. 3, pp. 178–185.

Hommes, T.G., "Supervision as Theological Method," *Journal of Pastoral Care*, September 1977, Vol. XXXI, No. 3, pp. 150–157.

Lapsley, J.N. "Practical Theology and Pastoral Care: An Essay in Pastoral Theology," in D.S. Browning (ed.), *Practical Theology*. San Francisco: Harper and Row, 1983.

Myers, R.L. "State Licensing and Pastoral Identity," *Journal of Pastoral Care*, June 1976, XXX, No. 2, pp. 76–82.

Prest, A.P.L. "By What Authority?" *Journal of Pastoral Care*, June 1976, XXX, No. 2, pp. 83–87.

Pruyser, P. "Assessment of the Patient's Religious Attitudes in the Psychiatric Case Study," *Bulletin of the Menninger Clinic*, July 1971, Vol. 35, No. 4, pp. 272–291.

Rader, B.B. "Supervision of Pastoral Psychology," *Journal of Pastoral Care*, September 1977, XXX, No. 3, pp. 178–185.

"Standards for Membership," *American Association of Pastoral Counselors Handbook* (adopted April 24, 1965—amended November 20, 1976).

Taggert, M. "The AAPC Membership Information Project," *Journal of Pastoral Care*, December 1972, XXVI, No. 4, pp. 219–244.

The Book of Order, The United Presbyterian Church in the United States of America, 1982–1983.

Vande Creek, L. "A Statistical Profile of the American Association of Pastoral Counselors and the Association for Clinical Pastoral Education," *Pastoral Psychology*, Spring 1983, Vol. 31, No. 3, pp. 170–178.

Ross H. Trower

Military

The Chaplain as Counselor

"Counseling" for the military chaplain may well be his chief ministerial function—at least from the perspective of his commanding officer as well as from the descriptions by his people of what it is that the chaplain does. It is the most pervasive notion among "outsiders" of the chaplain's professional activity. Moreover, it may be that his effectiveness is determined largely by the reputation he enjoys as a counselor. His place on the "team" (a critical concept in the military denoting both the structure and the dynamics of its societal units) is likely to be as a counselor (Hutcheson, 1975).

During World War II, when millions of men from all walks of life and some women came face to face with clergymen in uniform, they found that chaplains had official relationships within command, in addition to their having—supposedly—some kind of direct connection with the "Man Upstairs," who would hear out their complaints, their problems, their worries. Their enlisted superiors had impressed upon them early in military indoctrination that if they, the sergeants and the petty officers, could not help them, the chaplain would. He'd work a miracle! At the least, he'd give them sympathy.

"Go see the chaplain" might have been a "put-off" or "put-down," a joke, scornful derision of the "client" and the "padre," or a genuine referral, even a real desire to assist the soldier or sailor. One would need carefully to sort through tones, gestures, and the personality profile of the players to ascertain what was intended by these "referrals." In any case, a popular operant function was validated by which chaplains became known quickly in their important role as counselor. Two or three assumptions were made by those who advised, "Take it to the chaplain": (1) the chaplain had the desire, time and skills to give assistance to the troubled; (2) the chaplain would give every soldier, sailor, marine, or coast guardsman a fair hearing regardless of his religious preference; (3) the chaplain dealt with areas usually beyond the range of matters administrative authorities claimed for themselves.

It is an enormous tribute to the largely anecdotally described work of the many clergymen who served in uniform during World War II, when personnel were drafted into military service for combat and faced countless disjunctions in their lives and almost unspeakable fears, that "counseling" in these terms was reinforced as such an accepted ministry of military chaplains. Even today, then, counseling, perhaps more professionally structured and theologically oriented, is still the chaplain's stock-in-trade with all of his people.

All this is not to say that the military chaplain abandons the teaching of scripture, preaching the word of the Lord, administering the sacraments of his church, or visiting the sick and imprisoned. Rather, counseling is what he does along with these functions. It becomes his more rabbinic style. It may be his more "secular" work—even when he does it from his religious posture. It is what he can do for everyone. It is likely what only he in the unit does well. It is his "shingle," his professional calling card—the "religious" work he is expected to do for the adherents of his own spiritual community and in behalf of the entire organization.

This view of the chaplain as counselor is seldom examined theoretically within the military community. It is a practical solution to needs, a determination of functions among those which are felt should be done by officers. It is necessary and it fits. That the chaplain does counseling for military persons and members of their families, their dependents, is thus a primary expectation of persons who would desire his assistance. A military member might never receive the benefits of a chaplain's specifically liturgical functions; he would take it for granted that the chaplain would be his counselor if he came to him in need.

Counseling as Pastoral

Chaplains at times have struggled to define their counseling as pastoral. In recent years, each of the military services has provided a variety of counselors for its military members. Today, there are persons designated—and, often, rather well trained—as educational counselors, drug abuse counselors, alcohol counselors, benefits counselors, career counselors, family counselors. The list is lengthy in large military complexes. Many of these counselors are both experienced and credentialed; some are uniformed while others are civil service employees. Although chaplains are able to refer individuals to such specialists where they are available, greater numbers of people are likely to see their chaplains first, for many personnel are not located in large military centers. Chaplains, moreover, are usually more accessible to them.

The counseling of chaplains is pastoral because it is incorporated into their total religious program of caring for their personnel. Their counseling arises out of religiously grounded convictions about the needs of military people and is given sanction by their appointments as chaplains and their assignment to duties as chaplains. Chaplains may have gained expertise in specific areas of human illness and may participate in programs having relevance and potential for ministry. Their pastoral counseling begins in the needs of people whose military service tends to cut them off from the ministries of religion normally available in civilian life.

Command authorities, pressed with immediate concerns and often isolated from the centers where specialists are present, may ask the chaplain simply to provide the help he can. Such authorities expect the chaplain to be a generalist, not a specialist—except in the area of religion! That the chaplain counsels out of a framework that has spiritual and moral concerns is not challenged. He is never asked to abandon his religious convictions, those matters that are the focus of his specialty. He may only need to ask himself whether a religious intervention is appropriate and whether his religious view takes into account respect for his "client's" convictions.

The chaplain is generally held to be professionally able and accountable to determine the orientation of his counseling processes. It is expected by the military services that they will be coherent with the religious body of which the chaplain is a member. They must also be comprehensive enough to include all persons.

What the chaplain does then in meeting the expressed—or barely expressed—needs of those who seek his assistance in one-to-one or small group encounters will be described as pastoral counseling unless the chaplain himself defines his work differently. If he does, he will find himself finally defending his stance against common perceptions and expectations, his religious body, and, very likely, the majority of chaplains.

Beginnings

Pastoral counseling in the military environment most frequently begins with a simple plea from a military person or dependent member, "Chaplain, may I talk with you?" It may be asked in the setting of an office; it is as likely to be asked by a sailor standing on the deckplates of an engine room, an airman in the corner of an aircraft hangar, a soldier relaxing around the edges of a bivouac area, during a long flight—anywhere. It is the opening move of someone who, recognizing the corps insignia of a chaplain, seeks assurance, clarification, assistance, support, relief from the isolation of his or her life.

Obviously, the chaplain must decide whether the plea is casual, a kind of whiling away of time, or whether the plea bubbles up from a troubled soul. It is helpful to learn early what strength of effort has been made to ask that simple question, "Chaplain, may I talk with you?" Asked in an office by one who is likely to be unfamiliar with seeking professional assistance, it is hardly casual but rather the cry of an individual desperate in his need.

Information-gathering is vital in the first stages of counseling in the military setting, especially when referral data are not available and the client is unknown. If the chaplain has an assistant, he may want, in an office, to use a brief information card to gather some pertinent data ahead of his meeting with the counselee.[1] The early stages of pastoral counseling ought to be marked by concreteness, not with abstractions concerning morality or religion. They ought to determine, if possible, whether the presenting need is acute or chronic. They should explore what solutions toward resolution have already been attempted, and, perhaps, include an inquiry into what expectations the counselee has of the chaplain.

The chaplain, in turn, should engage enough in these first stages to express what he might do for the counselee, what kinds of time allocations can be given, and something of himself. He will probably convey quickly to the counselee whether he is interested or not in him, whether he feels for him or rejects him. The chaplain should ask himself, amidst the communications of these early interviews, "What is the problem?" His answers to himself should be tentative and amenable to ready modification.

Little will be said in this chapter about the developing dynamics of pastoral counseling, for they are not too different from pastoral counseling in environments other than the military. It needs to be stressed, however, that in the military setting the term of pastoral counseling is, more often than not, brief. Extended terms are possible if the military situation permits, but the chaplain learns that although he may be able to arrange many meetings with a counselee he had better move with a certain deliberateness toward accomplishing what he can in not more than three or four meetings. He needs also to affirm for the counselee, as well as for himself, that his ministry or "work" in these circumstances can be helpful. He will develop realistic objectives for "changes" in individuals; he will also recognize the necessity for referrals and for the utilization of resource networks in the military and in the civilian communities, where available, as his limitations for time and in such specialized training as may be indicated become more explicit.

Characteristics of Military Personnel

Some general characteristics of the military population may be useful for considering the features of pastoral counseling in the military environment. These characteristics are likely to be similar for the family member as well. It is not usual that the chaplain would be brought into counseling with dependent members of service personnel such as fathers or mothers or guardians. The chaplain may be asked to assist with children, especially teenage children. In military communities, where familes are numerous, he would probably be teamed with school counselors and family social workers of various kinds. Unless unusually well-equipped and specialized, the chaplain is generally not a pastoral counselor to children nor should he be.

Military men and women—and their spouses—are *young*. At the end of 1982, according to a Department of Defense report (1983), of the 1.8 million enlisted personnel on active duty in all the services, more than one-third were between the ages of 21 and 25. One-fourth were 20 and younger; almost one-fifth were between the ages of 26 and 30. In sum, then, nearly 80 percent of all enlisted personnel were between 17 and 30 years of age.

Of the almost three hundred thousand officers on active duty at the same time, a fourth were 26 through 30. Eighty percent of all officers were under the age of 40.

The chaplain's counseling clientele are not only young; they can be considered *healthy* people. Except where the chaplain's ministry is directed primarily to hospitals or rehabilitative units, where separation from the services is the outcome of the treatment, chaplains do not deal with physical or mental handicaps in the problems presented by their personnel. They may see healthy, active men and women who experience some fear or threat of failure because they do not measure up to competitive measurements or whose identity as achievers has been challenged by those who achieve even more. They indeed may find severe handicaps among family members.

Military men and women are educated, that is, among the general population they are mostly high school graduates—and more. Less than 8 percent of enlisted personnel did not have a high school diploma or equivalent certificate. Ninety-three percent of the officers had baccalaureate degrees; many of the degree holders had one or more advanced degrees (Department of Defense, 1983).

Diplomas and degrees are seen by military personnel authorities not only as achievements in subject mastery or requirements for certain kinds of performance but also, significantly, as indicators of the individual's proven ability to complete tasks. Thus, military people might be said to be generally successful, if success is thought of as the ability to carry through with a significant project.

Some images of military personnel tend to portray the soldier or the sailor as unattached, carefree. The likelihood is much greater that the serviceperson is *family-related*. Demographic descriptions of the military family require detailed discussion, not altogether appropriate here, but it is safe to state that 75 percent of all active duty officers have responsibilities relating to spouses and perhaps children and that 50 percent of all active duty enlisted personnel count their families among their responsibilities in life (Department of Defense, 1983). Most military men and women have family attachments which are currently a vital aspect of their lives. The pastoral counselor would do well to learn what attachments to family members or friends are of special significance to his counselee and how the significance matters.

It is my personal observation that military people are inquiring, curious, apt to learn about life, themselves, others, behaviors, improvements in their own sense of worth. Questions concerning values and discussions about value conflicts are attractive to them. At the edges and at the centers of these matters are religious concerns.

Military men and women cannot altogether be classified as "white collar"and "blue collar" in the terminologies that applied to industrial life in less technological times, but most have job requirements that make them *technicians* in their employment, certainly *specialists* of some kind in their work. Their preparation for what they do in military performance is often long-term and extensive. They may be assumed to be skilled in some ways. The unskilled, moreover, are usually on their way to becoming skilled.

Finally, military men and women, unlike their counterparts in the verbal academic world, are often less articulate in their readiness to describe feelings of anger, hurt, loneliness. They are more likely to act them out. One military psychiatrist, for example, found it more productive to ask his patients "What does *this* (activity) do to you?" than to reflect "How do you feel about *this* (activity)?" He received ready responses to the former question, hesitation to the latter. It might be said that service personnel are *activity-expressive*.

The characteristics described above shape the tenor and tone of pastoral counseling in the military environment. They distinguish the styles of chaplains from the styles of pastors in small-town settings, whose parishioners are older, more settled in their relationship objects and patterns, or from those in community agencies whose clients are among the spectra of persons in large urban areas. The chaplain as pastoral counselor is well advised to make observations about the sociological and demographic characteristics of his own unit or area in which he is located, for he is aided by an understanding of the environment from which his clients come.

Times for Counseling

There are times and situations in the lives of military persons which are conducive for pastoral counseling. They are not entirely dissimilar from those of young men and women in civilian settings but they bear enumeration, for the skillful and wise chaplain will make himself available and accessible for these times and he will be attuned to the "triggers" that propel his charges to seek his counsel. (Again, the chaplain's knowledge of the social structure of his unit and the dynamics implied in that structure will be helpful to his ministry in pastoral counseling.)

Every military person experiences an orientation phase, called "boot camp," "recruit training," "basic training," indoctrination. For most men and women it is a limited time (four to eight weeks) of considerable stress and sudden changes in their sense of identity. It is a period in which physical and psychological limits are pushed out to their maximal borders of containment. Individuals are expected to adapt to highly structured routines. Group performances are rewarded; personal efforts are approved only insofar as they contribute to the success of the team. Status within non-military communities (of the former state) mean little; position in the military hierarchy is all-pervasive.

Homesickness during indoctrination, of course, wells up like a knot in the stomach or an unswallowable obstruction in the throat and can overwhelm even the most unsuspecting victim. Different food, different clothing, different people, different sounds, and a compression of both space and time make life seem alien and isolating.

Chaplains are busy among recruits. Their ministry may seem largely directed toward adapting and caring for acute symptoms among their bewildered flock. They may tire of hearing the same "songs" of distress and they may themselves grow calloused to the pain around them. Yet they need to be aware of symptoms which persist, sounding alarm to greater than normal disturbances. They need as well to be sensitive to the needs of young men and women to make commitments as they start new careers and to learn spiritual exercises which can persist through lifetimes. These are "decision times," when often old behaviors are set aside and new ones are put into place. Lasting impressions are formed during military indoctrination. Poor pastoral counselors establish patterns for those who seek and are spurned or clumsily treated. Wise pastoral counselors open doors that are entered later in hope and confidence.

Another critical time involves the experience of death and loss by the military member. Many individuals in the military environment for the first time, it seems, come face to face with real grief. Away from home, the young soldier, sailor, airman, or marine comes to feel all the more helpless in the grip of his loss. He cannot share family feelings or the expressions and emotions of his own friends. He wants to move mountains and the sea to place himself alongside of the fallen parent or sister or brother or spouse. He may go home. He may be unable by reason of distance or duty to do so.

The death of a friend in one's own unit is very painful—and often dealt with in the gathered strength of the unit or, strikingly, in severe isolation. Personal feelings are submerged. Shared comments tend to be guarded. Yet, every member experiences loss and, in combat or high risk situations especially, identification.

Many times, the chaplain as pastoral counselor will be brought into the depths of tragedy. He may be the "breaker" of the news of death, more frequently than any professional person or military commander who serves in the area of his responsibility for people. His pastoral counseling at this moment may be minimal in the development of relationships, as mourners turn to family and clergypersons or move to pick up their lives again in new places of residence, but his manner and style will convey the quality both of his pastoral care and of his training. The chaplain will walk through the protocols of burial both as officiant and as spokesperson for the community's grief; he will attend as coordinator of the arrangements for burial. All the time he will be alert for danger signals in the early, shocking grief. The chaplain may also provide longer-term care for widows, children, and other significant persons such as "buddies" and co-workers.

Death and the consequent reactions of loss, so often unfamiliar to a youthful population, who are not keepers of the traditions, are important events for the pastoral counselor in a military environment.

As death is an infrequent experience, courtship, engagement, and marriage are frequent "times" among the young men and women of the military. Chaplains should be well prepared in their knowledge of the religious requirements for marriage, which are consonant with their own faith communities. They need to recognize that military persons are used to ceremonial evolutions and may expect "ceremony" in weddings. They can articulate preparatory requirements—even informally for a prospective bride and groom of faith communities other than their own. Then, chaplains must also prepare themselves for youthful impetuosity and involvement with persons who have little understanding of religious requirements, who have never been in close contact with a minister, priest, or rabbi, but who feel somehow that they want a chaplain to solemnize (a word rarely, if ever, uttered by them) their marriage. The chaplain should encourage them in their growth even if he is unable to comply with their expressed wants.

The pastoral counselor must take into account, furthermore, that disappointments in romance and rejections by lovers are also times for care and understanding. "Dear Johns," communications which terminate the fantasies of romance as well as the realities of courtship, can be devastating when they are delivered to those who are thousands of miles away from the loved ones. Again, chaplains may be called upon to foster hope as they work with the imaginings of the jilted and tend the wounds of the hurt.

"Rotations" and deployments, those periods when units move from their bases and home ports to operating areas overseas or distant from family, are times of great stress upon military personnel and their family members. They usually arrive with scheduled regularity, so that individuals are prepared for them. In international emergencies, they can develop rapidly, come suddenly. Returns home may be predictable; they are frequently delayed, postponed.

Before rotations, the anxieties surrounding separation—even for the single person—may cause chronic problems to become exacerbated acutely, imagined situations to become real. Coping mechanisms of military members and their spouses may seem to fail at these times. Hardships arise like duststorms over the homes of functioning family units, and requests to see the chaplain about getting transferred or remaining in the rear increase as official requests are denied by officers and supervisors who need every trained "body" for the forthcoming maneuver. Neighbors, friends—and pastors too!—may be brought into the anxious pre-deployment anticipations.

Not all military members and their family members, of course, experience severe problems prior to departures of the military person from home. It is a time of stress, to be sure, but most go about their preparations with a sense of purpose and resolution together with confidence in the network of support at home. Military members draw upon their obligations to duty. Chaplains will become inundated by "problem" members and will need to sort through facts carefully and feelings understandingly. They must be well acquainted with official policies and practices and have a knowledge of the military requirements, but they must also have the confidence of organizations that they are responsible in their judgments and competent in their assessments of potentially hazardous situations.

Times of return of military men and women are, likewise, occasions when chaplains will be sought out for crises in marriage, disappointments in relationships, and angry outbursts in readjusting experiences.

Many requests for the counseling of a chaplain begin out of the pain associated with a variety of life experiences: dissatisfaction with work, with bosses; anxiety about indebtedness, the illness of family members; boredom, irritability; disciplinary difficulties; failure of promotion, in qualifying examinations. They seem unrelated to religious experiences, but may be the areas where the hurt is evident, the "sickness" unknown and unrealized. They may provide the "talking edges" of emptiness, alienation, or interest, on the other hand, in what it is that chaplains believe, for the counselee too wants to believe. The chaplain may not count every counseling "case" as pastoral, but he should be alert to young men and women in their development, encouraging them in their wholistic growth with the Lord and members of the human family. Many military people like to "talk about things," discovering how others see life, what their views are. The chaplain's stance is one that has particular interest for many.

There are countless paradigms in the Christian scriptures, particularly the gospels, of those encapsulated, apparently singular meetings of Jesus of Nazareth with named and nameless persons which deserve the reflection of military chaplains upon their roles as pastoral counselors. The biblical accounts report "meetings"—"encounters" may be too strong a term to use for them though The New English Bible gives the subhead of "Journeys and Encounters" to Luke 9:51—18:30—that made enormous differences in the lives of those with whom Jesus spoke. There was that meeting of Jesus with the Samaritan woman at the well; with the young man who asked a "religious" question, "Master, which is the greatest commandment?"; with the men on the road to Emmaus; with a short fellow who climbed into a tree in order to see Jesus. Chaplains should not compare themselves to The Rabbi—or should they?—but they can see cries for help and "innocent" questions as having the potential for ministry for lifechanging as well as relief from the burdens of guilt.

Civilian Pastoral Counselors and the Military

Pastoral care-givers in civilian settings may be responsible for some military members, numbers of military families, and, certainly, veterans of military service within their congregations. Because military service is such an encompassing vocation, these clergypersons will find that their understanding of attitudes and behaviors among their people who now serve or have served and the sensitivities of family members is worth cultivating. Chaplains are happy to work with civilian clergypersons and to give and receive their referrals for pastoral counseling. They are used to cooperative efforts for the sake of the ministry to military people.

Confidentiality

Some comment should be made about the confidentiality of communications in pastoral counseling in the military setting. It is a topic of considerable interest today, one which bears more extensive treatment than can be given in an introductory volume.

In the rules of evidence for military judicial proceedings, found in the Manual for Courts-Martial, the communications of a penitent to his clergyman are held to be "privileged" when they are made "either as a formal act of religion or as a matter of conscience." The clergyperson cannot disclose them unless released by the one who made the communications. It is held that such privilege (given only for communications to spouse, lawyer and clergyman in the federal statute) is for the good of the community. It should be noted that privilege devolves upon the communicator, not the recipient of the communications, who is obliged to keep them in trust.

Generally, courts have been reluctant to test the rule of privilege, but there are comments and opinions on the rule with which chaplains should be familiar. In addition, chaplains should know the policies and rules, if any, for confidential communications which are held by their own faith communities as pertaining to clergy. They ought to be acquainted with the laws of the state in which they reside and have some feel for the issues of jurisdiction in matters where confidentiality might be involved.

In these things, as in many issues which project the military chaplain into the field of legal obligations as he counsels, he is well advised to discuss confidentiality with his command's legal counsel, supervisory and other chaplains. He might also take occasion to talk about confidentiality with his commanding officer early in his duty assignmment. It is a mistake for the chaplain to be naive about the legal ramifications of confidentiality; it is likewise a fatal error to be unprofessionally gossipy about one's counseling.[2]

Conclusions

This chapter began with the assertion that counseling may well be the chief ministerial function of a chaplain. There is no suggestion that other ministerial and priestly functions are less important. The point is rather that counseling can be the form of a relationship of the chaplain to his people that brings him into daily life and activity with all of them. It is an expression of the chaplain's charter to care for them even when religious symbols and ceremonies are not shared by all of them. His care, of course, is expected to include appropriate referrals for specific religious administrations when the circumstances demand, so that the free exercise of religion is maintained within the military institution. Yet every chaplain can do much for others in pastoral counseling that respects the freedom of individuals to make responsible decisions about their lives and values and faith systems.

Pastoral counseling is an instrumentality through which the chaplain can address wounded spirits with the word, with words, or with a helpful—or healing—action. It meets young, active, eager men and women at the points of their needs—in more personal, voluntary relationship—and through processes of interpersonal exchange invites their growth. Pastoral counseling indeed can encourage hope, faith, and love among persons who seek greater freedom from their fears and larger confidence in their strengths.

Notes

1. The chaplain who keeps records of counseling interviews must become knowledgeable of the requirements of the Privacy Act of 1974. He should seek the opinions and counsel of the command's legal authority.

2. The following two articles will stimulate thought and discussion about the rule of privilege and confidentiality in counseling:
Melvin R. Jacob, "Confidentiality: Reexamined and Reapplied." *Military Chaplains' Review*, Department of the Army Pamphlet 165–134, Summer 1982. U.S. Army Chaplain Board, Myer Hall, Bldg. 1207, Fort Monmouth, N.J. 07703, pp. 31–38, including comment by Israel Drazin; Carl E. Creswell, "Privileged Communication and the Military Chaplain." *Military Chaplains' Review*, DA Pam 165–128, Winter 1981, pp. 7–16.

Bibliography

Department of Defense. *Defense 83*. Superintendent of Documents, U.S. Government Printing Office, Washington, D.C., September, 1983, p. 30.
Hutcheson, Richard G., Jr. *The Churches and the Chaplaincy*. Atlanta: John Knox Press, 1974, pp. 32–34.

James J. Gill, S.J., M.D.

Anxiety and Stress

Anxiety and stress are part of everyone's life, including that of pastoral counselors as well as their clients. Both phenomena are experienced ubiquitously—in the city and on the farm, on the highway and at the airport, in the hospital and on the playing field, at work and in the home. No one is totally exempt from them, although some lives are afflicted by these conditions far more overwhelmingly and painfully than others. Fortunately, both can usually be mitigated through the expenditure of considerable personal effort, and often with the help of a counselor required. It would be unrealistic and undesirable to expect or attempt to eradicate them from one's life entirely.

Some writers in the fields of psychology, sociology and psychiatry employ the terms anxiety and stress synonymously. Others carefully distinguish between them, regarding anxiety as merely one of the forms in which stress can be endured. I personally find it useful to follow the latter practice and will do so in the pages that follow. The two terms also lend themselves to a wide range of definitions. Those which I will be presenting are not claimed as the best, but rather as the ones which appear to me as potentially most helpful to the pastoral counselor in his or her ministry.

Since anxiety is generally considered the principal manifestation of stress, it would seem sensible to give this basic emotion our first consideration here. If there is any single affect that qualifies as one of the best blessings and also one of the worst scourges in human existence, it is anxiety. The same multiform emotion that can stimulate an outstanding operatic or astronautical performance, a life-saving medical innovation, or a heroic rescue from fire is equally capable of preventing a person from speaking in public, flying in a plane, entering a crowded place of worship, or even driving a car to work. Anxiety can be felt as mild or severe, acute or chronic, energizing or paralyzing. It acts as a spice that heightens the enjoyment of life for some people but, like physical pain, takes away joy from all the days of others.

Anxiety's power to afflict human nature was perhaps best described by Søren Kierkegaard in *The Concept of Dread*. He wrote: "And no Grand Inquisitor has in readiness such terrible tortures as has anxiety, and no spy knows how to attack more artfully the man he suspects, choosing the instant when he is weakest, nor knows how to lay traps where he will be caught and ensnared, as anxiety knows how, and no sharpwitted judge knows how to interrogate, to examine and accuse as anxiety does, which never lets him escape, neither by diversion nor by noise, neither at work nor at play, neither by day nor by night."[1] Anxiety, Kierkegaard knew from experience, can be fierce as well as relentless.

On the other hand, a constructive function of anxiety was pointed out by O. Hobart Mowrer in *Learning, Theory and Personality Dynamics*. He affirmed, "Anxiety . . . is not the course of personal disorganization; rather it is the outcome or expression of such a state. The element of disorganization enters with the act of dissociation or repression, and anxiety represents not only an attempted return of the repressed but also a striving on the part of the total personality toward a re-establishment of unity, harmony, oneness, 'health.' "[2] Anxiety can, therefore, be regarded as a sign that human nature is trying to heal itself and make itself whole, just as it can be understood as a signal that an individual is experiencing threat and thus suffering.

Following the example of Sigmund Freud, most psychiatrists and psychologists today recognize a difference between anxiety and fear, the two emotions that result from perceiving oneself as being threatened. Experiencing fear, one's attention is directed principally toward the person, object, or situation regarded as imperiling one's well-being (e.g., a ferocious animal, beserk assailant, or engulfing fire); it is a reaction to a specific danger to which a person can make a definite adjustment, such as by fleeing. Anxiety, in contrast, is a reaction to the apprehension of a threat that is vague, one that produces a feeling of diffuseness, uncertainty, and helplessness in the face of unspecific danger.

In the case of fear, once the threat is ended, whether by running away or by gaining reassurance, all apprehensiveness vanishes. In anxiety, an individual is afraid but at the same time uncertain about what he or she is afraid of. It tends to fix one's awareness on oneself; the more severe it is, the more one's awareness of objects in the external world is obscured.

In *The Meaning of Anxiety*, Rollo May notes that anxiety and fear are emotional reactions that occur at different depths. He regards anxiety as "a response to threat on the basic level of the personality" (i.e., existence and values), whereas fears are "the response to threats before they get to this basic level."[3] May believes that if people can learn to react adequately to the specific dangers that threaten from outside, they can successfully avoid experiencing anxiety. He maintains that anxiety always results from a threat to some value that the individual regards as essential to his or her existence as a personality; it might be to physical life, to psychological existence (e.g., loss of freedom, meaninglessness), or to any value that one identifies with one's existence (e.g., success, someone's love).[4]

Another useful distinction made by Freud separates "neurotic" from "objective" (normal) anxiety. The neurotic kind is a reaction to threat that is (1) disproportionate to the objective danger, (2) involves intrapsychic conflict, and (3) is managed by retrenchment of activity and awareness, use of unconscious defense mechanisms, and development of symptoms. May calls neurotic "that [anxiety] which occurs when the incapacity for coping adequately with threats is not objective but subjective—i.e., due not to subjective weakness but to inner psychological patterns and conflicts which prevent the individual from using his power."[5]

Normal anxiety is a reaction that (1) is not disproportionate to the objective threat, (2) does not involve intrapsychic conflict, (3) does not require defense mechanisms for its management, and (4) can be confronted constructively on the level of conscious awareness or relieved if the objective situation is changed.[6] Pastoral counselors can help their clients to use such anxiety creatively. For instance, they can help young persons experiencing anxiety when moving away from their parents' home to invest their talents and energies in fashioning a new living environment for themselves. Counselors can similarly assist people suffering anxiety while contemplating their mortality to develop strong and deep relationships with other people and with God while they still have time.

Anxiety that is normal can be put to use in solving the problems that cause the anxiety, as opposed to neurotic anxiety that results in defensive avoidance of such problems. Thus, normal anxiety about contracting pneumonia can prompt us to dress warmly on a cold day. But neurotic anxiety in a person afraid of marriage can prompt a decision to choose celibacy and deny (defensively) that conjugal life is even worth considering.

Anxiety as Symptom

Most pastoral counselors, as psychiatrists do, generally use the term "anxiety" as meaning the neurotic kind. They regard this type of anxiety as a *symptom* exhibited by an individual who has a feeling of apprehension or uneasiness, usually with no clear cause. Among the various clinical settings in which the symptom of anxiety can be seen are physical diseases (e.g., epilepsy, thyrotoxicosis), psychiatric disorders (e.g., schizophrenia, depression), drug intoxication (e.g., stimulants, including amphetamines and caffeine), and withdrawal states (e.g., from barbiturates or alcohol).

Other conditions in which the pastoral counselor will occasionally observe anxiety in a client include the "major anxiety disorders" classified in the *Third Edition of the Diagnostic and Statistical Manual* (DSM-III) of the American Psychiatric Association:

1. *Agoraphobia*, the fear of being alone or in public places.
2. *Social phobia*, the fear of public scrutiny, or of being humiliated.
3. *Panic disorder*, recurring panic attacks without an appropriate trigger or stimulus.
4. *Generalized anxiety disorder*, the persistence of a state of anxiety without panic attacks, in the absence of other diagnoses.
5. *Obsessive-compulsive disorder*, anxiety associated with recurrent thoughts that the person recognizes as foreign and thus resists (obsessions), accompanied by ritualistic actions that follow these recurrent thoughts (compulsions).

Another diagnostic category applies to many people who appear to be suffering from a state of anxiety related solely to a recent situational event. In such instances, the emotion may have a clear-cut focus or may be free-floating, but in either case *situational anxiety* is considered to be the appropriate term for it. One example would be a motorcyclist who has just come within a hairbreadth of a collision that could have proved fatal. In such a case, the person's anxiety symptoms are likely to decrease gradually, together with an increase in the ability to function, over the subsequent two to three weeks. Pastoral counselors who give their clients a chance to repeatedly verbalize their accounts of such episodes and to express their related emotions (ventilate) help them to keep their recovery time to a minimum.

A final category is that of *post-traumatic stress disorder*. Stressors responsible for anxiety in relation to this classification include earthquakes, military combat, rape, airplane crashes, and fire. Such traumatic events are outside the range of usual human experience and would be expected to evoke symptoms of distress, including anxiety, in most people. The degree of impairment is variable, as is the clinical course. Ventilation of the feelings is, again, usually therapeutic.

Signs of Anxiety

The pastoral counselor will encounter anxiety manifested in a variety of ways. *Spells of anxiety* experienced by some clients will occur suddenly, spontaneously, without warning, and for no apparent reason. Victims feel as if a part of their body has for a brief time gone out of control. Symptoms include one or several of the following: lightheadedness, faintness, dizzy spells, a faintly sick feeling, sensation of fading out from the world, a feeling of imbalance while standing or walking, "jelly legs" (as if they are giving out), difficulty breathing, awareness of the heart pounding or racing, chest pains or pressure, choking sensation, nausea, hot flashes or flushes (sometimes with blotching of the skin), cold chills, diarrhea, headaches with associated pain in other parts of the body, derealization (things around become strange, unreal, foggy, detached from you), depersonalization (feeling outside or disconnected from your own body or a part of it).[7]

In *panic attacks*, which are sudden episodes of intense apprehension, fear, or terror (often accompanied by feelings of impending doom), some of the symptoms just listed may be present along with one or more of the following: tingling in hands or feet, sweating, trembling or shaking, choking or smothering sensations, fear of dying, going crazy, or doing something uncontrolled during an attack. These episodes usually last only minutes; rarely do they continue for hours. Reassurance from the pastoral counselor is generally helpful during these periods. Since such attacks are likely to recur, appropriate medication (usually an antidepressant) is prescribed by physicians, and supportive psychotherapy or behavior modification therapy is used as a follow-up.

Some anxious clients present themselves as hypochondriacs. These individuals unrealistically interpret their physical signs or sensations as abnormal, and then become preoccupied with the fear of having a serious disease. Thorough medical evauation does not support the diagnosis of any actual physical disorder, but the preoccupation persists despite medical reassurance. Often the patient consults a variety of physicians as one body system after another is believed by the person to be diseased. Firm but kind handling on the part of the counselor is required. Hypochondriacs should be referred to a physician who will provide long-term care and the reassurance of physical exams, supportive drug (psychopharmacological) therapy, and regularly scheduled visits.

Anxiety is also felt by some people who experience a persistent and irrational need to avoid certain objects, situations or actions. These phobic individuals sometimes become either homebound or immobilized to such an extent that, for them, relatively few ordinarily encountered situations remain unlinked to fearfulness. They may dread open or crowded places, public transportation, crossing a bridge, or entering a tunnel. Usually, their most intense and incapacitating fear is of undergoing an attack of panic in such situations. Drugs prescribed by a psychiatrist can usually block further panic attacks, and behavior therapy is ordinarily required if these persons are to learn to overcome their fear.

The behavior therapy employed to treat phobic persons comprises a variety of methods, including systematic desensitization, flooding, cognitive restructuring, and exposure treatment. All these have much in common: they are based on the assumption that responses are learned (or "conditioned"), and they attempt to reverse the process. They are methods of relearning more normal responses and are sometimes called "deconditioning" techniques. Many clinical psychologists are skilled in using these approaches; not very many psychiatrists or pastoral counselors have achieved a mastery of them. But it is important to keep in mind that successful use of one or more of these methods of removing a client's phobias does not imply that the underlying illness has been effectively treated. Frequently, a physical defect (probably neurobiological and endocrine) lies at the center of a person's anxiety disorder, and the core of the disease must be controlled by medication if the phobias are to be permanently eradicated.

Ways of Being Helpful

Pastoral counselors can do a number of things that can be helpful to persons suffering the pain of anxiety when it is more intense, frequent, or prolonged than human beings would ordinarily experience. For example:

1. Remind these anxious persons that relief is possible and available.
2. Encourage them to consult a physician for evaluation of their medical condition, which may be related to their symptoms.
3. Inform them that a great deal is known scientifically about anxiety and about ways of treating it. Recommend books such as Rollo May's *The Meaning of Anxiety*, Isaac Marks' *Living With Fear*, and David Sheehan's *The Anxiety Disease*.
4. Get in touch with an experienced librarian who will provide information that can be useful to anxious clients as well as their family or religious community. Don't discourage them from reading the journals and textbooks available to psychologists, physicians, counselors and other clinical specialists.
5. Accompany anxious patients to their physician's office, if necessary.
6. Encourage patients to take their medications and perform their treatment exercises (e.g., relaxation drills) as prescribed.
7. Tell the patient's doctor what side-effects of drugs you observe. Signs might include agitation, restlessness, tremors, unsteadiness, poor coordination, confusion, irritability, sadness, decrease in appetite, weight loss, increased eating, weight gain, sweating, jaundice, forgetfulness, or talking too much.

8. Be available to help phobic patients go into situations they have feared. Ask their therapist's advice about the best way of accompanying and supporting them.

9. As people in treatment for anxiety become less anxious and less dependent on others, they often become more demanding and aggressive; understand and welcome this as a sign of progress. As they struggle for independence and freedom, they tend to make those who have helped them feel rejected and unappreciated. Accept such behavior; disapproval could impede further improvement.

10. Once anti-panic medication has been prescribed, taken, and adjusted over a several-week period, encourage patients to do the things they have been avoiding, gradually assisting them to become more independent.

11. Encourage patients to take notes or use a tape recorder during treatment sessions if they are having difficulty remembering their physician's instructions or therapist's advice.

Anxiety Is Stressful

Anxiety has in recent years come to be identified with the term "stress." According to most behavioral scientists, it is usually this emotion which people are experiencing when they talk about the stress in their lives. Other affective states, such as anger, hostility, fear, and depression, can also be stressful. What they all have in common is their occurrence in reaction to some stimulus that triggers a psychophysiological arousal in response to the demand it places on the person. This "stress response" can be elicited by a stressor that is physical (e.g., excessive heat, cold, noise) or related to digestion or metabolism (e.g., caffeine, nicotine, amphetamine). Most often, however, it is a reaction to a stimulus interpreted by a person as being threatening, frustrating, challenging or otherwise aversive. Such events as an automobile accident, the death of a spouse, or losing one's house keys could provide occasions for experiencing anxiety, depression, or anger that are stressful. In each case, the way the individual interprets the event will determine which emotion or form of stress will be felt.

Response Is Similar

Underlying every type of stressful reaction is a pattern of physiological activity that is quite constant, no matter what specific emotion is sustained. Physiologist Walter Cannon called it the "fight or flight" response.

Both the autonomic nervous system and the endocrine system are involved, with manifold changes in tissues and organs throughout the body resulting. Once the neocortex of the brain recognizes a stimulus as a threat to the person's well-being, neural impulses release hormones from the adrenal, pituitary, thyroid and other glands which prepare the individual for vigorous action. They bring about dilation of the pupils of the eyes, accelerate the heart and strengthen its pumping action, increase blood flow and oxygen supply to the arm and leg muscles, curtail the process of digestion, add more sugar to the bloodstream—all for the sake of immediate, aggressive, physical reponse to the stressful situation.

Unfortunately, the hormones released into the bloodstream (epinephrine, norepinephrine, ACTH, cortisol, etc.) which bring about these changes that ready the body for action are likely to damage various organs and their tissues if the substances remain in circulation too long. When stress is experienced repeatedly at frequent intervals, there is medical evidence galore that such physical disorders as peptic ulcers, ulcerative colitis, coronary heart disease, strokes and arthritis are likely to be the outcome. If these illnesses are the result of prolonged or excessive stress, they are given the generic label of *psychosomatic* or *psychophysiological* disease. Even cancer in many of its forms, infections of various types, and episodes of high blood pressure and headaches are often attributable to stress.

Not all stress is harmful. Dr. Hans Selye, the world's foremost authority on the subject of stress, found in his research that some stress experiences are positive in their life consequences whereas others are detrimental. He called the former "eustress" and the latter "distress." Eustress is experienced by persons who perceive themselves as winning; it is accompanied by a sense of achievement, triumph, and exhilaration. People who feel they are losing undergo distress. Disappointment, helplessness, desperation, insecurity, or inadequacy produces stress of this type.

Cognition Related to Stress

Richard Lazarus is another major contributor to the field of research into stress and ways of coping with it. He emphasizes the important role played by cognition (i.e., thought, or perception) in the individual's stress response. Lazarus regards situations or events as being neutral; they become stressful only when perceived or appraised negatively.[8] Thus, for a stress response to occur, a person must become aware of an exterior or interior demand that calls into question his or her ability to cope with it successfully and painlessly. An example of an exterior demand would be a spouse threatening divorce; an interior one would be the knowledge that one has begun to show serious signs of losing one's memory.

Evidence of Stress

Pastoral counselors should be aware of *signs* of stress in the lives of their clients as well as in their own. Dr. Selye has suggested the following list: (1) general irritability, hyperexcitation or depression; (2) pounding of the heart (an indication of high blood pressure); (3) dryness of the throat and mouth; (4) impulsive behavior, emotional instability; (5) the over-powering urge to cry or run and hide; (6) inability to concentrate, flight of thoughts, and general disorientation; (7) predilection to become fatigued, and the loss of *joie de vivre*; (8) "free-floating anxiety" (i.e., afraid, but unable to recognize why); (9) emotional tension and alertness, a feeling of being "keyed up"; (10) trembling, nervous tic (i.e., brief, recurrent, irresistible movement of a small segment of the body); (11) tendency to be easily startled by sounds that are not loud; (12) high pitched, nervous laughter; (13) stuttering and other speech difficulties; (14) gnashing or grinding of the teeth; (15) insomnia; :(16) sweating; (17) the frequent need to urinate; (18) diarrhea, indigestion, queasiness in the stomach, and sometimes even vomiting; (19) migraine headaches; (20) premenstrual tension or missed menstrual cycle; (21) pain in the neck or lower back; (22) loss of appetite or compulsive eating; (23) increased smoking; (24) increased use of legally prescribed drugs, such as tranquilizers or amphetamines; (25) alcohol and drug addiction; (26) nightmares; (27) neurotic behavior; (28) psychoses; (29) a marked proneness to accidents.[9]

Other noteworthy signs of stress are absenteeism (avoidance of contact with the stressful situation), poor work performance (slipping obviously below the person's ordinary level of competence), and excessive use of defense mechanisms (such as denial, rationalization, or projection) which unconsciously enable one to fail to recognize, explain away, or find in someone else the flaws in one's self.

Modes of Assisting

There are many things that pastoral counselors can do in order to help their clients under stress. In a non-judgmental way, they can first of all assist them to realize that they are responsible for most of the stress in their lives. It is self-initiated and self-propagated. It is the client who *interprets* a neutral stimulus as possessing stress-eliciting characteristics. As George

Everly, Jr., and Robert Rosenfeld have suggested in *The Nature and Treatment of the Stress Response*, "Having the client realize and accept responsibility for the cause and reduction of excessive stress can be a major point in the therapeutic intervention."[10]

An alteration in a client's environment can sometimes be effected in an effort to prevent the occurrence of events that are likely to result in stress. The counselor can help clients to find ways to make changes in their own lives which will enable them to avoid, minimize or modify their occasions of stress (e.g., to take a new job and thus escape the hostility of an irritating foreman). At other times, pastoral care will be equally beneficial when it is channeled into urban planning, social protest and other political and legal directions (e.g., to reduce the level of aircraft noise causing stress to students in classrooms near an airport).

Clients need their counselor's help to understand the way their stress has been developing. They need to be taught (1) that the events in their lives which are resulting in painful emotions and potential (if not yet actual) disease are not *causing* these results, but only providing occasions for them, (2) that their interpretations of these events are what cause the emotions and damage, (3) that these interpretations are based on their beliefs (i.e., convictions formed through past experience, whether personal or vicarious), and (4) that when a stressful situation or event cannot be avoided, it is possible to reduce distress by modifying one's beliefs and interpretations. For example, an always hurrying, perfectionistic, competitive, Type A executive who is driving himself rapidly toward a heart attack by taking on too many time-consuming responsibilities is experiencing frequent anger and impatience because he believes deep in his soul that people are unworthy and God will reward them only if they accomplish in their lifetime all the things of which they are capable. He needs to come to recognize that as long as this belief is maintained and work opportunities are interpreted as unrefusable, his stress will continue and his life will be imperiled. Such a belief was probably learned early in life from achievement-oriented parents and other adults. To help him cut down the stress he is experiencing, the pastoral counselor is well situated to help him develop the belief that to be a good human being and one loved by God a person doesn't have to work excessively; it's all right to say no at times.

Everly and Rosenfeld recommend that the person helping stressed clients should discuss with them, early in the course of intervention, the most common misconceptions concerning the stress response. These authors list seven, and suggest that the counselor correct whatever erroneous understandings the client displays. The misconceptions are:

1. "Stress-related symptoms and psychosomatic diseases are all in my head; therefore they can't really injure me."

2. "Only weak people suffer from stress."
3. "I'm not responsible for the stress in my life—stress is unavoidable these days—we're all victims."
4. "I always know when I begin to suffer from excessive stress."
5. "It is easy to identify the causes of excessive stress."
6. "All people respond to stress in the same way."
7. "When I begin to suffer from excessive stress, all I have to do is sit down and relax."[11]

In working with their stress-afflicted clients, pastoral counselors can help them considerably by teaching them to develop self-awareness of the specific ways in which they manifest the stress response (i.e., by what signs or symptoms) and also to identify their personal stressors. Only when they recognize the sources of their stress can clients take successful steps to avoid them, or to prepare themselves to encounter them in a less stressful way.

Knowledge of such techniques as dietary modification, neuromuscular relaxation, assertiveness training, meditation, time management, social skills training, and conscious avoidance of stressors that are not amenable to modification are recommended to counselors of clients suffering from stress. Also, biofeedback, physical exercise, voluntarily controlled respiration, self-hypnosis, systematic desensitization, and a number of other techniques are employed by specialists treating their clients for stress, and these, too, can be learned and applied by pastoral counselors or provided by people to whom they might prefer to refer their clients for additional therapy.

Counselor as Social Model

Clients can be helped to modify their unrealistic or irrational beliefs about themselves, life, work, people, and God, and thus prepare themselves to live less stressfully, if their pastoral counselors present themselves transparently as persons whose own beliefs do not cause them to experience excessive stress. Clients will more easily reject their harmful ideals, values and convictions by being given a chance to clearly recognize and freely adopt those of the counselor. (I am certainly not recommending that the counselors *impose* these on their clients.) For example, when a counselor who spends some time at prayer every morning before going to work reveals this fact, together with his belief that this practice enables him to deal better with the difficulties that arise during the workday, there is a good chance that a highly stressed workaholic client who has believed that the earliest hours of the day were meant to be spent in his store may modify this belief and, like his counselor, thus begin to live less stressfully.

Suggestions for Counselors

Finally, I want to make six recommendations to persons who are becoming pastoral counselors. These are based on two decades of opportunities I have had to provide psychiatric consultation for men and women involved in the ministry of counseling. In order to keep the stress in your own life to a desirable minimum, I would suggest the following:

1. Strive to accept and to like yourself as you are. To accomplish this, it helps to clarify your ideals and values and live according to them. If you *enjoy* being you, it will be easy for you to spontaneously show esteem for your clients. When they (and you) feel esteemed, research shows that they (and you) will experience less stress in everyday life.

2. Maintain your own support networks. To do so, you will have to invest your leisure time regularly in social activities with your family, neighbors, colleagues, friends, and community members. You need such social supports to be able to express your feelings, survive crises, receive the esteem and affection of others, develop realistic goals, and get honest feedback. Again, research reveals that such networks serve to minimize the stress in a person's life.

3. Balance your life, not overloading it with work. Effective and popular pastoral counselors run the risk of being in such demand that they neglect their own well-being. Time should be set aside on a regular basis for spiritual exercises, physical exercise, intellectual and cultural development, social and creative activities, and professional improvement. Members of small support groups are often able to assist one another in seeing that all these needs are met, thus keeping each one as healthy and vigorous as possible, with immunity to excessive stress maximized.

4. Take vacations regularly and set aside some time for leisure every day. To prevent chronic stress, time for rest and relaxation must be alternated with time spent working for others, especially when they are troubled with family, marital, financial, emotional, addiction, or medical problems.

5. Be realistic. Ideals are wonderful to pursue *gradually*, but too many idealists are angry, and thus in a state of stress, too much of the time because their own performance, that of others, and the condition of the world around them at present are all falling short of that goal. The secret of mental health is to keep striving to improve oneself and the world while at the same time seeing the good in the way people and things are now.

6. Live today and love the moment. The past cannot be undone, so let go of memories that are distressing. The future doesn't exist, so don't spoil

the present hour by worrying over what is ahead. Just look for the
beauty in the faces, flowers, skies, and lives that surround you. Love is
the ultimate antidote for excessive stress.

Notes

1. *The Concept of Dread*, p. 139.
2. O.H. Mowrer, A.D. Ullman, *Time as a Determinant in Integrative Learning, Psychol. Rev.*, 1945, 52:2, pp. 61–90.
3. *The Meaning of Anxiety*, p. 225.
4. Ibid., p. 205.
5. Ibid., p. 214.
6. Ibid., p. 209.
7. *The Anxiety Disease*, pp. 21ff.
8. *Stress, Sanity and Survival*, p. 5.
9. *Managing Stress*, pp. 81ff.
10. *The Nature and Treatment of the Stress Response*, p. 6.
11. Ibid., p. 66.

Bibliography

Adams, J.D. *Understanding and Managing Stress: A Workbook in Changing Life Styles*. San Diego: University Associates, 1980.

Adams, J.D. (ed.). *Understanding and Managing Stress: A Book of Readings*. San Diego: University Associates, 1981.

Davis, M., E.R. Eshelman, and M. McKay. *The Relaxation and Stress Reduction Workbook*. Oakland: New Harbinger Publications, 1982.

Everly, G.S. and R. Rosenfeld. *The Nature and Treatment of the Stress Response*. New York: Plenum Press, 1981.

Freud, S. *The Problem of Anxiety*. New York: W.W. Norton and Co., Inc., 1964.

Goldberger, L. and S. Breznitz (eds.). *Handbook of Stress*. New York: Free Press, 1982.

Kutash, I.L., L.B. Schlesinger, and Associates. *Handbook on Stress and Anxiety*. San Francisco: Jossey-Bass Publishers, 1980.

Marks, I. *Living with Fear*. New York: McGraw-Hill, 1978.

May, R. *The Meaning of Anxiety*, rev. ed. New York: W.W. Norton and Co., Inc., 1977.

Meichenbaum, D. *Coping with Stress*. London: Century Publishing, 1983.

Selye, H. *The Stress of Life*. New York: McGraw-Hill, 1956.

Selye, H. *Stress Without Distress*. Philadelphia: Lippincott, 1974.
Selye, H. *Stress in Health and Disease*. Reading: Butterworth's, 1976.
Sheehan, D. *Anxiety Disease*. New York: Charles Scribner's Sons, 1983.
Wender, P. and D. Klein. *Mind, Mood and Medicine*. New York: Farrar, Straus and Giroux, 1981.
Yates, J. *Managing Stress*. New York: AMACOM, 1979.

Robert E. Neale

Loneliness:
Depression, Grief and Alienation

Thinking about loneliness and the lonely requires courage. Our thoughts recall the mood and we become caught and enveloped by it. Loneliness may even appear as an active power that pursues, overtakes, and destroys. Such reactions are understandable. But, as the experience of anxiety is a most powerful warning to us that there is danger to be confronted, so also is loneliness a useful warning. We who are lonely may feel overwhelmed because we do not know how to see loneliness or respond to it. So we explore loneliness and the lonely now in order to understand what it is and how it functions in our lives. First we will define what loneliness is. Then we will explore care of loneliness and the lonely. Finally, we will consider pastoral care of this condition and those who experience it.*

Loneliness and the Lonely

Loneliness is usually defined as a condition in which something is missing. We are aware of absence as a most powerful presence. My lack of something can influence me more than anything I possess. Recall the empty chair of a loved one who is dead. This emptiness can be an overwhelming presence that rules over all else that is present. In addition to this feeling, we sense that a change has taken place. Something has happened so that we are removed from a relationship (Gubrium, 1973, pp. 116ff). This break in accustomed connection lowers our morale: we wonder if and how we have failed, whether we are worthwhile. This preoccupation, in turn, helps to lower our coping ability. So what is significant in our lives

*This essay is adapted from *Loneliness, Solitude, and Companionship,* by Robert E. Neale. Copyright © 1984 Robert E. Neale. Adapted and used by permission of The Westminster Press, 925 Chestnut Street, Philadelphia, PA 19107. (This work includes exercises for individual and study groups which can be used by pastors for care and counseling.)

is not the sheer amount of social support we have, but sufficient regularity in relationship. Some of us have minimal relationships in a life-style of independence and are not lonely very much, whereas others of us who are maximally connected with others can become most lonely when separation occurs. This change need not be an exterior one. Rather than experience the loss of a relationship by physical severance from another, we can experience an interior change that creates loneliness. This is illustrated by the growing awareness of the adolescent in Carson McCullers' play, *The Member of the Wedding*, who is surprised into the observation: "The trouble with me is that for a long time, I have been just an 'I' person. All other people can say 'we.' Not to belong to a 'we' makes you too lonesome" (McCullers, 1951, pp. 51–52). The change that fosters loneliness can be interior growth that is a discovery of possibilities of relationship.

But loneliness is more than the passive and unhappy submission to separation. The other basic element is search. It is a consequence of our powerful faith that relationship is possible. Loneliness is not a passive and static condition, but a most active one. It is an attempt to right the wrong of absence. We illustrate this most clearly in the extreme, when strong absence is matched by strong faith. As lonely children, we had imaginary playmates. As lonely adults, we have cats, dead heroes, trees, a poem, nearly anything as our companion. What would we do without the fantasies that create some sense of relationship when none may appear for the moment or longer? These bizarre outcomes we see in others (and that others see in us) should not blind us to the strength of the inner faith that is a part of loneliness.

Loneliness may be defined as having two aspects, each of which must be present for the condition to occur: the experience of separation and the search to overcome it. Without the separation, loneliness will not occur. But separation may not lead to loneliness when we either experience separation affirmatively or with hopelessness. In neither case is there motivation for search. This combination of separation and search is lively. Loneliness is a full engagement in the battle to participate in relationship. And since it is a common daily experience, our struggle is a continual aspect of our lives. We may forget how concerned we are about relationship. Our experience of loneliness is a reminder.

Definition of loneliness as separation and search reveals its negative and positive aspects. Our experience of loneliness generates feelings of pain and helplessness, yet it is an action toward relationship. If our leading concern is the elimination of these feelings, we can try to survive with a minimum of relationship. But if we are able and willing to endure these feelings, we are attempting to change ourselves and/or our environment for the sake of relationship. We can conclude then that loneliness in general serves a good purpose. Unfortunately it never occurs in general. In an individual case there can be so much loneliness that the mood offers only a blow to the head that shocks us to a standstill. And even when not so paralyzed, our inappropriate responses to separation and search can be damaging to relationships.

Our typical response to separation is negative. This is reasonable because such a loss is a threat to our well-being. But separation is a reality built into our environment. Our life is a series of separations. For all the danger involved, this series encourages development. How could we grow up without it?

Our typical response to search is affirmative. This is reasonable because the threat to our well-being is acknowledged and countered. But a positive response to search is not always useful. We may enter only into a chronic promiscuous searching of quick, intimate relationships. Or we may chronically substitute God or a dog for the possibilities of intimacy with a human being. The leap to relationship from loneliness can be shallow, destructive of self, and abusive of others.

We get ourselves into unnecessary suffering when we do not react to the negative and positive aspects of both separation and search. Relationship involves the self and the other one. One of these poles disappears when our responses are one-sided. When separation is viewed positively and search negatively, the focus tends to be on the self only. When we believe that nothing worthwhile has been lost and nothing worthwhile can be gained, indulging ourselves is a likely outcome. In such "doing your own thing," the despair is barely concealed. This indulgence can be useful, but as a chronic state of mind, it is a perversion of loneliness that creates most unhappy gods.

The contrary also occurs. When separation is viewed negatively and search positively, the focus tends to be on the other pole only. When we believe that there is nothing worthwhile about ourselves, then the group can take over. We abandon ourselves and find life in a family, church or political movement. At worst, we live only by means of an "*ism*," and the despair is barely concealed. Such loss of self can be useful, but as a chronic state of mind, it also is a perversion of loneliness that creates most unhappy zombies.

Our conclusion is that we should accept both the positive and negative aspects of both separation and search. A balanced approach allows neither denial of separation nor despair about search, but does foster realism about the old and hope about the new. Denial and despair can serve us well when we are overcome, enabling us to endure until other means of coping can occur. They need to be, but need not be everlasting. We are moved quite naturally into them and then away from them toward realism and hope. Accepting both separation and search eventually works to prevent our flight from ourselves and others. We can then remain engaged in the battle to participate in relationship. Too much loneliness creates an inner tension that can destroy us, but too little allows for laxity in relationship. Courage is required so we can let the tension increase, if necessary, and then use it for full exploration of our condition.

Discussion of loneliness can expand its meaning beyond usefulness. It is not the only suffering we endure, and it is hardly the worst. To deem it a catch-all for all our negative experience not only overemphasizes but obscures its nature. We know that loneliness and isolation are not identical. We have been alone and not lonely, and we have been in the midst of others, yet lonely. However, we do experience loneliness in association with other conditions such as alienation, depression, and grief. Comparison with these will clarify what loneliness is and is not.

Alienation and loneliness can go hand in hand. What is alien is foreign and wholly different. To be estranged is to be detached and broken off from others or from oneself. We feel "out of it." But this is not identical to loneliness. Impersonal work conditions may lead us to alienation from others, and then, in turn, to loneliness. And when we are lonely, we may become alien to ourselves if we hide from the loneliness, or alienated from others if we try to manipulate them in order to remove our loneliness. But we can be lonely and not estranged. Separation as a result of a death may cause loneliness without alienation, whereas separation as a result of a divorce may cause both conditions together with each contributing to the other. When we are partially alienated, we are likely to be lonely, and vice versa. The conditions are distinct, yet make good companions.

We must also beware of the danger of equating loneliness and depression. Both conditions give rise to sadness, anger, guilt, worthlessness, and helplessness (Gaylin, 1968). We focus so much on depression that we may miss those occasions when the symptoms really indicate loneliness. We can be depressed about matters other than separation, and we can be lonely without being greatly angry or guilty or worthless. Yet depression is a likely consequence, for loneliness is the "sweet sorrow" that comes from parting. It is most important to understand, however, that total helplessness is not involved, for this would mean abandonment of the search. We may feel ourselves to be helpless in loneliness, but our cry of despair is a cry for help based on faith in its possibility.

Another distinction to make is between loneliness and grief. Grief also gives rise to feelings of sadness, anger, guilt, worthlessness, and helplessness. Grief is the consequence of a loss and is the process of moving from shock and inability to surrender the past, into deep distress over the reality of the loss, and then into an integration of what is valuable from the past into a new, meaningful pattern of relationship (Maris, 1975). Certainly loneliness can be involved in our grieving. But the amount of it will differ, depending on the importance of the specific relationship in comparison to others that have not been broken. In addition, we should note that whereas our loneliness is about loss of relationship, grief can pertain to other kinds of losses such as health and stages of life cycle. Finally, as already noted, discovery of the very possibility of relationship fosters loneliness. Grief over loss is not involved. Like alienation and depression, loneliness and grief go together easily but not necessarily.

This attempt to define loneliness and the lonely is likely to inflate the condition beyond all reason. We do need to be related to our environment in order to survive. We have awareness of this need as a tool for our use. Loneliness, then, is not an incidental aspect, but an essential part of being human. Still, the danger remains of separating loneliness from other conditions entirely. Even more dangerous is the assumption that loneliness takes priority over all other conditions at all times. This is not the case. We will risk our lives out of loneliness sometimes, but we will also risk loneliness in order to eat and sleep. Loneliness will help us to move toward another human being in spite of our anxiety, but not always, for we will often endure separation in order to feel and be safe with our habitual self-esteem. The conclusion is that loneliness is not a driving force that knows no obstacle and rides roughshod over every other human condition. Loneliness can be harnessed, directed, subdued, or even nearly extinguished. For some of us, loneliness can become the most significant condition. For others of us, it may never be so. The mood loneliness creates in us tends to overemphasize its power. So also does our self-pity. Our understanding of what loneliness is should help us resist such temptation.

Care of Loneliness and the Lonely

Lonely people suffer and need to be cared for. Loneliness can be destructive or creative and so it also needs to be cared for. Care is many things, but first and foremost it is exploration. The care of loneliness and the lonely involves exploration of the concrete case. When we are lonely, we cry out, "Why me?" This is a protest about being forsaken. It also is a question about causes of loneliness. Both prompt reflection that can deepen our understanding of relationship and of the nature of our participation in it. When we are lonely, we also cry out, "What happened?" This is a protest about what has been lost or not yet obtained. It is also a question about realms of relationship. Both prompt reflection that can deepen our understanding of possibilities of relationship and of the variety of our participation in it. Since care is exploration of loneliness, our tools are understanding of the four causes of loneliness and the five realms of relationship. We will outline the causes and realms and then mention some of the possibilities of explorative care that are raised.

The first and deepest cause of loneliness is the human condition itself. We are separate selves and know it. We know it most when we are companionable with another, the very strength of the relationship making the gulf so apparent. We are lonely because we are both separate from each other and participants in each other. To be both, and to know that we are both, is to be lonely. There is no return or advance to time and place of no loneliness. But we are not above trying. To only know ourselves as separate individuals, to be totally unaware of the possibilities of participation and community, is to be nearly without loneliness. Or to know only ourselves as members of community, to be totally unaware of ourselves as individuals, is to be nearly without loneliness. With these flights, we are attempting escape from our humanity. So the first cause of loneliness is the human condition itself. We may exist at times outside of loneliness, but we are never beyond it.

The second cause of loneliness is what normally comes to our minds. The focus is on a person or object that has been lost. We add to this the understanding that loneliness occurs also over what has not yet been gained, discovery of a potential for relationship. These constitute the cause of loneliness due to changes in relationship. Such changes are inevitable. Even if accidental, they are well within the order of things. Our average expectable environment includes friends who move to another part of the country and even death due to automobile collision. We even state, after a falling out of relationship, "Ah well, people change." Note that this second cause is different from the first. Both reflect the human condition, but the first is about the permanent situation of being both individual and participant, while the second involves change as occasional, and not continual. The latter can be overcome, the changes which cause loneliness also offering possibilities of new relationships or prompting search of them. We do make new friends, buy another car, and adopt children. This is not to suggest that all loneliness from this cause can be overcome. The end of a fifty year marriage through death of a spouse most likely leaves a permanent loneliness, and our lonely hope for some kinds of relationships may never be fulfilled. But we should not assume that changes in relationship necessarily and inevitably leave permanent loneliness. This would be a defensive reaction that only protects us from the anxieties of exploring possibilities of new relationships.

The third cause considers what is neither fundamental nor accidental, but is exceedingly common, problems in self and society. There are individual and group traits that foster loneliness. Some of us are loneliness-prone. These may include those of us whose relationships are uncertain, unclear, and hesitant. We who are this way are likely to seek relationship continually and yet maintain all specific relationships in a state of flux. The need for security forbids clear commitment and requires continual testing. Others of us are shy, distant, wistful outsiders who long to dive into the communal swim and either do not know how or are held back by some re-straining forces. And still others of us may be not only uncertain or shy, but also strange to others. A shy or uncertain one who is relatively "normal" can attract other shy or uncertain people at least. The strange one who is either outgoing or certain of relationships can move into a connection. But we who are both strange and shy or uncertain are nearly helpless ones from whom others keep their distance. Of course, such proneness is most likely a consequence of families that have fostered loneliness by ignoring chil-dren, overprotecting them, or giving them mixed signals on how to be-have. Larger groups can foster loneliness also. They vary in the amount of change in relationship caused by assorted customs. The high degree of mo-bility in American culture is a likely example. The physical mobility, social mobility, and mobility of value change in social morality all are sources of options that generate uncertainty and tentativeness. However beneficial the options, they are likely to increase our uncertainty, lessen support from others, and increase our loneliness. Consideration of this third cause of problems in self and society should not lead us to assume that our selves or societies are necessarily destructive. The issue is one of degree. Too much uncertainty, shyness, individuality, and loneliness can lead to se-vere problems in relationship, but too little can lead to stagnation at im-mature levels of relationships.

The fourth cause of loneliness is the most superficial, yet a source of great and unnecessary suffering. The cause is that of increasing loneliness that is already there. We who are already lonely find it increased by the responses of others and by our own responses as well. This exacerbation is usually caused by responses based on flight from, and protection against, loneliness rather than on acceptance, understanding and movement to-ward companionship. Loneliness is a condition that does not always call at-tention to itself, others tending to be less aware of it than we are ourselves. When our loneliness is perceived, others will often flee or fight it. They will remove themselves from us, as from a contagious disease. Or they will attack, either belittling the loneliness by arguing that it is not so large as is believed, or by encouraging relationship forcefully and prematurely. Yet separation and loneliness must be embraced before overcome. Exacerba-tion of our loneliness by others is matched by our own faulty responses. We can contribute to our problem by a variety of partial renunciations of relationship which sustain and increase loneliness. For example, we can deceive ourselves by trying to relate to someone who is not attracted to us, lowering our expectations by relating with distance and disengagement of the "new intimacy," or being attracted to people in general and working for the human race in relatively safe, one-way relationships of the professional providers of human services. Such flight and fight by others and ourselves is what so spoils the creative side of loneliness.

Our exploration of loneliness tends to focus on our intimate connections with loved ones. But there are other realms of relationship—groups of people, generations, things, and the world. Because we can relate in all these vast areas, the ways in which we experience loneliness are innumerable. But a review also can remind us of all the possibilities of relationship.

The first two realms of relationship are those of the individual and the group. When we experience loneliness in these realms, we have the driving restlessness and yearning search of relationship. But the symptoms differ (Weiss, 1973, pp. 17–22). When we are lonely over the absence of a close attachment to an individual, the stress reminds us of a small child who fears she has been abandoned by her mother. We are tense and vigilant. Our world seems desolate and barren, and we appear to ourselves as empty and hollow. This occurs to us as small children who have lost their mother and as adults who have lost a spouse. The symptoms of group loneliness are different. Our reactions remind us of the older child whose friends are away. We are bored and aimless, feeling on the margin of real life. This group loneliness can be as deep as that over loss of an individual. Seeing ourselves, or believing that others see us, as boring, odd, or worthless is terrifying because it is the group as well as the individual that tells us who we are. Reviewing these two realms of relationship together should not lead us to conclude that they are so similar that one can substitute for the other. The remedy for loneliness in one realm is not the remedy for loneliness in the other. The death of a spouse, for example, does cause group loneliness as well as individual loneliness because the social network is upset. But finding a new social network will not fill the gap left by the death of the spouse. The two realms of relationship affect each other but remain distinct. We know this in our heads, but our grieving hearts can be surprised.

The third realm of the generations begins with our family and extends to history and to the human race as a whole. Through our dependence as children on our parents and as elderly parents on our middle-aged children, we are given the possibility of becoming aware of the generations immediately before and after our own. To discover these and more distant possibilities of relationship is to experience the separation and search of loneliness. From whom have we come and toward whom are we going?

We remain lonely, or less than lonely, until we find our beginnings and endings. This is especially important in times of transition. To move somewhere, we have to know where we have been and can go. This realm is not just a luxurious possibility, but a social and individual necessity. The young, the old, and the middle-aged can feel cut off from the past or future and those who represent it. Without connections with the generations, there is no care, and without care, there is no survival. Our loneliness occurs to prompt us to join up with the human race. Perhaps some of us could stand a little more generational loneliness rather than less.

The fourth realm of relationship consists of all our companions that are not people—both the natural and artificial objects in our lives. Given the importance of our non-human environment for survival, it is not surprising that we become quite attached to a variety of things. These vary enormously: house or apartment, trees, cars, clothing, furniture, city buildings, books, jewelry, tools, and pets. We may fail to see that we have such material companions. If we do see ourselves as having them, we are likely to disparage the relationships. We do this in two ways. On the one hand, we refer to materialism and conspicuous waste, assuming that modern adults should be less attached to things. On the other hand, we can disparage our attachments by assuming that they occur because of deprivation of human connections and are not really two-way companionships anyway. But objects are important to us and we can relate to things just because they are there and are of interest to us in their own right as people are, and not just because we are deprived of some other kind of relationship. So object-loneliness occurs, and we are homesick, scene-sick, toy-sick, and so on. We can be as thing-deprived as we can be people-deprived.

The fifth and last realm of relationship is that of existence as a whole where the world is companion and the loneliness is a world loneliness. We want to respond to life with both wonder and welcome, to be astonished and yet at home. Companionship with various parts is not sufficient. We want to know if our world is against us, or indifferent to us, or for us. Religion is the traditional institution whose primary purpose is to call attention to our disconnection, and then to establish, maintain, and renew our relationship with the world. God is the ultimate symbol of the world as companion and the ultimate loneliness is, therefore, the absence of God. For this symbol to lose its power is a catastrophe. The gifted few who experience this can recover and bring back to us new revelations about relationship with the world. Out of this comes the body of myth and ritual which remind us that the world is our home. Myth is our affirmation of the world as companion and ritual is our participation in the friendly world.

This concern about the world as a whole is never outgrown. Modern versions of the concern appear in the growing interest in Oriental philosophy and religion, in the widespread fascination with the occult, in humanistic psychology, and even in some discussions of theoretical physics. We are pushed and shoved into a discovery of the whole. This grants us the courage to be lonely and continue the search for relationship to the parts of the world. Indeed, it may prompt us to awareness of possibilities we have not realized before. Companionship with the world is the affirmation of the possibility of relationships in all other realms. Our traditional religious myth and ritual assist us in this coming face to face. If we are without a living tradition of this sort, it is likely that we have developed, however rudimentarily, our own, individual traditions.

We began this section with the observation that both loneliness and the lonely need to be cared for. This care involves exploration of the concrete case. The tools for this are the four causes of loneliness and the five realms of relationship. We conclude with some summary of the kinds of exploration possible. When confronted with loneliness, our own or that of someone else, what can we look for?

1. We can look for the causes of the loneliness. There may be one or there may be several. The cause most readily acknowledged may not be the most significant one.

2. We can look for the realms involved in the loneliness. More than one realm is likely to be involved. For example, the death of a loved one deprives the survivor of an object as well as of a person. Since any part can symbolize the whole, there can be world loneliness as well. When such a death occurs, relationships to the generations are affected also. Any loneliness is likely to include more realms than is immediately apparent.

3. We can look for the variety of searching that occurs in loneliness. Separation within a realm should involve a search within it, and loneliness within a realm is resolved only by a new relationship with it. However, since any experience of loneliness can involve disconnection from more than one realm, we can discover more about the nature of the loss by the kind of searching that occurs. If a man who loses a wife purchases a pet dog, for example, he may not just be searching for a substitute for a human relationship, but primarily replacing the material object that his wife was in part.

4. We can look for the new possibilities uncovered. Loneliness prompts us to such discoveries. To lose a member of our family and then become concerned about the generations does not replace the lost relationship, but it does open us to another realm that can serve us well. To appreciate only one realm and become separate from one member of it is

quite different from knowing all five realms and becoming separate from a member of one of them. The separation is not ended necessarily, but it is put in its place when we are fully aware of and living in all five realms.

5. We can look for the combinations of the five realms of relationship with the four causes of loneliness. Note that loneliness in any of the five realms can be at any one of the four levels of cause. Typically, we ignore this possibility and limit certain kinds of loneliness to certain causes. Yet we are kindly suspicious with some justification about the adolescent philosopher who asserts awe about the universe and ignores his troubled shyness. The point is that any cause can be related to any realm, and loneliness in any realm related to any cause.

6. Having made the above point, we can remind ourselves that any number of both realms and causes can be participants in a single experience of loneliness. Our loneliness with regard to one specific person may have several causes, and our loneliness with regard to another may have several other causes. Moreover, the specific causes related to one realm in a single experience may be different from the causes related to another realm in the same experience. This last point is: we can look for the great complexity that exists in the loneliness experience due to the great variety of combinations of causes and realms.

To care for loneliness and the lonely is to fully explore the experience of separation and search. To do so is to discover the richness of loneliness. It is to face harsh reality, but the unbearable and impossible are made tragic and comprehensible. It is also to face realistic possibility. Loneliness is about the possibilities of relationship.

Pastoral Care of Loneliness and the Lonely

Loneliness can be unending, but if we discover that we are concerned, not just about ourselves or about what has been lost or unattained, but about relationship, we are moved from loneliness into solitude. The very discovery that we have lost a relationship is, at the same time, a possibility of discovery of relationships and of their existence in our lives. Solitude is the new condition in which relationship is recognized. It is likely to occur when we have fully faced the challenges of loneliness: facing our loneliness; seeing both our separation and our search and working for balance between them; acknowledging the five realms of relationship and the four causes of loneliness. Such exposure to the richness of our own loneliness fosters movement into transcendence of it by a deepening and broadening of our relationship-awareness. We will examine this understanding by suggesting more on the nature of solitude, psychotherapy, and pastoral care.

Solitude is a condition of exploring what has happened or is happening in relationships. Rather than getting away from it all (or them all), solitude is getting right into the heart of the matter. At times we try to enter this condition deliberately, feeling the need for understanding. At other times we only realize we are in the condition after it has been going on for a while. And when solitude occurs quite fully, there are surprises about relationship that happen to us. We think about someone we have not thought about in years. We miss someone more than we knew before. We discover we no longer feel about someone. When solitude rules, we are surprised by attitudes and insights that simply pop into our consciousness. These are our recognitions of relationship. They may be painful or joyous, strong or weak, sure or uncertain. But whatever the case, there is a quality of discovery of them to which we respond with "Aha." The fundamental discovery is that we are not alone in our aloneness. Absence makes the heart grow fonder, not in loneliness, but in solitude. This can even happen when reunion is not possible. After separation due to death, for example, loneliness occurs first, but as the loss is explored in the grief process, loneliness is replaced largely by appreciation of the loved one and of the relationship per se. Eventually the meaning and value of the relationship becomes overwhelmingly real, actually as if it has been discovered for the first time. Grief is ended when this new appreciation occurs. Of course, solitude occurs in the presence of others as well as apart from them. The occurrence and discovery of a relationship are distinct, and may occur together or separately. Finally, we note that the relationship being discovered and explored can occur in any of the five realms of relationship. We experience recognition of, and reflection on, relationship with individuals, groups, generations, things, and the whole as a whole. When this experience rules in our consciousness, it is likely that we have fully plumbed the experience of loneliness first.

Solitude is a way station between loneliness and companionship to which we return again and again throughout our lives. This is so because our relationships change. It is precisely the best of companionships that foster development of the individuals and of the relationship itself, and so foster loneliness as well. So solitude is a valuable condition that we do not outgrow any more than we outgrow loneliness. Some of us may even respect solitude more than either loneliness or companionship. This may be true of those of us in many walks of life. But, for our purposes, consider the psychotherapist. He or she is exposed to actual relationships with other human beings. But this is a one-way affair wherein the patient relates to the therapist as a human being in a more normal fashion than the therapist does to the patient. Further, the therapist focuses on recognition of their relationship, what it is and how it works, matters of transference, counter-transference and the like. The task of the therapist, I suggest, is to get into and remain in the condition of solitude. Solitude is the tool for understanding and helping the patient. The therapist enters into his or her work with this understanding of the method. The patient has to learn the method. So we can understand solitude as a way of defining the peculiar nature of psychotherapy. It is a form of parallel solitude in which one teaches the other to reach it and use it. In effective therapy, the patient who has begun with loneliness explores it fully and is moved gradually into solitude.

From this perspective on psychotherapy, we can affirm that the task is deepening and broadening relationship-awareness. Depth in solitude refers to our experience and acknowledgement of just how fundamental relationship per se is to us. We can live in many kinds of relationships for years without very much awareness of them, just as infants do. In the adult years, we have opportunity and natural demand for conscious appreciation of this fundamental fact of life. It is recognition of how fully bound we are to the other, that we do not and cannot exist without the other, and that we find our fullest satisfaction in linking with the other. Full acknowledgement of the brute and glorious fact is no easy achievement. We may be tempted to place far more stress on independence, even to the extent of granting ourselves the illusion of absolute freedom to choose or reject relationship per se whatever the circumstances. Such beliefs can serve to support our frightening entries into the precariousness of adult responsibilities. But we come to see our humble captivity, to respect it, and to embrace it as a need that is really beyond our control. Full experience of solitude grants us this depth of understanding of relationship. Paradoxically, it is just this depth experience of relationship that moves us out of solitude into concrete experiences of companionship.

The task also involves broadening our relationship-awareness. We are free to extend relationship as much as we can, and this is our natural propensity—to seek new relational stimulation. The possibilities are endless. They occur both within our customary realms of relationship and within those we have previously ignored. If our social network has been primarily associates on the job, then the possibility in solitude is the discovery and exploration of relationships in other groups. If we have found friendship primarily with a spouse, then the challenge is to extend the range to friendship with other people. Whatever our focus, there is room for expansion and the possibility for it. This includes other realms that may be somewhat foreign to us. We can, in solitude, be surprised by an interest in the material realms via nature or art, the historical realm of the generations via interest in the forebears of our family, or an interest in the world as a whole via the meaning of life. Real solitude, then, does not dwell only on the familiar. It is a lively condition, full of surprises.

These perspectives on psychotherapy as providing depth and breadth to the patient's solitude bring us to consideration of pastoral care. Surely the pastor and pastoral counselor can take care of loneliness and the lonely as others can, using the tools that have been discussed. They also can train those they seek to comfort and cure in the deepening and broadening of their recognition of relation in solitude. But they are in a position to carry this process on still more fully. Solitude is an awesome condition because recognition of relationship is a fundamental source of our own faith, hope, and love—of our capacity to live. Tradition recognizes it as connected with discovery of the holy.

What tends to elevate solitude in our thinking is the mood that accompanies discovery of relationship. It is the revelation to human beings. All ultimate revelation is, whatever its guises, essentially identical in message. Revelation is always revelation of relationship. The revelation is that relationship is. Life at any level depends upon it for survival and human life is not different, except in that its capacity for consciousness makes awareness of this necessity possible. Recall Samuel Johnson's celebrated remark to the woman who ventured to accept the universe: "Gad, she had better!" This is clever. It is also limited. This is the task, but it is not automatic for us and not automatically maintained. So loss of world acceptance occurs and so does rediscovery of it in solitude. It is this necessity, and the awareness of it, that renders the mood of solitudinal discovery so powerfully positive. The revelation is that relationship rules and, therefore, that we can relate to individuals, groups, the generations, objects, and to the world itself. To encounter the holy is to discover relationship as necessary and possible.

The oneness of the revelation of relationship is seen by us in different ways. Some of us do so traditionally with reference to God. So Thomas Merton speaks first of solitude and silence, but then the silence becomes a presence, and he can assert, "As soon as you are really alone, you are with God" (Merton, 1976, p. 113). Others of us receive the revelation with a focus on people, our personal and social saints, or on humanity itself. A wise old woman, Florida Scott-Maxwell, takes humanity into her heart, examines it, marvels over it, and then asserts, "I see man rise to such noble heights in his fateful struggle, that more often than we guess the gods may regard him with brotherly awe" (Scott-Maxwell, 1973, p. 81). She sees and responds to humankind as a whole. It is her ultimate companion with whom she struggles. Some of us are religious humanists like this wherein mankind is our ultimate concern. We then have moments of humble awe about this strange beast's existence in the universe that renews our capacity to relate. Such discovery of the world as a whole may occur to some of us through nature. Thoreau's discussion often indicates a nature mysticism. When asked if he is lonely in his life at Walden Pond, he responds that he lives where we all want to dwell near to, "the perennial source of our life" (Thoreau, 1966, p. 176). Like him, we can survey the heavens or fields of grass with an inner vision provided by solitude that somehow communicates to us that everything is "all right." So our discoveries of the holy will vary considerably in the parts of the world by which they are revealed and in the language we choose to respond with.

These experiences of the revelation of relationship and our responses to them can provide occasions for pastoral care and counseling. Some of us will make much of such experiences, while others will make little, but most of us do experience the world as a whole and so have some sense of what we mean by "holy." Some of us may lack these experiences or have them appear to be invalidated by experiences of loneliness in this realm or other realms. If those of us who offer pastoral care and counseling can transcend our own specific variants of the revelation of relationship, fully respect the variants of others, and encourage exploration of them, it is likely that we will gain new appreciation not only of loneliness and solitude, but also new appreciation of companionship. For as loneliness naturally leads to solitude, so does solitude lead to companionship. Of course, it follows that companionship leads to loneliness. Courage remains necessary. But the source of this is our experience of the revelation of relationship. Caring for loneliness and the lonely should include caring for them at the very source—in the loneliness, solitude, and companionship of God's relationship with creation.

Bibliography

Gaylin, W. *The Meaning of Despair.* New York: Science House, Inc., 1968.

Gubrium, J.F. *The Myth of the Golden Years.* Springfield: Charles C. Thomas, 1973.

Maris, P. *Loss and Change.* Garden City: Anchor Books, Doubleday & Co., Inc., 1975.

McCullers, C. *The Member of the Wedding.* New York: New Directions, 1951.

Merton, T. *Thoughts in Solitude.* New York: Farrar, Strauss & Giroux, 1976.

Scott-Maxwell, Florida. *The Measure of My Days.* New York: Alfred A. Knopf, 1973.

Thoreau, H.D. *Walden.* New York: Thomas Y. Crowell Company, Inc., 1966.

Weiss, R.S. *Loneliness: The Experience of Emotional and Social Isolation.* Cambridge: MIT Press, 1973.

David W. Augsburger

Anger and Aggression

Anger and aggression are among the most crucial elements in pastoral counseling and psychotherapy. Anger as emotional energy, aggression as its physical expression emerge in all humans in covert and subtle or overt and visible forms. Viewed as emotions to be *released*, the anger underground of persons nurtured in a culture of "niceness" must be brought to awareness, its hidden messages deciphered, and appropriate actions chosen. Viewed as emotions to be *reduced*, the anger overload of persons trapped in cyclical processes of collecting resentments, reviewing grievances, escalating rage, exploding in ventilation can be interrupted and new means of managing the chronic hostility can be learned. Viewed as emotions to be *invited* or encouraged, the anger energies of persons experiencing injustices or desiring change in restrictive relationships can be directed creatively for restructuring old binds.

In the therapeutic process, anger is crucial in both persons and in process. For the therapist, anger must be owned, appreciated, channeled, utilized to summon the inner resources of feelings, both positive and negative, into the interaction with the other; for the counselee, anger must be welcomed, its impact valued, its dignity prized, its demands clarified, canceled or negotiated; for the therapeutic process, anger is a crucial signal that growth, maturation, and autonomy from the therapist is occurring. (When there is no negative transference, there is no authentic growth.)

In this paper we will examine the theoretical understandings of anger and aggression, the clinical application of each in pastoral counseling and psychotherapy, and the theological grounding which can illuminate and integrate the contributions of each.

Theories of Anger and Aggression

Theories of the nature of human aggression have emerged from three contrasting perspectives—those seeing aggression as an inborn instinctive drive which, like the sexual instinct, seeks spontaneous periodic expres-

482

sion, those observing aggression as a learned behavioral response to noxious stimuli or frustration, and those viewing aggression as a basic power
thrust of the person toward the environment which can be either creative
or destructive.

Any adequate treatment of the nature of anger and aggression must
deal with the contributions of the psychoanalytic-instinctual theories
(group one), the behavioral aggressive-drive and social learning theories
(group two), and the phenomenological-perceptual theories (group three).

The first of these, the psychoanalytic, instinctual, ethological group
finds its most influential roots in Freudian theory of the nature of humans.
From Freud's early (Freud, 1905, p. 276) formulations of aggression as the
element of desire which is subjugated in sexuality to his final formulation
of self-destructive *thanatos* projected outward in aggression (Freud, 1937,
p. 139), the urge to aggress has been viewed in psychoanalysis as an instinctual, innate drive of essential human nature compounded by the nurture of a hostile environment or inhibited by the sanctions of society (Storr,
1968, p. 27). Freud writes: "If we are to take it as a truth that knows no
exception that everything living dies for internal reasons—becomes inor-
ganic again—then we shall be compelled to say that 'the aim of all life is
death'. . . ." (Freud, 1955, p. 38).

Although the majority of psychoanalysts, while following Freud in
other ways, refused to accept the theory of the death instinct, they did acknowledge a "destructive instinct" as the other pole of the sexual instinct
(Fromm, 1973, p. 15).

The second stream of theorists such as Rotter and Bandura emerged
from behaviorism. In contrast to the instinctive hereditary approaches of
the psychoanalytic perspective, the behavioralists saw aggression as environmentally induced.

"Aggression is always a consequence of frustration . . . the occurrence
of aggressive behavior always presupposes the existence of frustration and
contrariwise, that the existence of frustration always leads to some form of
aggression" (Dollard, 1939, p. 1).

No opinion was offered on the origins of this correlated occurrence.
Whether it was innate or learned, the behavior was seen as a measurable,
predictable human response to any frustrating interference with goal directed activity. Further research altered the theory significantly as it became clear that instigation to aggress is only one of a number of possible
responses to frustration and that frustration is not the only motivation to
aggression, as in instrumental aggression which overwhelms another dis-
passionately to obtain another goal.

Social Learning theorists, though sharing common learning theory
principles, have focused on those factors which facilitate or impede the

learning of aggressive habits. Thus the focus of causal analysis shifted from hypothesized internal determinants to a careful examination of external influences on responsiveness to the social environment, the stimulus events that evoke and the reinforcing consequences that alter aggressive acts (Bandura, 1973, p. 42).

The third stream includes the existential, phenomenological, perceptual theorists such as May, Rogers, Maslow and Perls, who stress that the individual reacts to the world in terms of that person's perceptions of it, that the subjective reality of each is crucial in understanding the nature of the anger felt or the aggression expressed.

Typical of the constructs of this group is the thought of Rollo May who sees "the origins of power as also the origins of aggression, for aggression is one use—or misuse—of power" (May, 1972, p. 123). Power is the ability to cause or prevent change which exists in two dimensions: (1) potentiality—latent power with the ability to cause change at some future time, and (2) actuality—the ability to be, to affect, to influence, to produce change (May, 1972, pp 99–100).

The process of self-affirmation and self-assertion is the existential experience of being, the expression of the power to be. May quotes Paul Tillich in clarifying this: "Every being affirms its own being. Its life is its self-affirmation—even if the self-affirmation has the form of self-surrender" (Tillich, 1952, p. 39).

Emerging from this body of analytic, behavioral and phenomenological theory are the following working definitions.

Anger is an emotional response with several component parts: (1) a physiological state of bodily arousal with autonomic, facial, respiratory and metabolic manifestations, (2) a cognitive state defining the arousal with internal demands focused on both internal and external events, (3) an energizing state with drive properties. It intensifies aggressive acts, while disorganizing non-aggressive responses such as concentration, attention and impulse control. At low levels anger is a tension state which acts as a reinforcer, but tends at high levels to be adversive and a decrease in tension acts as a reinforcer.

Aggression is an angry or instrumental response that adminsters punishment, pain or coercive force from one organism to another, delivering noxious stimuli in an interpersonal context (or to inanimate objects). Instrumental aggressive responses may be reinforced by the rewards of satisfactions such as food, water, sex, and desired objects; or securities such as approval, dominance, submission, prestige; or escape from adversive stimuli whether internal or external. Angry aggression is reinforced by the observation of the victim's pain.

The dynamics of these may be visualized by Figure A, showing the

Figure A

INSTINCTUAL THEORY
(Psychoanalytic, Instinctivist, Ethologist)

AGGRESSIVE ⟶ TENSION ⟶ AGGRESSIVE
INSTINCT   (Viewed in Hydraulic   BEHAVIOR
              Model Requiring
(Innate)   Tension Reduction
              by Ventilation/Action)

AGGRESSIVE DRIVE THEORY
(Behaviorism)

FRUSTRATION ⟶ AGGRESSIVE DRIVE ⟶ AGGRESSIVE
            (Organism—The   BEHAVIOR
            Motivation to Initiate
(Stimulus)   a Learned Sequence   (Response)
            of Behavior)

SOCIAL LEARNING THEORY

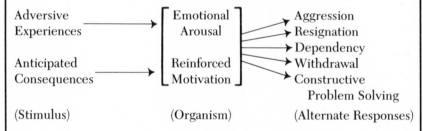

Adversive   ⟶ ⎡ Emotional ⎤   ⟶ Aggression
Experiences   Arousal   ⟶ Resignation
                        ⟶ Dependency
Anticipated   ⟶ Reinforced   ⟶ Withdrawal
Consequences   ⎣ Motivation ⎦   ⟶ Constructive
                               Problem Solving

(Stimulus)   (Organism)   (Alternate Responses)

PHENOMENOLOGICAL THEORY
(Client-Centered, Existential, Gestalt)

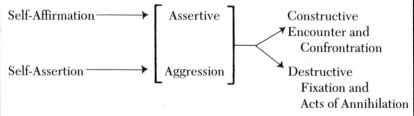

Self-Affirmation ⟶ ⎡ Assertive ⎤   Constructive
                           Encounter and
                           Confrontation
Self-Assertion ⟶ ⎣ Aggression ⎦   Destructive
                           Fixation and
                           Acts of Annihilation

(Power To Be)   (Motivation to Powerful Action) (Choice of responses)

linear causation of instinctual and behavioral theories, and the more complex models of the social learning and the existential theories.

The instinctual theory is a tension reduction model requiring ventilation or action for any satisfactory resolution. It is a hydraulic model, maintaining that anger and aggression accumulate from innate drives and must be expressed or it will be necessarily displaced into other parts of the personality, converted into somatic complaints, or emerge in projection, reaction formation, attribution, or other mechanisms of defense against the explosion of the pressures within.

This model deserves appreciation for its illumination of the hidden and unconscious dynamics of denial and distortion by which we recirculate anger into other emotional and physical responses. Clinically selected samples show persons who are operating in hydraulic accumulating of energy requiring discharge, although representative samples of any population reveal that this is not the nature of all humans, but of those who learned to process frustration and irritation in cyclical ways.

The behavioral theories are true learning theories, postulating little within the person beyond the internalized learnings of positive and negative expectancies. These perspectives instruct us to examine the sequences of learned behavior, to chart the instigations to aggress, to note the positive and negative reinforcers, and to define the differences between non-assertive behavior styles, assertive behavioral negotiating and relating styles, and aggressive coercive behaviors.

The existentialist theories prize the inner urgencies of the human as the thrusts for self-affirmation and self-assertion which as they emerge contain the possibility of creating or destroying, of constructive or destructive behaviors, of benign or malignant uses of power. They offer the clinician the possibility of affirming the power capacities of the person, of clarifying the process that turns it toward positive or negative ends, of developing or enhancing responsibility and choice, of redirecting or relearning defective sequences, of liberating the self from ineffectual patterns to discover effectual relationships.

Theologically, the dualism of the instinctual theories has a long and distinguished tradition. The suspicion of the body with its dark drives or impulses and the thrust of rational thought have ruled theological understandings of anger from St. Augustine in the fifth century to many theologians in the twentieth. The legacy of Plato's separation of the real and the ideal, the contribution of the Gnostic's division between the body and the spirit, and the impact of the ensuing gap in Christian thought between the flesh and the soul joined to alienate emotion from cognition.

The mind-body split, demanding that the body be repressed by the will, the mind renewed by the spirit, became the predominant psychology of Christian experience. The Hebraic unity of personhood as animated body was lost. The early Christian understanding of the essential goodness of our bodily humanness as confirmed by the incarnation was devalued. Sexuality and aggression were seen as the two undeniable evidences of evil within. So anger was seen as sinful evidence of fallen nature rather than as vital energy for living productively when channeled appropriately.

In reuniting what has been erroneously divided, integrative theological work strives toward the following:

One, anger has been rooted in the body, not in the whole self. Anger is an expression of bodily arousal, mental appraisal, and resulting emotional energies. All of these are worthful component parts of the whole self. No split is possible in theology of human nature, or psychology of the self.

Two, anger has been rooted in the evil of humanness we express as resulting from "the fall." Anger must be seen, in the biblical vision, as rooted in creation. We are created with the capacity for power, anger and assertiveness. These are essential parts of the image of God in us, and of the expression of God revealed to us.

Three, anger has been seen as the opposite of love, and as an abusive exercise of power. Anger can be, when creative, a form of active love, but, when destructive, an abuse of power. All justice in human relationships is worked by a balance of love and power. "Love and power are often contrasted in such a way that love is identified with a resignation of power and power with a denial of love. Powerless love and loveless power are contrasted" (Tillich, 1954, p. 13). Authentic, creative anger unites loving power and powerful love to demand justice in relationships and mutuality in the resolution of differences.

Anger Management in Pastoral Counseling

Pastoral psychotherapy, since it is rooted in a theology of human personhood rather than in any particular theoretical model—whether psychoanalytic, behavioral or existential—is free to draw on the insights offered by any or all of these as appropriate to the particular persons being treated. Since each theory, although it claims to be a comprehensive explanation of human behavior, is best seen as an analysis of part process, it may be utilized productively when the part in question is the portion of the person best illuminated by that particular theory. Anger displaced into unconscious processes or converted into somatic symptoms may be best understood in psychoanalytic perspectives. Aggression emerging from overcontrolled non-assertiveness responds best to assertiveness training, and anger in interpersonal conflict, marital relationships, and intrapersonal resentments responds more rapidly to existential interventions.

Anger is an emotional response which may be expressed creatively or destructively. Constructive anger energizes the person, interrupts the denial process, expresses needs, defends against imposition, mobilizes coping behaviors and assists the person in discriminating the character of relationship requiring renegotiation (Novaco, 1975, p. 6).

Each of these elements can be dysfunctions as energy overloads, the disruption of attention confuses, the expression becomes ventilation, the defense escalates in negative spiraling, and self-defeating behaviors may be mobilized and the discriminatory function may become hyperalert to threat whether real or imagined (see Figure B).

Constructive forms of anger seek to (1) cut through barriers to relationship, (2) confront not to injure the other but to penetrate into consciousness, (3) defend against threats to one's integrity, and (4) actualize one's ideas and identity in a hostile situation, ultimately aiming to overcome the blocks to reconciliation and healing. Destructive anger seeks to create distance, to destroy, to annihilate the other. Where constructive anger seeks to move into the other's territory to accomplish a restructuring of power, destructive anger seizes power over the other to usurp, exploit or exterminate (May, 1972, p. 151).

Unlearning destructive forms of anger management and relearning creative experiencing and expressing calls for differentiating from past behaviors and choosing new alternatives. In the socialization processes of childhood and adolescence, personal worth and performance success become seen as one. Self-worth is then dependent on interpersonal success, and the goal orientation is easily overwhelmed by personal esteem needs.

The therapeutic goal in anger training is to facilitate differentiation of anger awareness from six key areas of personality functioning. Anger awareness can be differentiated from arousal awareness so that bodily arousal (arousal may mean excitement, anxiety, fear, loss instead of anger) can be appreciated, owned, and channeled to its appropriate goal rather than result in anger flooding in any threat situation. In like steps, anger awareness must be differentiated from self-esteem, goal orientation, self-instructions, personal power and the reinforcers and rewards. Let's examine these therapeutic growth steps in sequence.

One: Differentiate between anger and arousal: When I am aware of my arousal and own it as excitement, energy and emotional investment, I am less likely to immediately identify the body-arousal as anger. The more immediate my awareness, the more open I am to experiencing my own arousal, tension and excitement, the less likely I am to become upset, agitated and impulsive.

Figure B

ANGER FUNCTIONS

Functions	*Dysfunctions*
I. ENERGIZING	
Anger energizes behavior by body-arousal. In challenging or competitive situations the burst of excitement released in anger increases vigor and drive.	The escalation of energy in arousal stimulates anxiety as a primary emotional response, triggering mind-appraisal and reappraisal in secondary emotions.
II. INTERRUPTING	
Anger interrupts the steady stream of ongoing behavior by focusing attention on the significant threat or issue in demand.	Anger disrupts attending, perceiving, retention, integration, thus interferring with normal information processing and reducing impulse control.
III. EXPRESSING	
Anger elicits the expressing of disappointments, frustrations, expectations and demands which might not be disclosed and discussed unless one party becomes angry about the situation.	Anger excites the ventilation of irritation, frustration, negativism, hostility and powerful demands which reduces tension in the sender while raising it in the receiver.
IV. DEFENDING	
Anger reduces anxiety by counterbalancing feelings of inferiority with instant feelings of power. It offers a sense of being able to take charge or control a deteriorating situation.	Anxiety is externalized and frequently escalates in a rebound effect as the intrapersonal conflict becomes interpersonal when the angry person places the issue on another or between self and other.
V. MOBILIZING	
Anger instigates the active mobilization of assertive behavior. It can elicit the release of more powerful responses to cope with a provocation or frustration.	The learned association which often links anger and aggression can lead to the automatic expression of verbal or physical assault in the breakdown of effective relating.
VI. DISCRIMINATING	
Through trained awareness of one's own arousal states, the experience of anger can signal the need for conscious choice of a learned course of action to achieve a desirable outcome in relationships.	Through hypersensitivity to provocation or threat, a person can perceive threats and respond in a learned pattern of irritability. The response of living in low-grade emergency reduces ability to cope effectively with stress.

Affirmation: "I can appreciate my body arousal and affirm my freedom to make accurate mind-appraisals of my own situation."

Two: Differentiate between anger and self-esteem: When I allow my self-esteem to be threatened, or measure my self-respect by my interpersonal success at the moment, or ground my self-worth in how another is responding to me, I am more likely to feel anger.

Affirmation: "I am a worthful person when feeling positive or negative, when succeeding or when being stymied, when receiving respect or disrespect."

Three: Differentiate between anger and goal-orientation: When I allow my focus of concern in a threat situation to move from a goal orientation to a personal orientation, I am more likely to get angry. When I begin to take threats personally or insults subjectively, I get side-tracked into self-defensiveness and baited into a hassle. I am less likely to be flooded by anger as I stay focused on what I want (goal), what I am negotiating now (task), and what I hope to achieve (desired outcome).

Affirmation: "I can recognize another's provocation without losing my focus on issues or orientation to the goal and task."

Four: Differentiate between anger and old self-instructions: When I am aroused, I am less likely to interpret and express the excitement as anger when I reject self-negations such as "I am powerless, I am losing control, I am about to be belittled, abused, ignored, exploited," and replace them with self-affirmations such as "I am capable, I am adequate for this moment, I am excited and able to channel my energies for power, I am in control of myself, we can reach a mutually satisfactory solution."

Affirmation: "I can track down my old patterns of negative self-instructions, and replace them with new affirmative self-statements."

Five: Differentiate between anger and personal power: When I am aroused, my awareness is sharpened, my energy levels are accelerated, my emotions become more potent and I feel powerful, I want to take charge. However frustration and the antagonism of the other may arouse fear that I am losing control. As I manage my anger in affirmative self-instructions, I am in control of my part of the situation.

Affirmation: "I am most powerful when I am taking charge of only my part of any situation and not fulfilling another's expectations that I be upset."

Six: Differentiate between anger and negative reinforcers: When I am evaluating a conflict I will reverse the natural process of over-rating resentments, frustrations, or failures and under-rating the agreements reached and effective relating achieved. I will congratulate myself on each step of growth and celebrate each effective response. I will share mutual appreciations with the other person for our new levels of understanding and the agreement we reached.

Affirmation: "I kept my cool, I owned my arousal, I expressed my perceptions, I asserted my expectations, I achieved the most satisfactory solution possible for us at the moment. Yea for me, hooray for us!"

Differentiation must occur between the cognitive-emotive processes and the automatic flooding of feelings, between the self as responsible agent and the impulsive preconscious reserves of negative self-statements and self-defeating instructions. The more differentiated the cognitive-emotive process in maturation, the more capable the person will be of experiencing rich feelings and of expressing them in intimacy. This motif is shared implicitly in all three streams of anger theory. For the analytic theory, it is differentiation between ego direction and impulsive action. For the Social Learning theorist it is the unlearning of old expectancies and their reinforcers and the relearning of new. For the existential perspective it is bringing behavior into awareness to facilitate responsibility, choice, and free expression of the self-regulating wisdom of the whole organism.

Therapeutically, the focus is of ventilational therapy as more than an awareness technique, and turns instead toward an assertive-affirmative expression of anger which negotiates, models and reinforces responses that can create solidarity with others. There is value in the free uncensored expression of rage in the safe environment of the therapeutic situation. Such catharsis is often an effective means for bringing the unaware into awareness, and can release pent up emotions so that further ownership and direction of the anger demands can be facilitated. However, the practice of ventilation as a therapeutic end models and reinforces the explosive behavior we hope to eventually limit or eliminate. One of the most recognized researchers on anger concludes a decade of intensive research on aggression in this way: "The evidence dictates now that it is unintelligent to encourage persons to be aggressive, even if, with the best of intentions, we want to limit such behavior to the confines of psychotherapy" (Berkowitz, 1973, p. 24).

Catharsis is effective as it leads to increased openness to the inner experience of the organism, and to more complete ownership of the demands which direct it. Since emotion exists as the conjunction of body arousal and mind appraisal, both discharge of arousal and change of appraisal are necessary for anger reduction (Schachter, 1962, p. 232). But the former without the latter leads to increase of anger. The latter step, in clarifying, confronting or canceling demands, is the crucial element in dissipating anger or aggression. Catharsis of emotional energies, without negotiation of possible demands and cancellation of impossible expectations, is powerless.

In clarifying the multiple layers of demands that empower anger in the conscious, pre-conscious and the repressed unconscious levels, one must uncover them layer by layer. The obvious levels of interpersonal conflict lie on the surface, beneath them are the self-esteem and performance demands, and below these are buried the pretentious levels of arrogant demands which extend the grandiose illusions of childhood. These range from "do what I want, when I want it, without my needing to ask it," to "honor my wishes, fulfill my dreams, satisfy my desires."

As the demands are clarified, two options emerge—confrontation with those demands that are just and cancellation of those which are unjust.

This clarifying, confronting, canceling is the process of claiming responsibility for anger emotions. The central therapeutic work with anger is essentially becoming aware of the implicit demands, making them explicit and taking the appropriate actions.

A parallel process for tracking down anger expectancies and the internal reinforcements given is offered by cognitive behaviorism's use of self-instructions. We use language to formulate plans of action and to guide our behaviors. It is a sort of internal dialogue we carry on with ourselves in preparation for a confrontation, in the midst of a conflict, and afterward.

The simplest such conversations begin at the morning mirror when self-image is reflected more clearly than facial image,

"Look at yourself—see how you look?"

"Yea, pretty terrible."

"Boy, are you right. You're overweight too."

"Well, I could lose a few pounds."

"A few? Well, it wouldn't matter if that were your only problem."

"You mean . . ."

"I don't have to tell you how badly you blew it yesterday . . ."

Our self-concept is based in part on the ratio of negative to positive things we say about ourselves in such internal conversations. The statements we make to ourselves about ourselves can trigger a wide range of reactions: anxiety, shame, guilt, envy, anger, resentment, and low self-esteem (Meichenbaum, 1977, p. 95).

The self-instructions we use to warn ourselves against the worst or discourage ourselves from seeking the best are the key to inviting change within. These self-instructions are frequently recorded announcements from our family of origin. If one listens closely, the inflections of parents and grandparents can be clearly heard. Along with these voices from the past instructing us on how to think, feel, and act are the recorded pronouncements of our own early learnings. The conflict behaviors of child-

Figure C

I. OPENNESS

I am open to the free spontaneous
flow of my responses to my world.

Irritation can occur as well as excitation,
anger can emerge as well as acceptance.

I trust the flow of thought and feeling
until it proves ineffective or unsatisfying.

I affirm my anger responses as my choices.
Your action does not determine my response.

You cannot make me angry; I make me angry
by seeing you with demands.

II. OWNERSHIP

I won my angry thoughts, feelings, actions.
I am responsible for my negative perceptions.

I affirm my anger, feelings are chosen
although all feelings are chosen indirectly.

As I perceive you rejecting, attacking, withholding,
I demand that you conform to my prescriptions.

And I then feel anger toward you and your acts.
So I do choose anger, indirectly, by demanding.

I often feel anger before I am aware of my demands.
Anger signals I must own my experience,
affirm my perceptions, identify my demands.

I affirm my response-ability to own my anger
and use it to signal my need to either

One: cancel my demands and relate in loving ways
or Two: express my demands for negotiated change.

hood, youth, and young adulthood remain with us in the warnings we repeat within, the guidelines we lay down as anxiety rises.

Tracking down the internal self-statements made, and replacing the negative ones with more positive, more effective self-instructions is a process of teasing out the tangled thoughts and rewriting the self-defeating sentences. Examining your own repertoire of positive and negative comments—learned or inherited, setting new alternatives afloat in the unconscious, and keeping new instructions aware in the conscious all work together in building new conflict behaviors (Augsburger, 1983, p. 32).

The Management of Aggression

Aggression, as the angry or instrumental action that inflicts pain or exerts force on another, seeks to unilaterally achieve one's desired ends. Aggression as a coercive action is a violation of self, of other and of the relationship. As an overt use of loveless power, it betrays justice.

Pastoral intervention, valuing the union of love and power, recognizes that the person who reacts too strongly (aggressive behavior) or too weakly (non-assertive behavior) is self-defeating either in yielding to or in usurping of another. Between these extremes lies a balanced response (assertive behavior) that expresses loving power. This behavioral paradigm provides a framework for the necessary steps in interrupting the angry aggression process in interpersonal, parental and marital relationships.

The assertiveness training paradigm views behavior on a three-point continuum from passive non-assertive through the midpoint of active assertive to the extreme of explosive aggressive behavior. Individuals may act consistently from any one of these three positions, or follow the more common explosive cycle from the non-assertive extreme to the aggressive outburst, followed by a contrite return to the non-assertive passivity (Faul and Augsburger, 1980).

Practicing non-assertive behavior necessitates the denial of one's own rights, thoughts or needs. Through withholding one's wants and allowing others to violate oneself, or through offering one's position in an apologetic acquiescence which allows others to ignore it, the non-assertive individual invites misuse.

Expressing aggressive behavior denies the other person's rights, values or needs by seizing power in a way which intimidates or violates the other, to meet one's own ends.

Exercising assertive behavior seeks the mutuality of balanced concern for both self and other. In the union of loving power anger can be expressed creatively and goals can be negotiated powerfully while relationship is affirmed as non-dispensable, as consistently prized and pursued.

Figure D

SELF-INSTRUCTIONS CHECKLIST

Old Self-Instructions   New Self-Instructions

Preparation

Old Self-Instructions	New Self-Instructions
"I just know the other guy will be testy, nasty, or pushy."	"I can be firm without being irritable or blunt."
"I'll get so frustrated I'm likely to lose my cool and blow my top."	"I know what I want to do so I can manage the emotions."
"I'm so fed up I can't hold this in much longer."	"Three deep breaths and I'll be relaxed no matter what he says or does."
"One more dig and I'll give him what he's asking for."	"This could get a bit tense but I can stay with the task and negotiate my goals."

Excitation

Old Self-Instructions	New Self-Instructions
"Oh-oh. I'm getting really bugged. He's not going to get away with pushing me around."	"I'm feeling warm in the face, my muscles are getting tight. I'm more aroused than I knew."
"I'm so tight inside I'm going to explode and get it off my chest."	"It's reasonable to get annoyed, but my real concern is to get things clear between us."
"Boy am I furious. How dare you treat me like this, you . . ."	"I really do care how this comes out. I'll take time to talk to myself so I'll not flip out."

Confrontation

Old Self-Instructions	New Self-Instructions
"You're all negatives, you insensitive clod. All you can offer is criticism."	"I'll look for positives and potential agreements without assuming the worst."
"Obviously you're out to get me, so why shouldn't I give you a bit of the same . . ."	"As long as I keep my cool, I'm in control of my half of the confrontation."
"If I don't stand up for me . . ."	"I don't need to prove myself."

Reward

Old Self-Instructions	New Self-Instructions
"Well, at least I was honest about how I felt."	"I did it. I kept my cool and focused on the issue."

Pastoral therapy of aggressive behavior can utilize theory, skill and technique from psychoanalytic and existential perspectives to combine with the behavioral schema to design intervention strategies for breaking into the cycles of coercion and violence in human relationships.

To demonstrate such proactive interventions we will examine in depth one particular instance of aggressive behavior, spouse abuse. The parallel forms of aggression in child abuse, aged parent abuse, interpersonal aggression et cetera deserve equal treatment, but within the limits of this chapter only one will be examined.

Aggression Intervention Applied

Angry cyclical aggression, as a particular human dilemma requiring pastoral care and intervention, is an interpersonal tragedy of such severity, and frequency that it dare not continue to be overlooked by clergy and people in a "conspiracy of denial."

One-fourth of American couples engage in an episode of violence in the course of their relationship, 16 percent report an abusive episode each year, and 10 percent experience extreme admitted physical abuse. Out of 47 million couples, 3.3 million wives and a quarter million husbands receive severe beatings. Husbands and wives are comparable in occurrence of violence with objects and committing homicides. Marital violence occurs in all social classes, and is privately perpetrated by publicly exemplary citizens.

Causes of abusive aggression in families include biological, psychological, metabolic, sociological and substance abuse factors. Among the biological contributions: (1) minimal brain dysfunctions, whether developmental or acquired, can lead to episodic dyscontrol; (2) a brain insult: severe head injury, encephalitis, stroke, Alzheimer's disease, tumor, although these cause a very small proportion of those with dyscontrol of aggression. The psychological factors reach from the antisocial personality disorders who use aggression without compunction to gain an objective, the psychotic hostility of acting-out episodes in the course of various mental disorders, and the episodic explosions of passive-aggressive personalities. Metabolic disorders include reactive hypoglycemia, sometimes combined with alcoholism, and the premenstrual syndrome. Sociological causes occur in families and cultural subsystems in which violent outbursts are commonly tolerated means of resolving conflict. Substance abuse is the single most common, most powerful precipitant of episodic violence, with alcohol being the most common triggering agent (Elliott, 1982).

The high correlation between alcoholism and battering need not be construed as inevitably predictable causation. There are (1) men who batter only when drunk, (2) men who are alcoholics and batter drunk or sober, (3) social drinkers who batter, (4) teetotalers who batter. The relationship between alcoholism and battering should be assessed for each situation.

Just as the roots of the aggressive tendencies are viewed in sharply different ways by those like the ethologists and analytic thinkers who see it as an inborn drive and the behavioral-existential who see it as learned, many pastoral therapists have been divided on this central issue. Some preferred to encourage ventilation, expression and catharsis. Others chose to teach anger dissipation, demand cancellation and negotiation of differences.

The impact of psychoanalytic theory on the management of family violence has led some pastoral therapists to continue to view aggression as an instinctual drive which needs periodic discharge to reduce the possibility of an uncontrolled violent outburst. This hydraulic model assumes that the innate tendency is to produce anger energy which must be expressed as anger or it will be converted, displaced, distorted in other transactions within the marriage and the family.

The most influential contribution to pastoral intervention in family violence has come from the approaches of Social Learning, existential, and behavioral theorists who see aggression as learned behavior. The conjunction of perceptions, beliefs, expectancies, coercive models, and aggressive behaviors are learned responses to frustration. Thus the recognition of anger, the clarification of perceptions, the cancellation of self-defeating beliefs, the incorporation of non-coercive models and the learning of effective problem solving skills allow for dissipation of anger emotions and aggressive impulses.

Aggression, whether in the family or in the community, is a complex behavior, dependent on the interaction of multiple factors. Aggression occurs when there is (1) some impetus or instigation to aggress, (2) a reduction or overwhelming of inhibitions against aggression, (3) a situation which combines opportunity, ability, and an available target. Many learnings converge in the aggressive act. Long term learnings: (1) the modeling of family of origin, (2) socialization of males and females, e.g., the values, norms, attitudes, beliefs, expectations instilled and reinforced, (3) the situational factors, including alcohol, drugs, emotional binds, habitual triangles and relational cycles.

In marriage, there is a wide range of kinds of aggression that occurs, and with varied intensity. The scale offered in Figure E provides a measure of the passive and active forms which vary both within and between marriages.

The abusing marriage may move cyclically through the stages indicated in the marital abuse scale with the warning signals of one, the ominous broodings of two, the psychological abuse of three, the economic deprivation of four (which victimizes, keeps dependent, removes alternatives, prevents escape) and the assault of five which terrorizes, and evokes shame, guilt and marred self-esteem (scale adapted from Monfalcone, 1980).

This cyclical movement toward battering behavior charts and explains the sequence of tension, explosion and calm which occurs with high frequency in abusive marriages, although the length of stages and the triggering events vary between persons and between stages of the life cycle for the same person.

Stage one: tension building phase. Minor battering incidents are handled by the partner through overlooking, calming, nurturing, absorbing, hoping, through a blend of denial and rationalization, that the cycle will not repeat.

Stage two: Explosion of acute battering. The complete lack of control is typified by (1) the batterer justifying the violence as teaching a necessary lesson, righting an inexcusable wrong, (2) loss of recall of what actually happened during the blind rage. The woman may precipitate this stage, when the intolerable tension shows abuse is inevitable, "to get it over with."

Stage three: Calm of kind loving contrition. Charming and gentle, the batterer is thoroughly repentant, offering gifts and promises of change and future dependability. His wonderful reasonableness matches her ideals of marital relationship making separation unlikely and belief in his transformation possible. Temporary acceptance of help may induce both to continue the relationship leading to the recurring cycle (Walker, 1978).

Intervention in Family Aggression

Abusiveness is a learned process. It is a myth that abusiveness is usually the result of irrevocable disease process, or personality disorders, or inherited disabilities that are unresponsive to all interventions. This relieves one or both spouses of responsibility for the abusive anger displays. Both the pastoral therapist and the couple must contradict the notion of indelible traits. They can discover the stimuli that elicit abusiveness and the events that intensify this interaction. As these sequences of behavior are tracked down, new means of anger management are learned, new patterns of conflict resolution acquired, the cycle of accumulation-explosion can be reversed.

Abusiveness is a joint problem. The myth that one party is solely and totally responsible for the situation emerges from the correct designation

Figure E

Marital Abuse Scale

	1	2	3	4	5	6
BEHAVIORS	Ignoring Silence Overwork	Withdrawal Absence Evasion	Blaming Accusing Berating	Depriving Physical Neglect	Violence Assault Attack	Homicide Suicide
MINIMUM EFFECTS	Loss of Intimacy Communic. Contact	Loss of Intimacy Companion- ship	Loss of Self-Esteem Crazymaking	Loss of Safety & Security	Injury Shame Guilt	Death Prison Mental Hospital
MAXIMUM EFFECTS	Alienation Rejection Divorce	Separation Acting Out Divorce	Mental Breakdown Divorce	Sickness (Phys. Ment) Divorce	Injury Impairment Death Divorce	Death Prison Mental Hospital

of one as batterer and the other as victim. In spite of the accuracy of the labeling and the differential of responsibility, the joint participation of both contributes to the process which must be reversed. The interaction of verbally assaultive and physically abusive behaviors between the two must be interrupted if cooperation is to be achieved. It takes two to continue a cycle, it takes one to quit, it takes both to break and remake it.

Abusiveness is a cyclical problem. The myth that abusiveness is a totally self-destructive process with no purposeful functions emerges from a negative valuation of conflict. Violence is a desperate but unsuccessful attempt at effecting change in relationships. The relearning of new positive spirals of behavior transactions can replace the negative spirals with effective cycles of problem solving skills (Margolin, 1979).

Summary

In this chapter we have attempted to demonstrate that a theological foundation of love and power united in justice allows the pastoral psychotherapist to affirm the polar thrusts for both interpersonal relationship and personal goals. This results in the channeling of love and anger creatively and the interrupting of aggression and coercion by reinforcing bonding behaviors and balancing personal and interpersonal responsibility. This theological base allows the integration of insights, techniques and strategies from psychoanalytic, behavioral, social learning and existential approaches to human change and growth. These perspectives are viewed as part processes which correct and complete each other when employed as methodologies for enhancing development and growth toward full humanness as creatures called of God to receive the gift of grace we call wholeness.

Bibliography

Augsburger, D. *Anger, Assertiveness and Pastoral Care*. Philadelphia: Fortress, 1979.

Augsburger, D. *When Caring Is Not Enough*. Ventura: Regal, 1983.

Bandura, A. *Aggression*. Englewood Cliffs: Prentice-Hall, 1973.

Berkowitz, L. "The Case for Bottling Up Rage," *Psychology Today*, July 1973.

Dollard, J. *Frustration and Aggression*. New Haven: Yale Univ., 1939.

Elliott, F. "Biological Contributions to Family Violence," *Clinical Approaches to Family Violence*. Rockville: Aspen, 1982.

Freud, S. *Beyond the Pleasure Principle*. London: Hogarth, 1955.

Freud, S. *New Introductory Lectures on Psychoanalysis*. London: Hogarth, 1937.

Freud, S. *Three Essays on the Theory of Sexuality*. London: Hogarth, 1905, 1950.

Faul, J. and Augsburger, D. *Beyond Assertiveness*. Waco: Word, 1980.

Lester, A. *Coping with Your Anger*. Philadelphia: Westminster, 1983.

Margolin, G. "Anger Management and Spouse Abuse," *American Journal of Family Therapy*, Vol. 7, No. 2, 1979.

May, R. *Power and Innocence*. New York: Norton, 1972.

Meichenbaum, D. *Cognitive-Behavior Modification*. New York: Plenum Press, 1977.

Monfalcone, W. *Coping with Abuse in the Family*. Philadelphia: Westminster, 1980.

Novaco, R. *Anger Control*. Lexington: Lexington Books, 1975.

Rotter, J. *Social Learning and Clinical Psychology*. Englewood Cliffs: Prentice-Hall, 1954.

Schachter, S. "How Emotions Are Labeled," *Psychological Review*, 69, 1962.

Storr, A. *Human Aggression*. Baltimore: Penguin Books, 1968.

Tillich, P. *Love, Power and Justice*. New York: Oxford, 1954.

Tillich, P. *The Courage To Be*. New Haven: Yale Univ., 1952.

Walker, L. In Chapman and Oates, *The Victimization of Women*. London: Sage, 1978.

James E. Royce, S.J.

Alcohol and Other Drug Dependencies

Most pastoral counselors today possess good counseling skills, yet even these tend to shy away from problems involving alcohol and other drugs. The reasons for this vary. One is the stereotype of the alcoholic as a skid-row bum, in spite of widespread knowledge that these constitute only 3 percent of alcoholics. The other 97 percent are women and men representing a cross-section of parishioners: rich and poor, old and young, devout or inattentive to religion. One is tempted to think of a drug addict as a "dope fiend" you would not allow in your living room; yet when we say "drugs" we mean prescription drugs like Valium or diet pills or sleeping medications every bit as much as we mean street drugs like heroin or PCP or cocaine. And of course marijuana is getting to be as common as beer or martinis in many segments of society, especially among adolescents and young adults.

Another reason why pastoral counselors have misgivings is that their seminary training usually did not include skills and knowledge precisely in this area. Like most older physicians, they were sent out to minister to a populace where alcoholism is epidemic, yet in one informal survey 85 percent of the respondents reported that they felt that their seminary training was inadequate here. (One physician, an American Board diplomate in his specialty, stated after taking our survey course in alcoholism that "80 percent of what I thought I knew about alcoholism was wrong.") It is only recently that alcoholism has been recognized as a primary illness, and indeed the number one public health problem in America, so it is not surprising that in most professions including the clergy preparation to deal with it has lagged far behind need.

Still another reason is the myth that alcoholics are hopeless or incurable. While it is true that there is no known "cure" for alcoholism in the sense of restoring their ability to drink socially, the fact is that alcoholism is our most treatable major illness, and success rates are excellent in those treatment centers which have abandoned the old psychiatric approaches and treat the addiction for what it is. One million members of Alcoholics Anonymous, according to a projection from their latest survey, attest to the fact that with God's grace and their psychologically sound twelve-step program they are happily sober and would not want to drink even if science made it possible for them.

In addition, alcoholism is almost always a family problem, and dealing with an angry spouse or a sick family system is taxing or threatening or both. Most often it is not the alcoholic but a family member who approaches the clergy or pastoral associate for help. The counselor then gets caught in the middle of a family fight, which as any policeman can attest is never a comfortable situation.

Lastly, it should be mentioned that addiction, to alcohol or any other drug, is a complex problem requiring an interdisciplinary approach which diverges from the pastor's all too frequent desire to play God, to be "all things to all men" instead of cooperating with several other agencies and professions whom they often do not know or know how to deal with. This is all the more important when we realize that many people in trouble go to their pastor first. If we take the oft-quoted figure from the old Midtown Manhattan study (Srole, 1962) that 42 percent of problems are seen first by the clergy, the distressing fact is that only 3 percent of admissions to alcoholism treatment centers come from referral by the clergy. Does the other 39 percent represent lost parishioners?

The purpose of this chapter, therefore, is not to teach basic counseling skills but to help reduce the frustration many feel in dealing with this special population, so that they may become more effective in counseling with this group and thus experience the joy of healing in this ministry.

Diagnosis

Objections to calling alcoholism a disease usually stem from the fact that we tend to construe the term "disease" too narrowly. As will be seen in the course of this chapter, it must be understood as a physiological, psychological, and spiritual illness: the whole person is sick. It is in the spiritual aspects that the pastoral counselor may be most helpful, but it is usually a mistake to start with that. First a diagnosis must be accepted.

Alcoholism is known as a disease of denial, whose chief symptom is inability to see that one has it. We say inability rather than unwillingness, for this is not denial in the sense of any rational, conscious rejection of the idea but an emotional blocking which is largely subconscious. This denial has been called "honest self-deception."

Moreover, denial has become so big a topic in the alcoholism field that counselors are now seen calling their clients a liar when the trouble is not so much conscious denial as just confusion. Contrary to what alcoholics have read or heard, they do not get drunk every time they drink, nor experience unpleasant effects on every occasion. Many report periods of normal social drinking in between binges. All have some happy memories of boisterous good times; this is due in part, of course, to retroactive falsification whereby any of us tend to remember the good and repress the unpleasant. They live in the futile hope that somehow they can find the magic formula whereby they can drink again like everybody else. Ironically, the more intelligent are not more open to reason here, but rather are more skillful at rationalization and denial.

Alcoholics do lie about their drinking, of course. They also get confused or have blackouts and do not remember how many drinks they had. Although a diagnosis can never be based solely on amount consumed rather than what happens when they drink, a drinking history must be taken and a basic rule might be to double whatever amounts they report. Thus "a couple of drinks" probably means four or five, and "a drink" can mean a waterglass full of hard liquor, six or eight times the traditional one-ounce jigger. One woman who was obviously in advanced-stage alcoholism kept telling her doctor, a physician well experienced in alcoholism, that she never had more than two drinks. In spite of his skill it took him fifteen days to uncover that she bought a full quart of gin each day and poured a pint into each of two large glasses, one for before dinner and one after: two drinks.

Denial is not restricted to the alcoholic. Society, including professionals, would rather look the other way or put some other label on the problems. "Your wife is a fine upstanding member of this parish, Mr. Jones; she couldn't possibly be an alcoholic"—meaning a skid-row bum, of course. Yet there are more alcoholics in our country clubs than on skid row, and more among our vestrymen and clergy and other professionals than in the average population. One pastor who insisted there were no alcoholics in his parish discovered that three members of his parish council had just taken a fourth member to their Alcoholics Anonymous meeting. Husbands tend to have more denial than wives; he will either be more defensive and likely to cover up for her, or be more rejecting and likely to divorce her. (It is commonly accepted now that the ratio of men to women alcoholics is equal, not the four or five to one that appears in the older books.)

Given all this denial, it is wise not to attempt to hang the label "alcoholic" on anyone. Better simply to talk calmly about whether drinking may be causing some life problems (Willoughby, 1979). Otherwise defenses go up and nothing is accomplished. The actual drinking history is perhaps better taken as part of a routine check on health habits: smoking, coffee, exercise and the like. We know that alcohol and/or other drugs may be involved in 60 to 90 percent of all cases of battered wives, divorces, abused children, rape, incest, bad checks, traffic and home accidents, employment problems, gastrointestinal complaints, and many other things the counselor hears about. Some of the following questions should be asked in every initial interview, whether or not excessive drinking is the presenting problem.

- Has anyone ever complained about your drinking?
- Have you or someone else worried that you drink too much?
- Does discussion about excessive drinking annoy you?
- Have you ever cut down on your drinking, or quit for a while? (Most do not realize that "going on the water wagon" is not a sign of control but a symptom of alcoholism; the true social drinker does not play these games of control.)
- Have you noticed that you can handle more liquor now than you used to? (Again, many will boast about being able to drink everybody else under the table, not realizing that good tolerance is a classic symptom of alcoholism rather than assurance that one is immune. Only in very late stages of the disease is there a sharp drop in tolerance.)
- Do you drink more when under pressure or after a disappointment or a quarrel? Do you find yourself giving reasons for having a drink? (A social drinker may *enjoy* a drink; the alcoholic *uses* it to cope.)
- Do you sometimes drink more than you intend or promise, even though you don't get drunk? (A myth is that the alcoholic gets drunk every time he drinks; just drinking more than one intends is an early sign of beginning to lose control.)
- Do you think about your next drink, or whether there will be enough to drink? Do you find yourself ready for the next round ahead of the others? Are you sometimes uncomfortable if no liquor is available?
- Do you wish to continue drinking after the others have had enough?
- Do you do or say things while drinking that you regret later?
- Were there any problem drinkers in your family? grandparents?
- Have you ever said or done things when drinking that you can't remember the next day?
- Do you remember the first time you had a drink? (Most of us can't, but the alcoholic often can, and reacts with a smirk or a smile or a frown.)
- Do you ever enjoy an eye-opener (a drink the morning after)?
- Have you ever switched beverages to control your drinking?

- Does the availability of drink affect your choice of recreation places or persons?
- (For spouse) Do you see a notable personality change after a few drinks?

The person who answers yes to two or three of the above questions is probably at least in early-stage alcoholism. Five "yes" answers would be a certain diagnosis, and indicative of at least early-middle stage. Heavy smoking and coffee drinking are often indicative signs.

Contrary to the social science in vogue for decades which stressed environment, it is now well established that some alcoholism can have a hereditary basis. Note that we do not ask about alcoholism but rather problem drinking in the ancestry, since in older generations it would not have been so identified. Also, we do not ask just about parents, since alcoholism like many hereditary diseases can skip a generation. One way is to ask what parents and grandparents died of: cirrhosis? driving accident?

Anxiety and depression are often self-medicated with alcohol, which in turn causes one to be more anxious and depressed. Drinking alone is a misleading question; many are very alone even in a crowded bar or tavern. Morning drink is likewise ambiguous: many alcoholics have heard this is a symptom and will deliberately wait until noon just to prove they are not alcoholic. Defensiveness, minimizing, "I'm not that bad" and accompanying body language often betray denial.

All the above symptoms usually appear long before gross bodily deterioration, but sometimes there are physical signs which even the non-medical professional can pick up: sweating, sticky palms, fatigue, sleep disturbances, slight hand tremor, acid stomach (use of Tums or Rolaids, etc.), morning cough, elevated blood pressure and pulse, small veins on nose and chin, yellowish tinge to skin or whites of eyes, puffiness, tendency to bruise or bleed easily, difficulty in fighting off infections, skin disorders, and high or low blood sugar. (Hypoglycemia is not a cause of alcoholism, but it may be a complication and can contribute to relapse because the low blood sugar is mistaken for a need to drink.)

A major step in the diagnosis is to link the drinking to the client's problems. Since most alcoholics are "con artists" it is all too easy for them to convince even the experienced professional that a string of bad luck or the spouse or the boss is the cause rather than that these problems are the effect of the drinking. Asking an alcoholic "Why do you drink?" is a waste of time because most alcoholics start drinking for the same reasons that we all do: to relax, to be sociable, out of custom, whatever. That is not the question. Why do they continue to drink, to the destruction of family, job, health, and life itself? Current research (Milam, 1981; Vaillant, 1983) says simply: because they need a drink; they are addicted to alcohol. Rather than face that, they develop marvelous skill in finding reasons to drink, and any counselor who gets drawn into playing that game will be taken on a long ride to nowhere. The counselor becomes an enabler, prolonging instead of treating the real problem.

Counselors are trained to analyze causes of behavior, usually past causes of present behavior. Carl Rogers made a great contribution to psychotherapy with his client-centered therapy. Neither approach has had much success with alcoholics. Most alcoholics are self-centered enough as well as highly skillful in self-deception; a non-directive mode can be very useful to draw out a neurotic, but it plays right into the hands of an alcoholic. As for analyzing reasons, this mode misses the important difference that in an alcoholic the psychopathology is mostly the result of the drinking rather than the cause of it. Clients would much rather talk about their sex life than their drinking.

The focus must be on alcoholism as a primary pathology in its own right, not a symptom of some underlying psychological conflict which does not exist in some 80 percent of the cases just as all researchers agree that there is no such thing as "the alcoholic personality" which lies at the root of alcoholism (see Royce, 1981, chapters 9 and 10 and sources cited therein). Earlier research which reported spikes on the MMPI or other signs of abnormality was done in alcoholics too soon after initial sobriety. CAT scans, brain waves (EEG) and other evidence now show that after blood alcohol has been detoxified, it may require even six months to two years for the residual toxic effects of alcohol to fully disappear from the brain. After that, repeat testing of most alcoholics reveals a personality score well within normal range. In sum, people are not drinking because they are abnormal, but are acting abnormally because they drink. Alcoholism therapy using this concept as a basis is getting remarkable high success rates.

The counselor must always be alert to the minority whose alcoholism is linked with sociopathic personality, schizophrenia, clinical depression or manic-depressive (affective) disorder, or neurosis which requires psychiatric care. But referral should be made only to a psychotherapist who understands alcoholism and other addictions. Even then, the alcoholism must be treated first: one cannot do successful psychotherapy on a brain which is toxic with alcohol or pills.

Intervention

The counselor must understand that this compulsion to drink in spite of all reasons to the contrary is not within the client's choice. The alcoholic has resolved, prayed, promised and "learned his lesson" a thousand times. The spouse says, "Why don't you drink like other people?" That is exactly what the alcoholic is trying to do. Neither understands that the nature of the illness makes this impossible, that the alcoholic's liver and brain react differently to alcohol than other people's. The husband says, "If she really loved me, she wouldn't *have* cancer." And the alcoholic's response is equally inane, much like saying, "All right darling, I promise: after tomorrow, no more cancer."

The problem is to get alcoholics to face this loss of control. "I can quit any time I want to" could be answered with "Why quit if it's no problem?" Actually, that phrase is almost a definition of alcoholism. If they really can "take it or leave it alone," *do* they leave it alone? For short periods, perhaps. That means nothing.

One way to let them prove to themselves their loss of control is to contract with them to have only two drinks a day, but every day, no more and no less. Explain that there is the same alcohol in a beer or glass of wine as in a shot of whiskey. They must agree to be absolutely honest, as they are the sole judge. They agree never to transfer one day's ration over to the next, nor to use more than a one-ounce measure for "a drink." It is not a valid test if someone else doles it out, or makes sure they stop, or if they have to take means such as leaving a party in order to keep within the quota. If they can take two drinks thus understood every day for six months they are probably not alcoholic. They must agree to come back if they exceed two drinks even one time, for whatever reason or in whatever way. This may seem like sending an alcoholic out to do more drinking, but for those who are in deep denial and for whom all other attempts have failed, this method may force a diagnosis and is better than letting the client leave without any commitment.

But the current wisdom favors a group intervention rather than the individual counselor trying to break through the denial and obtain an agreement to go to treatment or A.A. or both. The older word was confrontation, but that is too harsh and masks the fact that the process must be done with love, not to satisfy anyone's power needs. Although we were advocating the idea thirty years ago, the major impetus came from Dr. Vernon Johnson (1973) in the films and literature developed by the Johnson Institute in Minneapolis. A key fact is that forced treatment works: the old idea that you could not help alcoholics until they hit bottom or wanted help has been thoroughly disproved, especially in the alcoholism programs developed by business and industry and now usually called Employee Assistance Programs (EAP)—a term which ignores the fact that it may just as well be the employer as the employee who has a drinking problem.

Any pastoral counselor can obtain the skill to guide a group through a successful intervention. This involves several sessions with the family and others deemed appropriate, including the children over five. They know what's going on anyway, so there is no danger of hurting them by this exposure. Daddy's little girl or a mother's favorite son can be very effective by putting in just a few words at the right time. All must rehearse presenting specific instances of the alcoholic's drinking which distressed them, not vague general allegations. They must agree to maintain a united front and settle for nothing less than an agreement to go to treatment, or to regular A.A. with the proviso that even one more drinking bout signals entry into treatment without further debate. The alcoholic will try to divide the confronters by manipulating or playing one off against another. The counselor must warn them in the preparatory sessions to expect this and other ploys: the alcoholic will cry, accuse them of ganging up or being unfair or exaggerating, threaten to leave them or not love them anymore, etc. They must learn that they will lose the alcoholic anyway if the drinking continues, whereas they will win undying gratitude later in spite of anger now. A debriefing session should be scheduled for after the intervention, as it is an emotionally draining experience for all and there is always the possibility of failure just now which must be faced. The process rarely fails in the long run if properly done, and the intervention team becomes a support group after treatment.

A warning is in order: this method has achieved such vogue that like any good thing it is being abused. Amateurs are rushing into confrontation without adequate preparation or the guidance of a professional, or at an inappropriate time. Needless to say the diagnosis of alcoholism must be certain, or a family can be destroyed. But the very nature of alcoholism with its denial and inability to use will power effectively throws more responsibility on others to get the person to do something about the problem.

Since the spouse is often the first to contact the pastoral counselor, in individual counseling it is first necessary to establish rapport with the alcoholic in a manner which eliminates the feeling that initiative is coming from the spouse. "I realize, Mr. Jones, that your wife sort of pushed you into coming here. But what I really want to know is how you yourself feel about this problem." Needless to say, there is no use trying to talk to an alcoholic when he or she is drunk. But during a hangover is often a very good time, or shortly thereafter.

Counseling

If the person pours out a tale of discouragement and failure, it is a mistake to reassure too soon. At this point the client is not helped by being told that things are not really that bad. The client needs to feel that the counselor understands just how bad it is. Negative feelings need to be expressed and accepted before positive ones can replace them. Later the counselor can assure forgiveness and begin to help the person to build a new self-image, new goals in life. But catharsis usually must come first.

We said earlier in discussing denial that alcoholics suffer a great deal of confusion. A sense of hopelessness is common. They have been told it's a matter of will power, yet they have resolved ever harder and harder only to fail again and again. Nobody explained to them that an alcoholic obviously has the strongest will in the world when it comes to getting a drink, so it's not a matter of weak will but of physiological differences which science has discovered in both brain and liver. They are confused because they know they are quite competent in other areas; they need to learn that they are neither bad nor crazy any more than one who is subject to diabetic coma or epileptic fits.

Their self-esteem sinks very low, and their occasional bravado and grandiosity probably masquerades a tottering ego. Besides being confused, alcoholics usually experience remorse, guilt, shame, and self-hatred. For this reason the old preachy, moralizing approaches of the prohibitionistic religions did little for the alcoholic, except to furnish him with yet another reason to get drunk. The alcoholic will sense rejection by the counselor with amazing perspicacity. He is not a criminal but a lost sheep looking for the good shepherd. Hope does not come easily to one who feels, or has been called, "hopeless." Note that we do not use the words "reformed" and "recidivism" which imply moral or criminal guilt, but "recovered" to imply illness. One does not speak of a "reformed tubercular."

Another characteristic of many alcoholics is perfectionism, especially in those who are also children of alcoholic parents as many are. They tend to have low frustration tolerance anyhow, but are most prone to be unable to tolerate imperfection in themselves. The apparent arrogance we see is probably denial and an attempt to cope with their sense of helplessness. It often takes the form of projection on others. It is always the boss, the spouse, the police, "the system" or anyone or anything except alcohol which causes their miseries.

Pride is a major problem, as it is for all of us. Bill W., co-founder of Alcoholics Anonymous, wrote a great deal about humility, which we know to be the fundamental virtue of the spiritual life—and the most difficult. Alcoholics need help in understanding that humility is not saying they are no good. That is a lie, and humility is truth. The truth is that they are good enough that God made them, and loves them even if nobody else does. But the truth is also that they are not perfect, and what good they are is more due to God and their parents or others than to themselves. Kurtz (1979) conveys a brilliant insight in the title of his classic history of Alcoholics Anonymous: *Not-God*. It is the history of one million people who discovered that they are not God.

Guilt is a major problem for both alcoholics and family members, and one needing the ministration of the pastoral counselor. Psychiatrists and psychologists for years have talked about guilt, but all too often have confused true guilt with neurotic guilt-feelings. The former is objectively based, and often discussed under the term responsibility even by those who repudiate guilt as being all subjective and neurotic. The ones who have done wrong for which they are responsible need the assurance that an infinitely loving God can and gladly does forgive, regardless of the intense guilt feelings of the client. The pastoral counselor must learn how to assist an A.A. member in doing the Fourth and Fifth Steps. See, for example, Sellner (1981).

The person who feels guilty for something he or she did not do, or did not know was wrong at the time, or could not have done otherwise, needs explanation and catharsis, not forgiveness. An example is the recovering alcoholic woman who hears about the Fetal Alcohol Syndrome and says, "What a bad mother I am to have exposed my child to mental retardation and deformity," when the fact is that she never even heard of F.A.S. until she was in the alcoholism treatment center and hence could not possibly have been guilty of this. She can be helped to understand that she does indeed have responsibility to avoid drink if she gets pregnant in the future, but there in no question of her having sinned in the past on this point. Subjective feelings are not objective guilt. Similarly, one must distinguish guilt from regret. If I kill a little girl who runs out from between parked cars in spite of all vigilance on my part, I may regret this deeply but I am not guilty of murder. Children of alcoholics are particularly prone to false guilt feelings; they have been made to feel it is their fault that the parent drank. But all, alcoholic and family, need help sorting out their guilt problems.

Another frequent problem is loneliness. Discouraged, fearful and alienated from others, alcoholics tend to withdraw more and more into the inner world of self. Even in a crowded tavern or lively cocktail party, they are very much alone. Alcohol becomes their only trusted friend and source of comfort, even though it betrays them every time. This loneliness is probably a major reason for the success of Alcoholics Anonymous. The counselor simply cannot be with them constantly, whereas they can always call their A.A. sponsor or go to a meeting. It has been said that an A.A. meeting is the closest thing there is to first-century Christianity. The phony is usually unmasked quickly; there is a lot of genuine love. These people really care for each other.

Despite a wide range of differences, and with the admitted danger of unscientific generalizations, these problems seem to be common to most alcoholics. They of course take varied forms, but an understanding counselor can recognize them. Calling alcoholism a disease does not eliminate responsibility, but we must distinguish between being an alcoholic and doing something about it. Nobody chooses to be an alcoholic any more than one chooses to be a diabetic, or to have cancer. This is not a sin. But just as the diabetic must take insulin and follow a diet, so the alcoholic may be obliged to take the means to avoid drinking, be it treatment or A.A. or whatever. Even here their moral responsibility is diminished by the nature of the illness with its blinding denial and the power of obsessive-compulsive habit. Ironically, during the bitter battles which led to prohibition the most moralizing was done over the area where there is least moral responsibility: drunkenness by the alcoholic.

Since the drinking of alcoholics is not a matter of choice but the symptom of a disease, there is no use in appealing to good will or exhorting them to use will power. That is like telling a tubercular patient not to cough. Drunkenness is a sin, of course, for those who deliberately choose it. But alcoholics do not choose to get drunk; they get drunk in spite of intending not to. They are not morally depraved, they are sick. They are sinners, but aren't we all? Prayer is needed, but just praying with them may only drive them away. Better that we pray for guidance on how best to help them, just as the answer to acute appendicitis is not just to pray but to pray that God will guide the knife of the surgeon.

Just as we who are not surgeons must focus on getting the patient to a hospital, so those who are not alcohol specialists need to work on getting the alcoholic to the best sources of help. There is much the pastoral counselor can do: diagnosis, motivation to accept help, explanation of the disease and its treatment, introducing them to the warm fellowship and deeply spiritual program of Alcoholics Anonymous, supporting them during treatment and long-term recovery, and ministering to their spiritual needs throughout these various phases. They are indeed sick spiritually, and there is much the pastoral counselor can offer who understands the illness and the A.A. program.

The mistake is to think we can do it all. We must not look on A.A. as competition for our church, but as a means to enhance and deepen their religious commitment. During intervention and the early stages of treatment and recovery, we often must be patient and hold off from pushing the God of organized religion at them too fast. They have been alienated from God and church, full of guilt and remorse. We do not need to add to their guilt, but should stress the forgiveness of a loving God. They are groping their way back to that God through the alcoholic fog of confusion and shame, and may find him first under the vague A.A. phrase of a Higher Power. This may seem unsatisfactory to us, but to the alcoholic estranged and even hostile to denominational religion, "God as we understand him" in A.A. is far less threatening. If we handle it right, eventually they will find that this is the same God of their church.

Many recovered alcoholics make the statement, shocking in view of all the misery they have gone through, "I'm glad I'm an alcoholic." They go on to explain that if they were not alcoholic, they would never have joined Alcoholics Anonymous, and hence would never have discovered how much God loves them and how much they love God. Old but worth repeating is the story of the A.A. member explaining the twelve-step program to a small group of bishops, who listened attentively, but at the end one of them said, "That is a fine spiritual program, but we have all that already; what do you have that we don't?" The A.A. member thought a minute, then answered: "Success!" It is true that they succeed where we have so often failed. Even though A.A. itself says that it is not necessary to be an alcoholic in order to work successfully with them, there is something about a fellowship where all have the common understanding and warm emotional acceptance evident in any A.A. meeting. Professionals are urged strongly to attend some open A.A. meetings to see that it works.

One feature that might surprise the visitor is the laughter. Sometimes alcoholics will insist that they can do it alone, to which the A.A. member replies, "Maybe, but do it with us and it will be fun." Instead of spending the rest of their lives crying over spilt milk, they turn the past over to a loving God and live one day at a time and even learn to laugh at themselves—a sure sign of mental health. If humor is the recognition of incongruity, then what Kurtz (1979, p. 249) calls "the shared honesty of mutual vulnerability, openly acknowledged" at the heart of this fellowship can be the basis for not only acceptance but a good laugh.

Although the author is not a member, this discussion on counseling the alcoholic is shot through with references to Alcoholics Anonymous, simply because these meetings are the best single source of knowledge about what works with alcoholics. This is attested to by eminent psychiatrists like Harry M. Tiebout, M.D., said to know more about alcoholism than any other psychiatrist, Joseph Pursch, M.D., and many other professionals who admit they learned most (and "unlearned" their misconceptions) by attending open A.A. meetings and *listening* carefully, not lecturing. Any counselors who are uncomfortable about being seen going in to an open (as opposed to closed meetings for members only) meeting should probably re-examine their attitudes about alcoholism and seriously consider whether they should be counseling them.

Retrospectively, many alcoholics tell that one of the turning points in the development of their disease was when they stopped praying. When one is alienated from God, this is spiritual dis-ease; one cannot function with ease in relation to God, just as the physical dis-ease of alcoholism is that one cannot function with ease in relation to alcohol. Health is integral functioning; disease is lack of it: dys-function whether physical, mental or spiritual.

Prayer then is an area in which the counselor can be of great help to the recovering alcoholic. The eleventh step of the A.A. program says that they "sought by prayer and meditation to increase our conscious contact with God as we understood Him, praying only for knowledge of His will for us and the power to carry that out." The very mention of prayer and meditation is enough to terrify some alcoholics on the threshold of recovery, so some explanation and assurance is in order. The counselor can help them see that prayer is not folding one's hands and reciting long formulas, but just talking with God as a friend to a friend. And meditation is nothing more than quietly thinking about some truth or fact or passage from a book in God's presence, trying to see it from his perspective and talking it over with him.

A real challenge is the alcoholics who are willing to do something about the alcoholism but are repelled by "all the God talk" in A.A. Show them the fourth chapter entitled "We Agnostics" of the A.A. beloved "big book" *Alcoholics Anonymous* (1939) and assure them that A.A. is very tolerant of the professed atheist or agnostic. Nobody will force God on them, and each is allowed to think of God in any way one chooses. This is also true of the God of the great southern black spirituals which are an important part of our American musical heritage, or the Great Spirit of our native American Indians. It is simply not true that A.A. favors a white man's God or any other kind. Sometimes it is helpful to distinguish between spirituality and religion. Alcoholics Anonymous is an intensely spiritual program, but it is not sectarian religion and carefully avoids affiliation with any particular creed or church although they often rent meeting space in church basements.

The professed atheists are asked to consider that there is a Power greater than themselves, and it can be pointed out that at least alcohol seems to be more powerful than they are, since it is running their lives. One old-timer says that nobody can be so egotistical as to think that there is no power in existence greater than himself. We are all dependent on oxygen, but admission of this is not considered neurotic, just realism. We actually all depend on many others: for water, food, clothing, electricity. So dependence on God is not escapism but facing reality. Again, turning our lives over to the care of God does not mean that we dump everything on him and take no responsibility ourselves. God gave us talent and intelligence which he expects us to use. And "one day at a time" refers to not taking a drink; it does not mean that you don't buy fire insurance until the day your house burns down.

But it is not just atheists who have need of help in sorting out their thinking. We have seen priests drink themselves to death while believing that if they just prayed harder and resolved more firmly they could lick the problem. They need to understand the nature of the disease: that in addition to the whole psychology of habit, there is the concrete evidence of changes in both liver and brain and some of these are irreversible. This is not a moral issue, except the obligation to get help—and even that is confused in the alcoholic fog. The real sin may be our failure to educate both the alcoholic and ourselves as to the true nature of the illness.

A question still comes up about "taking the pledge" not to drink for a year. This author remembers naively administering the pledge to an alcoholic shortly after ordination. The man stayed sober for a year, but during the last few weeks the tension started building up, and as soon as the year was up he went off on a horrendous binge. Alcoholics Anonymous has the wisdom to avoid this with its "one day at a time" approach, saying that anybody can avoid having a drink for just twenty-four hours. Better direct the energies of both counselor and client toward identifying high-risk situations and devising alternative strategies for coping, to avoid relapse into drinking.

As for a pledge taken at confirmation or ordination or some similar time, this may have value if done without coercion and with full understanding of what is involved, especially if such persons know that hereditary predisposition means that they are statistically more likely to have problems if they drink. Although old-timers in A.A. find it useful to say that it is like an allergy, alcoholism is not an allergy in the technical sense of antigens. But if one is born with a disposition to break out in ugly red hives every time strawberries are eaten, it is obviously better not to eat strawberries. The parallel with alcohol is well founded in contemporary research, which has eliminated the influence of the alcoholic environment in identifying heredity as a factor in much alcoholism but not all.

Even for those not so disposed, a pledge can be motivated by the desire to set a good example for others and break the stereotype in our society of alcohol being associated with manliness or hospitality. The Pioneers are a group originating in Ireland who give up alcohol although they do not have the problem, to help those who do and as a witness of their concern. This is long-range prevention, but a counselor must have some concern for prevention, just as a physician would not be considered to be practicing good medicine who didn't believe in preventive medicine and left all that to the Center for Disease Control in Atlanta. We all have responsibility to change the social climate of attitudes toward the kind of drinking which causes such a large portion of our social ills. We need not favor neo-prohibitionism: drinking is not morally wrong for the non-alcoholic, but it is a known fact that alcoholism and alcohol problems are far more prevalent in those cultures which condone drunkenness, and we in America do just that with our humor and ideas of partying. Comedians notwithstanding, a "drunk" is not funny if alcoholism is involved.

A Family Illness

A major reason for this mention of prevention is the fact that alcoholism is a family disease. The spouse and family need help as much as or more than the alcoholic. Some do not like the term co-alcoholic, and certainly the word should not imply that the family illness is the same as alcoholism. But it can be just as devastating. The pastoral counselor needs to have a good grasp of the alcoholic family system, brilliantly described by the Episcopal clergyman Kellerman (1969) as "A Merry-Go-Round Named Denial" and by Jackson (1954) in a classic study, as well as by many more recent authors. Al-Anon family groups and literature are extremely important here; they are not just for wives of alcoholic men but for husbands of alcoholic women and any adult close to the problem. Alateen is for children of alcoholics, and both use the same twelve-step program of A.A. but with their own proper applications.

Note that all this is aimed at helping the family with their own emotional problems, regardless of whether the alcoholic is even still around, drinking or not. There are always residual problems for the one close to the problem regardless of whether the alcoholic has recovered, separated, divorced, died, or is still drinking and living with the family. Of course, if the alcoholic recovers as an indirect result of the family getting help, this is a welcome by-product; but it must be remembered that the family deserves help in its own right. More recently we have Adult Children of Alcoholics (COA, or ACOA) groups also using the Twelve Steps, along with literature describing the 40-year-old who is still struggling with the unresolved emotional problems and habits resulting from having grown up in an alcoholic family: guilt, perfectionism, need to control others, inability to enjoy, excessive sense of responsibility, mistrust, and many other problems (Black, 1981).

The connection with prevention is the stark reality that over half the children of alcoholic parents will become alcoholics themselves. The fact that it is not 100 percent shows that it is not necessary, but the frequency alerts us to the need for preventing it from happening as often as it does.

If proof were needed that alcoholism is not a matter of will power, we could point to the fact that these children all say "It Will Never Happen to Me" as the title of the book about them by Black (1981) so dramatically relates. They become alcoholics in spite of choosing not to. Knowledge of the alcoholic family dynamics will also be of great help in counseling with these grown-up children of alcoholics when seeking recovery for their own alcoholism. Again, guilt will be a major problem requiring pastoral help.

The family has its own ways of denying the problem. The wife will insist that her husband is too intelligent to be an alcoholic. In her mind this probably means a skid-row bum; little does she realize the number of doctors, attorneys, bankers, and even priests on skid row. "He's the finest husband and father in the world when he isn't drinking" is not merely emotional loyalty. Alcoholics seem to be on the average more intelligent and more talented. The husband of an alcoholic wife seems even more prone to denial. He cannot accept the fact that his beautiful bride whom he idealized is now a fallen angel. Moreover, it may be a matter of male pride that he cannot control his wife's drinking. The children are taught, more by example than by word, not to talk about it, not even to feel the emotions they are having about either the alcoholic parent or the spouse's irrational reactions and adjustments to the situation. The child from the alcoholic home is stereotyped as a juvenile delinquent, but more often they are the quiet, withdrawn child or the super-responsible over-achiever.

The counselor needs to understand that recovery by the alcoholic does not signal an instant state of health for the family. They have developed their own homeostatic adjustment to the drinking: the spouse controls the money and is the sole authority figure, has taken on the martyr role, and has taught the children to ignore the alcoholic and obey only the sober spouse. This reversal of roles will not be overthrown readily. Some families get so adjusted to an alcoholic environment that they think this is normal and cannot live out their proper roles in sobriety. It is easier to go along with the ways they have learned to adjust. This probably explains why so many daughters of alcoholic fathers end up marrying an alcoholic. As one of them explained, "I know what buttons to push." This is an example of what is meant by the whole family being sick, which is important to avoid usng just one member as a scapegoat, whether the alcoholic or the acting-out juvenile delinquent or the nagging wife. Al-Anon and Alateen are an important resource here.

Subconsciously the spouse may even sabotage the recovered alcoholic's sobriety to maintain the power or martyr role. This seems to happen even more often when the wife is the alcoholic. When she is drinking, the husband can be the superior one as well as the martyr; when she sobers up and becomes a person in her own right, perhaps with an I.Q. of 20 points higher than his, his male ego can't take it and he will set her up for a relapse. The car is never fixed when she has an A.A. meeting to go to, or he badgers her into having "just one" with him, or even says, "You were better in bed when you were drinking."

Fear of relapse is a major problem in the recovering alcoholic's family. As in any chronic illness, it is always a possibility and should not be discounted entirely. On the other hand, the family must learn that this is the alcoholic's responsibility and they should be neither over-protective nor guilt-ridden about it. A big point is that one relapse after treatment is common, and rather than looking on it as failure they all should realize that it is the beginning of a long and happy life of sobriety: the clincher argument that proves to alcoholics that they cannot drink socially. They heard this in the treatment center or at A.A. meetings, but didn't quite believe it applied to them until they tried one last time.

To conclude, we must emphasize that recovery is the bright side of alcoholism. Our major public health problem is also our most recoverable major illness. Contrary to the older attitudes among therapists, the fact is that work with this population is very gratifying. It is a joy to see recovered alcoholics getting well, looking and feeling good again, growing psychologically and spiritually. Alcoholism counseling is different from other counseling, both in method and because of the specialized knowledge required, but the rewards are great. The pastoral counselor has a special contribution to make because of the characteristics portrayed in this chapter.

Bibliography

Alcoholics Anonymous: The Story of How Many Thousands of Men and Women Have Recovered from Alcoholism. New York: Alcoholics Anonymous World Services, 1939; 3rd ed. 1976.

Alcoholics Anonymous, *A Clergyman Looks at A.A.* New York: Alcoholics Anonymous World Services, 1961.

Black, C. *It Will Never Happen to Me.* Denver: Medical Administration Co., 1981.

Jackson, J. "The Adjustment of the Family to the Crisis of Alcoholism." *Quarterly Journal of Studies on Alcohol*, 1954, 15, 562–586 (chapter 8 in Royce, 1981).

Johnson, V. *I'll Quit Tomorrow.* New York: Harper and Row, 1973.

Kellerman, J. *Alcoholism: A Merry-Go-Round Named Denial.* New York: Al-Anon Family Group Headquarters, 1969.

Kurtz, E. *Not-God: A History of Alcoholics Anonymous.* Center City: Hazelden, 1979.

Milam, J.R. *Under the Influence.* Seattle: Madrona, 1981.

Royce, J.E. *Alcohol Problems and Alcoholism: A Comprehensive Survey.* New York: Free Press,. 1981.

Sellner, E.C. *Christian Ministry and the Fifth Step.* Center City: Hazelden, 1981.

Srole, L. *Mental Health in the Metropolis: The Midtown Manhattan Study.* New York: McGraw-Hill, 1962.

Vaillant, G. *The Natural History of Alcoholism.* Cambridge: Harvard University Press, 1983.

Willoughby, A. *The Alcohol Troubled Person: Known and Unknown.* Chicago: Nelson-Hall, 1979.

Kenneth Byrne

Sexual Dysfunctioning

The issue of sexuality has become increasingly prominent in our society in the last two decades. The impact of this on the church was inevitable. It was only a matter of time before the question of sexual difficulties in marriage was to surface and challenge the pastoral counselor.

The expression of our sexuality is one of the most fundamental expressions of our relationship with God and our relationship to one another. It is a concrete representation of our need to reach out to others and to embrace them. "Indeed, our sexuality—in its fullest and richest sense—is both the physiological and psychological grounding of our capacity to love" (Nelson, 1978, p. 8). The most deeply satisfying sexual experiences always emerge from a context of an intimate, committed and loving relationship in which people have made a deep and lasting promise to know one another, with all of the implications of that knowing. As Norman Pittenger so eloquently points out, "Our sexuality is the ground or base . . . for our capacity to enter into relationships which are life-enhancing, life-enriching, and provide the possibility for humans to *become* what God would have them become: namely, fulfilled, integrated, sharing, and free recipients of the divine love" (Nelson, 1978, p. 6).

Unfortunately, many Christians were not lucky enough to be raised with such a positive and affirming view of sexuality. There have been innumerable interpretations of Christ's message which have reduced sexuality to the realm of the sinful, an experience to be shunned—perhaps even fearfully fled—as the embodiment of Satan's work. Thus, many who would wish to experience God's love through the challenge and mystery of a warm, loving and fully sexual relationship are handicapped by distorted ideas of what sexuality is. In many cases, this leads to difficulties—ranging from the mild and situational to the profound and potentially crippling— in the expression of sexuality. It becomes clear then that those suffering a sexual dysfunction also suffer a problem in their relationship with God.

The purpose of this chapter is to provide an introduction to the understanding and treatment of sexual dysfunctions. The pastoral counselor has a unique and powerful role in the treatment of these problems. The counselor is challenged to integrate a theology which affirms the expression of sexuality in the context of a loving and committed relationship as a celebration of Christ's lessons to us, with the modern psychological treatment of these disorders.

Human difficulties with sexuality have probably existed since our creation. Treatment for sexual incapacities are as old as recorded history. "Almost every imaginable 'witch's brew' and magic 'love potion' as well as innumerable physical manipulations . . . were tried without notable or predictable success" (Tyler, 1974, p. 409). Similarly, early psychiatric approaches to sexual dysfunctions met with uneven results at best. Beginning in the early 1960's and continuing through the present, significant advances have been made in a definition, description and treatment of sexual dysfunctions.

It is important to distinguish between sexual variations and sexual dysfunctions. Sexual variations describe sexual activity which has as its aim or focus some activity which differs from the norm in our society. No difficulty in actual functioning is implied. The fetishist, for example, who can only be sexually excited while fondling ladies' underwear, will be able to enjoy adequate erections and will achieve a full and enjoyable orgasm. The woman who can only be aroused in positions of bondage or humiliation can be easily aroused, lubricate and be orgasmic. Also called deviations or perversions, these kinds of sexual practices are more amenable to more traditional therapeutic methods.

In contrast, sexual dysfunctions cause difficulty in achieving or enjoying coitus. There are three syndromes seen in males, three seen in females, and one which is common to both.

Male Sexual Dysfunctions

Erectile Dysfunction. In this condition the man is unable to have an erection in a sexual situation. He may be sexually aroused and excited, and want to make love, but his penis does not become erect. Some men are able to ejaculate despite their flaccid penis. The precise point at which the man becomes anxious and then loses his erection varies widely. Some men can have erections with a mistress but not with a wife, or vice versa. Others have erections while clothed but not while undressed, or during foreplay but not when intercourse is expected. The only commonality is that the symptom prevents sexual intercourse. Men with *primary impotence* have never been successfully potent with a woman. Often, they can have erections either spontaneously or through masturbation. Those who have enjoyed a period of satisfactory functioning with a woman and then have difficulty are described as having *secondary impotence.*

The man who suffers with erectile dysfunction typically feels frustrated and humiliated. The symptom strikes at the heart of the physical representation of male self-esteem: the erection. It is not surprising to find that many clients with this symptom are also depressed. The problem also can have a serious impact on the marital relationship. Some wives experience their husbands' impotence as a personal rejection, and then pressure the husband into performing in order to reassure themselves, invariably worsening the situation.

Premature Ejaculation. Men with premature ejaculation are unable to exercise voluntary control over the reflex to ejaculate, reaching orgasm soon after becoming sexually excited. With some men this can occur with minimal foreplay. Many are able to insert their penis into the woman's vagina, but ejaculate quickly afterward. Many attempts have been made to quantify what constitutes "premature." Kaplan overrides these approaches in noting that " . . . the crucial aspect of prematurity is the *absence of voluntary control* over the ejaculatory reflex, regardless of whether this occurs after two thrusts or five, whether it occurs before the female reaches orgasm or not. Prematurity can thus be said to exist when orgasm occurs reflexly, i.e., when it is beyond the man's voluntary control once an intense level of sexual arousal is attained" (Kaplan, 1974, p. 290).

Like impotence, this problem is vexing and humiliating to the man who suffers from it, and frequently causes no end of distress for him and his partner. Often, the man tries a series of "distraction" devices, such as thinking about baseball scores, counting backward from one hundred, or pinching himself to cause minor pain. Often the wife is unaware that what appears to be her husband's coldness or detachment during love making is actually an attempt to minimize his excitement to avoid premature ejaculation.

Retarded Ejaculation. This condition is the exact opposite of premature ejaculation. The man is sexually aroused, achieves a firm erection, and has intercourse successfully. However, despite his urgent desire for the release of orgasm, he is unable to, despite what should be adequate stimulation. The severity of this condition can vary widely. In the mildest form, the man can have trouble ejaculating only in a specific situation, such as with a mistress. More commonly the problem occurs regularly with his wife. The man cannot achieve orgasms during intercourse, but can often do so with manual or oral stimulation by the wife. In some cases the man can only reach a climax by self-masturbation, typically engaging in fantasy as a distraction. The next step in the continuum is the man who cannot have orgasms in the presence of a woman, and, for example, must go into the bathroom to masturbate in order to climax. Finally, a small number of men have been so inhibited that they have never experienced orgasm. *Primary retarded ejaculators* have had this problem since their first attempt at intercourse. *Secondary retarded ejaculators* have enjoyed a period of satisfactory sexual functioning and then developed difficulty. As with the other conditions, men who suffer from this are quite distressed. Some will actually feign orgasm to avoid revealing their difficulty to their wife. In some cases, the man's anxious anticipation of failure can lead to secondary impotence. Wives have as disturbed response to this situation as to the other dysfunctions. Not uncommonly, the wife assumes that the problem is her lack of ability to "turn on" the man sufficiently, a quite incorrect conclusion.

Female Sexual Dysfunctions

General Sexual Dysfunction. This term generally replaces the outmoded and pejorative label of frigidity. Women with this difficulty describe experiencing virtually no sexual feeling. Their physical response varies from no lubrication to very mild lubrication with the stimulation of foreplay or intercourse. There are some clients who have never experienced sexual pleasure with a partner, and others who have been somewhat responsive in the past, but no longer are. Typically, this is seen in the woman who was aroused by touching or caressing before marriage, when intercourse was considered out of the question. After marriage, when intercourse becomes expected, the woman then becomes non-responsive.

The reaction to this condition varies widely. At one extreme is the woman who simply accepts her lack of feeling with patient resignation, and submits to intercourse to appease her spouse. Others can become saddened and dismayed, leading to a secondary depression. A not uncommon response is building resentment toward the man, both for the expectation he has and the pleasure he derives from sex. This response is often accompanied by a passive avoidance of intercourse. Some husbands are untroubled by their wives' lack of response, while others take it as a personal challenge to their artfulness as a lover. To reassure himself, the husband sometimes subtly or overtly pressures his wife for a more rewarding "performance," which only worsens matters.

Orgastic Dysfunction. This is undoubtedly the most common sexual difficulty among women. The term orgastic dysfunction means that the woman suffers from a specific inhibition in the total sexual response, namely, the ability to achieve orgasm. The woman may never have achieved an orgasm or may have begun having trouble after a period of having enjoyed successfully reaching climax. In *absolute* conditions the client cannot reach orgasm either with intercourse or other stimulation. In situational conditions she can have an orgasm, but only in circumscribed ways, such as masturbation. The woman who has trouble reaching orgasm is usually warm, loving and responsive to her husband. She typically enjoys sexual intercourse and her physical response is in all ways unimpaired. For these women the one problem is getting "stuck" at or near the plateau phase of the sexual response (Kaplan, 1974, p. 375).

Some women try to adapt to this difficulty by rationalizing its unimportance, often accompanied by a feigning of a climax. This can lead to a decreasing interest of lovemaking with a secondary depression. In some cases a generalized sexual dysfunction develops as a reaction. Other women are overtly unhappy and disturbed by their difficulty, and, as such, are more likely to seek help.

Vaginismus. This is a relatively rare condition in which the vaginal entrance involuntarily closes tightly when penetration is attempted. This reaction often extends to other situations, and not uncommonly gynecological exams are impossible without anesthesia. The situation is often accompanied by a deeply held, sometimes unconscious fear of penetration. This is a common cause of unconsummated marriages.

As would be expected, the response to this situation is typically an intense one. Many clients are shocked at their own response, having been previously interested in and excited by sexual play prior to first attempting intercourse. Their complete inability to tolerate intercourse often comes as a painful blow to their self-esteem.

The client seeking treatment is caught in a difficult dilemma: she is afraid of intercourse, and equally afraid of being cured, since by definition this means experiencing penetration. The spouse who suffers from marked sexual inhibition will be surprisingly tolerant of this situation. Others will attempt to force intercourse, which is almost impossible. Still others develop secondary impotence in reaction to their wives' inhibition.

Inhibited Sexual Desire: A Shared Symptom

The one sexual dysfunction found in both men and women is inhibited sexual dysfunction (ISD). People suffering from this difficulty complain of a lack of interest in sex. There is a notable absence of fantasies about sex. In situations which would be expected to evoke a sexual response there can instead be irritability, fear or tension. In Primary ISD the person has a life-long history of the absence of sexual feeling or fantasy. Not surprisingly, it is rare in the general population. Secondary ISD occurs when a period of sexual awareness is followed by a loss of sexual drive. With Global ISD there is no interest in sex at all. Most common is Situational ISD, where the client is aware of sexual drive in certain limited situations, and there is a distinct and surprising lack of libido in others—for example, the man who is sexually aroused by fantasies when he is alone, but feels no sexual attraction toward his loving and responsive wife, with whom he otherwise enjoys a satisfactory relationship.

Clearly, one difficulty in making the diagnosis of ISD is the question of what is normal sexual desire. The concept of normality is obviously relative, and to make a reasoned judgment the counselor must take into account factors such as the age, sex, physical health, current situational stressors, and previous patterns of adjustment of the client. It must also be noted that asexuality, in and of itself, does not constitute psychopathology. "Asexuality is certainly not always abnormal. . . . Some persons' sexual appetite falls on the low side of the normal distribution on the basis of constitutional determinants. Such persons are not bothered by the infrequency of their need for sex unless external circumstances exert pressure" (Kaplan, 1979, p. 68).

The response of the client and spouse to the problem of ISD varies widely. Some people accept the situation quite calmly, and live for years with no sexual activity. For others, the problem is a dramatic and painful challenge to their self-esteem. Some spouses are relieved by their mates' lack of desire, since this pattern complements their own anxieties about sexuality. Others are bitterly frustrated, and attempt a variety of strategies to help the situation, including extramarital affairs. Still others experience their mates' lack of interest as a personal rejection and become depressed.

ISD is probably the most frequent of all sexual dysfunctions. A review of cases at several programs for the treatment of sexual dysfunctions showed that approximately 40 percent of people requesting help suffered from ISD (Kaplan, 1979, p. 57). It should be noted that this is a sample of people who stepped forward and acknowledged a problem. The number of people who suffer in silence is as yet unknown, but may well be extremely high.

The Sexual History

There are three elements necessary to take a good sexual history, and they are presented here in their order of importance: a comfort with one's own sexuality, knowing what to ask about, and rudimentary interviewing skills.

Learning to talk with clients about sex usually raises strong feelings in the counselor. It offers myriad opportunities for errors deriving from the counselor's own anxiety. At the same time, it provides a wealth of opportunities to enhance the counseling relationship and to provide meaningful help to troubled clients.

The counselor's anxiety is revealed in many disguises. The most obvious in a bland denial of the subject, as is sometimes seen in the treatment of a married couple, where the counselor simply does not ask about their sexual relationship. The conclusion is then erroneously drawn that they don't have any sexual problems. A second version of this is the "hot potato" approach. The counselor asks one question, usually something like, "You don't have any sexual problems, do you?" The answer, not surprisingly, is a resounding "No!" and the counselor, feeling quite justified, moves on to other things. A third approach is the overly intellectualized interviewer, who speaks about sex as a philosophical discourse. This is usually complemented by a sprinkling of references to learned texts. All of this serves to help the interviewer get a large dose of emotional distance from his or her own feelings. Faced with this, the clients may talk about sex, but no real therapeutic work will get done. A more subtle disguise is the "show and tell" counselor, who gives the appearance of competence by bombarding the client with a host of questions about sexual matters, but then doesn't use the information to make constructive therapeutic interventions. The questions are motivated more by the counselor's sexual anxiety which is transformed into professional voyeurism, and the information being elicited is used only to titillate the counselor rather than to help the client. An equally smooth disguise is the "pass the buck" strategy. A client is troubled by a specific sexual dysfunction, such as premature ejaculation. The counselor discovers in the first interview that the client had a conflictual relationship with his mother. This is described to the client as the "real problem" and the discussion is henceforth limited to talking about the mother, leaving the symptom in the dust. While the mother may indeed have a good deal to do with the problem, this does not justify not talking about the symptom, or taking specific measures to alleviate it.

To talk meaningfully about sex with clients it is obviously essential that the counselor be reasonably at ease with his or her own sexuality. Supervision of one's work by a seasoned therapist is often helpful in detecting more subtle messages given to clients which may suggest that sex is "off limits" for discussion. It is also important that the therapist have knowledge of and appreciation for the wide breadth of human sexual behavior.

Most clients come to counseling with a pre-conceived idea about how the counselor will act and speak. These early transferences are often rooted in the client's association with friends who have had counseling, or by television and movies. Some clients may choose a pastoral counselor out of their own unconscious desire to avoid sex, reasoning that someone associated with the church wouldn't be interested in sex, or might be shocked by some of the sexual difficulties, thoughts or feelings that the client has. This pre-formed attitude provides an important opportunity for the counselor. By speaking openly and directly about sexuality, the counselor communicates a sense of comfort with sex, and indicates that this is an acceptable area for discussion and exploration. In this process, the counselor can reveal his or her own humanity and break up the transference of the client that a religious counselor is "above all of that."

For the purposes of organization, the history taking is divided into two sections, though in practice these naturally overlap. First, we need a clear and complete understanding of the specific symptom. Second, we need an understanding of the sexual development of the client and the spouse, and the attitudes and feelings which were engendered during this process. This information is usually gathered during the first few interviews, along with other data typically obtained at the start of counseling.

The most useful approach is to be direct and frank in inquiring about the difficulty. Virtually all clients will appreciate and respect the counselor who seriously and directly investigates a problem, rather than settling for a surface explanation. (The only exception to this is a client who is frankly paranoid, with whom a more indirect course must be taken.) There are a number of guidelines which will facilitate the process.

Don't settle for vague descriptions, such as "messing around" or "touching each other," since these provide little useful information. Respond by saying, "I'm afraid that's a bit vague—can you be more specific and tell me exactly what you mean?" If the client is unable to do this, follow-up questions can be more focused such as "Where do you like to be touched?" or "How long do you have foreplay before having intercourse?"

Begin with topics which are easier to discuss, and then move to ones which may provoke more anxiety. When clients have difficulty answering a question because of obvious embarrassment or anxiety, it is helpful to reassure them that they needn't worry about editing their response, or choosing what they feel are "the correct" words. If this doesn't help, simply inquiring along the lines of "Are you worried what I'll think of you if you were to tell me what's on your mind now?" can be helpful.

Precede questions with a statement about how commonplace or ordinary some experiences are. This both educates and reassures the client. For example, you might say, "Most people begin to masturbate as a child or an adolescent. Can you tell me when you first masturbated?"

Explain to the client why you are gathering certain information. This invariably helps in developing rapport, and enables the person to more readily tell you what you need to know. For example, "In order to get the best understanding of this difficulty, I need to learn more about your background and your sexual development."

In understanding the specific symptom, we want to know "when, where, who and what." The following questions can be useful, but are offered as only a guide, not a rigid format.

1. When did the problem first begin?
2. Where were you and whom were you with?
3. What was happening? How did you feel during this?
4. When does the problem occur now? How often is this?
5. Was there ever a time when you didn't have this problem?
6. Does the symptom change under different circumstances (e.g., different room, different time of the day, different partner if available)?

We also want to understand the clients' sexual history—how did they come to develop their feelings and attitudes about themselves, their body, sexuality, and their intimate relationships with others. The following questions again are offered as a guideline:

1. What was it like growing up in your house?
2. Can you describe each of your parents to me as people?
3. How did your parents deal with sexuality in your family? What impressions did you gain from them?
4. When did you first become aware of sex?
5. When did you begin to masturbate? Do you recall what you thought about that was exciting to you? Do you masturbate now? What do you usually think about?
6. Did you date as a teenager? What was it like for you?
7. What was your reaction to your first "wet dream" (males) or to the start of menstruation (females)?
8. When did you first have intercourse? How was it?
9. What was the most pleasant sexual experience you've had? The most unpleasant?

All of these questions should serve only as a tentative guide, and must be modified as necessary with each couple. Frequently, the more detailed sexual history will be taken with each spouse alone, and some aspects of it may be reviewed with the couple to clarify any misunderstanding, or to provide needed background information that they may not have shared with one another. Naturally, this is an area where extreme tactfulness must be exercised.

Finally, it should be kept in mind that no amount of technical interviewing skill, or knowledge about sexuality, can replace a genuine sense of personal comfort with oneself in the area of sexuality, and a warm concern for interest in helping other people.

Treatment of Sexual Dysfunctions

Kaplan (1974, 1979) provides a thorough discussion of the etiology of all of the sexual dysfunctions, including a variety of theoretical understandings. Most of these dysfunctions may be brought on by some undetected physical illness or as a response to medication. It is only when the symptom is clearly and unarguably situational that a psychological cause can be presumed without physical examination. Such a case would be the man who repeatedly suffers premature ejaculation with his wife, but not with a mistress.

Many sex therapy practitioners routinely begin treatment with a physical and/or gynecological examination, usually by a medical consultant. Tyler (1974) notes that in approximately 5 percent of cases the etiology is partially or wholly related to some physical cause. He recommends a general physical exam, including thorough observation by the physician of genital anatomy prior to treatment, which is certainly a reasonable approach. To the contrary, he cautions against undertaking a series of highly specialized investigative procedures on a routine basis.

A wide variety of approaches to treatment have become popular in the last decade. These include the use of artificial devices, such as penile splints and vibrators, a range of behavioral therapy approaches, hypnosis, and a variety of medications. In the majority of cases the underlying problem is a psychological one. "Overwhelmingly, human sexual-incapacity problems presented by patients are the consequences of (1) faulty learning, (2) inadequate knowledge, (3) inexperience, or (4) anxiety. Only a therapy program addressing itself to these defects has any chance of consistent success" (Tyler, 1974, p. 411). One symptom common to many clients is that they have little or no awareness of their own bodies' sexual feelings and responses.

The Sensate Focus approach pioneered by Masters and Johnson (1970) has emerged as the cornerstone of sex therapy. Typically, the couple is given detailed instructions for sharing mutual body massages for set periods of time under certain constraints. For example, the couple is instructed to set aside 30–45 minutes of uninterrupted time. They are to lie on a bed together nude, and take turns massaging one another. One is initially "the giver" and the other "the receiver." In the first phase they are typically forbidden by the therapist to have any sexual stimulation or to have intercourse. This prohibition is designed to eliminate performance anxieties by either partner. The purpose of the exercises is to help each person develop a keener, more focused appreciation of their own sexual responses. Contrary to popular belief, people with sexual dysfunctions are usually quite insensitive to their own responses. A common schedule would be to do this exercise every other evening between once-weekly therapy sessions. Response to the exercise is typically rather dramatic, often producing a wealth of dynamic material and sometimes a decrease in anxiety and improvement in the relationship. A covert benefit of the exercises is that in order to comply, the couple is forced to spend a considerable amount of time alone together, relaxing, something which troubled couples rarely experience.

Kaplan (1974, 1979) describes a detailed approach to treatment which is an integration of carefully prescribed sexual exercises, including Sensate Focus, and psychotherapy. The treatment format is kept flexible and responsive to the specific needs and symptoms of the couple. Thus, there may be one or two therapists, and the couple may be seen together at times or individually as necessary. The behavioral exercises are an integration of a vast amount of previous work, and are kept highly flexible and individualized. The treatment can be a largely supportive-educational approach, focusing mainly on a specific symptom with almost no interpretation of dynamic or unconscious issues. This could be seen in the treatment of certain premature ejaculators. Kaplan reports that " . . . on the average, premature ejaculation is relieved in 6.5 sessions conducted over a period of 3 to 6 weeks" (Kaplan, 1974, p. 200). Other cases may require an extended period of treatment, with a good deal of effort spent in gradually helping one or both partners to overcome long-standing personality traits which block sexual responsiveness. One of the significant features of Kaplan's contribution is the detailed reporting of a variety of case studies.

There is an old joke which underlines an important aspect of sexual dysfunctions. A man asks his wife, "Why don't you ever tell me when you have an orgasm?" The wife responds, "You're never around." The joke points out that in the majority of cases the sexual dysfunction takes place in the context of an ongoing relationship between two people. Most often, the counselor will also find difficulties in how the two people communicate, about sex and about lots of other issues. It is essential then that the counselor also provide help in improving communication skills of the couple. It is often useful to coach the partners on communicating clearly what they experience sexually, and what they would like the other person to do. They should avoid blaming and accusing the other. Similarly, most couples tend to "mind read," assuming they know what the other is thinking without bothering to "check it out." Teaching the couple to avoid this pitfall and to rely on clarifying what the other is saying—either verbally or non-verbally—can be quite useful in alleviating communication problems. Finally, educating them about the nature of the sexual dysfunction, and the probable reasons for it, and providing reassurance that they can be helped goes a long way in reducing anxiety.

It should be noted that the specific goal of the treatment for sexual dysfunction is the alleviation of the symptom. This therapy is quite different than either marital counseling or individual psychotherapy, insofar as the goals are much more limited. Commonly, a couple will achieve improvement in a sexual relationship, and then request further help alleviating other troubles between them.

Questions Clients Ask

The pastoral counselor should anticipate and be ready for the common questions which clients will pose, either in the context of initially discussing their sexual dysfunctions, or during the course of treatment with either the pastoral counselor or another therapist. Some of the more common ones are listed here, with some possible approaches for handling them. This is in no way a complete list, and the answers are provided only as starting points to be refined as the individual counselor finds necessary.

"Isn't devoting all this time 'working on' our marriage pretty self-centered? As Christians, shouldn't we be more concerned with helping others?" Here, the client must be helped to view their own marriage within a larger context. It also must be pointed out that when suffering with an unhappy marriage, one is ill equipped to be of service to others. In discussing this question, Clinebell makes the following point: "Enrichment of individual marriages is potentially a powerful resource for enriching life in society. The impact can be like a pebble dropped in a pond. The first circle beyond the marriage pair is the immediate family. Parents are the architects and builders of a family; whatever makes their marriage better will strengthen the personality health of their children. The outreach of enriched couples can help build a network of mutual support among families. This gradually strengthens the wholeness-sustaining fabric of a congregation and community. Couples who have mutually-satisfying marriages have the inner resources to reach out to even wider circles" (Clinebell, 1975, p. 26).

At times, treatment for sexual dysfunction includes either individual or mutual masturbation. This leads to another question: "Isn't masturbation always sinful?" Masturbation may well be the one sexual practice which has produced the most shame and guilt. Although there is no medical or psychological evidence that masturbation in and of itself produces any physical or psychological damage, it is still widely thought to be evil or harmful. In a thoughtful consideration of the subject, Nelson concludes: ". . . masturbation *can* be that occasional gift through which we are graced to break through the sexual dualisms that beset and alienate us. We need to pass beyond the preoccupation with the physical act itself and to inquire with greater sensitivity about its meanings" (Nelson, 1978, p. 173). In the context of therapy for sexual dysfunctions masturbation needs to be seen as a step toward achieving a more satisfying and rewarding marital relationship.

In a similar way, the encouragement of sexual fantasy is often essential in the treatment of sexual dysfunction. Some clients may say: "I'd rather not have these impure thoughts." Along with this is the common anxiety about the kind of sexual fantasies the client has, with the fear that they are either sinful or in some way abnormal. In fact, a certain degree of sexual fantasy is normal and desirable. In therapy, the use of fantasy is usually directed toward helping clients overcome an inhibition of sexual feeling which blocks the joyful communion of the couple. "It (fantasy) can enrich times of intercourse with the beloved not only by enhancing one's own sexual excitement, but also, in shared fantasies, it can create moods of sheer delight together. Fantasy can allow outlet of a compensatory kind for sexual feelings and desires which our value commitments do not permit us to act out. Paradoxically, it can bring freeing and enriching qualities to the convenanted relationship by refusing to insist that the partner be the sole source of satisfaction for the varied sexual desires one might have" (Nelson, 1978, pp. 161–162).

Virtually everyone has sexual fantasies at one time or another, and the only choice we have is to acknowledge this part of our humanity or to deny and repress it. To follow the second course is generally unwise, since it relegates the sexual feelings to the unconscious, where they will seek expression in some other way. It is important to reassure the client that sexual fantasy is just one part of who we are, and that the preferable course is to welcome these fantasies as an expression of our humanity and our interest in embracing others. They can be used creatively in the therapy to strengthen the marital relationship. Regarding the content of sexual fantasy, the specific details are diagnostic of the client's view of human relationships and sexuality. It is therefore important to reassure the client that any kind of fantasy he or she may have is acceptable and welcomed, and that thoughts or ideas aren't wrong or sinful. By the same token, allowing oneself to have sexual fantasies does *not* make it more likely that these will be translated into actual behavior. For many clients, it is helpful to explain that if one is aware of sexual impulses or feelings, and accepts them readily for what they are, it is actually less likely that they will be impulsively acted on. To the contrary, once known, they can be put to constructive use in improving one's marital relationship.

For successful sex therapy, there is often a period of frequent sexual contact guided by constraints placed on the couple by the therapist. The purpose of this sexual activity is to improve the functioning of one or both partners. This can sometimes lead to the question, "I thought the primary purpose of sex was reproduction. Why should we be putting all this emphasis on pleasure?" Contained in this question is a rejection and even hatred of one's bodily self, surely not what God wants for us. The theological question of the ultimate purpose of sexuality is a complex one, and for the purpose of this paper, is perhaps best left with the individual counselor. The attitude of rejecting pleasure is another matter. The particular danger here is that this attitude, often deeply held, can be used to work against the treatment goals of improvement in sexual functioning. The job of the counselor is to help the clients see that, though they may have been taught this by the church, this represents misguided thinking. The experience of sexual pleasure is a force created by God, intended to be used productively and lovingly by human beings. Pleasure aids us in experiencing our sensual unity, and leads directly to being more open to our spouse. To be truly loving in a marriage one must be free to welcome and enjoy the physical pleasures of sexuality.

Case Examples

John, age 28, and Mary, age 26, had met with their pastor for several visits prior to being married by him. Both had declined having intercourse prior to marriage, though they had enjoyed a good deal of petting. A modest two-week honeymoon led to quite enjoyable and satisfactory sexual relations, especially considering the natural stresses of such a time. After marriage they lived with Mary's parents for two months, and then moved into their own home. After moving in with his in-laws, John immediately began to experience premature ejaculation. Puzzled and humiliated, he said little to Mary. Shortly thereafter he had trouble getting an erection at all. When they moved to their own home, things did not improve. John consulted his family doctor, who offered some general reassurance which did not seem to help. John did not ask his physician for a referral, and when he was finally able to discuss the subject with Mary, she suggested returning to their pastor.

In the initial interview both were rather nervous and reluctant to directly discuss the problem. With warm but direct questioning the following history emerged. While at the home of Mary's parents they had slept in a room above the parents' bedroom. John had been quite anxious that they would be overheard making love. When pressed by the pastor John acknowledged that he was afraid that Mary's father in particular would be "disgusted and mad" to know John was having intercourse with his daughter. Mary's parents had not been in complete agreement with her decision to wed John, and had let her know this unequivocally. It emerged that she viewed John's difficulty, at least in part, as God's punishment for disobeying her parents. Both partners had a reasonably healthy outlook on sex, and neither showed signs of any other psychological difficulty. Their relationship had been a bit difficult in the area of sex, but was otherwise quite satisfactory to both.

The pastor explained that John's anxiety while living with Mary's parents was quite understandable. The symptom of premature ejaculation was a natural result of the anxiety. He was trying—without being aware of it—to get things over as quickly as possible, lessening chances that Mary's father would overhear them. The secondary impotence occurred because he became more and more anxious about his performance. The pastor discussed Mary's feeling of guilt, and reassured her that it was understandable but unreasonable to view the symptom as God's revenge.

Next, the pastor instructed the couple in the "stop-start" treatment for premature ejaculation. This involves the male relaxing on his back, nude, while his wife strokes his penis. As he begins to feel an orgasm approaching he signals her and she stops. They both relax while the urge to ejaculate subsides. The man is instructed to focus all of his attention on the sensations which lead up to the feeling of orgasm and is specifically instructed not to focus attention on his wife, and not to try to control the experience of orgasm. The exercise is repeated several times, following which the man may ejaculate. Attempts at intercourse are forbidden at this stage. After several sessions of this exercise, the wife is instructed to use vaseline in stroking the penis, a sensation which more approximately simulates intercourse. After several sessions of this method, the couple is usually ready to attempt intercourse, since by this time the man has achieved quite good control of the ejaculatory reflex.

The couple completed the homework exercises as instructed over a period of several weeks. By this time John had resumed his earlier ejaculatory competence, and counseling sessions were discontinued.

This case demonstrates the treatment of a relatively straightforward and uncomplicated symptom. The essential elements in the "cure" were the pastor's accepting and reassuring attitude, coupled with his friendly but determined interviewing style. He was able to indicate to the couple his own acceptance of sexuality, and knew exactly what information to ask for. The pastor was also able to assuage Mary's guilt feelings. The "stop-start" method reduces anxiety in the couple by taking the emphasis off of intercourse, and rapidly builds the expectation of success, since the male is able to withhold and control the ejaculatory response.

Bill, age 31, and Nancy, age 28, have been married for eighteen months. Prior to marriage they had attempted intercourse several times but were unsuccessful because "Nancy just tightened up" and couldn't permit penetration. She had reassured Bill that this was because premarital intercourse made her feel very guilty, and that things would improve after they were married. Instead, the situation had become worse and they had as yet not had intercourse. There had been a good deal of crying, bitterness and anger between the two, about almost every aspect of their life together. This represented a worsening of a pattern which existed before marriage.

Mary also suffered from a series of anxieties and periodically had panic attacks. Bill was a highly compulsive, rigid man, with little capacity for warmth or sharing relationships with others. The parents of both clients had a moderately severe psychiatric history.

Both people were quite devoted and active in their church life. They had both known their pastor well and enjoyed great confidence in her. After several visits in which she tried unsuccessfully to improve the couple's communication skills, the pastor decided that a long period of treatment would be needed. She referred the couple to a therapist in private practice with whom she was acquainted and who she knew had specific expertise in the treatment of sexual dysfunctions. Somewhat reluctantly, Bill and Nancy accepted this referral.

The couple made a satisfactory beginning in treatment, but as soon as the Sensate Focus exercises were prescribed, Mary raised objections, primarily on religious grounds. She complained that it was un-Christian to be so indulgent. With some probing, she also confided in feeling guilty about having sexual fantasies, saying that she preferred to simply "not think about that stuff."

Sensing these arguments as a smokescreen for Nancy's anxiety, the therapist suggested that the couple have a consultation with their pastor, and requested permission to call her. He shared his concern with the pastor, and asked her to see what she might do to help things along. In the consultation the pastor was able to allow Nancy to fully discuss her concerns, while at the same time clarifying that her thinking was not entirely in line with the church's beliefs. This enabled the pastor to gently confront Nancy with her reluctance to face the anxiety which the "homework assignments" generated. She encouraged Nancy to review this with the therapist.

This consultation set the format for several more which took place over the next two years. Whenever the therapist found himself running into the religious beliefs of either partner, he suggested such a consultation. Occasionally, the pastor could agree with the couple, and advised the therapist of the specific teachings in question. On other occasions, her discussion with the couple led to similar confrontations like the first one. Eventually the couple's relationship could be improved to the point where Nancy could participate in the behavioral exercises. She gradually became able to tolerate penetration, though it took a much longer time before she was able to be orgasmic with intercourse.

Further Recommendations

Understanding the concepts outlined in this article will provide the pastoral counselor with a basic grasp of sexual dysfunctions. Two caveats must be considered when applying these concepts to work with clients. First, working with sexual dysfunctions doesn't suit the temperament of everyone, and under most circumstances it would be a mistake to undertake the treatment of these disorders unless this is something one really wants to do. This means that there is readiness to face whatever anxieties there are regarding sexuality, and making a commitment to resolve them, through supervision, personal psychotherapy, or both. Second, in order to undertake the actual treatment of sexual dysfunctions, further study and training is required. There are, however, those counselors who practice in more remote areas with little professional support who have clients desperately in need of help. In this case, the pastoral counselor is "the only game in town" and must rely on reading as the primary source of instruction.

Clearly the major texts by Kaplan, and Masters and Johnson referred to throughout this chapter would be the natural starting place. *Masters and Johnson Explained* (Lehrman, 1970) will be a welcome addition for most readers. A starting point for further instruction on the sexual variations would be the articles by Bieber (1974), Money (1974), and Bak and Stewart (1974).

Some interesting and practical suggestions for integrating Christian concepts with the treatment of sexual dysfunctions are described by David and Duda (1977). Cavanagh (1983) reviews normal sexual development and discusses its role in marriage and religious life. In his book *Embodiment: An Approach to Sexuality and Christian Theology* (1978), Nelson offers a scholarly and insightful discussion of topics such as "Sexual Salvation: Grace and the Resurrection of the Body" and the "Morality of Sexual Variations," to name only two. He bravely takes on some of the otherwise neglected topics, such as Homosexuality and the Sexually Disenfranchised, including the physically disabled, the aged, the seriously ill and the mentally retarded. This work is highly recommended. Small (1974) describes his book *Christian: Celebrate Your Sexuality* as an "evangelical" approach to human sexuality. In a brief review Hiltner (1975) considers this a competent and basically conservative book, and notes: "The author's constructive arguments are always provocative of serious reflection, whether one accepts them in entirety or not" (p. 36).

Some counselors might like to approach the question of sexuality in a broader context. Clinebell (1975, 1977) offers two very practical guides for conducting both marriage counseling and enrichment retreats and groups. These books will be quite useful to any pastoral counselors participating in or considering either kind of work. Finally, the *Journal of Sex and Marital Therapy* will provide an ongoing source of excellent articles on all aspects of sex and marital therapy. It is a clinical and therapeutically oriented journal which reports on new therapeutic techniques, research on outcome and special clinical problems.

There are an endless number of continuing education workshops on the current scene. Unfortunately, the area of sexuality has had more than its share of exploitive charlatans holding themselves out as "experts." The one watchword in seeking further training is "Caution!" When considering taking further training, don't be reassured by the usual credentials in the helping professions, such as psychiatry, psychology, social work or nursing. Be certain that the educators have had thorough and responsible education specifically in the treatment of sexual dysfunctions.

It is hoped that this paper will be a springboard to counselors to more skillfully understand the sexual difficulties of clients, and to integrate this understanding with a theology which affirms sexuality as one of God's most precious gifts. The pastoral counselor is in a powerful and unique position to bring relief to the many people troubled by sexual difficulties. To be informed of the nature of these problems, and ready to deal with them, either by active counseling or by appropriate referral, will provide an invaluable service to those who place their trust in us.

Bibliography

Bak, R.C. and Steward, W.A. "Fetishism, Transvestitism and Voyeurism: A Psychoanalytic Approach." In Arieti, S. and Brody, E. (ed.), *The American Handbook of Psychiatry*, Vol. III. New York: Basic Books, 1974.

Bieber, I. "Sadism and Masochism: Phenomenology and Psychodynamics." In Arieti, S. and Brody, E. (ed.), *The American Handbook of Psychiatry*, Vol. III. New York: Basic Books, 1974.

Cavanagh, M.E. "The Impact of Psychosexual Growth on Marriage and Religious Life." *Human Development*, 1983, Vol. 4, pp. 16–24.

Clinebell, H.J., Jr. *Growth Counseling for Marriage Enrichment.* Philadelphia: Fortress Press, 1975.

Clinebell, H.J., Jr. *Growth Counseling for Mid-Years Couples.* Philadelphia: Fortress Press, 1977.

David, J.R. and Duda, F.C. "Christian Perspectives on the Treatment of Sexual Dysfunction." *Journal of Psychology and Theology,* Vol. 5 (4), 1977, pp. 322–336.

Hiltner, S., Ph.D. "Three Contributions to Understanding Human Sexuality." *Pastoral Psychology,* Vol. 24 (228), Fall 1975, pp. 30–39.

Kaplan, H.S. (ed.). *The New Sex Therapy.* New York: Brunner/Mazel, 1974.

Kaplan, H.S. (ed.). *Disorders of Sexual Desire.* New York: Brunner/Mazel, 1979.

Lehrman, N. (ed.). *Masters and Johnson Explained.* Scranton: Playboy Press, 1970.

Journal of Sex and Marital Therapy.

Money, J. "Intersexual and Transexual Behavior and Syndromes." *The American Handbook of Psychiatry.* New York: Basic Books, 1974, pp. 334–351.

Nelson, J.B. *Embodiment: An Approach to Sexuality and Christian Theology.* New York/Philadelphia: The Pilgrim Press, 1978.

Small, D.H. *Christian: Celebrate Your Sexuality.* Old Tappan: Fleming H. Revell Company, 1974.

Tyler, E.A. "Sexual-Incapacity Therapy." In Arieti, S. and Brody, E. (ed.), *The American Handbook of Psychiatry,* New York: Basic Books, 1974, Vol. III.

Coval B. MacDonald

Loss and Bereavement

The scope of research and literature related to loss and bereavement has significantly increased since the original impetus on this topic in the United States by Lindemann (1944), and now encompasses numerous disciplines and helping professions. Parameters to the current discussion before us, therefore, are essential. This discussion will draw on recent contributions to our subject from three disciplines: social psychology, psychiatry and pastoral theology. These contributions are not only recent but also distinct. The state-of-the-art on loss and bereavement will be our focus.

A recent and distinct contribution from social psychology is *Bitter, Bitter Tears: Nineteenth-Century Diarists and Twentieth-Century Grief Theories* by Paul C. Rosenblatt (1983). Using quantitative research methodologies of the social sciences, Rosenblatt goes beyond the useful but limited anecdotal material and vignettes frequently cited as clinical examples of loss and bereavement. He examines 56 diaries which include 140 deaths and 178 separations. In addition, the longitudinal and nineteenth-century data shape the distinct nature of his research, and introduce something other than anecdotes and vignettes on grief. His findings are necessary to any current discussion on grief.

In the field of psychiatry, *Time and the Inner Future: A Temporal Approach to Psychiatric Disorders* by Frederick Towne Melges (1982) introduces a distinct understanding to Time which has a direct bearing on experiences of loss and their associated grief. Although Melges applies his understanding of Time to a variety of emotional dysfunctions, his chapter on grief-resolution is both distinct and representative of the state-of-the-art. His contribution to our discussion is essential.

The prime and explicit focus of the discussion, however, is pastoral counseling with its associated disciplines: pastoral care and pastoral theology. Kenneth Mitchell and Herbert Anderson in *All Our Losses, All Our Griefs* (1983) provide perhaps the best single text on loss and bereavement from the theological perspective. Their concern for the "genesis" of loss in relation to the reality of finitude clearly makes a distinct contribution to the state-of-the-art on grief. This discussion, therefore, will proceed with Mitchell and Anderson as the organizing parameter, consonant with a focus on pastoral work. The special contributions of grief by Rosenblatt and Melges will enter that discussion at the appropriate places. It is hoped that pastoral ministry to persons who grieve will, thereby, be enriched.

Grief: What It Is Not, What It Is

Mitchell and Anderson stress the importance of viewing grief from a new perspective. That is, grief is not a disease. "We do not regard it as a disease entity." With a vivid image (p. 57), they state, "Grief is a part of life in a way that measles are not; to be wounded is not to be sick." A prevalent view that grief is to be overcome, with its implicit notion of cure, is rejected. As an essential component of life, grief is "lived through," neither overcome nor cured. Second, the process of bereavement is not characterized by certain stages, particularly, the stages of dying. The general confusion between grieving and dying is confronted directly by Mitchell and Anderson (p. 60) when they state, "Dying and grieving cannot, therefore, be taken as identical. It is an error to imagine that the stages of dying made familiar by Elisabeth Kubler-Ross—denial, anger, bargaining, depression and acceptance or resignation—are necessarily the stages of grieving. . . . The two processes do not tend toward the same end." This error, however, is widespread in the helping professions. Furthermore, if there are general "stages" to grieving, they are so broad as to render them meaningless as stages per se. Third, grief cannot be reduced to a single or primary emotional state, such as anxiety. Bringing into question any form of reductionism at this point, Mitchell and Anderson (p. 56) remind us: "So to reduce the feelings we experience does not give us an approach comprehensive enough to cover the almost infinite variety of loss experiences in human life." Finally, grief is not limited to death experiences alone. We tend to think of grief in such limited terms, and thereby miss the impact of all our losses and all our griefs.

The basically linear view that grief passes through general stages is questioned by Mitchell and Anderson. Rosenblatt's research on diaries of the nineteenth-century also questions this linear view. As he states (p. 21), ". . . the detailed data from the diaries seem to indicate that grief comes and goes recurrently. It does not seem, in the thoughts and feelings of the typical diarist, to wane gradually but to be absent some of the time and present some of the time. The diary data show that, rather than grief or thoughts of the lost person becoming steadily weakened, times of remembering alternate with times of no mention of the lost. . . . The intensity, duration, and some qualitative aspects of grief probably change over time, but the peaks of emotional intensity, even after several years have passed, may still be quite elevated." In short, the diaries do not show a gradual decline of the grief experience over time, with the associated implications of "stages of grief." On the contrary, and depending on the circumstances of the grieved person, intense grief can be experienced even several years after the loss. In a time when we tend to think of stages in many areas of the psychological disciplines, the experience of grief tends to resist the general flow of any stage approach and confronts us with the erratic and unpredictable power of loss itself.

If grief is not a disease, is not reducible to one primary emotion, is not to be characterized by stages and is not limited to the loss of a loved one through death, then what is grief?

Grief, above all, is ordinary, an essential part of human experience. It is not a disease to be cured. Mitchell and Anderson stress (p. 56): "Our intention is to maintain the ordinariness of grief." Thus, grief is brought back into the mainstream of life itself, without apologies and without the fear of disease. But why is grief ordinary? It is ordinary due to the genesis of grief. As a fundamental thesis, Mitchell and Anderson affirm (p. 20), "The genesis of grief lies in the inevitability of both attachment and separation for the sustenance and development of human life." Grief is ordinary to the degree that attachment and separation are both inevitable. "There is no life without attachment or loss; hence there is no life without grief." Grief is inevitable. Grief, therefore, is ordinary. The *genesis* of grief makes grief ordinary.

Drawing from the work of Margaret Mahler, the psychological "hatching" of the infant at three months is cited as a fundamental experience of loss. This ordinary experience of infants, with its associated reduction of activity and increased withdrawal, reflects a universal and primary experience of loss and bereavement. In the acute experience of grief in the adult, reduction of normal activity and withdrawal tap into this root loss of the hatching experience. The manifest "selfishness" of acute grief experiences are, therefore, ordinary and understandable. Mitchell and Anderson also cite the work of Melanie Klein as they develop the genesis of grief. As the infant differentiates between "Me" and "Not-Me," the infant gives up various attachments to its loved objects but then builds internal constructs which permit continued attachments to those loved objects. Referring to Klein, they point out (p. 24), "The development of a lively sense of self depends on having an internal world of reliable images to which one is attached." That "world of reliable images" is ordinary in the human world; the loss of those and other attachments precipitates the ordinariness of grief in that human world. Bereavement is not a disease. The genesis of grief is further established in Mitchell and Anderson by reference to the attachment theory of John Bowlby (1969). The primary, autonomous and lifelong character of attachment behavior places any loss of attachment squarely in the domain of ordinariness.

Individuation in the infant at three months and setting in place reliable images which modify attachments to loved objects continues throughout life. While psychological "hatching" is crucial in individuation, it is not absolutely determinative. Because attachment and separation from attachments continue in the life span of a person, grief is pervasive and persistent. This pervasive and persistent experience occurs at the loss of a pet, the series of "lasts" in the senior year of high school (Hayes, 1981), the loss of a job, the loss of property, the loss of power by persons who have been sexually abused, the loss of mobility expressed by older persons, the loss of a spouse in divorce, etc. During a life span, grief from such losses is unique, unpredictable and really never ends totally. In this sense, the ordinariness of grief, with its genesis in infancy, keeps before us *all* our losses and *all* our griefs and not just grief related to the death of loved persons.

The task of building "reliable images" during experiences of loss provides dynamic linkages to grief-resolution. This link is one of the most exciting state-of-the-art components in understanding and treating grief experiences. Mitchell and Anderson (pp. 125–131) develop at length the importance of remembering in grief-resolution, but do not explicitly link this to building reliable images; it is assumed this is implied. However, remembering, and its dynamic tie to setting in place reliable images of the lost object, needs to be made more explicit. Melges (pp. 195–214) in his chapter on grief-resolution makes this tie more explicit, though not completely so, in his use of guided imagery in the treatment of grief. It is here suggested that both remembering and guided imagery are essentially experiences of "building reliable images" with which to enter one's future. This point will be discussed further under the treatment of grief. It is mentioned here to highlight the importance of reliable images for both diagnosis and treatment of grief.

In addition to being ordinary, loss can be classified by six major types according to Mitchell and Anderson (pp. 36–51): material, relationship, intrapsychic, functional, role and systemic. However, the ways in which these losses are experienced will also shape our experience of the loss itself. Loss may be avoidable or unavoidable, temporary or permanent, actual or imagined, anticipated or unanticipated, or one might leave or be left. New knowledge on loss and bereavement now focuses on the last way of experiencing loss: leaving or being left. Rosenblatt (pp. 81–87) devotes special attention to Leavers vs. Left since data from the diaries deal with this special experience rather extensively, no doubt because it was a common phenomenon in the frontier days. Rosenblatt (p. 83) found that "the person who was left was much more likely than the leaver to mention the lost person" in the entries of the diaries. There was a small difference between leavers and left; but within that difference two variables stand out: the diarist's age and residence with the lost person. Those under thirty were equally high in their grief response whether they left or were left; but the older diarists, who tended to cope with separations, "reacted more strongly when they were left (when reminders were present) than when they were leavers. This was true when the older diarist was living with the person at the time of leaving." Mitchell and Anderson introduce the subtle but powerful differences in leaving or being left. Rosenblatt's diaries introduce data, especially age and residence, which further challenge our understanding of loss and bereavement. The importance of further work in this area, Leavers vs. Left, is clear when we know this is the experience of most persons who experience divorce, a major issue in our time (cf. Weiss, 1975).

Grief is ordinary. Grief is associated with a process of attachment and separation which is buffered by reliable images. Third, however, grief manifests significant distortions of Time. Mitchell and Anderson (p. 92) briefly refer to time distortions as time passing slowly or quickly in a grief experience, as the future and past without meaning. Melges makes clear that distortions of time, in grief as well as other emotional stresses, include more than the rate of Time—it passes slowly or quickly—or the meaning one gives to it. Distortions also include sequence and temporal organization, succession of events and large spans of awareness involving both past and future. Melges (p. 1) proposes that distortions of rate, sequence and temporal organization disrupt the "interplay of future images, plans of action and emotions." When this happens, "lack of anticipatory control and vicious cycles (spirals) may ensue." Time distortions in loss and bereavement properly include rate, sequence and temporal organization as components of psychological time which have significant impact on the course of grief work itself. Grief can become a vicious spiral downward deriving its power from distortions of psychological time, including but not limited to rate. The extensive and sustained analysis of psychological time by Melges provides crucial factors for understanding the time distortions in grief which Mitchell and Anderson briefly address. More specific contributions by Melges follow in the next section.

Grief: Working with The Bereaved Person

If the ordinariness of grief means anything, it means that all persons experience significant grief. That includes helpers, be they psychologists, psychiatrists, pastoral counselors, social workers, genuine friends. To work with bereaved persons, therefore, the helper needs to come to personal terms with his or her own experiences of loss. Referring to Norman Paul, Mitchell and Anderson (p. 110, p. 178) select two quotations which are worth repeating here: "Before a person can empathize with someone who has those feelings [of grief], he must have been able to accept those feelings in himself." "The ability of the therapist to empathize with grief and other painful states seems related to his capacity for reflective review of feelings generated by comparable situations in his own life." To this add the words of Melges (p. 212) in working with persons who grieve and need help, "Short term complications include . . . emotional draining of the therapist in empathizing with the relived scenes" and "The patient, the therapist, and the social network often have to be prepared for the patient to get worse, in terms of increased emotional turmoil, before getting better." The pastor and the pastoral counselor who want to help persons in their grief need a "capacity for reflective review" on personal loss and grief as well as "preparation" for a journey that is difficult for all concerned. In short, helping persons who grieve requires more than good intentions and a warm heart. Since pastors are in repeated situations to help grieving persons, the above observations are particularly pertinent. This section begins with these observations to highlight the importance of the pastor as a person in helping the bereaved.

The goal of helping bereaved persons must be clear. As Mitchell and Anderson (p. 65) state: "Loss of any kind requires reaffirmation of the self." The primary goal is that the grieving person reaffirm that self which is still there, continuous though changing. Reaffirmation of that self occurs in a "painful process of embracing a future." The goal has a direction: the future of the person. Melges (pp. 206ff) also endorses this primary goal: ". . . grief-resolution therapy involves helping the patient reconstruct his identity into the future." However, much needs to happen before the person claims that identity for his or her own future. Impediments to this personal search are real and sometimes frequent.

As Mitchell and Anderson (p. 97) indicate, the principal impediment is a reluctance or even refusal on the part of the grieving person to permit feelings of loss to emerge or to express powerful feelings about the loss. This can lead to an unhealthy pre-occupation with events which occurred immediately prior to the loss itself. In addition to proscriptions by society against expressing deep feelings of grief, particularly if the loss was sometime in the past and avoided at the time, a person's intolerance of pain or a need for control dictated by the situation or religious beliefs or the lack of affect in a family system might create impediments in dealing with personal grief. Rosenblatt's diaries consistently point out social isolation, which was frequent on the frontier, as another impediment.

Of the impediments to grieving listed above, the need for control is currently a significant source for debate. The diarists of the nineteenth century manifest various ways of controlling their grief. Rosenblatt (pp. 99–121) devotes an entire chapter to this phenomenon. He cites four major methods of that control: "(1) acting inconsistently with feelings, (2) self-instruction to behave in a controlled fashion, (3) avoiding reminders of the loss, and (4) cognitive minimizing of the loss." He then comments, "These means of control are generally congruent with contemporary behavior modification approaches to self-control." Rosenblatt, on the basis on his research, suggests various "amendments" to twentieth-century theories of grief work. One of these amendments centers on the issue of control. His findings show "that people are disposed to control their emotions some of the time." And he continues (p. 153), "Although some writers on grief argue that a bereaved person's turning away from grief is a sign or a cause of pathology, such turning away seems to be normal (in the sense of being common), to be rarely associated with pathology, and to be typically a sign of coping." His amendment concludes (p. 154), "Thus, it seems an appropriate amendment to the theory to state that people will typically withdraw at times, that this withdrawal is related to social and subsistence demands and perhaps to the demands of the grief process itself, and that a periodic withdrawal may facilitate grief work." Rosenblatt clearly introduces the positive function of control, in its delimiting function, for consideration in current grief theory. By suggesting it is basically consonant with behavior modification methods may make it palatable to some theorists and therapists, and lend his point some degree of respectability in the twentieth century.

Mitchell and Anderson also speak to the issue of control but bring into question cultural prescriptions against expression of grief, in spite of "social and subsistence demands" endorsed by Rosenblatt. As they state (p. 98), cultural, social and familial rules on control of feelings of grief "clearly limit grieving." The parameters of the current debate are obvious. Moreover, Mitchell and Anderson approach the issue from the theological perspective. Referring to Luther (p. 85), they remind us that he recommended moderation and control of one's grief. Luther suggests this approach to grief so that the one who grieves does not forget the sufferings of Christ on his or her behalf. "Luther's intent is comfort and moderation, but the effect is more one of control than one of comfort." They continue

(p. 90), "The problem with Luther's admonition is that not to grieve deeply is to grieve inadequately. . . . Freedom to grieve intensely from the onset of loss is what makes space later for a remembrance of Christ's suffering. . . ." While Rosenblatt might find support for his amendment to current grief work from behavior modification and Luther, there tends to be little support from Mitchell and Anderson, even though they respect some degree of control and recognize that an excessive lack of control "leads to stultifying self-absorption." The four major methods of control reflected in Rosenblatt's diaries might also reflect Luther's theology at this point, reminding us that the theology of Luther was a dominant force in the midwest during the time of the writing of the diaries. The fact that these methods of control were "common" might reflect the "common" theology of Luther and, therefore, might be an impediment to the process of grief. Most would agree with Rosenblatt that one needs to "draw back" from grief to assimilate the process, but what *methods* are to be used in that drawing back? Rosenblatt does not question the methods of his diarists nor does he suggest the possible theology of Luther reinforcing those methods.

Melges, on this issue of control, introduces an understanding of control which is different from that of Rosenblatt as well as that of Mitchell and Anderson. If Rosenblatt implies that we help those who are bereaved by an acknowledgment of their need for inconsistencies with feelings, self-instruction on control, avoidance and minimizing, and if Mitchell and Anderson imply that cultural, social and familial proscriptions on grief clearly limit grieving, then Melges directs us to consider "the loss of control" as a major component in grieving and gaining control of one's future as a major resolution to the grief experience. In short, Melges suggests increased psychological and emotional control in the person which, in turn, make possible a future-oriented identity reconstruction of the self. His method for treatment is clear and will be discussed soon. His focus, however, on the loss of inner controls and the dynamics which inhibit normal grief, which create the bondage of a downward spiral, is unique in the current work on loss and bereavement.

If the goal of grief counseling or therapy is the reaffirmation of the self of the bereaved person, then how is this brought about? Mitchell and Anderson (pp. 111-137) suggest four modes of help: intervention, as an initial helping response where one steps in; support, as a recognition and rehearsal of feelings; insistent encouragement, as appropriate invitations to remember; and reintegration, as re-establishing relationships to significant communities. Intervention is, in effect, only "an interim mode of care." It is remembering, however, which is their major therapeutic tool for the bereaved. They describe remembering as "tied to the task of creating cherishable memory." In the light of the foregoing discussion on the infant's experience of individuation and its need to maintain attachments to loved objects through building internal constructs of the loved objects, it might be more precise and helpful to say that remembering in the grief process actually "builds reliable images." This finer point is important, expecially when we come to discuss Melges and his critical use of "guided imagery" in grief-resolution.

Mitchell and Anderson (p. 126) state, ". . . one gains emotional release from what is lost by actively making it a memory." Hence, remembering is the tool to build memory which, in turn, releases one from the destructive power of loss. Unfortunately, they do not become sufficiently specific on how a helper assists the bereaved to "actively" make a memory of the loss which then releases. Fortunately, Melges is quite specific, as will be seen. Mitchell and Anderson suggest some broad, common and important general directions for building memories for the bereaved: preparations for the funeral, family rituals, scrapbooks. They remind us of the kinds of resistance which might be employed to avoid memory-making: repetition of the moment just before the loss, making the person a saint, talking in the present tense. Hence, their rationale for "insistent encouragement" to remember. They make occasional reference to the images that are present in remembering, but make no linkage to guided imagery—a prevalent technique in the therapeutic field today. Unfortunately, the absence of the linkage between imagery and remembering, at the therapeutic level, makes their treatment method only partially clear. Melges, again, completes that linkage. However, their general therapeutic direction is remarkably close to that of Melges (pp. 92–93): "Reminiscing is intended to liberate the bereaved from emotional claims of the past in order to think hopefully about the future." Remembering is a kind of rhythm in the counseling of grieving persons. In the clearest statement of their fundamental method, they state (p. 92): "In order to assist in the painful process of embracing a future without the lost object, we will suggest than an alternation between remembering and hoping is the proper focus of the work." This alternation between remembering and hoping is stated in general terms. Melges becomes more precise on what has to be remembered and how it is to be remembered. With that precision, one sees how hope is born. Again, the broad direction of Mitchell and Anderson is consonant with that of Melges, but Melges is more specific on his treatment of the bereaved person.

It is here suggested that Melges provides the best resource available in helping helpers with the clinical aspects of understanding release from the grief experience. Since his chapter on grief-resolution appears in a book whose title might not draw one to it for clinical help on grief (*Time*

and the Inner Future: A Temporal Approach to Psychiatric Disorders), a
comprehensive review will be presented here. His contribution is unique
and merits a wide audience, particularly in pastoral counseling. As a psychiatrist who helps the bereaved, Melges works primarily with persons
who live with unresolved grief. Although grief is ordinary, grief can also be
distorted. However, Melges (p. 196) suggests that his method of treatment
might have implications for helping those in normal grief situations: "Although our method of treatment is designed for clinicians dealing with
classical unresolved grief reactions, it may also have some usefulness in facilitating the grief-hope process in those suffering from 'normal' grief."
Current work in pastoral counseling with the bereaved would do well to
consider this invitation as a state-of-the-art helping modality for those who
seek pastoral help on their personal losses. It is important to remember
that his contributions are set in his broader model which deals with Time
as it relates to a lack of personal control which precipitates emotional spirals. That model cannot be presented here. This reminder, however,
might reduce the possibility of viewing Melges' treatment of grief merely
as an interesting technique. His theory is just as important as his practice.

The core of his treatment method is precise (p. 196): "The treatment
method makes use of present-time guided imagery for the facilitation of
normal grieving processes through the imaginary removal of obstacles,
such as binds with the deceased and blocks to emotional expression, that
previously have inhibited the detachment necessary for finding new images and plans of action." Insofar as Melges stresses the use of "present-
time" imagery after obstacles are removed, he introduces a unique helping
plan. Commenting on other uses of guided imagery with grieving persons,
Melges (p. 213) refers to his own approach: "This method of grief-resolution therapy deals with similar dynamics outlined in Volkan's (1975) 're-
grief therapy,' but differs from it since we emphasize reexperiencing the
grief in present-time imagery with the previous obstacles removed. Talking about the loss in the past tense is used only for initial history taking,
since it has been found that the binds and affects emerge more vividly
when the patient is actively encouraged to use the present tense and to
reexperience the loss in the here-and-now." The purpose of this process is
to facilitate the normal grieving process and the consequent detachment
which, in turn, makes possible a future orientation of the bereaved person.
The thrust of this method would receive strong support from Mitchell and
Anderson, as can be noted from their position stated earlier. However, the
unique point of Melges' method, present-time imagery, tends, in general
terms, to receive a negative review by them. Mitchell and Anderson (p.
88) consider the use of the present tense by a grieving person to be a possible symptom of "time-freezing" which keeps the person "stuck" at the

moment just before the loss. Again (p. 130), the use of the present tense might suggest resistance to the important task of remembering. "The moments immediately after a loss are not occasions for grammatical purity, but a sentence such as 'Carl is a good husband' when Carl has been dead for eighteen months suggests that Carl is being held as a present reality rather than a cherished memory. An occasional reminder that the past tense is the appropriate verb form when referring to someone who has died is usually all that is needed." The overall intent of Mitchell and Anderson would be supported by Melges, but the method of getting to the point of release would be different for Melges. A reminder to use the past tense would not be enough. In fact, just the opposite would be true. It is the use of the present tense, following a prescribed method, which releases from the bondage of grief, whether that bondage be acute (immediately after the loss and the weeks that follow) or chronic (eighteen months later). Indeed, "time-freezing" and resistance may be factors in the use of the present tense *in another way* which releases. What is that way?

A question of ethics arises at this point. Does a helper proceed in grief counseling or therapy and simply assume consent of the client, patient, parishioner? The answer is: No. Mitchell and Anderson (p. 166) state: "But grieving is and must be optional even though the feeling response to grief is not. Theologically and pastorally, it is important to honor a person's freedom not to grieve. . . . Instead, we write to remind ourselves and all helpers that we dare not violate an individual's freedom even for the sake of that person's health." The person chooses to work on grief or not; the helper does not make that decision. In fact, Melges begins working with a bereaved person by helping him or her to make a "firm decision to regrieve." As he remarks (p. 204), "the patient's decision to regrieve is often therapeutic in itself. How much time is devoted to the regrief work depends on the clarity of the patient's decison, his ego-strength, and the extent of his binds with the deceased." The patient has to decide to regrieve; the firmness and clarity of that decision is directly related to how long the work of regrieving will take. Hence, ethically and clincially, one does not proceed to help a bereaved person without the person knowing what is going on and without that person's decision to enter that journey to their personal future.

If a person makes a firm decision to do grief work, the therapist first tries to detect the obstacles to grieving. For Melges (pp. 198–200), these obstacles include: yearning for the lost object, overidentification with the deceased, a wish to cry or rage but unable to do so, misdirected anger toward the deceased, current grief reaction interlocked with previous grief reactions, unspoken contracts with the deceased, unrevealed secrets, lack of a support group, and secondary gains from not working on the grief. The decision to regrieve, therefore, plays an important role in reducing the defensive behavior of the person at the point of revealing the obstacles. To facilitate the process of detection, Melges suggests that the person "discuss positive exchanges with the deceased that occurred shortly before the loss." Melges (p. 203) comments: "Reexperiencing the depth of attachment in this way often revives the bereaved's lost sense of self and, although painful, engenders hope for the reemergence of parts of his or her identity." Overcoming the loss of control begins by getting in touch with that sense of self again. This technique for removing obstacles, tied to the decision to regrieve, introduces a process in which the person's defensive avoidance of the obstacles is reduced. Conversation about those obstacles can then proceed.

A second technique is guided imagery in the present tense. With various obstacles removed to a significant degree, the person is freer to gain control over events which, at the time of the loss, he or she could not control. Guided imagery involves visualizing "scenes of the loss as though they were happening in the here-and-now. This is done in the mind's eye of the patient whose eyelids should be closed." Recreating the sense of the presence of the deceased, for example by viewing the body in the funeral home, precipitates "silent dialogues" with the deceased and makes possible response from the loved one. It also makes possible the emergence of additional obstacles which need to be addressed. But this is *guided* imagery, not free-floating imagery: the therapist guides the experience, following—and in some situations directing—the person through the dialogue. Feelings of anger toward the deceased will emerge and these become opportunities for mutual forgiveness. Melges (p. 202) has "found that expression of anger is usually necessary before the patient forgives the deceased for some past wrongdoing. My patients with unresolved grief remain attached to the deceased not out of love but through anger. The anger has blocked the full realization of the love they also hold toward the deceased. For this reason, grief-resolution therapy promotes the full expression of anger as a prelude to forgiveness and understanding." If, as Rosenblatt's work on the diaries suggest, control in grief is proper and even therapeutic, Melges' work suggests that control of anger toward the deceased is highly undesirable and destructive of the emergence of forgiveness itself. From a theological perspective, expression of that anger is a necessary "penultimate" experience which makes forgiveness (a strong theological word!) possible.

The focus of present-time guided imagery is threefold: (1) reliving sequences, (2) revising the scene, and (3) revisiting the revised scene. These "stages" are *progressive*. The ordering is important. Reliving sequences of loss, as if they were happening now, provides opportunities for the person to actually feel again the original feelings "instead of 'talking about' them in the past tense." Viewing events in the funeral home or the funeral itself also helps the person get in touch with that sense of self once again, however shattered. In the revising stage, as Melges (p. 205) describes it, "the patient is asked to remove the obstacles from the scene. Usually this involves creating solitary scenes with the deceased in which highly private material (for example, anger, secrets, binds) can be worked out in the absence of competing relatives and social constraints." In revisiting the revised scene, "the patient is encouraged to engage in 'dialogues with the deceased' in order to acknowledge the finality of the loss." The various "obstacles" listed by Melges are worked through at this point in a concentrated way in which the bereaved gets "permission from the 'presence' of the deceased to look for new relationships and options, especially those that seem to flow naturally from what the deceased would have wanted for the bereaved." Melges (p. 205) then makes a critical suggestion which focuses on detaching the person for release into his or her personal future: "Toward the end of each of the revisited scenes in which dialogues with the presence have taken place, the therapist encourages the patient to exchange last words and asks whether the patient is ready to say goodbye to the deceased." If the person is not ready, encouragement to say "goodbye for now" is made. When the point of saying goodbye does come in the therapeutic process, and the deceased is lowered into the grave with the earth then covering the grave, and in imagination the bereaved has "walked away" about fifty yards, "he is asked to 'turn around and look back' in order to 'feel if there are aspects of the deceased's personality that you choose to develop in yourself.' Most often these are images of strengths, strands from the past that can serve as bridges to the future." It can be seen now that the specificity of remembering and hoping which Melges provides is consonant with the method suggested by Mitchell and Anderson, "alternation between remembering and hoping." The dynamics of that "alternation" are clear and are set in a strong theoretical framework consistent with what we have come to know about the grief experience itself. The consistent and focal use of present-time in Melges suggests the possibility of reevaluating the caution placed on present tense usage in Mitchell and Anderson. Perhaps the present-time issue might be compared to vaccines: the serum that caused a possible life and death situation is the very same serum that heals if used in the right amount and in the right way.

The decision to regrieve and present-time guided imagery are followed by a process of helping the person to "reconstruct his identity into the future." After the graveside scene noted above, the therapist asks "in what ways the patient chooses to be different from the deceased. The patient's choices to be similar or different are then recorded. The word choices are then later used as spurs to imaging the self in the future." The person is also helped to "time-distance" himself or herself into the future, imaging a return to a memorable place shared with the deceased. To be able to live in that image without being overcome by the loss would be "a test of the adequacy of the grief-resolution work." At this point, we might refer to Melanie Klein's reference to reliable images providing stable linkages to the lost object. Here Melges' present-time guided imagery builds those very images which link the bereaved person to their continuous past in such a way that the bereaved is attached to the deceased through love and not anger, which, in turn, permits the person to live "out of" their future. Again, Mitchell and Anderson suggest that the "cherished memory" is a positive sign of grief-resolution. It is that, of course; but grounding the cherished memory in the dynamic of reliable images provides a more comprehensive understanding of what actually is going on in the process of grief-resolution.

Melges stresses the importance of adjunctive therapies and proper use of medications with his method. The pluralism of his approach is important to note. He does not recommend present-time guided imagery for acutely manic or schizophrenic patients. For those who recently experienced a loss, it is also not necessary to employ guided imagery. However, facilitating the *processes,* "such as mobilizing anger, weeping, forgiveness, and undoing binds, can be helpful in dealing with acute grief." It is here recommended that the state-of-the-art of helping persons with loss and bereavement include, without question, the recent contributions of Melges.

Mary's Story: A Brief Comment

The following vignette provides an example of some of the principles of Melges' model which are also supported by Mitchell and Anderson. Mary was referred to this writer for pastoral counseling by her pastor. Mary is a seventy-one year old widow who, in the first session, spoke of an inexplicable "fear" which would come over her during the day, particularly in the early morning or on awakening. The counseling process is currently active and, to date, has included eleven sessions.

During the early phase of counseling, Mary described multiple losses in the preceding eighteen months. She lost her house in which she lived for many years: she was offered four times the original cost of the house and found the sale of her house to be a financially secure decision. She lost her neighborhood with its conveniences and attachments to friends. She lost a family member who was brutally murdered (the local papers covered the tragedy), a person whom Mary loved in a very special way. Her employer had to cut back staff, and Mary had to do not only her own work but the work of another person: in a sense, a loss of her own job which she liked very much. And during the course of counseling, her only child announced plans to buy a house a fair distance from where Mary lives. Two months prior to counseling, Mary had a massive surge of "fatigue" and was hospitalized. The fatigue was characterized by dizziness as well. A thyroid problem was detected. On release from the hospital, she was treated with four or five medications. The dizziness and the overwhelming fear persisted.

Counseling also began with Mary's report that she could not stand the thought of retiring. Remarkably, after having worked through a major depression in her mid-forties with psychiatric help, Mary began to work full-time for the first time in her adult life at age fifty-four. For seventeen years, then, Mary was a strong worker. Retirement was unacceptable because she did not know what she would do. She found her job difficult, however, because coping with essentially two jobs was overwhelming and distracting. She had to go back to work, but she was too weak and afraid of the continuing dizzy spells. Family and friends reinforced the idea that it would be best for her to go back to work. In her treatment with the psychiatrist some years back, Mary found that she tended to use illness as a means of not doing something she was expected to do.

As her stories of multiple grief unfolded one by one, it was pointed out to her that, in addition to some real medical issues, she was experiencing grief from many losses in the preceding eighteen months. Naming this experience was met with disbelief by Mary. The problem had to be physical. Slowly, Mary returned to her stories of loss. She was encouraged to explore these in her mind's eye. On each return to a story, Mary began to feel the grief in each one. She felt that her main grief was facing the possibility of never going back to work again. As she put it, "I am grieving over the loss of my *self*!" With continued pressure to go back to work, from herself and others, Mary went back for one morning around the sixth session. It was a disaster. At that point, she acknowledged to herself that she did not want to work, not that she was fleeing an unpleasant situation, but that she wanted something else for herself and did not know what. Some of the obstacles to grieving were being removed and having their effect, and the modest guided imagery in the counseling was helping her to detach herself in a controlled setting, making possible the emergence of new images and plans for her own future. The primary obstacles that were slowly removed included: interlocking griefs, sorting out each one and looking at them separately; unspoken contracts with family and friends that working full-time at age seventy-one was best for her; secrets, that she had a special love for her grandniece; the double-bind of saying "I can't be weak" and "I'll be weak if I don't want to do something"; anger toward her son who did not understand her griefs.

As Mary reaffirmed herself in this process, she described how she was alone most of the time in her new, big house. The contrast between the noise and hub-bub of her workplace and the quiet of her home was compared. For almost three months, she was not around much normal noise. When she did go out to dinner with friends, she felt dizzy. To use Melges' understanding of Time, Mary was having problems with rate, sequence and temporal organization, resulting, in part, from a reduction of stimulation of her five senses. About the same time, her son said that he and his wife were expecting their second child. To assist in the reestablishment of appropriate rate, sequence and temporal organization, it was suggested that Mary go to a mall once a day for twenty or thirty minutes, to hear the normal sounds and see the colors and movements (rate and sequence) but with a purpose: she would go to a store for infants and just look at yarn and patterns for an outfit for her coming grandchild, something she wanted to make for the child (increasing "span of awareness" in temporal organization). She did this, found satisfaction in it, and controlled her own patterns of doing it for a week or more.

Mitchell and Anderson speak of the loss of role as a significant loss. Mary was moving away from her role as a full-time employee, but what roles were before her? Work was still important to her. What "work roles" might there be for her? The work of being a grandmother was introduced; the span of awareness in temporal organization had increased to the point that new roles might be reviewed. Resistance was there at first: she had not been around children much, she would respond to the needs of her son and daughter-in-law on request but not interfere with their lives by initiating grandmotherly acts. She was encouraged to image making a meal for her three year old grandchild, with just her and the child present. The meal was spaghetti-o's and muffins made by Mary and milk, from 4:00 P.M. to about 8:00 P.M. After the imaging, Mary said, "I suppose I could do that easily enough." She did, and did it again: the "work" of grandmother and grandchild, alone, together. It was at this point that her son announced their move to a new home about forty-five miles away. Initially upset, Mary quickly found herself understanding their family needs; the "loss" was not incapacitating. To use Melges' point, in a certain sense Mary was able to "distance" herself from a loss and go on with her life.

And go on she did. Her identity reconstruction continued to focus around work. This time she discussed her interest in being a volunteer in a resale shop of her church, something she had thought she would like to do a few years ago. In the tenth session, she made plans to visit the shop and check it out. In the next session, the most recent one, Mary reported how she arose the day of that visit and caught herself playing the sick role to avoid going, and stopped that game. She liked the visit, but was uncertain about "what they would expect." Then she said, "I think I feel that if I get really well, people will expect me to work the way I used to." A major integration for further identity reconstruction! Review was made of how she can take charge of her volunteer hours as well as take control of what she expected of herself and others in that situation. Near the end of the most recent hour, Mary said with some relief, "I know one thing. I don't have that fear anymore." That "fear" now can be seen as a fear of losing control of her own future. As she slowly experienced increased control of her own future, through removing the obstacles noted above and through modest guided imagery on multiple interlocking griefs, she found the fear gone.

Mary is continuing counseling, a remarkable woman who is willing to move into her own future, not without some anxiety but with a firmer sense of her new roles. Some of these will no doubt emerge as she continues to build new images of herself and with the "reliable images" of her past more stable.

Theological Reflections

Pastoral counseling requires a theological base from which it draws its own identity. Without a theological base, it has no resource to shape its specialty; without a clinical base, it loses resources which can inform its theological contributions. It is instructive to note that a psychiatrist, Melges, and pastoral theologians, Mitchell and Anderson, approach clinical issues on loss and bereavement with a major theological construct: Time. Melges' clinical use of Time can and will inform a theological understanding of Time: rate, sequence, temporal organization, future-orientation. Mitchell and Anderson bring a theological understanding of Time, in its dimension of finitude, to clinical data. We see here the importance of Time as a critical factor in understanding and helping persons in stress and emotional dysfunction. This writer suggests that the issues of rate, sequence, temporal organization, future-orientation, and finitude are not exclusive to the issue of Time in a therapeutic context. Time can also be viewed as a "mode of being in one's world." In this sense, Time can be "lived" in contraction, abstraction, adaptation and rhythm. Rate, sequence, temporal organization, future-orientation, finitude—all these can be "lived" in each of these modes. Neither Melges nor Mitchell and Anderson address this view, but Time as a mode of lived contraction, abstraction, adaptation or rhythm introduces factors which have theological, theoretical and clinical usefulness. This writer, with contributions from Brian Snyder, has developed a model entitled "Theological Diagnosis: A Pastoral Approach" which is in process for publication and which complements emerging discussions on Time in the resolution of emotional dysfunction. The reader is encouraged to consider Time, both theologically and clinically, as a primary variable in helping persons. Serious reflection in this area has just begun, and Melges has drawn our attention to it as no other therapist has. Pastoral counselors, with their theological resources in place, would do well to integrate a theological view of Time—more precisely, a biblical view of Time—with the clinical practice of pastoral counseling itself. The centrality of Time in the experience of loss and bereavement perhaps will stimulate that task.

With respect to loss and bereavement, in particular, Mitchell and Anderson provide a powerful theological context in which to understand more fully the experience of grief and grieving. The works of Mahler, Klein and Bowlby stand on ther own merit; but Mitchell and Anderson (p. 29) remind us that attachments and their derivatives (reliable images) are, theologically, "a continuation of God's love for creation." The structure of the human world is sustained by God's love through imaging, or more broadly stated, imagination. They further stress that the loss of "things"— houses, jobs, property, dreams—violate the sacredness of a person's life as does the loss of a loved person violate that sacredness. Their theological call is that all of life is to be preserved because all of life is sacred. If this theological point, based in creation, is not honored, then the apathy of Stoicism will reign, as, unfortunately, it tends to do in the experience of many Christians. When creation ruptures, as it will, in the loss of things or persons, a sign of our final acceptance of that rupture is our gratitude. This is a surprising and interesting contribution by Mitchell and Anderson (p. 131): "The capacity for gratitude makes it possible to bring closure to a life, or a relationship, however long or short." Melges (p. 198) reminds us of the words of John Bowlby (1963, 1973) that weeping is a "biologically ingrained" response which helps us to accept the finality of the loss. From a theological perspective on grief-resolution, Mitchell and Anderson remind us that gratitude for a relationship to a lost thing or person is also a sign of our acceptance of the finality of the loss. Melges approaches the concept of gratitude when he has the patient, fifty yards away from the graveside, turn and reflect on what he or she wants to continue with the deceased. But he does not draw it to the theological level of gratitude. Mitchell and Anderson do this through a theological understanding of creation and the sacredness of all life.

The central theological thrust, however, of Mitchell and Anderson is to "force a recognition of finitude." As they state (p. 79), "Traumatic loss upsets our illusion that we live in an orderly world. If we can find someone or something to blame, we can continue to avoid the fact that life is uncertain and precarious." The avoidance of the fact of our finitude sustains the comfort of our illusion of orderliness. As they continue to press their point (pp. 163–164), "Finitude, including the physical death of our flesh, is a necessary part of life. . . . If we must organize our lives to deny the reality of finitude, then it is death rather than life which is the primary power in our lives." Grief and grieving, therefore, become responses of *human* love *for God's creation*. It is in this human suffering for God's world that we prevent apathy toward God's creation. Paradoxically, it is suffering which makes us alive to the sacredness of all life! In short, they conclude (p. 172), "Our finitude is evidence of providence."

The powerful theological underpinnings of their position on loss and bereavement raise an interesting question for Melges: Future-orientation for what? He does not address that question. Mitchell and Anderson do: for the *mutual* benediction of humans and God on the sacredness of creation itself. Both humans and God "make sacred" all Time in which the tragedies of finite space occur.

Finally, Anderson and Mitchell (pp. 96, 97, 169) remind us that the work of grief can change our belief system about God. "The principal theological question when we are confronted by loss and grief is not Why do we suffer? but Who suffers with us? . . . The affirmation that God suffers with us shifts the focus from resolution to mutuality. The question about God which grief raises is not God's power or goodness but God's faithfulness." And (p. 170), "To address God even in anger is an act of confidence that one's sorrow and suffering have not driven God away." With such theological precision on a massive issue, Mitchell and Anderson invite pastoral conselors to push beyond the temptation to stop at the *resolution* of grief to the *mutuality in grief* with God who suffers with us. In this sense, they answer the question: Future-orientation for what? As pastoral theologians, their theological contribution to the clinical issues on loss and bereavement enrich the state-of-the-art in helping persons with their journey through the many valleys of the shadow of death.

Bibliography

Bowlby, J. "Pathological Mourning and Childhood Mourning." *Journal of the American Psychoanalytic Association*, 1963, 11, pp. 500–541.

Bowlby, J. *Attachment and Loss, Volume I: Attachment*. London: Hogarth Press, 1969.

Bowlby, J. *Attachment and Loss, Volume II, Separation.* New York: Basic Books, 1973.

Hayes, R.L. "High School Graduation: The Case for Identity Loss." *The Personnel and Guidance Journal,* February 1981, pp. 369–371.

Lindemann, E. "Symptomatology and Management of Acute Grief." *American Journal of Psychiatry,* 1944, pp. 101, 141–148.

Melges, F.T. *Time and the Inner Future: A Temporal Approach to Psychiatric Disorders.* New York: John Wiley & Sons, 1982.

Mitchell, K. and Anderson, H. *All Our Losses, All Our Griefs.* Philadelphia: The Westminster Press, 1983.

Rosenblatt, P.C. *Bitter, Bitter Tears: Nineteenth-Century Diarists and Twentieth-Century Grief Theories.* Minneapolis: University of Minnesota Press, 1983.

Volkan, V.D. " 'Re-Grief' Therapy." In B. Schoenberg (ed.), *Bereavement: Its Psychosocial Aspects.* New York: Columbia University Press, 1975.

Weiss, R.S. *Marital Separation.* New York: Basic Books, 1975.

David A. Steere

Supervising Pastoral Counseling

Supervision is the principal method of teaching pastoral counseling. Our grasp of counseling theories tends to fade with each step we take away from a formal classroom, unless these ideas take on reality in concrete instances where they apply. Both the conceptual tools and the specific techniques needed to work effectively with others can be mastered only through ordered reflection upon the counseling process itself. And that is what supervision is designed to accomplish— the acquisition of knowledge within the specific context of its use.

The term "supervision" broadly designates the process of overseeing someone else's work. If you agree to supervise me, you assume some responsibility for helping me perform a job, whether it be upholstering a chair, teaching a class, or doing pastoral counseling. Usually, you will have some expertise in the task at hand and some authority in the structure of what is going on. You will assign, regulate, and evaluate my activities with some say-so about my qualifications and advancement.

When it comes to the work of the pastor, supervision is nothing new. It may be as old as Jesus sending out the seventy-two to spread the good news and then talking with them about what happened when they returned. And just as the pastoral task of giving counsel has changed from one age to another, the style of supervising its practice also changed with the beliefs that governed the times. (Clebsch and Jaekle, 1964). The church adopted a Thomistic psychology based upon Aristotelian thought in the twelfth and thirteenth centuries. Pastoral counselors embraced the "faculty psychology" of sense, imagination, passions, and reason that followed the Enlightenment. Theological education seized the notion of apprenticeship from the guild system of the Middle Ages and made supervised practice under a tried cleric of higher rank standard in the preparation for priesthood. Pastoral training not only drew upon the existing psycho-

559

logies of the day to understand its task. It made use of the best supervisory practices of every age to accomplish it.

It comes as no surprise, then, that contemporary theories that govern the supervision of pastoral counseling are the product of a dialogue with professionals in the fields of psychiatry, social work, clinical psychology, education, and marriage and family therapy. This chapter will (1) identify four major traditions in the current practice of supervision in pastoral counseling with some of their varying emphases, (2) advance a model for supervision sufficiently comprehensive to contain and integrate these differing approaches, and (3) discuss three basic dimensions of the supervisory task common to them all.

Four Supervisory Traditions

The word supervision can have both broad and narrow meanings. It can mean the oversight of an entire educational process in the clinical setting: designing, administrating, and implementing a training program. It can also designate one particular part of this teaching/learning process—systematic reflection with trainees on the actual process of their clinical practice. Supervision in this latter sense became the core teaching method in the clinical setting and began to develop a theory all its own. Four separate theoretical traditions converge to make up contemporary theories of supervision in pastoral counseling, each with its own distinct approach to the task: Clinical Pastoral Education, the psychodynamic tradition, the humanistic tradition, and the systemic tradition.

Clinical Pastoral Education

Current supervisory practices in pastoral counseling are the clear product of interprofessional cooperation in the clinical setting. The term "clinical" literally means "at the bedside." (Schuster, Sandt, and Thaler, 1972, p. 1). It derives from the Greek word *kline* for the couch in the Temple of Aesculapius where the Greeks went to find a cure for their ills. A clinician is one who gathers data "at the bedside." Clinical medicine is concerned with the actual observation and treatment of disease among patients rather than its study through experimental research in the laboratory. The term was adopted by clinical pastoral educators in the 1920s the way Richard Cabot used it in a famous lecture entitled "A Plea for a Clinical Year in the Course of Theological Study" urging that the clergy be trained to practice theology in the same way physicians learn to practice medicine in the clinical setting. (1926, p. 7) Anton Boisen, who conducted what was probably the first program of clinical pastoral education as we know it today, put it another way: the theological student should learn how to read "living human documents" as well as the traditional documents of the church's faith. (1951)

The CPE tradition learned and incorporated much from other supervisory traditions in the clinical setting. But it managed to preserve this central focus upon a clinical method of theological inquiry. For Cabot and Dicks, this meant the study of verbatim records of the pastoral conversation in which religious beliefs became the substance of what is done or acted out in the actual process of pastoral care with the patient. (1936) What they envisioned was a *clinical theology* setting forth specific ways the pastor's body of theological belief takes shape in concrete methods such as "creative listening." Boisen's emphasis on the study of *living human documents* involved the observation of how the actual beliefs people hold function to direct the course of their lives, for illness or for health, for sin or for salvation.

It remained for Seward Hiltner to draw together these initial commitments to ordered reflection on the pastoral conversation into a formal discipline of *pastoral theology.* (1958) Pastoral theology was defined as a branch of theological knowledge and inquiry that brings the pastoral perspective to bear on concrete helping operations drawing conclusions of a theological order from systematic reflections upon them. We begin with theological hypotheses about what will actually be of help to human beings, then reflect on the caring process step-by-step, and emerge with conclusions of a theological order about the theories that govern it. This made the actual task of supervisory reflection a valid and legitimate source of theological knowledge. As Hiltner put it, "The truth about how the truth operates is part of the truth itself." (1958, p. 220)

Supervision in the CPE tradition developed an intense personal relationship between supervisor and student. Its hallmark is the presentation of verbatim records of the pastoral conversation constructed by recall. The case study of religious histories of patients is also important along with a form of group supervision (interpersonal relations group) which deals with the trainee's personal reactions to the entire experience. There has been much debate whether the focus of supervision lies in the acquisition of pastoral skills or in the personal growth of the trainee or both. (Steere, 1989) But from the 1920s on, supervision in the CPE tradition saw itself as a theological discipline and not simply as a practice shared with other helping professions. Genuine knowledge about theology itself is acquired, reformulated, and tested again in the crucible of human experience.

The Psychodynamic Tradition

The American Association of Pastoral Counselors (AAPC) was formed in 1963 in order to recognize and credential a rapidly expanding number of pastoral counselors. Most of its founders came out of the CPE movement, and one-quarter of CPE remains a requirement for membership to date. An important difference, however, was present in the situation that spawned it. Standards for the reliable training of pastoral counselors were sought among existing secular disciplines in psychotherapy. Supervision from professional figures in the fields of psychiatry, psychology, or social work was required. This made sense as pastoral counselors sought to raise their expertise to levels comparable to those of their colleagues. In the process, both the psychodynamic and the humanistic traditions of long-standing influence were formally integrated into supervision in pastoral counseling.

The psychodynamic tradition has its roots in psychoanalytic theory where the task of dealing with our unconscious motivations or forces (dynamics) outside our awareness is central to all human change. Sigmund Freud considered anyone making use of the twin phenomena of *resistance* and *transference* to be doing psychoanalysis. (1938, p. 9, 39) Resistance is the term for that mental mechanism by which we shut out of our conscious awareness traumatic or seemingly unacceptable aspects of our personal experience. We push from our memory the painful roots of the problems we address. We make constructive changes in our life when someone assists us in circumventing our resistance to bring these repressed experiences to consciousness, thereby gaining insight into how they determine our present striving. For Freud any technique that helps one achieve this is a psychoanalytic one.

The term "transference" was given to the phenomenon of reexperiencing childhood emotions toward significant others with someone else in the present. In its narrowest definition, transference is restricted to instances in the psychoanalytic relationship where the patient projects onto the analyst infantile feelings of libido (love, sexual attraction) and aggression (hate, primitive rage) originally experienced toward a parenting figure. Broader definitions are more common today in which the phenomenon of transference is expanded to include the whole range of relationships in which we may project "the face" of someone significant from our past onto the person we interact with currently with similar affect and behavior.

Both these elements of resistance and transference are prominent in psychodynamic theories of supervision. Therapists in training can be expected to resist awareness of how earlier experiences are determining their present striving, just as their patients do. Their own countertransference toward persons with whom they work can distort their perceptions and inhibit their effectiveness. Learning to do psychotherapy required a corresponding self-encounter in depth on the part of therapists-in-training to manage the whole process.

Accordingly, some form of personal analysis or "didactic analysis" has always been a part of psychoanalytic training. The issue is whether it belongs within the context of supervision. Early in the movement, some argued that the same analyst should analyze and supervise the trainee because you could only supervise people properly if you knew them well enough through conducting their own personal analysis. Others insisted upon separating the two completely. Supervision should be a didactic experience focusing sole attention on how to treat patients and not address issues of personal therapy.

The problem is that psychotherapists-in-training never seem to get all their personal issues settled in therapy and then go to supervision with no further need for insight into their own unconscious motivations and transference. Most psychodynamic supervisors separated the two, but not so completely. Rudolph Ekstein and Robert Wallerstein's *The Teaching and Learning of Psychotherapy* became the classic text in the psychodynamic tradition by mid-century. (1958) The authors rejected a patient-centered approach in which the therapist brings technical problems with the patient to the supervisor and is given advice. They also rejected a therapist-centered approach which focused on the therapist's blind spots and countertransference reactions to patients. Instead, they proposed *a process-centered* emphasis on the interaction between patient, therapist, and supervisor with a clear focus on what is happening in this whole system of relationships.

This involved psychodynamic supervision in a number of things that paralleled the psychotherapeutic relationship it addressed. There were points where the therapist's own personal difficulties got in the way of treatment. Ekstein and Wallerstein called these "learning problems" because they continually stood in the way of the student's acquisition of psychotherapeutic skills. Moreover, a similar set of difficulties also appeared in the relationship between the supervisor and the therapist-in-training. In spite of whatever good intentions occupied their conscious minds, students were found to resist learning from supervision. These characteristic resistances to supervision, termed "problems about learning," originated in each trainee's own "unique transference" toward the supervisor.

To make the situation even more complex, psychodynamic theories of supervision soon began to observe a *parallel process* at work between these two sets of problems that were always cluttering up the psychotherapeutic situation and the supervisory relationship at the same time. (Doehrman, 1976) Psychotherapists-in-training may give the patient in therapy what they desire from their supervisor, or they may read into the patient elements of their own anxiety in the supervisory relationship. What students see and present from a therapeutic relationship frequently parallels comparable problems they themselves experience in supervision. It is as if the supervisory conversation addresses a constant metaphor in which the patient's problem in psychotherapy may be used to express the therapist's problem in supervision and vice versa. More often than not, resolution of the problem in supervision is accompanied by a similar breakthrough or gain in the therapeutic relationship.

The hallmark of supervision in the psychodynamic tradition is continuous case presentation of the same patient, week by week, following progress across this parallel process we have been considering. Systematic reflection is not confined to the therapeutic relationship the trainee presents, and regularly expands to address the trainee's resistance to the learning process of supervision itself. Since most important data that supervisees bring are personal data concerning their own attitudes, approaches, and feelings toward patients, verbal description, process notes, and personal reflection are the primary means of presenting material. Audio and video recording, while helpful, find their principal use in stimulating immediate recall of one's internal attitudes and intentions at the point of intervention. Ekstein and Wallerstein favored the separation of supervision from administrative oversight of the patients' treatment. They wanted the supervisor free to encourage maximum learning at the supervisee's own initiative and readiness and not be tempted to "treat the patient" through the supervisory process.

The Humanistic Tradition

The humanistic tradition in supervisory theory finds its roots in the work of Carl Rogers and his approach known as "client-centered therapy." (1951) Rogers became the first non-medical practitioner to effectively challenge the reign of psychoanalytic helping theory. His approach was soon labeled "non-directive counseling" because of the permissiveness that characterized it in which the counselor listened, clarified what was being said without interpretation, and attempted to help people arrive at their own solutions to their problems. Rogers himself preferred the term "client-centered therapy" to indicate that the significant activities in therapy were those of the client, not the therapist. In essense:

If the counselor:

1. places a high value on the worth and capacity of the individual,
2. operates on the hypothesis that the individual is capable of self-understanding and self-direction,
3. creates an atmosphere of genuine acceptance and warmth,
4. develops a sensitive ability to perceive experience as it is seen by his client,
5. communicates to the client something of his understanding of the inner world of the client;

then the client:

1. finds it safe to explore fearful and threatening aspects of experience,
2. comes to a deeper understanding and acceptance of all aspects of himself,
3. is able to reorganize himself in the direction of his ideal,
4. finds it more satisfying to be his reorganized self,
5. discovers that he no longer needs the counselor.

(Rogers and Becker, 1950, pp. 33–34)

Rogers' approach had immediate appeal to pastoral counselors, both theologically and practically. Theologically, it expressed in human paradigm the force of God's forgiveness as personal acceptance. Practically, it freed training and supervision from the cumbersome necessity of psychoanalytic methodology. By mid-century, the reigning theory of pastoral counseling expressed a marked affinity to this tradition. Seward Hiltner's "eductive counseling," Paul Johnson's "responsive counseling," and Carroll Wise's "non-coercive counseling" (although he steadfastly refused any label for it) were all constructed along lines similar to Carl Rogers' client-centered therapy. (Hiltner, 1949, Johnson, 1953, Wise 1951) The normative helping act was that of "evoking" or "calling forth" resources that were internal to the person receiving help. The same tradition is preserved by Barry K. Estadt, John R. Compton, and Melvin C. Blanchette in their definitive work on the supervision of pastoral counseling: *The Art of Clinical Supervision: A Pastoral Counseling Perspective.* (1987) Here, the *core process of supervision* is defined around Robert Carkhuff's helping skills of attending, exploring, and personalizing which embody the primary client-centered orientation of the humanistic tradition. (1987)

Supervisory theory in the humanistic tradition soon established itself around modeling the experience it sought to teach. Client-centered therapy turned upon what came to be known as the "therapeutic conditions" of *empathy, understanding, respect,* and *genuineness.* Wherever these conditions prevailed, positive change was facilitated. Not only were they curative factors in psychotherapy; they were found to stimulate creative efforts to develop therapeutic skills in supervision. They were equally applicable to patterns of interaction in groups, so client-centered therapists were increasingly trained as group therapists and supervised in the group setting.

Central to the humanistic tradition in supervision is its faithfulness to the scientist/practitioner model in psychology which undertook extensive research in the implementation and effectiveness of client-centered therapy. Careful one-on-one supervision buttressed by extensive research in techniques that bring effective therapeutic outcomes governed training programs. (Rogers and Dymond, 1954) Wide use was made of electrically recorded data in supervision. Rogers believed that only careful study of the actual interview, preferably with a sound recording and a transcript available, made it possible to determine what purposes were actually being accomplished by the therapist. At the core of supervisory reflection was the task of determining how each response to the client can congruently convey the therapist's fundamental orientation toward that individual's worth as a person. Effective supervision modeled the empathetic understanding, respect, and genuineness which the supervisee was being taught to implement with the client.

The Systemic Tradition

Since mid-century a fourth tradition in supervision has emerged among marriage and family therapists which can be characterized by its emphasis upon systems theory. Proponents cut across traditional lines separating the professions uniting to treat the family system rather than the individual. Regarding a linear, cause-and-effect approach to understanding emotional problems to be too narrow, the systemic tradition began working with concepts of circular causality within the family unit where psychopathology both originated and was sustained. The symptomatic person or the identified patient was found to provide an important role either in maintaining stability or in bringing about change in that system—or both. Treatment came to be conceived in terms of measures that intervened in or altered constructively the way the family system operates as a whole, eliminating whatever within its relationships produced symptomatic behavior. Along with the practice of family therapy came new ways of doing supervision indigenous to its experience of working with relational systems.

One principal innovation was the practice of live supervision that grew up among marriage and family therapists. In general, the term "live supervision" describes any process in which the supervisor guides the therapist during the actual course of treatment itself. The most common way is to observe from behind a one-way glass. Contact with the therapist is maintained throughout the session in any number of ways. Some supervisors knock on the door or interrupt with a buzzer asking therapists to step out for consultation. Others call in on the telephone for a conversation in the midst of treatment. Still others have experimented with putting a "bug" in the ear of the therapist, permitting a running commentary and step-by-step instructions during the whole process. Some supervisors on occasion walk into the room and join the therapist for brief periods of time to undertake specific interventions. Two recent volumes afford the best introduction to supervision from the systems perspective: *Handbook of Family Therapy Training in Supervision,* edited by Howard A. Liddle, Douglas C. Breunlin, and Richard C. Schwartz, and *Family Therapy Supervision: Recent Developments in Practice,* edited by Rosemary Whiffen and John Byng-Hall. (Liddle, 1988, Whiffen, 1982)

Live supervision has many advantages. Trainees may provide a higher quality treatment if their supervisors can guide therapy at strategic points. It eliminates fruitless periods in reflective supervision of sitting through long segments of previously recorded material after therapy has gone awry and the session "lost" in an unproductive direction. Potentially irrelevant and damaging sequences of interaction may be interrupted, building the therapist's confidence through success early in training. Some systemic supervisors are critical of its emphasis upon technique to the neglect of teaching trainees a comprehensive theory of life that organizes their behavior as therapists. Others insist that while live supervision may prove effective in the short run, it can stifle the trainee's long-term growth and autonomy. But some balanced and measured use of it is a growing part of most training programs.

There are wide variations in the use of live supervision throughout the systemic tradition. Structural/strategic supervisors who see issues of power and hierarchy as paramount give authoritative directives to the therapist concerning interventions and the next steps in treatment. Groups behind a one-way mirror may observe and discuss what is going on, but the supervisor directs the entire process, assuming responsibility for its outcome. Supervisors from the Milan School have the group observing behind the window take an active part in the treatment, writing prescriptions, designing rituals and paradoxical directives which are delivered to the family as messages from the "team" behind the glass. Other supervisors with stronger humanistic leanings, who make a larger place for personal choice among members of the family system, may place the team in the treatment room with the family. Instead of issuing authoritative prescriptions and strategies from behind a one-way mirror, team members openly discuss different ways of looking at the family process in a "reflective dialogue," making supervision an open procedure conducted in the presence of the family and part of the actual course of treatment. The family's responses to the discussion by the supervisor and team members then constitute the next step in therapy.

Systems theorists soon encountered a phenomenon in supervision they called *isomorphism* which proved analogous to what the psychodynamic tradition called *parallel process.* Isomorphism is the tendency for patterns to repeat themselves at all levels of the family therapy system. A particular pattern in the parent/child relationship begins to reappear in the relationship between therapist and parent. Suddenly the same therapist/parent pattern reappears in the supervisory relationship itself. The father in the family is over-solicitous and placating, reluctant to assert his ideas and take initiative toward his son. The therapist ignores this behavior and fails to recognize and confront it for fear of driving him further into the background. The supervisor is reluctant to intervene, with a vague sense that the therapist lacks the confidence to make a potent demand that the father behave differently. One and the same problem plays itself out at each level of the system of family therapy that confronts it.

Resolution of the isomorphic issue will cascade down the treatment hierarchy from supervisor to therapist to family member. The same parallel process is operative. As the supervisor is successful in assisting the therapist to overcome blocks to self-assertion, the therapist begins to succeed in helping the father engage in appropriate assertive measures with his son who in turn stops apathetically flunking out of school.

To an already existing complexity of supervisory theory and methodology the systemic tradition contributed its practice of live supervision in which both supervisor and supporting group or team can take part in the treatment process itself. Supervision remains a reflective process, but the interval of time between reflection and return for implementation of supervisory decisions is reduced to the immediate present. Supervision has traveled full circle from Ekstein and Wallerstein's separation of it from administrative responsibilities for treating the patient. Now everybody involved may take an active and responsible role in what goes on in the treatment room.

A Reflective Model

Our next step is to advance a model for supervising pastoral counselors that is broad enough to encompass this diversity of contemporary approaches, yet focused enough to provide clarity and integrity to the task. It is constructed from a general model that has been in use at Louisville Presbyterian Seminary for a number of years. (Steere, 1969) It has proven sufficiently comprehensive to encompass supervision at both beginning and advanced levels together with its varied forms and formats, whether one is addressing counseling relationships with individuals, groups, couples, or families.

Definition

Supervision in pastoral counseling is a teaching/learning process conducted through an extended relationship in which supervisor and supervisees agree to engage in systematic reflection upon the trainees' concrete practice of pastoral counseling in order to focus all available resources on the supervisees' personal growth in their professional role. The terms of this definition bear some explanation.

1. Supervision takes place in an *extended relationship* that develops across time. It is not a one-shot affair as consultation sometimes

is. We benefit through regular engagement in it. There is an accumu-
lative effect, as we learn to use it, which increases over time and
experience.

2. Supervision is founded upon a *mutual agreement* between supervisor and supervisee. This involves a clear contract, verbal and
usually written, outlining responsibilities and culminating in
evaluation.

3. Supervision involves *systematic reflection* upon *concrete practice*. The actual events of the counseling relationship are presented as
precisely as possible. There are many ways to do this. They range
from simple recall and verbal reconstruction to the use of verbatim
records, process notes, case studies, audio and video tape recordings,
and various forms of live supervision. Whatever the method, the essence of supervision is disciplined reflection upon the raw data of
concrete practice.

4. The supervisory conversation *focuses all available resources*
upon understanding what transpired in the data addressed. For pastoral counselors, these resources include the best conceptual understandings available to supervisor and student from the range of theological knowledge they share, on the one hand, and the knowledge of
such human sciences as psychology, sociology, and anthropology, on
the other. Whatever helping theories are adopted from contemporary professional disciplines must be constantly placed in mutually
critical correlations with the pastoral counselor's own theological assumptions. The notion of shared *availability* between supervisor and
student is crucial in such efforts. Both parties must possess conceptual
tools with sufficient mastery of their meaning and relevance to make
them useable in concrete applications to practice.

5. It follows that supervision cannot impart all the information
necessary for understanding the resources it employs. It must rely on
the larger context of theological education for this. As conceptual
resources are increased in the supervisee through seasoned learning
and use, so will the depth of that person's experience in supervision.

6. The aim of supervision is *personal growth in one's professional
role*. These words are carefully chosen. As in all good education personal growth is an important goal. No one can engage in such close
personal reflection upon efforts to counsel others without wrestling
with personal changes that are required to increase effectiveness.
These often involve basic patterns in attitude or behavior. Whatever
the case, supervision concentrates on making these changes in one's

professional role as a pastoral counselor. This distinguishes it from pastoral counseling or psychotherapy.

Three Clinical Poles

Any effort to engage in constructive reflection upon the raw data of counseling will immediately involve participants in what we term the *three clinical poles.* The focus is clearly upon the concrete process of interaction between counselor and counselee, exchange by exchange, transaction by transaction. This is the first pole for clinical reflection. What went on, step by step, in the counseling relationship? What helped accomplish its purposes? What hindered or got in the way? This will inevitably involve a shift of reflective attention between the second and third clinical poles: the pole involving the counselor and what is going on within his or her internal process and the pole involving the counselee or counselees and what is going on inside their internal systems.

The situation is depicted in Figure 1. The focus of supervisory conversation is clearly on the counseling relationship itself (I—Process Pole). This is represented by the larger circle in the center which encompasses everything that transpires within a particular counseling process between the parties involved. Whatever lies within its boundaries is germane to and admissible within supervisory reflection. This, however, necessitates commensurate amounts of attention to the other two clinical poles.

To understand fully what is going on we must know something about what happens inside the counselor (II—Internal/Counselor(s) Pole). What history, attitudes, intentions, beliefs, and behaviors are brought to the counseling relationship? How do they influence participation in this specific transaction? What previous personal issues come into play? Effective supervision will address any factor in the counselor's own life experience that this particular helping process draws within the circumference of attention. This is represented by the shaded elliptical portion of the circle standing for the pastoral counselor overlapping the area of the larger circle designating the process of pastoral counseling. It represents that part of the counselor's personal life that impinges upon this particular pastoral event. The situation becomes even more complex when we add a second counselor (co-therapy) or a team behind the window (live supervision). What goes on within these relationships is an equally important

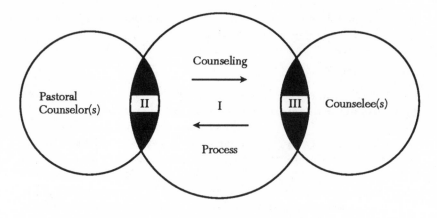

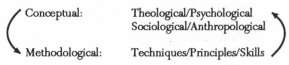

Figure 1

part of the second clinical pole. But here our model draws a boundary to the domain of supervisory conversation. We address only those issues in the internal life process of counselors to which the counseling event at hand gives rise. Other matters from their personal lives in general are the domain of counseling or psychotherapy proper.

By the same token, it is equally necessary to concentrate attention upon the person or person receiving counseling (III—Internal/ Counselee(s) Pole). We need to know enough about their history, attitudes, beliefs, intentions, and behaviors in order to understand their response to the specific transaction at hand. The deeper the grasp of these factors, the more effective the supervisory conversation in framing strategies, interventions, and interpretations of the process. This becomes even more complex when supervision addresses the internal system of a group, a couple, or a family. Reflective attention to these issues is represented by the elliptical area of the circle designating counselee(s) overlapping the larger circle representing the counseling process itself. It represents what supervision must determine about these persons in order to develop theoretical and methodological skills to provide them with effective pastoral counseling. Research in general about the character of these persons' lives, the structure of relationships that sustain them, or the nature of their beliefs, attitudes, values, and the like belongs beyond the boundaries of supervision and within the domain of some other discipline of study, be it theological, psychological, sociological, anthropological, or whatever. Again, supervision cannot generate within itself the resources upon which it draws.

Among the supervisory traditions we have been considering, we can observe different measures of attention to one or another of these three clinical poles. Anton Boisen's emphasis upon the study of *living human documents* as a source of knowledge about how beliefs function for persons in crisis focused upon Pole III—Internal/Counselee(s). Cabot and Dicks, through concentrating clinical study on verbatim records of what transpired in the counseling relationship, stressed Pole I—Process. Supervision in the psychodynamic tradition shifted a great deal of attention over to the second clinical pole—Internal/Counselee(s)—as supervisors focused upon the therapists' resistance to learning and countertransference to patients. Yet each approach demands that supervision pay attention to all three. The humanistic tradition, for example, may concentrate supervision on the actual process (I) of counseling through the use of audio and video records of what transpired. But the counselor's congruence in reflecting an inner attitude (II) of belief in each individual's personal worth and capacity to pursue self-chosen solutions to life problems is measured in each counselor-response. And so is the counselor's *empathy* in terms of its accuracy in responding to what is intended in each communication by the counselee (III). Psychodynamic supervisors address their supervisees' unconscious motivations and distortions through countertransference (I) in order to enable them to make accurate interpretations (II) of their patients' internal dynamics (III).

Among supervisors in the systemic tradition there is the same breadth. Structural/strategic supervisors may direct their main attention in live supervision to frame specific interventions in the family system at crucial points (I). Others from the systemic school (systemic, proper) may have the supervisory team engage in a "reflective dialogue" in the family's presence, inventing various accounts of what currently governs its relationships (III) and positively connoting the strategies of individual members. Supervisors who emphasize transgenerational influences may send supervisees back to their families of origin with particular tasks to differentiate themselves from the grips of its emotional process (II), so they may learn how to help clients engage in similar therapeutic missions of their own (III).

Whatever the theoretical tradition of the supervisor, Figure 1 attempts to depict the circular character of supervision as a teaching/ learning process as it addresses its conceptual and methodological resources. Any conceptual understandings of the counseling process that come into play are subjected to their concrete function in understanding the actual process of counseling at hand. Theoretical knowledge finds immediate expression and expansion within the use of each professional skill it dictates, and vice versa, each continually reshaping the other as a certain integrity grows deep within.

Three Dimensions of Supervision

We turn now to identify three dimensions of the supervisory task common to all the approaches we have been considering. Whatever their varying degrees of attention to the three clinical poles, all of them share: (1) a dimension of *administrative oversight* which has to do with maintaining the welfare or treatment of counselees or clients together with whatever institutional structure supports the services that are rendered; (2) a *therapeutic dimension* of personal growth which focuses attention on whatever insight, behavioral change, or other personal conditions must be met by the supervisee in order to increase personal effectiveness; and (3) a dimension of the *working alliance* in the supervisory relationships themselves between supervisee, peers, and supervisor which requires periodic attention to make the whole process work.

Each of these three dimensions provides an essential element to the supervisory conversation. Yet each can become a hook upon which the supervisory process gets caught and subverted. Any one of the three, if permitted to dominate the others to the point of their exclusion, can render the process ineffectual. Yet each is so vital in its time that its neglect disestablishes supervision, giving rise to the clinical axiom: when supervision is stuck in one dimension, switch to another and see where that leads.

Administrative Oversight

In all supervision, there is an inevitable tension between the desire to train the student and a sense of responsibility to oversee the care of clients or patients. What distinguishes supervision from ordinary administrative oversight in general is its central commitment to teach a way of thinking and acting in accord with conceptualizations from a professional role. Its disciplined reflection will always go beyond merely devising more effective strategies and methods. The supervisor is an educator out to create a climate of intensely personal learning in which patterns of thinking and responding are developed that may last a lifetime.

So this first dimension of the supervisory conversation begins with a focus on the task of delivering effective pastoral counseling to the client. But it may take many turns along the way. Allowances may be made for students to learn at their own pace, to make their own mistakes and benefit from them. New concepts may require tentative periods of incubation; new skills may result in awkward periods of uncertain efforts to try on new methods for size to see how they fit. Most good supervisors will make a conscious choice at times to permit supervisees to struggle with their partially-formed understandings that are less than state of the art. In supervision it is always more important that trainees learn to do things for themselves rather than that these things be done as quickly and effectively as possible—for example, by the supervisor stepping in and doing it for them which is a common pitfall in live supervision.

Clinical supervisors from any tradition constantly balance their attention between concerns for personal learning and concerns for the welfare of the patient. There are times when concerns for a counselee's well-being will override personal learning. For example, severely depressed persons who are at risk of suicide require well-established procedures that refrain from excessive nurture, obtain clear contracts against harming themselves, and make appropriate referral which no responsible supervisor would leave to a process of trial and error. There are limits in the minds of most supervisors having to do with protecting counselees from excessive control and domination by a trainee who talks too much or protecting particular individuals who are vulnerable from excessive confrontation or harmful criticism. As liability increases along with litigation against malpractice in the field of mental health, no supervisory program in pastoral counseling will ignore this dimension of administrative oversight in order to protect the services it renders at the institutional level.

Within some traditions where instructions, directives, and demonstrations by the supervisor are a normal part of supervision, there is minimal conflict between administrative and supervisory concerns.

Structural/strategic supervisors doing live supervision of family therapy assume full responsibility for the course for treatment and intervene from behind the one-way glass with clear directives to supervisees about what they should do ("Give them my voice"). Their
assumption is that competence is learned by being empowered to act
effectively rather than left to founder in search of one's own
resources.

In other situations, however, a subtle tension between administrative and supervisory concerns follows each step of the way. Take
live supervision of a co-leader in group counseling, for example. Will
supervisees learn more if the supervisor interrupts and guides at crucial points when the group is at a loss or if the supervisor permits
supervisees to struggle for a while to find their own way? How effective is learning when the supervisor takes over at a particular point
and demonstrates an alternative when the supervisee is stuck? And
how long should the supervisor refrain from doing so in order to give
supervisees a chance to discover things for themselves without abdi-
cating shared responsibility in the overall course of the group's life?

It is clear that excessive concern in this dimension of administrative oversight can disestablish learning, particularly if permitted to
eclipse the other two dimensions of supervision. But one wonders if
any form of supervision can ever be free from some tension between
the desire to let supervisees learn by trial and error and the desire to
ensure the highest quality of practice the supervisory system can
muster, moment by moment. Supervision is always conducted within
the context of a larger system of administrative relationships constantly triangling others into its procedures. We have cited examples
where our supervisor may represent the welfare of a particular patient or serve as interpreter of institutional policies. At other times
the open nature of the supervisory relationship calls for the freedom
to question and challenge existing regulations, theories, and practices. Sensitive supervisors will not permit the administrative dimension of their role to dominate it to the exclusion of such concerns.

The Therapeutic Dimension

In the intensely personal task of pastoral counseling, strong measures of self-confrontation are unavoidable. We use ourselves as an
instrument to bring about change. In supervision we are faced continually with some personal impasse that gets in our way when we set out
to be of help to others. Things happen that demand that we change,
too. The therapeutic dimension of supervision focuses attention upon
whatever insight, behavioral change, or other personal conditions

need to be met by the supervisee in order to function effectively in the role of pastoral counselor.

There are a number of ways to look at this therapeutic dimension. One is to recognize a certain inner integrity that all good counselors have. It makes us reluctant to expect others whom we counsel to deal with anything we must avoid or have not yet mastered in our own lives. We cannot help a counselee unearth a hidden rage that has been denied for years if we fear or deny a similar anger in our own experience. We cannot counsel a couple deeply divided over parenting their children without encountering the difficulties marking the relationships in our own marriage and family. In supervision we are always bumping into our own unfinished business. In this sense, each new troublesome client bears a gift of self-confrontation that brings us up short before our next issue of personal growth, regardless of how experienced we think we are.

Consequently, each supervisory tradition allowed for this therapeutic dimension in particular ways. Supervisors in the psychodynamic tradition sought to provide the same intensely personal relationship that the therapist provides in psychotherapy, permitting trainees to identify and work through personal issues that inhibited both their learning and their effectiveness with clients. In many schools of group therapy, a treatment experience as a member of a therapy group became a standard part of supervisory training to lead one. Supervisors in the humanistic tradition founded the supervisory experience upon providing supervisees the same therapeutic conditions of empathetic understanding, respect, and genuineness their trainees were taught to extend to clients. From the beginning the CPE tradition included a group experience for supervisees as a formal part of supervisory efforts to address personal issues evoked by training.

For supervision within the tradition of systems theory, the issue has not been so clear-cut. Transgenerational schools had no difficulty including specific tasks of differentiation from the therapist-in-training's family of origin within supervision. But systems theorists who always address the marital and family unit as a whole had no place for dealing with personal behavior apart from its context. They confronted specific relational issues among trainees within the isomorphic character of their appearance through the system of supervised therapy which we described earlier. The therapist's problem with the family becomes the supervisor's problem with the therapist in supervision, permitting necessary changes in relational behavior to be dealt with in the context of the supervisory relationship itself.

It is no accident that all of our supervisory traditions set out to model in the supervisory relationship the essence of what they regard to be curative or therapeutic in the psychotherapy they supervise. This is more than practicing what you preach or demonstrating what you teach. It is a necessary step in the training of effective counselors. It is one thing to go off in private and to get our act together in personal psychotherapy. It is another to keep that act together through continual entry into and involvement in the many personal and interpersonal systems of others we seek to help. The latter constitutes the therapeutic dimension of supervision.

The therapeutic dimension of our model maintains a clear boundary between these two domains of psychotherapy and supervision. Any personal issue that supervision addresses must originate within the supervisee's professional relationships. The supervisory conversation need not impose an unnatural restriction on discussing its specifics. Supervisees are free to generalize to the presence of similar conflicts throughout their lives, fitting their present experience into the larger mosaic of their own personal history. But our model limits the attention given to working for personal change in those professional relationships to whatever is occurring here and now. It does not extend attention to one's personal past or present family life or other non-professional relationships. Within these boundaries anything therapeutic that can be accomplished within supervision is a responsible use of time and energy. Supervisors may model good counseling procedures in identifying and exploring the problem. Specific strategies to work through its grips in the present sphere of clinical relationships with administrators, peers, supervisors, and patients are well within the bounds of supervisory conversation.

The therapeutic dimension of supervision can also become a hook that subverts its process. Occasionally a trainee's personal problems become so great that they dominate the supervisory hour. The focus of reflection upon concrete clinical practice is surrendered and supervision is converted into personal therapy. We have identified this as a supervisory game called "Sick" in training workshops for supervisors. In its common form, both supervisor and supervisee subtly agree at a covert level that the supervisee is so "troubled," "mixed up," "stressed," or "confused" that each supervisory hour is converted into counseling regarding these problems. Responsible presentation and assessment of clinical materials is avoided. The student is "Sick" and cannot be expected to perform competently. The supervisor gets to demonstrate the role of "Wonderful Counselor." In its more subtle forms, clinical learning is undermined by referring everything to one's current personal issue, excusing oneself from substantial, critical reflection upon the work at hand. This is a temptation for more seasoned players who would rather be "Sick" than "Stupid." Resolutions are found through referring the trainee's personal issues to a proper setting for psychotherapy outside supervision where they can receive adequate time and attention. Supervision then may reestablish its focus in the first dimension of administrative oversight.

The Working Alliance

The third dimension of supervisory reflection is the working alliance in the supervisory relationship itself. The term is borrowed from the psychodynamic tradition to describe a quality of collaboration in supervision similar to the one in psychotherapy between analyst and patient. (Bordin, 1982) At the heart of this collaboration for change is a bonding aspect of working together in cooperative endeavor. It is like the rhythmic "Heave Ho!" through which a team of persons moves a heavy object. It demands that the parties succeed in building up, repairing, and maintaining this working relationship.

Supervisors can count on experiencing some substantial resistance from each person entering supervision with them. Psychodynamic supervisors offer a vivid description of characteristic forms of resistance encountered among psychotherapists-in-training. (Ekstein and Wallerstein, 1958, pp. 142–156) Some students approach learning through vigorous denying, warding off the impact of supervision by reducing it to the familiar or refusing to acknowledge that any help can accrue. Others learn only through submission, the too easy manner of adopting the supervisor's offerings, leading to an imitative assumption of external trappings of content without truly effective learning. Still others react with a *"mea culpa"* attitude which constitutes a response with embarrassment and readied acknowledgement magnifying one's own feelings to the point of caricature and learning only by being beaten. Still others evade supervision by awarding the supervisor the task of achieving results, refusing to accept a role of responsible participation. Others have problems finding a problem to discuss or escape through over-involvement by maintaining so many conflicting interests that training is obtained "on the run."

There are any number of ways in the literature on supervision to conceptualize the particular forms this resistance may take. Supervisors from several traditions have elected to use Eric Berne's metaphor of psychological games to identify a number of "supervisory games" that can be observed between supervisors and supervisees. (Kadushin, 1968; Steere, 1969; McCarty, 1978) Such games involve supervisor and student in an unconscious collusion to avoid the demanding task of supervision through a repetitive series of transactions (moves), governed by an ulterior and complementary alliance of which they are unaware, progressing to a predictable outcome (payoff) that frustrates the professed aims of both parties. (Berne, 1964) A typical example is "Look What You Made Me Do" in which the supervisee shifts increasing responsibility to the supervisor ("You're the Super") who eventually designs some strategy for the supervisee's counseling. The supervisee meticulously executes the task, unsuccessfully returning with clinical data to the effect of "Look What You Made Me Do," disestablishing the professional and personal well-being of both parties.

Others conceptualize resistance in terms of "irrational beliefs" and "self-defeating philosophies" with which supervisees needlessly upset themselves. The three most common ones are: (1) "I *must* do well in supervision and be approved by my supervisor"; (2) "My supervisor *has to* be competent and treat me fairly"; (3) "The supervision program *must* be well arranged and effective, and I *can't stand it* if it isn't." (Wessler and Ellis, 1982)

Whatever one's perspective, some reflection upon the character of the supervisory relationship itself proves necessary to establish and maintain its working alliance. Whatever self-defeating patterns of feeling, thinking, and acting its parties carry into everyday life will eventually emerge to disrupt collaboration and mutual trust. If permitted to go unattended, the quality of this working alliance deteriorates, yielding unvoiced frustration with one another and increasingly ineffective supervisory hours.

Whenever the supervisory conversation addresses this dimension of its working alliance, it also enters the fertile field of exploring what we have described as *parallel process* and the *isomorphic character* of the entire system surrounding the therapeutic relationship. We have noted this recurrent tendency of the therapist's issues in the treatment relationship to reappear in the supervisory relationship and vice versa. For example, an otherwise cooperative and forthright trainee presented in a somewhat defiant and obscure way his work with a client who himself was rebelliously nondescript about his own life experience in the counseling hour. Before either party was aware of it, the supervisor was probing for information that was missing and not forthcoming from the supervisee who became more defensive and guarded, replicating the frustrating experience in the counseling relationship upon which the two reflected.

Psychodynamic explanations of this parallel process view the counselor as identifying with the counselee and unconsciously presenting this emotional material to the supervisor in the way it was encountered. Such efforts can persist for lengthy periods of supervision when the counselee's issue is sufficiently similar to something in the counselor's own personal life that persists and begs for resolution. First dimension efforts at clinical reflection are increasingly frustrated and ineffective as both the treatment and its supervision become bogged down in this impasse of parallel process. Third dimension resolutions through reflection upon the supervisory relationship not only serve to restore effective collaboration but present the counselor-in-training with a corrective experience that is normally accompained by a similar breakthrough with the counselee in counseling.

The experience of *isomorphism* reported by systemic supervisors, however, suggests that we are dealing with an even broader phenomenon. This same parallel process appears to manifest itself throughout the entire system of relationships surrounding marriage and family therapy. For example, during a session of live supervision, therapy with a family behind the glass suddenly became confusing and chaotic as both parents criticized each other. Anxiety rose and communication became tangential. The hapless co-therapists emerged from the room for consultation with the "team" behind the glass with mounting anxiety, feeling both confused and critical of each other. Conversation among team members was equally chaotic, and efforts by the supervisor to focus feedback were met with tangential responses. The supervisor became critical of the team and anxious about restoring some order and potency to the therapy. It was as though the whole system of relationships surrounding the family therapy had been unwittingly inducted into one and the same problem-determined system.

I have come to regard such isomorphism as not only common but inevitable among sensitive and caring human systems. There are a number of metaphors by which to comprehend its effect and contemplate appropriate awareness, detachment, and intervention. The *hypnotic* metaphor is one. Through involvement and joining efforts we are inducted into the family system at some level of its emotional fusion, thereby beginning to feel the way its members feel, think the way its members think, and respond the way its members do to the problems at hand. Constructive intervention demands that we somehow break this trance.

Another is the metaphor of the *game* as it is used by Berne and Palazzoli. (Berne, 1964; Palazzoli, Cirillo, Selvini, and Sorrentino, 1989) The game metaphor preserves the notion of a number of players beneath their level of ordinary awareness being drawn into an elaborate system of interaction which progresses to a repetitive and well-defined outcome. It effectively integrates the notion of general rules governing the players' interactions (systemics—holistic thinking) and moves made by individual subjects (strategic thinking) embodying ideas of conflict and deception. Whenever we address a human problem with any depth and reflect upon it in supervision, we all become players from our own specific vantage point: therapists, supervisors, referring parties, administrators, families, supporting figures, etc. To become involved is to enter the game at some point as a player with a position and a role. To change the outcome involves supervision in the necessary task of reflection in this third dimension with sufficient detachment and differentiation from present rules and personal strategies to function as part of the solution rather than part of the problem.

I am reminded of the old German fairy tale in which a boy steals the magic goose and becomes stuck to it. Subsequently, anyone who touches the boy or the goose or anyone touching the boy or the goose also becomes stuck. Any effort to extricate or free participants involves the next person becoming stuck, and what we encounter in such a problem-determined system as a game are numbers of people wandering across the countryside all stuck together. Supervision begins and ends with the search for effective means by which supervisor and supervisee can unstick themselves, so that they can help other people in the system to unstick themselves.

Bibliography

Berne, E. *Games People Play.* New York: Acove Press, 1964.

Berne, E. *Principles of Group Treatment.* New York: Oxford University Press, 1966.

Boisen, A.T. "The Challenge to Our Seminaries," *Journal of Pastoral Care,* Spring 1951, pp. 8–12.

Bordin, E.S. "A Working Alliance-based Model of Supervision," *The Counseling Psychologist* 11 (1):35–42 (1982).

Cabot, R.C. *Adventures on the Borderline of Ethics.* New York: Harper & Brothers, 1926.

Cabot, R.C. and Dicks, R.L. *The Art of Ministering to the Sick.* New York: Macmillan Co., 1936.

Carkhuff, R. *The Art of Helping VI.* Amherst: Human Resources Development Press, 1987.

Carter, E.A., "Supervisory Discussion in the Presence of the Family," in R. Whiffin and J. Byng-Hall, eds, *Family Therapy Supervision.* London: Gruss and Stratton, 1982, pp. 69–90.

Clebsch, W.A. and Jaekle, C.R. *Pastoral Care in Historic Perspective.* Englewood Cliffs, N.J.: Prentice-Hall, Inc., 1964.

Doehrman, M.J.G., "Parallel Process in Supervision and Psychotherapy," *Bulletin of the Menninger Clinic,* March 1976, pp. 9–104.

Ekstein, R. and Wallerstein, R.S. *The Teaching and Learning of Psychotherapy.* New York: Basic Books, 1958.

Estadt, B.K., Compton, J.R., and Blanchette, M.C., eds., *The Art of Clinical Supervision: A Pastoral Counseling Perspective.* Mahwah: Paulist Press, 1987.

Freud, S. "The History of the Psychanalytic Movement," in *The Basic Writings of Sigmund Freud,* trans. and ed. A.A. Biell. New York: Random House, 1938.

Hiltner, S. *Preface to Pastoral Theology.* Nashville: Abingdon Press, 1958.

Hoffman, L.W. *Old Scapes, New Maps: A Training Program for Psychotherapy Supervisors.* Cambridge: Milusik Press, 1990.

Kadushin, A. "Games People Play in Supervision," *Social Work,* July 1968, pp. 23–32.

Laing, R.D. *Politics of the Family.* New York: Vintage Books, 1972.

Liddle, H.A., Breunlin, D.C., and Schwartz, R.C., eds., *Handbook of Family Therapy Training and Supervision.* New York: London: Guilford Press, 1988.

McCarty, D. *The Supervision of Ministry Students.* Atlanta: Southwest Baptist Home Mission Board, Southern Baptist Convention, 1978.

Mead, D.E., ed. *Effective Supervision.* New York: Brunner/Mazel, 1990.

Palazzoli, M.S., Cirillo, S., Selvini, M. and Sorrentino, A.M. *Family Games.* New York and London: W.W. Norton & Co., 1989.

Practical Applications in Supervision. A Manual Written by the California Association for Marriage and Family Therapists Educational Foundation, 1990.

Ritterman, M. *Using Hypnosis in Family Therapy.* San Francisco: Jossey-Bass, 1983.

Rogers, C.R. *The Clinical Treatment of the Problem Child.* Boston: Houghton Mifflin Co., 1939.

Rogers, C.R. *Client-Centered Therapy: Its Current Practice, Implications, and Theory.* New York: Houghton Mifflin Co., 1951.

Rogers, C.R. and Becker, R.J. "A Basic Orientation for Counseling," *Pastoral Psychology,* February 1950, pp. 26–34.

Rogers, C.R. and Dymond, R.F., eds. *Psychotherapy in Personal Change.* Chicago: University of Chicago Press, 1954.

Schuster, J.J., Sandt, J.J., and Thaler, O.F. *Clinical Supervision of the Psychiatric Resident.* New York: Brunner/Mazel, 1972.

Simon, R. "Behind the One Way Mirror: An Interview with Jay Haley," *Family Therapy Networker,* Sept.–Oct. 1982, pp. 18–25, 28, 29, 58, 59.

Simon, R. "Deeper, Deeper, Deeper . . . The Family's Hypnotic Pull," *Family Therapy Networker* 9 (March–April 1985), pp. 20–28, 69–71.

Steere, D.A., "An Experiment in Supervisory Training," *Journal of Pastoral Care,* December 1969, pp. 202–217.

Steere, D.A., *The Supervision of Pastoral Care.* Louisville/Westminster: John Knox Press, 1989.

Wessler, R. and Ellis, A. "Supervision in Counseling: Rational Emotive Therapy," *The Counseling Psychologist* 11 (1):443–449, 1982.

Whiffin, R. and Byng-Hall, J. Jr. eds. *Family Therapy Supervision: Recent Developments in Practice.* London: Grune and Stralton, 1982.

Whittaker, C.A. "Hypnosis and Family Depth Therapy," in *Eriksonian Approaches to Hypnosis and Psychotherapy,* Jeffrey K. Zeig, ed. New York: Brunnen/Mazel, 1982.

Carolyn J. Bohler

Essential Elements of Family Systems Approaches to Pastoral Counseling

This chapter conveys some of the essential elements of family systems approaches to pastoral counseling. These elements are introduced and explained through several case examples from possible pastor-parishioner situations. After the case material, there is a brief overview of the schools of family systems from which these theories and practices have evolved. Finally, emerging issues—gender, faith, ethnicity, and societal dimensions—are examined regarding their effect upon family systems therapy.

Cinderella or Paper Bag Princess?

A family of four had been active members of a particular local church for the entire life of the children, a son, now twenty-one away at college, and a girl, seventeen, who is a senior in high school. The mother comes to the pastor in desperation. The daughter has a difficult relationship with her boyfriend—so up and down that nightly the whole family is in distress as the daughter cries, the father withdraws from her upsetting behavior, and the mother struggles to shelter the daughter and soothe the father. The mother wants the pastor to talk with the daughter, to help her to see that she must give up this boyfriend who is mistreating her and ruining their lives.

"Identified Patient"

If a pastor were to look with eyes attentive to systems, she would virtually never see just an individual; the focus for attention is the pattern of interaction within the whole system. Problems, solutions, and resources are embedded in the family context. The pastor would immediately reframe the issue in her own mind as a family dilemma, not as the daughter's problem alone. This would affect the pastor's response to the mother, which could be:

—"You are all so concerned about this. Why don't you and your daughter, and even your husband, come in together to tell me more about the situation."

—"May I come by this evening, when all of you are home, to talk about this situation?"

—"It seems to me that your daughter will need a lot of family support to get through this. Would you and your husband (and your son, if possible) be willing to come in with her to express your support?"

Even if the pastor only manages to talk with the daughter, she can *think* of the situation in family terms, not isolating the daughter in her own mind as the sole person with a "problem" which needs to be fixed. It is important that the healing resources of the family be emphasized. Families easily feel blamed when they are seen as the focus of counseling; their immediate reaction is often to deny their involvement in the "identified patient's" personal situation.

Resistance to Change—Desire to Change

Whereas much of psychodynamic therapy places the responsibility for resistance to change in the client ("he is resisting therapy"), family systems therapists take very seriously their own responsibility to finesse the family's resistance to change. A good deal of the therapeutic strategy involves how to maneuver the resistance so that it can be circumvented. The family counselor seeks to befriend the resistance to change, rather than to fight it or deny it.

Families are quite wedded to repeating their patterns of interaction, the family's *homeostatic cycle,* even if the current situation is quite painful. The members of the family want help and may be only dimly aware that they cannot change the situation without adjusting the family's whole set of interactions.

Two professors of psychiatry who counsel from a family systems perspective, Carol M. Anderson and Susan Stewart, have provided an excellent book, *Mastering Resistance: A Practical Guide to Family Therapy.* They use family systems analyses to describe how family members may resist counseling in ongoing treatment, challenge the therapist's competence, or encounter complications that are created by the helping systems themselves. (Anderson and Stewart, 1983)

The Symptom Is Connected to the System

From a systems' point of view, all individuals are interconnected so that a change in one person affects all other persons. The way a person behaves, thinks, or feels affects other family members, while at the same time the other family members have an effect on that person's behaviors, thoughts and feelings. This circular view of causality will be expanded upon in the next section.

In a family, the symptom helps to maintain the system (as it is currently functioning) at the same time that the system maintains the symptom. (Papp, 1983, pp. 17–19) That is why the symptomatic behavior cannot be removed or "healed" without affecting the whole system; it also explains how the symptom will be affected if members of the family other than the symptom-bearer make significant changes in their part of the system.

In this case, the pastor needs to ask herself immediately, and to reevaluate frequently, how the symptom(s) is (are) intertwined with other behaviors. She can ask the family to *describe exactly* what occurs on a given night. The scenario unfolds: The teenage girl expects a call from her boyfriend; she had seen him with another girl at school and is worried. No call comes by 9:30 p.m., so she calls his home. After the boyfriend's dad says he's not there, the girl becomes panicked, starts crying, and continues to cry for quite a while.

The mother worries about the daughter and tries to comfort her, but the daughter screams that the mother can't understand. The mother says the daughter is ruining her life waiting for this no-good boy, that the daughter must stop crying, and that she is disturbing the family's peace and quiet. The mother leaves the daughter's room to find the father angry that the mother has doted upon the daughter's tears once more. He says he cannot tolerate their daughter's behavior and wishes the mother would put her foot down. The mother tells her husband that she doesn't know what to do. She begins to feel badly about what she said to the daughter, so she massages the daughter's back until finally the episode wanes for the night. The mother and father are cool to each other as they get into bed, certainly not romantic toward each other as they are frustrated and upset.

It should be noted that family approaches to counseling have *focused upon behaviors*, precise behaviors. Family members will tend to give generalizations. It is important to get the exact sequence of behaviors, such as: a whiny daughter triggers an angry withdrawing dad which leads to a placating mother which perpetuates the daughter's whining.

It is quite possible to ask the family to *enact* an evening tribulation right in the counseling session. The pastor could visit the family in their home, with the advantage that she can ask the family to reenact what happens in the setting in which it actually occurs.

Even without the prompting of the counselor, families inadvertently show what does occur in the family on a regular basis. If the counselor is attentive, she may note how the family sits, who talks with whom, who uses active or passive verb tenses, and what tones of voice are present. An *enactment* may not be repeating what tends to occur, but could be simply asking the members to talk to each other right now in the counseling session.

One way to think about the *connection between the system and the symptom* in this case is as follows. The unkindness of the boyfriend, and to some extent the daughter's subsequent upset, is defined by the family as a problem—the symptom. This family system is one in which members trip over each other to care for each other. Family members (perhaps especially the females) are not encouraged to resolve their own problems, but are expected to be highly dependent and affected by others in the family. Mother and father are currently trying to solve their daughter's problem. They tell her what to do, but perhaps they do not back up enough to let her live with her own choices (even the choice to be hysterical) before telling her again what to do or not to do. *The parents try to prohibit her upset, but they do it by becoming upset themselves.*

In their exasperation, the parents fear that they are not managing to solve the daughter's problem, so they decide that someone else may be able to solve it—the pastor. This is tricky, for the daughter needs to trust her own abilities to make decisions as she grows up. Intervention by the parents or the pastor may suggest to her that she is not able to be trusted to make wise decisions. Yet she may benefit from wisdom evoked by parental or pastoral care. If she becomes too dependent upon external authorities for advice or the opportunity to rebel at advice, this pattern of interactions may inadvertently help to maintain the daughter's dependency upon the boyfriend (another external authority). She may be unable to leave—boyfriend or parents. She may maintain both sets of relationships through dependency and upset. The boyfriend's unkindness to, but dependency upon, the teenage girl, and the daughter's upset but dependency upon him, keep this system functioning. But, also, the whole system, functioning as it does, fosters dependency and upset for all members.

Circular Causation

Systems theory shuns linear thinking, accepting as its cardinal rule *circular causation.* X does not cause Y. Rather, one event triggers another which triggers another, etc. The events which are thought of as "effects" are really also "causes" of the earlier events. X leads to Y leads to Z leads to X. Rather than eliminating "X," an isolated event (identified patient's behavior), the family therapist's goal is to interrupt the cycle any place in the chain of events. Intervention in the cycle is what is necessary—it does not have to start with the so-called identified-patient.

Hearing the family's scenario, one realizes that there is no simple cause and effect in the family's system. The boy's behavior during the day and evening have not "caused" the panic in the household, though it has been a contributing factor. The girl's withdrawal yet insistent neediness has not caused the mother's feeling of being tugged in two directions and the father's withdrawing behavior, though the girl's behavior is a contributing factor. The father's withdrawing and resentment do not make the daughter and mother explode, but these are contributing elements. The mother's sense of responsibility for two lives other than her own does not cause the upset, but does help to maintain the cycle of dependency. The mother's putting up with being screamed at by the daughter may lessen the mother's wavering self-esteem while at the same time models for her daughter tolerance with being emotionally mistreated (as the daughter is by the boyfriend). The older brother's exit and independence does not cause this daughter's present stuckness, but each sibling's behavior affects the other's. All the causes move together to *create and maintain* the effect, the symptom which is painful for all. Those with the most power in the system may be the strongest factors in maintaining the system.

Certainly it is possible to counsel the teenager about self-respect, to encourage her to speak up to her boyfriend, to get her needs met. It is crucial to hear the daughter's story—how she feels about herself and what this boy means to her. It is important to ask what her level of involvement is with the boy. Do they have sexual intercourse? If they do not, she can be congratulated for a mature decision, given her values, their ages, and the shakiness of their relationship. If they do, she should be asked if this is something she genuinely wants to do, how it fits with her beliefs and values, and what possible effects it may have upon her, her relationship with the boy, and their future. Birth control and concern for AIDS should be faced squarely. The pastor should explore what the teenage girl expects in a relationship and how she is able (or unable) to tell her current boyfriend what she wants. But a systems counselor will not just focus upon the girl's feelings or behaviors—counseling will not aim at changes she alone makes. The system itself needs to be interrupted.

One of the most direct ways to transform this system may be to talk with the teenage boy and girl together. If the girl is asked to invite the boy for counseling, she might be empowered to take charge of her part in their relationship, as she would be suggesting to her friend that changes are necessary. The present dynamics could be discussed with them in a mood of helpful interchange, not blaming either one. If the girl does not want to invite her friend, or if he declines her request, these behaviors become important focal points for the counseling.

Interventions, used to interrupt a system, can be made at any point in the system. The parents can be coached to react in unpredictable, even odd ways, so that the daughter will discover that she cannot expect the same family patterns to follow her upset.

The mother could agree to choose not to follow the crying daughter into the room. She could start reading a good book or do something else which is worthwhile when she starts to feel she must console her daughter. The father could calmly knock at the daughter's door, then sit down, sharing with the daughter some of the events he has had during the day, then thank her for listening and leave. The parents could (if the weather and environment are conducive) take a walk together whenever the daughter goes to her room crying. Or they could agree to interact with each other (talk, play a game) whenever one of them is inclined to pacify the daughter or withdraw from the other. Then, whenever they hear the crying subside, they could, using a *non-anxious demeanor,* interact with the daughter.

The brother could be contacted by the pastor (with the other family members' permission) and told that his brotherly words of wisdom may be beneficial for his sister. (His grasp of his parents' behavior may be helpful insight for the parents, too.) Perhaps he could call, visit, or write a note. This might strengthen the sibling relationship by involving the brother and loosen the tight connection between the other three. It also functions to communicate that males' involvement is just as essential as that of females to solving family and friendship dilemmas.

In these ways the cycle is interrupted. The parents do not foster the repetitious events. Rather than ineffectively trying to solve the daughter's problem, they are communicating that the family is *not* going to *revolve around* those issues. They are *staying in touch* with the daughter, but only in constructive ways, *reinforcing* her positive interactions, not her negative ones.

The parents and brother, by implementing these new behaviors, are acting *unpredictably*. In this way they open the door to the teenage girl's behaving in a new way. In the cycle which has become repetitious, the daughter's actions do not vary; she can't think of any other response. But if the other family members show alternative responses during their part of the cycle, the implicit message is that the daughter can respond differently, too.

Family Cohesion and Boundaries

When we attend to the *boundaries* which families exhibit, we see that many families in our culture are *enmeshed*, so close that there is not a clear boundary between what one member or another feels and thinks. At the other extreme is the *disengaged* family, which exhibits only little emotional connection between family members. Family therapists recognize that families function healthfully with varying degrees of closeness. What would be too much for some families is just right for others. There is not a specific norm which is best for all families.

However, when there is strong enmeshment and a symptom present, the therapist may seek to make interventions which realign the family members' interactions to create more *permeable boundaries*. In this way, each member would not *escalate* the concerns of the other members.

The counselor in the case we are looking at can observe and state that each member is strongly affected by the others. This family can be encouraged to explore the meaning of their value of "closeness." "When one suffers, we all suffer," says the mother, showing congruence between her theology and behavior. "We have time for each other," says the father, who is not feeling close to the mother right now.

Now the therapist has the opportunity to use *reframing*. Closeness can be maintained as a value, but framed quite differently. The pastor explains, "When I hear your kind of closeness, I get the image of a soccer team which stays so close to the ball that they end up kicking each other's legs—there's no room to move the ball forward when they're all kicking each other. I wonder whether closeness could also be the AT&T 'reach out and touch' kind—where you play your positions, but keep an eye on each other and the goal of the game from some distance, giving each other room to move."

Here the counselor has helped the family to reflect upon its values, to look at its theme of "closeness," and to gently give that theme a different frame. It would be possible to maintain the value, but to have it look quite different. If the parents were told *not* to be so close, or not to be so involved with their daughter's relationships with her friends, they would surely resist the advice (for that goes against their deeply held parental values and the worries of their own life-stage crises). But if the family is shown, using images, metaphors, or stories, how closeness can be expressed differently (and differently as their children grow), they may be able to entertain a more gentle, more empowering closeness.

Perhaps the girl could use more of her own resources and knowledge if she were given more emotional room. Closeness may be a positive value for the adults (pastor included). However, it is important not to dismiss the chance of some form of abuse in the girl's past or present experience. Abuse often goes under the guise of secretive, false closeness. How is it that the girl is willing to stay in a relationship in which she admits she is being emotionally abused?

Attitudinal or behavioral *themes* can be passed down from one generation to another. (Family therapists vary in their emphasis upon generational data.) A counselor may inquire into the way in which the parents' families of origin were "close" and the presence of any abuse in those extended families.

Another action which a family-systems oriented pastor might take is to prescribe *homework assignments* aimed at changing the *boundaries* within the system. The daughter is trying to grow up while the parents are negotiating "empty nest" transitions; it is a natural time of boundary reformation. In this case, the pastor may view the situation like this: father temporarily isolated, trying to pull the mother back from the daughter, but fearful of losing both daughter and mother; mother using her caring skills, striving to keep the family "together." The teenage girl may need reassurance that she will have mom and dad with her, even as she leaves home and makes her own decisions. Parents may be requested to focus on their being with their daughter, not just at times when they are correcting her.

The pastor could assign the daughter the *task* of asking the father and mother out, separately. The pastor asks what the interests are and determines that the daughter and father enjoy bowling. She can suggest that the daughter ask the father to go bowling. The girl and mother used to bicycle together, so the daughter is coached to ask the mother for a Saturday bike ride. The pastor can prohibit the family members from talking about the boyfriend during these events. A new, more flexible set of boundaries is being sought in which each person has access to the others and offers support for the others. In addition, it brings back reminiscences of earlier times, when there was that access within each dyad. Paradoxically, prescribing times together with people who are currently feeling separated in the system enables those individuals to leave the system when the time is right.

Because the mother says that she wants to use her talents more fully, but doesn't know what to do, the mother can be encouraged to share with the pastor what is happening in her own life. She works part-time, but knows she will soon have a lot of time on her hands. The mother is anxious about her life without children at home. She can be encouraged to take up activities which are important to her, but do not revolve around the growing children. She may be given a homework assignment to explore some of these specific options.

Also, the two adults need to give themselves permission to strengthen their relationship with each other, to do things as a couple. Soon they will live together as a twosome again after two decades of raising children in the home. They can nurture their relationship more fully now; that very nurturance often simultaneously benefits the children.

The Use of Metaphors and Images for Reframing

When the pastor/counselor comments about her image of the family playing soccer, she is using a *metaphor* to describe the family. Some schools of family systems use metaphors quite intentionally, since metaphors communicate what words cannot. In this case the counselor has provided the image. It is also possible to ask the family members to find the images of themselves. (Bohler, 1987, pp. 63–71)

Peggy Papp uses a technique she calls "Couples Choreography" both to make a tentative *diagnosis* about a couple's relationship pattern and to observe what *progress* has been made, when the end of the counseling is in sight. (Papp, 1983, pp. 142–164) The husband of one couple with which Papp used this approach "saw his wife as a fleeting person in the fog—a disappearing phantom. He would try to follow her and capture her but she was always just out of his reach." The wife saw her husband "as a 200-pound rock. She was autumn rain, which gently pattered against the rock in the hope of drawing him out. She wanted him to 'stop being a rock and open up and become a flower.' "

Papp assessed the central theme of this couple: "I want you to see me," was the husband's stance; the wife's reciprocal position was "I'm afraid to look."

At the end of therapy Papp asked that couple to explore fantasies which represented their current relationship. The dismal, distant images transformed into life-giving ones. The husband's was "heavily laden with images indicating the change in their sexual relationship: 'We are either stones or pieces of drift wood lying on the beach, half buried by the sand. We are peeking out so we can see the beautiful ocean. The waves come in and crash over us—they are constantly rolling in and rolling out and rolling in and rolling out. We are enjoying it together. It is a peaceful feeling. I particularly like the rhythmic envelopment of the waves.' " The wife's fantasy "took place in a park on a windy, sunny day. They were two balloons tied together with a string: 'We've been let go. We bob up and down with the wind, but we've been tied together. It's a free-floating feeling.' " (Papp, 1983, pp. 156–159)

Stories Which Inform

Another possibility, in working with the teenager, would be to hear or to discover what stories inform her. The counselor encourages the girl to describe her relationship with her boyfriend more fully. In the midst of that discussion the counselor reflects, "You seem to act rather like Cinderella. You had a great dance with this prince at the ball. Now you're waiting for him to bring the shoe, but he never does." The girl confirms this with a knowing smile, saying she is convinced that he will start acting like a prince again some day, if only she waits.

Now the pastor can introduce new stories, or discuss different endings to old stories, supposing that the underlying stories the girl holds function as guiding—and limiting—realities for her. It is helpful if the pastoral counselor is full of stories (historical, imaginary, biblical, fairy). One which might be provocative for this teenager is *The Paper Bag Princess*. In this children's book, the princess, Elizabeth, is engaged to Prince Ronald. A dragon carries off Ronald, creating general havoc. The princess survives, but has no clothing and is covered with dirt. She finds a paper bag, which she puts on. Courageous and intelligent, Elizabeth goes to the dragon's cave and knocks at the door. She cleverly gets the dragon to show her how he can fly around the world, several times. She has the dragon demonstrate his fiery abilities, too. Finally, the dragon drops, exhausted, into sleep.

The girl opens the door to let Prince Ronald out, but he is not grateful. He is upset that she does not look like a princess. She concludes, "Ronald, your clothes are really pretty and your hair is very neat. You look like a real prince, but you are a bum." And they don't get married after all. (Munsch, 1980)

The teenager, amused, may not name the insight she has derived. *Insight is not the goal* of family counseling nearly so much as the *introduction of novelty* into intact systems of interaction. As she is introduced to Elizabeth and Ronald, this young woman has images which are in discord with her Cinderella motif. Choice has been introduced, subtly, with humor, in a take-it-or-leave-it kind of way, assuming that the girl has inner resources which can guide her in choosing.

Life Stage Issues

Life Stage issues, both of the individuals and of the family, are significant in family therapy. (Carter and McGoldrick, 1980) The patterns of interaction are altered greatly when a member leaves the household, as when a child leaves home, an adult leaves a marriage, or a person dies. A brand new set of interactions needs to be negotiated. Change is likely to be threatening to each member of the family, especially if the family has been emotionally so close that challenges for one become equally challenging for the others.

This lengthy scenario offers many opportunities to see family systems counseling in practice in a way which is feasible for the pastor of a church. Access into families, their behaviors, their myths/themes/images, their fears and longings are natural for the pastor. A pastor who is immersed in systems thinking can pick up a photograph during a pastoral visit and comment upon dynamics apparent in the photo. For example, "I notice you're always in the middle," the pastor can say to the family member around whom interactions revolve.

We will look at another case, then name the various schools of family systems.

Catching Up with the Joneses

The pastor well remembered the sincere soul-searching of Mrs. Jones, who had caught his ear at the annual family retreat several years ago. Mrs. Jones was then fifty. She had a seven year old boy, Tony, whom the pastor assumed was her son. Mrs. Jones called him "the light of my life." The pastor, new to this church, seemed caring, so Mrs. Jones felt she could talk. She told him that this boy was really her grandson. She had three children, the youngest a son, Brian. When Brian was eighteen, he had a child by a woman who did not want to raise the child. Brian would not let the boy be adopted, so he tried to rear the boy himself, but Brian was not able to cope. Mr. and Mrs. Jones had then agreed to raise Tony.

At that retreat Mrs. Jones had explained that she and her husband were deeply appreciative of Tony—he was indeed a blessing. However, they had expected to have time to be with each other, and they longed for that.

Four years passed—the light of the Jones' life was eleven. Brian, who was now twenty-nine, had grown up, married, and begun to earn a living. He and his wife Louise now wanted to raise Tony. Brian had always had custody of the boy, even though he went months without seeing him. Mr. and Mrs. Jones were glad that their son was ready to take on this responsibility. They believed that their many prayers were being answered; their grandchild would come to know his father. However, how would they manage to relinquish parenthood?

All knew changes were to occur; none knew how to guarantee that those would go well. A year later they asked the pastor to help. The new parents were trying very hard to parent; the grandparents were trying equally hard not to parent. The boy was respectful of his parents, but called Mrs. Jones nightly to help him with his homework. He sat with his grandparents in church, as he had for years (Tony's parents did not attend, but Tony begged to be allowed to go).

Louise had begun to talk with Mrs. Jones, trying to learn about Tony. Mr. and Mrs. Jones did their best to update Brian and Louise on the boy's life, giving them various scrapbooks and telling them of childhood events.

The realistic-optimist approach is best when working with "blended" families and families which undergo the addition of members. (Lindblad-Goldberg, 1989) It is unrealistic to act as if the past has not happened. The past needs to be embraced, but not so tightly that it dominates the present. Parents are the ones who are most likely to experience gains and choices, when "blending" occurs; children often fear loss and experience lack of choice. (Lindblad-Goldberg, 1989)

Three stages are apparent in the assimilation of a family: the honeymoon, during which there is often denial of problems or negative feelings; reality sets in, when each member becomes more aware of his or her own needs; then either there is adaptation to the new or a symptom (a problem) arises. (Lindblad-Goldberg, 1989)

This family has a very difficult transition to make, but the necessity of such transitions is not at all rare today. Numerous families have to negotiate and renegotiate parenthood and care-taking. The Jones family was intentional about what was happening; many families are not clear about what is happening, much less about what they want to happen.

Triangles; Direct Communication; Behavior Emphasis

What could the pastor do to help? One of the most significant elements of family counseling is attention to *triangles.* Systems work best when people talk directly to one another. Brother talks to sister about brother-sister concerns; grandchild and grandfather talk to each other directly. Triangles emerge when two people communicate to a third rather than each other.

If a child calls home from a friend's house, the father answers, and the child asks to talk with the mother (to get permission to stay at the friend's home for dinner), there may be a triangle present. If the mother is the one who makes rules about visiting friends and this role is acceptable and known by all members in the family, there is no triangle, but a clear understanding of roles and rules. However, if the mother talks with child and with father, but the father and child talk to the mother instead of each other, then there is a triangle.

As the Joneses try to interpret Tony to his new parents, a triangle emerges within the extended family. All, in good faith, participate in creating and maintaining the triangle. Pastoral care would *prescribe direct communication.* Brian and Tony could profitably spend their time with each other rather than learning about each other exclusively from the older generation. The church time could be genuine time with grandparents. But the homework time could be assigned to be with current parents (assuming that they are able to help). In this way the parents take on their appropriate responsibilities on a daily basis.

Negotiation about who does what with whom, the *assignment of straightforward tasks,* and focus upon *direct communication* are essentials in family systems therapy. There is a realism about the *messiness* of families. (Way, 1988) Ideal pictures are not painted, but the daily ambiguities and difficulties are faced matter-of-factly. There is hardly any searching for the "whys" of feelings or behaviors, for the attention is on "what" is happening and "how." The contention has been that if behavior changes, feelings and attitudes will follow. There has been, in family systems therapy, very *little attention to intrapsychic events.* Currently some female family therapists who are looking at gender patterns are reintroducing the relevance of feelings. (Walters, 1988)

Friedman, in *Generation to Generation,* cites numerous examples of triangles not only in family systems, but also in churches and synagogues. (Friedman, 1985) A student in one of my classes at seminary presented this dilemma: His church had been forming caring teams, clusters of people who would visit newcomers and shut-ins in pairs. One member of such a pair called the student pastor to tell him that she would not be going out with her partner—she would be visiting alone. This member further requested that the student tell the partner. The pastor suggested that the woman tell the partner herself, but the woman said she did not want to and hung up the phone. The student, learning about triangles, was acutely aware that he was in one. He did not want to call the partner himself, for that would maintain the triangle. However, he believed that there was no other way for him to function, since the partner "had to be told."

Another member of the class, who had grasped and begun to embody Friedman's points, suggested that the fellow student could simply not tell the partner. The student, and many others in the class (including myself), worried that he would then be blamed in front of the whole team for not carrying out her request. The class member who had grasped the truth of triangles responded, "Then you can say, in front of everyone, 'See, now you all know not to trust me with messages to someone else which you should take yourself.' " The point was made.

Triangles do not work. People must talk directly to the people with whom they relate. The way to get ourselves out of triangles is to facilitate their not working, to frustrate the system in such a way that the only thing which *will* work is direct interaction. Here, *humor* and a *non-anxious presence,* two significant qualities for systems work, are helpfully enlisted.

In the Jones' case, the boy and his dad could be asked to look at the scrapbook together during the counseling session. The counselor can comment with a twinkle of humor that the real live boy can say more than the photo about the events depicted in the picture. The father and son can be coached in their talking with each other—now. An *enactment* is used: the two are asked to talk with each other in front of the counselor. The counselor can reflect upon what he sees is occurring. He can encourage and ask for changes in tone, words, or behavior which might help the interaction.

Partial Realities—No Search for "the" Reality

A guiding perspective for work with families is to uncover *partial realities*. Sometimes a hard task for the minister, but essential for family counseling, is to relinquish the notion that there is one true "reality" in the family. There is no one truth; a search for one suggests that the system is not taken seriously. Tony has one reality, Brian another, Mr. and Mrs. Jones have their own, and Louise develops her own reality. None of these realities is more correct than the others. If each view of reality is shared in the presence of the others, all views take on relativity.

Tony shares why he thinks his father asked his parents to raise him for eleven years. Brian explains the story in his way. The Joneses express their perceptions. As each reality is shared, these are acknowledged and valued verbally by the counselor. But the counselor does not create an atmosphere in which a correct scenario is to be pieced together. There is none. To express rather than to hide partial realities is important. To value and live with the ambiguity created by knowing that each member lives with different interpretations is humbling and offers growth-potential for all.

Secrets

Seldom do family systems approaches to therapy condone the maintenance of family secrets. Many "*secrets*" in systems are actually "known secrets." They are in the mental closets of the members, not allowed to be named. They function as ghosts if they are allowed to haunt current family interactions. When this happens, naming the ghosts can disempower them. In this case, the genetic mother may be a "secret." All the members of the current family would benefit from being allowed to express their feelings about and memories of this teenage girl from over a decade ago.

Rituals

The pastor is in a prime position to make use of *rituals*. Secular family therapists enlist the aid of rituals in order to say goodbye to a member whose memory continues to haunt the family, to celebrate and affirm one member's ethnic background, to formally join family members who have been grafted onto the family, or to facilitate any other movement which has gotten stuck.

Pastors have access to a variety of rituals from our tradition. We can connect the wisdom of both therapeutic and religious disciplines to create appropriate rituals for families. In this case a ritual of rebirth (or commitment) to parenting for Brian and one which would "baptize" Tony into the new parental family could be effective. The rituals could include a time of gratitude for the grandparents and a sacred letting-go of their responsibility as primary parents.

Rituals have enormous power over the psyches of individuals and communities. Long lectures on what a family "should" do are wearisome and most often ineffective, whereas well-planned brief rituals can transform a family for a lifetime.

Now that we have observed a number of dynamics which are useful to the parish pastor as he or she works with families, we will look briefly at how these practices fit into the various therapeutic approaches.

Schools of Family Systems Approaches

In the 1970s, as practitioners began to explore the family as the locus of therapy, centers developed which took on different approaches according to the populations which were the primary clients, the training of the psychotherapists, and the research being done. Writers on family systems approaches do not classify these "schools" in the same manner, but there are general agreements regarding the cluster of people who have developed and followed the various approaches.

For this explanation, I will describe briefly six dominant approaches: "Structural Family Therapy," "Structural-Strategic," "Strategic," "Experiential," "Systemic," and the "Bowenian Intergenerational Approach." Consultation, debate, ferment, dialogue, and refinement take place within each approach and between approaches. There are some basic premises and techniques which virtually all family therapists ascribe to, but there are differences in flavor, emphasis, and style.

"Structural Family Therapy" receives that name because there is a strong emphasis placed upon discerning the structure of the family; therapy often revolves around restructuring the family so that it promotes healthy functioning. Salvador Minuchin pioneered in developing this approach, especially when he was director of the Philadelphia Child Guidance Center. One of his most influential books was *Families and Family Therapy* in 1974.

Families are perceived to be open social systems which are constantly undergoing structural transformations. Boundaries between individuals may be flexible or rigid; families can be enmeshed (with weak boundaries) or disengaged (uninvolved). Diagrams are often drawn to form a hypothesis about the family dynamics. Triangles are observed, power is located, and rules are discerned. All this is discussed with the family. It is typical to suggest enactments, interactions between family members, during the therapy session.

"Structural-Strategic Therapy" is linked primarily with Jay Haley, who wrote a book called *Problem-Solving Therapy*. Haley's model focuses upon hierarchies, power relationships and problem-maintaining interactions along with transitions in the family life cycle. He has written a good deal about how the therapist "joins" the family, and he identifies practical ways for the family to solve its problems through enactments, prescriptions, and tasks.

The "Strategic" approach was first developed by a group of researchers and therapists in Palo Alto, California, at the Mental Research Institute (MRI). Gregory Bateson, Don Jackson, Jay Haley, Lynn Hoffman, and Virginia Satir were some of the most notable in the group who observed and researched family communication, homeostasis, and circular causation. This approach has evolved into a brief therapy model that is practiced in many locations in the United States (Milwaukee, Dayton, Chicago). The focal point of this model is to identify the vicious cycles of interactions that develop when people try to solve a problem—a problem-maintaining cycle.

Another set of therapists, including Paul Watzlawick, John Weakland, and Richard Fisch, were members and associates of MRI during the period 1965–1974. These people developed what they called "The Interactional View" and wrote of paradoxical observations of change in *Change: Principles of Problem Formation and Problem Resolution* in 1974.

Today a cluster of therapists may be classified as "Experiential," within the family systems umbrella. Virginia Satir, who was the first director of MRI, did not stay with that group, but proceeded to develop an emphasis upon social systems, communication, and feelings of worth. Carl Whitaker is another prominent therapist who would now be seen as experiential.

A number of people, such as Peggy Papp, at the Ackerman Institute for Family Therapy, carry on what has come to be known as the "Systemic" model. Papp, who has been in practice since 1966, served as co-director of the Brief Therapy Project at the Ackerman Institute, but she also held faculty positions at the Philadelphia Child Guidance Clinic. One of her major works carries on the notion of change in the title, *The Process of Change*. She uses paradox, myths, and rituals as she helps a family to untangle the tight connection between the system and the symptom.

Some of these systemic therapists are influenced by the approach of a group in Milan, Italy, which itself was influenced by the MRI and Bateson, but has developed emphases in positive connotation, prescriptive rituals and circular questioning.

The final "school" is called the "Bowenian Intergenerational Approach," because it was influenced by Murray Bowen. It is developed now by people such as Monica McGoldrick and Harriet Goldhor Lerner. McGoldrick has made major contributions to the field with her study of ethnicity (*Ethnicity and Family Therapy*) and more recently, with Carol Anderson and Froma Walsh, of gender (*Women in Families*).

Pastoral counseling has been dramatically influenced in the past few years by the publication of a book by Edwin Friedman, *Generation to Generation*, which follows primarily the Bowenian model. The emphasis in the Bowenian approach is upon multi-generational influences. What is unfinished or is carried on as a theme in one generation perpetuates itself in later generations if it is not completed or acknowledged and changed. Differentiation or self-definition, in conjunction with genuine staying-in-touch with other members, is seen as the most effective approach to leadership in families.

When family systems approaches began to impact the therapeutic world, elaborate explanations about the connectedness between individuals' problems and the family were abundant. Now most psychotherapeutic approaches have incorporated (in theory at least) the awareness of this truth. We find gestalt family therapy approaches, psychodynamic family orientations, T.A. family approaches, and behavioristic family approaches.

Ethnicity, Gender, Faith, and Societal Issues

Whether a family systems therapist emphasizes the impact of generations, the structure of the current family, or the myths and themes which are unspoken but pervasive, family therapists have placed more emphasis upon the *functions* of interactions than they have upon the *content* of the interactions.

For example, one might notice that an adult live-in boyfriend interrupts a woman almost every time she tries to speak. The question can be raised, in the counselor's mind, "What *function* does the interruption play?" Does the interruption serve to keep the man thinking of himself as essential in the family? Does it help to keep the woman unsure of her own opinions? Less attended to, but now recognized as important, are such questions as: "What kind of power does this couple assume that males and females should have in families?" "How do each of the adults experience power?" "How does society's gender biases foster their behavior?"

During the past two decades there has been an ethos of neutrality regarding *content* in family therapy. Basically, if a family manages to change over time and to face the inevitable crises of family life without the creation of symptoms within family members, then that family has been considered relatively healthy. Therapists tended to believe that they were not imposing their values upon families regarding race, gender, social or faith issues.

Rachel T. Hare-Mustin and others are currently challenging the possibility of holding a neutral stance. "Despite a therapist's presumed neutrality, family therapy is not value-free, whether it involves a psychodynamic stance or a systems approach. Even neutrality itself represents a value. The idea of therapeutic neutrality denies the fact that all therapists hold normative concepts of good and poor functioning, growth and stagnation, male and female." (McGoldrick, Anderson and Walsh, 1989, p. 62)

Recently, more attention has been given to ethnicity factors in family systems therapy; gender issues are now being recognized as significant content issues, too. A few therapists have encouraged family counselors to raise social and ethical issues, such as the impact of nuclear threat upon families. (Winawer, 1989)

The Pastoral Care Network for Social Responsibility, modeled after the organization, Physicians for Social Responsibility, has taken a lead in encouraging pastoral counselors to attend to social and environmental issues. However, in this movement there has not been much intentional connection with family systems.

To date there has not been much weight given to faith issues amidst family counseling. Rizzuto, in *The Birth of the Living God*, provided an object-relations psychoanalytical approach which encouraged therapists to consider people's concepts of God and the role of faith in the counseling process. She takes the family dynamics of early childhood seriously, as she theorizes how children develop their God concept and their orientation toward religion. (Rizzuto, 1979)

The time is ripe for family systems approaches to take seriously faith issues and family members' images of God in current families. These issues and images do function as crucial elements in a family system. God is sometimes even in a triangle with a couple, so that one or both partners relate more to their "God" than to each other.

Gender

Numerous women who have been practicing family systems therapy for two decades are now writing about the importance of gender issues in counseling. (McGoldrick, Anderson, and Walsh, 1989; Walters, Carter, Papp, and Silverstein, 1988; Bepko and Krestan, 1990; and Hochschild, 1989) The authors of *Women in Families* explain, "For the first 20 years the field operated in a gender-blind fashion, as if family members were simply interchangeable units of a system. Gender was one of those 'content' areas regarded as less significant than the 'process' of interaction in a system." (McGoldrick, Anderson, and Walsh, 1989, p. 9)

Virginia Golder writes, "There is no such clinical entity as a 'gender case' any more than there is a unique clinical entity, a 'generation case.' Even to ask, 'What are the gender issues in this family?' misses the point. . . . Gender and the gendering of power are not secondary mediating variables affecting family life; they construct family life in the deepest sense." (McGoldrick, Anderson, and Walsh, 1989, p. 56)

These observations have immense practical importance. For example, many family therapists have, buying into the circular model of causation, accepted as a premise for interventions the rule: "Get the pursuer to back off so that the distancer can move in." That is, if one member in a family is distant and another very close, the one who was acting very close has often been told to back off, so that the distancer might move forward. This seemed to many therapists a "neutral" stance in the midst of circular behavior patterns. Now we realize how often this results in blaming women, who are likely to be the "pursuers," labeled "over-involved," "loving too much," or "enmeshed." The distancers, often men, have been gently encouraged to engage more fully with their families rather than being challenged to be more responsible. Women have tended to accept the blame as a trade-off for change in the family dynamics. Women therapists are now seeing that although this treatment plan may reduce immediate and obvious symptoms, it is not worth the price paid for the women's loss of self-esteem and long-term relational outcomes. Betty Carter suggests that a better rule, if a rule is needed, would be: "Validate the concerns of the more involved one and challenge the distance of the one less involved." (Walters, Carter, Papp, and Silverstein, 1988, p. 347)

In the first, long, case presented in this chapter it matters greatly whether scenario one or two is taken: 1. The mother is told to back off; the father is encouraged to take charge; and the daughter is asked to get to know the father more. 2. The mother is validated in her concern for the daughter; the father is challenged to participate in dialogue with daughter and wife; and both mother and father are encouraged to spend time separately with their daughter (as well as with each other). In the first scenario the mother easily feels blamed (she already experiences self-blame). In the second, the father's responsibility to interact and his capacity to care are taken seriously, and the mother is acknowledged as caring, but needing help and attention to self, too.

Another practical difference that recognizing gender biases makes in family therapy relates to the connection between power and circular causation.

A man and woman may have developed a circular pattern of actions which continues to maintain itself. He abuses her, she insists she is getting out of the relationship, he apologizes, she forgives, they celebrate, live with equanimity for a while, then the pattern continues. A strictly circular analysis views the woman as partially responsible for her abuse, for she stays in the system and (by her behavior) helps to maintain the cycle. However, what this analysis misses is the imbalance of power in the relationship and society in which the two live. If this woman has only a minimal income, is frightened of the man's strength, is protecting children, and perceives that she has no place to go, she is not an equal in the circular pattern. This example is horrible, but makes the point. Counselors often assume that participants in families have equal power and base their judgments and guidance for families upon that; given our society today, this assumption is false.

An attentive counselor might say to a woman, "I notice that when you speak, your children do not act as if they hear you." "I don't have a voice," says the mother. "Now if their father would say something, they'd listen." The pastoral counselor would be foolish to focus solely upon this one voiceless mother, as if she were idiosyncratically unable to get her words heard. The pastor needs to name the gender issue: women in our culture are not heard—some are quiet, some speak, some yell, but a great majority are not heard. We *cannot assume* that this particular mother is *making the connections* to her cultural sisters' dilemma. Experiencing powerlessness, she may be blaming herself for not speaking properly. (Bohler, 1990, pp. 67–69)

Hochschild shows how family myths can revolve around gender issues, in her book, *The Second Shift: Working Parents and the Revolution at Home.* She describes the relationship of couples who were chosen for study because both wife and husband work outside the home and because they represent a wide spectrum of families, economically, educationally, and ethnically. The woman in one couple needed to believe that she and her husband shared in the household tasks equally. After much frustration and some fear of losing her husband over the issue, she developed a myth (which she believed) that in fact things were equal. "I do the upstairs, Evan does the downstairs." The "upstairs included the living room, the dining room, the kitchen, two bedrooms, and two baths. The downstairs meant the garage, a place for storage and hobbies. . . . Evan would take care of the car, the garage, and Max, the family dog." (Hochschild, 1989, p. 43)

Ethnicity

Churches are one of the most segregated segments of our population today. Therefore, we have less opportunity to work with diverse ethnic populations when we are a local church pastor than we would if we were in some secular settings. However, every pastor needs to be attentive to ethnicity issues, for these affect *every* person in our society.

Let us consider Ms. Black and Mr. White who go to their pastor for pre-marriage counseling. Ms. Black's father, who is a member of the congregation, suggests that her pastor would probably be glad to officiate at their wedding.

The minister has counseled one hundred other couples prior to their marriages. She has developed a several-week set of counseling procedures which she believes works quite well. Ordinarily, she does not attend to ethnicity issues. Now she is aware, when this couple arrives, that they will be known as a "bi-racial" couple. However, after two sessions, the couple has not mentioned anything to do with ethnicity. She is tempted not to mention it either; after all, she believes that race is not important to a good marriage, and this couple clearly is serious and responsible in their relationship.

In terms of *function* and *structure* race and ethnicity may be irrelevant. But in terms of *content*, the impact of *society* upon the couple, and the effect of the *historical memory* of their families, ethnicity and race are essential elements of the counseling.

This couple responds, when the pastor asks how their marriage will be affected by their being from different ethnic backgrounds, by saying, "We've talked about it and it won't be a problem." The pastor knows that she is now called on to be very authentic herself. After all, she has a particular skin color and ethnic background. Even the couple's interaction with her is "colored" by each of the three of their own skin colors. She can share some of her experience as Afro-American, Hispanic, Anglo, or whatever her ethnic background is. She can name opportunities and challenges which she knows will be present for the couple. She prods them to see the real issues ahead. (Anderson and Stewart, 1983, pp. 120–150 for discussion of resistance due to therapist's particularity)

With all issues, but most obviously those of ethnicity and gender, the therapist needs to be alert to *joining* the family and to the *therapist's own use of self.*

Joining is the process of entering into the family system enough to get a flavor of that family and to enable the members to sense that the therapist is seeking to get their frame of reference. One of the trickiest factors of joining is getting out, for the system must continue to function without the therapist. The therapist joins temporarily to experience the family. But the therapist must also not make himself essential to the process and must maintain a sense of his own identity separate from the family.

Most family therapists seek to use themselves in an authentic, genuine fashion to build what bridges they can between members. A counselor can briefly comment, "As a woman, Jane, I can feel your frustration about not being able to speak up, but as an extrovert, John, I can identify with your impatience when it takes Jane a while to get her thoughts expressed." In this way the counselor has used her own experience to join with both members of the couple and to subtly enable the couples to empathize with each other. She has not, however, shifted the focus to herself, but used herself to stay focused upon the others.

Boyd-Franklin writes regarding the *use of self* with black families. (Boyd-Franklin, 1989, pp. 95–120) Far more important than gathering knowledge about other cultures, races, classes, and genders than our own is the sense of relativity of experience and the willingness to ask and listen. (McGoldrick, 1982) Counselees will tell us what it is like to be black or white in their families, their experience, and their dreams. We need to read the situation afresh, not to place ethnic stereotypes upon particular persons; yet we need to name the issues which are present. The more familiar we are with various ethnic groups, the better we may know the issues to name.

It is important for family members to express their feelings regarding working with a female or male counselor and to name their lack of trust in a white counselor or their uncertainty about working with a black one. Here the counselor can, sometimes with humor, accept his or her finitude while maintaining a non-anxious presence about having of necessity to be one gender and to have one particular combination of ethnic heritages. (Anderson and Stewart, 1983, pp. 120–150)

Boyd-Franklin suggests that in working with black families, the structural approach (following Minuchin) is useful at the beginning stages of therapy. It provides concrete solutions and, with its emphasis upon engagement and problem-solving techniques, helps in the restructuring of the family system. She suggests that the Bowenian model is useful in the mid-phase of therapy. Talk of families of origin and the making of genograms are intimidating and not immediately relevant in the initial phase of therapy, but later they are helpful for including the extended family and to encourage the family members to deal directly with their families of origin. She proposes that the paradoxical/strategic/systemic approaches, though not at all appropriate at the beginning stages of therapy, where there is not sufficient trust, are helpful in the later stages of therapy with families which are very resistant to change. (Boyd-Franklin, 1989, pp. 131–132)

The Preacher, the Prophet, the Pastoral Care-Giver

"Rub-a-dub-dub," three were in the tub and were all called knaves. We pastors are called to multiple roles in our churches. We are the preacher, the prophet, and the pastoral care-giver. I believe we are knaves only if we deny one role at the expense of the others. Thus far, we have examined the usefulness of systems approaches in the clear counseling functions of the pastor. However, systems thinking needs to be applied to our prophetic and preaching roles as well. There are families in our churches who have difficulty finding safe housing, affordable health care, appropriate educational assistance, or productive jobs. Here the prophetic role can be combined with the care-giving one. We need to incorporate larger community systems into our counseling.

I observed (through a one-way mirror) a family therapist who spent several sessions helping a family to alter their behavior patterns as the three children took responsibility for caring for themselves, doing homework, and maintaining the apartment while the mother worked late afternoons and evenings. The housing unit in which this family lived was a high rise which was unsafe, so the mother would not let the children leave their tiny unit. I could not help but think that no matter how many times this set of four people tried to negotiate their behavior patterns, to ease the tensions among them, it was impossible to create a healthy environment when they were so cramped and afraid to exit their domain even for a breath of air.

The pastoral counselor—even more than other family therapists —needs to see bigger systems, to work for systems change in communities as well as in domestic spheres. This is not only to fulfill the prophetic function of ministry, but also because therapy cannot be effective when the larger system is ignored. Forgetting the bigger systems is parallel to blaming the identified patient. This family should not be seen as an "identified patient" of the housing unit, implicitly blamed for its own problems. The community housing complexities themselves help to create the problem, maintain it, and could be a resource for this family's (and many other families') healing.

On numerous occasions pastors who attend to systems issues will find it helpful to use the resources of the community which are already in place. An example of this is referral to drug and alcoholic rehabilitation programs and twelve step programs. There are a variety of excellent resources which can guide a pastor to gain help in facilitating an intervention into a family system which calls for chemical abuse treatment. (Wegscheider, 1981, and Vaughn, 1989)

How the pastor preaches, offers pre-marriage counseling, makes hospital visits, and suggests referrals can be transformed by thinking oriented toward families. The preacher might not avoid the messy family issues prevalent, especially in the vibrantly religious people of the Hebrew Bible, if he saw preaching on these passages as opportunities to bridge to the messiness of families as they interact today. Rather than avoiding rape, affairs, incest, or other painful dimensions of human interactions recorded in the Bible, these can be named in sermons, along with a call to specific systems changes in the present.

Pre-marriage counseling could take families of origin seriously. The bride and groom can be asked to find out a great deal about their parents and each other's families. (Friedman, 1985, pp. 91–99) The pastor can begin an educational task, enabling the couple to start thinking of themselves as a system. When pastors work with families to prepare funerals, they can remind themselves that, again, there is not one grieving spouse or child, but a whole grieving family which probably has some unresolved family issues. Essential to the healing process are follow-up visits in which focus is not just upon the grief, but upon the restructuring of the family now that a member is absent.

Hospital visits are transformed if the pastor who sits by the relative of the person who is in surgery realizes that pastoral care can take place right then, with the relative. Family dynamics become quite apparent in stressful times; these can be noticed and named. Often the healing of the "patient" is bound up with his or her interactions with that very relative with whom we sit. Likewise, when we are called upon to make referrals for in-depth counseling, we have an opportunity to plant the idea that the whole family might benefit from seeking counseling together. The minister should anticipate resistance, but can assist the counselor to whom the referral is made (advisably one who is attentive to systems) by reframing the issue as a family one.

Once a member of the congregation I served told me that she was wondering whether she had to get sick for me to visit her. She made her point clearly. Pastors do not want to reinforce sickness by visiting only the sick! Visits to healthy functioning people are essential. Likewise, visits which could be labeled "healthy-family interviews" provide an avenue for dialogue with the whole family unit without a focus upon pathology. These interviews function as "check-ups," underscoring the importance of the whole as well as individuals.

Throughout all pastoral work, when one names family issues it is important to be clear that families need not be nuclear ones. Whoever live together or have strong emotional and behavioral ties can be considered a family. Some "single" people like to consider themselves families of one, while others consider themselves as members of a friendship-family-network. Individuals are made vulnerable if they are left out of "family" events at a church. There needs to be consistent and clear defining of families to include everyone.

Implicit in all pastoral work is the awareness that the minister is influenced by his or her own family of origin. Herbert Andersen suggests that the pastor's experience in his or her family of origin is "the primary authority for understanding the dynamics of family life. . . . The kind of role we played in our families affects our pastoral impulses. It is probably even instrumental in our being called to be helpers." (Anderson, 1984, p. 106)

Whether it is a brief comment about families in a sermon, an allusion to the pastor's own family of origin, the naming of a systems dynamic which is witnessed in an administrative board meeting, or an intervention made through formal counseling sessions, the pastor has enormous authority to transform the way in which people experience interactions—problems and their solutions. We not only have the power to make a difference, but the natural access into families at crucial moments in their forming and growing.

Bibliography

Anderson, Carol M. and Susan Stewart. *Mastering Resistance: A Practical Guide to Family Therapy.* New York: The Guilford Press, 1983.

Anderson, Herbert. *The Family and Pastoral Care.* Philadelphia: Fortress Press, 1984.

Augsburger, David W. *Pastoral Counseling Across Cultures.* Philadelphia: The Westminster Press, 1986.

Bepko, Claudia and Jo-Ann Krestan. *Too Good for Her Own Good: Breaking Free From the Burden of Female Responsibility.* New York: Harper and Row, 1990.

Bohler, Carolyn. "Metaphors for God in Pastoral Counseling." *Circuit Rider,* April 1987, 3–4.

Bohler, Carolyn. "The Use of Storytelling in Pastoral Counseling." *The Journal of Pastoral Care,* 1987, Vol. XLI, No. 1, 63–71.

Bohler, Carolyn. *When You Need to Take a Stand.* Louisville: Westminster/John Knox Press, 1990.

Boyd-Franklin, Nancy. *Black Families in Therapy: A Multisystems Approach.* New York: The Guilford Press, 1989.

Capps, Donald. *Reframing: A New Method in Pastoral Care.* Minneapolis: Fortress Press, 1990.

Carter, Elizabeth A. and Monica McGoldrick (eds.). *The Family Life Cycle: A Framework for Family Therapy.* New York: Gardner Press, Inc., 1980.

Chodorow, Nancy. *The Reproduction of Mothering: Psychoanalysis and the Sociology of Gender.* Berkeley and Los Angeles: The University of California Press, 1978.

Colomb, Herman D. *Stepfathers—Struggles and Solutions.* Louisville: Westminster/John Knox Press, 1989.

Dornbusch, Sanford M. and Myra H. Strober (eds.). *Feminism, Children, and the New Families.* New York: The Guilford Press, 1988.

Ferber, Andrew, Marilyn Mendelsohn, and August Napier. *The Book of Family Therapy.* Boston: Houghton Mifflin Company, 1972.

Friedman, Edwin H. *Generation to Generation: Family Process in Church and Synagogue.* New York: The Guilford Press, 1985.

Gurman, F. and D. Kniskerd (eds.). *Handbook of Family Therapy.* New York: Brunner/Mazel, Inc. 1981.

Haley, Jay. *Problem Solving Therapy.* San Francisco: Jossey-Bass Publishers, 1978.

Hochschild, Arlie. *The Second Shift: Working Parents and the Revolution at Home.* New York: Viking, 1989.

Hyde, Margaret O. and Elizabeth Held Forsyth. *Parents Divided, Parents Multiplied.* Louisville: Westminster/John Knox Press, 1989.

Judson, Stephanie (ed.). *A Manual on Nonviolence and Children.* Philadelphia: New Society Publishers, 1984.

Kriesel, Harold T. "Marriage and Family Counseling," in Stone, Howard W. and William M. Clements (eds.). *Handbook for Basic Types of Pastoral Care and Counseling.* Nashville: Abingdon, 1991.

Lindblad-Goldberg, Marion. Lectures given at The Philadelphia Child Guidance Clinic for the Summer Intern Program, June 1989.

McAdoo, Harriette Pipes (ed.). *Black Families: Second Edition.* Newbury Park: Sage Publications, 1988.

McGoldrick, Monica (ed.). *Ethnicity and Family Therapy.* New York: The Guilford Press, 1982.

McGoldrick, Monica, Carol M. Anderson, and Froma Walsh (eds.). *Women in Families: A Framework for Family Therapy.* New York: W. W. Norton and Co., Inc., 1989.

Minuchin, Salvador. *Families and Family Therapy.* Cambridge: Harvard University Press, 1974.

Munsch, Robert N. *The Paper Bag Princess.* Toronto: Annick Press, Ltd., 1980.

Olson, Richard P. and Joe H. Leonard, Jr. *Ministry with Families in Flux: The Church and Changing Patterns of Life.* Louisville: Westminster/John Knox Press, 1990.

Papp, Peggy. *The Process of Change.* New York: The Guilford Press, 1983.

Patton, John and Brian H. Childs. *Christian Marriage and Family: Caring for Our Generations.* Nashville: Abingdon Press, 1988.

Rassieur, Charles L. *Pastor, Our Marriage Is in Trouble: A Guide to Short-Term Counseling.* Philadelphia: The Westminster Press, 1988.

Rizzuto, Ana-Maria. *The Birth of the Living God: A Psychoanalytic Study.* Chicago: The University of Chicago Press, 1979.

Satir, Virginia. *Conjoint Family Therapy: A Guide to Theory and Technique* (rev. ed.). Palo Alto: Science and Behavior Books, 1967.

Streiker, Lowell D. *Fathering: Old Game, New Rules: A Look at the Changing Roles of Fathers.* Nashville: Abingdon, 1989.

Trebilcot, Joyce (ed.). *Mothering: Essays in Feminist Theory.* Savage: Rowman and Littlefield Publishers, Inc., 1983.

Vaughn, Joe. *Family Intervention: Hope for Families Struggling with Alcohol and Drugs.* Louisville: Westminster/John Knox Press, 1989.

Walters, Marianne, Betty Carter, Peggy Papp, and Olga Silverstein. *The Invisible Web: Gender Patterns in Family Relationships.* New York: The Guilford Press, 1988.

Watzlawick, Paul, John Weakland, and Richard Fisch. *Change: Principles of Problem Formation and Problem Resolution.* New York: W.W. Norton & Co., Inc., 1974.

Way, Peggy. Lectures presented to the Kansas Area Seminar on Professional Ministry, January 5–7, 1988, Wichita, Kansas.

Wegscheider, Sharon. *Another Chance: Hope and Health for the Alcoholic Family.* Palo Alto: Science and Behavior Books, 1981.

Winawer, Hinda. Discussion at an Ackerman Institute Workshop, New York, November 1989.

Melvin C. Blanchette

A Philosophical Foundation for Professional and Ethical Issues in Pastoral Counseling

"The attitude you should have is the one that Christ Jesus had." (Philippians 2:5)

"What we mean by ethics is what has traditionally been thought of as the 'ought' questions, as distinguished from the 'is' questions. 'You are here' is a fact. 'Ought you to be here?' is an ethical question." (Willard Gaylin, President, The Hastings Center, 1988, p. 3)

In a May 1987 issue of *Time* magazine, the cover story began with the question: "What Ever Happened to Ethics?" by Ezra Bowen, the senior writer. The author went to great lengths to explore the rules and practices of American politics, business, and society at large. Combined with the breadth of coverage was also an in-depth analysis of the people and the events of that time. The reader may recall that it was during this time that Ivan Boesky pleaded guilty to trading on inside information, Jim Bakker was defrocked because of a tryst with a church secretary, and former National Security Advisor, Robert McFarlane, testified about the secret Contra funding scene. There are many more people who could be added to this list. Those mentioned are included only to illustrate the above-named categories. Violations of ethical behavior have a recent as well as a remote history.

Even in the Bible (2 Sam 11), we are told how King David, an ancestor of Jesus, while remaining at home in Jerusalem as other determined Israelites were waging war, seduced the wife of one of his most dedicated soldiers. Only the prophet Nathan, through a small but effective case study, was able to get the king to reflect on his moral and ethical behavior. Nathan fulfilled his task and spoke to the king in God's name so that justice might be served and the king's conscience might be reconciled. Nathan tells the king a story about a poor man who had a lamb as a family pet until on a certain day a wealthy neighbor made off with the animal, killed it, and then served it for dinner. The king was enraged by this injustice and was stirred to compassion for the poor man. The king went so far as to say that the wealthy man should die. At this point in the story, Nathan declared to the king the resounding moral message of the story: "You are the man."

Whether in examples taken from this morning's newspaper or those contained in the collective accounts of the scriptures, the question "What Ever Happened to Ethics?" is both relevant and meaningful. It is relevant because these issues touch the lives and work of pastoral counselors. It is meaningful because clients bring into the consulting room manifold examples of how they were either the victims or the perpetrators of unethical or immoral behavior.

This chapter places a high value on ethical judgment and conduct for the ministry and profession of pastoral counseling. Rather than bemoaning the question "What Ever Happened to Ethics?" which is really more symptomatic than problematic, two prior and interrelated questions will be asked. First, "Why and what are ethics?" In order to provide answers to these questions, there will be an exploration into the moral philosophy of Immanuel Kant. After answering "Why and what are ethics?" we will turn our attention to "How are ethics applied?" from the theoretical world of moral philosophy to the everyday world of people's lives and professionals' behavior. Lastly, the chapter will discuss some pastoral and practical reflections dealing with the lives and ministry of pastoral counselors. There is an underlying conviction that an ethical culture and society will result only when there is a harmony between the sciences and humanities.

Part I. Philosophical Foundation

"Techniques without theory are blind, and theory without techniques is empty." (Kant, quoted by Ekstein, 1956)

The insight provided by this inspirational quotation will inform the two sections for this chapter. To answer the questions "Why ethics?" and "What are ethics?" it will be necessary to review philosophically what constitutes good or bad, right or wrong. The study of ethics finds its origin in moral philosophy. History records to what degree, and what importance, ethics has held at any particular point in time. To paraphrase Dickens, the era can be the best of times or the worst of times—more recently, "it has been the worst of times, it has been the worst of times." Gerard Piel, the recent editor of *Scientific American*, explained why our time has been "the worst of times" for ethical and moral behavior. What Piel (1972) said does not result in peace of mind, but it does give a perspective permitting a context for understanding:

> It was a cowardly and costly truce in the academics of the nineteenth century, at the close of the great Darwinian scandal, that set up the false dichotomy between the sciences and humanities, that is, if truth can be sought in the absence of concern for values, or values cherished without courage to face the truth.

At that time, ethical concerns were given renewed emphasis because of a changing view in the philosophy of science. From 1930 to 1965 in the behavioral sciences, there was a disinterest in the scientific study of moral philosophy. This phenomenon was traced by Warwick (1980) to the triumph of logical positivism. This school of philosophy held that evidence was meaningful only when it was empirically verifiable or when it served as a needless repetition of an idea in logic or mathematics. Hence, during the positivism period, ethical statements, which are experiential and are expressions of values, but which cannot be deducted from logical and mathematical argument, lost their currency of meaning because they did not fulfill the definition of what is verifiable by empirical observation. This fallacy was pushed to the extreme, and is evidenced in this statement by Nielsen (1972): "We have physical tests for tone deafness or color blindness, but not for moral blindness."

More recently, there has been a decline in the excessive dominance of logical positivism. What is becoming more apparent is simply the fact that the nature of evidence in ethics is different in degree and kind from that provided in the study of sensory problems similar to those noted.

Along with this new awareness of difference, a renewed focus is being given to the construction of ethical principles within the philosophy of science. On a more practical level, since 1987, when the *Time* magazine article signaled a clear and present danger caused by the absence of ethics, three major professional associations—the American Association of Pastoral Counselors (1990–1991), the American Psychological Association (1987, 1991), and the American Association for Counseling and Development (1988)—have given a considerable investment in terms of time and energy in developing ethical guidelines for their members and other professionals engaged in helping relationships.

There are reasons, many and compelling, for a renewed interest in the theory of ethics. One, very visible, is the attention caused by the media which has heightened public awareness of ethical issues. A less subtle but no less important force is a renewed interest in moral philosophy. Ethics, a synonym for moral philosophy, includes the analysis, evaluation, and development of criteria for judging moral problems. Accordingly, the study of ethics reviews three types of theories: normative, meta-ethical, and good-reason theories. The first type, the normative theory, is the one of greatest concern to pastoral counselors. According to the *Encyclopedia of Philosophy*, "Normative ethics tries systematically to establish the general principles for determining right or wrong or good or evil" (Nielsen, 1972). The term *normative* refers to what the behavior of professional counselors *ought* to be rather than what it is.

Immanuel Kant (1785/1969) is perhaps the most important critical thinker and proponent of normative ethics. His seminal book, *Foundations of the Metaphysics of Morals*, is foundational for pastoral counselors, not only because of its historical value on ethical reasoning, but also because of its practical value as a foundation for pastoral counselors to examine the implications of their ethical behavior.

In *Foundations*, Kant investigates the fundamental and integrative principle of morality. It is important to bear in mind that moral actions institute actions governed by reason rather than passion. They are undertaken because of the principle or maxim they embody rather than from some ulterior motive or drive. Hence, actions are good or bad not because of their effects, but rather because of the maxim from which they are undertaken. This maxim must be in keeping with fundamental ethical requirements. Kant will be remembered for his formulation of the "categorical imperative" expressed through individuals asking themselves whether they would want their principle for action to become a universal law grading the actions of all other individuals faced with similar situations. This famous categorical imperative is expressed as follows: "I should never act in such a way that I could not also will that my maxim should be a universal law" (Kant, 1785/1969). Pastoral counselors faced with ethical decisions must begin the process of self-examination with this basic question: "Would I want my action to become a universal law?"

The two interrelated questions "Why ethics?" and "What are ethics?" have been answered through the Kantian principle of universality. Kant's sound and seasoned reasoning provides the foundation from which action can be judged to be either good or bad, right or wrong. Moral philosophy defines ethics as being a science which deals with the analysis, evaluation, and development of criteria for deciding moral problems and situations. Gerard Piel's sage advice must be remembered, for only when there is a coherent relation between the sciences and humanities can there be a contemporary ethical culture. In the next section, "How are ethics applied?" will be discussed using as a context the Code of Ethics for the American Association of Pastoral Counselors (AAPC) in which normative ethics are embodied and through which ethics are expressed. A brief historical account of pastoral counseling and its becoming a profession will provide necessary introductory background.

Part II. Professional and Ethical Issues

As a profession, pastoral counseling does not enjoy the time-honored position it has held within the history of the church. Pastoral counseling is a specific form of individual pastoral care in which ministers utilize the knowledge and skills from the contemporary helping profession within a ministerial and theological framework.

Historically, individual pastoral care has been a rich part of the tradition of Christian ministry. Clebsch and Jaekle, in *Pastoral Care in Historical Perspective* (1983), provide an excellent overview of the various functions of ministry and pastoral counseling in particular. For the reader who is interested in a more detailed account of how pastoral counseling is both a ministry and a profession, please confer my chapter in *Pastoral Counseling* (1991). James W. Ewing (1991) describes the role of pastoral counseling by using the metaphor of a bridge:

> Because the field links together religion and behavioral science and consequently sacred tradition and secular lifestyle, it functions as a structural bridge over the chasm of contemporary compartmentalization of knowledge and professional activity. Those persons attracted to the field usually function with multiple intellectual and professional commit-

ments. At a time when our Western culture is witness to rapid change and fragmentation, pastoral counseling is attempting to bridge such through attention to the integrative and holistic process of human living and knowing.

Accordingly, pastoral counseling hinges on the tradition of ministry as well as being a profession among the other helping professions.

As a profession, pastoral counseling is a twentieth century phenomenon. This recognition of its professionalism is evidenced through the publication of the AAPC Code of Ethics. Ethics code development is a necessary and essential step in the professionalization of any occupation (Wilensky, 1964). A profession such as pastoral counseling requires a code of ethics because society maintains a different relationship with professions than with a business enterprise. As a profession, the underlying notion of pastoral counseling is its proclivity to profess, that is, to claim to have some knowledge, special training, or skill not shared by the non-professional. It is, however, insufficient for the professional simply to profess in any helping relationship. What is professed must also be believed by the public. Thus, the over-arching concern of all professions is the adage *credat emptor*—freely translated as "that the client may believe." This expression is quite different from the more familiar one which governs the sale of goods, *caveat emptor*—"let the buyer beware." It is of the greatest importance that members of the public believe or trust in the claims made by the professional. This is especially true in a profession such as pastoral counseling when clients are expected to disclose the most intimate details of their lives, those not ordinarily shared with others.

After reviewing the ethical codes of the American Psychological Association, the American Association of Pastoral Counselors, and the American Association of Counseling and Development, one is struck by the similarity among them. The principles of each code are primarily directed toward ensuring the safety of the public served by the counseling professional. Through ensuring the public's safety, the ethical principles provide a climate and foundation of trust from which helping professionals can build a therapeutic and healing relationship. Hence, the significance of trust in the helping relationship gives additional conviction and speaks to the absolute necessity of "Why ethics?" Ethical principles inform the practice of counseling professionals and protect the trust upon which any relationship is based; conversely, whenever there is a violation of this trust, the public as well as the reputation of the profession is harmed.

In terms of code development, the American Psychological Association (APA) created an ethics committee in 1938; however, a formal ethics code was not adopted until 1953. The first code was developed using a quasi-empirical method. Input from the membership was requested and this information was utilized to develop the code. The fact that this code has undergone change and significant revision through the years indicates how ethics codes must be adaptive to the cultural context and circumstances of the times. The most recent edition was issued and amended June 2, 1989 (*American Psychologist*, July 1990). At this writing, after almost three years of revising the prior document, a new code will be issued probably within a year of this publication.

The most recent American Association of Pastoral Counselors' (AAPC) Code of Ethics was adopted by its Board of Governors on recommendation by the Association's Ethics Committee during the Annual Convention on April 11, 1986. However, during its recent meeting (1990) in the historic city of Williamsburg, Virginia, the Association's Ethics Committee presented for review a new Code of Ethics to the Board of Governors. This proposed new code, when compared and contrasted with the 1981 edition, can only be described as—transformational. This new code commanded the attention and is the result of hard and tireless work on the part of the Association's Ethics Committee. They are to be commended for their effort in generating a document of such elegance in style and substance, yet doing so with an economy of words. During the coming year, Principles I–VII of the proposed new code will be used as a study document. It is recommended that these principles be read with care, and responses be sent to the regional or national Association Ethics Committee. Principle VIII, entitled "Procedures," was appended to the current Code of Ethics and was voted on to take effect immediately.

With this historical overview and in light of Kant's ethical imperative, we now consider the AAPC Code of Ethics as normative ethics. According to the Prologue of the Code of Ethics (1990), pastoral counselors are committed to a vision of what constitutes their identity as ministers and competent mental health professionals:

Principle I—Prologue

As members of the American Association of Pastoral Counselors we are committed to the traditions and values of our faith communities and to the dignity and worth of each individual. We are dedicated to advancing the welfare of those who seek our assistance and to the maintenance of high standards of professional conduct and competence. As members of AAPC we are accountable for our ministry whatever its setting. This accountability is expressed in relationships to clients, colleagues, students, our faith communities, and through the acceptance and practice of the principles and procedures of this Code of Ethics.

Flowing from this Prologue (1990), seven foundational premises are derived which serve as the means for members to uphold these standards. They are as follows:

In order to uphold our standards, members of AAPC covenant agree to accept the following foundational premises:

A. As pastoral counselors we maintain association with the faith group in which we have ecclesiastical standing.

B. We seek to remain abreast of new developments in the field through both educational activities and clinical experience. We agree to continue post-graduate education and professional growth, including supervision, consultation, and active participation in the meetings and affairs of the Association.

C. Recognizing that isolation can lead to a loss of perspective and judgment, at all levels of membership we agree to seek out and engage in collegial relationships.

D. We agree to manage our personal lives in a healthful fashion and agree to seek appropriate treatment for our own personal problems or conflicts.

E. We do not attempt to diagnose or provide treatment for problems or issues that are outside the reasonable boundaries of our competence.

F. We agree to maintain supervision and/or consultation at all levels of membership.

G. We agree to establish and maintain appropriate professional relationship boundaries (see Principles III, G. & H. and V, A.–D.).

Professional responsibilities are delineated in terms of general principles, leaving room for pastoral counselors to use discretion and moral reasonableness in handling individual situations. The remaining principles are: Principle II—Professional Practices; Principle III —Client Relationships; Principle IV—Confidentiality; Principle V—

Supervisee, Student & Employee Relationships; Principle VI—Interprofessional Relationships; Principle VII—Advertising; and Principle VIII—Procedures. When several principles apply to a given situation, as they often do, pastoral counselors must balance one principle against the other. When faced with balancing principles, pastoral counselors should consider the problem in terms of the universal principles.

These ethical principles (AAPC, 1991) are both deontological and teleological. Deontological theories of normative ethics insist "that certain kinds of actions are inherently right, or right as a matter of principle, because of their being the kinds of actions that they are or because of their conforming to some formal principle" (Gewirth, 1975). Accordingly, these ethical principles pass the test of deontology because they conform to the fundamental ethical principles.

The ethical prologue conforms to the categorical imperative's test of universality and expresses one of the mandates that follows from the imperative: "Act so that you treat humanity, whether in your own person or in the person of another, always as an end and never as a means only" (Kant, 1785/1969). Teleological theories of normative ethics purport "that actions are right because of the goodness of their consequences" (Gewirth, 1975). This importance of the consequences of behavior is in keeping with the term teleology; however, it has a different meaning for pastoral counselors, who employ this term to describe purposive behavior rather than the consequences of behavior. In this sense, the ethical principles of the AAPC Code of Ethics are congruent with Kantian ethics in which an action is or is not ethical because of its purpose or maxim, rather than because of its effects.

The AAPC Ethics Committee on both regional and national levels deals with ethical complaints and adjudicates cases. Principle VIII—Procedures reflects a concern for the seriousness of the behaviors involved in a situation. Accordingly, in addition to considering the potential harm involved, which would be a teleological consideration, it also evaluates the behavior in terms of its deontological significance. Hence, the ethical principles and their use in applying sanctions against the inappropriate or unethical behavior of pastoral counselors reinforce the obligations of pastoral counselors and the consequences of their behavior—reflecting the interrelationship between the deontological and teleological aspects of normative ethics.

The ethical principles of the AAPC Code of Ethics enable pastoral counselors to reflect on their intentions and what motivates their behavior as those who continue the healing ministry of Jesus. All pastoral counselors have the same ultimate goal for their clients, namely: ". . . to make the best of him that his inherited capacities will allow and so to make him as efficient and as capable as is possible" (Freud, 1923).

In addition, pastoral counselors would enter into a helping relationship in order (1) to enable a person to become free in order to become responsible, and (2) to enable a person to deal with pain in its many forms in order to understand the deeper significance it plays in life (Blanchette, 1991). Although pastoral counseling is a ministry practiced in faith by religiously oriented people, the AAPC Code of Ethics plays an important role in framing what pastoral counselors ought to do in various situations. The Code of Ethics is the embodiment of what constitutes ethical behavior, and provides in practical and pragmatic terms how theory is made operational through clear statements of objectives and goals.

A unique feature of the AAPC Code of Ethics is its explicit affirmation that pastoral counselors are committed to a belief in God and in the dignity and worth of each person. Aside from this explicit declaration of a belief in God and the dignity and worth of each individual made in God's image, the AAPC Code of Ethics closely parallels the Ethical Principles of the American Psychological Association. While these codes vary in length and specific content, they contain similar themes: to promote the welfare of the consumer, to maintain competence, to protect confidentiality and/or privacy, to act responsibly, to avoid exploitation, and to uphold the integrity of the profession. To appreciate the full meaning and the converging nature of these ethical codes is to generalize their content into two broad moral categories:

I. *Care of the Public:* Direct care for the public underlies the ethical standards of the American Association of Pastoral Counselors and the American Psychological Association. These principles are: *responsibility, moral and legal standards,* and the *welfare of the consumer.* According to each of these principles, two related questions are being asked: Did the pastoral counselor honor the trust of the client? Did the pastoral counselor take unfair advantage of the client, either intentionally or unintentionally through negligence or ignorance? Whether the lack of care resulting in offensive behavior was intentional or unintentional, the effect on the client or other person is almost always the same.

II. *Care for Pastoral Counselor's Education and Training:* The remaining principles concern the professional's ability and competence to serve the public properly. These include: specific discussions of the meaning of professional competence; the ethical issues involved in the making of public statements; the issue of confidentiality of the professional relationship with clients; the issue of dual relationships; the use of various assessment techniques; and for the APA Code of Ethics, the ethics of the use of animals in experimentation. Pastoral counseling is governed by a standard of caring expressed through a Code of Ethics. Thus far we have established the philosophical basis for these codes.

In turn, the AAPC Code of Ethics and the APA Ethical Standards embody and apply these standards of care through explicit principles and procedures. Now we turn our attention to some pastoral and practical reflections regarding the lives and ministry of pastoral counselors.

Pastoral and Practical Reflections

1. Pastoral counselors are mandated to live lives of exemplary conduct. Remember that the ethical code applies to members not only in their roles as pastoral counselors, but also in their lives as well. There can be no ethical gap between the life and the work of the pastoral counselor.
2. Pastoral counseling continues the healing ministry of Jesus and so comes under the greatest and most severe sanctions imposed by God spoken through the prophet Ezekiel (see especially chapter 34). Note the adjective *pastoral*. As shepherds, pastoral counselors are called to be not only co-pilgrims, but also guides for those who are searching for meaning and purpose.
3. Pastoral counselors are not simply counselors with additional training in theology and in the pastoral arts and sciences. Pastoral counselors are mandated to be members in good standing with their supporting faith groups. As such, pastoral counselors maintain a vital denominational connectedness with a religious body.

   Pastoral counselors function within a unique context. This context alone gives a correct understanding of what the ministry and profession entails. Pastoral counseling is pastoral because its origin is rooted within the religious ministry of the *cura animarum*, a tradition of care and cure of souls. Accordingly, pastoral counselors derive their authorization to practice this religious ministry from their respective religious bodies or denominations. From this empowerment comes the energy and vitality of the pastoral counseling ministry, a work done in faith within the community of believers.

4. As members of a helping profession which seeks to establish human relationships and techniques for bringing about personality and behavioral change, pastoral counselors must be eminently aware of those principles which guide the beginning, continuation, and termination of any therapeutic alliance. These principles are clearly delineated in the ethical codes referred to above. Accordingly, pastoral counselors are encouraged to have an organizing structure which can guide their conduct and influence their practice throughout the therapeutic process. An excellent article which provides such an organizing structure is provided by DePauw (1986).

5. During the contractual phase of building a therapeutic alliance, pastoral counselors are directed to secure "informed consent." This is basically a strategy for the pastoral counselor to provide potential clients with necessary and sufficient information about their initial evaluation, treatment plan, and projected length of counseling so that clients can make an informed judgment regarding their participation in the process. A practical article dealing with this issue and guidelines is provided by Rodgerson (1991).

6. Pastoral counselors frequently serve as ministers in a local congregation. As such they are in a position to counsel parishioners. In this regard, pastoral counselors would do well to review Principle II—Welfare of Others, A-5, 6, and 7 in the Ethical Principles of Psychologists, and Principle III—Client Relationships, G., and Principle V—Supervisee, Student & Employee Relationships, A.–D. and sexual behavior with former clients (Principle III, H. of the AAPC Code of Ethics). Each of these principles speaks of the necessity for avoiding dual relationships with current or former clients. This is the clearest and most direct declaration that sexual behavior with a client is both illegal and unethical. It is unfortunate that this ethical principle is the most frequently cited in ethical misconduct charges (*American Psychologist*, July

1990). Young has an excellent article entitled "Professional
and Ethical Issues for Ministers Who Counsel" (1989).

7. Confidentiality is the foundation and the bedrock upon
which is built the counseling relationship. Under confidentiality's protective cover clients freely discuss their most private lives. Pastoral counselors must be aware of the duties
and limitations of confidentiality. Confidentiality prohibits
any disclosure of communication made to a pastoral counselor by a client during the course of professional employment. While confidentiality originated in professional ethics
codes, it has been incorporated in legislation and court rul-
ings. Hence, disclosure of a client's communication may
subject the pastoral counselor not only to an ethical reprimand, but also to civil or criminal liability (DeKraai and
Sales, 1982).

A concept which is closely aligned with confidentiality is
that of privileged communication. As such, privileged communication is a legal term involving the right not to reveal
confidential information in a legal procedure. Privileged
communication is granted by statute and protects clients
from having their communications revealed in a judicial setting without explicit permission. The privileged information
belongs to the client and is vested in the client by legislative
authority. Pastoral counselors are encouraged to explore the
statutes regarding privileged information of their respective
states. Unless the state has a law that says communication
between counselor and client is privileged, then judges can
force pastoral counselors to provide information about their
clients. Accordingly, it is very important that pastoral counselors clearly and directly inform their clients that private
communication ceases when public peril begins. This would
involve issues of suicide, homicide, and child physical/
sexual abuse. In these circumstances, pastoral counselors,
because they are mental health professionals, must exercise
their responsibility as mandatory reporters.

8. Being a competent pastoral counselor means having the
knowledge, skills, and abilities necessary to perform the
functions relevant to the ministry and profession of pastoral
counseling. It always involves a judgment between the ability of the pastoral counselor to practice in a given setting and
the needs of the person receiving a specified standard of

care. Areas where pastoral counselors must make an ethical judgment regarding competence are those of cross-cultural concerns and issues involving gender, race, and culturally distinct groups (Cayleff, 1986).

9. Pastoral counselors are encouraged to know the laws and statutes relevant to counseling within their respective states and jurisdictions. While the meaning as well as the often strict enforcement of ethical principles may make them appear to be synonymous with law, there is one important difference between laws and ethical principles. An important legal principle is the qualifying factor of degree of negligence or intention. Determining a violation of an ethical principle rarely involves consideration of such a qualifying factor. Ethical principles and violations tend to be absolute. This is because of the nature of the population governed by ethical codes, namely well-trained professionals from whom the public demands such exemplary conduct.

10. Lastly, an issue which has been surfacing in a number of professional meetings is whether or not pastoral counselors should be certified or licensed as professional counselors. It would seem reasonable that as long as pastors are doing short term counseling in their parishes, there is no obligation to seek further legitimacy since that counseling is an integral component of the *cura animarum* expected of the pastor by the congregation. However, if a pastoral counselor is doing counseling in a state or private mental agency, that counselor should receive certification as a professional counselor even though the adjective *pastoral* might be expressed only through an attitudinal presence. In addition, pastoral counselors who are practicing in their parishes and seeing people from the wider community should be regulated by the prevailing laws of certification and licensure in the same way as other professionals since they are offering mental health services to the general public, an activity which is becoming increasingly regulated by the state. This issue of certification or licensure is intimately related to the identity of pastoral counselors. A decision must be made regarding one's professional work. Am I a pastor who counsels? Am I a counselor who is also a pastor? If pastoral counselors are functioning within the boundaries of their parish ministry, such is clearly a ministry done for God. If pastoral counselors

are working within a state agency and outside parish boundaries, this is an activity clearly under the activity of state regulation.

This chapter has founded the philosophical and theoretical basis for ethics in the moral philosophy of Immanuel Kant. The interrelated question of "Why and what are ethics?" has been established through the Kantian principle of universality. How these theoretical principles become expressed in ethical terms is through a Code of Ethics for respective professions. Certain ethical and professional issues of pastoral counseling as a ministry and profession were reviewed.

Some pastoral and practical reflections provided a framework to respond to some specific issues of pragmatic and immediate significance in the lives and ministry of pastoral counselors.

In conclusion, pastoral counselors, like all mental health professionals, are called to have a current and comprehensive understanding of the ethical principles which govern their lives and infuse their work. In addition, pastoral counselors are invited to have the attitude that Christ Jesus had, because pastoral counseling is a continuation of the healing ministry of Jesus. Moreover, pastoral counselors need to possess the compassion and courage of Jesus, who was able to stop an outraged crowd from stoning to death a woman whose behavior they considered immoral. Jesus stepped forward and stopped the revenge while exhorting values such as compassion, understanding, forgiveness, and reforming one's life. The pastoral counselor can do nothing more—and certainly nothing less.

The Clients' Rights[1]

Listed below are some of the rights generally agreed upon as belonging to clients seeking and engaging in therapy. Consumer rights may differ from state to state.

Clients have the right to:

—have full and complete knowledge of the therapist's qualifications and training
—be informed fully regarding the terms under which service will be provided
—discuss their therapy with anyone they choose, including another therapist
—have a detailed explanation of any procedure (whether psycho-

logical or medical) or form of therapy that the therapist or any other professional recommends prior to treatment

—refuse evaluation or treatment of any kind unless the right of refusal is limited by law (as in instances of court-ordered evaluation or commitment)

—request summaries of or, in many states, direct access to their files or to have pertinent information in their files shared with another therapist, an organization, or any other party, assuming that the clients provide signed consent if requested to do so

—question the therapist's competence and, if they so desire, to complain to the therapist's superior or to file formal complaints with pertinent professional bodies or legal bodies

—request a copy of ethics codes and other guidelines and procedures that govern the therapist's practice

—terminate therapy at any time or, in the case of court-ordered treatment, refuse to participate in therapy (recognizing that the client may have to face legal consequences as a result of his or her refusal)

Note

See B.K. Bennett, B.K. Bryant, G.R. Vandenbos, & A. Greenwood, *Professional Liability and Risk Management.* American Psychological Association, 1990.

Bibliography

American Association of Pastoral Counselors. Proposed AAPC Code of Ethics. Fairfax: *American Association of Pastoral Counselors' Newsletter*, Summer 1990, Vol. 28, No. 3.

American Psychological Association. Committee on Science and Professional Ethics and Conduct. May 1984. Ethics Statement issued, *APA Monitor*, 36.

American Psychological Association. *Ethical Principles of Psychologists.* Washington, D.C.: APA, 1981.

American Psychological Association. *Standards for Providers of Psychological Services.* Washington, D.C.: APA, 1977.

American Psychologist. *Journal of the American Psychological Association,* July 1990, No. 7, 873–875.

Blanchette, M.C. "Professional and Ethical Issues in Pastoral Counseling," in B. Estadt, M. Blanchette, & J. Compton (eds.), *Pastoral Counseling*. Englewood Cliffs: Prentice-Hall, Inc., 1991.

Cayleff, S.E. "Ethical issues in counseling gender, race, and culturally distinct groups," *Journal of Counseling and Development*, January 1986, Vol. 64, 345–347.

Clebsch, W. & C. Jaekle. *Pastoral Care in Historical Perspective*. New York: Jason Aronson, Inc., 1983.

DeKraai, M.B. & B. Sales. "Privileged communications of psychologists," *Professional Psychology*, June 1982, Vol. 13, No. 3, 372–388.

DePauw, M.E. "Avoiding ethical violations: A timeline perspective for individual counseling," in *Journal of Counseling and Development*. January 1986, Vol. 64, 303–306.

Ekstein, R. "Psychoanalytic techniques," in *Progress in Clinical Psychology*. New York: Greene & Stratton, 1956, 2, 79–97.

Ewing, J.W. *Pastoral Counseling*. Englewood Cliffs: Prentice-Hall, Inc., 1991.

Freud, S. *Psychoanalytic Psychotherapy*, T.J. Paolino Jr. (ed.). New York: Brunner/Mazel, 1981, 13.

Gaylin, W. *Ethics in America*. Cultural Information Service and the Corporation for Public Broadcasting. P.O. Box 786, Madison Square Station, New York, NY 10159.

Gewirth, A. "Ethics," in *The New Encyclopaedia Britannica*, 1975, Vol. 6, 976–998. Chicago: Encyclopaedia Britannica.

Habermas, J. *Communication and the Evolution of Society* (T. McCarthy, trans.). Boston: Beacon Press. Original work published 1976.

Habermas, J. *Theory of Communicative Action* (Vol. 1), T. McCarthy, trans.). Boston: Beacon Press. Original work published 1981.

Kant, I. *Foundations of the Metaphysics of Morals*, R.P. Wolff (ed.), L. Beck (trans.). Indianapolis: Bobbs-Merrill, 1969. Original work published 1785.

Kohlberg, L. "Moral stages and moralization," in T. Lickona (ed.), *Moral Development and Behavior*. New York: Holt, Rinehart & Winston, 1976.

Nielsen, K. "Problems of Ethics," in P. Edwards (ed.), *The Encyclopedia of Philosophy* (reprint ed.), Vol. 3, 117–134. New York: Macmillan, 1972.

Piel, G. *The Acceleration of History*. New York: Knopf, 1972.

Warwick, D. *The teachings of ethics VI: The teaching of ethics in the social sciences*. Hastings-on-Hudson: Hastings Institute of Society, 1980.

Wilensky, H.L. "The Professionalization of Everyone?" *American Journal of Sociology,* 1964, 70, 137–158.

Young, M. "Professional and Ethical Issues for Ministers Who Counsel," *The Journal of Pastoral Care,* 1989, Vol. XLIII, No. 3, 269–275.

Joanne Marie G. Greer

Research in Pastoral Counseling: Definitions, Methods, and Research Training

Introduction

According to Strunk (1985), *modern* pastoral counseling is tied both to theology and to a group of human sciences which were non-existent during much of the history of pastoral counseling. This highlights a specific research dilemma in pastoral counseling: to what extent is the pastoral counseling researcher to be guided by belief, and to what extent by state-of-the-art science? The answer to this question is neither obvious nor simple, but is an important first step in delineating the nature of pastoral counseling research. In this chapter I will attempt to identify some reasonable responses to this global definitional question, and will also survey the armamentarium of social science research techniques to identify those techniques most congenial to the pastoral counseling research effort. Finally, I will address the training of future researchers in pastoral counseling.

Section I. Can Pastoral Counseling Be Simultaneously "Pastoral" and "Scientific"?

Pastoral counselors represent a recent-day rapprochement between (psychological) science and religion. It is useful to consider an earlier rapprochement between these two fields: the shaman-healer evolved into the physician-healer. It is noteworthy that clinical psychology and psychiatry, as the heirs of the religious shaman, still retain some qualities of the religious side of humankind. Even the secular mental health worker is to some vestigial extent influenced by the religious heritage of mental health work. For example, it is difficult to persevere in the work of psychotherapy without something very like the religious virtue of hope. But the greater weight of influence for the secular mental health worker comes from the secular scientific world. What is the appropriate balance between religion and secular science for the pastoral counselor, and, more specifically, for the pastoral counseling *researcher?*

The worldview of the pastoral counselor is somewhat different, and may be *very* different from that of the secular health professional. A number of decades have been dedicated to studying the interface of faith and psychological science for the practitioner pastoral counselor. While these clarifications and reflections can partially inform pastoral counseling research, other important issues remain to be addressed. These questions are specific to the triple interface of the *pastoral* role, the *counselor* role, and the *researcher* role.

The most simplistic approach to structured research is found in the straightforward application of laboratory scientific method: the formulating and testing of hypotheses and the rejection of (or failure to accept) unsupported beliefs. This research process appears to be, in its narrowest form, antithetical to the life of faith, which consists *precisely* in the acceptance of unsupported beliefs. Where, then, can there be a rapprochement between the scientific method in behavioral science research and the faith basis in pastoral counseling? This is the most difficult question which this chapter will attempt to address.

There are several types of pastorally-oriented research to consider in attempting to define "pastoral counseling research":

1. Studies of believers as sociological groups. An example might be "A comparative study of child-rearing practices of believers and non-believers." This type of study is not pastoral counseling research, but rather belongs to the sociology of religion, an academic field. While certainly these studies are often interesting to religious persons (what group does not enjoy reading about itself?), they are of only peripheral use in the professional work of the pastoral counselor. These studies may expand a counselor's knowledge of the individual subculture within which a client lives, but these studies do not add to the knowledge of how best to perform pastoral counseling, or how to assess the *intrapsychic* outcomes of pastoral counseling.

Precisely because sociological studies are *sociological* rather than religious, they are easier to execute with technical precision. Sociology-of-religion researchers do not have to struggle with the interface of faith and their academic discipline, and deal only in a limited way with intrapsychic life. Rather, they simply follow good general research practices to observe the presumed effects of faith or church membership and activities in their area of interest: social behavior.

2. Research aimed at proving, through psychological or behavioral observations and measurements, the positive effects of various beliefs and belief systems on the mental health status and social behavior of believers. These studies are similar in abstract structure to well-known studies of relationships between belief systems and *physical* health: e.g. the studies showing positive health impact of the dietary practices of the Seventh Day Adventists.

Such studies belong to a type of research I would like to designate by the term "motivated research." A flippant formulation of the hypotheses of such studies might be "Jesus cures" (either instead of or in addition to "Jesus saves"). Clearly, motivated research reaches out toward the non-believing community with a variation of what an Anglican pastor of my acquaintance calls "rice Christianity," i.e. the practice of missionaries in feeding non-believers in order to later convert them. Motivated research strives to *prove* that believers are better off (better fed) in the here-and-now than the non-believers are, with the evident intent of promoting esteem for and interest in religion. Therefore, motivated research has a type of open or covert apologetics function. One might almost call it marketing research on behalf of God as the good psychological product. Critiquing the theology behind such research hypotheses is beyond the scope of my paper. But it is important to understand that purposeful studies of this ilk are generally disrespected in the secular academic community because such studies violate long-standing principles of scientific research. A key ideal of secular scientific research is a neutrality toward the outcome of a study; properly designed and executed research does not seek so much to prove a pre-conceived position as to explore what might be so. In my opinion, motivated research has no reasonable audience. To the educated non-believer this research is likely to be an object of ridicule, while for the believer this research could easily be understood as offering a false set of reasons for the continued practice of faith, hope, and love, and could therefore actually be deleterious to faith development. Both of these outcomes seem highly undesirable.

For all these reasons, I feel that motivated research should not be practiced in the pastoral counseling community any more than it should be practiced in medical or scientific studies.

3. Theoretical psychological studies which seek to *identify psychological factors* that facilitate or hamper the life of faith or the identification of and fulfillment of one's place in creation in the here-and-now. Concomitantly, one must also include research seeking to identify efficient pastoral-therapeutic strategies to *remove intra-*

psychic obstacles to the life of faith or to the identification of and fulfillment of one's place in creation. This latter research would correspond to what is known in secular psychology as "research on technique."

These types of research seem most appropriate to designate as "pastoral counseling research" because such studies represent an appropriate melding of the psychological and the faith knowledge bases found in pastoral counseling. An example of the first category might be "a study of the environmental and developmental factors *which may facilitate* the life of faith within a marriage commitment." An example of the second category might be "a study of optimal psychological distance and intimacy within the pastoral counseling dyad for *facilitating* progress of the client." The phrasing of hypotheses in terms of *facilitating* rather than *causing* a spiritual/psychological outcome seems an important distinction which should be found throughout pastoral counseling research. The pastoral counselor presumably believes in the primacy of God as the ultimate source of human spiritual, social, and psychological growth. At the same time, the pastoral counselor as mental health worker is also involved in a human apostolate, in furthering the work of God, and thus may reasonably turn to research in order to identify better ways to carry out his or her human collaboration in the work of God.

Section II. Some General Ideas About Method in Research: What Is "Methodology"?

Methodology in any research field consists of a few broadly defined activities: (1) development of statements of models to explain data of interest to the particular discipline; (2) development of formal definitions and measures of the constructs in the model(s); (3) development of formal tests of the explanatory power of any model, as compared with competing models; (4) extension of knowledge by application of inductive and deductive reasoning to make extrapolations from validated models. Specifics of this process are necessarily influenced by the particular discipline's accumulated body of knowledge. However, the general structure of necessity conforms to certain basic rules of logic, no matter what the discipline.

What is a "model"? Our intuitive idea is sound when we think of a "model airplane" or a "model community mental health center." A model unites into a formal relationship all the parts which we find necessary to some idea such as "airplane" or "mental health center." The model airplane is a better example because it has an element of *simplification* which is ordinarily found in a research model. A research model is a statement of the essential relationship(s) among a set of concepts and/or objects of interest. The non-essential is stripped off, to better examine the underlying skeleton.

As the reader may immediately suspect, a regular area of contention among researchers in any particular field is whether or not this or that attribute is essential. Such disputes are negotiable, based on further research. Here is a pleasing example, from educational research. For many years educational researchers maintained that class size was an important variable in any school-based learning model. A researcher who suspected that class size was irrelevant did a naturalistic study of class sizes in public schools. He gathered achievement data on the children in various class sizes found in public school, ranging from fifteen to forty children per class. He found no difference in their achievement, after statistically adjusting for differences in IQ, social status, etc. A dissenting researcher replicated the study, looking at class sizes between five and fifteen. He found that class size *in that range* was a significant factor in learning. These two researchers were able to resolve their dispute, based on one's partial replication of the other's research.

This is a particularly nice example because it conveys the spirit of testing models with data—a process which is cumulative and to a great extent collaborative. It is unlikely that any one researcher will have all the relevant insights on a specific problem. Therefore, a necessary aspect of methodology is the *standardization* of descriptive and inferential processes to make communication with other researchers possible. Such standardization also makes possible parsimonious and elegant variations, replications, tests, challenges, and extensions to another researcher's work.

An essential aspect of the standardization of method is the *abstracting* of both the model and hypotheses into some form of notation. Math-haters in any field usually have to be persuaded that this translation is necessary. A Danny Kaye joke gets this point over very effectively:

Two Persons at a Cocktail Party
Speaker 1: How did you like the Himalayas?
Speaker 2: Loved him; Hated her.

The point is, words don't mean the same to different people. Before you and I can either argue or agree, we must unambiguously communicate. We must struggle with the process of setting down our hypotheses in a mutually understood, standard form. Research methodology gives us the tool for this. During this century, logicians, mathematicians, statisticians, philosophers, operations research analysts, linguists, psychologists, engineers, and others have evolved a set formal vocabulary with which to explicate and debate models. Pastoral counseling has absolutely no choice but to master this language. Further, it is certainly possible for pastoral counselors to do so. This is clearly so because the needed material is being taught at the master's level in almost all post-bachelor's curricula in social sciences, behavioral sciences, and education.

On the other hand, research courses need not be *heavily* mathematical, and indeed should not be, at all levels of instruction except the most advanced. Mathematical foundations are necessary for the average user only to the extent that they help a person understand what to do. As Roberts notes,

> The essence of statistics is only incidentally mathematical: It embraces the systematic formulation of decision and inferential problems, including the recognition that there *is* a problem; the formulation of tentative statistical models to guide data analysis, which requires understanding of the assumptions or specifications required for proper application of the models; and the diagnostic checking and fitting of these tentative models. In the process of teaching these things we need to stress real problems, not finger exercises for arithmetic. . . . Further, the tools of statistics given highest emphasis should be those of highest potential in the student's field of application. (Roberts, 1978)

Non-mathematicians often think that mathematics as a discipline is both inflexible and exact. John Von Neumann noted that these are in fact misconceptions, and mathematicians actually disagree about what constitutes adequate proof, and which parts of the discipline are proven beyond doubt. He felt that a more important contribution of mathematics to our thinking is that it has demonstrated an enormous flexibility in the *formation of concepts*, a degree of flexibility to which it is very difficult to arrive in a non-mathematical mode. (J. Von Neumann, 1963)

One aspect of testing models where mathematics is both unavoidable and extremely helpful is the process of devising measures. A measure can be as simple as a tally of occurrences of a certain type of material in a client's sessions. Other measures are simply categories:

male/female, child/adult, etc. Some measures are relatively continuous like IQ, income, and age. The process of manipulating and combining measures without violating logic is a tricky business, because the measures are only imperfect representations of the idea being measured.

Elementary measurement theory is easily mastered by beginning research design students, and most also find it very interesting. This is another area where it is most efficient to learn a little for oneself, even when consultants are available. After all, no consultant will have a truly personal insight into one's own data and one's own planned comparisons and contrasts.

A pastoral counselor researcher-to-be must learn to state an unambiguous research hypothesis, identify relevant data with which to test it, evaluate alternative measures, select a technically adequate measure, take proper account of competing explanations of change, and decide whether the results of the study support or disprove the hypothesis.

Section III. Does Correct Methodology *Really* Matter?

Methodology is sometimes scorned as mere "number-crunching." One cannot deny that research methods are but the handmaiden of the research itself. Nevertheless, proper research design always elucidates the truth, while slapdash designs may hopelessly obscure it. Several humorous books have built upon this fact, including *How to Lie with Statistics* (Huff, 1954) and *Science Is a Sacred Cow.* (Standen, 1950) Good methodology makes a disciplined researcher.

If the content of one's discipline is of emotional importance, it becomes difficult to remain aware of the line between facts and beliefs. (Martin, 1983) Methodology converts beliefs, hunches, clinical judgment, and accumulated experience into testable hypotheses which can then be *objectively* validated. Method is the researcher's protection against self-deception. The author of *Science Is a Sacred Cow* twits the biased researcher with an apocryphal tale of the research subject who gets drunk on whiskey and soda water on Monday, brandy and soda water on Tuesday, gin and soda water on Wednesday, etc. What caused his drunkenness? Obviously the common factor, soda water. What is the methodology lesson in this tale? Competing explanations for the same data must be given a fair chance to emerge. (Standen, 1950, at p. 25)

A more subtle example of a poor research design is the following. A mental health researcher looked at the correlation between certain brain scan data and characteristics of the "Multiple Personality" diagnosis. To do this the researcher repetitively reused a small sample of twelve subjects to compute fifteen correlation coefficients, one by one. It requires a fairly good knowledge of statistical research methodology to recognize that these computations are fatally flawed and therefore the results are uninterpretable. The results are meaningless because a relative balance must be preserved between the number of computations to be extracted from the data and the number of research subjects, known as degrees of freedom. Ignoring requisite degrees of freedom for one's desired computations will give results which are indeterminate, i.e. uninterpretable.

Even if there were an adequate number of subjects, this particular study also has a second design flaw. It reuses the same subjects fifteen times for fifteen simple computations, rather than using a more complex overall significance test. As a result, the probability levels for the fifteen statistical tests will be incorrect and misleading. This second example was deliberately selected to have less obvious flaws, in order to bring home the impossibility of relying on untutored logic to develop a viable research design. Issues such as degrees of freedom and repeated reuse of the same subjects are sometimes complex, and are best taken care of by including a statistician on the planning team for a research project. However, for many small studies this is not practical. Consequently, any researcher must master the general concepts and a few rules of thumb about sample selection.

A basic course in research design can be thought of as a map to the mine field which lies in the researcher's way as he or she struggles to concretize and test hypotheses. Teachers of these courses sometimes joke about the sincerity model, i.e. the attitude that "I have a worthy hypothesis and I am sincere in seeking the truth, therefore I need not worry about all these technicalities." (Patton, 1978) The pursuit of probable truth is a harsh business. It *does* matter whether or not the data are sufficient to support the hypotheses. If not, the researcher's situation is similar to that of the person who believes he can walk safely out of a tenth-story window. Disaster strikes just as surely whether he believes he is safe or not.

A philosophical side benefit of formal research designs is their unrelenting reminder that a model is just a model, and not a reality. The reification of constructs such as ego, superego, id, or self is an ongoing problem in mental health theorizing. Such failures of logic can be avoided by recalling the fact that the data and not the model is the ultimate reality. Theorists from a wide variety of fields find themselves struggling against the wish to reify constructs. Noted psychometric researcher Lee Cronbach once commented, "The true IQ is a hero-figure as well known to us as the Lone Ranger; we try to tell about it and suddenly realize that not even Wechsler himself knows what the "true Full Scale IQ" might mean." (Cronbach et al., 1972)

Testing of treatment models for efficacy and specificity can only be accomplished by formal confrontation of model with data. In the process one grasps firmly that models and constructs are not *things* but *ideas.* In the end, the model must bow to the data. As one enthusiastic statistician's T-shirt proclaimed, "Data Is Everything!" Respect for the data is the most important principle of research. If the data don't fit the model, it is the model that is suspect, because the model is only an idea, while the data are a part of reality.

It is also extremely important to insist upon precise variable definitions. Here we will find the solution to such seeming dilemmas as research studies which purport to prove that untrained counselors are as effective as highly trained ones, or that short-term behavioral modification is as effective as long-term insight oriented counseling. The treatment situations are most probably *not* equivalent in their outcomes. They may seem so simply because the data gathered are too simplistic for an accurate test of the hypotheses. When the correct contrasts are identified, and the appropriate data has been gathered, it will be possible to demonstrate the differences we hypothesize to exist. For example, studies which purport to prove that short-term behavior modification is equal to long-term insight-oriented therapy use a less complex model of human functioning. Few pastoral counselors would be satisfied with a treatment regimen which merely got a client to go to work every day and stop making trouble at home. Yet these are two common criteria for short-term mental health treatment success.

Section IV. Hypothesis Testing: "Did Anything Really Happen?"

A very major concern of methodology is separating random fluctuation, often called "error" or "noise," from *meaningful* ups and downs in the data. The central classical data-analytic technique, Analysis of Variance (ANOVA), separates the fluctuations in the data into

(1) variations within groups and (2) variations between groups. This permits the researcher to consider whether the differences *between* two groups (either treatment-1 versus treatment-2, or treatment versus control) are considerably greater than the differences among the clients *within* each of the groups. If the subjects are assigned to their groups randomly, then the variation *within* any group represents expectable human variability, as opposed to variability due to treatment. In contrast, the variability *between* two groups will represent the true differences due to treatment. The ratio of these two types of variability is "tested for significance." If the ratio is favorable, the treatment is promising.

If the data do not show a difference, however, the formal method merely withholds judgment. For this reason, careful researchers speak of "failing to reject the hypothesis of no differences" rather than "accepting the hypothesis of no differences." This is an important point for pastoral counselors to grasp, because it is quite possible that finding ways to study pastoral counseling with formal scientific method may take time. The learning process may involve some failures, and it is important to understand that these should in no way be taken to prove that pastoral counseling is without a unique impact.

To make clearer the advantages of formal comparisons across randomized groups, let's consider the most commonly used defective research design, the "one group pre-test/post-test study." The usual form of such comparative studies is a pre-treatment and a post-treatment measure. As Rogosa and Willett (1985) note, however, designs with only two observations are usually inadequate for the assessment of systematic individual differences in growth. This is because the subtle movements forward and backward during the period of change are lost when measures are taken at only the beginning and the end of the treatment period. Further, this design offers no means to measure and to separate out the common human variability from the variability due to the treatment effect. This design was often seen a generation ago in mental health treatment research. Introduction of a second group, a control group, has led to the surprising finding that some people get well with no treatment at all! Consequently, any claims for treatment efficacy must be superior to the effect of simply leaving the client alone. To demonstrate this incremental efficacy, one needs a control group.

Other kinds of variability besides unwanted random variability must also be controlled. For example, an intake process before counseling may have a biasing effect on the measure of counseling effectiveness. The "Solomon four-group design" controls for this problem:

		Time	
Group-1	Intake	Treatment	Post-test
Group-2	Intake	No Treatment	Post-test
Group-3	No Intake	Treatment	Post-test
Group-4	No Intake	No Treatment	Post-test

Here the effects of the post-test can be measured on Group-4, and the effects of the pretest can be measured by Group-2 minus Group-4. The effect of the treatment will be measured by the scores of Group-1 minus Group-2, while the effect of the treatment plus the post-testing process can be seen in Group-3. This kind of sophisticated control is important in treatment research, because evaluation and interviewing are known to have some short-term therapeutic effect. It is necessary to control for this short-term artifact in order to measure the effect specifically due to the treatment under formal consideration.

In another example, consider the evaluation of different styles of supervision and/or specific supervisors for effectiveness. In such a study the order of exposure to supervisors and also the learning stage of the trainee must be controlled. These are two sources of variability which are extraneous to the matter of real interest, i.e. the comparison of supervisory techniques. This particular design problem has surfaced over and over in educational research, where the personal style of a teacher may interact with a teaching method. Further, a personal attribute of the learner may also interact with a teaching method. When the interfering variable is an easily identifiable one, such as gender, its effect can be anticipated and controlled by manipulations of the data during the planning and data analysis. If the effect is unique, such as one supervisor's personality, it can be controlled by spreading it evenly across the whole study, e.g. by rotating each trainee through the entire supervisor roster. A further problem which will then arise is whether it makes a difference whether a trainee gets Supervisor A before or after Supervisor B. An elegant research design which takes care of all these problems is the so-called Latin Square. In the supervision research example, supervisors would be arrayed across columns, and trainees down the rows of the research protocol. The sequence of pairing for supervisor/trainee pairs would then be randomized by a third code at the row and column intersections:

Supervisor 1	Supervisor 2	Supervisor 3	Supervisor 4	
a	b	c	d	Trainee 1, 5, 9, etc.
b	c	d	a	Trainee 2, 6, 10, etc.
c	d	a	b	Trainee 3, 7, 11, etc.
d	a	b	c	Trainee 4, 8, 12, etc.

The order of supervisors for the first group of trainees would be 1, 2, 3, 4 because their cells are coded a, b, c, d. For the second group of trainees, the order of supervisors would be 2, 3, 4, 1 because their cells are coded b, c, d, a. And so on. All of the following can be studied via this design:

—comparisons of technical approaches a, b, c, and d
—comparisons of supervisors 1, 2, 3, and 4
—comparisons of *order* of presentation of approaches
—comparisons of *order* of presentation of supervisors.

Furthermore, the comparisons of supervisors are controlled (balanced) for method and for trainee maturity, while the comparisons of methods are controlled (balanced) for individual characteristics of supervisor and trainee maturity. To study the impact of the order of presentation of the four supervisory styles, you would sum trainee ratings across the four rows, while to compare the supervisory styles themselves, you would sum ratings down the four columns. Unfortunately, this design does not give a direct measure of random fluctuation, but this might not be a concern in a study in which the participants had been so carefully screened.

The Latin Square must be square, but the dimensions are optional. It could be 5×5, 6×6, etc.—all depending on the number of treatments, approaches, or styles one wanted to compare. This is an excellent example of the usefulness of a planned design even for a research undertaking which will not yield any numerical data at all! The data gathered in such a study could well be purely impressionistic ratings, based on expert judgment. The rotational pattern would nevertheless serve to control extraneous factors in the study, whether they are due to attributes of the supervisor or trainee, or to the order of presentation of each supervisor to trainees.

Much of the technical work in designing a particular research study is the identification and control of *unwanted* causes of fluctuation, so that the fluctuation due to the effect to be studied can be teased out and exposed if it is present. Statisticians focus a great deal of their research on developing research designs which minimize unwanted fluctuation and maximize meaningful information, while holding down costs and numbers of subjects needed. Optimizing the research design is a process of minimizing the variation in the data which is due to unwanted fluctuation, while maximizing the variation in the data which is due to the variables of research interest. In situations where the data are expensive to gather, a further concept of efficiency of design comes into play: the relative payoff in control of unwanted fluctuation for the cost of the various design possibilities is computed. In this way the researcher can choose the design which gives the most experimental control for the project funds available. Design efficiency will be an area of great importance in designing pastoral counseling studies, because the natural form of the data is costly, involving both long periods of time and highly trained observers.

Section V. Using "Standard" Methodology: How To Begin?

Any researchers in need of formal methodological skills can take one of two approaches. They can either study the topic area or seek a consultant. Consultation may prove difficult for pastoral counseling researchers, since some consultants have neither the interest nor the patience to understand the multiple facets of pastoral counseling data. Conversely, the pastoral counselor will almost certainly find it a strain to understand and defer to the consultant's technical concerns. This difficulty occurs in other esoteric fields as well; ultimately many content areas develop their own methodologists to solve this problem. Many graduate school programs attempt to place the potential researcher in a middle ground; they give enough training in methodology so that the candidate can design simple studies and can also function as an intelligent shopper for data-analytic services. This approach appears desirable for the potential pastoral counseling researcher. Conceptualizing a workable research project and getting the best service from consultants is laborious or even impossible without minimally "speaking the language."

Section VI. Not All Useful Theories Can Be Proved

It is important that pastoral counselors begin to systematize their theories and chip away at validating them. Such a validation process will yield not only confirmation of the familiar, but discovery of the unknown. In the process, pastoral counselors can take comfort in the fact that no reasonable person expects any discipline to function solely on a basis of fully proven theory. All disciplines also rely for everyday operation on insight, hunch, approximation, and expert opinion.

The pastoral counselor modifies use of scientific research studies in yet a further way, beyond insight and hunch. He or she relies also upon faith and divine guidance. It is important for the growth of pastoral counseling as an academic discipline and a professional field to realize that there is no inherent conflict between careful research about pastoral counseling work and the life of faith as a pastoral counselor. Simply because the insights about pastoral work gleaned from research will be seen "in a glass darkly" does not mean that this limited vision will not be useful in the here-and-now.

Not only pastoral counseling data, but any form of mental health data has a high level of complexity and ambiguity. Further, the learning of the therapist's or counselor's role and tasks consumes great time and energy. Pastoral counselors, often lacking even basic methodology skills, are perhaps insufficiently aware of how simple, and sometimes how flawed, the methodology approaches are in some published treatment research (Salsburg, 1985). With relatively little further investment in training time, pastoral counselors could become recognized participants in the general mental health research community.

Is it important for pastoral counseling to come in this way under the dominance of formal research methodology? Yes, it is, for several reasons. The isolation of pastoral counselors from the mental health research community would suggest to critics a shrinking back from the tests to which other treatment researchers submit their procedures. Undoubtedly, critics would be underestimating the work involved in formal tests of such complex hypotheses, but their point would be nonetheless valid. Pastoral counselors must learn and use the methodology of statistical evaluation, rather than proclaiming it irrelevant to their special theories and hypotheses. At the same time, a part of their identity as pastoral counselors will be to remain aware that the explanations of human change which they find within their research about their counseling methods are only part of the whole story. In summary, good pastoral counseling research will embody a continual reflection on, and alternation between, the poles of faith and action in carrying out God's work in the psychological world.

Bibliography

Cronbach, Lee J., Goldine C. Gleser *et al. The Dependability of Behavioral Measurements: Theory of Generalizability for Scores and Profiles.* New York: John Wiley and Sons, 1972, p. 387.

Huff, Darrell. *How to Lie with Statistics.* New York: Norton, 1954.

Martin, James A. "Science and Democracy in the Age of Technology: Separating Fact from Value," *American Statistician,* 37, No. 4, Part 2, 1983, pp. 367–373.

Patton, Michael Quinn. *Utilization Focused Evaluation.* Beverly Hills: Sage Publications, 1978, p. 13.

Roberts, Harry V. "Statisticians Can Matter," *American Statistician,* 32, No. 2, 1978, pp. 45–51 at 50.

Rogosa, David R. and John B. Willett. "Understanding Correlates of Change by Modeling Individual Differences in Growth," *Psychometrika,* 50, No. 2, June 1985, pp. 203–228.

Salsburg, David S. "The Religion of Statistics as Practiced in Medical Journals," *American Statistician, 39, No. 3, 1985, pp. 220–223.*

Standen, Anthony. *Science Is a Sacred Cow.* New York: E. P. Dutton and Company, 1950.

Strunk, Orlo, "A Prolegomenon to a History of Pastoral Counseling," in Wicks *et al., Clinical Handbook of Pastoral Counseling.* Mahwah: Paulist Press, 1985.

Von Neumann, John. "The Role of Mathematics in Science and Society," in *Collected Works,* Volume VI. New York: Macmillan Co., 1963.

William A. Barry, S.J.

Spiritual Direction

In their history of pastoral care Clebsch and Jaekle (1964) opined: "There is no place in the structure and rhythm of the life of modern congregations where a serious discussion concerning the state of one's soul is expected." They went on to speak of the malaise of clergy who often feel like amateur psychiatrists and continued:

> Part of the reason for this anxiety may be the feeling that usual pastoral routines provide no contact with alienated people face to face in situations that define the minister as one who is alerted to and talented in a certain kind of spiritual conversation that can knit together broken bonds between God and man. This extemporizing virtually deprives the church of its ministry of pastoral reconciling at a time when alienation is at the root of much human woe and anxiety. (p. 66)

At the time they published their historical survey the Roman Catholic Church had the confessional as a place where such conversations could happen. How often they did is hard to tell. The fact that most Catholics gave up frequent confession as soon as it became known that they did not have to go could be an indication that confession, for them, had not been a positive experience of such a spiritual conversation. Yet over the centuries the confessional has been and still is a place where many people found such healing spiritual conversations. It is, of course, not the only place where such conversations are found either in the Roman Catholic Church or in other denominations. But the conversations which Clebsch and Jaekle see as lacking and which many people found in the confessional and elsewhere in the pastoral ministry are called spiritual direction. For these conversations had as their purpose the knitting together of the broken bonds between God and the human person, in other words, helping the person to union with God. As Kenneth Leech (1980) says: "Union with God is not a peripheral area of interest for the Christian, and it is union with God which is the central concern of spiritual direction." (p. 2) Leech himself laments that so few ministers and clergy feel competent to engage in such conversations and writes his book because the "church at the present time is in desperate need of spiritual guides, men and women who are steeped in prayer and in the spirit, and who can therefore be bearers of the spirit to our age." (p. 2) I have a similar purpose in writing this chapter.

What is spiritual direction? In a sense all pastoral care which has as its purpose helping people to union with God can be called spiritual direction. Preaching, liturgy, teaching, admonishing, pastoral visiting, feeding the hungry, etc.—all these ministries of pastoral care can be undertaken with the purpose of helping people to union with God. Over the centuries, however, spiritual direction has taken on a specialized (and sometimes a very esoteric) meaning. Leech (1980), in his chapter on the history of spiritual direction, notes, "The term 'spiritual direction' is usually applied to the cure of souls when it involves the specific needs of one individual." (p. 34) For purposes of this chapter I want to define spiritual direction as a form of pastoral counseling "given by one Christian to another which enables that person to pay attention to God's personal communication to him or her, to respond to this personally communicating God, to grow in intimacy with this God, and to live out the consequences of the relationship." (Barry and Connolly, 1982, p. 8; see also Culligan, 1983 for similar definitions)

Before we go further, let me say a word about the terms "spiritual" and "direction" since both can lead to false conclusions. By the term "spiritual" we refer to the inner life, to the heart as biblical writers understand that word, "the personal core out of which come the good and evil that people think and do." (Barry and Connolly, 1982, p. 10) "Direction" does not mean leading another by the nose but rather implies that the person who seeks "direction" is on a journey and wants help finding his or her way. As a form of pastoral counseling, spiritual direction uses all the listening and counseling skills associated with that professional practice. Just as the term pastoral counseling can be misused to denote the equivalent of "brainwashing," so too the term "spiritual direction" can be misused. But if the purpose of spiritual direction is union with God, then the question of what kind of pastoral counseling is appropriate can only be answered by asking a further question, "What kind of union does God want with us?"

It seems clear from scripture and tradition that God wants a relationship of intimacy with human beings that corresponds to their level of maturity. Two scriptural examples will suffice. In the Abraham cycle of stories in the book of Genesis Abraham seems to develop from a man of blind obedience in chapter 11 to an adult friend of God in chapter 18. There God decides to tell Abraham what he intends to do to Sodom and Gomorrah. This revelation allows Abraham to haggle with God and even to tell God that he cannot do an unjust thing. In chapter 15 of John's gospel Jesus says: "I call you servants no longer; a servant does not know what his master is about. I have called you friends, because I have disclosed to you everything that I heard from my Father." (Jn 15:15) If God wants an intimate relationship with adults, then the spiritual direction which is help to such intimacy must treat the people directed as adults. It must respect their freedom and their integrity. Moreover, such spiritual direction must be able to deal with each individual as an individual and each relationship as unique. So the spiritual director must be open to the mystery that is the human person, especially when the person engages in the relationship with God.

To say that spiritual direction is about union with God presumes that God and the human person encounter each other. The spiritual director helps people to pay attention to the encounter with God in their lives. Paying attention means being attentive to experience. If, with John E. Smith (1968), we define experience as an encounter between a being that exists and another being who can be conscious of what is happening in the encounter, then experience does not have to be construed as something purely subjective. Moreover, experience thus defined has many dimensions. If the two beings who encounter one another are encountered in the physical world, then there is a physical dimension to the experience. If the one who is conscious of the encounter is a biological being, then the experience has a biological dimension. So too for the psychological, the sociological and the cultural dimensions of experience. However, the person who is conscious may not be aware of these dimensions; hence for him or her the experience does not have these dimensions. For example, a man who has just read a ghost story hears a breeze rustle the leaves on a dark night, looks up in fright, sees a ghost and runs away screaming. In reality there is no ghost, but he will not believe it because he is unaware of the psychological dimension of his experience. The psychological dimension does not exist for him, at least in this moment.

Does human experience have a religious dimension? What is required is the existence of God who is both transcendent to and immanent in this world and a person who believes in and is alert for the encounter with God. If the transcendent God is immanent in this world he creates, then God is encountered, indeed, is encountered at every moment of our existence. But human beings, even believers, are not always alert for the encounter. Hence many, if not most, of our experiences do not have a religious dimension. People who want to become more aware of the encounter with God and to develop their relationship with God need help to develop that awareness, and that help, I would contend, is that form of pastoral counseling I have called spiritual direction. The first requisite, therefore, for anyone who would be a spiritual director is an experience-based belief in the religious dimension of experience. In other words, the spiritual director must have personal experience of the relationship with God, something stressed throughout the history of the church. (Leech, 1980)

Not everyone will agree that spiritual direction is a form of pastoral counseling. Some might say that pastoral counseling focuses on problems whereas spiritual direction focuses on the person's call to union with God. Yet I would maintain that a pastoral counseling that does not have as at least one of its purposes helping people to a deeper relation with God does not deserve the adjective pastoral. Pastoral counseling that is merely licensed psychological counseling done by someone who is ordained or in a church-related setting is not, to my mind, pastoral. Some might say that spiritual direction is the practical application of the principles of ascetical theology to the individual. To them I would say that if the practical application is to be really helpful to an adult relation with God, then it must be done by a skilled helper who can help others to make sense of their experience in the light of the principles of ascetical theology. In other words, the practical application will have to use the skills of pastoral counseling. Ultimately the one who does spiritual direction has to decide whether help to union with God means help with a relationship or not. If it is help with a relationship, then the spiritual director will help people to engage in the relationship, pay attention to what happens when they do, talk about what happens in order to discern what is of God from what is not of God in their experiences. In other words, the spiritual director needs to help people to discern the religious dimension from all the other dimensions of any experience. Moreover, the tradition holds that one of the actors in the pot of our experience is the evil one who tries to disrupt our journey to union with God. However, the trail of Satan's influence can only be discerned if the one who is being directed describes his or her experience as openly and fully as possible. Once again, the director must have the skills to foster such an exploration of experience. The spiritual director must be, in the words of Egan (1986), a "skilled helper."

The Particular Focus of Spiritual Direction

If spiritual direction is a form of pastoral counseling, how can we distinguish it from other forms? I believe that the central focus of spiritual direction distinguishes it from other forms. The central focus of spiritual direction is the relationship itself between the person seeking direction and God. Let me explain. In pastoral counseling with a married couple experiencing trouble in their marriage the central focus will be the relationship between the couple themselves. Of course, the pastoral counselor will try to help the couple to see their relationship in terms of the relationship with God and the church, but the central focus will be what happens between the two people themselves. In pastoral counseling with a person whose neurotic patterns of behavior are having serious negative repercussions in life and work, the central focus will be the experience of the client and the dynamic understanding of the reasons for the self-defeating behavior. The pastoral counselor will use the resources of the relationship with God to help the person toward inner healing, but the relationship with God is not the central focus. In spiritual direction the focus is the relationship between God and the person. The directee is encouraged to pay attention to the religious dimension of experience, to note times when he or she feels the presence of God, to try to discern what is of God from what is not of God in these experiences. To paraphrase Barry and Connolly (1982), the religious dimension of experience "is to spiritual direction what foodstuff is to cooking. Without foodstuff there can be no cooking." Without the religious dimension of experience "there can be no spiritual direction." (p. 8) Once again I want to underline the necessity of personal experience of this religious dimension for spiritual directors. If they do not have such personal experience, then their direction will not focus on the religious dimension of experience because they will not know what it is.

Other Needed Qualities in Spiritual Directors

Spiritual directors need all the qualities of any skilled helper. They must have what Braaty (1954) calls a "surplus of warmth," a real love for others which shows itself in commitment, effort to understand and spontaneity (Bordin, 1968).

> Commitment is the spiritual director's willingness to help the directee grow in union with God and to commit his time, his resources, and himself to that end. Effort to understand means that the spiritual director tries to maintain a contemplative attitude to the directee, tries to perceive how he is experiencing the Lord and life. Spontaneity means that the spiritual director is himself not controlled and inhibited by his role as a spiritual director, but is able to express his own feelings, thoughts, and hopes when expressing them will be helpful to the directee. (Barry and Connolly, 1982, p. 126)

They need a quiet trust and confidence in God's desire and ability to help directees to grow in the relationship. Humble self-confidence is also a requisite for good spiritual direction, the kind of self-confidence that allows the director to speak the truth without fear of consequences. In general, spiritual directors need to be the kind of persons others will trust with their hearts.

In the history of the church spiritual direction was often given by ordained clergy. Ordination, however, is neither a sufficient nor a necessary condition for being a spiritual director. Throughout history lay men and women have been effective spiritual directors. (de Guibert, 1956; Leech, 1980) Many of the spiritual directors of the desert were not ordained. Catherine of Genoa, Teresa of Avila and many other non-ordained women were remarkable spiritual directors. Ignatius of Loyola was a most effective spiritual director long before he became a priest. Moreover, many ordained men and women would make very poor spiritual directors. (Barry and Connolly, 1982, pp. 122–123) In point of fact, there is no office of spiritual direction in the church. (de Guibert, 1956) Spiritual direction is a charism, a gift of God to the church in the form of people who can do the work and are trusted by those who seek them out. Even though office in the church does not make them spiritual directors, nevertheless spiritual directors need to be deeply rooted in the church. Spiritual direction is an ecclesial charism.

The Skilled Helper

In this section I want to use the general outline provided by Egan (1986) to indicate how the spiritual director uses the skills of the counselor to help people to develop their relationship with God. Egan delineates three stages of the helping process. The first stage aims at identifying and clarifying problem situations and unused opportunities. The skilled helper uses the skills of attending to and respect for the client, accurate empathy, genuineness, concreteness and helpful challenging to help the client to explore what Egan calls the "present scenario" and to tell his or her story. In spiritual direction the "present scenario" is the religious dimension of experience since the last session of direction. The spiritual director uses all the skills of the counselor to help the directee to explore his or her experience of the relationship with God since the last session. In effect, the director helps the directee to tell his or her story of God. (Ruffing, 1989) This exploration is extremely important. Many people need a great deal of help to pay attention to the religious dimension of their experience and to believe that they have experiences worth the effort of attention and description. Too often people downplay their experience, finding it hard to believe that God could be communicating with them or that their experience would be interesting to explore with another person. Moreover, all of us are highly ambivalent about our relationship with God; in the depths of our being we are attracted to union with God, and at the same time we strongly resist the pull toward union with God. (Barry, 1990; May, 1982) Thus those who seek spiritual direction need all the help of the skilled helper to explore their present experience. Before they make judgments about the meaning of their experience, they need to pay attention to it, to savor it, to describe it. They will only do this with a skilled helper who genuinely wants to listen to and empathize with that experience.

Only after the person's experience has been sufficiently explored is it time to evaluate it, to look at it from the point of view of whether and to what extent the experience is of God. Here we touch upon what has traditionally been called the discernment of spirits. (Sampson, 1979; Sweeney, 1980; Barry and Connolly, 1982, ch. 7; Toner, 1982; Delaney, 1987) We have already noted that every experience is multidimensional. There are physical, physiological, psychological, social, and cultural dimensions to every experience. Hence, discernment must try to distinguish these dimensions from the religious insofar as such distinguishing is possible. Moreover, Christian tradition has held that the human heart is a battleground where Satan tries to draw the person away from union with God. It would take us too far afield to discuss in detail all the ramifications of the discernment of spirits here. The interested reader can find helpful material in the sources cited above. Discernment helps the directee not only to decide what is of God in his or her experience, but also to recognize resistances and blind alleys and to realize what he or she most deeply desires. This discernment leads to the second stage of the process of skilled helping.

Egan's second stage looks toward a change in the present scenario on the assumption that it is not the preferred scenario. So the skilled helper helps the client to create new scenarios and to set goals. In spiritual direction the preferred scenario may be a change, but it also may be "more of the same." In other words, the directee may come to the realization that he or she wants a deepening of the experience that has already occurred. For example, a young man has been asking God to assure him that God still loves him even though he had refused to help his mother when she was dying of cancer. During the past week he has experienced Jesus as looking on him with love just the way he looked at the rich young man. (Mk 10:17–22) He felt great remorse for his neglect of his mother, but also greatly relieved because Jesus seemed to be communicating to him not only that Jesus still loved him, but also that his mother forgave him as well. In the spiritual direction session he comes to the conclusion that he needs to let this experience sink in more because even after the experience he occasionally reverted to depression. However, in the course of a spiritual direction session or of a few sessions a directee may come to realize that he or she has been resisting a new development in the relationship with God and desire to be more open to it. Then the preferred scenario would be to let God come closer in prayer and in life. The director would help the directee to envisage this new development and figure out ways to let it happen. Let me give an extended example.

Ruth comes to the realization that God wants to free her of fear of vulnerability. The fear showed itself when she sensed that God wanted to put his arms around her. She quickly stopped praying and began to distract herself with work and reading. During the past few sessions of direction she has also become quite uncomfortable when the spiritual director brings the conversation back to this experience. During these sessions she discovers some of the roots of the fear and also strong anger at God for not having protected her at earlier times of vulnerability. She wants to overcome the resistance and realizes that she would be much freer if she could let God come closer. The spiritual director helps her to envision what steps she can take to move toward her goal or preferred scenario. In her anxiety about the giant step of letting God embrace her she misses seeing that she can tell God how afraid she is and ask him to help to overcome the fear.

With this example we come to Egan's third stage, helping clients to develop strategies for action. The director has been helping Ruth not only to set her goal, but also to begin to look at the steps she can take to reach the goal, or at least to keep the relationship with God alive and moving in the desired direction of greater closeness. The task of the spiritual director here will be to help the directee to be creative and inventive in approaching God. Often enough the resistance to a new scenario can be so strong that a head-on attack is counter-productive. Then the director needs to help the directee to look at courses of action that are actually possible to undertake. Ruth, for example, could not let God take her into his arms, but she could tell God that she was terrified of his doing that and then ask his help to overcome the fear. Sometimes, too, directees need help to take steps to change their lifestyle which is interfering with union with God. Here again, the director uses the skills of the pastoral counselor to help the directee make effective plans in order to attain a deeper union with God.

The Development of the Relationship with God

In the history of spirituality many attempts have been made to describe the development of the relationship with God. Teresa of Avila used the image of a castle with many mansions, the person progressing from the outermost mansion into the inner sanctum. A traditional progression describes the movement from the purgative way to the illuminative way to the unitive way. In his *Spiritual Exercises* Ignatius of Loyola uses the image of weeks to describe the development of the relationship with the mystery we call God. For readers of this handbook a description of the development of the relationship with God precisely on the analogy of a developing human relationship may be helpful.

A relationship of growing intimacy begins with mutual attraction between the two people. We do not seek to develop a relationship with someone whom we dislike or of whom we are afraid. Many people are afraid of God. For them God is a snoop or a tyrant ready to catch them out for the least fault (Guntrip, 1957). Such people need a great deal of help to have an experience of God that will change their image of God, or, to be more precise, their self-God schema. They need an experience of God as loving creator, as desiring them into existence and keeping them in existence out of love. (Moore, 1985) Only such an experience can ground a real desire to get closer to God. The psychiatrist J.S. Mackenzie says it well:

> The *enjoyment of God* should be the supreme end of spiritual technique; and it is in that enjoyment of God that we feel not only saved in the Evangelical sense, but safe: we are conscious of belonging to God, and hence are never alone; and, to the degree we have these two, hostile feelings disappear. . . . In that relationship Nature seems friendly and homely; even its vast spaces instead of eliciting a sense of terror speak of the infinite love; and the nearer beauty becomes the garment with which the Almighty clothes Himself. (Guntrip, 1957, pp. 194–195)

This enjoyment of God is like the experience of a desire for "I know not what," a desire C.S. Lewis called joy. (1955) I believe that this kind of experience is available to everyone and is the reason we can affirm that everyone is created to praise, reverence and serve God and thus be happy with God forever. Union with God is the deepest desire of the human heart, but many people need help to experience that desire because they have been hurt by life.

After the initial experience of attraction and, perhaps, a honeymoon period, human relationships face a number of hurdles. When the bloom is off the rose, disagreements and fears arise that cloud the development of the relationship. "Will she still love me if I tell her that I don't like her mother." "I don't really like the way he talks to me. If I tell him, will that end the relationship?" "I broke his favorite record. Will he forgive me?" If the relationship is to progress and deepen, the two people will have to work through these dark times together. Otherwise the relationship will wither on the vine. So too with the relationship with God. After the euphoria of the initial or continuing experience of God's great goodness people begin to wonder whether it really was a pipe dream. They feel ashamed before God as they remember their past. "Could God really want to be close to me when he knows that I lied about a friend?" "If God is so good, how could he let me be physically abused by my father? Can I tell him how angry I am at him?" In the presence of the holy mystery human beings feel their own unholiness and quake. Isaiah cried: "Woe to me! I am ruined! For I am a man of unclean lips, and I live among a people of unclean lips, my eyes have seen the King, the Lord Almighty." (Is 6:5) When Peter saw the miraculous catch of fish, he said, "Go away from me, Lord; I am a sinful man!" (Lk 5:9) At this stage of the developing relationship with God, people can be overwhelmed by the fear that God has turned his back on them because of their sins. Of course, it is an illusion since Jesus died not to save the just, but sinners. The truth that people at this stage need to experience is that God loves them unconditionally, warts and all. People who do not know in their bones that they are loved sinners need directors who help them to ask God to remove the blinders that keep them from experiencing God's unconditional love.

When two people have developed their relationship to the point where they are relatively sure that their love of one another is built on a solid foundation, then they can begin to look outward together. They enter what Erikson called the generativity stage. A married couple plan on children, for example. Two friends begin to think of something they can do together. A community of friends discuss how they can improve their neighborhood. A similar shift happens to people who have come to believe through deep experience that they are unconditionally loved by God, that they are loved sinners. Where before the questions in the relationship with God revolved around the self, now the questions become other-directed. In a sense people become more apostolic in orientation, wondering how they can spread the good news that has so changed their own lives. For Christians this stage is often called the stage of following or imitating Christ. Earlier they wanted to know that Jesus still loved them; they wanted to be sure that Jesus looked on them with love; the focus was inward. Now they are sure of that love. One image that describes this stage is that of two friends walking or working together; the focus is outward. There are resistances to a deepening intimacy with Jesus at this stage, but they spring from more realistic fears. Those who grow close to Jesus and become like him often suffer the same fate as Jesus suffered. Indeed, in the gospels Jesus promises that his disciples will be treated just as he was treated. Spiritual direction at this stage helps people to recognize the rationalizations and fears that can keep them from pursuing their desire for a more intimate friendship with Jesus. Spiritual directors can be the agents of what Macmurray (1961) calls "real religion."

All religion . . . is concerned to overcome fear. We can distinguish real religion from unreal by contrasting their formulae for dealing with negative motivation. The maxim of illusory religion runs: "Fear not; trust in God and He will see that none of the things you fear will happen to you"; that of real religion, on the contrary, is "Fear not; the things that you are afraid of are quite likely to happen to you, but they are nothing to be afraid of." (p. 171)

But they can only be such agents if they maintain a stance of letting people deal directly with the Lord in the manner recommended by Ignatius of Loyola in his *Spiritual Exercises.* (Puhl, 1951) "Therefore, the director of the Exercises, as a balance at equilibrium, without leaning to one side or the other, should permit the Creator to deal directly with the creature, and the creature directly with his Creator and Lord." (p. 6) Spiritual directors, in other words, must help their directees to discern the spirits and make free choices, not push them in one direction or the other.

People who develop a relationship of deep intimacy also suffer with one another. Indeed, the pain of one's dearest friend may cause one more pain than one's own suffering. People who get close to Jesus often find themselves feeling much more deeply the suffering and pain of others, almost as though they now see the world through Jesus' eyes. Yet painful though it is, they find themselves strangely consoled. At times they may want to turn their eyes away from what they now see, but they also realize that they do not want to move away from closeness to Jesus. In other words, they sense that intimacy with Jesus means suffering with him and being with him in his ongoing passion. And of course, they also experience in and through this compassion with Jesus the joy of the resurrection. This joy is deep and real, probably because the people who experience it have been willing to accept life whole as Jesus did and does with all its pains and sufferings and tragedies. "Did not the Christ have to suffer these things and then enter his glory?" (Lk 24:26)

People whose relationship with God moves to such depth often find themselves not needing many words in their prayer. Like friends who have grown old together they commune with God silently and deeply. They also seem able to discover God rather easily in their daily lives of work and leisure. God is not far from their minds and hearts. In the terminology of Ignatian spirituality they have become contemplatives in action, able to find God in all things. (Barry, in press)

Often enough when stages of the spiritual life are described, it can seem that the movement from one stage to another depends only on the willingness of the person to enter into the new stage. First, we need to remind ourselves that the process we have been describing is a process of grace. Only God can give the increase. Second, it is well to remember that the development of any relationship depends on many factors, not the least of which is the capacity of the individual for deeper intimacy. Moreover, the possibility of moving more deeply into the relationship with God will also depend on what cognitive developmental psychologists in the tradition of Piaget call states of disequilibrium, where there is some dissatisfaction with the present level of development. People can settle for a plateau in their relationship with God, a plateau which may be quite comfortable. (Liebert, in press)

Transference and Countertransference and Supervision

Since spiritual direction is a form of pastoral counseling, it is to be expected that the relationship between the director and directee will be affected by the self-other schemata which in counseling relationships lead to transference and countertransference reactions. Such reactions can derail the purpose of spiritual direction and cause real harm to the directee if they are not handled with professional skill by the spiritual director. Moreover, spiritual directors themselves put up resistance to developing a more intimate relationship with God; hence their own resistances can get in the way of their being able to help certain directees. As a result, spiritual directors need supervised training to be able to carry on this demanding ministry (Edwards, 1980; Barry and Connolly, 1982). But they also need to seek out ongoing supervision. Such supervision can be obtained through peer group interaction as well as through an individual. This supervision must, however, focus on the experience of the directors in their work as spiritual directors and not on their directees. It is far too easy to focus on the persons who are absent, namely on the directees.

Conclusion

I have argued that spiritual direction is a form of pastoral counseling and have shown how the skills of such counseling are used to help people to become more aware of the religious dimension of experience and to develop their relationship with God. Let me here make some final observations. Spiritual directors will need some knowledge of personality development in order to be helpful to people at various stages of such development. Studzinski (1985) gives an example of the application of the psychology of midlife development to spiritual direction. Direction with different personality types also requires flexibility on the part of directors. (Clarke, 1983; Osiek, 1985) Directors will also have to be aware of the differences between men and women and take these into account in their ministry. Feminist writers are making us aware that much of the spiritual tradition has been handed on by men and has had a decidedly patriarchal cast. (Fischer, 1988; Seelaus, 1977) The psychology of C.G. Jung has a strong influence on some significant figures in the modern movement for training spiritual directors. This trend can best be seen in the work of Morton Kelsey. (1984) Anyone familiar with the spiritual tradition will recognize that my contribution to this volume comes from what is called the "kataphatic" way, one that pays attention to images, feelings, and thoughts as a way to God. The "apophatic" way in the tradition tries to avoid images and thoughts through concentration on a prayer word or mantra. For an introduction to this tradition of spiritual direction see Main (1988) or Pennington (1986). Finally, I have said nothing about group spiritual direction because I have had no experience with it nor have I seen any significant writing on the subject. I do know that some directors do work with groups, and I hope that we will soon see descriptions of what happens and how it goes.

Bibliography

Barry, W.A. *Paying Attention to God: Discernment in Prayer.* Notre Dame: Ave Maria, 1990.

Barry, W.A. *In All Things To Love and Serve God: The Spiritual Exercises of St. Ignatius of Loyola.* Notre Dame: Ave Maria, in press.

Barry, W.A. & Connolly, W.J. *The Practice of Spiritual Direction.* San Francisco: Harper & Row (Seabury) 1982.

Bordin, E.S. *Psychological Counseling* (2nd ed.). New York: Appleton-Century-Crofts, 1968.

Braaty, T. *Fundamentals of Psychoanalytic Technique.* New York: Wiley, 1954.

Clarke, T.E. "Jungian Types and Forms of Prayer," *Review for Religious,* 42, 1983, 661–676.

Clebsch, W.A. & Jaekle, C.R. *Pastoral Care in Historical Perspective: An Essay with Exhibits.* New York: Harper Torchbook, 1964.

Culligan, K.G. (ed.) *Spiritual Direction: Contemporary Readings.* Locust Valley: Living Flame Press, 1983.

de Guibert, J. *The Theology of the Spiritual Life*. New York: Sheed & Ward, 1956.

Delaney, W.K. "Discernment of Spirits in Ignatius of Loyola and Teresa of Avila," *Review for Religious*, 46, 1987, 598–611.

Edwards, T. *Spiritual Friend: Reclaiming the Gift of Spiritual Direction*. New York: Paulist Press, 1980.

Egan, G. *The Skilled Helper: A Systematic Approach to Effective Helping* (3rd ed.). Belmont: Brooks/Cole, 1986.

Fischer, K. *Women at the Well: Feminist Perspectives on Spiritual Direction*. New York/Mahwah: Paulist Press, 1988.

Guntrip, H. *Psychology and Religion*. New York: Harper & Row, 1957.

Kelsey, M.T. *Companions on the Inner Way: The Art of Spiritual Guidance*. New York: Crossroad, 1984.

Leech, K. *Soul Friend: The Practice of Christian Spirituality*. San Francisco: Harper & Row, 1980.

Lewis, C.S. *Surprised by Joy: The Shape of My Early Life*. London: Geoffrey Bles, 1955.

Liebert, E.A. *The Developmental Context of Spiritual Direction*. Mahwah: Paulist Press, in press.

Macmurray, J. *Persons in Relation*. London: Faber & Faber, 1961.

Main, J. *The Heart of Creation*. London: Darton, Longman & Todd, 1988.

May, G. *Care of Mind/Care of Soul*. San Francisco: Harper & Row, 1982.

Moore, S. *Let This Mind Be in You: The Quest for Identity Through Oedipus to Christ*. Minneapolis: Winston, 1985.

Osiek, C. "The Spiritual Direction of 'Thinking' Types," *Review for Religious*, 44, 1985, 209–219.

Pennington, M.B. "Centering Prayer: Refining the Rules," *Review for Religious*, 45, 1986, 386–393.

Puhl, L.J. (ed.). *The Spiritual Exercises of St. Ignatius*. Chicago: Loyola University Press, 1951.

Ruffing, J. *Uncovering Stories of Faith: Spiritual Direction and Narrative*. New York/Mahwah: Paulist Press, 1989.

Sampson, W. "Discerning the Spirits in Prayer," *Review for Religious*, 38, 1979, 229–235.

Seelaus, V. "New Approaches and Needs for Spiritual Direction of Women in the Catholic Church," Albany, *CRUX Extra*, June 27, 1977.

Smith, J.E. *Experience and God*. New York: Oxford, 1968.

Studzinski, R. *Spiritual Direction and Midlife Development.* Chicago: Loyola University Press, 1985.

Sweeney, R.J. "Discernment in the Spiritual Direction of St. Francis de Sales," *Review for Religious,* 39, 1980, 127–141.

Toner, J.J. *A Commentary on St. Ignatius' Rules for the Discernment of Spirits: A Guide to the Principles and Practice.* St. Louis: Institute for Jesuit Sources, 1982.

Notes on the Contributors
(follow the order of the articles)

ROBERT J. WICKS is Professor and Director of Program Development of the Graduate Programs in Pastoral Counseling at Loyola College in Maryland. He has been a Visiting Lecturer at both Princeton Theological Seminary and Washington Theological Union. In addition, he is on the Editorial Board of *Human Development* and the Editorial Committee of *The Journal of Pastoral Care* (1991). His recent books include: *Self-Ministry Through Self-Understanding, Living Simply in an Anxious World, Availability: The Problem and the Gift*, and *Seeking Perspective.*

M. SCOTT PECK, M.D. is recognized as a leader in the current movement toward the integration of psychology and spirituality. He was educated at Harvard University and Case Western Reserve, and served in the Army Medical Corps from 1963 to 1972. He now has a private practice in New Preston, CT.

DONALD BROWNING is Alexander Campbell Professor of Religion and Psychological Studies at the Divinity School of the University of Chicago. He is the author of five books, including *Generative Man* and *Practical Care.*

ORLO STRUNK, JR. is Professor of Psychology of Religion and Pastoral Psychology in the Division of Religious and Theological Studies of the Graduate School of Arts and Sciences, Boston University, and in the Boston University School of Theology. His most recent book is *Privacy: Experience, Understanding, Expression.*

CLYDE J. STECKEL is Academic Vice President and Professor of Theology and Psychology at United Theological Seminary of Minneapolis/St. Paul. He holds a Ph.D. from the University of Chicago and is the author of numerous articles and the book *Theology and Ethics of Behavior Modification.*

JOANN WOLSKI CONN is Associate Professor of Religious Studies at Neumann College, Aston, PA. She received her Ph.D. in Religion from Columbia University/Union Theological Seminary, New York. Currently she is preparing a book on inter-disciplinary resources for women's Christian development.

BERNARD JAMES TYRRELL, S.J. is Professor of Religious Studies and Philosophy at Gonzaga University in Spokane, WA. He is the author of three books, including *Christotherapy* and *Christotherapy II.* Fr. Tyrrell has lectured widely and offered many institutes on Christotherapy.

RICHARD D. PARSONS is Associate Professor of Counselor Education, West Chester University and has a private practice in West Chester, PA. Dr. Parsons holds a Ph.D. in Psychology from Temple University. Dr. Parsons has published nine books and over fifty articles in the area of mental health prevention and intervention. His most recent books include *Valuing Sexuality* (W.C. Brown), *Adolescence: What's a Parent To Do?* (Paulist Press) and *Counseling Strategies* (Allyn & Bacon).

EDGAR DRAPER, M.D. is Professor and Chairperson of the Department of Psychology at the University of Mississippi Medical Center. Dr. Draper received his medical degree from the Washington University Medical School and has received advanced training at the Institute for Psychoanalysis in Chicago. He is the author of several books including *Psychiatry and Pastoral Care.*

BEVAN STEADMAN, M.D. currently serves as staff physician and Director of Undergraduate Education in Psychology and Human Behavior of the University of Mississippi Medical School. Dr. Steadman also serves as consultant to a number of rehabilitation and treatment centers in the Jackson, MS area.

DAVID K. SWITZER is Professor of Pastoral Theology at Perkins School of Theology, Southern Methodist University. He regularly presents workshops on Crisis Counseling and Loss and Grief throughout the United States and many other countries. Among the books he has authored are *Pastor, Preacher, Person* and *The Minister as Crisis Counselor.*

MADONNA MARIE CUNNINGHAM, O.S.F. holds a Ph.D. in Clinical Psychology from Fordham University. Since 1970 she has been the congregation psychologist for the Sisters of St. Francis of Philadelphia of which she is a member. At Neumann College, Aston, PA, she was successively an associate professor of psychology, Director of the Counseling Center, and President.

RICHARD R. OSMER is an ordained United Methodist minister. He is an instructor of Christian Education at the Candler School of Theology and research associate of the Theology and Personality program at Emory University. He attended Harvard Divinity School and Yale Divinity School.

JAMES W. FOWLER is a United Methodist minister from the Western North Carolina Conference. With degrees from Duke, Drew, and Harvard Universities, he is presently Professor of Theology and Human Development and Director of the Center for Faith Development at Candler School of Theology, Emory University. His latest book titled *Becoming Adult, Becoming Christian* was published in the fall of 1984.

DONALD CAPPS is William Harte Felmeth Professor of Pastoral Theology at Princeton Theological Seminary. He received his Ph.D. from the University of Chicago and holds an honorary Th.D. from the University of Uppsala, Sweden. He is past-President of the Society for the Scientific Study of Religion. He has authored several books in Pastoral Theology, including *Deadly Sins and Saving Virtues, Reframing: A New Method in Pastoral Care,* and *The Depleted Self: Sin in a Narcissistic Age.*

JAMES N. LAPSLEY was Egner Professor of Pastoral Theology at Princeton Theological Seminary until his retirement. He holds a doctorate from the University of Chicago, and is the author of *Salvation and Health* and editor of *The Concept of Willing.*

LOY O. BASCUE is a counseling psychologist who received his Ph.D. from the University of Maryland. He is currently the training director of the Pennsylvania Foundation of Pastoral Counseling, Inc., and is an Associate Professor of Psychiatry and Human Behavior at the medical college of Thomas Jefferson University in Philadelphia.

ROY LEWIS, an ordained United Methodist pastor, is the Executive Director and founder of the Pennsylvania Foundation of Pastoral Counseling. He holds a Doctor of Ministries degree with special studies in pastoral psychotherapy from Drew University.

EMMA J. JUSTES is Associate Professor of Pastoral Psychology and Counseling at Garrett-Evangelical Theological Seminary, Evanston, Illinois. She received her Ph.D. from Princeton Theological Seminary and is an ordained American Baptist minister. She is working on a book on the pastoral care of women.

EDWARD P. WIMBERLY is an Associate Professor in the Graduate School of Theology at Oral Roberts University. He received his Ph.D. in Pastoral Psychology and Counseling from Boston University. An ordained United Methodist minister, Dr. Wimberly has pastored several churches and led many seminars and workshops on Pastoral Care throughout the Eastern United States.

LOWELL G. COLSTON is Professor Emeritus of Pastoral Care at Christian Theological Seminary, Indianapolis, IN. Professor Colston received his Doctor of Philosophy degree from the University of Chicago. He is an ordained minister of the Christian Church (Disciples of Christ) and is a diplomate of the American Association of Pastoral Counselors. He is the author of several books including *Pastoral Care with Handicapped Persons*.

RALPH L. UNDERWOOD, a United Methodist minister, is Associate Professor of Pastoral Care at Austin Presbyterian Theological Seminary. Dr. Underwood attended Asbury Theological Seminary, Princeton Theological Seminary, and the University of Chicago from which he holds a Ph.D.

GERALD FATH, O.P. received his Doctor of Ministry degree in Psychology and Clinical Studies from Andover-Newton Theological School. Following several years as a staff psychotherapist for the House of Affirmation in Hopedale and Boston, MA, Fr. Fath is now the Director of the Florida House of Affirmation.

CAROLE A. RAYBURN is a clinical psychologist with a degree in ministry. President of the Maryland Psychological Association (1984–1985), she is also President of the Section on the Clinical Psychology of Women of the American Psychological Association Division of Clinical Psychology. Dr. Rayburn has written numerous papers in journals and books on pastoral counseling and on women and religion.

SAMUEL M. NATALE is Professor of Management and Industrial Relations at the University of Bridgeport, CT, and is also a managerial consultant and psychotherapist. He received his doctorate from Oxford University, England. He is the author of four books, the most recent of which is entitled *Ethics and Morals in Business*. Dr. Natale is a Visiting Fellow at St. Edmund House at the University of Cambridge, England.

SHARON PARKS is an Assistant Professor at Harvard Divinity School where she teaches courses in Religion and Psychology, Pastoral Counseling, Spirituality, and Education. She received her doctorate from Harvard University.

F. CLARK POWER is an Assistant Professor in the Program for Liberal Studies at Notre Dame. His research and publishing are focused on issues in Moral Development and Education and Faith Development. He holds a Ph.D. from Harvard's Graduate School of Education in Human Development.

BRIAN H. CHILDS, who received his Ph.D. from Princeton Theological Seminary, is a senior clinical staff member and Director of Advanced Pastoral Studies at Trinity Counseling Service in Princeton, NJ, and also a lecturer in Pastoral Theology at Princeton Theological Seminary.

REAR ADMIRAL ROSS H. TROWER, D.D., Chaplain, U.S. Navy (retired), completed his thirty-eight years in the Navy as the Chief of Chaplains. He served in Korea and in Vietnam and was awarded the Distinguished Service Medal by the President of the United States. He was the Director of the Navy Chaplains School.

JAMES J. GILL, S.J., M.D., is a priest, physician, and psychiatrist. He is founder of the Jesuit Educational Center for Human Development and editor-in-chief of the journal *Human Development*. He has worked at the Harvard University Health Services during the past fifteen years.

ROBERT E. NEALE was educated at Amherst College and Union Theological Seminary and is an ordained minister of the United Church of Christ. He is Professor of Psychiatry and Religion at Union Theological Seminary. His most recent book is *Loneliness, Solitude, and Companionship: An Essay on Welcoming Strangers.*

DAVID W. AUGSBURGER is Professor of Pastoral Counseling at the Associated Mennonite Biblical Seminaries, Elkhart, IN. He is an ordained minister of the Mennonite Church and received a Ph.D. in Pastoral Psychotherapy and Personality from the School of Theology at Claremont, CA. He is a diplomate of the American Association of Pastoral Counselors, and is the author of fifteen books.

JAMES E. ROYCE, S.J., is a Professor Emeritus of Psychology at Seattle University and Director of the Alcohol Studies Program. His *Alcohol Problems and Alcoholism,* which has won two national awards, is the textbook for the "Symposium on Alcoholism" which he has taught since 1950. His other books include *Man and His Nature* and *Man and Meaning.*

KENNETH BYRNE, is Assistant Clinical Professor, Department of Mental Health Sciences, at Hahnemann University, Philadelphia, and has a clinical practice in Bala Cynwyd, PA. Dr. Byrne studied psychoanalysis at the Hampstead Clinic in London with Anna Freud.

COVAL B. MACDONALD is a graduate of Fuller Theological Seminary, Harvard Divinity School, and holds a Ph.D. from the Divinity School of the University of Chicago in Pastoral Care and Counseling. He is currently a counselor at Interface in Houston, TX. Dr. MacDonald is a Presbyterian minister. He has extensive experience counseling couples and families going through divorce.

DAVID A. STEERE is Professor of Pastoral Care and Counseling at Louisville Presbyterian Theological Seminary. He is a Certified Supervisor with the Association for Clinical Pastoral Education, a Diplomate with the American Association of Pastoral Counselors, an Approved Supervisor for the American Association of Marriage and Family Therapy, and a Clinical Teaching Member of the International Transactional Analysis Association. He is the author of *Bodily Expressions in Psychotherapy* and the editor of *The Supervisor of Pastoral Care.*

CAROLYN J. BOHLER is the mother of two children and the Emma Sanborn Tousant Professor of Pastoral Theology at United Theological Seminary in Dayton, Ohio. She has authored *Opening to God: Guided Imagery Meditations on Scripture* (1977), *Prayer on Wings: A Search for Authentic Prayer* (1990), and *When You Need to Take a Stand* (1990). She is co-editor of the *Journal of the Society of Pastoral Theology*.

MELVIN C. BLANCHETTE is a priest of the Society of St. Sulpice. He received his doctorate in professional psychology from United States International University, San Diego, California. His professional interests are in teaching developmental psychology, professional ethics, and courses in psychological testing. Helping to bridge the gap between theology and psychology has been a long-term source of reflection and exploration. He has been associated with the Department of Pastoral Counseling at Loyola since 1977. Recently, he became Personnel Director for his religious community.

JOANNE MARIE G. GREER, Director of Research for the Pastoral Counseling Department at Loyola College in Maryland, has dual specialties of research methodology and psychoanalytic psychology. She received a B.S. in mathematics from St. Mary's Dominican College, New Orleans, and a Ph.D. in Research Design and Statistics from the University of Maryland, where she concentrated on psychological measurement. She also holds a post-doctoral diploma in psychoanalysis from the Washington Psychoanalytic Institute. Formerly with the U.S. Department of Health and Human Services, she is the author of numerous journal articles and government monographs on various technical subjects in health services research.

WILLIAM A. BARRY, S.J. is presently provincial of the Jesuits of the New England province. He has a doctorate in clinical psychology from the University of Michigan and taught courses in pastoral counseling and spiritual direction at Weston School of Theology, Cambridge, MA. He was co-founder of the Center for Religious Development in Cambridge. He co-authored *The Practice of Spiritual Development* and authored a number of books including *Paying Attention to God: Discernment in Prayer* and *"Now Choose Life": Conversion as the Way to Life*.

Appendix

American Association of Pastoral Counselors Code of Ethics Approved April 27, 1991

Principle I—Prologue

As members* of the American Association of Pastoral Counselors we are committed to the various theologies, traditions, and values of our faith communities and to the dignity and worth of each individual. We are dedicated to advancing the welfare of those who seek our assistance and to the maintenance of high standards of professional conduct and competence. We are accountable for our ministry whatever its setting. This accountability is expressed in relationships to clients, colleagues, students, our faith communities, and through the acceptance and practice of the principles and procedures of this Code of Ethics.

In order to uphold our standards, as members of AAPC we covenant to accept the following foundational premises:

A. To maintain responsible association with the faith group in which we have ecclesiastical standing.

B. To avoid discriminating against or refusing employment, educational opportunity or professional assistance to anyone on the basis of race, gender, sexual orientation, religion or national origin.

(Violations alleged to have occurred prior to the approval of this Code shall be considered under the Code and procedures in effect at the time of the alleged violation.)

* The use of "member", "we", "us" and "our" refer to and are binding upon all levels of individual and institutional membership and affiliation of AAPC.

C. To remain abreast of new developments in the field through both educational activities and clinical experience. We agree at all levels of membership to continue post-graduate education and professional growth, including supervision, consultation, and active participation in the meetings and affairs of the Association.

D. To seek out and engage in collegial relationships, recognizing that isolation can lead to a loss of perspective and judgement.

E. To manage our personal lives in a healthful fashion and to seek appropriate assistance for our own personal problems or

F. To diagnose or provide treatment only for those problems or issues that are within the reasonable boundaries of our competence.

G. To establish and maintain appropriate professional relationship boundaries.

Principle II—Professional Practices

In all professional matters members of AAPC maintain practices that protect the public and advance the profession.

A. We use our knowledge and professional associations for the benefit of the people we serve and not to secure unfair personal advantage.

B. We clearly represent our level of membership and limit our practice to that level.

C. Fees and financial arrangements, as with all contractual matters, are always discussed without hesitation or equivocation at the onset and are established in a straight-forward, professional manner.

D. We are prepared to render service to individuals and communities in crisis without regard to financial remuneration when necessary.

E. We neither receive nor pay a commission for referral of a client.

F. We conduct our practice, agency, regional and Association fiscal affairs with due regard to recognized business and accounting procedures.

G. Upon the transfer of a pastoral counseling practice or the sale of real, personal, tangible or intangible property or assets used in such practice, the privacy and well being of the client shall be of primary concern.

1. Client names and records shall be excluded from the transfer or sale.

2. Any fees paid shall be for services rendered, consultation, equipment, real estate, and the name and logo of the counseling agency.

H. We are careful to represent facts truthfully to clients, referral sources and third party payors regarding credentials and services rendered. We shall correct any misrepresentation of our professional qualifications or affiliations.

I. We do not malign colleagues or other professionals.

Principle III—Client Relationships

It is the responsibility of members of AAPC to maintain relationships with clients on a professional basis.

A. We do not abandon or neglect clients. If we are unable, or unwilling for appropriate reasons, to provide professional help or continue a professional relationship, every reasonable effort is made to arrange for continuation of treatment with another professional.

B. We make only realistic statements regarding the pastoral counseling process and its outcome.

C. We show sensitive regard for the moral, social and religious standards of clients and communities. We avoid imposing our beliefs on others, although we may express them when appropriate in the pastoral counseling process.

D. Counseling relationships are continued only so long as it is reasonably clear that the clients are benefiting from the relationship.

E. We recognize the trust placed in and unique power of the therapeutic relationship. While acknowledging the complexity of some pastoral relationships, we avoid exploiting the trust and dependency of clients. We avoid those dual relationships with clients (e.g., business or close personal relationships), which could impair our professional judgement, compromise the integrity of the treatment and/or use the relationship for our own gain.

F. We do not engage in harassment, abusive words or actions, or exploitative coercion of clients or former clients.

G. All forms of sexual behavior or harassment with clients are unethical, even when a client invites or consents to such behavior or involvement. Sexual behavior is defined as, but not limited to, all forms of overt and covert seductive speech, gestures and behavior as well as physical contact of a sexual nature; harassment is defined as but not limited to, repeated comments, gestures or physical contacts of a sexual nature.

H. We recognize that the therapist/client relationship involves a power imbalance, the residual effects of which are operative following the termination of the therapy relationship. Therefore, all sexual behavior or harassment as defined in Principle III, G with former clients is unethical.

Principle IV—Confidentiality

As members of AAPC we respect the integrity and protect the welfare of all persons with whom we are working and have an obligation to safeguard information about them that has been obtained in the course of the counseling process.

A. All records kept on a client are stored or disposed of in a manner that assures security and confidentiality.

B. We treat all communications from clients with professional confidence.

C. Except in those situations where the identity of the client is necessary to the understanding of the case, we use only the first names of our clients when engaged in supervision or consultation. It is our responsibility to convey the importance of confidentiality to the supervisor/consultant; this is particularly important when the supervision is shared by other professionals, as in a supervisory group.

D. We do not disclose client confidences to anyone, except: as mandated by law; to prevent a clear and immediate danger to someone; in the course of a civil, criminal or disciplinary action arising from the counseling where the pastoral counselor is a defendant; for purposes of supervision or consultation; or by previously obtained written permission. In cases involving more than one person (as client) written permission must be obtained from all legally accountable persons who have been present during the counseling before any disclosure can be made.

E. We obtain informed written consent of clients before audio and/ or video tape recording or permitting third party observation of their sessions.

F. We do not use these standards of confidentiality to avoid intervention when it is necessary: eg., when there is evidence of abuse of minors, the elderly, the disabled, the physically or mentally incompetent.

G. When current or former clients are referred to in a publication, while teaching or in a public presentation, their identity is thoroughly disguised.

Principle V—Supervisee, Student & Employee Relationships

As members of AAPC we have an ethical concern for the integrity and welfare of our supervisees, students and employees. These relationships are maintained on a professional and confidential basis. We recognize our influential position with regard to both current and former supervisees, students and employees, and avoid exploiting their trust and dependency. We make every effort to avoid dual relationships with such persons that could impair our judgement or increase the risk of personal and/or financial exploitation.

A. We do not engage in ongoing counseling relationships with current supervisees, students and employees.

B. We do not engage in sexual or other harassment of supervisees, students, employees, research subjects or colleagues.

C. All forms of sexual behavior, as defined in Principle III, G, with our supervisees, students, research subjects and employees (except in employee situations involving domestic partners) are unethical.

D. We advise our students, supervisees, and employees against offering or engaging in, or holding themselves out as competent to engage in, professional services beyond their training, level of experience and competence.

E. We do not harass or dismiss an employee who has acted in a reasonable, responsible and ethical manner to protect, or intervene on behalf of, a client or other member of the public or another employee.

Principle VI—Interprofessional Relationships

As members of AAPC we relate to and cooperate with other professional persons in our community and beyond. We are part of a network of health care professionals and are expected to develop and maintain interdisciplinary and interprofessional relationships.

A. We do not offer ongoing clinical services to persons currently receiving treatment from another professional without prior knowledge of and in consultation with the other professional, with the clients' informed consent. Soliciting such clients is unethical.

B. We exercise care and interprofessional courtesy when approached for services by persons who claim or appear to have inappropriately terminated treatment with another professional.

Principle VII—Advertising

Any advertising by or for a member of AAPC, including announcements, public statements and promotional activities, is undertaken with the purpose of helping the public make informed judge-ments and choices.

A. We do not misrepresent our professional qualifications, affilia-tions and functions, or falsely imply sponsorship or certification by any organization.

B. We may use the following information to describe ourselves and the services we provide: Name; highest relevant academic degree earned from an accredited institution; date, type and level of certification or licensure; AAPC membership level, clearly stated; address and telephone number; office hours; a brief re-view of services offered, e.g., individual, couple and group coun-seling; fee information; languages spoken; and policy regarding third party payments. Additional relevant information may be provided if it is legitimate, reasonable, free of deception and not otherwise prohibited by these principles. We may not use the initials "AAPC" after our names in the manner of an academic degree.

C. Announcements and brochures promoting our services describe them with accuracy and dignity, devoid of all claims or evalua-tion. We may send them to professional persons, religious institu-tions and other agencies, but to prospective individual clients only in response to inquires.

D. We do not make public statements which contain any of the following:

1. A false, fraudulent, misleading, deceptive or unfair statement.

2. A misrepresentation of fact or a statement likely to mislead or deceive because in context it makes only a partial disclosure of relevant facts.

3. A testimonial from a client regarding the quality of services or products.

4. A statement intended or likely to create false or unjustified expectations of favorable results.

5. A statement implying unusual, unique, or one-of-a-kind abilities, including misrepresentation through sensationalism, exaggeration or superficiality.

6. A statement intended or likely to exploit a client's fears, anxieties or emotions.

7. A statement concerning the comparative desirability of offered services.

8. A statement of direct solicitation of individual clients.

E. We do not compensate in any way a representative of the press, radio, television or other communication medium for the purpose of professional publicity and news items. A paid advertisement must be identified as such, unless it is contextually apparent that it is a paid advertisement. We are responsible for the content of such advertisement. Any advertisement to the public by radio or television is to be pre-recorded, approved by us and a recording of the actual transmission retained in our possession.

F. Advertisements or announcements by us of workshops, clinics, seminars, growth groups or similar services or endeavors, are to give a clear statement of purpose and a clear description of the experiences to be provided. The education, training and experience of the provider(s) involved are to be appropriately specified.

G. Advertisements or announcements soliciting research participants, in which clinical or other professional services are offered as an inducement, make clear the nature of the services as well as the cost and other obligations or risks to be accepted by participants in the research.

Principle VIII—Procedures

As members of the American Association of Pastoral Counselors we are committed to accept the judgement of other members as to standards of professional ethics, subject to the procedures that follow. Refusal or failure to cooperate with an ethics investigation at any point may be considered grounds for dismissal.

As members of AAPC we are bound by ethical standards to take action, according to the procedures outlined herein, when it appears that another member has violated the Code of Ethics. Whenever ethical questions arise and the answers do not appear to be clear, we consult with the Regional Ethics Committee for information and clarification.

A. General Procedures

1. While all ethical violations are recognized as serious, if an alleged violation is not threatening to the well-being of the member or others, we are encouraged first to approach the member in question to see if the matter can be resolved through clarification or remonstrance.

2. If this fails, or if an alleged violation appears to be a serious threat to the well-being of the member or others, the matter is immediately referred to the Regional Ethics Committee. This constitutes a formal complaint and shall be made in writing to the Regional Ethics Committee, which begins an investigation as soon as possible and in a deliberate and careful manner.

3. If members receive complaints of unethical conduct against them, they shall promptly report the complaints to the Regional Ethics Committee.

4. Regional Ethics Committees shall consult with the Association Chairperson or Committee immediately upon receipt of a complaint. The Executive Director of AAPC shall be notified by phone of the complaint.

5. A Regional Ethics Committee begins an investigation as soon as a complaint from a primary party has been received. A copy of the complaint (or a summary or a portion of it which indicates the nature of the complaint) is sent to the member against whom it is directed.

6. A Regional Ethics Committee may also begin an investigation based upon information obtained from other sources, including but not limited to:

   a. Notification of suspension or dismissal from another professional organization or from the member's endorsing faith group.

   b. The media.

   c. Knowledge that a member has been convicted of, or is engaged in conduct which could lead to the conviction of, a felony or of a misdemeanor related to the member's qualifications or functioning as a pastoral counselor.

   d. Knowledge that a member has had a professional license or certificate suspended or revoked.

   e. Knowledge that a member has shown a lack of competency to practice pastoral counseling due to impairment through physical or mental causes or the abuse of alcohol or other substances.

7. When a Regional Ethics Committee proceeds on its own initiative (in lieu of the receipt of a written complaint), it shall prepare a statement concerning the factual allegations against the member; a copy of this shall be sent to the member.

8. Complaints may be brought by anyone. Complaints by members shall be brought promptly, with due regard for client confidentiality.

9. Investigations usually include separate personal interviews by the Regional Ethics Committee with the person(s) who has made the complaint, with the member against whom the complaint has been made and with anyone else deemed necessary to obtain needed information. All parties involved are to be supported while at the same time not given unnecessary information or promises.

10. Notes are to be kept which include dates and brief summaries of all phone calls and meetings. These notes are to be kept confidential, including the use of initials instead of names whenever feasible. These notes should be clear enough to enable a reasonable person to conclude that the

Regional Committee's investigation was adequate and its findings sufficient to sustain its determination(s).

11. At the discretion of the Regional Chairperson, legal counsel may be obtained to ensure that these procedures are followed accurately. The member against whom a complaint has been made may also seek legal counsel, at his/her/its own expense, but under no circumstances shall legal counsel be present at any Ethics Committee meeting or investigative interview.

12. Any member of a Regional Ethics Committee who has or has had a close personal or collegial relationship with the member under investigation shall be excused from the investigation and deliberations of that case. If this includes the chairperson, a chair pro-tem shall be named. Regional Ethics Committees may recruit any member(s) of AAPC, from any region, for a specific investigation.

13. Confidentiality is crucial. However, when it is deemed to be in the best interest of protecting the public and the Association and its members, if a Regional or Association Ethics Committee is approached by a member of AAPC or of the public and is asked about allegations against a particular member, the committee member or chairperson may reveal to that person that a) an investigation of the alleged violation(s) is in process, or b) that the member is under probation or either is or has been recommended for, suspension or dismissal. No other details are to be revealed.

14. Any member under investigation, probation or suspension who moves to another region during the course of these actions shall notify in writing the chairpersons of the Ethics Committees of both the former and new regions. A copy of each notification shall be sent to the other chairperson. In the case of suspension, a copy shall also be sent to the Association Ethics Chairperson.

    a. Investigations shall be conducted and completed by the Ethics Committee of the region in which the alleged violation occurred.

b. A copy of the complete file shall be sent to the ethics chairperson of the region into which the member relocates. That chairperson shall be responsible for the management of the ongoing process until it is resolved, in consultation with the original Ethics Chairperson.

c. Responsibility for the management of the case shall be transferred to the Ethics Committee in the new region at a time that is deemed appropriate by both Regional Ethics Chairpersons.

15. Investigations can be held and disciplinary actions can be taken only against those members who were members at the time the alleged violation of the Code took place. Conversely, if a member resigns during or after such violation, during the course of an investigation, or during a term of probation or suspension, ethics procedures shall proceed to completion.

B. Actions

When an investigation is complete, there are six courses of action that an Ethics Committee may take:

1. Advice that the complaint is unfounded.

2. Admonishment. This action is meant to be educational, when a member has been unaware of having violated the Code of Ethics.

3. Reprimand. This action is a serious reproof or rebuke of the member. It is based upon an assessment that the member has accepted responsibility for the violation and that the reprimand is adequate to ensure that it will not reoccur.

Actions 2 and 3 may be taken only in those cases in which the violation is deemed not to be threatening to the well-being of the member or others.

4. Probation. This action is based upon an assessment that the member needs to work on certain issues, spelled out in writing to the member by the Ethics Committee, in order to

reasonably ensure that the violation will not reoccur; also, that the member's continued ministry, whatever its setting, will not pose a threat to the well-being of the member or others. The length of the probation may be extended if deemed appropriate by the Ethics Committee. Likewise, at any time during a probation the Ethics Committee may change its action and require a different action, based upon new information, a new understanding of previous information, non-compliance with the terms of the probation or non-cooperation with the committee.

These first four actions are taken by the Regional Ethics Committees. The following two are recommended by the Regional Ethics Committees for action by the Association Ethics Committee.

5. Suspension. This action is the same as probation, except it requires that the member cease all functioning as a pastoral counselor, whatever the setting, unless otherwise spelled out in writing to the member by recommendation from the Regional Ethics Committee and enacted by the Association Ethics Committee.

6. Dismissal. This action may be taken in any case but is mandated when a member has been found guilty in a court of law of a felony, or of a misdemeanor which is related to the member's functioning as a pastoral counselor.

C. Appeals Process and Records

With each of the six actions above, the action is communicated to the complainant and to the member by certified mail, return receipt requested, with notification that the decision may be appealed. In cases of probation and suspension only that fact, not the terms, is communicated to the complainant.

1. Actions 1 through 4 may be appealed to the Association Ethics Committee, at which point the Regional Ethics Chairperson forwards the complete file along with a summary of the case to the Association Ethics Chairperson.

   a. The Association Ethics Chairperson decides upon and organizes any additional investigation that may be necessary.

b. When this is accomplished, the Association Ethics Committee reviews the case and meets either in person or by conference call to discuss the appeal and to reach a decision.

c. If no appeal is received within 30 days of this receipt, a chronological summary (without names) of the case is sealed in an envelope with only the member's name on the outside. It is then sent to the Executive Director for safe keeping. In the case of a probation, this is done following the completion of the probation.

d. The summary is to be kept by the Executive Director for a period of twenty years, or longer if another investigation is begun. In the event another investigation of that member begins, the summary may be sent upon request to a Regional or Association Ethics Committee.

2. Actions 5 and 6 may be appealed to the Board of Governors, at which point the Association Ethics Chairperson forwards the complete file along with a summary of the case to the Secretary of the Board.

a. The Secretary, in consultation with members of the Executive Committee of the Board, decides upon and organizes any additional investigation that may be necessary.

b. When this is accomplished, the Executive Committee of the Board shall review the case and meet either in person or by conference call to discuss the appeal. It then recommends a decision to the full Board of Governors, which makes a decision about the appeal.

c. If no appeal is received within 30 days of the above mentioned receipt, the procedure is the same as in 1, c, with "suspension" being substituted for "probation".

d. The file, with summary, shall be kept by the Executive Director indefinitely and shall be destroyed one year after the Association learns of the member's death. A Regional or Association Ethics Committee may request this file if another complaint is received or investigation is begun regarding the member. In addition, in the case of dismissal, the file may also be sent upon request to a Regional or Association Membership Committee if the person reapplies for membership.

e. If a member appeals a decision for dismissal, the member shall cease all functioning as a pastoral counselor during the appeal.

f. If the decision for dismissal is upheld in the appeal process, the member shall immediately send the membership certificate to the Executive Director.

3. Decisions by the Board of Governors regarding appeals are final.

D. Notifications

1. When placed on probation the member shall report this status in writing to a present or prospective employer, including supervisors and consultants, and copies shall be sent to the Regional Ethics Chairperson. Notification of probationary status (only) shall be sent by the Regional Ethics Chairperson to the member's endorsing faith group, relevant state regulatory agencies and any and all other professional organizations to which the member belongs.

2. Determinations of suspension or dismissal, once the appeal time or procedures are over, are publicized to the membership in the next Newsletter. The announcement is limited to the member's full name and highest earned degree, geographical location, the fact and date of suspension or dismissal and the specific Principle(s) of the Code violated. If a member is dismissed for violation of Principle VIII, first paragraph (refusal or failure to cooperate with an ethics investigation at any point), all other Principles alleged to have been violated shall also be listed. In the case of suspension, the announcement shall state that the member is "suspended from all activity as a pastoral counselor" and shall state the length of time for the suspension.

3. In the case of dismissal or suspension, the Association Ethics Chairperson, once the appeal time or procedures are over, shall notify the member's endorsing faith group, relevant state regulatory agencies, and any and all other professional organizations to which the member belongs. The specific information communicated is the same as above.

Name Index

Adler, A., 28, 62
Aist, C., 1
Aldrich, C.K., 119
Alexander, K.L., 416
Allen, W.R., 304, 307
Anderson, C.M., 586, 602, 603, 604, 607
Anderson, H., 539–49, 551–52, 554–57
Anderson, H., 610
Andreasen, N.J., 363–64
Aponte, H., 271–72
Arasteh, R., 382
Argyle, M., 106
Aronoff, M.S., 98, 101
Attneave, C.L., 159
Augsberger, D., 494
Augustine, St., 8, 60, 183, 486

Bach, G., 275
Back, K., 11
Bak, R.C., 536
Bakan, D., 223, 391
Baldwick, J., 284
Baldwin, B.A., 134, 138, 146, 156, 158
Baldwin, J.M., 172
Baldwin, J.W., 332
Balint, M., 127
Bandura, A., 483–84
Barbour, I., 195
Barker, R.G., 412
Barry, W.A., 50, 53, 648, 651, 652, 653, 658, 659
Barth, K., 17–18
Bateson, G., 601, 602
Beardslee, W., 206–07
Becker, R.J., 565

Bepko, C., 604
Berenson, B.G., 98, 101, 104
Berkowitz, L., 491
Berne, E., 579, 580, 582
Bieber, I., 536
Black, C., 516–17
Black, M., 195
Blanchette, M.C., 566, 623
Blanck, G., 98
Blatt, M., 197
Blumstein, P., 288
Bohler, C., 606
Boisen, A.T., 17, 20–21, 561, 573
Boosco, A., 269
Bordin, E.S., 579, 652
Boszormenyi-Nagy, I., 270
Bowen, E., 614
Bowen, M., 602
Bowlby, J., 542, 556
Bowles, S., 411
Boyd-Franklin, N., 607, 608
Braaty, T., 651–52
Breunlin, D.C., 567
Broderick, C., 268–69
Brodsky, A., 91
Bronfenbrenner, U., 192
Brown, R.E., 54
Browning, D., 30, 33, 339, 402, 434
Butler, R.N., 245, 260
Byng-Hall, J., 567

Cabot, R.C., 20–22, 560–61, 573
Calvin, J., 340
Candee, D., 418
Cannon, W., 458

Subject Index

694